*New Security Challenges Series*

General Editor: **Stuart Croft**, Professor of Inter
Politics and International Studies at the Univ
the ESRC's New Security Challenges Programm

The last decade demonstrated that threats to s
manifestations, and that they invite interest a
sciences, civil society and a very broad policy community. In the past, the avoidance of war was the primary objective, but with the end of the Cold War the retention of military defence as the centrepiece of the international security agenda became untenable. There has been, therefore, a significant shift in emphasis away from traditional approaches to security to a new agenda that talks of the softer side of security, in terms of human security, economic security and environmental security. The topical *New Security Challenges Series* reflects this pressing political and research agenda.

*Titles include*:

Jon Coaffee, David Murakami Wood and Peter Rogers
THE EVERYDAY RESILIENCE OF THE CITY
How Cities Respond to Terrorism and Disaster

Tom Dyson
NEOCLASSICAL REALISM AND DEFENCE REFORM IN POST-COLD WAR EUROPE

Håkan Edström, Janne Haaland Matlary and Magnus Petersson (*editors*)
NATO: THE POWER OF PARTNERSHIPS

Christopher Farrington (*editor*)
GLOBAL CHANGE, CIVIL SOCIETY AND THE NORTHERN IRELAND PEACE PROCESS
Implementing the Political Settlement

Kevin Gillan, Jenny Pickerill and Frank Webster
ANTI-WAR ACTIVISM
New Media and Protest in the Information Age

Andrew Hill
RE-IMAGINING THE WAR ON TERROR
Seeing, Waiting, Travelling

Andrew Hoskins and Ben O'Loughlin
TELEVISION AND TERROR
Conflicting Times and the Crisis of News Discourse

Paul Jackson and Peter Albrecht
RECONSTRUCTION SECURITY AFTER CONFLICT
Security Sector Reform in Sierra Leone

Bryan Mabee
THE GLOBALIZATION OF SECURITY
State Power, Security Provision and Legitimacy

Janne Haaland Matlary
EUROPEAN UNION SECURITY DYNAMICS
In the New National Interest

Michael Pugh, Neil Cooper and Mandy Turner (*editors*)
WHOSE PEACE? CRITICAL PERSPECTIVES ON THE POLITICAL ECONOMY OF PEACEBUILDING

Brian Rappert and Chandré Gould (*editors*)
BIOSECURITY
Origins, Transformations and Practices

Brian Rappert
BIOTECHNOLOGY, SECURITY AND THE SEARCH FOR LIMITS
An Inquiry into Research and Methods

Brian Rappert (*editor*)
TECHNOLOGY AND SECURITY
Governing Threats in the New Millenium

Ali Tekin and Paul A. Williams
GEO-POLITICS OF THE EURO-ASIA ENERGY NEXUS
The European Union, Russia and Turkey

Lisa Watanabe
SECURING EUROPE

---

**New Security Challenges Series**
**Series Standing Order ISBN 978–0–230–00216–6 (hardback) and ISBN 978–0–230–00217–3 (paperback)**

You can receive future titles in this series as they are published by placing a standing order. Please contact your bookseller or, in case of difficulty, write to us at the address below with your name and address, the title of the series and the ISBN quoted above.

Customer Services Department, Macmillan Distribution Ltd, Houndmills, Basingstoke, Hampshire RG21 6XS, England

# Whose Peace? Critical Perspectives on the Political Economy of Peacebuilding

Edited by

Michael Pugh
*Professor of Peace and Conflict Studies, University of Bradford, UK*

Neil Cooper
*Senior Lecturer in International Relations and Security, University of Bradford, UK*

and

Mandy Turner
*Lecturer in Conflict Resolution, University of Bradford, UK*

palgrave
macmillan

© Selection, editorial matter, introduction and conclusion © Michael Pugh, Neil Cooper and Mandy Turner 2008, 2011
Foreword © Mark Duffield 2011
All remaining chapters © respective authors 2008, 2011

All rights reserved. No reproduction, copy or transmission of this publication may be made without written permission.

No portion of this publication may be reproduced, copied or transmitted save with written permission or in accordance with the provisions of the Copyright, Designs and Patents Act 1988, or under the terms of any licence permitting limited copying issued by the Copyright Licensing Agency, Saffron House, 6-10 Kirby Street, London EC1N 8TS.

Any person who does any unauthorized act in relation to this publication may be liable to criminal prosecution and civil claims for damages.

The authors have asserted their rights to be identified as the authors of this work in accordance with the Copyright, Designs and Patents Act 1988.

First published 2008
Published in paperback 2011 by
PALGRAVE MACMILLAN

Palgrave Macmillan in the UK is an imprint of Macmillan Publishers Limited, registered in England, company number 785998, of Houndmills, Basingstoke, Hampshire RG21 6XS.

Palgrave Macmillan in the US is a division of St Martin's Press LLC,
175 Fifth Avenue, New York, NY 10010.

Palgrave Macmillan is the global academic imprint of the above companies and has companies and representatives throughout the world.

Palgrave® and Macmillan® are registered trademarks in the United States, the United Kingdom, Europe and other countries.

ISBN 978–0–230–57335–2 hardback
ISBN 978–0–230–28561–3 paperback

This book is printed on paper suitable for recycling and made from fully managed and sustained forest sources. Logging, pulping and manufacturing processes are expected to conform to the environmental regulations of the country of origin.

A catalogue record for this book is available from the British Library.

A catalog record for this book is available from the Library of Congress.

10  9  8  7  6  5  4  3  2  1
20 19 18 17 16 15 14 13 12 11

Printed and bound in Great Britain by
CPI Antony Rowe, Chippenham and Eastbourne

# Contents

| | |
|---|---|
| List of Figures and Table | viii |
| List of Contributors | ix |
| List of Abbreviations and Acronyms | xiv |
| Preface and Acknowledgements | xvii |
| Foreword by Mark Duffield | xviii |

Introduction     1
*Michael Pugh, Neil Cooper and Mandy Turner*

## Part I   The Political Economy of Liberal War and Peace

1   The Political Economy of Peace Processes     13
    *Jan Selby*

2   The Gendered Impact of Peace     32
    *Donna Pankhurst*

3   Neoliberalism Versus Peacebuilding in Iraq     49
    *Eric Herring*

## Part II   Trade

4   Trading with Security: Trade Liberalisation and Conflict     69
    *Susan Willett*

5   Corporate Social Responsibility     87
    *Salil Tripathi*

6   As Good as it Gets: Securing Diamonds in Sierra Leone     105
    *Neil Cooper*

## Part III   Employment

7   From Waging War to Peace Work: Labour and Labour Markets     123
    *Christopher Cramer*

| 8 | Employment, Labour Rights and Social Resistance<br>*Michael Pugh* | 141 |
|---|---|---|
| 9 | Securitising the Economy of Reintegration in Liberia<br>*Kathleen M. Jennings* | 159 |

## Part IV  Diasporas

| 10 | Three Discourses on Diasporas and Peacebuilding<br>*Mandy Turner* | 175 |
|---|---|---|
| 11 | Diaspora Engagement in Peacebuilding: Empirical and Theoretical Challenges<br>*Kenneth Bush* | 193 |
| 12 | Rwandese Diasporas and the Reconstruction of a Fragile Peace<br>*Rebecca Davies* | 208 |

## Part V  Borderlands and the Cartography of Violent Economies

| 13 | War, Peace and the Places in Between: Why Borderlands are Central<br>*Jonathan Goodhand* | 227 |
|---|---|---|
| 14 | Microfinance and Borderlands: Impacts of 'Local Neoliberalism'<br>*Milford Bateman* | 247 |
| 15 | Potential Difference: Internal Borderlands in Africa<br>*Stephen Jackson* | 268 |

## Part VI  Civil Society

| 16 | Welfare and the Civil Peace: Poverty with Rights?<br>*Oliver P. Richmond* | 289 |
|---|---|---|
| 17 | Peace Constituencies in Peacebuilding: The *Mesas de Concertación* in Guatemala<br>*Cécile Mouly* | 304 |
| 18 | El Salvador: The Limits of a Violent Peace<br>*Mo Hume* | 320 |

## Part VII  Global Governance

19  Post-Conflict Statebuilding: Governance Without
    Government                                                    339
    *David Chandler*

20  The UN Peacebuilding Commission: The Rise and Fall
    of a Good Idea                                                358
    *Mats Berdal*

21  Material Reproduction and Stateness in Bosnia and
    Herzegovina                                                   375
    *Berit Bliesemann de Guevara*

Conclusion: The Political Economy of Peacebuilding – Whose
Peace? Where Next?                                                392
*Michael Pugh, Neil Cooper and Mandy Turner*

*Index*                                                           402

# List of Figures and Table

**Figures**

6.1 Official Sierrra Leone diamond exports 106
6.2 The diamond pyramid in Sierra Leone 112

**Table**

4.1 Statistical profile of vulnerable LDCs, 2003 and 2004 74

# List of Contributors

**Milford Bateman** is a freelance consultant specialising in issues of sustainable local economic and social development, mainly working in the countries of Southeast Europe and the Middle East. He is also Visiting Professor of Economics at the University of Juraj Dobrila Pula, Croatia.

**Mats Berdal** is Professor of Security and Development, Department of War Studies, King's College London, and Visiting Professor, National Defence and Command College, Oslo. From 2000 to 2003 he was Director of Studies at the International Institute for Strategic Studies. He has focused on the UN, peacekeeping and the political economy of armed conflict and is the co-editor with Spyros Economides of *United Nations Interventionism, 1991–2004* (2007). He edited *Studies in International Relations: Essays by Philip Windsor* (2002) and is completing a book on *The UN and the Search for International Order*.

**Berit Bliesemann de Guevara** is Research Assistant and PhD candidate at the Institute of International Politics, Helmut Schmidt University, Hamburg, and Head of the German Political Science Association working group on Orders of Violence. Her publications include articles on post-conflict statebuilding in Bosnia and Herzegovina, war economies and violent orders in Peru and northeast India, and Columbian guerrilla websites.

**Kenneth Bush** is Associate Professor of Peace Studies, St. Paul University, Ottawa, Canada. He has worked widely with non-governmental, governmental and multilateral actors in conflict-prone areas, particularly Sri Lanka. He was Special Adviser on Humanitarian Issues to the Canadian Government when it served on the UN Security Council (1998–2000). He is the author of *The Intra-Group Dimensions of Ethnic Conflict* (2003) and of numerous chapters on peacebuilding and development. He has published in *Global Governance*, *Canadian Foreign Policy* and the *Canadian Journal of Development Studies*.

**David Chandler** is Professor of International Relations, Centre for the Study of Democracy, University of Westminster. He is the founding editor of the *Journal of Intervention and Statebuilding*. His research focuses on new forms of international intervention and regulation, particularly those projected in the language of ethical foreign policy, the rule of law, human security, empowerment, democratization, state capacity-building, human rights, civil society development, anti-corruption, country 'ownership' and 'pro-poor' development. His most recent publication is *Empire in Denial: The Politics of State-building* (2006).

**Neil Cooper** is Senior Lecturer in International Relations and Security, Department of Peace Studies, University of Bradford. His research interests include the arms trade, the arms control and the political economy of civil conflicts. His recent publications include an edited special issue on war economies of *Conflict, Security and Development*, co-authorship of *War Economies in a Regional Context: The Challenges of Transformation* (2004), and articles in *Security Dialogue, Contemporary Security Policy, Review of International Studies* and *Development and Change*.

**Christopher Cramer** is Professor of Political Economy of Development and Chair of the Centre of African Studies, School of Oriental African Studies, University of London. He has been a consultant for the International Labour Organisation, UN Development Programme, UN Commission on Trade, Aid & Development, Food and Agriculture Organisation, International Fund for Agricultural Development, the European Commission, Swedish International Development Agency, the World Bank and the Ethiopian Government. His publications include *Civil War is Not a Stupid Thing: Accounting for Violence in Developing Countries* (2006) and co-authorship of *Supporting Ownership: Swedish Development Cooperation with Kenya, Tanzania and Uganda*.

**Rebecca Davies** is Senior Lecturer, Department of International Relations, University of Plymouth, and Research Fellow at the Centre for International and Comparative Politics, University of Stellenbosch, South Africa. She has published articles in *Third World Quarterly* and the *Review of African Political Economy* concerning the political economy of diasporas under conditions of globalisation.

**Mark Duffield** is Professor of Development Politics and Director of the Global Insecurities Centre, University of Bristol, UK. He researches development as security; the NGO movement; the changing nature of humanitarian intervention; the political economy of internal war; human security and 'the responsibility to protect'; migration and development; and reconstruction of war-affected societies. His latest book is *Development, Security and Unending War: Governing the World of Peoples*, Polity Press, 2007.

**Jonathan Goodhand** is Senior Lecturer in Development Practice, Department of Development Studies, School of Oriental and African Studies, University of London. He has extensive experience in managing humanitarian and development programmes in Afghanistan/Pakistan and Sri Lanka, and as a researcher and adviser in South and Central Asia for a range of NGOs and aid agencies and international organisations. His interests include the political economy of aid and conflict, NGOs and post-conflict reconstruction. His recent publications include *Aiding Peace: The Role of NGOs in Armed Conflict* (2006) and co-authorship of *Aid, Conflict & Peacebuilding in Sri Lanka 2000–2005*.

**Eric Herring** is Senior Lecturer in International Politics, University of Bristol. His books include *Iraq in Fragments: The Occupation and its Legacy* (2006) with Glen Rangwala; *The Arms Dynamic in World Politics* (1998) with Barry Buzan; and *Danger and Opportunity: Explaining International Crisis Outcomes* (1995). He has also published many articles on critical security issues. He was Specialist Adviser to the Select Committee on Economic Affairs of the House of Lords for its enquiry into economic sanctions in 2006–2007.

**Mo Hume** is Lecturer in Politics, University of Glasgow. Her research focuses on issues of gender and violence in post-war El Salvador, addressing issues regarding the social meaning and visibility of violence and crime, particularly at the micro level. Previously, she worked for several years with the women's movement in El Salvador on gendered processes of local development and women's political participation.

**Stephen Jackson** is a special adviser to the Deputy Special Representative of the Secretary-General with the UN Mission in the Democratic Republic of the Congo. Previously, he was Deputy Director of the Conflict Prevention and Peace Forum in New York and Director of the International Famine Centre at the National University of Ireland, Cork. During the 1990s he worked in the humanitarian sector in Central Africa. He holds a PhD in Cultural Anthropology from Princeton University and has published in *Politique Africaine*, *African Studies Review* (special journal issue, co-edited with Peter Geschiere) and the *Review of African Political Economy*.

**Kathleen M. Jennings** is a researcher at the Fafo Institute for Applied International Studies, Oslo, and coordinates its New Security Programme. Recent and forthcoming publications include articles in *International Peacekeeping*, *Global Governance* and the *European Journal for Development Research*. She was previously a research associate at the Council on Foreign Relations in Washington DC.

**Cécile Mouly** holds a PhD in International Studies from the University of Cambridge. She previously worked in the Department of Political Affairs and the Department of Peacekeeping Operations at the UN. She also served as Civil Affairs Officer with the United Nations Operation in Burundi and as a member of the Nepal project committee of Peace Brigades

International. Her main research interests are peacebuilding and civil society.

**Donna Pankhurst** is Professor of Peacebuilding and Development, Department of Peace Studies, University of Bradford. She researches on gender, conflict and peace issues and peacebuilding in Africa. She has worked with NGOs and international organisations as adviser and consultant. Her publications include *Gendered Peace: Women's Struggles for Post-war Justice and Reconciliation* (2007); 'Sex Wars and Other Wars. Towards a Feminist Approach to Peacebuilding' in *Development in Practice* (2003); 'Women and Politics in Africa. The Case of Uganda', *Parliamentary Affairs* (2002); and a chapter in *Women, Politics and Change* (2002).

**Michael Pugh** is Professor of Peace and Conflict Studies, University of Bradford, and editor of the journal *International Peacekeeping* and the Cass Peacekeeping book series. He was a member of the ESRC-funded Transformation of War Economies team. He edited *Regeneration of War-torn Societies* (2000), and co-authored with Neil Cooper and Jonathan Goodhand *War Economies in a Regional Context* (2004).

**Oliver P. Richmond** is Professor of International Relations, School of International Relations, and Director of the Centre for Peace and Conflict Studies, University of St Andrews. His publications include *Peace in International Relations Theory* (2008) and *The Transformation of Peace* (2005). He edits a Palgrave Macmillan book series, 'Rethinking Peace and Conflict Studies', and has co-edited special issues of *Review of International Studies* and *Global Society*.

**Jan Selby** is Senior Lecturer, Department of International Relations, University of Sussex. His research centres on peace processes, resource conflicts, and international and social theory. He is the author of *Water, Power and Politics in the Middle East: The Other Israeli-Palestinian Conflict* (2003) and *The Global Politics of Oil* (forthcoming 2008), and co-editor (with Feargal Cochrane and Rosaleen Duffy) of *Global Governance, Conflict and Resistance* (2003). His articles have appeared in *Review of International Studies*, *Third World Quarterly*, *Government and Opposition*, *International Relations*, *Interventions* and *New Political Economy*.

**Salil Tripathi** is Senior Policy Adviser at International Alert, London, and on the governance group of 'Voluntary Principles for Security and Human Rights'. He is a member of the human rights working group at the UN Global Compact, the International Advisory Network of the Business and Human Rights Resource Centre, and is an adviser to the corporate complicity project at the International Commission of Jurists. He was Amnesty International's Researcher for economic relations and human rights (1999–2005), and represented Amnesty International at the Kimberley Process, Voluntary Principles, the Global Compact, and the World Economic Forum.

**Mandy Turner** is Lecturer in Conflict Resolution, Department of Peace Studies, University of Bradford. She is assistant editor of *International Peacekeeping* and has published articles on peacebuilding, regulating the trade in conflict goods, diasporas and peacebuilding, and statebuilding in Palestine in *Conflict, Security and Development, Democratization, Journal of Corporate Citizenship, The World Today* and *The Guardian*.

**Susan Willett** is a security and development consultant, formerly Director of the 'Cost of Disarmament' programme at the UN Institute for Disarmament Research, Geneva. Reports include 'Military Expenditures, Arms Procurement and Corruption in Sub-Saharan Africa' (2007). Publications include *Mortgaging the Future; The South Asian Arms Race* (2003); *Participatory Monitoring of Humanitarian Mine Action: Giving Voice to Citizens of Nicaragua, Mozambique and Cambodia*, edited for UNIDIR (2003); 'New Barbarians at the Gate: Losing the Liberal Peace in Africa', *Review of African Political Economy* (2005).

# List of Abbreviations and Acronyms

| | |
|---|---|
| AEP | Afghanistan Expatriate Programme |
| *AFP* | *Agence France Presse* |
| AP | Associated Press |
| AU | African Union |
| BiH | Bosnia and Herzegovina |
| CB | Census Bureau (United States) |
| *CETIM* | *Centre Europe Tiers Monde* |
| CIA | Central Intelligence Agency (United States) |
| CPA | Coalition Provisional Authority (Iraq) |
| CPA | Comprehensive Peace Agreement (Liberia) |
| CRS | Congressional Research Service (United States) |
| CSO | civil society organisation |
| CSR | corporate social responsibility |
| DACO | Development Assistance Coordination Office (Sierra Leone) |
| DD/DDR | Disarmament, Demobilisation/and Reintegration |
| DDI | Diamond Development Initiative |
| DFID | Department for International Development (UK) |
| DoD | Department of Defense (United States) |
| DoS | Department of State (United States) |
| DPA | Dayton Peace Agreement |
| DRC | Democratic Republic of Congo |
| ECOSOC | Economic and Social Council (UN) |
| EPIC | Education for Peace in Iraq Center |
| ETU | Economic Transition Unit (BiH) |
| Fafo | Norwegian Institute of Applied Social Science |
| FAO | Food and Agriculture Organisation |
| FATA | Federally Administered Tribal Areas of Pakistan |
| FBiH | Federation of Bosnia and Herzegovina |
| FDI | foreign direct investment |
| FIAS | Foreign Investment Advisory Service (United States) |
| FLEGT | Forest Law Enforcement Governance and Trade |
| FMLN | Farabundo Martí National Liberation Front (El Salvador) |
| *FN* | *Forces Nouvelles* (Côte d'Ivoire) |
| *FPI* | *Front Populaire Ivoirien* |
| *FSLN* | *Frente Sandinista de Liberacion Nacional* (Nicaragua) |
| GAO | Government Accountability Office (United States) |
| GDP | gross domestic product |

| | |
|---|---|
| GEMAP | Governance and Economic Management Assistance Programme (Liberia) |
| GNP | gross national product |
| HLP | High-level Panel on Threats, Challenges and Change |
| HR CAS | House of Representatives Committee on Armed Services (United States) |
| HRW | Human Rights Watch |
| I-BIZ | Iraq-Based Industrial Zone |
| ICG | International Crisis Group |
| ICISS | International Commission on Intervention and State Sovereignty |
| IDMP | Integrated Diamond Management Program |
| IDS | Institute of Development Studies (Sussex) |
| IFI | international financial institution |
| IFOU | Iraqi Federation of Oil Unions |
| IFRC | International Federation of Red Cross and Red Crescent Societies |
| ILO | International Labour Organisation/Office |
| IMF | International Monetary Fund |
| IoM | Institute of Medicine (United States) |
| IOM | International Organisation for Migration |
| IPDWG | Iraq Peace and Development Working Group |
| IRIN | Integrated Regional Information Networks |
| ITA | Indirect Tax Agency (BiH) |
| KPCS | Kimberley Process Certification Scheme |
| KRG | Kurdish Regional Government |
| LDC | less/least developed country |
| LTTE | Liberation Tigers of Tamil Eelam (Sri Lanka) |
| MDGs | Millennium Development Goals |
| MFI | microfinance institution |
| MINUGUA | United Nations Verification Mission in Guatemala |
| MIT | Massachusetts Institute of Technology |
| MRU | Mano River Union |
| MSI | Management Systems International |
| NAM | Non-Aligned Movement |
| NMJD | Network Movement for Justice and Development |
| NORAD | Norwegian Agency for Development Cooperation |
| NSCSE | New Sudan Centre for Statistics and Evaluation |
| NURC | National Unity and Reconciliation Council (Rwanda) |
| OBN | Open Broadcast Network (BiH) |
| ODI | Overseas Development Institute (UK) |
| OECD | Organisation for Economic Cooperation and Development |
| ORB | Opinion Research Business |
| Oxfam | Oxford Famine Relief |

| | |
|---|---|
| PAC | Partnership Africa–Canada |
| PBC/F/SO | Peace Building Commission/Fund/Support Office |
| PDA | Peace Diamonds Alliance |
| PDCI | *Parti Democratique de Côte Ivoire* |
| PEPP | Palestinian Expatriate Professional Project |
| PNC | National Civil Police (El Salvador) |
| PRSP | poverty reduction strategy paper |
| PRT | Provincial Reconstruction Team (Afghanistan) |
| RCD | *Rassemblement Congolais pour la Démocratie* |
| RDR | *Rassemblement des Républicains* (Côte d'Ivoire) |
| RPF | Rwandan Patriotic Front |
| RS | Republika Srpska (BiH) |
| RUF | Revolutionary United Front (Sierra Leone) |
| SAARC | South Asian Association for Regional Cooperation |
| SIDA | Swedish International Development Agency |
| SLDC | Sierra Leone Diamond Company |
| SLIP | Sierra Leone Investment Forum |
| SME | small and medium-sized enterprise |
| SSCR Net | Network for Economic, Social and Cultural Rights |
| TRC | Truth and Reconciliation Commission |
| UMU | United Mineworkers Union (Sierra Leone) |
| UNCTAD | United Nations Conference on Trade and Development |
| UNDP | United Nations Development Programme |
| UNHCR | United Nations High Commissioner for Refugees |
| UNICEF | United Nations Children's Fund |
| UNIDIR | United Nations Institute for Disarmament Research |
| UNIFEM | United Nations Development Fund for Women |
| UNITA | *União Nacional para a Independência Total de Angola* |
| UNODC | United Nations Office on Drugs and Crime |
| UNRISD | United Nations Research Institute for Social Development |
| UPI | United Press International |
| URNG | *Unidad Revolucionaria Nacional Guatemalteca* (Guatemala) |
| US A&MC | Army and Marine Corps (United States) |
| US SIGIR | US Special Inspector General for Iraq |
| USAID | US Agency for International Development |
| USIP | US Institute of Peace |
| WFP | World Food Programme |
| WHO | World Health Organisation |
| WOTCLEF | Women Trafficking and Child Labour Eradication Foundation |
| WTO | World Trade Organisation |

# Preface and Acknowledgements

The genesis of this book lay in a realisation that the economic dimensions of political and social issues in peacebuilding were either silenced or left to the field of econometrics under the aegis of International Financial Institutions (IFIs). To redress this dearth of academic interest, Neil Cooper and Michael Pugh (in International Relations) began joint work under the auspices of the International Peace Academy (now Institute) in New York in 2002. The Institute provided generous assistance and encouragement which led to the publication of *War Economies in a Regional Context: Challenges of Transformation* (Lynne Rienner, 2004) with Jonathan Goodhand from the field of Development Studies. This provided a basis for a more comprehensive project on the 'Transformation of War Economies After Conflict', based at the University of Plymouth and also involving Jo Spear and Greg Kent, as part of the UK's Economic and Social Research Council's 'New Security Challenges Programme'. The research later transferred to the University of Bradford, where Mandy Turner, a sociologist with expertise in political economy, joined the team and was instrumental in fostering a network of scholars, developing the website (http://www.brad.ac.uk/acad/twe) and bringing that phase of the research to a productive conclusion. This included a special issue of *Conflict Security and Development*. This research provided a solid platform for the much expanded agenda represented by this volume, for it was logical to 'mobilise' many other scholars in the network who were often working independently but were enthusiastic about contributing to a critical scholarship of peacebuilding.

The editors register their thanks to the ESRC for award Res. 223.25.0071. Our thanks are also extended for the help and encouragement of the many people who attended seminars and workshops and shared their expertise, as well as to the International Peace Institute for funding a mid-project conference at the University of Plymouth. The contributors individually also acknowledge the many people who assisted them in their specific areas. In addition, we owe particular thanks to Simon Payne, Head of Law and Social Science, University of Plymouth, for supporting initial development of the project; Professor Stuart Croft, University of Warwick, who encouraged us to develop this publication; and Professor Mark Cleary, Vice-Chancellor, University of Bradford, who helped us to structure the research.

Michael Pugh, Neil Cooper and Mandy Turner
University of Bradford

# Foreword

*Mark Duffield*

If Afghanistan is anything to go by, the strategic defeat of liberal interventionism in Iraq has not led to any serious pause for thought. Indeed, it appears to have raised the stakes. When put together with the business-as-usual response to the 2008 financial crisis, it increasingly looks as if politicians have lost any rational attachment to the world around them. For the average person, experiencing a setback usually results in reflection and a change of behaviour. Our political and economic culture, however, is oblivious to this possibility. As Naomi Klein has pointed out, we now live in a world where disasters – whether from invasion, conflict, economic collapse or extreme weather – are no longer experienced as something to be avoided and protected against. To the contrary, they are regarded as somehow offering singular, not-to-be-missed opportunities to clear away all manner of infrastructural, institutional and political obstacles, creating a clean sheet to work on. The name of this opportunistic and essentially authoritarian ethos is neoliberalism. From seeing disaster as an opportunity, the distance of travel necessary to experience failure as success is minimal; in a neoliberal world, the bigger the catastrophe, the greater the opportunities and thus rapture of accomplishment. How else can we explain two decades of liberal interventionism that, even to those in the driving seat, has failed to solve the political problems used to justify it? Indeed, it has compounded these dilemmas, deepening ethnic divisions, propagating widening insecurity, entrenching unequal North–South relations, creating greater aid dependency, and has been complicit in the death of growing numbers of civilians and aid workers alike. Yet the commitment to a neoliberal crusade to dissolve the public realm and entrench market fundamentalism remains essentially unchanged.

Western aid policy seems trapped within its own hegemonic world view. It promotes belief in its universalism and its appeal to the masses – even though its horizon stretches no further than basic needs – and that, in truth, there is no other way. However, if neoliberalism is in a state of denial, life has continued to change around it. While universalism is a seductive illusion from within the aid bubble, outside things look different. The contrarian economic rise of China, India and Brazil, when added to the wide-ranging and multilevel practices of resistance, evasion and desertion that liberal interventionism has evoked within its own self-appointed fiefdom of fragile states and 'ungoverned spaces', befits a mood of crisis rather than hegemony. If we imagine neoliberalism as having an external sovereign frontier strung out across the global borderlands beyond the homeland ramparts of the US, Europe and Australia – a frontier measured in terms of influence and attraction rather than fixed crossing-points – we would see a contested and moving frontier of loosely demarcated zones of market fundamentalism and accumulation through dispossession. In some places, and at some levels, the frontier is collapsing and being pushed back, elsewhere it is under siege. While violent expansion is taking place in a few areas, everywhere liberalism's sovereign frontier is disputed. The double walls, razor-wire, blast-barriers, gated communities and private security guards that together define the signature architecture of the UN integrated mission – a built environment now ubiquitous from the Caribbean through Africa to the Middle East and Asia – are a material expression of where North meets South in the global borderlands.

Sudan is an example of this crisis. Western influence, at least non-military influence measured as political sway, economic presence and cultural attraction, has never been weaker. With regard to oil, under the weight of Western restrictions, Sudan has been turning east since the 1980s, especially towards Asia, for investment and technology. The effects of 9/11 have deepened this reorientation. The Sudanese elite that still banked in Europe, for example, soon felt they were not welcome. The result was a final decamp to the Middle East and a consolidation of existing economic and political ties. Sudan now has what one could call a modern form of 'dual economy' composed of 'gloom' and 'boom' elements. Guided by Sudanese statecraft, the West is confined to the gloom economy of humanitarian assistance, so-called sustainable development and purported state-building. It is restricted to the disaster zones, failing projects, serial emergencies and fortified aid compounds of Darfur and South Sudan. Viewed from a distance, Western influence is peripheral. The boom economy is located in the central regions of northern Sudan. Based on oil, real estate, telecommunications and agri-business, Khartoum has attracted levels of investment and material assistance from the Middle East and Asia that far outstrip Western aid budgets. Through an architectural 'Dubaification', in less than a decade the skyline of Khartoum has changed significantly. The effects of this boom economy, its origins and dynamics, have been to push back the liberal frontier. While deeply ambiguous, with its own winners and losers, the boom has encouraged nuanced, multi-levelled and often unexpected forms of resistance and desertion. After leading the rush to urban gated communities and walled off by their own security protocols in the gloom economy, Western aid agencies now occupy a parallel world.

In the mid-1970s, villages along the Blue Nile to the south of Sennar, except for the scattered houses of notables and merchants, lacked electricity. Most of the 250-mile journey from Khartoum was on unsurfaced roads that became impassable at times during the rains. Water was drawn straight from the river and, reflecting the cost and lack of power, TV sets or refrigerators in people's homes were rare. In the intervening years, these villages have changed dramatically. A surfaced road now connects them to Khartoum and some have become small towns in their own right, complete with India-style rickshaw scooters. Like much of the central region, most compounds draw electricity from the grid. While mud is still the major building material, within households TV sets, refrigerators and even washing machines are common. Water comes from artesian wells and, as with the rest of Africa, even those on modest incomes have mobile telephones. Compared to three decades ago, the average material standard of living has visibly improved. An important driver of this change is Asian capitalism. The Chinese in particular have flooded the market with cheap consumer goods of every description. Throughout wide areas of northern Sudan, small farmers, petty traders, lorry drivers and migrant workers now find these goods within their reach.

Besides material changes, there has also been a profound cultural shift. The Islamic republic that came into being in 1989 had a definite, if internationally controversial, social agenda. While conducting a destructive war in the south and west, it promoted a modernist programme of national salvation in its north and central heartlands. The place of women has been central to this project. Although, it is true, women are privileged only in relation to the family ideal, female education has received a significant boost. At least half of the students at Khartoum University, for example, are women. Compared to even a decade ago, women are now the visible mainstay of office and clerical work in Khartoum. Given the emphasis on the family, there is no contradiction here. For the new middle class, working women are essential for realising the consumerist potential of the boom economy. These include new leisure activities, such as the growing popularity of dining out, that embrace families as a whole. Even women's fashions have changed. Rather than the traditional *tobe*, a body wrapping made from a single piece of colourful material, head scarves, blouses and long fitted skirts are now the preferred work dress. This easing of social codes also extends to the above-mentioned villages on the Blue Nile. In the 1970s, a male visitor would not usually speak to married women or visit the private rooms of a compound. This conservatism has eased. Married women expect to have their say and invitations into kitchens and living quarters are common. Whether from better education or, as some would have it, the effects of Egyptian TV soap operas, or even the desire to show off a fridge-freezer, things have changed.

These developments are not problem-free and all come with their own contingencies. Importantly, they underpin a social shift that the current regime had not planned or anticipated, and even now may not be able to contain. Taken together the interconnected improvement in material conditions and weakening social conservatism is a good example of 'actually existing development'. While actual, in the sense of being observable, very little of it – perhaps none – can be attributed to Western aid or influence. Indeed, through its restrictions and sanctions policies, the West is more likely to undermine rather than support these modest advances. Because of its axiomatic linking of development and security, social advance within an Islamic state sits rather awkwardly as something more likely to invoke fear rather than favour. These gains have occurred through a combination of Islamic resistance, Asian capitalism, local entrepreneurship and hard work. They reflect the vulnerability of liberalism's external sovereign frontier to resistance, evasion and desertion. Since the West now makes few cheap consumer goods, its influence largely rests on its ability to project military violence; an ability that is underpinned by the hollow moral relativism of the gloom economy. However, despite the mirage of universalism that pervades the liberal peace project, the crisis of the external frontier is being registered at some level of political consciousness. Without this, it would be difficult to explain why some of the most secure nations in the world, on any reasonable measure, have embarked upon deeply paranoid programmes of homeland hyper-security in response to cultural difference and distant political autonomy.

This collection of studies seeks to break out of the policy bubble of liberal peace. In focusing on the political economy of transition, including the conditionalities in donor policy, they challenge its premises and assumptions and, as such, provide a basis from which North–South relations can be rethought. In this respect, the editors have called for a need to move beyond a conventional problem-solving response. That is, the belief that more research, a better circulation of 'good practice' and incremental reform will redress the malaise into which the development–security nexus has sunk. Instead, they call for a paradigm shift in which nothing is left unquestioned. In adding to this call, perhaps rather than intervention, we need a politics of 'letting go'. This is not an isolationist position but an active politics intimately connected with issues of difference and autonomy, and what constitutes trust and friendship in our present world; nor would a politics of letting go duck the immense problems associated with climate change and managing the biosphere. Any genuine approach to issues of difference, autonomy and trust would, of necessity, have to explore questions of decentralisation, ownership and negotiation. If current trends continue, the problem-solving approach will oversee a deepening polarisation between those inside the gated communities, secure corridors and zones of privileged access and movement, and those outside these secure archipelagos. The real danger is a widening gap between those cities and elite enclaves able to selectively connect with the world, including guaranteeing their own food security, and the redundant and bypassed populations now surplus to requirements. Liberal peace has done nothing to counter these trends, indeed, it is actively driving them.

Global Insecurities Centre<br>University of Bristol

# Introduction

*Michael Pugh, Neil Cooper and Mandy Turner*

Since the mid-1990s academics and policymakers have become increasingly concerned to understand the political economy of contemporary (so-called) 'civil conflicts', particularly given the way in which groups such as the Revolutionary United Front in Sierra Leone and the Revolutionary Armed Forces of Colombia have traded resources to fund conflict. The advent of the UN's Peacebuilding Commission, formally inaugurated in July 2006, also testifies to a growing international interest in reconstruction and conflict transformation.

Indeed, there is now a significant body of literature examining various dimensions of the conflict–resources–political economy nexus. Existing research has tended to focus on specific countries, regions or conflict goods and has addressed the now rather *passé* 'greed versus grievance' debate over the inception and duration of conflict. There has been much less in the way of cross-cutting thematic analyses of key variables that influence the political economies of peacebuilding.

The legacies of conflict are not ignored here. Whether peace is fragile, as in Timor-Leste, the Democratic Republic of Congo and Afghanistan, or relatively well established, as in Sierra Leone, Angola and Bosnia and Herzegovina, the economic landscapes are usually characterised by the legacies of disruption to production and exchange, by population displacement, unemployment and poverty, and by 'criminality' and re-configured economic incentive structures. It is in these contexts that agencies of international humanitarianism, security and development operate in an attempt to reform the local institutions, policy strategies and incentive structures – generally equipped with a combination of standard operating procedures and a level of hubris unjustified by earlier experience of economic transformations after conflicts. Rather than investigating the inception and maintenance of conflict, the main focus of our research is on the attempt to transform war economies. This usually occurs after a peace settlement, however vulnerable, but as in Afghanistan and Iraq, can also commence while war continues.

In contrast to the traditionally limited activities of peacekeeping and peacemaking, peacebuilding involves a raft of intrusive practices intended to ensure long-term stability after, even during, conflict. The character of the intrusions has been defined and analysed by Mark Duffield (2001) as a form of international liberalism. US President, George W. Bush provided a short description of this 'liberal peace', which became a mantra in US, EU and UN doctrine: 'We seek a just peace where repression, resentment and poverty are replaced with the hope of democracy, development, free markets and free trade' (Bush, 2002). International assistance for transition has been elevated to new levels of administration, while often largely disregarding local bodies of knowledge and struggles against universalising presumptions of a particular liberal–capitalist economic order. Regardless of whether intervention has been initially consensual or coercive, *all* peacebuilding operations involve the exercise of power and illustrate relations of power between actors at the global, regional and local levels.

At first sight it seems paradoxical that the political economy of transitions has been neglected in much of the peacebuilding literature, relative to issues of statist security sector reform, democratisation and rule of law. It is an odd sort of silence that seems to derive from a parody of Marxism based on an economic determinism that disqualifies local, non-conceptualised knowledge and privileges technicist frameworks and discursive practices as 'scientific' (Foucault, 1976 [2003]: 7–8). In part this reflects what Richard Ashley refers to as 'economism', the notion that the economic sphere invades, directs and exists independently of the political – a charge incongruously levelled by realists and liberals against theories that *contest* the inevitability and universal applicability of capitalist ideologies of value. Economism 'produces a perspective in which political practice is devoid of all independent capacities to reflect upon or to check economic processes... an apology for the worldwide hegemony of a deadly logic of economy in determining social and political outcomes' (Ashley, 1983: 465). Furthermore, the realist emphasis on statebuilding and the ontology of statism represses politics from below: 'interests that are not reducible to state interests... enter the political realm only insofar as they are mediated by state interests' (Ashley, 1983: 470).

The silences and disqualifications fostered by a host of commentators from Kenneth Waltz to Francis Fukuyama and Jeffrey Sachs presume an *a priori* economic geology, universal in its supposed immunity to political shaping. This is structured in the institutional governance of the global economy, and has been taken to an extreme in the conditionalities introduced by the phalanx of aid agencies and international organisations engaged in post-conflict recovery programmes. Donors and purveyors of economic guidance have considerable clout in peacebuilding. For example, the World Bank has a seat in the UN Peacebuilding Commission, uses Trust Funds to exercise leverage when it has no direct role, drives the donor conferences and, backed by International Monetary Fund conditionalities, places state institution building at the top of its agenda so that neoliberal political economies can be institutionalised. The UNDP and donors have varied degrees of emphasis on what needs to be done, but the culture of structural adjustment and conditionality is all-pervasive. In a review of IMF agreements with 41 countries during the period of global recession 2007–09 (including stand-by arrangements, poverty reduction and growth facilities and exogenous shock facilities), the Center for Economic and Policy Research found that pro-cyclical economic policies were in place in 31 cases, including war-torn countries such as Afghanistan (Weisbrot *et al*, 2009).

Another school, more critical of the liberal emphasis on democratisation and marketisation, though without seeing a contradiction between the two, proposes statebuilding to resurrect 'effective' institutions as a condition of social stability. The true purpose of the state, however, would be not only to reassert instruments of state coercion to underpin the rule of law, but to 'reinforce and "lock in" liberalizing political and economic reforms' (Paris, 2006: 435). In other words, the state as a protector and regulator of society, and its economic development, reclaims a dominant role in engineering the liberal peace, whose basic tenets are democracy and 'free markets'. It is nothing less than a bid to rescue the liberal peace from its crisis of hegemony (see Chandler, 2006; Duffield, 2001; Richmond, 2005). For defenders such as Roland Paris, liberal peacebuilding is the only viable solution for rebuilding war-torn societies: '[t]he challenge today is not to replace or move "beyond" liberal peacebuilding but to reform existing approaches within a broadly liberal framework' (Paris, 2010: 362; also Burgess and Begby, 2009). While defenders are sometimes prepared to acknowledge the myriad problems of liberal peacebuilding including the limited knowledge of local conditions and insufficient local ownership, these are usually regarded as merely technical problems of implementation rather than basic flaws in the model. Moreover, the claim that there is 'no alternative' to liberal peacebuilding is over-deterministic and rests on similar assumptions to Francis Fukuyama's *End of History and the Last Man* (1992), that Western liberalism represents the ultimate evolutionary direction for all societies, as if local societies have no agency (see Richmond, this volume).

The traumatic experiences of Iraq and Afghanistan have certainly dented such assumptions. There has also been a rolling back of the commitment to implement specific elements of the liberal peace model. In particular, the democratisation and human rights agendas have been substantially downgraded as oil and security considerations in the Middle East, Central Asia and sub-Saharan Africa have led to serial accommodation with autocratic governments and rejection of uncomfortable democratic outcomes such as the election of Hamas in Palestine (Baxter and Akbarzadeh, 2008). At the same time, the economic crisis in Western neoliberalism has caused profound unease about its viability as a model of development, and the transfer of economic and political power to non-liberal states such as China has become more pronounced (Hutton, 2008).

Nevertheless, as Naomi Klein (2007) has noted, one of the ironies of the neoliberal economic model propagated by liberal interventionists is that every crisis is treated as an opportunity to impose or extend the model even further. Thus donors and international financial institutions have retained an evangelical faith in the transformative powers of neoliberal economics, and the neoliberal component of the liberal peace project has proved remarkably resilient in the face of its own crisis and may even (in the short-term at least) experience a brief renaissance as crisis produces more opportunities for 'shock therapy' (Weisbrot, et al., 2005). More generally, while the liberal peace model is certainly no longer as unquestioned as it was in the 1990s, it is still the dominant paradigm articulated by powerful donors, UN agencies, IFIs and academics such as Paris. Ultimately a failure to appreciate the extent to which liberal peace intervention is predicated on ignoring the local and dismissing the everyday experiences of people as either irrelevant or as forms of deviance, represents a potent combination of hubris and denial, as illustrated by the comments of a US Lieutenant Colonel, who on the withdrawal of US combat troops from Iraq in August 2010, reportedly claimed: '[w]hat has been achieved is going to echo throughout the region: prosperity, peace, truth and freedom, the works' (cited by Chulov, 2010).

Peacebuilding strategies pursued after peace settlements and after conquest have had a core of common presumptions: neoliberal policies of open markets, privatisation and fiscal constraint, and governance policies focused on institutions and enhancing instruments of state coercion and capacity building based on the now near-universal conceit that 'development requires security'. There is little space to (formally) dissent from these policy prescriptions whether international peacebuilders were originally invited in or arrived in the wake of an external invasion. This is one of the reasons why liberal prescriptions often fail – because concern for local everyday life is limited and the incentives for obstruction, co-option or evasion of neoliberal governance mechanisms commensurately high.

## Purpose of the book

The book offers an innovative exploration of the question: 'what constitutes a political economy of peace and who shapes it?' Currently, policymakers and some commentators assume that what is to be constructed is either self-evident or unproblematic, and the issue of 'whose peace?' tends to be treated as either again unproblematic or answered with the phrase 'the stakeholders', as if they are unmistakable. Other academics engaged with security, development and humanitarian issues have been critical of external imposition (e.g., Caplan, 2005; Chesterman, 2004; Easterly, 2006; Klein,

2007; Krause and Jütersonke, 2005; Paris, 2004). This book offers more critical perspectives that reach beyond the technicist approach of international financial institutions and the cadres of international capital. Indeed, one of the aims of the book will be to interrogate and critique the necromancy of the supposedly 'a-political' economic technicians who favour war-torn societies with standard panaceas for recovery.

The field remains remarkably under-theorised, and there is certainly space for critiques of the supposedly neutral economic governance that betrays disciplinary and security functions bound up with the promotion of global capital. Some of the critiques here engage with the claims made by liberal economic determiners and statebuilders.

Such claims have been expressed by Paddy Ashdown, former High Representative in Bosnia and Herzegovina, a peacebuilding *vizier* who announced,

> Ironically, as a politician I campaigned against many of her [Thatcher's] reforms, arguing that they would lead to lost jobs and the selling off of the national wealth; only to find myself instituting very similar reforms in Bosnia and facing the same arguments and opposition. What makes matters worse in most post-conflict countries is that they are poor, not rich – so the pain can be far greater. There is not much the interveners can do about this, except understand it and recognise that by insisting on accelerated reforms we are often asking local politicians to take responsibility for a level of social disruption which our own politicians at home would reject without a second thought.
>
> (Ashdown, 2007: 83)

The statement is remarkable for its economic determinism and political abdication. What is fine for Tuzla (Federation, Bosnia) would have been unacceptable in Yeovil (Somerset, UK). Responsibility for the impact of tough measures introduced from outside is shuffled onto local politicians. This economic determinism has been possible only as a Utopian experiment because populations are economically disenfranchised, and statist engineering of free markets placed beyond any democratic reach (Cox, 1992; Gray, 1998 [2002]: 16–18). But the quest for a 'free market' is a political project not an iron law of economics, and reformers have to step in to mitigate the social instability (sometimes expressed as nationalism and fundamentalism) trailed by dynamic capitalism in its unending quest for profitable outlets for accumulated surplus (Gray, 1998 [2002]: 210; Harvey, 2003). Thus peacebuilding as currently practised privileges private over public goods, while at the same time attempting to reconcile communities on the basis of a modern version of Adam Smith's 'hidden hand', the aggregation of private needs and goods. One can add employment, livelihoods and social capital to Keynes's aphorism concerning self-regulated financial speculation: 'When the capital development of a country becomes a by-product of the activities of a casino, the job is likely to be ill-done' (Keynes, 1936 [1967]: 158–9; see also Strange, 1986).

The claim for liberal statebuilding lacks sufficient reflection on the limitations of building states. Indeed, peace processes have had the opposite effect, destroying the state, as in Iraq. And peacebuilding conditionality is predicated on artificial stimulation of state (re)creation where it was a factor in conflict and where continuing, and legitimate, quests for a non-unitary state are dismissed as wrecking strategies by foreign embassies, as in Bosnia and Herzegovina (MIA, 2007).

In constructing the book, space for a variety of approaches has been created, whereby 'critical', as for Keith Krause and Michael Williams, represents a general orientation that departs from the conceptual limitations of orthodox thinking (1997: xix) – in this context the dominant conceptions and practices of political economy in peacebuilding – including the possibilities of moving from problem-solving perspectives to a paradigm shift in the treatment of post-conflict political economies, as outlined in the conclusion.

## Structure of the book

The book has an original format. There is a broad division into sections based on interrelated issue areas: liberal war and peace, trade, employment, diasporas, borderlands, civil society and governance. Each issue area is then addressed in three dimensions. The first is a general conceptual and theoretical analysis, at a global or discursive level. The second element of each section is a deeper analysis of a particular theme. The third element is a case study in a spatial setting to offer detailed analysis of how the issue influences local political economies.

Part I surveys the political economy of peace processes that, as Jan Selby shows, have considerable influence on the direction of securitisation. This is followed by the theme of gendered peace (Donna Pankhurst) with particular attention to the backlash experienced by women when fighting stops. The case study by Eric Herring provides a timely analysis of the tensions between nationalism and peacebuilding in Iraq.

Part II sets the context of war-torn political economies in the global economic system, beginning with the stresses engendered by trade liberalisation as analysed by Susan Willett. Given the high expectations among peacebuilders for foreign direct investment in war-torn societies and for corporate responsibility, Salil Tripathi's thematic chapter is a valuable assessment of the reliance on voluntarism in regulation and the often overestimated potential of corporate power in building peace. The case study on the Sierra Leone diamond sector by Neil Cooper contends that while the security dimension of the security–development nexus has been pursued relatively successfully in Sierra Leone, the neoliberalised economy has only marginally ameliorated the devastating human consequences stemming from legacies of the conflict and the country's position in the international system.

Part III focuses on employment, with an opening chapter by Christopher Cramer on the impact of transitions from war to peace on labour markets. This is followed by an investigation into socio-economic (primarily labour) rights and the role of informal working as a signifier of resistance to liberalisation (Michael Pugh). The case study is a critique by Kathleen M. Jennings of the securitisation of reintegration of former combatants in Liberia, an approach that suppresses the economic welfare of former combatants.

Diasporas are often overlooked as transnational networks with peacebuilding potential. In Part IV Mandy Turner contrasts three discourses on diasporas (as development actors, security risks and peacebuilders), concluding that their roles are subordinated to liberal peace policies and processes. The economic contribution of diasporas to homeland reconstruction is assessed by Kenneth Bush, who advocates a nuanced approach to cultivating diaspora capacities that shuns the lens of western security interests. The role of the Rwandese diaspora forms the basis for the case study by Rebecca Davies, illustrating the limits of reconstruction dominated by Tutsi returnees and internationals.

Part V highlights the spatial dimensions of political economies of conflict and peace. Jonathan Goodhand places borderlands in the centre of his analysis and investigates the impact of borderlands on the mobilisation of coercion, legitimacy and capital. One of the most frequently touted mechanisms for the recovery of borderlands after conflict is micro credit facilities. Milford Bateman questions its effectiveness and argues that micro credit is a way of making the poor responsible for circulating poverty. Stephen Jackson's case study of internal borderlands shows that they share a common ability to present 'potential difference' to neighbours and develop incentives to use political power or violence to leverage profit across borders.

Issues relating to civil society are examined in Part VI, beginning with Oliver P. Richmond's critique of the neoliberal incarnation of peacebuilding that discounts welfare relative to an empty institutionalism which prevents the formation of a social contract with the state. In a slight departure from the general pattern, this is followed by two case studies: of peace constituencies in Guatemala by Cécile Mouly and the prolongation of violence in El Salvador by Mo Hume. The former shows how spontaneous local social movements have the potential to enhance ownership of peacebuilding; the latter shows how in spite of gains for civil society the neoliberal peace has not fostered alternative structures to violence.

In Part VII, David Chandler's chapter contends that virtual states have been created in the aftermath of conflict, their 'sovereignty' removed under the guise of partnership with external actors who thereby avoid responsibility and accountability for their coercive regulation. The disappointing outcome of the attempt to develop an international peacebuilding competence through the Peacebuilding Commission is the subject of Mats Berdal's chapter, his contention being that it was partly a victim of the deeply politicised environment surrounding the 2005 World Summit with its potential damaged by linkage to wider UN reform. Berit Bliesemann de Guevara's case study of Bosnia and Herzegovina shows that governance through precepts of neoliberalism has not only failed as a statebuilding project but has left local communities little space for determining their economic future.

The book's conclusion offers further interpretations of the empirical material and some recommendations for engaging with war-torn societies. It also tenders deliberations on problem-solving within the global framework of neoliberal capitalism and a shift towards a de-securitisation of the political economy of peacebuilding through the adoption of a life welfare approach. It develops three core arguments. First, it draws on the various critiques of the securitisation of underdevelopment presented in the book to argue not just for a de-securitisation of the political economy of peacebuilding, but for a new paradigm and associated language within which to consider the challenges of peacebuilding. In particular, it postulates the concept of 'life welfare' as an advance on the 'human security' paradigm, to embrace alternative notions of life (the individual, community, the biosphere and planetary environment). It also places welfare rather than security centre stage, with welfare understood in two ways. First, welfare as well-being – the optimisation of life potentials – and second, welfare understood as a social contract that embraces mechanisms of redistribution, insurance and positive discrimination for the poor.

A further aspect of this concept of life welfare is its recognition of heterodoxy, particularly in the economic sphere, and the consequent need for peacebuilding to move from the imposition of an assumed universal model to negotiations on the means of arriving at an emancipatory global and local political economy of peace. This may imply a scaling back of projects of massive economic and social change inside war-torn societies. Conversely, it also implies a scaling up of the willingness to interrogate and transform global economic structures and institutions that limit the potential of war-torn societies.

Ultimately, therefore, while the book offers deliberations on problem-solving approaches within the existing global framework of capitalism, it also represents an argument for a de-securitisation of the political economy of peacebuilding and the adoption of an approach which places life welfare at the heart of local and global policy.

# References

Ashdown, Paddy, 2007, *Swords and Ploughshares: Bringing Peace to the 21st Century*, London: Wiedenfeld & Nicholson.
Ashley, Richard K., 1983, 'Three Modes of Economism', *International Studies Quarterly*, Vol. 27, No. 4, pp. 463–96.
Baxter, Kyle and Shahram Akbarzadeh, 2008, *US Foreign Policy in the Middle East: The Roots of Anti-Americanism*, Abingdon: Routledge.
Begby, Endre and J. Peter Burgess, 2009, 'Human Security and Liberal Peace', *Public Reason*, Vol. 1, No. 1, pp. 91–104.
Bush, George W., 2002, 'Securing Freedom's Triumph', *New York Times*, 12 Dec.
Caplan, Richard, 2005, *The International Governance of War-Torn Territories: Rule and Reconstruction*, Oxford: Oxford University Press.
Chandler, David, 2006, *Empire in Denial: The Politics of State-Building*, London: Pluto.
Chesterman, Simon, 2004, *You, The People: The United Nations, Transitional Administration, and State-Building*, Oxford: Oxford University Press.
Chulov, Martin, 2010, 'From Shock and Awe to a Quiet Exit – US Troops Pull Out of Iraq', *The Guardian*, 20 August 2010, p. 1.
Cox, Robert W., 1992, 'Globalization, Multilateralism, and Democracy', John Holmes Memorial Lecture to the Academic Council on the United Nations System (at: www.acuns.org/publications/Cox/Cox.TOC.shtml).
Duffield, Mark, 2001, *Global Governance and the New Wars: The Merging of Development and Security*, London: Zed Books.
Easterly, William, 2006, *White Man's Burden: Why the West's Efforts to Aid the Rest Have Done so Much Ill and so Little Good*, Oxford: Oxford University Press.
Foucault, Michel, 1976, *Society Must Be Defended*, David Macey (trans.), London: Allen Lane, 2003 edn.
Gray, John, 1998, *False Dawn: The Delusions of Global Capitalism*, London: Granta, 2002 edn.
Harvey, David, 2003, *The New Imperialism*, Oxford: Oxford University Press.
Hutton, Will, 2008, *The Writing on the Wall: China and the West in the 21st Century*, London: Abacus.
Keynes, John M., 1936, *The General Theory of Employment, Interest and Money*, London: Macmillan, 1967 edn.
Klein, Naomi, 2007, *Shock Doctrine: The Rise of Disaster Capitalism*, London: Allen Lane.
Krause, Keith and Michael C. Williams (eds), 1997, *Critical Security Studies: Concepts and Cases*, London: UCL Press.
Krause, Keith and Oliver Jütersonke, 2005, 'Peace, Security and Development in Post-Conflict Environments', *Security Dialogue*, Vol. 36, No. 4, pp. 447–62.
MIA (Media Intelligence Agency), 2007, 'Reforms in BiH: Homogenization on the Up'. 4 Sept. wire provision, Sarajevo.
Paris, Roland, 2004, *At War's End*, Cambridge: Cambridge University Press.
Paris, Roland, 2006, 'Bringing the Leviathan Back In: Classical Versus Contemporary Studies of the Liberal Peace', *International Studies Review*, Vol. 8, No. 3, pp. 425–40.
Paris, Roland, 2010, 'Saving Liberal Peacebuilding', *Review of International Studies*, Vol. 36, No. 2, pp. 337–65.
Richmond, Oliver P., 2005, *The Transformation of Peace*, London: Palgrave Macmillan.
Strange, Susan, 1986, *Casino Capitalism*, Oxford: Blackwell.

Weisbrot, Mark, Dean Baker and David Rosnick, 2005, 'The Scorecard on Development: 25 Years of Diminished Progress', Center for Economic and Policy Research: Washington DC, September (at: www.cepr.net/index.php/publications/reports/scorecard-on-development-25-years-of-diminished-progress/).

Weisbrot, Mark, Rebecca Ray, Jake Johnston, Jose Antonio Cordero and Juan Antonio Montecino, 2009, 'IMF-Supported Macroeconomic Policies and the World Recession: A Look at Forty-One Borrowing Countries', Center for Economic Policy Research, Washington DC, 5 October (at: www.cepr.net/documents/publications/imf-2009-10.pdf).

# Part I

# The Political Economy of Liberal War and Peace

# 1
# The Political Economy of Peace Processes

*Jan Selby*

When, during the summer of 2007, the Catholic Primate of All Ireland and Archbishop of Armagh, Sean Brady, attended a celebration of Irish culture in Milwaukee, he had more to speak on than the usual subjects of social breakdown and sexual abuse; his other main concern was to promote inward investment to support the Northern Ireland peace process. Echoing pleas by political, economic and cultural leaders across the Northern Irish political spectrum, he called on the British government to bring down corporation tax in the North to the same 12.5 per cent level as in the Irish Republic, and urged American companies to increase their investment in Northern Ireland (Cooney, 2007). His call was made at a time of growing concern within the Republic about the potential economic repercussions of the resumption of power-sharing in Belfast – a concern that economic growth may become increasingly concentrated in the Dublin–Belfast corridor, crystallised above all by an Aer Lingus decision to open a new Belfast flight hub at the expense of established routes from Shannon (Connolly, 2007). And his call was also made against a backdrop of ongoing discussions in the North, and with London, over a plethora of economic issues – about water bills, house prices, public sector investment, cross-border cooperation and much more besides.

As this illustrates, issues of political economy not only can be, but I would argue always are, absolutely pivotal to the form and functioning of peace processes. These issues do not simply pertain to natural resources, to poverty and criminality or to any of the other development–security problems so commonly identified by 'post-conflict' peacebuilders, but also include issues ranging from corporation tax to credit ratings. Moreover, as the concerns above indicate, peace processes are disparate and divergent in their economic and social impacts – benefiting some while harming others, or at the very least raising troubling questions about who they might leave behind.

This chapter provides a summary critical perspective on the political economy of peace processes. I use the term 'peace processes' rather than 'peacebuilding' because the former are quite distinct from the latter, and pose quite distinct analytical challenges. Moreover, I say a 'critical perspective' because, while mainstream discourse on peace processes is informed by a range of liberal assumptions about the relations between political and economic change, this chapter submits these liberal assumptions to critique, and points towards an alternative historical materialist reading of peace processes. The chapter draws primarily upon evidence from the Middle East, but also from peace processes in South Asia, Latin America and, with the case of Northern Ireland, Europe. The bulk of the chapter first sets out the liberal orthodoxy on the political economy of peace processes, and then proceeds to critique it. Beforehand, however, we need to clarify precisely what 'peace processes' are, how they differ from 'peacebuilding', and why they merit close scrutiny.

## Peace processes

The notion of 'peacebuilding' has moved to the centre of academic and practitioner discourse on how to end wars and promote peace (Boutros-Ghali, 1992; Paris, 2002, 2004; Richmond, 2005). And yet in mainstream public and high political discourse, the more common focus has been 'peace processes'. Certainly, centrist British and US media outlets such as the BBC and the *New York Times* discuss peace processes much more than they do peacebuilding. The term 'peace process' has become a standard part of the global political lexicon, applied to contexts as different as Northern Ireland, Sudan, Columbia, the Basque country, the Middle East and India–Pakistan.

In conflict resolution accounts, peace processes are understood as phased processes for negotiating and nurturing peace. They can be either intra-state (as in Sudan or Columbia) or inter-state (as in the cases of the Arab–Israeli or India–Pakistan processes). They can involve extensive mediation from international actors and significant international peacebuilding support (as in the Israeli–Palestinian peace process), or barely any such third party involvement at all (as in India–Pakistan, where India resists all efforts to internationalise resolution of the dispute). Peace processes are first and foremost between the immediate parties to a conflict. They commonly begin with unofficial and secretive negotiations, undertaken by academics, businesspeople, religious leaders and other non-state or third-party actors, within the context of ongoing conflict and often government prohibitions (or fear of hostile public response) to formal negotiations. If productive, such back-channel talks then typically open the way for public and formalised negotiations, either around skeletal framework agreements or around public statements, letter exchanges and/or agreed negotiating frameworks – on condition of some sort of ceasefire. A series of accords then usually follow, the early ones full of general statements of principles, confidence-building measures and agreements on issues with positive-sum dimensions (such as pledges to pursue joint economic development programmes); the later ones more concerned with the details of implementation, as well as attempts at resolution of the most contentious political issues separating the parties, which are typically left unresolved, even unaddressed, within earlier negotiations. These developments are accompanied by economic and social reconstruction programmes funded by international peacebuilders or state authorities, which, in combination with the resolution of outstanding political differences, hopefully usher in a final peace settlement and a happy conclusion to the peace process (Darby and Mac Ginty, 2003; Guelke, 2003).

To such mainstream liberal conflict resolution depictions of peace processes, further points can be added. First, peace processes are a historically novel political phenomenon or institution: the term 'peace process' was first used only in the mid-1970s, when American diplomats coined it as a label for the tentative thaw in relations between Israel, Syria and Egypt (Quandt, 2001: 1; Saunders, 1985: 3), and the practice of making peace through a staged and protracted process of negotiation between enemies is likewise historically unique. Second, peace processes usually fail: as with most of the examples listed above – though with the striking exception, at least for now, of Northern Ireland – peace processes typically end by stalling, collapsing or dying altogether (Mac Ginty, 2006). Third, a good part of the reason for this is that peace processes are inter-elite political accommodations whose aim is often not so much 'peace' as the reconfiguration of domestic hegemony and/or international legitimacy; peace processes are reformist, conservative and far from revolutionary phenomena, and often therefore do not provide a basis for the social transformations necessary for sustainable peace. And fourth, because they are so protracted, peace processes furnish plenty of opportunities for participants to both 'have their cake and eat it too' – that is, for the parties to peace processes to on the one hand claim and display their commitment to peace and accrue various benefits as a result, while on the other hand avoiding, often for many years, having to make substantive political compromises. (For further discussion of the nature and late twentieth-century emergence of peace processes, see Selby, 2007.)

Peace processes, then, differ from peacebuilding in several key regards. First, whereas in peacebuilding it is international organisations and liberal Westerners who are usually considered the primary agents of peace, in peace processes it is local elites who occupy centre stage. So while peacebuilding is founded on a neo-colonial civilising mission, as Paris (2002) observes, this is not true to nearly the same extent of peace processes. This does not mean that peace processes are purely local exercises – indeed as indicated below this is far from being the case – merely that local dynamics, situated within their global context, need to be our main concern. Second, while peacebuilding is an essentially liberal exercise, an attempt to transplant liberal democratic structures into post-conflict societies, peace processes are typically informed by a sharply realist power politics. It is surely no coincidence that the very first peace process was born out of a US administration whose key foreign policy figure was that doyen of realist diplomacy, Henry Kissinger (Quandt, 2001). Third, whereas peacebuilding is concerned, relatively narrowly, with transplanting templates for social and economic reconstruction, peace processes are broader and more complex political phenomena, home to bewildering and unique transitional political arrangements (a Palestinian Authority, for instance, which under the Oslo peace process was responsible for administering over 200 non-contiguous pockets of West Bank territory) as well as final-status political differences which remain intractable for most of their duration. And fourth, whereas peacebuilding is usually thought of as being a 'post-conflict' activity, peace processes attempt to span the whole temporal divide between protracted conflict and sustainable peace. In all of these respects, peace processes are both distinct from and much more complex than peacebuilding.

## The liberal orthodoxy on peace processes

Given the specificity and complexity of peace processes, there are, as one might imagine, numerous ways in which economic transformations might be thought to affect them. Indeed there are five main strands to mainstream liberal thinking on the political economy of peace processes: a broad equation of economic liberalisation, globalisation and peace; a liberal functionalist understanding of the route to regional stability; a belief that globalisation is ushering in new styles of politics and identity; an emphasis on the importance of fighting poverty and supporting the economic reconstruction of war-torn societies; and a generous faith in business actors as important agents of peace and social transformation.

The belief that economic liberalism promotes peace is hardly new; indeed the idea has a powerful intellectual heritage, with Montesquieu, Kant, Cobden and Angell amongst its most celebrated advocates. But since the 1980s, it has been espoused with renewed vigour – as a plethora of policymakers and intellectuals have sought to examine, and by and large argue for, neo-liberal economic reforms. Economic liberalisation, it is argued, reduces barriers to the movement of goods and capital, increases levels of international trade and investment, deepens global interdependencies and, in turn, inspires a transformation of state and societal interests away from war towards commerce and peace. According to such arguments, there is a clear positive correlation between economic integration and peaceful inter-state relations. The existence of such a correlation is a well-established 'common-sense' within both academic (Russett and Oneal, 2001) and popular (Friedman, 2005: 515–39) liberal discourse. The moral seems abundantly clear: if states want sustainable peace, one crucial way for them to bring this about is by liberalising their economies and entering into the spirit of globalisation.

If this applies primarily at a global level, a second strand of liberal thinking – functionalism – is explicitly regional in emphasis. According to functionalists, regional cooperation on relatively insignificant 'low political' issues can create patterns of mutual interest and trust which will eventually 'spill over' into the 'high political' arena, nurturing both bilateral peace settlements and regional economic and political integration. It was just such a process, functionalists contend, which facilitated the emergence, growth and consolidation of the European Union out of those small seeds planted, in the early 1950s, by the European Coal and Steel Community (Haas, 1964; Mitrany, 1975). By the same token, it is argued, inter- and intra-state peace processes are best supported by broader processes of regional cooperation and integration – in places as disparate as the Middle East, South Asia and Northern Ireland. Thus during the early 1990s, the Israeli Foreign Minister Shimon Peres argued, in clearly functionalist terms, that the challenge was to construct a 'new Middle East', in which mutually reinforcing processes of democratisation, domestic political stabilisation, and regional economic and security cooperation would eventually effect regional political integration and sustainable bilateral peace settlements (Peres, 1993). Many other Israeli and international experts argued along similar lines, emphasising in particular the pacific effects of regional economic cooperation (Carkoğlu et al., 1998; Fishelson, 1989; Fisher et al., 1993, 1994; Merhav, 1989). In turn, the framework of the Middle East peace process was structured not only around bilateral negotiations, but additionally around a multilateral track which focused on low-level and regional issues, and oversaw a series of annual regional economic summits (Peters, 1996). In the South Asian context, similarly, Pakistani and especially Indian elites and commentators regularly identify links between the consolidation of the South Asian Association for Regional Cooperation (SAARC) and their bilateral peace process, and often depict their planned Iran–Pakistan–India gas pipeline, like the European Coal and Steel Community 50 years earlier, as a potential catalyst to regional cooperation and peace (Dixit, 2005; Khosla, 2005). Finally, in the case of Northern Ireland, it has often been argued that European integration and the resultant economic and political transformation of Britain and Ireland, and of their relations, have been crucial contextual factors behind the peace process and the winding down of 'the Troubles' (Cox, 1998; Guelke, 1988; Meehan, 2000).

The third strand within mainstream liberal thought holds that, quite aside from the direct causal impacts of commercial interdependence, globalisation is engendering various new styles of politics and identity which indirectly support peacemaking. Globalisation is thought to result in a softening of state boundaries and, in more extreme versions of this thesis, to herald their wholesale disintegration in the face of rising global flows of goods, capital and people (Ohmae, 2002). It is also often associated with increasingly pluralised structures of governance, as power is dispersed away from the sovereign state – moving both upwards to international organisations, and downwards to regional and local governments (Rosenau and Czempiel, 1992; Selby, 2003a). Finally, globalisation is also often said to inspire a decline in traditional state-centric national identities, to foster a concomitant upsurge in new forms of sub-national, ethnic and religious identities, and by contrast to stimulate the phenomenon of cosmopolitan post-nationalism (Habermas, 2001; Held, 1995). All of these supposed developments have been identified as having (or as being likely to have) profound effects upon peace processes. Thus in the South Asian context, analysts and political leaders alike have argued that the softening of state borders, courtesy of globalisation, provides an opportunity for resolution of the India–Pakistan–Kashmir dispute without the redrawing of state boundaries (Kumar, 2005). In the Middle East, Shimon Peres has argued that 'borders are irrelevant' within a global knowledge economy, and that this creates potential for the construction of a new Middle East and resolution of the Arab–Israeli conflict (Peres, 2000). In the Northern Ireland context, the expansion of the EU and its federal systems of governance are said to have reduced the significance of the question of sovereignty, and thus created space for North–South cooperation: in a post-sovereign world, it is claimed, the question of whether Northern Ireland remains part of the UK or becomes part of a united Ireland is increasingly redundant. In places as different as Ireland and the Middle East, global economic integration, the withering of state power and increased levels of cross-cultural interaction (as a result of improved communications and transport, as well as the growing size and self-confidence of diasporas) are said to lead to a decline in parochial forms of established national identity and a concomitant rise in liberal, cosmopolitan and post-national understandings of selfhood – which in turn engender a reduced commitment to nationalist narratives and struggles (on Ireland, see Hume, 1988; Kearney, 1997; on Israel, see Ezrahi, 1997; Nimni, 2003).

In the fourth strand of most contemporary liberal thinking, poverty is viewed as an accomplice to conflict, and thus as a problem that needs to be addressed for security as well as development reasons. Thomas Friedman's 'Golden Arches theory of conflict resolution' clearly illustrates the core assumptions: 'when a country reaches the level of economic development where it has a middle class big enough to support a McDonald's network, it becomes a McDonald's country', Friedman writes. 'And people in McDonald's countries don't like to fight wars anymore, they prefer to wait in line for burgers' (1999: 195). The middle class, so the argument goes, prioritise material prosperity and opportunity over war: they are an essentially peace-oriented class. The poor, by contrast, lack these opportunities, and are thus much more likely to be attracted by the lure of self-affirmation through violence: 'poverty and distress', as Peres writes of the Middle Eastern context, have given rise to 'fanaticism, fundamentalism and false messianism' (Peres, 1993: 45–6). This problem is deepened, according to liberal thinking, by the fact that protracted violent conflicts have crushing economic repercussions – typically including reduced levels of domestic and international investment; the flight of local middle classes and their capital; increased unemployment and poverty; and the growing economic importance of conflict-related and criminal activity, which in turn empower local interests dependent upon the continuation of violence and disorder. War-torn societies find themselves trapped within a vicious cycle of poverty, desperation and violence; and thus the task of foreign governments and international organisations is to help reverse these vicious dynamics into more virtuous ones, in which economic growth and stability will promote peace, and growing political stability will in turn provide the necessary foundation for ever-more sustainable economic growth. The existence of such powerful linkages between development, peace and security is now an unquestioned orthodoxy within international development and post-conflict reconstruction thinking (DFID, 2005; NORAD, 2004; SIDA, 2005; also Duffield, 2001). Indeed, together with the goal of creating functioning political institutions, the ambition of creating the foundations for sustainable economic development, and thereby peace, is the central stated aim of the contemporary liberal peacebuilding agenda.

The fifth and final strand of mainstream liberal thinking assumes that business actors are a powerful and essentially positive constituency for peace. Increased foreign and domestic private sector investment is vital, it is assumed, for societies emerging from conflict, helping those societies to reap the material rewards of peace, as well as to strengthen constituencies opposed to a return to war. Business ties are also viewed as crucial to functionalist 'spill-over', since business interactions are amongst those low-level forms of cooperation which slowly help to consolidate shared interests and understanding between erstwhile enemies. Finally, business actors' standard combination of high influence and (formal) political non-partisanship is such that they can often play, it is claimed, defining roles in formal and back-channel peace negotiations. As the Institute for Multi-Track Diplomacy has declared, typifying this orthodoxy, the 'business community has a great deal to contribute to any peace process', there being 'a natural partnership between business and peacebuilding' (IMTD, 1998; see also International Alert, 2006; Nelson, 2000; Wenger and Möckli, 2003). Or as Peres said at the 2007 World Economic Forum, during a 'feel-good' session on prospects for the Israeli–Palestinian peace process, 'the snow of Davos' is no less than 'the hope for the future' (Peres, 2007).

Such is the liberal orthodoxy on the political economy of peace processes – a series of interrelated claims which are so widely accepted, and treated as so compellingly commonsensical within global political discourse – that they are almost beyond the reach of questioning. But question them we must, for this liberal orthodoxy is almost entirely mistaken.

## The contradictions of globalisation

To start with, the liberal model of the nexus between peace and globalisation begins from the premise that economic liberalisation and globalisation create interdependencies which in turn help to forge ties of trust, interest and peace, both globally and across conflict regions. There are at least four major flaws in this model.

First, it is far from clear that there is indeed a positive relationship between commerce or economic openness on the one hand and peace or peace processes on the other. Among the world's most economically open and most globally penetrated societies are many countries in Africa, Asia and Latin America which are persistently home to civil and cross-border violence (Chossudovsky, 1997; Chua, 2004). At the other end of the economic spectrum, Great Britain during the nineteenth century and the United States during the twentieth and early twenty-first centuries have not only been the leading advocates of liberal free trade, but also the leading exponents and practitioners of war (Blum, 2006: 162–220; Carr, 1946). Close US–German economic relations during the 1930s and 1940s did little to build ties of trust and interest between the two rising hegemonic powers. Equally, the United States was the primary purchaser of Iraqi oil throughout the 1990s and early 2000s, but this hardly seems to have moderated US policy towards it. And if we consider peace processes specifically, the picture is no clearer. Peace processes have in some cases roughly coincided with periods of neo-liberal economic transformation: the Arab–Israeli peace processes of the mid-1990s followed hot on the heels of the liberalisation of Israel's capital markets (Nitzan and Bichler, 2002; Shafir and Peled, 2002), while the Northern Ireland process was likewise narrowly predated by the flood of largely US foreign investment into the Irish Republic (O'Hearn, 2001). And yet, the most startling period of liberalisation in Israel, during 2001 to 2003, coincided with heightened Israeli repression in the West Bank and Gaza and the effective cessation of the entire Arab–Israeli peace process (Peled, 2004). Similarly, Columbia and Sri Lanka have amongst the most open economies in Latin America and South Asia respectively, but neither have managed to successfully prosecute peace processes (Embuldeniya, 2003; Richani, 2002). Perhaps the best that can be said is that there is abundant counter-evidence to the liberal equation of commerce and peace.

A second problem with liberal discourse on the peace–globalisation nexus is that it is largely silent on questions of economic inequality and unevenness, and their political implications. For even if we accepted that there is indeed a generally positive relationship between commerce and peace, it would not necessarily follow that globalisation or liberalisation are inherently pacific – for the simple reason that global production, trade, investment and wealth are so unevenly distributed. Manufacturing remains heavily concentrated within Western Europe, North America and now also East Asia – the rise of the last being in many ways code for globalisation. Over 75 per cent of world trade and foreign direct investment are within or between this triad of developed capitalist regions. International income and wealth inequalities are as never before, having risen steeply since the early 1990s (Nederveen Piertese, 2002; Wade, 2004). Moreover, this highly uneven pattern becomes more striking still when one also considers the growing internal differentiation of societies and economies, especially within the post-colonial South – the growing divides between regions, between urban and rural areas, and between social classes that are the products both of economic development and of the limited capacity of state authorities, informed by neo-liberal ideas, to seriously pursue strategies of regional or social redistribution. The significance of these growing global and internal inequalities is twofold. Not only are they often a direct or indirect source of violent conflict – as in Colombia, where reduced tariffs on agricultural imports in the early 1990s led to a crisis in the small farming sector, to increased coca production, and to violent class-based conflict over its spoils (Richani, 2002); or in Indian-administered Kashmir, where the corrupt local political elite are fiscally dependent upon the Indian state, and opposed on both economic and political grounds by the majority populace of the Kashmir Valley (Bose, 2005). In addition, the unevenness of the contemporary global order is such that it is arguably characterised more by dependency than by interdependency. In the admittedly extreme case of the Israeli–Palestinian peace process, for instance, the Palestinians are dependent on Israel for most foodstuffs and manufactured goods, as well as for revenue collection; while for their part, Israel is dependent upon the Palestinians for next to nothing (West Bank and Gaza Palestinians used to constitute an important pool of cheap labour for the growing Israeli economy, but now Eastern European and Asian workers perform this function instead). Mainstream liberal thinking has it that interdependencies breed mutual trust, understanding and interests in peace. In contexts of structured economic subordination and dependency, however, this model can hardly apply.

Third, and most importantly, there is a striking contradiction between globalisation and the functionalist dream of peace through regional integration. There are good grounds for doubting whether liberal functionalist reasoning has ever had much value: even in the European case, integration was always a 'high political' project, led by France, facilitated by the occupation of Germany, within the permissive contexts both of the Cold War and of the internally homogeneous European nation-states produced through war-time genocides and post-war displacements (Judt, 2005). But if that was the case in the 1950s, then a half century later the project of peace through functional integration is even more transparently fantastic. In present-day India, for instance, while political and business leaders repeatedly emphasise in their public discourse the potential for SAARC to provide a regional context for bilateral peacemaking, the reality behind the rhetoric is actually quite different. For, quite understandably, Mumbai's or Bangalore's business elites are much more excited by the prospects for enhanced production, trade and investment ties with the United States, Europe and East Asia, than they are by the negligible benefits to be had from any rapprochement with Pakistan. In any case, while it is true that the India–Pakistan conflict prevents all but minor levels of official bilateral trade and investment, political restrictions are easily circumvented in a variety of ways: thus the Indian company Tata sells its tea in Pakistan under the name of its subsidiary, Tetley, while Indian goods destined for Pakistan are routinely shipped via, and relabelled in, Dubai (Khan, 2005). For their part, Delhi's foreign policy elites are much more preoccupied with India's place on the global stage than they are with the question of India's difficult regional relations (a May 2006 speech by India's foreign minister on India's place in the world failed to even mention Pakistan – see Saran, 2006). India's interest in regional integration is, in sum, fairly shallow. Similarly in the context of the Middle East peace process, while throughout the early and mid-1990s Israeli politicians and analysts spoke enthusiastically of the opportunities for regional integration and its potential 'spill-over' effects, the major opportunities for Israeli capital lay elsewhere. The central problem facing the Israeli corporate sector during the early 1990s was that diplomatic isolation and the secondary Arab economic boycott posed profound obstacles to the country's global penetration, making it more difficult for Israeli businesses to enter emerging markets in South and East Asia, or to attract investment from, and enter into, joint ventures with European and North American companies. Addressing this situation became a priority for Israeli business leaders, and the Oslo peace process was launched in part for this reason. Crucially, however, Israeli political and business leaders were only marginally concerned with the benefits to be had from regional economic integration: there were opportunities to be had from US-supported export processing zones in Jordan and Egypt, to be sure, but the Middle East was just too small and too heavily penetrated a market to be of any great economic significance to Israeli businesses. Much more enticing were the opportunities afforded by China, Japan, India, Europe and North America (Ben-Porat, 2005; Bouillon, 2004; Moore, 2003; Peled, 2004; Shafir and Peled, 2002). For, as both of these examples suggest, economic and political elites in the global South are generally more interested in expanding North–South ties than they are in consolidating intra-regional ones – which effectively means that there is little concrete support for the project of peace through regional integration.

Finally, it is simply not the case that globalisation is reducing the significance of borders and sovereignty, and thereby territorial disputes. For, counter-intuitively perhaps, the development of capitalism has been characterised by a social – and also spatial – differentiation of the political and economic spheres, in which political sovereignty and boundaries become more precisely defined and regulated at one and the same time that these boundaries are ever more routinely transgressed (Rosenberg, 1994, 2000). Absolute sovereignty and free trade developed together, as products and defining features of capitalist modernity, and not in opposition to one another; and equally since 1980, the increased global flows of capital and bodies that are the hallmarks of globalisation have been paralleled by a proliferation of new forms of border control, regulation and surveillance. At the extreme, the result has been the construction of towering militarised walls and electrified fences – along the US–Mexican border; around Spain's north African enclaves of Cueta and Melilla; between Indian- and Pakistani-controlled Kashmir; and most notoriously around and inside the West Bank and Gaza Strip (Davis, 2005). Such fortifications do not simply arise out of the failure of peacemaking: India's fencing of Kashmir occurred concurrently with its dialogue with Pakistan, and with its espousal of a 'soft borders' approach to the resolution of the Kashmir dispute, while the Oslo peace process was marked from its inception by an ever-tightening physical and bureaucratic 'matrix of control' of the Palestinians (Halper, 2005). Contrary to Peres's claim that a global knowledge economy is rendering borders irrelevant, the depth of contemporary conflicts and inequalities is such that – at least where states are capable of constructing and enforcing them – borders and barriers are more relevant than ever.

In view of this, the relationship between globalisation and peace processes needs radical rethinking in two ways. First, ontologically, economic liberalisation and increased global commerce do not necessarily help and may indeed hinder peace processes – because they are also paralleled by increased global and civil inequalities; because, in the global South at least, they impede regional integration; because they have been accompanied by the tightening rather than withering of borders and state sovereignty; and because, in any case, the liberal equation of commerce and peace is very much open to doubt. But second, discursively, both 'globalisation' and 'peace processes' need to be understood as narrative constructs which, to borrow from Robert Cox, are 'always for someone and for some purpose' (Cox, 1981). The discourse of 'globalisation' depicts a world in the liberal image, and through so doing can serve a whole range of functions (Cameron and Palan, 2004); more specifically, the argument that peacemaking is facilitated or rendered inevitable by globalisation, voiced so often by Peres and others, is less a statement of fact than a rhetorical positioning of peace processes on the right side of history. Equally, the discourse of 'peace processes' allows their participants to claim a commitment to the process of peacemaking, and reap great benefits in return, without necessarily having to make any substantive sacrifices – it allows their participants 'to have their cake and eat it too'. The consequences can be profound. By participating in that discursive construct called 'the Oslo peace process' during the early 1990s, Israel managed to transform itself into a dynamic high-tech globalised economy, without having to make any final status compromises with the Palestinians. Equally,

Pakistan's and India's participation in an even more fictitious 'peace process' since 2003 garnered them a degree of international space and legitimacy, without requiring them to make any progress on core issues – which, as a result, they have not. As both these cases illustrate, 'peace processes' are a means by which states can re-brand themselves in the hope of improving their position and competitive edge within the global political economy. Instead, then, of globalisation furthering peace, it may be more accurate to say that peace processes and the appearance of peace are amongst the competitive strategies of neo-liberalising states and societies in an era of global capital (Selby, 2007).

## Poverty, development and peace

So much for the liberal orthodoxy on globalisation and peace, but what of its parallel claims regarding the pacific impacts of economic development? The problems here are at least twofold.

First, contemporary liberal thinking is erroneously idealistic about the relationship between violence and development. To recall, the current orthodoxy has it that violence is an impediment to development, with severe economic consequences, and thus that the task of peacebuilding and peace processes is to transform vicious cycles of poverty and violence into virtuous ones of prosperity and peace. If only matters were so straightforward. For historically, large-scale violence has been a universal and arguably therefore necessary feature of the transition to capitalist modernity; and in the contemporary developing world, violence has been a commonplace effect and expression of those conflicts over patterns of accumulation resulting from development (e.g., Cramer, 2006; Moore, 1967). Not only that, but as the experiences of successful late- and late-late-developing societies in Europe and East Asia suggest, state power, coercion and the ensuing legitimacy offer crucial comparative developmental advantages – with internal state violence facilitating the swift destruction of traditional social structures, and geopolitical conflict and nationalism increasing the hegemonic power of development elites (e.g., Kohli, 2004; Weiss and Hobson, 1995; Woo-Cummings, 1999). Equally, in contemporary conflict zones there is plentiful evidence that violence and crisis can bring economic advantages. This is not only in contexts such as Columbia, Afghanistan or Liberia, where conflict provides a potent environment for the rise of shadow or criminalised political economies; it applies in other ways too. Thus the development of Israel's high-tech sector during the 1990s, for example, had its roots in the military industrial complex of the 1970s and IT training within particular units of the Israel Defense Forces (Levy, 1997). Equally, though very differently, Indian Jammu and Kashmir has become one of the more prosperous states in India largely on the back of federal government investment in the state – its funding of a huge security presence, plus its reconstruction programmes and annual payment of state debts – these all having been driven by political and security concerns (Habibullah, 2004). Protracted conflicts often give rise to the emergence of local political economies which, in their own terms or for certain social groups, are quite successful: in Indian Kashmir, Israeli West Bank settlements and also Northern Ireland, for instance, conflict has provided alibis for the maintenance of welfare state structures and spending that have elsewhere been largely abandoned. The usual liberal assumption, of course, is that peace ushers forth an era of peace dividends, and this may in some contexts be true; however, it is also the case that by challenging the political basis of (often quite successful) political economies of crisis, peace can be a threat to development (Cramer, 2006: 245). The benefit of peace processes in this regard is that they usually allow states to simultaneously accrue both economic peace dividends, and continued, even increased, international aid. For example, the Israeli–Egyptian peace process of the mid- and late 1970s saw both parties repeatedly demanding increased levels of military aid from the United States as a condition of accepting US proposals; equally, the Colombian peace process coincided with the start of the US Plan Colombia military intervention and aid programme – such are the contradictions of 'peace processes'!

Second, contemporary liberal thinking is overly simplistic in its understanding of which social groups support, and which tend to oppose, peace processes. For poverty is not a necessary or trans-historical cause of violence, and middle classes and business communities are not inherently pacific in inclination. Of course, poverty and worsening economic conditions can in many cases be linked to violence, but equally there are numerous counter-examples of cases where violence erupts in the contexts of rapid economic growth and declining poverty (as with the onset of the second Palestinian intifada in 2000). Likewise, while middle-class expansion can in certain cases be associated with a turn away from violence (the transformation of Sinn Fein's political strategy during the 1990s, for example, has often been linked with the expansion of Northern Ireland's Catholic middle class – Bew *et al*., 2002), in other contexts this is far from being the case. In some contexts, middle classes are the main upholders and disseminators of nationalist consensus, fearful of challenging and straying too far from accepted norms; elsewhere, as for instance in contemporary India, middle classes have been at the forefront of support for religious-nationalist parties and violence; and indeed historically, middle classes have typically provided the main leadership for revolutionary political mobilisation. The connections between class change, conflict and peace are, then, historically variable, socially specific, and decidedly not amenable to trans-historical generalisation. As if to indicate this, within a year of Friedman coining his Golden Arches Theory of Conflict Resolution, of claiming that 'no two countries that both had McDonald's has fought a war against each other', and of fretting that 'Pakistan is still – dangerously – a Macfree zone' (Friedman, 1999: 195) – Pakistan had not only attained a middle class large enough to support a

McDonald's network, but had also instigated a fourth war with India, over the heights of Kargil in the Himalayas.

Finally, similar doubts are in order about the learnings of business communities. Mainstream liberal discourse claims, to recall, that there is a natural partnership between business and peacemaking. And yet, business actors can gain in a plethora of ways from conflicts – from the opportunities they provide for illicit economic activity; from the markets they create for heightened defence and related spending; from increased inflation (which is typically uneven in its impact, allowing some actors or sectors to increase their economic power at the expense of others); and so on (Nitzan and Bichler, 2002). Moreover, corporate actors typically have a class agenda – an interest in minimising wages and limiting union activity which often leads them to ally with right-wing, nationalist and sectarian forces (see, for example, Foot, 1989, in relation to the development of sectarianism in Northern Ireland; and see also Chapter 8 of this volume). In the context of our highly mobile contemporary global economy, business people operating in conflict zones can readily relocate – this being a much easier option than entering the political fray and trying to contribute to peacemaking. Most importantly of all, corporate actors are for the most part heavily reliant upon state support and thus have a powerful interest in remaining comfortably within established nationalist consensuses. The fallacy of liberal political economy is that economic actors are properly autonomous from and opposed to the state – it being this that permits them to be a natural partner to peacemaking. The reality, of course, is very different. For instance, while Peres's overblown public rhetoric depicts 'the snow of Davos' as 'the hope for the future', the stubborn reality, as he himself has observed in interview, is that 'the [Israeli] business community benefits more from its relations with government than from peace' (Barsella, 2004: 30). As in Israel, so too elsewhere: business is not a natural partner to peace processes.

## Conclusion

In mainstream liberal thinking, economic development and globalisation are viewed as essentially pro-peace, and as pro-peace processes. This view is mistaken, first of all, because the contemporary global capitalist order does not conform to liberal ideals: corporate sectors are dependent upon states, not autonomous from them; middle classes and business communities are not inherently pacific; the global political economy is starkly and increasingly divided, including between a rich core and a subordinate periphery; and dreams of regional integration are for the most part obstructed by global inequality, opportunity and mobility. Given these and related shortcomings of liberal thinking, on balance it would be fairer to say that contemporary patterns of economic development and globalisation are impediments to peace. In addition, the liberal reasoning is mistaken because, in an ironic mirroring of classical Marxism, it is both reductionist and essentialist in its portrayal of the impacts of economic change upon patterns of war and peace – assuming that economic change determines political transformation, and that the direction of these transformations is historically and socially fixed. For while contemporary patterns of development and globalisation may (or may not) be on the whole conducive to peacemaking, the question of how these patterns play out in different contexts is a socially and historically specific one – for the simple reason that the distinct, though combined, developmental trajectories of different societies make them by and large impervious to trans-historical generalisation.

Finally, mainstream conflict resolution and peacebuilding discourse is mistakenly naïve about 'peace processes'. It is commonly assumed that peace processes involve a natural process of working towards peace, and therefore that liberal claims about the relations between economic change and peace apply with equal force to peace processes. However, peace processes are, as indicated above, historically novel phenomena, not natural or trans-historical ones; they are phenomena, moreover, which can quite readily provide breeding grounds for the entire gamut of regressive political developments. The militarisation of Israel and Egypt, the fencing of Kashmir, the creation of a ludicrously fragmented Palestinian Authority, Plan Columbia, the end of the Arab boycott without the agreement of any final peace, and much more besides, are all the products of peace processes. Peace processes, we might well say, involve simulations of peace (Selby, 2003b, 2003c, 2007). In view of this, it is not only the liberal political economy of peace processes, but also peace processes themselves that are in need of further critique.

## Acknowledgement

This chapter draws on research conducted in Israel, the West Bank and Gaza, and India and Pakistan during 2005 and 2006, as part of a UK Economic and Social Research Council funded project on 'The political economy of the Israeli-Palestinian and Indo-Pak peace processes' (RES-228-25-0010). Further information is available at: www.esrcsocietytoday.ac.uk/esrcinfocentre/viewawardpage.aspx?awardnumber=RES-228-25-0010.

## References

Barsella, Anat, 2004, *'Voice' and 'Loyalty': The Role of the Israeli Business Community in Peace-Building*, Essex Papers, No. 161, Colchester: University of Essex.

Ben-Porat, Guy, 2005, 'A new Middle East? Globalization, peace and the "double movement"', *International Relations*, Vol. 19, No. 1, pp. 39–62.

Bew, Paul, Peter Gibbon and Henry Patterson, 2002, *Northern Ireland 1921–2001: Political Forces and Social Classes*, 2nd edn, London: Serif.

Blum, William, 2006, *Rogue State: A Guide to the World's Only Superpower*, 3rd edn, London: Zed Books.

Bose, Sumantra, 2005, *Kashmir: Roots of Conflict, Paths to Peace*, Cambridge, MA: Harvard University Press.
Bouillon, Markus, 2004, *The Peace Business: Money and Power in the Palestine–Israel Conflict*, London: IB Tauris.
Boutros-Ghali, Boutros, 1992, *An Agenda for Peace: Preventive Diplomacy, Peacemaking and Peace-Keeping*, New York: United Nations.
Cameron, Angus and Ronen Palan, 2004, *The Imagined Economies of Globalization*, London: Sage.
Carkoğlu, Ali, Mine Eder and Kemal Kirişci, 1998, *The Political Economy of Regional Cooperation in the Middle East*, London: Routledge.
Carr, Edmund H., 1946, *The Twenty Years' Crisis, 1919–1939*, 2nd edn, London: Macmillan.
Chossudovsky, Michel, 1997, *The Globalisation of Poverty: Impacts of IMF and World Bank Reforms*, London: Zed Books.
Chua, Amy, 2004, *World on Fire: How Exporting Free Market Democracy Breeds Ethnic Hatred and Global Instability*, London: Arrow.
Connolly, Niamh, 2007, 'Shannon up in the air', *Sunday Business Post* (Dublin), 19 August.
Cooney, John, 2007, 'Archbishop urges more US investment in North', *Irish Independent* (Dublin), 18 August.
Cox, Michael, 1998, '"Cinderella at The Ball": explaining the end of the war in Northern Ireland', *Millennium*, Vol. 27, No. 2, pp. 325–42.
Cox, Robert, 1981, 'Social Forces, State and World Orders: Beyond International Relations Theory', *Millennium*, Vol. 10, No. 2, pp. 126–55.
Cramer, Christopher, 2006, *Civil War is Not a Stupid Thing: Accounting for Violence in Developing Countries*, London: Hurst.
Darby, John and Roger Mac Ginty, 2003, 'Conclusion: peace processes, present and future', in John Darby and Roger Mac Ginty (eds), *Contemporary Peacemaking: Conflict, Violence and Peace Processes*, Basingstoke: Palgrave, pp. 256–74.
Davis, Mike, 2005, 'The great wall of capital', in Michael Sorkin (ed.), *Against the Wall: Israel's Barrier to Peace*, New York: New Press, pp. 88–99.
DFID, 2005, *Fighting Poverty to Build a Safer World: A Strategy for Security and Development*, London: DFID.
Dixit, Kanak Mani, 2005, 'Within grasp: Persian gas for the South Asian engine', *Himal South Asian* (Nepal), July.
Duffield, Mark, 2001, *Global Governance and the New Wars: The Merging of Security and Development*, London: Zed Books.
Embuldeniya, Don, 2003, 'Corporate capital in contemporary Sri Lanka', in Ananya Reed (ed.), *Corporate Capitalism in Contemporary South Asia: Conventional Wisdoms and South Asian Realities*, Basingstoke: Palgrave, pp. 171–93.
Ezrahi, Yaron, 1997, *Rubber Bullets: Power and Conscience in Modern Israel*, London: Farrar Straus & Giroux.
Fishelson, Gideon (ed.), 1989, *Economic Cooperation in the Middle East*, Boulder, CO: Westview.
Fisher, Stanley, Dani Rodrik and Elias Tuma (eds), 1993, *The Economics of Middle East Peace: Views from the Region*, Cambridge, MA: MIT Press.
Fisher, Stanley, Leonard Hausman, Anna Karasik and Thomas Schelling (eds), 1994, *Securing Peace in the Middle East: Project on Economic Transition*, Cambridge, MA: MIT Press.
Foot, Paul, 1989, *Ireland: Why Britain Must Get Out*, London: Chatto & Windus.

Friedman, Thomas, 1999, *The Lexus and the Olive Tree*, London: HarperCollins.
Friedman, Thomas, 2005, *The World is Flat: The Globalized World in the Twenty-First Century*, London: Penguin.
Guelke, Adrian, 1988, *Northern Ireland: The International Perspective*, Dublin: Gill and Macmillan.
Guelke, Adrian, 2003, 'Negotiations and peace processes', in John Darby and Roger Mac Ginty (eds), *Contemporary Peacemaking: Conflict, Violence and Peace Processes*, Basingstoke: Palgrave, pp. 53–64.
Haas, Ernst, 1964, *Beyond the Nation-State: Functionalism and International Organization*, Stanford, CA: Stanford University Press.
Habermas, Jurgen, 2001, *The Postnational Constellation: Political Essays*, Cambridge, MA: MIT Press.
Habibullah, Wajahat, 2004, 'The Political Economy of the Kashmir Conflict: Opportunities for Peacebuilding and for US Policy', US Institute of Peace Special Report No. 121, Washington, DC.
Halper, Jeff, 2005, *Obstacles to Peace: A Reframing of the Israeli-Palestinian Conflict*, Jerusalem: Israeli Committee Against House Demolitions.
Held, David, 1995, *Democracy and the Global Order: From the Modern State to Cosmopolitan Governance*, Cambridge: Polity.
Hume, John, 1988, 'Europe of the regions', in Richard Kearney (ed.), *Across the Frontiers: Ireland in the 1990s*, Dublin: Wolfhound.
IMTD (Institute for Multi-Track Diplomacy), 1998, *Six Roles for Business in Peacebuilding*, Arlington, VA.
International Alert, 2006, *Local Business, Local Peace: The Peacebuilding Potential of the Domestic Private Sector*, London: International Alert.
Judt, Tony, 2005, *Postwar: A History of Europe since 1945*, London: Penguin.
Kearney, Richard, 1997, *Postnationalist Ireland: Politics, Culture, Philosophy*, London: Routledge.
Khan, Shaheen Rafi, 2005, *Quantifying Informal Trade between India and Pakistan*, Islamabad: Sustainable Development Policy Institute.
Khosla, I. P. (ed.), 2005, *Energy and Diplomacy*, New Delhi: Konark.
Kohli, Atul, 2004, *State Directed Development: Political Power and Industrialization in the Global Periphery*, Cambridge: Cambridge University Press.
Kumar, Radha, 2005, *Making Peace with Partition*, Delhi: Penguin.
Levy, Yagil, 1997, *Trial and Error: Israel's Route from War to De-Escalation*, Albany: State University of New York Press.
Mac Ginty, Roger, 2006, *No War, No Peace: The Rejuvenation of Stalled Peace Processes and Peace Accords*, Basingstoke: Palgrave.
Meehan, Elizabeth, 2000, '"Britain's Irish question: Britain's European question?" British-Irish relations in the context of European Union and the Belfast agreement', *Review of International Studies*, Vol. 26, No. 1, pp. 83–97.
Merhav, Meir (ed.), 1989, *Economic Cooperation and Middle East Peace*, London: Wiedenfeld & Nicholson.
Mitrany, David, 1975, *The Functional Theory of Peace*, New York: St. Martin's Press.
Moore, Barrington, 1967, *Social Origins of Dictatorship and Democracy: Lord and Peasant in the Making of the Modern World*, London: Penguin.
Moore, Pete, 2003, 'The Newest Jordan: Free Trade, Peace, and an Ace in the Hole', Middle East Report Online, 26 June (at: www.merip.org/mero/mero062603.html).
Nederveen Piertese, Jan, 2002, 'Global inequality: bringing politics back in', *Third World Quarterly*, Vol. 23, No. 6, pp. 1023–46.

Nelson, Jane, 2000, *The Business of Peace: The Private Sector as a Partner in Conflict Prevention and Resolution*, London: International Alert/International Business Leaders' Forum/Council on Economic Priorities.

Nimni, Ephraim (ed.), 2003, *The Challenge of Post-Zionism: Alternatives to Israeli Fundamentalist Politics*, London: Zed Books.

Nitzan, Jonathan and Shimshon Bichler, 2002, *The Global Political Economy of Israel*, London: Pluto.

NORAD (Norwegian Agency for Development Cooperation), 2004, *Peacebuilding: A Development Perspective*, Oslo.

O'Hearn, Denis, 2001, *The Atlantic Economy: Britain, the US and Ireland*, Manchester: Manchester University Press.

Ohmae, Kenichi, 2002, *The Borderless World: Power and Strategy in the Global Marketplace*, London: Profile.

Paris, Roland, 2002, 'International peacebuilding and the mission civilisatrice', *Review of International Studies*, Vol. 28, No. 4, pp. 637–56.

Paris, Roland, 2004, *At War's End: Building Peace After Civil Conflicts*, Cambridge: Cambridge University Press.

Peled, Yoav, 2004, 'Profits or glory? The twenty-eighth Elul of Arik Sharon', *New Left Review*, No. 29, pp. 47–70.

Peres, Shimon, 1993, *The New Middle East*, New York: Holt.

Peres, Shimon, 2000, Keynote address at the Washington Institute for Near East Policy, 15 September.

Peres, Shimon, 2007, address at World Economic Forum, Davos (at: http://gaia.world-television.com/wef/worldeconomicforum_annualmeeting2007/default.aspx?sn=19223).

Peters, Joel, 1996, *Pathways to Peace: The Multilateral Arab-Israeli Peace Talks*, London: Royal Institute of International Affairs.

Quandt, William, 2001, *Peace Process: American Diplomacy and the Arab-Israeli Conflict Since 1967*, 2nd edn, Washington, DC: Brookings Institute.

Richani, Nazih, 2002, *Systems of Violence: The Political Economy of War and Peace in Columbia*, Albany: State University of New York Press.

Richmond, Oliver P., 2005, *The Transformation of Peace*, Basingstoke: Palgrave Macmillian.

Rosenau, James and Ernesto Czempiel (eds), 1992, *Governance Without Government: Order and Change in World Politics*, Cambridge: Cambridge University Press.

Rosenberg, Justin, 1994, *The Empire of Civil Society: A Critique of the Realist Theory of International Relations*, London: Verso.

Rosenberg, Justin, 2000, *The Follies of Globalisation Theory*, London Verso.

Russett, Bruce and John Oneal, 2001, *Triangulating Peace: Democracy, Interdependence and International Organizations*, New York: W.W. Norton.

Saran, Shyam, 2006, 'India and the emerging world order', speech to the International Institute for Strategic Studies 25 May, (at: www.iiss.org/conferences/recent-key-addresses/shyam-saran-address).

Saunders, Harold, 1985, *The Other Walls: The Arab-Israeli Peace Process in a Global Perspective*, rev. edn, Princeton, NJ: Princeton University Press.

Selby, Jan, 2003a, 'Introduction' in Feargal Cochrane *et al.* (eds), *Global Governance, Conflict and Resistance*, Basingstoke: Palgrave Macmillan, pp. 1–18.

Selby, Jan, 2003b, 'Governance and resistance in Palestine: simulations, confrontations, sumoud', in Feargal Cochrane *et al.* (eds), *Global Governance, Conflict and Resistance*, Basingstoke: Palgrave Macmillan, pp. 118–34.

Selby, Jan, 2003c, 'Dressing up domination as "cooperation": the case of Israeli-Palestinian water relations', *Review of International Studies*, Vol. 29, No. 1, pp. 21–38.

Selby, Jan, 2007, 'Peace processes: a genealogy and critique', paper presented at Millennium annual conference, London, 21 October.

Shafir, Gershon and Yoav Peled (eds), 2002, *The New Israel: Peacemaking and Liberalization*, Boulder, CO: Westview.

SIDA (Swedish International Development Agency), 2005, *Promoting Peace and Security Through Development Cooperation*, Stockholm: Edita.

Wade, Robert, 2004, 'Is globalization reducing poverty and inequality?', *World Development*, Vol. 32, No. 4, pp. 567–89.

Weiss, Linda and John Hobson, 1995, *State and Economic Development: A Comparative Historical Analysis*, Cambridge: Polity.

Wenger, Andreas and Daniel Möckli, 2003, *Conflict Prevention: The Untapped Potential of the Business Sector*, Boulder, CO: Lynne Rienner.

Woo-Cummings, Meredith (ed.), 1999, *The Developmental State*, Ithaca, NY: Cornell University Press.

# 2
# The Gendered Impact of Peace[1]

*Donna Pankhurst*

Much has been written about women's experiences during wars and, after well over a decade of feminist lobbying, there has been generalised international recognition that women play key roles during wars, carrying heavy socio-economic burdens and themselves suffering casualties. Such a shift away from women being virtually invisible in analyses of conflict has been facilitated by a common understanding that so-called 'new wars' led to an increased vulnerability of civilians, and that women and children have become major casualties (Giles and Hyndman, 2004: 3–5). Nevertheless, more men than women continue to die directly from all violence in the world, as well as directly from war (Pearce, 2006; WHO, 2002). However, on average, more women than men die or suffer serious disease as a result of interstate and internationalised civil wars when the post-conflict period is included (Plümper and Neumayer, 2006: 3). Furthermore, because in the post-war context women survivors generally outnumber men as a group, they bear the greater burdens of post-war recovery (see, e.g., Turshen, 2001b: 58). In this context, and in highly varied cultural settings, women face distinct difficulties in seeking justice for crimes committed against them during wars and afterwards when they attempt to participate in 'truth and reconciliation' endeavours, and when they attempt to re-build their lives.

This chapter thus interrogates the ways in which the endings of war still often bring highly gendered, often violent, challenges from men and the state. It is split into five sections and a conclusion. The first assesses the post-war backlash against women – the attempt to force women into 'traditional' gender roles as well as the increase in gender-based violence in the post-war period. The second section focuses on the impact of the post-war political context on women, in particular the attempt to institute the rule of law. It concludes that transitional systems of justice fail to address the needs of women. This failure is also observed in post-war truth and reconciliation processes which are assessed in the third section. The fourth section outlines the struggle to enhance women's civil and political participation after war and concludes that while gains have been made, there is still much to be done. The fifth section focuses on the gender implications of post-war socio-economic policies in both rural and urban settings. The conclusion is that despite considerable institutional knowledge about the needs of women, they remain marginalised in post-war strategies.

## Post-war backlash against women

The post-conflict environment is not one in which life for women returns to 'normal' – even if a return to previous patterns of gender and social relationships were desirable or even possible. The upheaval of war, in which societies have been transformed and livelihood systems disrupted, in which women have assumed certain roles for the first time or come into contact with new ideas, has its own impact on inter-personal relationships and social expectations. Furthermore, evidence from gendered analyses of post-war situations in the former Yugoslavia, sub-Saharan Africa, Latin America, Asia and elsewhere shows that women face not only continuation of some of the aggression they endured during the war, but also new forms of violence (Rehn and Sirleaf, 2002). In the design of policies for post-war reconstruction, women's needs are often systematically ignored, and even deliberately marginalised (Cockburn, 2004: 41; El Bushra, 2004; Goldstein, 2001: 394–5; Meintjes *et al.*, 2001a).

Together, the continued and new forms of violence, and the attacks on women's newly assumed rights and behaviours, constitute what frequently amounts to a post-war backlash against women (Meintjes *et al.*, 2001b: 12; Pankhurst, 2003: 11; Pankhurst and Pearce, 1998; Turshen, 2001a: 84). This seems to be common across contrasting social, economic and geographical contexts although the specific forms vary (Meintjes *et al.*, 2001a). Two key common elements seem to be: an 'anti-women' discourse with associated restrictions on the life choices of women (El Bushra, 2004; Meintjes *et al.*, 2001b: 12–14); and violence against women which continues above pre-conflict levels and sometimes at a higher level than during war (Rehn and Sirleaf, 2002; Chapter 18 in this volume).

The backlash discourse is often about 'restoring' something associated with peace in the past – even where the change actually undermines women's rights in favour of an unambiguously male gender politics – and strongly associates women with cultural notions of 'tradition', motherhood and peace, using new and old cultural norms (Turshen, 2001a: 80).

Women can be targeted for having gained economic independence from men, for having been employed in 'male' roles, or for having adopted urban and educated lifestyles in predominantly rural societies. There are calls for them to be forced 'back' into kitchens and fields, even if they were not thus occupied in these areas before the war (Cockburn, 2004: 40). It is sometimes unclear whether these are spontaneous reactions from individual men, or orchestrated by the government (Luciak, 2001). In either case, at both social and individual levels there are forceful attempts to define women's roles and rights as secondary to those of men, and to restrict women's behaviour (Kelly, 2000: 62; Pankhurst and Pearce, 1998; Sideris, 2001a: 67).

Protests by women against such behaviour are often castigated as being 'Western-influenced' (El Bushra, 2004; Kandiyoti, 2007). In such an intense and sometimes violent moment, the state can bring to bear many of the policies used in 'normal times' to intervene in gender politics to favour men. The state becomes instrumental in enforcing controls over women's sexuality; fails to increase, or prevent a decline, in women's personal security; imposes legal, or supports social, restrictions on women's movement, access to housing, jobs and property (especially land), and marginalises women's health needs. As evidenced in Kosovo, such official policy outcomes are reinforced by the practices of international organisations which do not actively seek the opinions of women or fail to promote their interests where this might be deemed 'culturally insensitive' (Rehn and Sirleaf, 2002: 125).

Women also commonly find their contributions to the war and peace efforts marginalised in both official and popular accounts. Such backlash was experienced by women active in liberation struggles, for example in Algeria, Eritrea, Mozambique, Vietnam and Zimbabwe, where some of the women concerned had even risen to senior military ranks (Luciak, 2001; Sørenson, 1998: 37). In the post-war backlash in the Balkans, women's rights to abortion were reduced as compared with the pre-war situation. As these were wars in which mass rape was a key weapon, this constitutes a form of violence against women having to bear the consequences of giving birth to children conceived under horrific circumstances (Žarkov et al., 2007). In El Salvador, considerable social animosity and pressure was brought to bear on women who had challenged gender roles during conflict and those who wanted to continue to do so afterwards. This led many to choose a less politically active, public role. Political scandals resulting from the exposure of sexual abuse committed by Gen. Manuel Noriega in Panama and Daniel Ortega and other senior members of the Frente Sandinista de Liberacion Nacional (FSLN) in Nicaragua revealed the extensive social support that remained for condoning the sexual abuse of young girls and the social abuse and murder of women (Luciak, 2001).

A second major feature of post-war backlash is violence targeted at women, and sexual assault in particular, which often continue above the level of pre-conflict violence, and sometimes at a higher level than during war itself. After wars officially end, women continue to be raped by soldiers, policemen, former combatants (both strangers and partners) and even peacekeepers – those whose responsibility it is to safeguard and protect them in 'peace' environments (Rehn and Sirleaf, 2002; Väyrynen, 2004). In camps for refugees and the displaced, and in areas where livelihood systems have collapsed, they continue to be forced to sell sex as a means of economic survival. In addition, it is normal for domestic abuse to increase in the post-war setting, both from partners returning home from the war, and from partners who remained at home (Cheywa et al., 2004; Rehn and Sirleaf, 2002; Sørenson, 1998; Turshen, 2001a: 84). Even though men also suffer from high crime rates, as a group they are also the main perpetrators (Pearce, 2006). It has been observed, for example, that 'in Cambodia in the mid-1990s... many women – as many as 75 per cent in one study – were victims of domestic violence, often at the hands of men who... kept the small arms and light weapons they used during the war' (Rehn and Sirleaf, 2002).

The explanations offered for this backlash violence are varied, and often rather conjectural, but suffice to say that the backlash is a substantial obstacle to women's empowerment in post-war societies, particularly when added to the challenging political and socio-economic policy contexts in which women attempt to improve their post-war situations.

## Post-war political context for women

Some wars end in an atmosphere pervasive with the desire to build a new type of society, particularly where some kind of liberation struggle was fought and won (Sørenson, 1998: 41–2; Turshen, 2002: 891–2). Where gender issues were raised as part of the political agenda of the conflict (e.g., in South Africa), or where the situation of women received much attention during the conflict (e.g., in Afghanistan), there may be a greater potential for improving women's legal rights beyond the pre-war situation. Where many women gained sufficient confidence to articulate their needs during the conflict, they may be more effective campaigners and activists. Where the post-war period heralds a greater openness to learning from similar circumstances in other countries, governments may see more clearly the efficacy of supporting women. If unprecedented amounts of international funding become available, as is often the case in poor countries following a conflict, there may be external pressure for policies that support women, and funds may be directly available to women's organisations.

If women are to benefit from such opportunities, it is important to identify the strategies to promote and the issues to be given priority. These are bound to vary. Post-war contexts pose dilemmas about the extent to which they require special approaches, or merely represent normal challenges for social and economic development. Where production and communication have been devastated, and where large numbers of people have fled their homes, the need for 'exceptional' approaches to macro-policies for 'recovery', 'rehabilitation' and 'reintegration' is commonly perceived. In the political arena, there may likewise be 'exceptional' requirements, for example, for voter registration and the establishment of election machinery, and increasingly for some kind of exceptional judicial or 'truth and reconciliation' process.

Such exceptional and urgent activities may receive new streams of international funding and be given high priority by all parties. But in the immediate post-war stage, these exercises are more difficult to implement effectively since the state, so recently contested, is politically weak and its apparatus damaged or barely intact. Weakened state capacity tends to lead to outcomes that are detrimental to women's interests, thus adding to the cards stacked against them. In the absence of an effective state, these activities are largely controlled and determined from outside the country, as part of what has become known as the 'peace industry' (Pankhurst and Pearce, 1998).

Post-war administrations face the challenge of trying to (re-)build respect for human rights and for rights-based behaviour in the population at large, among former fighters, members of the security forces, and in the justice system. Despite significant improvements, women still access fewer political rights than men in the post-war context. Nurturing a human rights culture in the post-war context is complicated because all too often many of the perpetrators of abuses during the war are still at large, and may even be members of the government, the police or the armed forces. Even when perpetrators are prosecuted, these tend to be a relatively small number despite the necessary legal framework and evidence against suspects being available (Brownmiller, 1975: 31–2; Walsh, 2007). Furthermore, attempts to (re-)establish the rule of law in post-war contexts have proved extremely difficult in most places, even where large sums of money are invested, as was the case in Latin America (Seider, 2003).

Until relatively recently, women's rights in the post-war context seem to have been breached almost with complete impunity. In contexts where transitional systems of justice are used as part of a process to rebuild the rule of law, women's human rights are not given priority. For instance, the police tend to operate with a strong gender bias, even where post-war reform and political change means that men are no longer subject to arbitrary arrest and torture (Kandiyoti, 2007). It is not uncommon for women to be pressured not to report abuse by men, particularly if the men are members of key political movements, the government or where there is a shortage of men available for marriage. Where rape was widespread during war, it is extremely difficult to bring prosecutions in the post-war setting. Children's rights have been taken more seriously over the last decade, with the plight of former child soldiers receiving a great deal more attention and increasing international support, but the focus still remains on boys rather than girls. Many experiences of girls, such as sexual abuse by peacekeeping forces in Mozambique, remain hidden (Nordstrom, 1997: 15–19).

This continues despite the fact that we now have a consistent body of international jurisprudence that has established and re-affirmed rape as a war crime, a crime against humanity and an element of genocide. Much has also been learned about the actual processes required for women to access such justice frameworks in the post-war context, and particularly the lessons learned from the International Criminal Court for Yugoslavia. However, for many women access to such justice requires support from their state and knowledge of processes available to them (Walsh, 2007). For example, in the International Criminal Tribunal for Rwanda women survivors were treated poorly in the justice processes, the court gave a low priority to the prosecution of such crimes, and in some cases attempts by women to give evidence resulted in personal and material suffering on their return home (Nowrojee, 2007). This inability to address the needs of women is evident not only in transitional systems of justice, but also in post-war truth and reconciliation processes.

## Post-war truth processes, reconciliation and traditional conflict resolution

The linking of 'truth' and 'reconciliation' has become common in post-war contexts. 'Reconciliation' is about restoring congenial relationships, involving some level of forgiveness. There is considerable discussion about whether and how reconciliation might be possible (Bloomfield, 2003), but there has been virtually no discussion about 'gender reconciliation'. Women are often expected to identify themselves with reconciliation and peacebuilding interventions, in the same way that the idea of women's 'inherent peacefulness' may be co-opted or deployed to reduce hostilities during war-time (Pankhurst, 2003). But some of these interventions should be interpreted as being about reconciliation between women and men.

There have been more than 20 truth commissions since 1974 (see Hayner, 2001). Whatever their purpose, the most common abuses under-reported to truth commissions are those suffered by women, as indeed are those least prosecuted. In the South African Truth and Reconciliation Commission (TRC), although women constituted the majority of witnesses for acts of violence committed against others, only a few initially spoke about acts of sexual violence committed against themselves (Manjoo, 2007). After prompting from women activists, the TRC tried to create an enabling environment where women could feel safe to speak out; but even then, few could find the words or courage to speak publicly of sexual violation. Some women-only hearings were then held, which many women regarded as successful in addressing the problem (Goldblat and Meintjes, 1998: 29). Others that have tried to take women's concerns seriously include Peru, Sierra Leone and East Timor. However, the experience of the national TRC in Peru shows once again that it is very difficult to get testimonies from women survivors, and that the precise definition of the crime (i.e., in this case narrowly defined) dramatically affected the process of collecting evidence. In Sierra Leone and East Timor there was a greater commitment to investigating gender crimes, though there are risks that women's war experiences get restricted to sexual crimes and specifically rape (Dal Secco, 2007).

The ideal of a gender-aware truth process is not only to avoid omitting the particular sufferings of women, but also to integrate into the conflict narrative women's experiences as fighters, survivors of attack and torture, household managers and community leaders. To release such stories may require a different kind of truth process from a state commission. For example, in 2000 women's groups in Japan and neighbouring countries came together to hold an unofficial war crimes tribunal to look at the issue of sexual slavery by the Japanese army during the Second World War. Although the state failed to award compensation, it was forced to acknowledge the existence of a hidden narrative (Walsh, 2007).

Coming to terms with what happened during conflict has led people in Africa to increasingly turn to local 'traditional' processes. These mechanisms include rituals, and transfers of property and labour (individual and collective), intended to achieve a range of outcomes including retribution, compensation, forgiveness and building of trust (Pankhurst, 2002, 2003). These processes tend to reflect highly gendered local political and power relations, and by no means belong to some value-free traditional culture. They are also occurring at the same time as a process of 'retraditionalisation' in some African countries which is usually geared towards limiting women's rights (Turshen, 2001a: 80). Women are normally marginalised in practice and their needs not given any priority. Some traditional processes even have cultural roots in such practices as exchanging women as wives between different groups by way of compensation and repairing community relations, as in Afghanistan (Kandiyoti, 2007). In post-war contexts, the revival of 'traditional' practice can form part of the backlash that puts women back 'in their place'. And yet, where gender awareness is incorporated, it can be used to help build a new society. For example, the Rwandan government revived an old system of dispute resolution that had largely fallen into disuse, to assist with hearing genocide cases. The *gacaca* (community court), in its new form, has incorporated important roles for women. Among many other fundamental changes was the participation of women as judges. And the participation of women in civil and political life is a key to reducing the impact of the post-war backlash.

## Civil and political participation

Where there is a perception that women 'earned' new rights because of the war-time roles, there may be a new awareness in the post-war environment of what women can contribute politically, and of the moral imperative to let this happen. The chances of such perceptions influencing political structures are greater where there is a conscious attempt to build a 'new' society after a 'liberation', as in Nicaragua in the 1980s and in South Africa in the 1990s. It is less likely when the post-war context is dominated by a political ideology that does not recognise women's contribution or potential for public life.

In Kashmir, for example, it is unlikely that women will anticipate a moment of liberation. With the deepening of the conflict and the growing hold of religious fundamentalism among insurgents, the imposition of restrictions on women has forced them to submit to rigid patriarchal mores (Butalia, 2001). Yet even in deeply conservative environments such as Kashmir or Somalia, there can also be recognition during war-time of the ways women exercise old forms of 'influence-as-power'. In private, they may guide men's decisions; they may perform in public as singers or poets; they may give directions as elders or leaders in cultural activities; or act as informal negotiators whilst visiting kin or engaging in trade. From such gradual accretions of responsibility, the opportunity may emerge for basic legal and political rights to be developed in a post-war setting.

In the post-war situation, new constitutions and laws with radical provisions can be speedily affected; even though they initially exist only on paper, they may well be more progressive than if there had been no war or upheaval. For example, after the war of liberation in Zimbabwe, women's legal status was much improved. In Namibia and Eritrea women were given clear rights in the constitution. The establishment of formal legal rights for women is, however, only one step towards their realisation, particularly in post-conflict settings where war has been prolonged, illiteracy is widespread and access to the law may be confined to a handful of the elite. Moreover, the existence of such political rights does not protect women from a 'backlash'.

Even where the political and legal apparatus is in place to allow women to take part in political life, their level of political participation tends to remain lower than men's. They may be discouraged by the educational requirements for voter registration, or the long distance needed to travel in order to vote, as shown in a number of elections. Practical or cultural constraints, or family and community pressure, can bar women from exercising their right to vote, or to stand for elections. Similarly, attempts to encourage civil society organisations to participate in public debate, or consult with government, may marginalise the views of women if these organisations are dominated by men. Special activities to involve women may still be required and international proposals may not be implemented for many years (EC, 1995).

In El Salvador, the difficulties of building alliances and making tactical priorities around elections led to a reduction in the number of women elected after some initial success. In Nicaragua there was a greater success in getting women elected under the FSLN but women's issues were taken more seriously only after the Sandinistas lost power and the women's movement developed more autonomously. Women's groups were successful in getting gender issues written into the Guatemala peace accord in 1996, which had not been possible in the other two cases, though many had still not been implemented by 2007.

The issue of how to increase women's representation in politics remains challenging. The Beijing Platform for Action (1995) called for a 30 per cent minimum representation of women in decision-making bodies, while the UN Security Council Resolution 1325 (2000) urged the appointment of women in peace processes and subsequent political structures. There have been some striking successes in using these international frameworks to increase the representation of women. In post-war settings in particular there are sometimes opportunities for pushing forward reforms and innovative approaches where there is a coincidence between the desires of international donors and local women's groups.

Where women have gained stronger political voice through the experience of conflict, they may be able to leapfrog stages that elsewhere remain protracted. For instance in South Africa, the majority of African National Congress (ANC) leaders at the transition to democracy were men, even though gender equality was much discussed. Women fought for representation and succeeded, with the result that the first parliament of the Government of National Unity was made up of 15 per cent women in the Senate and 24 per cent in the National Assembly (Sørenson, 1998). Even in Afghanistan, the Constitutional Loya Jirga ensured that at least 19 per cent of the 500 seats went to women, who actually gained 20 per cent (Kandiyoti, 2007).

Sometimes measures to assist women's representation have been introduced post-war that would not be implemented in the donor countries promoting this agenda (Rehn and Sirleaf, 2002: 81). For instance, the UK government supported the reservation of seats for women in local and national government structures in Uganda – when women's quotas for political parties was deemed illegal in the UK (Tamale, 1999). These issues are felt across the world as women try to increase their engagement in formal politics, but in post-war societies where the conditions are ripe, changes can happen at an unprecedented rate. Rwanda offers a striking example. Elections to the national assembly in 2003 delivered 49 per cent of the seats to women, a higher proportion than in any OECD country, reflecting the high proportion of women among genocide survivors. Nonetheless, this massive change was by no means demographically inevitable, and will have consequences for political life in Rwanda that are as yet too early to judge.

## The gendered impact of post-war socio-economic policies

It is normal at the end of war to find women heavily represented in the most marginalised sections of society. They are the returnees with access to the fewest resources, the ex-combatants who tend to be overlooked, the heads of household with least support. Women tend to predominate in the most stigmatised and disadvantaged groups: rape survivors, orphans, disabled people and widows (who may constitute up to 30 per cent of a post-war population;

Sørensen, 1998: 38). They generally tend to be the least well-trained and educated, whether in urban or rural areas, and have specific health needs that are overlooked.

In spite of rhetoric, and even sincere political commitment, regarding support for women, macro-level policies for the post-war context tend to ignore what women are trying to do, or are designed to stop them doing it. For instance, many women continue with war-time economic strategies involving small-scale trade in the informal economy; such strategies tend to be ignored as being unsustainable or unimportant, rather than being evaluated as providing an important service, let alone the potential for successful business growth. In Mozambique, the post-war government restricted the informal 'grassroots economy', on which women had come to depend (Chingono, 2001: 116). Similarly, women also often attempt to re-build primary education and primary healthcare services as state services collapse; but these are often pushed aside in favour of bringing in qualified professionals, who tend to be men (Sørensen, 1998).

Deniz Kandiyoti (2007) shows how external donors have misunderstood the local cultures in Afghanistan, assuming that so-called traditions which oppress women are timeless when in fact they have a history of being contested and vary in intensity. In spite of a strong international commitment to improve the situation of women in the post-war context, women have a very difficult time trying to fight poverty and protect their livelihoods while also being subject to violence from men, including those in official positions.

At the end of most wars, health services are run-down or have collapsed entirely. High morbidity and mortality levels in a population from avoidable diseases constitute a serious development cost (Stewart and Fitzgerald, 2001: 236). However, expenditure on health has not yet been recognised by lending agencies as a high priority in considering the mechanisms for post-conflict reconstruction. Leading economists have called for public entitlements to health and education to be sustained during and after wars, as this would actually assist economic recovery, particularly as primary health and education only account for a fraction of social expenditure (Stewart and Fitzgerald, 2001: 237, 240). Virtually every report on women and conflict highlights the need for health programmes to be specifically geared towards women as a precondition for social recovery. Nonetheless, neglect of women's health needs during pregnancy, childbirth and for rape injuries tends to be common, and this neglect has a multiplier effect on their difficulties in meeting the needs of dependants and other community members, as well as undermining their ability to participate in public life.

Some general economic and social policies have more acute implications for women than others and significant change could be supported by focusing on a few key areas, depending on context. For example, where the majority of the surviving population relies on agriculture as the main source of livelihood, land reform is often crucial, and is especially important where levels of urbanisation and education are higher. Each of these sectors are explored below.

Agricultural economies are normally characterised by a strong gender bias. Women typically receive less of the income generated from their labour, and have less access to other people's labour and less control over their own, than men. Meanwhile, men are often accused of 'wasting' farm incomes in times of social change, and particularly during conflict. As a result, many women seek opportunities to sell their labour to others for very poor returns, sometimes in secret, to guarantee some minimum resources for household needs (Sørenson, 1998: 19–20; UNIFEM, 2001).

War disrupts established systems of land tenure without reference to local custom or law relating to ownership and use of land, which leaves a confused post-war land rights legacy. This happened in Mozambique, even though existing communal land tenure arrangements made the sale of land illegal (UNIFEM, 2001: 45–53).As a general pattern, women do not gain rights here and the more severe the land shortage, the more the pressure on women's rights. In many places women may be the majority of post-war adult survivors in the countryside, as in Mozambique (Chingono, 2001: 95), but discriminatory legal practices or entrenched social attitudes can prevent them from taking possession of family lands (Cockburn, 2001: 26; Meintjes *et al.*, 2001b: 16; Turshen, 2001b: 62–3). In Rwanda women were barred from claiming lands through inheritance under customary law, even though under the constitution they had the legal right to inherit. Some revisions were made to inheritance laws to try to address this problem, but these still do not provide women with secure tenure (UNIFEM, 2001: 38–44).

At the end of a conflict, there is often pressure to 'sort out' land tenure and land use from several directions. Reform promoted by international lending organisations is almost universally in favour of privatised, individual tenure arrangements. The almost universal outcome has been that women emerge with rights no stronger than previously, and frequently find them drastically reduced (Davison, 1998). There is a tendency to overlook the ways in which women accessed rights as family members, or as independent women. New land titles tend to be granted almost exclusively to men (Davison, 1998; UNIFEM, 2001), and even where there is no legal impediment to women purchasing such rights, men may actively discourage them from taking them up, as in Guatemala (UNIFEM, 2001:63).

Where women have some access in their own right, this is usually less secure than men's and often dependent on their marital status. There may also be a conscious prejudice on the part of planners involved in land allocations and titles, who may characterise rural women as poorly educated, more 'backward' than men, and therefore not as able to take advantage of land reform opportunities. Inequalities are compounded by the fact that post-war rehabilitation of agriculture (usually involving the distribution of seeds, tools and livestock) is usually organised on a household basis in which the man is always seen as the head, even where it is clear that women's agricultural production is important for food security and small-scale business (Chingono, 2001; Sørenson, 1998: 20). Undermining women's land rights and marginalising them in agrarian reform is thus unlikely to improve food security where women retain the main responsibility for meeting household food needs, especially where conflict has left them as heads of households. These gender-based impacts can also be seen in the urban context. The post-war environment provides an opportunity for states to consider employment strategies afresh, rather than merely seeking to recover the pre-war situation and 'reintegrate' returnees into a shattered economy. This is particularly important where towns and cities did not offer sufficient job opportunities before the war. Where wars are fought in the countryside, people tend to flee to urban areas, even while formal employment is severely constrained because of the disruptions of war.

With recovery, a prolonged shortage of male workers (due to death or absence) may lead to women taking up key positions and becoming a significant part of the workforce. However, this is unusual; returning men normally take up the best employment opportunities – for which on average they have better education and training (Sørensen, 1998). Cultural arguments about women's roles are often used to prevent them from trying to enter the formal sector. In some cases women's legal rights of access to employment may actually be curtailed by the state in the post-war context (Kelly, 2000: 62).

Women ex-combatants, even where they have held very responsible positions during war as in Eritrea, frequently find it harder than men to make a life in their rural homes or seek a living in town (Sørensen, 1998: 26). In the context of a backlash, they are particular targets for censure. Cultural constraints or newly coined political versions of them also keep women away from employment. The lack of adequate childcare can also be an obstacle to taking up jobs, as female ex-combatants in Eritrea found (Sørensen, 1998).

While these gender-based discriminations in the formal employment sector have a negative impact on women's lives, women's peace-time employment is predominantly in the informal economy anyway, based on trade in vegetables from the countryside, cooked food, beer, scarce goods from long-distance trade and handicrafts. These goods offer relatively quick returns for small investment and do not require access to land. In war-ravaged societies where formal trade has not yet recovered – if it had ever developed – these activities may be keeping society provisioned. Women entrepreneurs are often able to meet local urban demands for cheap food which governments cannot provide. In Somalia, for example, women have taken over men's traditional roles and became increasingly involved in economic activity, selling livestock and acquiring a virtual monopoly of the barter trade in food, clothing and other items (UNHCR, 1994). In Mozambique, they marketed fruit, fish, vegetables and beer. Yet none of these trading and retailing activities tends to be supported by post-war governments.

As part of the post-war backlash against women, their retailing can often be curtailed. Successful women may be socially castigated, their entrepreneurial activities treated as undesirable or illegal. In Zimbabwe, women created informal trade networks that spanned several countries in an attempt to supplement family incomes. However, this resulted in their being branded as prostitutes and harassed at international borders (Cheater and Gaidzanwa, 1996: 191). As they have become more successful economically, male-dominated state institutions have brought in regulations to undermine them. An alternative approach would be to investigate such activities and identify ways to support their development: many women's businesses fail due to insufficient capital and skills in business management. Relief and development organisations increasingly seek to work with women in the post-war context and are also able to offer sources of income – either as direct employment or to support women's organisations.

The last resort for women without other gainful employment is often prostitution. In post-war contexts formal and informal selling of sex flourishes, particularly where there is a market provided by international peacekeepers (Bedont, 2005) or tourists (Sørenson, 1998: 24). Post-war countries may see very fast growth in the numbers of women involved. The most effective strategy for limiting the numbers would be to support their alternative endeavours in small-scale production and trade, through the provision of training and small loans, and to ensure that they are included in general opportunities for training and education appropriate for formal sector employment. This plea has featured in major reports for many years, but women still find that they have little choice but to risk their lives in this way. Even those who are lucky enough to undergo training or education have to find ways to eat in the meantime (Rehn and Sirleaf, 2002).

## Conclusion

For more than a decade, the UN has proclaimed that women's needs deserve greater attention in the post-war context. Yet the problems, rights abuses and programme shortcomings documented in many old reports (UN, 1995–1998) remain commonplace. The plight of women during war, particularly the scale of their sexual violation, has attracted international attention, and is often used to characterise the barbarism of mankind or brutality of particular 'enemy' groups. Women's roles in working to end conflicts are increasingly celebrated – even if other roles are downplayed. As a consequence, women participants in post-war peacebuilding have been thrust into unprecedented prominence by international organisations. Yet for all this visibility, women usually remain marginal, as a group or as individuals, in peace negotiations, in consultations about post-war strategies, and in the public life of post-war societies.

The persistent reluctance of academic and policy analysts and advisers to incorporate lessons about gender analysis and embed them into policy processes in the post-war setting needs to be recorded, and further effort is needed to overcome this thoughtless, or deliberate, resistance. This can itself be seen as part of the backlash against women, helping to allow, if not facilitate, the playing out of intense gender politics in households, communities and the wider world. Feminist histories of conflicts, and feminist studies of development, provide a rich store of relevant experiences, both positive and negative. These have been collated and analysed for several years and comprise a significant literature; but they are still not taken sufficiently seriously by many international actors in post-war contexts.

In the future it is to be hoped that international agencies and donors will be better prepared to take opportunities to put these lessons about how to mitigate injustices for women centre-stage when advising and supporting the post-war recovery programmes – in political, governance, economic and social spheres alike. It is also to be hoped that post-war governments will more readily see the advantages in developing policies that not only support women's efforts to survive, but enable them to fulfil their potential in helping rebuild their societies closer to the image of gender equality and to move further away from a 'gendered peace'.

## Note

1. This chapter is largely based on a previous publication by the author, 'Introduction: Gendered War and Peace' (2007) in Pankhurst, D. (ed.) *Gendered Peace. Women's Struggles for Post-War Justice and Reconciliation*, New York and London: Routledge.

## References

Bedont, Barbara, 2005, 'The Renewed Popularity of the Rule of Law: Implications for Women, Impunity, and Peacekeeping', in Mazurana *et al.* (eds), *Gender, Conflict, and Peacekeeping*, Lanham, MD: Rowman & Littlefield.

Bloomfield, David, Teresa Barnes and Luc Huyse (eds), 2003, *Reconciliation After Violent Conflict. A Handbook*, Stockholm: International Institute for Democracy and Electoral Assistance.

Brownmiller, Susan, 1975, *Against Our Will. Men, Women and Rape*, New York: Simon & Schuster.

Butalia, Urvashi, 2001, 'Women and Communal Conflict: New Challenges for the Women's Movement in India', in Caroline Moser and Fiona C. Clark (eds), *Victims, Perpetrators Or Actors? Gender, Armed Conflict and Political Violence*, London: Zed Books.

Cheater, Angela P. and Rudo B. Gaidzanwa, 1996, 'Citizenship in Neo-Patrilineal States: Gender and Mobility in Southern Africa', *Journal of Southern African Studies*, Vol. 22, No. 2, pp. 189–200.
Cheywa, Spindel, Elisa Levy and Melissa Connor, 2004, *With an End In Sight. Strategies from the UNIFEM Trust Fund to Eliminate Violence Against Women*, New York: UNIFEM.
Chingono, Mark, 2001, 'Mozambique: War, Economic Change and Development in Manica Province, 1982–1992', in Frances Stewart and Valpy Fitzgerald (eds), *War and Underdevelopment*, Vol. 2, Oxford: Oxford University Press.
Cockburn, Cynthia, 2001, 'The Gendered Dynamics of Armed Conflict and Political Violence', in Caroline Moser and Fiona C. Clark (eds), *Victims, Perpetrators Or Actors? Gender, Armed Conflict and Political Violence*, London: Zed Books.
Cockburn, Cynthia, 2004, 'The Continuum of Violence: A Gender Perspective on War and Peace', in Wenona Giles and Jennifer Hyndman (eds), *Sites of Violence. Gender and Conflict Zones*, Berkley, CA: University of California Press.
Dal Secco, Alessandra, 2007, 'Truth and Reconciliation Commissions and Gender Justice', in Donna Pankhurst (ed.), *Gendered Peace. Women's Struggles for Post-War Reconciliation and Justice*, New York: Routledge.
Dubravka Zarkov, D., R. Drezgic and T. Djuric-Kuzmanovic, 2007 'Gendered War, Gendered Peace: Violent Conflict in the Balkans and its Consequences', in Donna Pankhurst (ed.), *Gendered Peace. Women's Search for Post-war Justice and Reconciliation*, London: Routledge, pp. 265–91.
EC (European Council), 1995, *Integrating Gender Issues in Development Cooperation*, Brussels.
El Bushra, Judy, 2004, 'Fused in Combat: Gender Relations and Armed Combat', in Haleh Afshar and Deborah Eade (eds), *Development, Women and War. Feminist Perspectives*, Oxford: Oxfam.
Giles, Wenona and Jennifer Hyndman, 2004, 'Introduction. Gender and Conflict in a Global Context', in Wenona Giles and Jennifer Hyndman (eds) *Sites of Violence. Gender and Conflict Zones*, Berkley, CA: University of California Press.
Goldblatt, Beth and Sheila Meintjes, 1998, 'South African Women Demand the Truth', in Meredeth Turshen and Clotilde Twagiramariya (eds), *What Women Do In Wartime. Gender and Conflict in Africa*, London: Zed Books.
Goldstein, Joshua S., 2001, *War and Gender*, Cambridge: Cambridge University Press.
Hayner, Priscilla B., 2001, *Unspeakable Truths. Confronting State Terror and Atrocity*, London: Routledge.
Kandiyoti, Deniz, 2007, 'The Politics of Gender and Reconstruction in Afghanistan', in Donna Pankhurst (ed.), *Gendered Peace. Women's Struggles for Post-War Reconciliation and Justice*, New York: Routledge.
Kelly, Liz, 2000, 'Wars Against Women: Sexual Violence, Sexual Politics and the Militarised State', in Susie Jacobs, Ruth Jacobson and Jennifer Marchbank (eds), *States of Conflict. Gender, Violence and Resistance*, London: Zed Books.
Luciak, Ilja A., 2001, *After the Revolution: Gender and Democracy in El Salvador, Nicaragua, and Guatemala*, Baltimore, MD: Johns Hopkins University Press.
Manjoo, Rashida, 2007, 'Gender Injustice and The South African Truth and Reconciliation Commission', in Donna Pankhurst (ed.), *Gendered Peace. Women's Struggles for Post-War Reconciliation and Justice*, New York: Routledge.
Meintjes, Sheila, Anu Pillay and Meredeth Turshen (eds), 2001a, *The Aftermath. Women in Post-conflict Transformation*, London: Zed Books.

Meintjes, Sheila, Anu Pillay and Meredeth Turshen, 2001b, 'There is No Aftermath for Women', in Sheila Meintjes, Anu Pillay and Meredeth Turshen (eds), *The Aftermath. Women in Post-conflict Transformation*, London: Zed Books.
Nordstrom, Carolyn, 1997, *Girls and Warzones. Troubling Questions*, Uppsala: Life and Peace Institute.
Nowrojee, Binaifer, 2007, ' "Your Justice is too Slow". Will the International Criminal Tribunal for Rwanda Fail Rwanda's Rape Victims?', in Donna Pankhurst (ed.), *Gendered Peace. Women's Struggles for Post-War Reconciliation and Justice*, New York: Routledge.
Pankhurst, Donna and Jenny Pearce, 1998, 'Engendering the Analysis of Conflict: Perspectives from the South', in Haleh Afshar (ed.), *Women and Empowerment*, New York: Routledge.
Pankhurst, Donna, 2002, 'Making a Difference? The Inclusion of Gender into Conflict Management Policies', in Marianne Braig and Sonja Wölte (eds), *Common Ground or Mutual Exclusion?* London: Zed Books.
Pankhurst, Donna, 2003, 'The "Sex War" and Other Wars: Towards a Feminist Approach to Peacebuilding', *Development In Practice*, Vol. 13, Nos. 2 & 3, pp. 154–76.
Pankhurst, Donna (ed.), 2007, *Gendered Peace. Women's Struggles for Post-War Reconciliation and Justice*, New York: Routledge.
Pearce, Jenny, 2006, 'Bringing Violence "Back Home": Gender Socialisation and the Transmission of Violence Through Time and Space', *Global Civil Society*, London: Sage.
Plümper, Thomas and Eric Neumayer, 2006, 'The Unequal Burden of War: The Effect of Armed Conflict on the Gender Gap in Life Expectancy', *International Organization*, Vol. 60, No. 3, pp. 723–54.
Rehn, Elisabeth and Ellen Johnson Sirleaf, 2002, *Women, War and Peace, The Independent Experts' Assessment on the Impact of Armed Conflict on Women and Women's Role in Peace-building*, New York: UNIFEM.
Seider, Rachel, 2003, 'Renegotiating "Law and Order": Judicial Reform and Citizen Responses in Post-War Guatemala', *Democratization*, Vol. 10, No. 4, pp. 137–60.
Sideris, Tina, 2001a, 'Problems of Identity, Solidarity and Reconciliation', in Sheila Meintjes, Anu Pillay and Meredeth Turshen (eds), *The Aftermath. Women in Post-conflict Transformation*, London: Zed Books.
Sørensen, Birgitte, 1998, *Women and Post-Conflict Reconstruction: Issues and Sources*, War-Torn Societies Project Occasional Paper No.3, June, UNRISD, Geneva.
Stewart, Frances and Valpy Fitzgerald, 2001, 'The Costs of War in Poor Countries: Conclusions and Policy Recommendations', in Frances Stewart and Fitzgerald Valpy (eds), *War and Underdevelopment*, Oxford: Oxford University Press, pp. 225–45.
Tamale, Sylvia, 1999, *When Hens Begin to Crow*, Kampala: Fountain Press.
Turshen, Meredeth, 1998, 'Women's War Stories', in Meredeth Turshen and Clotilde Twagiramariya (eds), *What Women Do In Wartime. Gender and Conflict in Africa*, London: Zed Books.
Turshen, Meredeth and Clotilde Twagiramariya (eds), 1998, *What Women Do In Wartime. Gender and Conflict in Africa*, London: Zed Books.
Turshen, Meredeth and Ousseina Alidou, 2000, 'Africa: Women in the Aftermath of Civil War', *Race and Class*, Vol. 41, No. 4, pp. 81–92.
Turshen, Meredeth, 2001a, 'Engendering Relations of State to Society in the Aftermath', in Sheila Meintjes, Anu Pillay and Meredeth Turshen (eds.), *The Aftermath. Women in Post-conflict Transformation*, London: Zed Books.

Turshen, Meredeth, 2001b, 'The Political Economy of Rape: An analysis of Systematic Rape and Sexual Abuse of Women During Armed Conflict in Africa', in Caroline Moser, and Fiona C. Clark (eds), *Victims, Perpetrators Or Actors? Gender, Armed Conflict and Political Violence*, London: Zed Books.

Turshen, Meredeth, 2002, 'Algerian Women in the Liberation Struggle and the Civil War: From Active Participants to Passive Victims', *Social Research*, Vol. 69, No. 3, pp. 889–911.

UN, 1995, *Platform for Action*, Beijing.

UN, 1996, *Report on the World Conference to Review and Appraise the Achievements of the United Nations Decade for Women: Equality, Development and Peace*.

UN, 1997, *Report of Expert Group Meeting on Adolescent Girls and Their Rights*.

UN, 1998, *Resolution on Women and Armed Conflict*, Commission for the Status of Women.

UN High Commission for Refugees (UNHCR), 1994, 'Women in Somalia', *Refugee Survey Quarterly*, Vol. 13, Nos 2&3, pp. 92–115.

UNIFEM, 2001, *Women's Land and Property Rights in Situations of Conflict and Reconstruction*.

Väyrynen, Tarja, 2004, 'Gender and UN Peace Operations: The Confines of Modernity', *International Peacekeeping*, Vol. 11, No. 1, pp. 125–43.

Walsh, Martha, 2007, 'Gendering International Justice: Progress and Pitfalls at International Criminal Tribunals', in Donna Pankhurst (ed.), *Gendered Peace. Women's Struggles for Post-War Reconciliation and Justice*, New York: Routledge.

World Health Organisation, 2002, *World Report on Violence and Health*, World Health Organisation: Geneva.

# 3
# Neoliberalism Versus Peacebuilding in Iraq

*Eric Herring*

The notion of peacebuilding, and within that ensuring sustained peace by economic means, is attracting increasing attention in international policy circles, including the UN. A critical literature has developed in response which argues that the practice of international peacebuilding in recent years has mostly been a neocolonial top-down imposition of a liberal peace which favours business over labour and welfare and which ignores public preferences (e.g., Pugh, 2006; Richmond, 2006; Turner and Pugh, 2006). The critical literature also argues that international practice has failed to demonstrate in places such as Afghanistan any real capability to conceptualise – never mind carry out effectively – peacebuilding through economic means (Goodhand, 2002).

This chapter broadly endorses those critical views and builds on them in several ways. First, it shows that building peace through economic means in Iraq continues to be at most a vague, unfulfilled aspiration rather than a serious policy instrument. Second, it argues that, in the case of Iraq, peace is being subordinated by the United States and key institutions of global governance to an attempt to impose a neoliberal political economy, with that attempt experiencing major setbacks. Third, it argues for more of a distinction between liberalism and neoliberalism. While the two are related and indeed overlapping, the most negative – anti-labour, anti-welfare and anti-democratic – aspects of economic policy in Iraq are associated mainly with the latter. Recommendations such as working with, rather than against, organised labour on the grounds that it will contribute more to building a political economy of peace are pointless when the policies are not mistaken and when the goal is not peace but neoliberal objectives such as the defeat of organised labour. Fourth, it argues for giving more thought to presenting a dynamic picture of the struggle for and against neoliberal peacebuilding and the inclusions and exclusions which that struggle produces. Finally, it shows that economic peacebuilding is as much about counter-insurgent war as it is about peace.

## Peacebuilding as an instrument of liberal global governance

The theory and practice of peacebuilding has developed primarily as an instrument of liberal global governance. Liberal is defined here as a formal and informal commitment to principles and practices of individual rights and responsibilities in the context of equality of opportunity, the rule of law, freedom of expression and association, a mainly market economy and governments chosen in multi-party free elections. That liberalism is propagated and implemented globally above, below and at the state level, and in a governance mode, that is by a diverse range of non-state and quasi-state as well as state actors. A substantial, though variable, amount of state ownership of industry, economic regulation and planning and social welfare have been a routine part of the class compromise between capital and labour to stabilise liberal governance (Harvey, 2005: 10–12). However, such features resulting in what is usually termed 'embedded liberalism' (Ruggie, 1982, 2003) are not necessarily part of liberal governance and all these features are targeted for dismantling by the neoliberal project.

In this context, peacebuilding is in effect defined as a deliberate attempt to create the sustained non-use of physical violence to achieve social and political objectives (especially non-liberal ones, with violence being an instrument of liberal governance that is accepted in principle even if disputed in particular cases). The idea of peacebuilding has long been a staple of liberal peace activists and is now attracting increasing attention in global governance forums, most notably the UN. In March 2005, then UN Secretary-General Kofi Annan in his report *In Larger Freedom* called for a new UN Peacebuilding Commission to help countries make 'the transition from war to lasting peace' (Annan, 2005: para. 114): it was established the following year.

While the US government has remained immune to explicit discourses of 'peacebuilding', economic or otherwise, in relation to Iraq, consideration has been given in liberal governance circles to the economic aspects of creating lasting peace (US DoS, 2007: 2). This follows on from concern about the problems posed by war economies in two senses – economic activities on which combatants rely to support their war effort, and, more perniciously, economic activity that is dependent on the continuation of war. In this context, war is defined loosely so as to include violence for primarily economic rather than political purposes, a distinction which is often difficult to make in practice. The economic dimension of peacebuilding is then defined in the liberal framing as giving people an economic stake in peace rather than war that is sufficient in scale or type to make war less likely. Those exploring the economic aspect of peacebuilding in Iraq explicitly are mainly think tanks and humanitarian NGOs. The US Institute of Peace (USIP) was granted $10 million in Congress in 2003 with the explicit goal of promoting peacebuilding in Iraq, but its focus has not primarily been on economic issues

(USIP, 2005). In contrast, the Iraq Peace and Development Working Group (IPDWG) of NGOs is arguing for much greater weight to be given to an economic approach to peacebuilding and claims that it can be vital in ending conflict (EPIC, 2007). The contrast between their approaches emphasises the lack of any agreed idea of what peacebuilding is, how it works or how it relates to contemporary trends in the global political economy.

## Peacebuilding, neoliberalism and exclusion

Peacebuilding takes place not in a vacuum but in the context of broader trends in political economy. In contemporary world politics, the main trends are, in sum, a shift from welfare to competition (or, synonymously, neoliberal) economies, with a significant proportion of humanity excluded from most of the material gains of either and reduced to self-help or 'bare life' (Agamben, 1998; Duffield, 2005, 2007; Harvey, 2000, 2003, 2005; Jessop, 2002, 2003).

The models of welfare and competition political economies have been set out superbly by Bob Jessop in particular (2002, 2003). In a welfare political economy in the advanced industrial world, the state aims for full employment and promotes it through government spending, demand management and regulation of collective bargaining between workers and employers in relatively closed national economies. The state promotes labour's acceptance of capital by encouraging consumption and providing welfare. Policymaking, including planning, regulation of business and correcting market failure, is primarily the affair of national governments. In a competition political economy, the state promotes flexibility, innovation and productivity in business and labour through incentives such as tax cuts, deregulation and privatisation. The dominant goal is competitiveness in markets that are never fully free. Many social factors such as skills, defined broadly, are seen as vital to competitiveness, and the value of social policies such as education is measured primarily in relation to their perceived contribution to the economic sphere. Similarly, social welfare is seen decreasingly as a right and more as a means to promote competitiveness, with social welfare that seems to discourage or not contribute to competitiveness stigmatised or eliminated (see Chapter 16 in this volume). Policymaking occurs at and across many levels – sub-national, national, regional and global – and with non-state and quasi-state actors as well as the state playing major policy roles. This multi-levelled governance does not herald the weakening of the state but instead its transformation. From this perspective, under neoliberalism, the state per se remains a central but transformed actor, rather than being transcended or merely weakened, as some perspectives on globalisation argue. Furthermore, the state seeks to exercise 'metagovernance', that is, influence over governance (Jessop, 2002: ch. 6) to secure a new class compromise through legitimation and material benefits.

This is not a simple, standardised transition with an end point. Different states have different national characteristics, different places within the global capitalist system and powerful dynamics that interact with these processes but are significantly independent from them and may overwhelm them, possibly for a long time. In addition, neoliberalism is itself evolving, with the replacement at the end of the 1990s of what was known as 'the Washington consensus' of structural adjustment (privatisation, deregulation and cuts in state spending) with 'the post-Washington consensus', which places a much greater emphasis on a role for the state and on social change and control to internalise acceptance of neoliberalism (Duffield, 2007: 98, 166–7). In the case of Iraq, there are many important features not captured in the phrase 'transition from a welfare to a competition political economy'. Before the invasion, Iraq was characterised by a state that, due to its oil income, was able to rely on bribes, extreme repression and towards the end increased tribalism and religiosity to stay in control. This created a huge challenge for any effort to transform its extensive but warped state-owned industries and state welfare provision, further distorted and undermined by corruption and many years of war and sanctions. Since the invasion, Iraq has become a fragmented state – that is, one in which actors dispute where overall political authority lies and in which there are no agreed procedures for resolving such disputes (Herring and Rangwala, 2006) – with myriad power struggles. This has created tremendous problems for efforts to neoliberalise Iraq as there is no coherent state to carry out that project.

While efforts to socialise the Iraqi elite into neoliberalism continue, those actors who control elements of the state and Iraqi governance more generally still have a major role in interpreting and applying it at national level, and in exercising tactical and strategic judgements about what serves their own interests. Neoliberal ideas and policies have to interact with Iraq's mix of secular and Islamic beliefs (on Islam and capitalism more generally, see Tripp, 2006). All of this is deeply intertwined with insurgent, sectarian, militia, criminal and Coalition violence so that disruption and instability is widespread. On top of this, the implications of US forces being withdrawn from combat in Iraq, even withdrawn entirely, are potentially dramatic and could lead in a number of different directions. Herbert Docena's newspaper article, 'How the US Got its Neoliberal Way in Iraq' (Docena, 2005), tracked a succession of drafts of the proposed new Iraqi constitution adopted by referendum in October 2005. It showed that the United States had managed to steer it away from initial commitments to state ownership of industry and natural resources, social justice and comprehensive economic rights and towards neoliberal ideas of privatisation, deregulation, free movement of capital and elimination of state subsidies. The Political Office for the Iraqi Resistance, announced in July 2007 as the political front of some of the largest Iraqi insurgent groups, stated that all agreements and institutions established as a product of the occupation would be repudiated (Milne, 2007). Thus far, relations between the mainly 'Sunni Arab Awakening' militias (which in 2007 accepted US arms and money to fight the Islamic State of Iraq) have generally been hostile: there is little sign of an accommodation with the Iraqi state (Spiegel, 2008). Hence the neoliberal constitution put in place in 2005 could be ripped up and replaced. That said, whatever political system emerges from the current conflict will have to interact with a significantly though unevenly neoliberal global economy.

Altogether, the road to a neoliberal Iraq is inevitably distinctive and, due to the characteristics of its situation with violent upheaval under way, particularly uncertain. The two ideal types – welfare system and competition system – have been discussed above in terms of their inclusive dimensions, that is, the ways that society is integrated into them. However, the battles for and between them can also result, intentionally and unintentionally, in exclusions. Mark Duffield argues that the contemporary project of development is now limited to ensuring that populations in the less developed world are mostly required to attempt to be 'self-reliant in terms of basic economic and welfare needs', while the developed world generally retains for itself 'the life-supporting technologies associated with mass society' (Duffield, 2005: 141, 2007). Similarly, Vanessa Pupavac (2005) argues that development now takes the form of 'therapeutic governance' in which the less developed world is assisted in coping with, and policed to enforce its acceptance of, marginalisation from capitalist production, consumption and welfare. Neil Cooper (2006) provides a complementary critique of 'chimeric governance' which claims to be enriching the poor and securing the rich but is actually doing neither. To this can usefully be added the category of bare life (Agamben, 1998). To be reduced to bare life is to be stripped of all rights, even the right and meaning of self-help. A person or group reduced to bare life can be acted upon by others who assert their right to do so without accepting any responsibility to that person or group.

A valuable contribution has been made by these authors in drawing attention to the exclusionary aspects of contemporary capitalism. However, the current operation of capitalism in the less developed world is not always primarily reducible to these exclusions. The fundamental logic of capitalism is the intensification and extension of the monetisation of human relations for the purpose of protecting and promoting profit. Keeping much of humanity marginalised is dysfunctional to that overall logic even if it is functional in particular places and at particular times for fractions of capital and/or elements of the systems of governance of which it is a part. Marginalisation may sometimes be what occurs but it is sub-optimal, and so this creates a systemic incentive to probe for new and profitable inclusions. On some measures Iraq has in the last few years slid towards the bottom of the developmental heap, but the pattern is a mixed one of capitalist inclusion and exclusion.

We need a much better understanding of the paths to inclusion versus exclusion, and hence what can be done to influence them in desirable directions. As a necessary first step, this chapter reframes these ideas of exclusion into an overall picture of the dynamics of contemporary capitalism and explaining major changes in it and providing ideas around which to map the ebb and flow of these spaces and relations.

The UK, United States, Iraq and Somalia are located at various places in the spheres of welfare, competition, self-help and bare life, and in relation to the degree to which their populations are included in or excluded from contemporary capitalist welfare and competition. Clearly, locating the political economies of particular states at specific points on such a representation can only be approximate. Furthermore, it does not consider their trajectories over time, and even if the general tendency is towards neoliberal competition, within that various sectors of society will be heading in different directions. Nevertheless, it helps to draw attention to the big picture: to give one simple measure, in 2002 there were almost 300 doctors for every 100,000 US citizens whereas Somalis only had 2, with large variation in the number of doctors from least to most developed countries (UNCTAD, 2007: 150). The figure for Iraq in mid-2007 was approximately 100 doctors per 100,000 citizens, calculated on the basis of figures in the Brookings Institution's *Iraq Index* (O'Hanlon and Campbell, 2007: 46).

The United States is the furthest down the road towards a society included in a competition system, with the UK retaining much more in terms of welfare. Iraq, too, has welfare systems (though of a different sort, such as food rations) but these are reaching the population to only a limited extent and the competition economy is failing to include more than half of the potential Iraqi workforce, as discussed further below. Somalia, the kind of society Duffield, Pupavac and Cooper seem to have in mind, is even further failed by contemporary capitalism, with self-help routines and even larger numbers of people than those in Iraq reduced to mere physical survival. A 2005 UK Department for International Development (DFID) study lists 46 low income 'fragile states', concentrated mainly in Africa, Southeast Asia and the Pacific, which it defines as 'those where the government cannot or will not deliver core functions to the majority of its people, including the poor' (UK DFID, 2005: 7). The word 'neoliberalism' is entirely absent from the study, as if the dominant economic ideology could not possibly have been a major factor in the existence of this disastrous exclusion.

Inclusion and exclusion can be measured in four ways. The first measure is the proportion of the population covered by welfare measures or able to participate in the competition economy. All Iraqis are entitled to food rations and fuel prices are subsidised. However, the internally displaced are forced to rely on emergency relief for basic needs, and, with unemployment extremely high, exclusion from the competition economy is the norm, even taking into account the informal economy. In 2007, 80 per cent of Iraqis did not have effective sanitation, 70 per cent did not have regular access to clean water, and 40 per cent lacked access to the Public Distribution System (PDS) of food and basic cleaning materials (WFP, 2007; WHO, 2007; O'Hanlon and Campbell, 2007: 45–47). Although some estimates of unemployment were much lower, the Iraqi Planning Ministry's range of 60–70 per cent was confirmed in a poll in February 2007, in which 59 per cent of those of working age said that they were unemployed (35 per cent of men and 84 per cent of women) and 32 per cent said no one in their household was employed (ORB, 2007: 67–68; O'Hanlon, J., 2007: p. 40; IRIN, 2007c).

The UN High Commissioner for Refugees (UNHCR) estimated that, by mid-2007, about 2 million Iraqis had fled the country, mainly to Jordan and Syria and also to Egypt, with another 2 million displaced within Iraq's borders. Most of the displacement has occurred since the invasion and especially since the 22 February 2006 bombing of the al-Askariya Shi'a shrine in Samarra, 60 miles north of Baghdad, which triggered a wave of sectarian attacks and intimidation (IRIN, 2007d). Although 300,000 Iraqis did return in the first two years after the invasion, returnees have been rare. Tens of thousands have returned since the last quarter of 2007, but this is still a tiny percentage of the total, and the returns are as much due to poverty and visa problems as to a reduction in violence of around two-thirds (Reuters, 2008). The industrialised countries have been highly successful in shutting out Iraqi refugees since 2003. Whereas 2000 Iraqis arrive in Syria every day, the United States has taken in only 831 Iraqi refugees since it invaded (AFP, 2007a; UNHCR, 2007). By 2007, the UNHCR had managed to raise only $100 million for all Iraqi displaced persons. It reports that humanitarian agencies and Iraq's neighbouring countries are overwhelmed and unable to provide for the burns victims, torture victims or those in need of prostheses. The 750,000 Iraqi refugees in Jordan are not legally recognised as refugees, cannot work legally and have had severe problems with access to medical care and education. When they go out to work, they risk arrest and deportation and some women have resorted to working in the sex industry. Protection of women and children from violence and abuse is practically nil, and care for the psychologically traumatised is non-existent (Women's Commission, 2007).

The second measure of inclusion and exclusion is the extent of that welfare provision, or opportunity to compete, within particular sectors and across them. Since the invasion, there has been a drastic decline in welfare provision despite near-universal formal entitlement across all sectors – health, education, employment protection and pensions. Notable exclusions from employment and pension entitlement have been former senior and often middle and lower ranking Ba'thists. In 2006, 15 per cent of the population were food insecure and in desperate need of a whole range of humanitarian assistance despite receiving rations through the PDS, and about 20 per cent of children were chronically malnourished. In a move probably being replicated elsewhere, Shi'a tribes in southern Iraq are setting up their own schools to provide free education for 2000 children, due to insecurity and overcrowding caused by families displaced from elsewhere in Iraq (IRIN, 2007a). They are providing armed guards for the schools and wages for teachers, all paid for by donations by local people.

The third relates to the distribution of wealth. The more uneven it is, the more exclusionary it is, whether in relative or absolute terms, because wealth is a prerequisite for effective participation in many activities. The pattern of unequal wealth distribution that existed in pre-invasion Iraq continues, but with important changes in its composition due to new patterns of rampant corruption, incomes increased many times over for some employees and the collapse of the incomes of many others, employed and unemployed. Iraq's distribution of wealth is more equal than average in the Middle East. In 2004 the richest 20 per cent received 44 per cent of total household income while the poorest 20 per cent received 7 per cent (UNDP, 2005: 150–6). However, this is in a context of extremely low average incomes: nearly 9 million Iraqis (about one-third of the population) are living below the poverty line (cited in IFRC, 2007: 3).

The fourth examines which social groups (class, ethnic, sectarian, gender, racial, political or any others) are formally or informally able or permitted to participate. Routinely, such groups are fluid, cross-cutting and socially constructed. Ethno-sectarian cleansing, displacement by war and de-Ba'thification have all played a role in new inclusions and exclusions.

The turn to sectarian violence in Iraq is not the only factor ensuring that the idea of class, indispensable to materialist understandings of politics, has been obscured and mostly ignored in discussions of the political economy of post-invasion Iraq. The other is the ideology of neoliberalism itself (Harvey, 2005: 201–2). The role of class in Iraq was explored at length by Hanna Batatu (1978) in a landmark study – with class seen as a stratification which was essentially economic and in particular related to inequalities of wealth that generated antagonisms. Such stratifications were, and still are, multidimensional and potentially cross-cutting and can be secondary to other stratifications such as those of sect, ethnicity and tribe. There is space here only to gesture towards the significance of class and its contribution to the current crisis of the neoliberal project in Iraq. For example, in late 2004, an opinion poll found that 65 per cent of Iraqis favoured a large role for the state in the economy and a mere 5 per cent wanted its role reduced, preferences which directly contradicted the actions of the Coalition and its Iraqi appointees. At the same time another poll among Iraqi business people in Baghdad, the mainly Kurdish city of Irbil and the largely Shi'a city of Hilla south of Baghdad, found them to hold remarkably consistent views irrespective of geographical location or ethnic and sectarian differences. The new laws and regulations were supported by 68 per cent as good for their businesses and only 3 per cent thought these would cause their businesses to suffer. The polls also showed the Iraqi business class to be sceptical of the Coalition countries as business partners and providers of security, and to doubt that the political parties that the Coalition propelled to power represented the views of business (Herring and Rangwala, 2006: 233–6). These few points counter the notion of a unified transnational and US-led capitalist elite controlling Iraq. Equally, the fragmentation of political power, including the primacy of local politics since the invasion, has meant that Iraq is a long way from having a coherent national capitalist class (Herring and Rangwala, 2006: ch. 3). It is fragmented across local, tribal, ethnic, sectarian and international dimensions, with accommodations and alliances crystallising only sporadically. Furthermore, the clash between what most Iraqis want and what the business elite want, and the view of the Iraqi business elite that the Iraqi political elite does not represent it is indicative of the lack of a legitimised, stable class composition to post-invasion Iraq.

In understanding inclusion and exclusion, the distinction between insured and uninsured life is helpful, as Duffield (2005, 2007) has emphasised. Patterns of insurance inequality across states draw our attention to global inequalities, and patterns of insurance inequality within states highlight the continuing relevance of class. The population is provided with state-funded healthcare, education, unemployment benefit, insurance and pensions in ideal-type welfare systems or have sufficient income to allow them access to state-regulated private provision in some or all of these sectors in ideal-type competition systems. In the United States in 2005, about 15 per cent of the population did not have health insurance (US CB, 2007). The result of non-insurance is unnecessary deaths, in the region of 18,000 a year (US IoM, 2004). State-subsidised health care in the United States is not intended to provide full coverage of medical care for those who cannot afford, or have chosen not to take out, private health insurance. Furthermore, having healthcare insurance does not guarantee against crippling medical bills, as the insurance normally covers only some aspects of healthcare. About half of those who filed for bankruptcy in the United States in 2001 did so due to illness and medical bills, even though some 75 per cent of those medical bankrupts had health insurance (Himmelstein et al., 2005).

Insurance coverage of any kind is almost impossible to secure for most Iraqis because of their extremely low incomes, while Iraq is a lucrative source of income from foreigners for the international insurance industry (BPL Global, 2004). The five Iraqi private and two state insurance companies combined in 2004 to offer insurance which, for a fee of $35 per year, will pay out $3500 (more than twice the average annual salary for the minority who actually have work) for someone killed as a result of the violence (Dreazen, 2005). However, only about 100 of the policies were sold in the first year, and so almost all Iraqis are uninsured against this threat. Many Iraqi academics continue to flee the country for fear of being targeted by insurgents, Islamic fundamentalists, sectarian death squads and kidnap and ransom gangs. In an effort to encourage academics to stay or even return, the Iraqi Ministry of Finance in 2007 began to offer academics funds to hire private bodyguards and life insurance from the State Insurance Company (IRIN, 2007b). Neoliberalised or not, insurance is beyond the reach of most Iraqis.

## Clear, hold and build US military bases

The United States claimed to have launched a new effort to address the various economic exclusions of Iraqis as part of its 'surge' that began in January 2007, encapsulated in its counterinsurgency slogan 'clear, hold and build' (US A&MC, 2006: paras 5.51–89). Much fanfare surrounded the adoption in December 2006 of the new joint US army and marines counterinsurgency manual (US A&MC, 2006) and the appointment of counterinsurgency expert Gen. David Petraeus in January 2007 to command the Multi-National Force-Iraq (MNF-I). Despite talk about undermining the insurgency and militias by giving Iraqis an economic stake in peace, the economic dimension of peacebuilding and counterinsurgency often comes a distant second to the use of force and repression by the United States and its Iraqi allies. For example, in the first four and a half months of 2007, US aircraft dropped 237 bombs and missiles in Iraq, more than double the rate of 2006 (AP, 2007).

The United States points to the completion of various reconstruction projects in Baghdad and its plans for further projects as evidence of an economic element to the surge (Gilmore, 2007; US SIGIR, 2007: 1, 5). However, the additional US funding is tiny – $1 billion to double the number of Provincial Reconstruction Teams (PRTs). In comparison, the United States committed $22 billion of its own, and $37 billion of Iraqi, funds for reconstruction up to 2005, though much of that was wasted, lost through corruption or diverted to security spending (Herring and Rangwala, 2006: 241–5). The PRTs up to the surge had been severely hampered in their work by security problems, staff shortages and lack of cooperation between US institutions (US SIGIR, 2006). The new PRTs, the key actors in promoting the US role in economic peacebuilding outside Baghdad, had made a little progress by mid-2007 but nothing that would have a serious impact on giving Iraqis an economic stake in peace (US SIGIR, 2007: 1, 5–6). Meanwhile, the few economic gains made from the previous commitment of vastly larger funds were seeping away. In Spring 2007, the US Special Inspector General for Iraq (SIGIR) found that, in 7 out of 9 reconstruction projects it assessed, the buildings and equipment involved were being run unsustainably, mainly due to lack of maintenance and spare parts (US SIGIR, 2007: 8).

In June 2007, the US military announced what it called the Iraq-Based Industrial Zone (I-BIZ) programme to build fortified, walled zones outside its bases to service them. With the aim of encouraging Iraqis to give up violence, these were to be Iraqi and not US or other foreign businesses (AFP,

2007b). The model up to that point had been to have its bases serviced by the huge US Halliburton subsidiary, Kellogg, Brown and Root, which then brought in thousands of foreign, mainly South Asian, workers. The pilot programme was operational for two years near the Polish base of Camp Echo at Diwaniyah in al-Qadisyah province, halfway between Baghdad and Basra. The first formal zone was planned for the vast Camp Victory base at Baghdad airport, with others to be built at Camp Speicher near Tikrit, Camp Taji north of Baghdad and at Talil near Nasiriyah in Dhi Qar province north of Basra. The United States has pressed on with building these 'enduring' bases despite overwhelming Iraqi opposition. Few Iraqis would want an economic stake in these bases, and instead of being a contribution to peacebuilding they will be what one might call 'mortar magnets', attracting continual attack. The US hope is to connect its base-building with its Department of Defense Business Transformation Task Force to revive Iraq's state-owned industries (*Conservative Voice*, 2007). However, almost no progress had been made when, in July 2007, the Ministry of Industry and Minerals reported that only 10 of the country's 200 state-owned major industries were operational at all, and that 60 per cent of these were almost idle. It reported that all plans to revive them had failed and that the Ministry of Finance had refused grants or even loans to help revive them, and it has repeatedly extended 'deadlines' for foreign investment (*Azzaman*, 2007). In contrast, Iraq's war economy is flourishing.

## Flexible and structural economies of war and peace

In addition to such policies as industrial zones linked to US military bases, efforts to create a political economy of peace in Iraq include negative efforts in the sense of identifying and shutting down the insurgent and militia war economy – that is, the means used by groups to raise money to fight the existing Iraqi government, its US-led Coalition backers or each other. Prominent among these means are oil smuggling, the informal economy more generally, extortion, kidnapping, misappropriation of state revenues, donations by the Islamic faithful and diasporas and the incomes derived from the day jobs of part-time fighters. As outlined above, the US surge also includes some efforts to give people and groups an economic stake in peace. Where this economic activity could in broad terms continue, even if war became peace, it can be termed flexible or adaptable. A war economy can be thought of, in a more restrictive and demanding sense, as a situation in which the economic base of elites and the livelihoods of ordinary people depend on the continuation of armed conflict, and in which they do not have an alternative means of making a living. This is a structural or rigid political economy of war. Targeting insurgent and militia funds has been advocated by Keith Crane, a senior economist at the RAND Corporation think tank who worked for the Coalition Provisional Authority (CPA) in 2003 (Crane,

2007). However, the financial bases of those fighting the Coalition, the Iraqi government and other Iraqi non-state actors are diverse and robust (Burns and Semple, 2006; Parker and Moore, 2007). This is partly because of the phenomenon of 'embedded insurgents' – those officially employed by the Iraqi state, including its security forces, but who are actually members or supporters of insurgent and militia groups (Herring and Rangwala, 2006: 195, 197).

The notion that there could be a liberal war economy is an area of almost complete silence in the liberal peacebuilding literature. When considered at all, it is treated as deviant or marginal, the work of local and international criminals in the black or informal economy, laundering funds and goods into the formal economy. In contrast, the liberal war economy is well understood in some strands of critical thought, most explicitly in older writings focused on the notion of a military–industrial complex and the permanent war economy and also in more recent writings on war as central to globalisation (Barkawi, 2006; Melman, 1974). The financial base of the US war economy in relation to Iraq is vastly larger than that of its armed opponents. The United States was spending $10 billion per month on the war in Iraq, with $450 billion to be spent by the end of the financial year in September 2007 (US CRS, 2007).

The United States has a structural war economy in that cuts in military expenditure would have major consequences for related political actors, corporations and civilian and military personnel employed in them, leading some to see this as so entrenched as to be a permanent war economy (Melman, 2003). Whether or not this is accurate, the structural war economy is not one that particularly requires the United States to keep fighting in Iraq, where US military personnel and equipment are under severe strain. Military spending could be kept at the same levels and reallocated. Nor does access to Iraqi oil require the United States to keep fighting – even if the oil remains in state hands, Iraq will need to sell it on the international market. Instead, the United States wants to ensure that the future of Iraqi oil is a neoliberal one. The Iraqi government that the United States relies on to ensure the passage of unpopular neoliberalising oil legislation is elected, but tottering and fragmented. It survives only because of the US military presence, despite the $19 billion spent by the United States on training 346,500 personnel in the Iraqi security forces (US GAO, 2007a; US HR CAS, 2007).

## Prioritising the neoliberalisation of oil over peacebuilding

The oil issue epitomises the conflict between neoliberalism and peacebuilding in Iraq, and US prioritisation of the former. The Bush administration, mandated by Congress, requires the Iraqi government to pass legislation on the oil industry as one of its benchmarks of progress. Many US officials (including President Bush himself) represented the law approved by the Iraqi government early in 2007 and submitted to parliament for approval in July 2007 as being aimed at ensuring the equitable sharing of oil revenues among the Iraqi people (Lando, 2007b). In fact, this hydrocarbon law would regulate the development of existing and new oil fields and in particular set out the relationship between central and regional governments and the roles that foreign companies will be allowed to play. The revenue sharing law on ownership of Iraq's oil and gas resources and distribution of the revenues is even further from being finalised, and other related laws are still to be drafted (US GAO, 2007b).

The underlying trend in the draft legislation is to weaken the role of the central government in relation to regions, open space for privatisation and limit Iraq's control over foreign oil companies (Jarrar, 2007; Visser, 2007). Possible provisions are for foreign oil companies to decide production levels, be represented within state institutions, have exclusive decades-long rights to specified oil fields that shut out the Iraqi nationalised oil industry and have limitations on taxation of their profits. The terms may end up being far more favourable to foreign oil companies than is normal in comparison with other oil producers. They may also lock future Iraqi governments legally into that position, with disputes decided not nationally but by binding international arbitration. Meanwhile, the Kurdish Regional Government (KRG) has been unilaterally doing deals with foreign oil companies, and exploration is already under way. The KRG sought to formalise this in August 2007 when its parliament passed its own hydrocarbon law which put up 40 exploration blocs for tender (Howard, 2007). In addition, the Iraqi parliament passed a law in July 2007 to allow domestic and foreign companies to build refineries in Iraq while still retaining the existing state-owned refineries, at least for a time (Lando, 2007c). Both of these steps show that piecemeal oil privatisation is under way.

The laws are being written in secret with the US government and oil companies intimately involved and the Iraqi oil unions and public completely excluded (Jarrar, 2007). When the Iraqi Federation of Oil Unions (IFOU) threatened to strike unless it was allowed to participate, the Iraqi Minister for Oil, Hussein al-Shahristani, asserted that Iraq's oil unions had no right to a say in the legislation because they were unelected and illegal: the latter point is a reference to a law from the Ba'thist era from 1987 which banned unions from public enterprises (Lando, 2007e). During the period of formal occupation, the US-led CPA endorsed this law, refused to talk to the unions when it drafted new labour laws and was actively hostile to the unions (Herring and Rangwala, 2006: 228). In July 2007, the Oil Ministry formally issued a legal notice banning all cooperation with the Iraqi oil unions (Al-Ghad, 2007). Meanwhile, oil workers faced a pay cut due to the cancellation of regular bonuses by the Iraq Pipelines Company. When the oil workers in southern Iraq responded by striking, Iraqi troops surrounded the workers and warrants were issued for the arrest of the union leaders for 'sabotaging the economy' (quoted in Lando, 2007a).

The United States claims that the oil legislation is an urgently needed element of national reconciliation and is vital for raising investment funds to modernise the Iraqi oil industry. In reality, the effort to push through the legislation is proving politically divisive and Iraq is not short of investment funds – as of December 2006, Iraq had spent only 3 per cent of its oil sector capital project funds (US GAO, 2007b: 14). Over a hundred Iraqi experts on oil, economic and legal issues wrote to parliament asking it not to pass the hydrocarbon law on the grounds that a stronger role was needed for central government than the law allowed for, and that there was no need for a hydrocarbon law until constitutional issues in relation to revenue sharing were resolved (Lando, 2007d). A country-wide opinion poll conducted in July 2007 found that 63 per cent of Iraqis (32 per cent strongly) preferred Iraq's oil to be developed and produced by Iraqi state-owned companies. Only 31 per cent (10 per cent strongly) preferred foreign companies to have that role; 91 per cent thought that the Iraqi government had supplied them with no, not very much or a little information on the hydrocarbon law and 76 per cent did not feel adequately informed about it (Davidson, 2007). There were differences of emphasis but no basic disagreement across region, ethnicity and sect. Correspondingly, support grew in parliament for the view that no oil legislation should be passed until US forces had left.

## Conclusion

Contemporary peacebuilding is primarily an instrument of global liberal governance, counterinsurgency and neoliberalism. In this process, a significant portion of the world's population have to rely for their survival predominantly and often unsuccessfully on what few resources they have outside of state welfare and outside of competitive integration into the wider economy. Some have been stripped, formally or practically, of all the rights associated with social being. Millions of Iraqis have joined the excluded. The United States has led a drive to open up the Iraqi economy, and there is a growing internalisation of neoliberalism among the Iraqi political and business elites despite the clear preference among the Iraqi public for a welfare state. Economic reconstruction has stalled due to corruption, reliance on mainly US-based multinational corporations which the US government has been reluctant to regulate effectively and most of all due to insurgents and militias. However, neoliberalisation is still proceeding at arm's length, via Iraq's integration into the institutions of global governance and the push for related legislation (Herring and Rangwala, 2006: esp. ch. 5).

What is good for neoliberalism can be good for dominant interests in the United States but Iraq's armed opposition sharpened the contradictions between them painfully (Stokes, 2005). The US government increasingly urgently perceives state provision of jobs and welfare as economically necessary for countering that opposition. This was symbolised early in 2007 by a new programme to revive state-owned industries rather than privatising them or leaving them to rot (Negus, 2007). It is no coincidence that this effort is being managed by the US Department of Defense rather than a civilian branch of government. Ironically, the new policy accentuates a contradiction between the United States and its Shi'a allies in the Iraqi state apparatus, some of whom shun the state-owned industries as hangovers of the era of Ba'thism. Such pragmatic compromises are not new in US policy in Iraq, as evidenced by the PDS and continued, albeit reduced, state subsidies for fertilisers, pesticides and fuel. However, the overall trend has been a negative one for neoliberalism in Iraq, especially when compared with the high point of grand declarations of intent in mid-2003 (Herring and Rangwala, 2006: 215, 222–5).

This does not mean that the attempt to neoliberalise Iraq is over or even suspended. It is still being implemented at various levels (e.g., in keeping business taxation low and regressive, as decreed by the CPA during the period of formal occupation) and is likely to reassert itself strongly as opportunities arise. It is being implemented at huge and unevenly distributed cost in the United States. The cost to the US government of the war in Iraq thus far has been calculated at $3 trillion (Stiglitz and Bilmes, 2008). Furthermore, whatever the constellation of forces that make up Iraq's government and broader governance, the continuing question of how to engage with an increasingly neoliberal global economy remains. The conflict between US-led neoliberalism and democratic peacebuilding is at its most stark in the case of oil. Instead of being the indispensable base of peacebuilding, the Iraqi public is being shut out, and the Iraqi trade unions – the most vigorous organised section of non-sectarian, non-violent Iraqi civil society – are being branded criminal and threatened by soldiers. Nevertheless, the content of the main pieces of oil legislation is in flux, important aspects have been left vague and the ability and will of the United States and its allies in the Iraqi government to enforce acceptance of its provisions is uncertain. From this, it can be seen that the crisis of neoliberalism in Iraq is not a one-off event but a dialectical, dynamic and contingent process. There are, therefore, 'spaces of hope' (Harvey, 2000, 2005: ch. 7) for inclusive and democratic peacebuilding in Iraq: neoliberalism is not an unstoppable force. The most notable of these are Iraq's free, non-violent and non-sectarian trade union movement; the support that its views and approach have among the Iraqi public; the many concessions made by the advocates of neoliberalism; and the consistent support among most Iraqis for a non-sectarian, democratic Iraqi state with a strong central government and control of its natural resources (ORB, 2007). Furthermore, these Iraqi struggles are connected to the worldwide and multi-faceted movement challenging neoliberalism (Harvey, 2005: ch. 7).

# References

AFP (*Agence France Presse*), 2007a, 'Only 133 Iraqi Refugees Allowed in US so Far This Year', 9 July.
AFP, 2007b, 'Zones For Iraqi Industry to Support US Military', 5 June.
Agamben, Giorgio, 1998, *Homo Sacer: Sovereign Power and Bare Life*, Stanford, CA: Stanford University Press.
Al-Ghad (Amman), 2007, 'How To Ban a Union', 7 August.
Annan, Kofi, 2005, 'In Larger Freedom: Towards Development, Human Rights and Security for All', UN doc., A/59/2005, 21 March.
AP (Associated Press), 2007, 'U.S. Doubles Air Attacks in Iraq', 6 June.
*Azzaman* (London), 2007, '60% of State Industries Idle', 13 July.
Barkawi, Tarak, 2006, *Globalization and War*, Lanham, MD: Rowman & Littlefield.
Batatu, Hanna, 1978, *The Old Social Classes and the Revolutionary Movements of Iraq*, Princeton, NJ: Princeton University Press.
BPL Global, 2004, 'Insurance Brief – Insurance for Iraq: 2004', 15 July.
Burns, John F. and Kirk Semple, 2006, 'U.S. Finds Iraq Insurgency Has Funds to Sustain Itself', *The New York Times*, 25 November.
*Conservative Voice*, 2007, 'Industrialization Revitalization Continues', 21 May.
Cooper, Neil, 2006, 'Chimeric Governance and the Extension of Resource Regulation', *Conflict, Security and Development*, Vol. 6, No. 3, pp. 315–35.
Crane, Keith, 2007, 'Put Insurgents Out of Business', *Christian Science Monitor*, 29 January.
Davidson, Christina, 2007, 'Poll Tests Iraqi Support for Oil Privatization' (at: www.IraqSlogger.com), 6 August.
Docena, Herbert, 2005, 'How the US Got its Neoliberal Way in Iraq', *Asia Times* (at: www.atimes.com), 1 September.
Dreazen, Jochi J., 2005, 'As Iraqi Terror Rises, One Industry Finds Niche', *The Wall Street Journal*, 19 August.
Duffield, Mark, 2005, 'Getting Savages to Fight Barbarians: Development, Security and the Colonial Present', *Conflict, Security and Development*, Vol. 5, No. 2, pp. 141–59.
Duffield, Mark, 2007, *Development, Security and Unending War. Governing the World of Peoples*, London: Polity.
EPIC (Education for Peace in Iraq Center), 2007, 'National Groups Join with EPIC in Calling for Humanitarian, Economic Surge to Help End Iraq War', 24 July.
Gilmore, Gerry J., 2007, 'Baghdad Revives as Surge, Economic Programs Take Effect', *American Forces Press Service*, 23 July.
Goodhand, Jonathan, 2002, 'Aiding Violence or Building Peace? The Role of International Aid in Afghanistan', *Third World Quarterly*, Vol. 23, No. 5, pp. 837–59.
Harvey, David, 2000, *Spaces of Hope*, Edinburgh: Edinburgh University Press.
Harvey, David, 2003, *The New Imperialism*, Oxford: Oxford University Press.
Harvey, David, 2005, *A Brief History of Neoliberalism*, Oxford: Oxford University Press.
Herring, Eric and Glen Rangwala, 2006, *Iraq in Fragments: The Occupation and its Legacy*, London: Hurst.
Himmelstein, David U., Elizabeth Warren, Deborah Thorne and Steffie Woolhandler, 2005, 'Marketwatch: Illness and Injury as Contributors to Bankruptcy', *Health Affairs* (Bethesda, MD), 2 February.
Howard, Michael, 2007, 'The Struggle for Iraq's Oil Flares Up As Kurds Open Doors to Foreign Investors', *The Guardian*, 7 August.

IFRC (International Federation of Red Cross and Red Crescent Societies), 2007, 'Iraq: Response to Humanitarian Crisis', 18 June.
IRIN (Integrated Regional Information Networks), 2007a, 'Iraq: Local Tribes in South Set Up Schools', *ReliefWeb*, 4 June.
IRIN, 2007b, 'Iraq: Ministry to Insure and Protect Professors', 12 July.
IRIN, 2007c, 'Iraq: Jobs Fair Aims To Reduce Unemployment, Insurgency', 10 July.
IRIN, 2007d, 'Iraq: Number of IDPs Tops One Million, Says Iraqi Red Crescent', 9 July.
Jarrar, Raed, 2007, 'The New Oil Law Will Increase Violence in Iraq', *In The Middle – Raed Jarrar's Blog* (at: http://raedinthemiddle.blogspot.com), 23 April.
Jessop, Bob, 2002, *The Future of the Capitalist State*, Cambridge: Polity Press.
Jessop, Bob, 2003, 'Globalization and the National State', unpublished paper, Department of Sociology, University of Lancaster, 5 December.
Lando, Ben, 2007a, 'Oil Strikers Met by Iraqi Troops', United Press International (UPI), 6 June.
Lando, Ben, 2007b, 'US Ignorant on Iraq Oil Law', UPI, 14 June.
Lando, Ben, 2007c, 'Iraq Oil Refineries Go Private', UPI, 25 July.
Lando, Ben, 2007d, '108 Iraq Experts Call for Oil Law Change', UPI, 18 July.
Lando, Ben, 2007e, 'Shahristani: Iraq Oil Unions Not Legit', UPI, 26 July.
Melman, Seymour, 1974, *The Permanent War Economy: American Capitalism in Decline*, New York: Simon & Schuster.
Melman, Seymour, 2003, 'In the Grip of a Permanent War Economy', *CounterPunch* (Petrolia, CA) (at: www.counterpunch.org), 15 March.
Milne, Seumas, 2007, 'Insurgents Form Political Front to Plan for US Pullout', *The Guardian*, 19 July.
Negus, Steve, 2007, 'U-turn as US Tries to Revive Iraqi State Industry', *The Financial Times*, 8 March.
O'Hanlon, Michael E. and Jason H. Campbell, 2007, *Iraq Index*, 23 July (at: www.brookings.edu/saban/iraq-index.aspx).
ORB (Opinion Research Business), 2007, *Public Attitudes in Iraq – Four Years On*, March.
Parker, Christopher and Peter W. Moore, 2007, 'The War Economy of Iraq', *Middle East Report*, MER 243, Summer.
Pugh, Michael, 2006, 'Post-war Economies and the New York Dissensus', *Conflict, Security and Development*, Vol. 6, No. 3, pp. 269–89.
Pupavac, Vanessa, 2005, 'Human Security and the Rise of Global Therapeutic Governance', *Conflict, Security and Development*, Vol. 52, No. 2, pp. 161–81.
Reuters, 2008, 'Red Crescent Says 46,000 Refugees Return to Iraq End 2007', 8 January.
Richmond, Oliver P., 2006, 'The Problem of Understanding the "Liberal Peace"', *Conflict, Security and Development*, Vol. 6, No. 3, pp. 291–314.
Ruggie, John G., 1982, 'International Regimes, Transactions and Change: Embedded Liberalism in the Postwar Economic Order', *International Organization*, Vol. 36, No. 2, pp. 379–415.
Ruggie, John G., 2003, 'Taking Embedded Liberalism Global: The Corporate Connection', in David Held and Mathias Koenig-Archibugi (eds), *Taming Globalization: Frontiers of Governance*, Cambridge: Polity Press, pp. 93–129.
Spiegel, Peter, 2008, 'U.S. Shifts Sunni Strategy in Iraq', *Los Angeles Times*, 14 January.
Stiglitz, Joseph and Linda Bilmes, 2008, *The Three Trillion Dollar War: The True Cost of the Iraq Conflict*, London: Allen Lane.
Stokes, Doug, 2005, 'The Heart of Empire? Theorising US Empire in an Era of Transnational Capitalism', *Third World Quarterly*, Vol. 26, No. 2, pp. 227–46.

Tripp, Charles, 2006, *Islam and the Moral Economy: The Challenge of Capitalism*, Cambridge: Cambridge University Press.
Turner, Mandy and Michael Pugh, 2006, 'Towards a New Agenda for Transforming War Economies', *Conflict, Security and Development*, Vol. 6, No. 3, pp. 471–9.
UK DFID (Department for International Development), 2005, *Why We Need to Work More Effectively in Fragile States*.
UNCTAD (UN Conference on Trade and Development), 2007, *The Least Developed Countries Report*.
UNDP (UN Development Programme), 2005, *Iraq Living Conditions Survey 2004. Vol. II: Analytical Report*, Iraqi Ministry of Planning and Development Cooperation.
UNHCR (UN High Commissioner for Refugees), 2007, 'Iraq Displacement: Host Countries Left in the Lurch', 6 July.
US A&MC (Army and Marine Corps), 2006, *Counterinsurgency*, FM 3-24 MCWP 3-33.5, December.
US CB (Census Bureau), 2007, *Census Bureau Revises 2004 and 2005 Health Insurance Coverage Estimates*, 23 March.
US CRS (Congressional Research Service), 2007, *The Cost of Iraq, Afghanistan, and Other Global War on Terror Operations Since 9/11*, updated June 28.
US DoS (Department of State), 2007, *Iraq Weekly Status Report*, 11 July.
US GAO (Government Accountability Office), 2007a, *Stabilizing Iraq: Factors Impeding the Development of Capable Iraqi Security Forces*, 13 March.
US GAO, 2007b, *Rebuilding Iraq: Serious Challenges Impair Efforts to Restore Iraq's Oil Sector and Enact Hydrocarbon Legislation*, 18 July.
US HR CAS (House of Representatives Committee on Armed Services), 2007, *Stand Up and Be Counted: The Continuing Challenge of Building the Iraqi Security Forces*, Subcommittee on Oversight & Investigations, June.
US IoM (Institute of Medicine), 2004, 'Insuring American's Health: Principles and Recommendations', 14 January.
USIP (Institute of Peace), 2005, 'Institute Focuses on Iraq', 15 December.
US SIGIR (Special Inspector General for Iraq Reconstruction), 2006, *Status of the Provincial Reconstruction Team in Iraq*, 29 October.
US SIGIR, 2007, *Moving Beyond the IRRF*, 30 April.
Visser, Reidar, 2007, 'Iraq's Draft Oil Law: The Federal Dimension', 6 March.
WFP (World Food Programme), 2007, *Iraq – Facts and Figures*.
WHO (World Health Organisation), 2007, 'Violence Threatens Health in Iraq', 17 April.
Women's Commission (For Refugee Women and Children) 2007, ' "Terrible Things Happened To Me": Violence Against Iraqi Women and Girls', 19 June.

# Part II
# Trade

# 4
# Trading with Security: Trade Liberalisation and Conflict

*Susan Willett*

The liberal peace agenda asserts that free trade and economic integration hold out the possibility of generating greater peace and stability in conflict-prone regions (Gartzke and Li, 2003; Nowak, 2004; Russett and Oneal, 2001). In theory, international trade enables an increase in the price of labour-intensive goods and thereby raises incomes and reduces returns to capital. In this way trade is thought to have a direct effect on poverty alleviation and thus has the potential to eradicate those economic factors, such as poverty and income inequality, which contribute to societal tensions and human insecurity (DFID, 2000). A growing number of economists, however, have argued that the links between international trade, poverty reduction and conflict are neither as straightforward, nor as inevitable, as neoliberal trade theory suggests (Barbieri, 2002; Winters, 2000). Mounting evidence suggests that trade liberalisation policies have generated highly destabilising adjustment costs in least developed countries (LDCs) that have disproportionately affected the poor (Meagher, 2003; Milanović, 2005; Stiglitz, 2003; UNCTAD, 2004a; Wade, 2005). These trends have intensified social tensions, weakened already fragile states, and in worst-case scenarios have contributed to conflict (UNCTAD, 2004a). In the light of the destabilising effects of trade liberalisation, Hegre (2000) has concluded that it can facilitate the liberal peace only when full development has taken place. Despite the re-conceptualisation of underdevelopment as a 'security threat' (UN, 2004), mainstream development policies continue to prioritise the imposition of trade liberalisation, deregulation and privatisation regardless of the levels of instability in low-income countries.

The aim of this chapter is to provide a more nuanced understanding of the impact of liberal peace policies on weak and fragile states in the developing world. By focusing on the effects of trade liberalisation and its impacts on security, we go to the heart of the contemporary development–security nexus, and explode the myth that current practices in trade liberalisation, symbolised by the Washington consensus, hold the key to peace and development. For the most part, the focus here is on the LDCs, as they are most in need of both sustainable development and security. As a group they have the highest statistical risk of conflict (UNCTAD, 2004a; Collier *et al.*, 2003). It is in these countries that trade policies need to be sensitised to the particular conditions of vulnerability and weakness if trade is to enhance, rather than undermine, security for all.

## Trade liberalisation and development

Modern trade theory is built upon Ricardo's theory of comparative advantage, which contends that if countries with different advantages in products and services trade with each other, both will become better off. Even if a country has no 'absolute advantage' in what it produces, if it specialises and exports those products in which it has a relative advantage (i.e., least cost advantage), both parties will benefit. Extrapolating from this, it is argued that developing countries that specialise in trade based on their comparative advantage will generate rapid rates of economic growth enabling economic convergence with advanced 'market' economies (Sachs and Werner, 1995). The precondition for growth and convergence is trade liberalisation predicated on the removal of trade barriers.

Trade liberalisation is a critical building block of the neoliberal development model. Under the auspices of structural adjustment programmes the majority of developing countries have been pressurised into liberalising their trade. The 'distorting' practice of government interventions in the market is minimised and trade specialisation predicated upon comparative advantage actively encouraged. It is assumed that these strategies will lead to factor price equalisation between countries (the Stopler–Samuelson theorem), which should improve the real wages of labour in poor countries. In this manner it is claimed that trade liberalisation is inherently pro-poor (Dollar and Kraay, 2001).

The enthusiasm for trade liberalisation was reinforced by the export-led model of development that had so dramatically transformed the fortunes of many East Asian economies and helped to lift 400 million people out of poverty (Dollar, 1992). Production for export markets was an important catalyst in generating employment, attracting foreign direct investment (FDI), enhancing technological innovations and linking local economies into the global market place (World Bank, 1993). However, blinkered by free market ideology the World Bank chose to ignore the model of *dynamic* comparative advantage that had typified the East Asian success, and instead promoted a *static* model of comparative advantage, which encouraged LDCs to specialise in commodity export trade (Shafaeddin, 2005).

Robust evidence from the East Asian experience has shown that the dominant process in successful development is not specialisation but diversification – the expansion of capacities across a wide range of products (Wade, 2004). The static model of comparative advantage offers little opportunity for low-income economies to diversify or upgrade their economies (Shafaeddin, 2005). Rather, it has trapped many developing countries into dependency on volatile commodity markets that provide few prospects for development or growth. This model has become a 'poverty trap' caused by the inevitable deterioration in the terms of trade for commodities.

As early as 1950, the Prebisch–Singer thesis warned about the long-term structural tendency for primary commodity prices to decline *vis-à-vis* manufactured goods that would result in the loss of relative purchasing power by developing countries. Between 1980 and 2002, the terms of trade in agricultural commodities declined by more than 50 per cent in relation to manufactured goods. As a result the ratio of trade to GDP in many LDCs remained flat or declined. The cumulative loss resulting from the deteriorating terms of trade over nearly three decades for non-oil exporting African economies amounted to 119 per cent of their combined GDP in 1997 (World Bank, 2000: 21–2).

Out of 141 developing countries, 95 are more than 50 per cent dependent on commodity exports, including oil. For most sub-Saharan African countries the figure is 80 per cent. Outside of the oil sector, commodity producers have little control over world price fluctuations. The 'openness model' imposed by the international financial institutions (IFIs) has made them even more vulnerable to trade shocks (UNCTAD, 2004a). Long insensitive to the effects of greater openness on the poor, the International Monetary Fund (IMF, 2003) has had to acknowledge that exogenous shocks tend to produce prolonged recessions that increase unemployment and contribute to social and political instability. Mainstream trade economists claim that while short-term costs are unavoidable in the long run, everyone will benefit eventually (Dollar and Kraay, 2001; Sachs and Werner, 1995). Evidence for this assertion is limited (Ghose, 2001). The negative employment effects tend to be greater in LDCs than other developing countries because they have less diversified economies with fewer alternative sources of employment (Polaski, 2006).

A surge in demand for primary commodities, stimulated by India and China, appears to be benefiting many primary commodity producers. According to the UN *World Economic Situations and Prospects*, 2007, report, LDCs experienced strong economic performance during 2006 with an average growth rate of 7 per cent. An increase in South-to-South trade and financial linkages was expected to maintain the trend. Notwithstanding this dramatic improvement, most LDCs remain vulnerable to a global slowdown and to volatility in international commodity and financial markets. The terms of trade for LDCs have not improved because of the persistent downward trend in the relative prices of commodities *vis-à-vis* manufactured goods (Maizels, 1996). Higher oil prices are a critical factor militating against improved terms of trade in all but the oil exporting LDCs. And while LDCs have experienced higher rates of growth than in the past, this has not been accompanied by an expansion in employment.

Locked into a model of comparative disadvantage and plagued by unsustainable levels of debt, LDCs have been unable to break out of their commodity dependency to establish the virtuous interaction between FDI, domestic capital formation, export-led growth and poverty reduction that underpins the convergence hypothesis of the 'openness model'. For the world's poorest countries 'divergence' rather than 'convergence' has become the norm. Economic regression or stagnation, declining per capita incomes, and economic, social and political instability have become entrenched (Ghose, 2001; UNCTAD, 2004a) – all factors which have greatly increased the risk of instability and conflict in low-income economies.

## Unequal terms of trade

The structural problems encountered by primary commodity producers have been compounded by the 'dumping' of subsidised agricultural goods produced by OECD countries. According to the Food and Agriculture Organisation (FAO, 2004), agricultural prices declined by 70 per cent between 1961 and 2001. Collier and Dehn (2002) found that this trend led to an average loss of 6 per cent of GDP for LDCs between 1984 and 2002. Consequently, the ratio of trade to GDP remained flat or declined in many primary commodity producers and many millions of peasant farmers lost their livelihoods. Terms of trade losses have been compounded by restricted market access to OECD countries. Tariffs, quotas, anti-dumping and countervailing duties imposed (at times arbitrarily) on imports, unfair sanitary and phytosanitary import restrictions, production, investment and export subsidies for agricultural and industrial goods, and corporate anti-competitive practices not only hinder exporting by developing countries but also harm their domestic markets (UNCTAD, 2004b).

The European Union (EU) responded to these criticisms by implementing an 'Everything But Arms' programme designed to provide LDCs with preferential access to EU markets. But EU quotas under this programme are very limited. For example, LDCs could only export a volume of sugar equivalent to 1 per cent of EU consumption; in effect, 49 of the world's poorest countries could supply one of the world's richest regions with just three days' worth of its sugar consumption (Oxfam, 2004).

The Doha Development Round of the World Trade Organisation (WTO) was designed to redress conspicuous imbalances in the global trading system. But in 2006 the talks stalled irrevocably, revealing a deep divide between the OECD countries and the developing world. The governments of rich countries constantly stress their commitment to poverty alleviation yet use their trade policies to conduct what Oxfam terms 'robbery against the world's poor' (Oxfam, 2002). When developing countries export to OECD markets, they face tariff barriers that are four times higher than those encountered by rich countries, and these cost the developing world $100 billion a year or twice what they receive in aid. The continued dumping of subsidised agricultural goods on third world markets at below cost of production has put tens of thousands of third world farmers out of work, galvanising a political backlash against trade liberalisation policies. In Latin America, which was forced to liberalise rapidly, dysfunctional inequality grew dramatically to undermine social cohesion (Justino et al., 2003). The loss of livelihoods produced political upheaval. Left-of-centre coalitions were elected in rapid succession, starting with Chavez in Venezuela (1998), 'Lula' da Silva in Brazil (2002), Kirchner in Argentina (2003), Tabare Vazquez in Uruguay (2004) and Evo Morales, Bolivia's first indigenous President (2005). All opposed the trade liberalisation regime.

If Africa, East Asia, South Asia and Latin America were each to increase their share of world exports by 1 per cent, the resulting income gains could lift 128 million people out of poverty. But under current conditions the benefits of trade liberalisation overwhelmingly flow to the rich countries, intensifying global income inequality (Ghose, 2001; IDS–Oxfam, 1999; Polaski, 2006; Wade, 2005). Some 14 per cent of the world's population in the rich countries account for 75 per cent of global GDP. For every US dollar generated through trade, low-income countries only receive 3 cents, a degree of trade exclusion increasingly acknowledged as a major challenge of this century (Annan, 2000; DFID, 2000).

## Poverty and conflict

Statistical data on poverty in LDCs is not comprehensive; however, UNCTAD's *Least Developed Countries Report 2002: Escaping the Poverty Trap* provides some detailed indicators (see Table 4.1 below). Based on national data for private consumption, it estimates the incidence and depth of poverty in 39 LDCs. Figures for the second half of the 1990s show that 4 out of 5 people in the selected countries lived on less than $2 a day, and half of the entire population lived on less than $1 a day. The number living on less than a dollar a day had more than doubled over the previous 30 years.

In African LDCs the proportion of the population living on less than a dollar a day had risen from 56 per cent in the second half of the 1970s to 65 per cent in the second half of the 1990s. Poverty rates were most marked in countries dependent on non-oil commodity exports (especially in mineral producing countries), with 69 per cent of the population living on less than a dollar in 1997–1999, up from 63 per cent in 1981–1983.

The poor have few assets with which to protect themselves during an economic downturn and are less able to absorb the adjustment costs than other segments of society (Bannister and Thugge, 2001; IDS–Oxfam, 1999; Winters, 2000). More significantly, severe shocks in so-called transitionary periods can foster permanent absolute poverty because the poor lose the

Table 4.1 Statistical profile of vulnerable LDCs, 2003 and 2004

| Country | GNI per capita $(2004) | Life expectancy at birth m/f (2003) | Agric. as % of GDP (2003) | Rural labour force % Total (2004) | Exports ($m) (2003) | Imports ($m) (2003) | Debt ($m) (2003) | Debt as % of GNI | Debt service as % of exports (2003) |
|---|---|---|---|---|---|---|---|---|---|
| Afghanistan | – | 41/42 | 52.0 | 66 | 2263.7 | 3441.0 | – | – | – |
| Angola | 1030 | 38/42 | 8.8 | 71 | 9407.0 | 8809.9 | 9698.4 | 90.4 | 14.2 |
| Burundi | 90 | 40/45 | 49.0 | 90 | 40.7 | 106.4 | 1309.7 | 227.7 | 71.8 |
| Cambodia | 320 | 50/57 | 34.5 | 69 | 2621.8 | 3013.0 | 3139.2 | 77.3 | 1.0 |
| CAR | 310 | 42/43 | 60.8 | 69 | 292.7 | 366.3 | 1327.8 | 111.2 | 0.2 |
| Chad | 260 | 44/47 | 45.6 | 71 | 458.9 | 846.8 | 1499.3 | 64.2 | 10.1 |
| DRC | 120 | 42/45 | 57.9 | 61 | 1047.5 | 1223.5 | 11,170.5 | 207.4 | 88.5 |
| Eritrea | 180 | 58/61 | 13.9 | 76 | 102.8 | 743.7 | 634.6 | 70.5 | 11.5 |
| Ethiopia | 110 | 49/51 | 41.8 | 81 | 1139.6 | 2430.6 | 7151.0 | 108.4 | 7.9 |
| Guinea | 460 | 51/53 | 24.6 | 82 | 799.3 | 891.8 | 3456.7 | 96.1 | 16.4 |
| Guinea–Bissau | 160 | 45/48 | 68.7 | 82 | 70.8 | 104.4 | 745.1 | 326.6 | 21.5 |
| Haiti | 390 | 52/54 | 27.9 | 60 | 479.3 | 1379.7 | 1307.5 | 45 | 10.8 |

| | | | | | | | |
|---|---|---|---|---|---|---|---|
| Lesotho | 740 | 35/40 | 16.6 | 38 | 471.3 | 1084.5 | 706.5 | 51.2 | 14.2 |
| Liberia | 110 | 40/43 | – | 66 | 132.7 | 184.2 | 2567.5 | 679.2 | 0.2 |
| Myanmar | – | 56/63 | 57.2 | 69 | 2810.0 | 2288.0 | 7318.4 | – | 4.3 |
| Nepal | 260 | 60/61 | 40.6 | 93 | 974.4 | 1683.7 | 3253 | 55.7 | 11.6 |
| Rwanda | 220 | 43/46 | 41.6 | 90 | 140.2 | 452.9 | 1540 | 92.7 | 15.1 |
| Sierra Leone | 200 | 37/39 | 52.7 | 60 | 178.1 | 392.5 | 1611.9 | 211.2 | 14.2 |
| Solomon Islands | 550 | 69/73 | – | 72 | 77.7 | 82.2 | 185.7 | 75.1 | 7.3 |
| Somalia | – | 43/45 | – | 69 | – | – | 2837.9 | – | – |
| Sudan | 530 | 57/62 | 39.2 | 57 | 2892.8 | 2152.6 | 17,496.1 | 107.0 | 1.2 |
| Timor-Leste | 550 | 55/61 | 26.3 | 81 | – | – | – | – | – |
| Uganda | 270 | 47/50 | 32.4 | 78 | 777.5 | 1662.0 | 4552.8 | 73.8 | 10.8 |

*Source*: UNCTAD Statistical Profiles of the Least Developed Countries, 2005.

opportunity to acquire human capital in the form of education, healthcare and nutrition, and this affects their ability to transcend poverty in the future.

Fearon and Laitin (2003) show the importance of rising per capita income in reducing the likelihood of violent conflict, whereas income inequality and low levels of development have been found to correlate positively with political instability and conflict (Collier *et al.*, 2003; Nafziger and Auvinen, 2002, 2004; Stewart and Fitzgerald, 2000; UNCTAD, 2004a). In the three decades to 2004, 87 per cent of the conflicts in the world had taken place in developing countries, 36 of them in LDCs. Although a highly heterogeneous group of states, LDCs share common characteristics in low income, primary commodity dependency, high levels of indebtedness and economic failure that renders them susceptible to conflict, perhaps more prone to conflict than to peace (UNCTAD, 2004a).

Most LDCs have been subjected to IMF structural adjustment programmes for at least two decades. Their economies were opened up to international trade, increasing their vulnerability to exogenous shocks, while cuts in public expenditure eroded public service provision, removed social safety nets and undermined the capacity of governments to manage their economies and deliver security to their citizens. The collapse in the rule of law and state security systems created power and legitimacy vacuums into which corrupt elites, warlords and criminal groups have been able to nurture shadow economies and illicit trade. The growth in illicit trade, its scale, global reach, complexity and diversity constitutes a shadow global economy that increasingly integrates and competes with the formal global economy (Naim, 2005).

## The case of Côte d'Ivoire

The case of Côte d'Ivoire offers a typical instance of the inequality–conflict nexus and illustrates the way that imposed trade liberalisation and other neoliberal reforms ignore the destabilising social consequences. Media coverage of the war in Côte d'Ivoire portrayed the conflict simplistically – as an ethno-religious schism between the prosperous Christian south and a predominantly Muslim north. But the descent into conflict in 2002 can be understood only in a political economy context. In a matter of two decades the country was transformed from being the most successful in West Africa to an impoverished, war-torn state. Since the colonial period, Côte d'Ivoire's economy has been based on agricultural exports. The country produces 40 per cent of the world's cocoa crop, and is a major exporter of coffee, bananas, cotton, palm oil, pineapple and rubber. During the 1960s and 1970s it became one of Africa's most prosperous and well-managed states, enjoying an average rate of GDP growth of 7 per cent per annum. Until his death in 1993, President Houphouet-Boigny was proclaimed to be Africa's most successful free-market capitalist and economists referred to as the 'Ivorian miracle'. The high rates of growth attracted migrants from poorer neighbours, principally Burkina Faso, Mali and Guinea. By 1980 non-Ivorians made up 41 per cent of the adult labour force, and in the 1990s about 30 per cent of the country's population. Government policy during the 1960s and 1970s was to encourage a 'land rush' by declaring that 'the land belongs to those who cultivate it'. Migrants who participated generated a sense of grievance among indigenous small farmers in the cocoa sector. In the mid-1980s cocoa revenues deteriorated as the world price crashed. Côte d'Ivoire's GDP plummeted, from 4.3 per cent in 1981 to –4.4 per cent in 1984. The economy entered a prolonged recession, which resulted in a reduction in GNP per capita from US$1000 in 1980 to US$670 in 2000. Relations between immigrants and Ivorians became highly aggravated and when the government attempted to 'renegotiate' land arrangements with migrants, violent clashes broke out in the countryside.

In 1989 the government entered an IMF standby agreement conditional on economic reforms. Six World Bank structural adjustment loans were made between 1989 and 1993, and in 1994, following a currency devaluation, the government was forced to go to the IMF for a stabilisation loan. The conditionalities involved a multi-year programme of economic reforms (including cuts in health and education spending and removing the bread subsidy) and trade liberalisation ostensibly designed to achieve stability and economic growth.

The state-managed cocoa industry was privatised. The state regulatory body was dismantled, thereby eliminating a stabilisation mechanism that had provided small farmers a guaranteed income and some security against fluctuations in world prices. The marketing of cocoa and coffee was deregulated and an auction system introduced. Thus the risks of price fluctuations were transferred from the state to small-scale farmers. Reforming the coffee and cotton sectors affected the basic foundations of society, as some 60–70 per cent of the population was engaged in agriculture. By 1992, an estimated 50 per cent of the total population was living in dire poverty. Small farmers went out of business or smuggled cocoa across the border to neighbouring states where they could command higher prices. High unemployment was followed by an expansion in shadow trade which became progressively dominated by criminal networks from both within Côte d'Ivoire and beyond.

Many of the rural poor were forced into the urban centres to look for work. But there were few opportunities to be found. Despairing young men living in appalling conditions with no future prospects became angry and restless. A crime wave hit Abidjan in the early 1990s (Wannenburg, 2005). Conflicts between locals and immigrants continued and were reflected in party politics. The newly formed *Front Populaire Ivoirien* (FPI) led by Laurent Gbagbo, representing mainly indigenous peoples in the cocoa areas, focused on the alleged reliance on migrants of the ruling *Parti Démocratique de Côte Ivoire* (PDCI). The PDCI responded with a xenophobia that played to sentiments stirred by the severe economic crisis. By the 1995 elections, the FPI was joined by a PDCI splinter group to form the *Rassemblement des Républicains* (RDR). Its leader, Allassan Ouattara, had cut short his Washington career as an IMF vice-president to help shake up the ruling elite. The PDCI launched a campaign against him to prevent his candidature on the grounds that he was not an Ivorian. Ouattara then led the RDR in an 'active boycott' to disrupt the election, which was held amidst widespread violence. The outcome was merely another PDCI victory and an even more embittered and resentful opposition.

The economy revived in 1995 after a 50 per cent currency devaluation and improved prices for coffee and cocoa. An average growth rate of 6 per cent in 1995–1998 did little to stabilise the political system. In 1998 the rural land tenure law was reformed to strengthen customary land rights, seen by many as a way of settling scores with 'foreign' landholders. When the price of coffee and cocoa again collapsed in 1999, growth declined to −2.4 per cent in 2000 (World Bank, 2000). Family farms were devastated and rural poverty exploded. Economic instability exacerbated the rising social tensions, and in September 2002 after a failed coup attempt by the *Forces Nouvelles* (FN) the country descended into war. Côte d'Ivoire became divided, with the south controlled by President Gbagbo and the north ruled by Guillaume Soro, the leader of the FN rebels. Elections that were to be held in 2005 were postponed. Foreign entrepreneurs left and external financing was suspended. Despite the deployment of thousands of UN and French peacekeepers, the country remains divided.

Following the signing of the Ougadougou Agreement of 5 March 2007 and the appointment of Soro as prime minister in a transitional government, the international community had high hopes for a durable peace settlement, but this optimism was short-lived. On 29 June 2007, Soro's plane was attacked and tensions increased. Also, the general failure of the disarmament, demobilisation and reintegration (DDR) programme suggests that there was little incentive for peace on either side. During the course of the civil war, elements within the presidential and rebel camps established networks of economic and political power that they have been unwilling to disband. In the south the elites seized the income and revenues generated by cocoa and oil, while the north has effectively become a free-trade zone for conflict trade. Illegal timber and rubber is smuggled in from eastern Liberia and shipped out of Côte d'Ivoire; cotton is illegally exported into Burkina Faso and Mali; and cheap cigarettes are smuggled in from Guinea. Cannabis production has become widespread and its trade is used to acquire weapons for the rebel army (Wannenburg, 2005).

Not having many exploitable natural resources, Côte d'Ivoire has become a major transit point for many forms of illegal trade in the region. It is on the human and drug trafficking route of notorious criminal gangs that operate out of Nigeria. Some of the 200,000–300,000 children enslaved and trafficked each year in West Africa end up working on the cocoa plantations in Côte d'Ivoire (Salah, 2001). Without a sustained peace in Côte d'Ivoire, the emerging shadow economy will become more deeply entrenched in the criminal economy of West Africa (UNODC, 2005). This will benefit a small coterie of conflict entrepreneurs, but leave the majority of the population facing an increasingly impoverished and insecure future.

## Shadow economies and conflict trade

Shadow economies and conflict trade flourish in situations where trade liberalisation fails the poor (Duffield, 2000, 2001; Meagher, 2003; Pugh *et al.*, 2004). In the 1980s economists predicted that the informal economy would disappear with the onset of economic reforms and trade liberalisation, but in reality shadow economies expanded and deepened as well as globalised, forming what some scholars refer to as shadow globalisation (Lock, 2005). Indeed, Schneider and Klinglmair (2004) estimate that shadow economies in 1999–2000 accounted for 41 per cent of official GDP in developing countries. In Africa work in the informal economy accounted for almost 80 per cent of non-agricultural employment, over 60 per cent of urban employment and over 90 per cent of all new jobs in the 1990s (ILO, 2002). Workers in the informal economy experience highly unstable incomes, very low and irregular pay and are vulnerable to all forms of exploitation and harassment. Where shadow economies flourish, the capacity of the state becomes diminished due to the decline in tax revenues and its inability to maintain adequate levels of public expenditures. In Colombia, Afghanistan, the DRC and the majority of West African states, the criminal economy and conflict trade generate significant (and probably growing) proportions of national income.

Shadow economies are prone to being usurped by violent actors and criminal entrepreneurs, obscuring boundaries between the informal and the criminal spheres of the economy. New forms of social control emerge alongside the state, which is losing a monopoly of violence. Such networks accumulate substantial human capital allowing them to carry out sophisticated transnational operations, often with a global reach. The complex networks of trans-border trade that emerge are multifaceted systems traversed by clusters of traders, financiers, fixers and carriers. They link remote peasant communities in the Andes to cocaine users in the capitals of the developed world.

Once a shadow economy based on illegal trade becomes established it is very hard to eradicate, as the US war on drugs has found in the Latin America. In 2000–2006 the United States spent $4.7 billion on 'Plan Colombia' attempting to eliminate the coca trade through aerial spraying and tough interdiction and law enforcement measures. This caused coca production to halve by 2003, but stimulated an increase in production in Bolivia and Peru. Total Andean supply has thus remained more or less constant (Forero,

2006). The multi-billion dollar cocaine business enables Andean criminal fraternities to control territories and act with impunity. They have powerful incentives to keep going, as do many of the small-scale producers who benefit from the illicit trade.

A similar pattern has arisen in Afghanistan where the eradication of the drug trade has failed abysmally and where the proceeds of the trade fuel a costly and destructive war. Two decades of war have seen opium production increase fifteen-fold since the 1979 Soviet intervention. In 2002 the UN Office on Drugs and Crime estimated that Afghanistan's opium output accounted for 15 per cent of GDP and was worth seven times the country's legal annual exports (UNODC, 2003). Extreme poverty increasingly drove the rural population into opium production as a means of survival, with the prospect of earning eight times the annual average wage (UNODC, 2003). As with cocaine, dismantling the opium economy is no easy task and cannot be done by military and authoritarian means: 'This implies aiding poor farmers, providing micro-finance, providing employment opportunities for women and itinerant workers, education for children especially girls and neutralising the power of warlords' (UNODC, 2003: 1). This challenge reaches into the geo-politics of terrorism and violence, but has its roots in a development crisis of immense proportions.

## Resource wars and conflict trade

Resource wars are rooted in the long-standing tradition of shadow trades that exploit differences in the economic and regulatory environments within regions in the developing world. These conditions and long-established trading networks have created opportunities for entrepreneurial warlords to use and improve the informal trade routes linking them into a globalised network. Shadow trade is rapidly able to reassert itself within each new regulatory context. Trade routes are adapted, new methods of trafficking invented new markets exploited and new forms of money laundering are identified.

Entrepreneurs trade their legally or illegally produced commodities on legitimate, but unregulated, global markets in order to obtain the financial resources needed to sustain war. Such trends reflect a symbiotic relationship between current patterns of globalisation and conflict, in which basic human security has become the main casualty (Bayart *et al.*, 1999; Duffield, 2000). Duffield argues that the entrepreneurial use of violence makes rational economic sense, not only because of the local status and wealth that entrepreneurs obtain, but also because it locates them within the power relations of the global *status quo*. The profitability and power derived from such trade helps to explain the durability of violence and conflict and the general resistance to international attempts to broker peace (Ballentine and Niztschke, 2003; Berdal and Malone, 2000). As shadow war economies become entrenched, the climate of insecurity and violence they engender spreads along smuggling routes and across borders, creating spill-over effects in neighbouring states.

An orthodox international response to 'resource wars' has been to adopt the 'greed thesis' (Collier *et al.*, 2003). This provides a scapegoat in that it lays the onus of culpability for the failure of development and the outbreak of conflict on local actors. At the same time it reinforces the international project for good governance and anti-corruption, and avoids having to modify the neoliberal vision of peace and development. Within this framework initiatives are aimed at sanctioning illicit trade and controlling supply. The most widely publicised initiative is the Kimberley Process Certification Scheme, a process designed to certify the origin of diamonds from sources which are free of conflict. The process was established in 2003 to prevent rebel groups and their rivals from financing their wars from diamond sales. The certification scheme aims to prevent 'blood diamonds' from entering the mainstream rough diamond market (Global Witness, 2004). So far these initiatives have largely failed to either control conflict trade or address the grievances and inequities which give rise to these forms of trade in the first place.

The econometric 'resource wars' hypothesis is anyway seriously flawed. Drawing upon the detailed analysis of ten cases of conflict in the developing world, Ballentine and Nitzschke (2003) conclude that access to natural or financial resources was neither the primary nor the sole cause of conflict breaking out, though predation may prolong hostilities and create serious impediments to conflict resolution. In general, they found that the outbreak of conflict is triggered by the interaction of economic motives and opportunities, with long-standing grievances over the mismanagement or inequitable distribution of resource wealth, exclusionary and repressive political systems, inter-group disputes and security dilemmas exacerbated by unaccountable and ineffective states. Poverty, inequality and exclusion are grievance factors that more often than not predate the emergence of greed as the motivation for conflict (UNCTAD, 2004a). Case studies confirm this critique. For example, the roots of the Rwandan crisis have been traced back to failed structural adjustment policies (Uvin, 1998). The origins of armed conflict in Nepal are related to the structural adjustment policies that marginalised a large segment of the rural population and minority groups from the mainstream of economic and social life (Pokhrel, 2004). Likewise, in the cases of former Yugoslavia and Sierra Leone, austerity and liberalisation programmes contributed significantly to the conditions for state decline and conflict (Pugh *et al.*, 2004).

## An alternative approach to trade and security

The need for conflict prevention that emphasises equitable forms of development does not appear to have created greater coherence in international trade policies. As Barbieri (2002) has argued, the liberal peace assumption that there is a positive correlation between international trade, global economic integration and conflict prevention has proved to be a costly illusion. Analysis of the trade and security relationship needs to be based upon a more nuanced and realistic understanding of how powerful economic, social and political forces generate international insecurities. Such an understanding tends to be missing from major international policy reports on security and development. Such analysis needs to be reflective and self-critical, all the more so as policy interventions in fragile or conflict-prone states can all too easily have adverse or self-defeating effects.

As this chapter has shown, externally imposed trade liberalisation policies can be highly destabilising in fragile, low-income states. Countries should be able to develop trade policies that best suit their priorities and needs. Trade liberalisation needs to be sequenced more carefully, recognising that there are different optimal degrees of openness at different stages of development. More to the point, trade liberalisation should not be regarded as a substitute for distributive and rights-based sustainable development strategies.

In Europe the liberalisation of trade occurred over decades and was accompanied by the building of institutional, administrative, legal, regulatory and financial mechanisms which supported the process of integration. In contrast, hasty and ill-conceived trade liberalisation policies have been imposed on developing states, and applied without appropriate sequencing, compensatory development strategies or increased levels of aid (Milanović, 2005; Stiglitz, 2003; UNCTAD, 2004a; Wade, 2007). In the developing world where institutional and administrative capacity is weak, infrastructure is underdeveloped and financial structures are frail, trade reform has been expected to triumph in a matter of years rather than decades. In many cases this has been highly destabilising. The sequencing of trade liberalisation needs to be more sensitive to the socio-economic impacts and pay greater attention to the adjustment needs of different sectors of the economy. Millions of vulnerable rural poor suffer as a result of inappropriate and poorly sequenced trade liberalisation policies. Yet the institutions, and economists, that promote these policies take no responsibility for the disastrous outcomes of their enforced reforms; rather they blame the collapse of states and subsequent chaos on corrupt and poor governance.

A different paradigm is needed for framing development and trade to enhance economic stability, socio-economic welfare and the security of vulnerable low-income societies. An architecture for development, which acknowledges the existence and consequences of market failure and is sensitive to the possibility of political and social destabilisation, is required, closer to the approach of the 1947 Marshall Plan (UNCTAD, 2006).

It is instructive to briefly examine the Marshall Plan's objectives, which provided a devastated and war-torn Europe with some US$12.4 billion in aid for post-war reconstruction. Disbursed over a four-year period, most of the aid took the form of grants rather than loans, and amounted to little more than 1 per cent of America's GDP. The Marshall Plan introduced organising principles to encourage policymakers to forge a new kind of social contract that would avoid the deflationary and dysfunctional policies that prevailed in the inter-war period. Quick fixes and shock therapy for a return to 'normal' market conditions were considered inappropriate and politically destabilising in the emergency conditions of post-war Europe. In trade, Europe was allowed to gradually dismantle direct and indirect controls in accordance with an agreement secured with the European Payments Union, which implemented the reforms between 1950 and 1958. This provided some protection against American competition and gave time for the reconstruction of enterprises potentially capable of competitive substitution. At the same time the United States agreed to a rapid improvement in access to its own markets for European exports, a policy of asymmetric liberalisation that stands in marked contrast to the current global trade system. In the current environment a priority should be to establish an effective link between trade reform and poverty reduction. According to UNCTAD (2004a), strategic intervention is required on several fronts simultaneously: mainstreaming trade and development in national poverty reduction strategies; more effective international financial and technical assistance for developing domestic production and trade capacities; an enabling trade regime to include a phasing out by OECD countries of agricultural support measures that adversely affect developing countries; new international mechanisms to reduce vulnerability to negative commodity price shocks; and more effective market access for LDCs complemented by new supply-side preferences. The instability and displacement risks of trade liberalisation need to be factored into trade models along with the possible trade-offs between growth and stability. In particular, there needs to be greater awareness about the way that trade reforms can shift the balance of power between groups and how these shifts may have long-term destabilising consequences. Rapid reforms induce dramatic changes in societies, placing strains on traditional, social, political and economic systems, which can undermine social stability. Where trade reforms unavoidably cause poverty and dislocation among certain sectors of society, social safety nets need to be strengthened or re-established.

Finally, the industrialised world needs to liberalise its own agricultural sectors. This is the most important measure that the developed world can undertake to support poverty alleviation and conflict prevention in the developing world. An increase in demand for agricultural exports and a possible increase in prices would boost rural incomes in the developing world and provide greater employment opportunities and work security. These measures need to be complemented by long-term strategies for economic diversification and industrialisation within the developing world. This can occur only if the static approach to comparative advantage gives way to a more dynamic approach that might provide LDCs with the opportunity to break out of their 'curse of primary commodity dependency', and with it the cycle of economic stagnation, instability and violence.

## References

Annan, Kofi, 2000, *We the Peoples: The Role of the United Nations in the 21st Century Millennium Report of the Secretary General*, New York: United Nations.

Ballentine, Karen and Heiko Nitzschke, 2003, *Beyond Greed and Grievance: Policy Lessons from Studies in the Political Economy of Armed Conflict*, New York: International Peace Academy.

Bannister, Geoffrey J. and Kamau, Thugge, 2001, 'International Trade and Poverty Alleviation', IMF Working Paper No. 01/54 (at SSRN: http:// ssrn.com/abstract=270440), May.

Barbieri K., 2002, *The Liberal Illusion: Does Trade Promote Peace?* Ann Arbor, MI: University of Michigan.

Bayart, Jean-François, Stephen Ellis and Beatrice Hibou, 1999, *The Criminalisation of the State in Africa*, Oxford: James Curry.

Berdal, Mats and David Malone (eds), 2000, *Greed and Grievance: Economic Agendas in Civil Wars*, Boulder, CO: Lynne Rienner.

Collier, Paul and Jan Dehn, 2002, 'Aid Shocks and Growth', World Bank Working Paper 2688, Washington, DC.

Collier, Paul, Havard Hegre, Anke Hoeffler, Marta Reynal Querol and Nicholas Sambanis, 2003, *Breaking the Conflict Trap: Civil War and Development Policy*, Oxford: Oxford University Press for World Bank.

DFID, 2000, *Making Globalisation Work for the Worlds Poor*, White Paper on International Development, London, December.

Dollar, David, 1992, 'Outward Orientated Developing Countries Really do Growth More Rapidly: Evidence from 95 LDCs 1976–1985', *Economic Development and Cultural Change*, Vol. 40, No. 3, pp. 523–45.

Dollar, David and Aart Kraay, 2001, 'Trade, Growth and Poverty', World Bank Policy Research Department, Working Paper No. 2615, Washington, DC.

Duffield, Mark, 2000, 'Globalisation, Trans-border Trade and War Economies', in Mats Berdal and David Malone (eds), *Greed and Grievance: Economic Agendas in Civil Wars*, Boulder, CO: Lynne Rienner, pp. 69–89.

Duffield, Mark, 2001, *Global Governance and the New Wars*, London: Zed Books.

FAO (Food and Agriculture Organisation), 2004, *The State of Agricultural Commodity Markets 2004*, Rome.

Fearon, James and David Laitin, 2003, 'Ethnicity, Insurgency and Civil War', *American Political Science Review*, Vol. 97, pp. 75–90.

Forero, Juan, 2006, 'Colombia's Coca Survives US Plan to Uproot It', *New York Times*, 19 August.

Gartzke, Erik and Quan Li, 2003, 'War, Peace, and the Invisible Hand: Positive Political Externalities of Economic Globalization', *International Studies Quarterly*, Vol. 47, No. 4, pp. 561–86.

Ghose, Ajit K., 2001, 'Global Economic Inequality and International Trade', ILO Employment Paper, Geneva: International Labour Office, December.

Global Witness, 2004, *The Key to Kimberley: Internal Diamond Controls Seven Core Studies*, London: Global Witness, October.

Hegre, Havard, 2000, 'Development and the Liberal Peace: What Does it Take to be a Trading State?', *Journal of Peace Research*, Vol. 37, No. 1, pp. 5–30.

IDS–Oxfam, 1999, 'Liberalization and Poverty', Final Report to DFID, August.
ILO, 2002, 'Decent Work and the Informal Economy', paper presented at the International Labour Conference 90th Session, World Development Unity, ILO, Geneva, June.
IMF, 2003, *Fund Assistance for Countries Facing Exogenous Shocks*, prepared by the Policy Development and Review Department, Washington, DC.
Justino, Patricia, Julie Litchfield and Leopold Whitehead, 2003, 'The Impact of Inequality in Latin America', PRUS Working Paper No. 21, University of Sussex (at: www.sussex.ac.uk/Units/PRU/wps/wp21.pdf).
Lock, Peter, 2005, *War Economies and the Shadow of Globalisation*, Berghof Handbook Dialogue Series, Berghof Research Centre for Constructive Conflict Management (at: www.berghof-handbook.net/uploads/download/dialogue3_lock.pdf).
Maizels, Alfred, 1996, 'New Evidence on the North–South Terms of Trade', *Southletter* No. 27, Vol. 4, South Centre, Geneva.
Meagher, Kate, 2003, 'A Back Door to Globalisation? Structural Adjustment, Globalisation and Transborder Trade in West Africa', *Review of African Political Economy*, Vol. 30, No. 95, pp. 57–75.
Milanović, Branko, 2005, 'Why Did the Poorest Countries Fail to Catch Up?' Carnegie Paper No. 62, Carnegie Endowment for International Peace, Washington, DC, October.
Nafziger, E. Wayne and Juha Auvinen, 2002, 'Economic Development, Inequality, and War and State Violence', *World Development*, Vol. 30, No. 2, pp. 153–63.
Nafziger, E. Wayne and Juha Auvinen, 2004, *Economic Development, Inequality, and War: Humanitarian Emergencies in Developing Countries*, London: Palgrave Macmillan.
Naim, Moises, 2005, *Illicit: How Smugglers, Traffickers and Copycats are Hijacking the Global Economy*, London: Arrow.
Nowak, Robert, 2004, 'Economic Integration as an Element of Conflict Prevention in Europe', Joint High-level Workshop, UN Economic Commission for Europe, 8 March.
Oxfam, 2002, *Rigged Rules and Double Standards: Trade Globalisation and the Fight Against Poverty*, Oxford: Oxfam.
Oxfam, 2004, 'Dumping on the World: How EU Sugar Policies Hurt Poor Countries', Oxfam Briefing Paper 61, April.
Pokhrel, Gokul, 2004, 'History of Conflict in Nepal' (at: www.fesnepal.org/reports/2004/seminar_reports/paper_conflict-reporting/paper_gokal.htm).
Polaski, Sandr, 2006, 'Winners and Losers: Impact of the Doha Round on Developing Countries', Carnegie Endowment Report, Washington, DC, March.
Pugh, Michael and Neil Cooper with Jonathan Goodhand, 2004, *War Economies in a Regional Context: Challenges of Transformation*, Boulder, CO: Lynne Rienner.
Russett, Bruce M. and John R. Oneal, 2001, *Triangulating Peace: Democracy, Interdependence, and International Organizations*, New York: Norton.
Sachs, Jeffrey and Andrew Werner, 1995, 'Economic Reform and the Process of Global Integration', *Brookings Papers on Economic Activity*, Washington, DC: The Brookings Institution.
Salah, Rima, 2001, 'Child Trafficking in West and Central Africa: An Overview', paper at the First Conference on Human Trafficking, The Women Trafficking and Child Labour Eradication Foundation (WOTCLEF), Abuja, Nigeria.
Schneider, Friedrich and Robert Klinglmair, 2004, 'Shadow Economies Around the World: What Do We Know?', CREMA Working Paper No. 0403, Department of Economics, Johannes Kepler University of Linz, Austria, April.

Shafaeddin, Mehdi, 2005, 'Trade Liberalisation and Economic Reform in Developing Countries: Structural Change or De-Industrialisation', UNCTAD discussion paper No. 179, Geneva.

Stewart, Frances and Valpy Fitzgerald (eds), 2000, *War and Underdevelopment*, Vol. 1, Oxford: Oxford University Press.

Stiglitz, Joseph, 2003, *Globalization and its Discontents*, W.W. Norton.

UN, 2004, *Report of the Secretary General's High Level Panel on Threats Challenges and Change*, New York: United Nations, 2 December.

UN, 2007, *World Economic Situation and Prospects 2007*, Geneva: UN World Economic and Social Survey.

UNCTAD, 2002, *Least Developed Countries Report 2002: Escaping the Poverty Trap*, Geneva.

UNCTAD, 2004a, *Least Developed Countries Report 2004, Linking International Trade and Poverty Reduction*, No. E.04 11.0.0.27, Geneva.

UNCTAD, 2004b, *Trade and Development Report 2004*, Geneva.

UNCTAD, 2006, *Economic Development in Africa: Doubling Aid: Making the 'Big Push' Work*, UNCTAD/GDS/AFRICA/2006, Geneva.

UNODC 2003, *The Opium Economy in Afghanistan*, New York: UN Office on Drugs and Crime.

UNODC, 2005, *Transnational Organised Crime in the West African Region*, New York.

Uvin, Peter, 1998, *Aiding Violence: The Development Enterprise in Rwanda*, West Hartford, CT: Kumarian.

Wade, Robert, 2004, *Governing the Markets: Economic Theory and the Role of Government in East Asian Industrialisation*, Princeton, NJ: Princeton University Press.

Wade, Robert, 2005, 'Is Globalisation Reducing Poverty and Inequality', in John Ravenhill (ed.), *Global Political Economy*, Oxford: Oxford University Press.

Wade, Robert, 2007, 'Globalisation: Emancipatory or Reinforcing?' (at: www.opendemocracy.ne.globalisation-institutions_government/globalisation_inequality_4292.jsp).

Wannenburg, Gail, 2005, 'Organised Crime in West Africa', *African Security Review* Vol. 14, No. 4, pp. 5–16.

Winters, Alan, 2000, 'Trade, Trade Policy and Poverty: What Are the Links', discussion paper No. 2382, Centre for Economic Policy Research, London.

World Bank, 1993, *The East Asian Miracle*, Washington, DC.

World Bank, 2000, *World Development Report 2000/2001: Attacking Poverty*, Oxford: Oxford University Press.

# 5
# Corporate Social Responsibility
*Salil Tripathi*

At an international seminar on business and human rights in London in December 2005, Luis Moreno Ocampo, who had assumed responsibility as the Prosecutor of the International Criminal Court, spoke eloquently about ways to bring peace to northern Uganda. He focused on young children being recruited into conflict in northern Uganda by the Lord's Resistance Army, which is accused of having abducted some 20,000 children over 19 years. The audience was a sympathetic one: it comprised senior executives of some of the largest multinational companies in the world, and included senior representatives of those companies that had come together under the Business Leaders' Initiative on Human Rights,[1] to 'road-test' the Norms and Responsibilities for Transnational Corporations and Other Business Enterprises with Regard to Human Rights.[2] Ocampo exhorted the corporate leaders to create jobs for these youths so that they did not return to a life of crime or violence. The executives found Ocampo's presentation moving, but were their companies ever going to be in a position to recruit disarmed child soldiers?

Northern Uganda is typical of many fragile states, where, according to peacebuilding orthodoxy, resurgence in productive economic activity could wean people away from destructive violence. Indeed, assessments and development plans prepared by donor agencies for post-invasion Iraq, south Sudan, Liberia, Sierra Leone, Bosnia and Herzegovina and other conflict areas, all recognise three factors as given. First, the state has limited resources; second, the international community has competing priorities; and third, responsible companies should therefore help jump-start economies by investing in employment-generating enterprises. There is an element of truth in each of these assumptions. Fragile states have limited resources and depend on aid; the international community has many other priorities; and responsible companies can create jobs by investing in these economies. But this reasoning overlooks the fact that companies are not peacebuilding institutions (even though they benefit from peaceful conditions and their conduct can contribute to peacebuilding). Companies do not have a legal obligation to invest in specific countries or regions. They tend to invest in stable economies, where their staff members feel safe and where a return of capital is guaranteed. Post-conflict societies are neither able to ensure safety nor is it certain – in post-conflict or in other countries – that they will be ensured a fair return on capital. The political economies of post-conflict emerging markets make returns risky and unpredictable.

The reluctance of businesses to sign up to Ocampo's appeal was unsurprising, even though those companies were at the forefront of the corporate social responsibility (CSR) movement. They have often signed up to international CSR instruments – the UN Global Compact, the Voluntary Principles for Security and Human Rights, the Extractive Industries Transparency Initiative, the Business Leaders' Initiative on Human Rights (discussed later). Assuming that such leading companies intend to be benign and avoid adverse social impacts, the scale of their activities requires levels of technological sophistication and access to infrastructure that fragile states cannot provide. In fact, the kind of companies most likely to act in a socially responsible manner are least likely to invest where responsible investment is most needed because the preconditions do not exist in such places. And the companies that are drawn to such regions are likely to lack exposure to the CSR movement or do not intend to adhere to its ideals. This issue will be accentuated in the future, as most of the new investment in fragile states comes from the emerging powers. For example, in the energy sector, the 2007 *World Investment Report* notes that 'The combined overseas production of CNOOC, CNPC, Sinopec (all China), Lukoil (Russian Federation), ONGC (India), Petrobras (Brazil) and Petronas (Malaysia) exceeded 528 million barrels of oil equivalent in 2005, up from only 22 million barrels 10 years earlier' (UNCTAD, 2007). Indeed, total foreign investment flows to Africa alone have doubled over two years, to reach US$36 billion in 2006. Often, companies from the newly industrialised nations invest in war-torn or politically unstable countries, such as Sudan. These investors have not necessarily experienced the pressures that made Western firms adopt CSR as a framework for their operations. Moreover, host governments in fragile states appreciate the absence of conditionalities, whereas local authorities are able to cast the conditions imposed on investment projects by Western companies, governments and NGOs in neo-imperialist terms.

This chapter has four sections. The first surveys the changing relationship between the economy and the state, particularly in terms of governance in the developing world and how business conducts itself. The second focuses on how businesses operate in zones of conflict. The third section assesses self-regulatory measures such as the Kimberley Process Certification System for diamonds. The fourth and final section argues that while self-regulatory initiatives are necessary, they are insufficient to ensure compliance with human rights responsibilities and cannot be seen as substitutes for regulation. This is even more important when tasks are taken away from the state and entrusted to the private sector. By encouraging that trend, the international community runs the risk of undermining the nascent state and its organs, and de-capacitating it before it has had an opportunity to function effectively. The state, as a regulator, cannot abdicate its responsibility, but a weak state is not an effective regulator. The 'international community' must therefore take responsibility in this realm and ensure that businesses become effective partners in promoting peace rather than promoting conflict.

## The role of governments

Corporate unwillingness to play the role of the state has been accompanied by states ceding their role in micromanaging the economy. The end of the Cold War and the decline in influence of the socialist paradigm has meant that governments are either unwilling or unable to intervene and regulate the economy, having ceded authority to supranational instruments, such as the World Trade Organisation (WTO), and through bilateral and multilateral investment agreements and treaties. In some cases, the pressure on governments to improve their public finance has forced them to reduce their economic role, requiring them to privatise functions, including the delivery of essential services. Some critics are sceptical about the state abdicating its traditional role (e.g., Harris *et al.*, 1995). Others have questioned the presumed efficiencies of the market and of privatisation (e.g., Greenwald and Stiglitz, 1995). Some, while not opposed to privatisation, are nonetheless concerned about maintaining the state's regulatory responsibilities and particularly its human rights obligations (e.g., Amnesty International, 2005c). It should be noted, however, that under their human rights treaty obligations, states are not required to deliver services but to protect human rights, by ensuring access to entitlements and regulating services.[3] Human rights law is ideologically neutral; it does not favour free market economics or the state-owned socialist model (though the application is highly political; see Chapter 8, this volume). Non-state suppliers of essential services do not have to be large Western companies. They can be workers' or farmers' cooperatives, NGOs, local companies or trade unions.

These issues acquire a sharper edge in zones of conflict, where civil society expectations are high and the state's capability to meet its needs is low. Governments and the 'international community', which expect responsible companies to lead recovery in fragile states, therefore, need to pay close attention to the potential conflict dynamic that could emerge from applying a policy that works well in a country without violent conflict.

The CSR instruments currently in place primarily cover Western companies rather than those from newly industrialising countries in Asia. Even if the CSR instruments are drawn from internationally ratified treaties, home governments are in a position to cite some CSR concerns – on labour standards and environmental standards – as the back door to protectionism.

The challenge is to ensure that whatever new framework or architecture is created to encompass the role of companies in zones of conflict, it should be universal and not represent values of particular cultural traditions. Companies have called for competition on an equal footing; one way to do so is by framing rules that apply to all entities. While it is true that certain practices in the CSR framework may appear to be 'Western', in essence they represent global values, as articulated by international treaties. For example, each of the ten principles of the Global Compact is drawn from international human rights law, environmental protocols and statutes, labour standards and the 2003 UN convention against corruption. Furthermore, international humanitarian law applies not only to states but also to non-state actors and, unlike human rights law, it is not derogable. This means that respect for local cultures, customs and traditions should always guide corporate conduct, but not if those customs, cultures and traditions violate the fundamental principles of international law.

More importantly, this architecture should make what are currently regarded as best practices to be *required* norms and not *voluntary* initiatives, to ensure stronger adherence to codes of conduct. And, most importantly, governments could recognise that while privatisation and a private sector role in jump-starting economies may be economically beneficial to a war-torn community, it cannot be the only or even the predominant strategy. The private sector is not designed to be a peacebuilder, and has different incentives from those that governments may seek to establish.

At root is the problem of asymmetry in the relationship between large corporations and states with weak governance mechanisms. International law applies to states that are assumed to possess legitimate regulatory authority over a specific territory. But a country in conflict, or emerging from conflict, either lacks control over the entire territory or is unwilling to exercise authority. In such contexts, large corporations influence the state rather than vice-versa. Such asymmetry was the basis of colonial expansion, when large trading companies operated abroad and the flag followed trade: the British East India Company, the Dutch East India Company and the businesses in Africa of the Belgian King Leopold are only some of the more glaring examples (see Chanda, 2007; Hochschild, 2000; Keay, 1993; Pakenham, 1992). The role of the Belgian mining company, *Union Minière du Haut Katanga*, in aiding the failed secession of Katanga from what is now the Democratic Republic of Congo (DRC) has been well documented (Litvin, 2004).

Companies now operate in a vastly different environment, with greater public scrutiny, stricter laws, better enforcement and a more egalitarian architecture of international law than that which prevailed in the colonial period. Companies today readily cede to the state the responsibilities and obligations to protect human rights, even as they lobby to reduce the regulatory reach of the state. Indeed, the nature of that relationship changed with the end of colonial empires and newly independent states, gaining the power to regulate the conduct of companies operating in their territory. But the balance has begun to shift again as economies have deregulated, and in this neoliberal environment OECD countries encourage companies in their jurisdiction to invest abroad, while host states do all they can to invite foreign investment.

International organisations, including the UN, expect the private sector to play a leading role in building the economic foundations of a post-conflict society, as if unaware of this fundamental asymmetry or the historical lessons. One of the unintended consequences of this asymmetry can be seen where a foreign company is the only major enterprise functioning in a remote area. The communities around the company expect it to fulfil all roles expected of the government, including providing education, healthcare, electricity, water and perhaps even law and order. The company may choose to offer such services to a few communities in its vicinity or sphere of influence, lacking the capacity, expertise, mandate or incentives to provide for the entire population. This is fundamentally discriminatory, and fuels future conflict in the region as communities deprived of the benefits express their wrath against the company or the benefiting communities. Universal service obligation applies to states, not to companies. A company's impact is rarely neutral and can be counterproductive to peacebuilding. By its very presence, as well as through its actions, it can exacerbate conditions (as indicated below) that create conflict or sow the seeds of future conflict.

Many, if not most, companies comply with the law and help to generate prosperity by creating jobs, paying taxes, producing goods and providing services. In the context of operating in a conflict zone, the Norwegian oil company Statoil has been praised for its operations in the Niger Delta, where its facilities have rarely been targeted by protestors.[4] In the textile sector, after being justly criticised for poor labour relations at their facilities in Southeast Asia, many leading apparel manufacturers from the United States have formed partnerships with the International Labour Organisation (ILO) and international NGOs, such as the Fair Labor Association,[5] to root out unfair labour practices from the factories of their sub-contractors. But some companies, through acts or omissions, contribute to or directly commit abuses. While considerable critical attention has focused on the role of multinationals in the developing world – from 1974 to 1992 the UN Conference on Trade and Development (UNCTAD) hosted the Centre for Transnational Corporations, whose role was to study the 'negative' effects of multinational investments in the developing world – insufficient attention has been paid to the role of local companies in this regard. The Draft Norms, prepared at the Sub-Commission for the Promotion and Protection of Human Rights at the UN, attempt to rectify this because multinational companies are not more likely to commit abuses (in fact, there is no correlation between the ownership of a company and the abuse committed). According to data from the Stockholm Institute for International Economics (Graham, 1994), a multinational or its affiliate pays twice the wages a local company pays in low-income countries (the ratio narrows in higher-income countries). But because of the perception that the balance of power is weighted in favour of global corporations, most debate and international attention has focused on the conduct of multinational companies that operate in the developing world.

Recognising that companies operating internationally are not adequately regulated by either home or host states, and there is no overarching treaty or law to regulate their conduct, NGOs began researching corporate conduct in the mid-1990s in order to lobby for binding accountability mechanisms. Among them, Global Witness, founded in 1993, focused on the links between natural resources and armed conflict, and through a series of investigations drew international attention to conflict commodities (Global Witness, 1998, 1999); Human Rights Watch produced an important report on the Niger Delta in 1997; Partnership Africa Canada reported in 1999 on links between rebel forces and the diamond trade; and in 1998 Amnesty International published human rights principles for companies. These accompanied the critiques of market-based capitalism and corporate power (e.g., Hertz, 2001; Klein, 2000) and the activities of social movements that had begun protesting against corporate globalisation. The World Social Forum met at Porto Alegre, Brazil, at the same time as world leaders and business executives tended to meet annually at the World Economic Forum in Davos, Switzerland.

The Draft Norms on Human Rights appeared in this context, in what NGOs saw as an effective way of regulating corporate conduct, in recognition of the need for a common global framework. But the norms were contentious and, except among human rights groups and other civil society organisations, did not enjoy support. No state or major industry organisation supported them. Only a group of companies operating under the banner, the Business Leaders' Initiative on Human Rights, was prepared to test aspects of the Draft Norms as they applied to their management practices. However, the debate created space for discussion about the role of business in society, and subsequently the then UN Secretary-General (Kofi Annan) had a mandate to appoint a Special Representative for business and human rights in 2005 (Harvard academic, John Ruggie, an architect of the UN Global Compact and the Millennium Declaration).

The Global Compact in 2000 had already initiated a policy dialogue on companies operating in zones of conflict. Since then, there have been numerous conferences, meetings and reports within and beyond the UN system to consider how to promote a more positive role for business in countries subject to violence, corruption and weak governance. In 2001, International Alert and the International Business Leaders' Forum published *Business for Peace*, followed by a ground-breaking UN publication in 2002 providing guidance to companies operating in conflict zones (Global Compact, 2002), which was then followed by guidelines for the extractive industry (International Alert, 2005).

Criticism of perceived corporate complicity in human rights abuses took a more aggressive form in the United States, where victims of human rights abuses initiated legal proceedings against companies under the Alien Tort Claims Act of 1789, which allows foreigners to sue in US courts for damages for violations of customary international law norms, such as the prohibition of slavery, genocide, torture, crimes against humanity and war crimes. While none of the almost 40 cases filed against companies has been successful as of mid-2007, and one case (*Doe v. UNOCAL*) was settled out of court, these cases have generated adverse publicity leading to reputational damage for the companies, besides raising legal, financial and management costs. Lawsuits are forcing companies to revise their position, and many would accept minimal rules to ensure 'a level playing field' and voluntary codes of conduct rather than regulation. A typical code would require companies to follow high standards, but there are also, typically, loopholes to make the interpretation of the code, as well as its application, ambiguous, and in any case legally unenforceable. 'Codes of conduct work only for the well-intentioned' is a remark made frequently by businesses and academics in the CSR sphere. Most of the time there are no mechanisms to verify or monitor the conduct, and by leaving the language vague there are few opportunities for external parties to assess performance.

The group of NGOs campaigning for Economic, Social and Cultural Rights – ESCR-Net – previously called for a binding corporate accountability mechanism, which could include a global treaty, so that victims of abuse are not dependent on vaguely worded CSR initiatives to protect their rights (ESCR-Net, 2006). Those advocating such a framework have argued that the hybrid systems that currently frame the debate lack rigour and authority; the failure of states to prosecute crimes is seen by such advocates not as evidence of corporate innocence, but as another example of states submitting to corporate power. However, dissenters, represented by NGOs such as *Centre Europe Tiers Monde* (CETIM) and legal scholars such as Usha Ramanathan in India, do not want human rights obligations transferred to companies for the sound legal reason that it would allow the state to reduce, if not abdicate, its own obligations to protect human rights (see CETIM, 2005; Ramanathan, 2001).

In the absence of such an overarching global treaty to establish clear rules regarding the roles and responsibilities of state and corporations, policymakers, companies, civil society groups and governments have created a variety of hybrid, multi-stakeholder instruments to address some of the common problems associated with corporate behaviour in zones of conflict. These include the conduct of security forces (Voluntary Principles on Security and Human Rights), revenue transparency (Extractive Industry Transparency Initiative) and the management of resources and trade mechanisms (Kimberley

Process Certification Scheme). Some are voluntary with a part-mandatory character (as in the Kimberley Process where states can be and have been expelled or suspended); some have become *de facto* mandatory through their inclusion in agreements between the state and the investor (as in British Petroleum's agreement with Indonesian authorities); and some are part of corporate codes of conduct (as in Exxon's security policies which draw from the Voluntary Principles and have, internally, become mandatory). But all initiatives fall short of NGO expectations for enforcement mechanisms.

The aim of each initiative is to improve conditions *in situ* by improving operating environments by promoting good conduct and declaring unequivocally that bad conduct will not be tolerated. In the absence of overarching rules these initiatives remain important – but such codes cannot substitute for binding rules and, depending on the companies involved, the initiatives are unlikely to advance peacebuilding alone. Well-intentioned companies can, at most, contribute to peacebuilding, but the entire agenda of job generation cannot be placed on their shoulders. It should also be noted that these initiatives, by their very nature and infancy, are inadequate to avoid the negative impacts of corporate conduct in war-torn societies. Of course, no declaration, including the Universal Declaration of Human Rights, can suffice to prevent human rights abuses. Likewise, companies adopting these hybrid forms of governance cannot assume that mere enactment of specific policies is enough. The codes simply show that a company *says* it is committed to apply the policies at all levels of its operations, and to its subsidiaries, collaborators, partners and associates, and that such codes will be verified independently and monitored, and corrective action taken to end abuses that do take place.

While states have played an important role in developing these initiatives, it should not be assumed that the states are 'in the driver's seat'. Participating officials often describe their role as enablers and facilitators, rather than regulators. As a result, the private sector has a large influence in drafting the language of the initiatives, perhaps appearing to compromise existing treaty obligations of the state. Amnesty International asserts, for example, that State Investor Agreements between companies and states may erode a state's ability to protect human rights (Amnesty International, 2003). While this remains untested, British Petroleum signed a deed poll in 2003 after Amnesty International campaigned on a stabilisation clause in the Baku–Ceyhan–Tbilisi pipeline agreement that could chill potential future regulation protecting human rights (Amnesty International, 2003, 2005b).[6] However, because treaties are signed by states they remain bound by them. But with the role of the state shrinking in many economies, there is a potentially significant governance gap, whereby the government has legal obligations but is absent, and the private sector, without obligations, is the only entity present. While there is broad agreement among companies, civil society groups and states about the goals of these initiatives, there are major differences between them about the meaning, reach and enforceability of these standards. Typically, companies assert that the voluntary initiatives are enough; NGOs see them as the starting point towards a regulatory framework. As such, these measures can only be considered temporary, while a global consensus emerges to ensure that corporate activity causes no harm to civilians and does not exacerbate conflict.

## Business in zones of conflict

Businesses (i.e., any private commercial entity, typically a non-state actor pursuing profit) operate wherever there is profit potential. The instabilities in zones of conflict present a conundrum because they are too risky for responsible investors, but offer greater rewards for other companies willing to accept risks. Premiums are high, too, and that attracts a particular kind of risk-taking investor, especially where valuable natural resources may be worth exploiting. For some businesses, operating in a conflict or fragile peace can represent an opportunity: companies providing logistical support to distribute relief or construction companies providing maintenance services for shattered infrastructure, for example. Others are compelled by resource location to operate in difficult areas, irrespective of the political persuasion of the host government. Then there is the perverse incentive: a rebel force needs revenues to finance conflict, and may sell resources to unscrupulous businesses.

Businesses have always operated in conflict areas, and have resisted regulation on the grounds that cumbersome procedures would force them to leave the field open to even less socially responsible businesses, thereby damaging the affected communities. Consider the case of Sudan. Human rights groups published extensive reports suggesting a link between conflict in the South and oil companies operating there (Amnesty International, 2000; Human Rights Watch, 2003). Activist groups targeted the companies, particularly Talisman Energy of Canada, to divest from Sudan, and the Presbyterian Church of Sudan sued Talisman Energy in the United States (though the company pulled out of Sudan in 2004 and the case was dismissed). Throughout the period leading up to Talisman's withdrawal, the company defended its conduct, and engaged a consultancy firm to report on its social development performance and pointed to various initiatives it had taken to improve the lives of local people (including provision of healthcare facilities). The company claimed that if it departed, other companies without any commitment to responsible conduct would take over the operations.[7] Eventually, that is exactly what happened: Talisman Energy's stake was ultimately bought by the Oil and Natural Gas Commission of India, which partnered Talisman Energy's earlier partners, Petronas Bhd of Malaysia and the Chinese National Petroleum Corporation. While there is no evidence to suggest that the conduct of the three Asian companies differs in any way from that of Western oil companies, none of them is active in CSR initiatives apart from Petronas which signed a joint declaration with others against corruption at the World Summit for Sustainable Development in Johannesburg, in 2002. Activist groups continued their campaign while the Sudan military continued to bomb in the south, allegedly sometimes using infrastructure built by Talisman Energy. Villages were razed, leading to mass displacement and an increase in refugees, thereby making it easier for oil companies to subsequently continue exploration activities. There is no evidence to link companies with the bombing missions, but in the lawsuit targeting Talisman Energy under the Alien Tort Claims Act (since dismissed) among the observations the plaintiffs made was that the company stood to gain from the removal of communities in oil-producing areas. Sudan activists have alleged that the state's interests were congruent with those of the corporation, a point that remains an assertion.

## Implementing self-regulating measures

Anticipating regulatory reach and governmental initiatives, some companies have developed their own voluntary initiatives, in order to reduce the likelihood of becoming complicit in conflict, as outlined above. However, a few caveats are in order: the initiatives focus primarily on the extractive sector, but the problem is not unique to that sector. Many extractive industries operate in peaceful or relatively conflict-free zones (Botswana, Malaysia and the Sultanate of Oman), whereas some non-extractive industries, including the finance sector, operate in zones of conflict and may have an adverse impact on it. But resources in conflictual parts of the world and headline-grabbing incidents have combined to ensure that attention remains focused on the extractive sector (Ruggie, 2006).

Where resources can be procured, secured and shipped out to blend in the mainstream of global trade, government forces or warring factions have an incentive to capture them and claim sovereignty. The worst form of human rights abuses – from forced labour, sexual abuse of women and girls, use of child soldiers, torture, extra-judicial executions, disappearances and abductions – often follow. In theory, if a particular product, industry or commodity is responsible for creating or contributing to a conflict, it should be possible to stop it. But in the post-Cold War environment of liberalised trade, where goods pass through many ports before being used or processed, stopping trade in a particular commodity is problematic. The potential to replicate the Kimberley Process Certification Scheme – a system established by all countries trading diamonds to ensure that rough diamonds from rebel-held areas of conflict zones do not enter the legitimate international trade after sanctions were imposed on diamonds from three African countries (see Chapter 6, this volume) in other industries – is limited for three reasons. First, a diamond is a unique product with an elastic demand: consumers have no compelling reason to buy one except for the allure created by the marketing surrounding it. Second, its supply chain – due to historical reasons – is unique with a few nodal points: De Beers, which for a long time acted as a monopsony and monopoly; Antwerp, as a global trading hub; the United States and Japan, which account for some 90 per cent of the global market; and the United States, India and Israel, as the main processing centres. This permitted regulation at the so-called 'choke points', as the industry was not as widespread as, say, the apparel industry or the oil industry. Some of that dynamic is changing, but the basic pattern remains. Finally, sanctions were imposed, making it inevitable that some collective action for enforcement was needed.

Given this background, what can a corporation do if it intends to act responsibly in a conflict zone? While international human rights law primarily applies to the state, international humanitarian law applies to companies as well. In regions where governance is weak and where the writ of the distant capital does not run, companies face a peculiar dilemma: should they ignore the poverty and inequalities around them, and continue to operate as if it were not their concern? Should a company step in and play the role of a government to provide essential services to communities? If so, what are the limits of their obligation? And who is to be held accountable if they fail to provide promised services?

The gap between what companies promise and what they deliver, as well as the gap between what the communities expect and what they actually get, is often a cause of friction leading to violence. In the Niger Delta, small fishing communities coexist with oil flow stations and storage tanks. The contrast in wealth and resources between the communities and company compounds and property is glaring. Chevron and Shell have provided services to communities near their area of operations, but they often fail to meet expectations or they arouse the animosity and envy of more far-flung communities. The latter have taken out their anger on the communities which benefit from the projects, or on the company by either attacking its infrastructure (such as oil pipelines) or abducting employees or contractors (Amnesty International, 2005a). Shell claims to have spent nearly US$140 million in 2005 on philanthropy in the Niger Delta (Shell Co., 2006), and Chevron $130 million in 1997–2007 (Chevron, 2007). Yet both companies have regularly been attacked by saboteurs and armed militia, as well as by peaceful protestors. As both companies are junior partners of the Nigerian National Petroleum Corporation, the Nigerian government has an obligation to protect its national assets, and has sent thousands of troops to the area, contributing to further violence.

Many companies operate in countries that have a poor realisation of economic, social and cultural rights, as measured in the UN Development Programme's *Human Development Index*. They are also the most likely to erupt in conflict where inhabitants live in poverty. Some industries stung by scandals – chocolates, extractives, toy-making and apparel – have joined with other stakeholders to deal with corruption, human rights, labour rights and revenue management. Typically, these structures are created to deal with specific problems and situations, and bring together entities – such as the state, companies and civil society actors – which accept common interests.[8] Other initiatives have severe limitations. The Extractive Industries Transparency Initiative is based on the publish-what-you-pay principle, revealing information about what a company has paid the government, but not about how the money has been used by the state. The Voluntary Principles aims to inspire companies to use their influence so that security forces, public and private, behave according to the law, particularly in areas where human rights protection is inadequate. But there are no real enforcement mechanisms here either. The EU's Forest Law Enforcement Governance and Trade (FLEGT) aims to preserve environmental integrity rather than inhibit conflict. In the case of the Kimberley Process, some governments, such as Namibia and South Africa, increasingly consider that the problem of conflict diamonds no longer matters because the conflicts are over. Companies, however, confront the problem of illicit artisanal mining. While companies would prevent stones within their territory being stolen, the conditions in which workers operate are miserable, and companies which sign up to international codes of conduct find it counterproductive to develop security mechanisms aimed at restraining such miners (International Alert, 2006) due to human rights abuses by security forces in the past (Amnesty International, 2002). And for civil society groups, such hybrid mechanisms are temporary, stop-gap arrangements towards reaching a treaty on corporate crime or a convention covering environmental sustainability, development, poverty alleviation and healthcare.

## The China challenge

The initiatives described above include Western firms and Western NGOs, but investment in fragile states also increasingly comes from China. Two-way trade between China and Africa had quadrupled to US$40 billion in 2005; and in 2007 China was Africa's third largest trading partner (World Bank, 2007). Chinese demand for commodities and diversification in apparel, food processing, telecom products and construction has driven investment priorities. At US$1.2 billion, Chinese foreign direct investment in Africa in 2006 was much smaller than the $29 billion invested by the United States, but had increased tenfold since 2003 (Alden, 2005). According to World Bank estimates (2007), trade volume will exceed US$100 billion within a few years. Chinese entrepreneurship includes uranium exploration in Namibia, manganese, iron ore and gold purchases in South Africa, oil drilling in the Gulf of Guinea and Sudan, and hardwood extraction from Congo (Turner, 2007). Press reports indicate that Chinese investment in oil production and ports and pipelines in Sudan alone amounted to US$4 billion by 2007; Angola supplied nearly a fifth of China's oil imports in 2006; China buys half the lumber exported by Gabon and 60 per cent of Equatorial Guinea's lumber; and in 2007 China offered US$5 billion to finance infrastructure in the DRC in return for preferential access to mining concessions (Lorenz and Thielke, 2007).

This is not to suggest that China's access to African commodities is illegitimate, and Africa has the right to exploit its natural resources. China's strategy is probably not so very different from the way European companies invested in Africa a century ago, but Western firms have now adopted codes of behaviour that aim to eliminate bad practices. Chinese companies appear to be less concerned with 'responsible investment' or human rights in their sphere of influence or area of operations (Ruggie, 2007).

## Conclusion: making peacebuilding a goal for the private sector

The crisis of development cannot be solved by one set of actors alone, and CSR processes are exemplary and worth attention for bringing together a wide range of stakeholders. But they are only as strong as the weakest link, and being consensus-driven often achieve minimum goals, making it harder to move beyond the most harrowing abuse, or the lowest common denominator. Given that the existing initiatives are largely voluntary and that companies are unwilling to make them mandatory, their scope remains limited. As more companies from newly investing countries show interest in weak governance zones, the effectiveness of these initiatives will weaken further unless elevated to an industry standard and made mandatory. It is only with mandatory performance requirements that corporate engagement will be equitable and credibly responsible, and the playing field will be level – not only for the companies but, more important, for communities and civilians around them, who will be ensured a level of human rights protection that would otherwise, in theory, vary, depending on the investor. Businesses have frequently sought regulation for non-discriminatory treatment from host and home states as well as other regulators, in laws governing investment, trade policy, taxation and competition. The same principle applies in regulations concerning corporate conduct in conflict zones. To restate international humanitarian law's cornerstone, it applies to every entity and is non-derogable (unlike human rights law, which under specific circumstances can be suspended).

But governments would have to take the lead, and this is unlikely except in extreme instances of threats to international peace and security as in the context of 'blood diamonds' in West Africa. The record of sanctions regimes suggests that while imposing sanctions is an easy first step, implementing, monitoring and prosecuting violations is considerably more difficult. States can play a more active role in two ways. One is through executive conditionality. If home government participation in loans or export credits were conditional on rights observance and CSR then companies would be forced to take these seriously. A more direct form of intervention would be the law itself: failure to comply would lead to punishment following prosecution.

In addition, if stock market regulations or loan covenants were to impose corporate reporting of investors' conduct in weak governance zones, and if credit rating agencies were to assess corporate conduct and correlate this with the likelihood of lawsuits, rating company bond offerings or loans accordingly, that would exact a price for bad behaviour. Companies operating within the framework of international law would be rewarded by the market, through cheaper loans, and companies operating outside such a framework would find credit more expensive.

However, there remain ambiguities about what is expected of companies and what is required. The Draft Norms made an effort to pin some human rights responsibility on companies, but the process stalled because responsibilities that were clearly not those of corporations, or hard to define as 'corporate', were also included. There is now limited appetite for global regulation, even as initiatives are proliferating. One encouraging sign is a growing consensus about what cannot be done. The 'Business and International Crimes' project of the Norwegian policy institute, Fafo and the International Peace Institute in New York indicate areas where companies can be held criminally liable: committing, or being complicit in, international crimes, such as war crimes, genocide and crimes against humanity. Non-state actors are being held liable for such abuses, and this is likely to get wider acceptance, the Fafo project gaining tacit acceptance in the work of the Special Representative for Business and Human Rights. Other developments include the International Committee of the Red Cross and Red Crescent's *Business and International Humanitarian Law* (2006), the Business Leaders' Initiative on Human Rights' *Guide for Integrating Human Rights in Business Management* (2005), the contested draft Norms; the safeguards developed by the International Finance Corporation for its lending to the private sector; the OECD's Risk Management Tool for companies operating in weak governance zones (2006); and the International Chamber of Commerce, the International Organisation of Employers, and the Business and Industry Advisory Committee's joint response to the Risk Management Tool (OECD, 2006).

The first building block of each initiative, and of International Alert's 'Conflict-Sensitive Business Practices', is to avoid causing harm. This means compliance with international laws and adherence to best practices where they exceed the law. In undertaking social investment projects, care must be taken to ensure that those activities do not cause further harm. Clarity regarding complicity is important because human rights abuses in conflict zones are committed by warring parties, and by security forces or armed groups in non-conflict settings as well. Ordinarily, companies do not commit such abuses, but some companies benefit from abuses and others may intend that specific abuses do take place so that they can gain access to a specific resource, although proving intent is extremely difficult. While being one step removed from the abuses, companies are not directly responsible, but could be held complicit, if certain conditions are met, such as aiding and abetting, constructive knowledge (known and should have known), intent, benefit and so on.

The proliferation of initiatives does not lead to clarity but practical ideas do thrive in a marketplace where specific efforts are piloted. Traditional conflict prevention and peacebuilding programmes consider the private sector in passing, as a source of investment or trade. But harnessing energy to build and sustain peace means including the private sector as a potential ally while also understanding the limits of the role it can play because of the different constituencies to which it responds, different value systems under which it operates, and different incentives to which it reacts.

There is a fundamental issue here: practitioners who work in peacebuilding are often driven by the public spirit, and their motives are often altruistic. State officials carry out functions and mandates determined by their foreign policy objectives. The instincts of capitalists, however, are different and to harness them for peacebuilding requires nuance and skill that sometimes eludes central planners. Asking companies to create jobs in environments without stable market conditions, or physical safety and infrastructure, will not work.

The basic principle of entrepreneurial activity is risk but at the same time companies do not have all the answers and often seek subsidies and benefits from the state or international agencies to generate economic activity. Engaging the private sector, then, requires understanding its incentives, limitations and potential and aligning its interests to the public good.

## Notes

1. The group includes leading multinationals from Europe and the United States (at: www.blihr.org).
2. The Draft Norms were adopted by the Sub-Commission for the Promotion and Protection of Human Rights in 2003 (at: www.unhchr.ch/huridocda/huridoca.nsf/(Symbol)/E.CN.4.Sub.2.2003.12.Rev.2.En?Opendocument). Many NGOs strongly supported them but they were vigorously contested and not formally adopted by the then Human Rights Commission. Although no company formally adopted them, BLIHR companies used them to guide the development of their management policies.
3. See the 1997 Maastricht Guidelines on Violations of Economic, Social and Cultural Rights (at: www1.umn.edu/humanrts/instree/Maastrichtguidelines_.html) and the 1987 Limburg Principles on the Implementation of the International Covenant on Economic, Social and Cultural Rights (at: www.unimaas.nl/bestand.asp?id=2453).
4. See in particular its Akassa Development Project, in collaboration with BP and the NGO Pro-Natura (at: www.pronatura-nigeria.org/adf.htm).

5. Better Factories Cambodia project of the ILO (at: www.betterfactories.org/about BFC.aspx?z=2&c=1).
6. See www.amnesty.org.uk/content.asp?CategoryID=10128#deed.
7. Confidential NGO–Talisman discussions during the period, including with NGOs seeking disinvestment.
8. Pims Brown (with inputs from Clean Clothes Campaign, Netherlands, and Ethical Trading Initiative, UK), 'Background Input Document: Principles that make for effective governance of multi-stakeholder initiatives', October 2007, draft at expert's workshop on improving human rights performance of business through multi-stakeholder initiatives, The Hague, 6–7 November 2007.

## References

Alden, Chris, 2005, 'Leveraging the Dragon: Towards an Africa that can say No', March (at: http://yaleglobal.yale.edu/display.article?id=5336).
Amnesty International, 1998, 'Human Rights Principles for Companies', ACT 70/001/1998 (at: http://web.amnesty.org/library/index/engACT700011998?open&of=eng-398).
Amnesty International, 2000, 'Sudan: The Human Price of Oil', AFR 54/001/2000 (at: http://web.amnesty.org/library/Index/ENGAFR540042000?open&of=ENG-398).
Amnesty International, 2002, 'The Democratic Republic of Congo: Making a Killing', AFR 62/017/2002 (at: http://web.amnesty.org/library/index/engafr620172002).
Amnesty International, 2003, 'Human Rights on the Line. The Baku–Tbilisi–Ceyhan Pipeline Project' (at: www.amnesty.org.uk/content.asp?CategoryID=10128).
Amnesty International, 2005a, 'Ten Years On: Injustice and Violence Haunt the Niger Delta', AFR44/002/2005 (at: http://web.amnesty.org/library/pdf/AFR440222005ENGLISH/$File/AFR4402205.pdf).
Amnesty International, 2005b, 'Contracting Out of Human Rights: The Chad–Cameroon Pipeline Project', POL/31/12/2005 (at: http://web.amnesty.org/library/index/engpol340122005).
Amnesty International, 2005c, 'Human Rights and Privatisation', POL/34/003/2005 (at: http://web.amnesty.org/library/index/engpol340032005).
Business Leaders' Initiative on Human Rights, 2005, 'Guide for Integrating Human Rights in Business Management', the Office of the High Commissioner on Human Rights, and the Global Compact Office, New York (at: www.blihr.org/tools).
CETIM, 2005, 'Transnational Corporations and Human Rights', Europe–Third World Centre, Geneva, November (at: www.cetim.ch/en/documents/bro2-stn-A4-an.pdf).
Chanda, Nayan, 2007, *Bound Together: How Traders, Preachers, Adventurers and Warriors Shaped Globalization*, New Haven, CT: Yale University Press.
Chevron, 2007, 'Nigeria Fact Sheet', November (at: www.chevron.com/documents/pdf/nigeriafactsheet.pdf).
ESCR-Net, 2006, 'Joint NGO Letter in Response to the Interim Report of the UN Special Representative on Human Rights and Business', 18 May (at: www.escr-net.org/actions_more/actions_more_show.htm?doc_id=430932&parent_id=430908).
Global Compact, 2002, 'Global Compact Business Guide for Conflict Impact Assessment and Risk Management', New York (at: www.unglobalcompact.org/docs/issues_doc/7.2.3/BusinessGuide.pdf).
Global Witness, 1998, 'A Rough Trade', London (at: www.globalwitness.org/media_library_detail.php/90/en/a_rough_trade).

Global Witness, 1999, 'A Crude Awakening', London (at: www.globalwitness.org/media_library_detail.php/93/en/a_crude_awakening).

Graham, Edward, 1994, 'The (Not Wholly Satisfactory) State of the Theory of Foreign Direct Investment and the Multinational Enterprise', Washington: Institute for International Economics.

Greenwald, Bruce and Joseph Stiglitz, 1995, 'Externalities in Economies with Incomplete Information and Incomplete Markets', *Quarterly Journal of Economics*, Vol. 101, No. 2, pp. 229–64.

Harris, John, Janet Hunter and Colin Lewis (eds), 1995, *The New Institutional Economics and Third World Development*, New York: Routledge.

Hertz, Noreena, 2001, *The Silent Takeover: Global Capitalism and the Death of Democracy*, London: Arrow.

Hochschild, Adam, 2000, *King Leopold's Ghost*, Oxford: Oxford University Press.

Human Rights Watch, 1999, 'The Price of Oil', New York (at: www.hrw.org/reports/1999/nigeria/index.htm).

Human Rights Watch, 2003, 'Sudan, Oil and Human Rights', New York (at: www.hrw.org/reports/2003/sudan1103).

International Alert, 2001, Jane Nelson, 'Business of Peace: The Private Sector as a Partner in Conflict Prevention and Resolution', International Business Leaders' Forum, and the Council on Economic Priorities (at: www.international-alert.org/publications/237.php).

International Alert, 2005, 'Conflict Sensitive Business Practice: Guidance for the Extractive Sector' (at: www.international-alert.org/our_work/themes/extractive_industries.php).

International Alert, 2006, Robert Powell and Mohamed Yahya, 'The Current State of Diamond Mining in the Mano River Basin and the use of Diamonds as a Tool for Peacebuilding and Development', June (at: www.international-alert.org/publications/281.php).

International Committee of the Red Cross and Red Crescent, 2006, 'Business and International Humanitarian Law', Geneva (at: www.icrc.org/eng/business-ihl).

Keay, John, 1993, *The Honorable Company: A History of the East India Company*, London: HarperCollins.

Klein, Naomi, 2000, *No Logo*, London: Flamingo.

Litvin, Daniel, 2004, *Empires of Profit: Commerce, Conquest and Corporate Responsibility*, London: Texere.

Lorenz, Andreas and Theo Thielke, 2007, 'The Age of the Dragon: China's Conquest of Africa', *Der Spiegel* (Berlin), 30 May (at: www.spiegel.de/international/world/0,1518,484603,00.html).

OECD, 2006, 'Risk Awareness Tool for Multinational Enterprises in Weak Governance Zones', OECD (at: www.oecd.org/dataoecd/26/21/36885821.pdf).

Pakenham, Thomas, 1992, *The Scramble for Africa*, London: Abacus.

Partnership Africa Canada, 1999, 'The Heart of the Matter: Sierra Leone, Diamonds, and Human Security' (at: www.pacweb.org/e/pdf/heart%20of%20the%20matter.doc).

Ramanathan, Usha, 2001, 'Business and Human Rights: The India Paper', International Environment Law Research Centre, Geneva (at: www.ielrc.org/content/w0102.pdf).

Ruggie, John G., 2006, 'Interim Report of the Special Representative of the Secretary-General on the Issue of Human Rights and Transnational Corporations and Other Business Enterprises', UN doc. E. CN.4/2006/97.

Ruggie, John G., 2007, *Human Rights Policies of Chinese Companies: Results from a Survey*, Harvard University.

Shell Co., 2006, 'Sustainability Report 2006' (at: http://sustainabilityreport.shell.com/responsibleenergy/localdevelopment/shell-foundation.html).
Turner, Mandy, 2007, 'Scramble for Africa', *The Guardian*, 2 May.
United Nations Conference on Trade and Development (UNCTAD), 2007, 'World Investment Report 2007', Vienna (at: www.unctad.org/Templates/webflyer.asp?docid=9001&intItemID=2068&lang=1).
World Bank, 2007, 'Africa's Silk Road: China and India's New Economic Frontier', Washington, DC (at: http://web.worldbank.org/WBSITE/EXTERNAL/COUNTRIES/AFRICAEXT/0contentMDK :21056305 ~menuPK :258666 ~ pagePK : 146736~piPK: 226340~theSitePK:258644,00.html).

# 6
# As Good as it Gets: Securing Diamonds in Sierra Leone

*Neil Cooper*

Three interrelated factors make Sierra Leone in general and its extractive sector in particular worthy of examination. First, since the formal declaration of peace in 2002 the country has emerged as a model of liberal peacebuilding.[1] The UN deployed one of its largest ever peacekeeping operations at a total cost of $2.8 billion.[2] Official development assistance to Sierra Leone (multilateral, bilateral and UN agencies) amounted to US$1.2 billion between 2003 and 2006 (DACO, 2006: 7) and in 2006 the country's $1.6 billion debt was forgiven (ICG, 2007: 8). In 2007 the country experienced its second successful post-conflict national election resulting in a transition of power to the opposition All People's Congress.

Second, while various factors contributed to, and sustained, the war in Sierra Leone (Gberie, 2005; Keen, 2005; Richards, 1996), the country has become indelibly associated with the trade in 'conflict diamonds'. Moreover, the emergence of several apparently diamond-related conflicts in the 1990s led to the creation in January 2003 of the Kimberley Process Certification Scheme (KPCS) – a global certification system which aims to prevent the trade in conflict diamonds. Although the regime operates under a rather restrictive definition of conflict diamonds, it includes virtually all the states involved in the global diamond trade and includes a commitment not to trade with non-members. The regime is thus considered to have 'regulatory teeth', in contrast to the more 'gummy' voluntary codes that have characterised other ethical trading initiatives (Turner, 2006). Furthermore, the Sierra Leone government anticipated Kimberley by introducing its own certification regime in September 2000, since when official diamond exports have risen dramatically (Figure 6.1). Sierra Leone therefore appears as a specific example of the generally beneficial effects of the Kimberley regime.

Third, the political economy of peacebuilding in Sierra Leone in general, and reform of the diamond sector in particular, reflects the merger of security and development highlighted by commentators as a feature of post-Cold War liberal interventionism (Duffield, 2001, 2005; Goodhand,

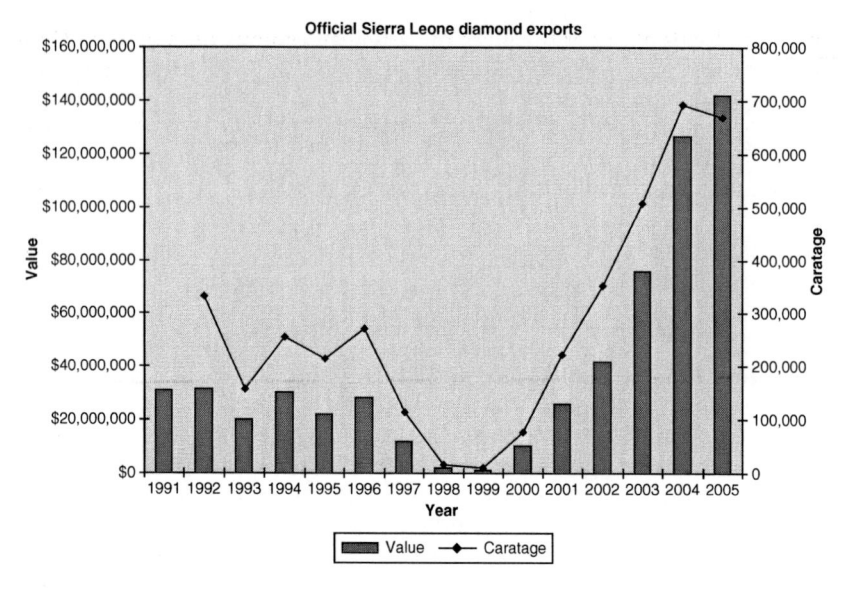

*Figure 6.1* Official Sierrra Leone diamond exports
*Source*: Government Gold and Diamond Office, Sierra Leone.

2006; Richmond, 2005). Two aspects of this merger are relevant here. First, underdevelopment, particularly when manifest in weak states, has been securitised as a threat to the *developed* world, as such states are deemed to be the source of numerous instabilities that threaten global order – disease, crime, terror and refugees (Cooper, 2006). For the 2005 UN's High Level Panel on Threats, this has given rise to the phenomenon of 'mutual vulnerability' in which both the rich and the poor worlds are threatened by poverty, thus creating a mutual interest in redressing the conditions of the poor in the global South (United Nations, 2005). Symptomatic of this is the apparent shift from the rigours of structural adjustment and general scepticism about the role of the state to a 'post-Washington consensus' emphasis on poverty reduction and the importance of state strength and state institutions in maintaining order and delivering development. For critics on the other hand, while the perception of threat may actually be misplaced (Hehir, 2007), it has nevertheless produced a policy response that Paul Rogers describes as 'liddism' (Rogers, 2000) – one designed to keep the lid on disorder rather than fundamentally transform the underlying conditions of the poor. Second, the merger of security and development rests on the notion that the two are interdependent, and mutually reinforcing. In contrast, I suggest that in Sierra Leone it has permitted the encroachment of security (in its narrow sense) into development, and continued 'neoliberalisation' under the guise of participatory poverty reduction. Consequently, whilst the security element of the security/development equation has been pursued relatively successfully, a particularly anaemic version of 'development as security' has been implemented. Thus, while Sierra Leone may well be a model of contemporary peacebuilding, it demonstrates the limits of a liberal intervention framework best characterised as 'liddism' in operation. This argument is first developed with respect to macroeconomic policy in general and then with respect to the diamond sector in particular.

## The political economy of peacebuilding in Sierra Leone

Liberal intervention in Sierra Leone has been relatively successful in re-establishing order. The state's monopoly of violence has been resuscitated (ICG, 2007: 12), with the army and the police, buoyed by various security sector reform initiatives pursued by donors, generally considered to be among the more effective institutions (personal interview, 2007). Security has also been underpinned by the UN peacekeeping force (withdrawn in 2005) and, initially at least, a British 'over-the-horizon' security guarantee to provide a military reaction to a crisis within 48 to 72 hours (ICG, 2001: 21).

However, six years after the final ceasefire and five years after the formal declaration of peace, poverty remains pervasive with a 35 per cent literacy rate and a 70 per cent unemployment rate (Lancaster, 2007: 10); only 7 per cent of the population is able to access electricity (UN Peacebuilding Commission, 2007) and the average life expectancy is 41. In real terms GDP per head in 2005 remained below the levels in 1990 prior to the outbreak of conflict (World Bank, 2007: 25) and Sierra Leone is ranked last in the UNDP's 2007 *Human Development Index* (UNDP, 2007: 229–32).

Donor influence on the country has been extensive: combining the use of old-fashioned conditionalities (Balogun and Gberie, 2005; Thomson, 2007: 30) with newer 'post-conditionality' forms of influence via more direct involvement in government (Chapter 19, this volume). In the diamond sector, for example, the UK's Department for International Development (DFID) funded the post of Director General of the Ministry of Mineral Resources – a position held (at the time of writing) by a Canadian expatriate consultant provided by Adam Smith International. Donor–government discussions on the diamond sector formally take place in the High Level Diamond Steering Committee, which includes representatives from the UK, United States, EU and World Bank (USAID, 2004: 2).

Nevertheless, the discourse on both broad macroeconomic policy and the diamond sector suggests a sea change from the structural adjustment prescriptions imposed on pre-conflict Sierra Leone. The emphasis, post-war, is on local participation, ownership and empowerment. For example, it is claimed that the development strategy reflects 'the outcome of extensive participatory consultations' (IMF, 2001: 2). However, not only has the extent of such consultations been questioned (Castañada, 2006: 97–8; Kamara with Nkaw, 2006), the macroeconomic prescription for post-conflict Sierra Leone bears a striking similarity to the 'one size fits all' prescriptions of earlier periods of international financial institutions (IFIs) tutelage and for other developing countries. The emphasis has been on reducing corporation and income tax, lowering tariff rates and promoting privatisation (World Bank, 2006: 106) – with consultants proposing that the last should be facilitated by ensuring that Highly Indebted Poor Country debt relief incorporates debt write-off for enterprises scheduled for privatisation (PricewaterhouseCoopers, 2007: 41). In addition, cuts in income tax have been offset with recommendations for introduction of a regressive sales tax as part of a policy to promote 'sustainable pro-poor growth' (IMF, 2005: 15; 2007: 29–31).

The debate over the government's decision to raise public sector salaries in response to a two-day general strike in 2005 is particularly instructive with regard to the role of donor influence, the intermingling of the security and development agendas and the co-option of apparently radical language to frame the promotion of neoliberal orthodoxies. Viewing the issue through the lens of security, the International Monetary Fund (IMF) agreed with the authorities that the strike 'threatened state security in a fragile, post-conflict environment, leaving the government with little choice [but to raise salaries]' (IMF, 2005: 16). Viewed from a development and poverty reduction perspective, however, the IMF has been equally adamant that the consequent increase in the wage bill 'weakened the government's ability to meet poverty-related expenditure targets' (ibid.) and insists it avoid a repeat of 2005. This is in a context where the World Bank has noted 'many civil servants have salaries that are close to or below the poverty threshold' (World Bank, 2003: 16).

Much the same phenomenon can be seen in the government's 2005 poverty reduction strategy paper (PRSP). The conceptual merger of security and development provided the context in which the PRSP could note 'almost all sectors and sub-sectors in the budget are poverty-focused including the security sector' (World Bank, 2005a: 107–8). Consequently, 16.1 per cent of projected PRSP expenditure for the period 2005–2007 was allocated to security initiatives that included restructuring the army and developing an intelligence service to support the army and police (ibid., annex 2: 138 and annex 4: 152–4). In contrast, projected funding on education and health accounted for 5.8 per cent and 8 per cent of overall expenditure, respectively. This is not to suggest that expenditure on the security sector in Sierra Leone is unnecessary but that legitimising it as intrinsic to poverty reduction obfuscates the hard decisions that need to be taken between spending on the security services and spending on other sectors that produce clear benefits for the economy. This is particularly the case given that spending on the security sector is generally considered to act as a drag on economic growth (Chan, 1985; Sandler and Hartley, 1995: 201–20) and may even increase the risk of a return to conflict (Collier and Hoeffler, 2004).

In broad terms, then, phrases such as 'development', 'poverty reduction' and 'job creation' have become substitutes for the continued application of neoliberal prescriptions that privilege privatisation, marketisation and the presumed trickle-down benefits of macroeconomic stability over emergency job creation, social welfare and subsidy and protection for strategic sectors of the economy. This is in contrast to World Bank research that suggests spending on social policies produces significant benefits for growth, even if this is done at the expense of a deterioration in macroeconomic balances (Collier *et al*., 2003: 155). Moreover, inherent in the merger of security and development is an implied teleology of peacebuilding in which the creation of security (understood as order and stability) can create the conditions for development actors to work their economic miracles. In Sierra Leone, however, the establishment of order has led most of them to withdraw or scale down their activities in favour of work in new security hot zones.

The combined effect of such policies has led Joseph Hanlon to ask whether donors are encouraging the reproduction of the conditions that caused the war (Hanlon, 2005: 471). While this overlooks the relative success in delivering security as order inside Sierra Leone and the removal of external security threats (such as Charles Taylor), it does highlight the profound limits to development policy in Sierra Leone, which has limited the direct promotion of alternative livelihoods outside of the alluvial diamond sector.

## The diamond sector

Reform of the diamond sector in Sierra Leone has notably reflected the broader emphasis on, and relative success of, policies designed within a security and law and order framework, compared with development initiatives.

The diamond industry has traditionally functioned as a mainstay of the country's economy, accounting for some 70 per cent of foreign exchange earnings in the 1960s and 1970s (PAC and NMJD, 2004: 2), but has also been characterised by significant levels of smuggling. The capture and control of this shadow trade by governing elites in the 1970s and 1980s contributed to a radical decline in official exports, further exacerbated during the civil war when the rebel Revolutionary United Front (RUF) gained control of the key diamond-producing region. However, the introduction of a national diamond certification system in 2000 and the inception of the global Kimberley regime in 2003 have coincided with a significant increase in official exports (see Figure 6.1).

In part, this is explicable by the fact that while the formal aim of the Kimberley regime is simply to prevent the trade in *conflict* diamonds, the creation of a global certification system designed to record the export and import of each package of rough diamonds means that it also functions *de facto* as a regime to prevent the illicit trade in diamonds more generally (PAC, 2006: 3). Thus, even post-conflict, post-RUF Sierra Leone would appear to have experienced the beneficial effects of Kimberley certification.

In reality, several other factors have also contributed to the rise in official exports, including reassertion of government control over the diamond areas, a rise in mining operations since the end of the conflict and a commitment by key actors in the diamond community to export through the official system. The imposition of UN sanctions on Liberian diamonds from 2001 through to May 2007 also created incentives for diamonds to be smuggled *into* the country (Global Witness, 2005: 16–17), as has the conflict in Côte d'Ivoire and the tightening of regulations concerning the import of cash in Guinea (World Bank, 2006: 63). Moreover, the extent of the local 'buy-in' to the official certification process compared with shadow trade is highly contingent on a range of risk/reputation/opportunity cost calculations that actors in the industry constantly make. For example, a proposal in 2005 to effectively raise the tax burden on diamond exporters resulted in a significant increase in official exports from Guinea (personal interview, 2007). Certainly, a substantial proportion of diamonds are still exported illicitly. Indeed, the literature on the post-conflict diamond sector evinces an almost obsessive concern with attempting to quantify this trade, although estimates vary widely (see, for example, IMF, 2005: 34; Zohar, 2003).

Nevertheless, the substantial rise in official exports cannot be totally discounted. It would therefore appear that the attempt to monitor and regulate diamond exports within the security and policing framework of the Kimberley certification system has, to date at least, been relatively successful. As Partnership Africa Canada has noted, though,

> The Kimberley Process is strictly about controlling the trade in rough diamonds, in order to ensure [they]...are not used to finance conflict. There is nothing in the KPCS requiring governments to improve the lot of diamond miners, to distribute the wealth from diamond mining to local communities, or to use the revenues from diamond mining for anything at all.
>
> (PAC, 2007: 6)

However, the global discourse on the diamond industry has evolved to incorporate a concern about the developmental impact of the rough diamond trade. The concrete manifestation of this at the global level came in October 2005 with the foundation of the Diamond Development Initiative (DDI), which aimed to 'optimize the beneficial development impact of artisanal diamond mining to miners and their communities within countries in which the diamonds are mined' (PAC website: DDI).

This broader agenda has also been reflected in the meetings and the work of the Kimberley system itself, most notably in the work of the KPCS Working Group on Alluvial/Artisanal Producers. Thus, while the DDI and Kimberley are notionally distinct, there is a degree of overlap in their espousal of the diamond development perspective. In one sense, then, this can be understood as an evolution of the broad agenda associated with Kimberley so that it *effectively* incorporates both the security (conflict diamonds/anti-smuggling) and development aspects of the trade in rough diamonds (DDI agenda). However, at the global level at least, the DDI has not really gone beyond holding conferences and producing papers to generate any concrete initiative. Inside Sierra Leone, though, donors have funded various initiatives rooted in the kind of development perspective that underpins the DDI, although most pre-date its formal creation. As in the case of the broader merger of security and development, the promise of this merging of the 'conflict' and 'development diamonds' frameworks is that it reflects and harnesses the symbiotic relationship between the two themes, particularly for post-conflict societies. Moreover, just as there is deemed to be a teleology of peacebuilding involving a gradual shift in emphasis from security to development, so the emergence of diamond development initiatives can be understood as reflecting a similar process at work on the specific issue of conflict diamonds as the diamond-related conflicts of the 1990s have formally concluded.

In contrast, policy in Sierra Leone is notable more for the way in which both the operation of Kimberley and the local reform initiatives aimed at the diamond sector have manifestly failed to promote development. There is insufficient space here to deal with the full range of policy issues pertinent to the diamond sector and what follows will necessarily represent a brief and simplified analysis. However, one way of illustrating this argument is to focus on three core development challenges for the diamond sector: raising the conditions and pay of the diggers, raising government revenue from diamond exports and addressing the problem of capital flight. The remainder of this chapter will therefore examine these issues.

## Raising the conditions and pay of the diggers

The diamond economy in Sierra Leone comprises an industrial mining sector mainly concentrated on the Kimberlite mining operations of Koidu Holdings and an alluvial diamond sector traditionally dominated by artisanal production – though the Sierra Leone Diamond Company (SLDC), for example, has plans for the industrial mining of alluvial diamonds (Levin and Gberie, 2006: 6). There are some concerns that production from the alluvial sector may decline in the future as traditional mining areas become exhausted. Nevertheless, this sector currently provides the majority of diamond exports from Sierra Leone.

The alluvial diamond economy incorporates a diverse range of actors and trading relationships. In its bare essentials, however, it is best depicted as a

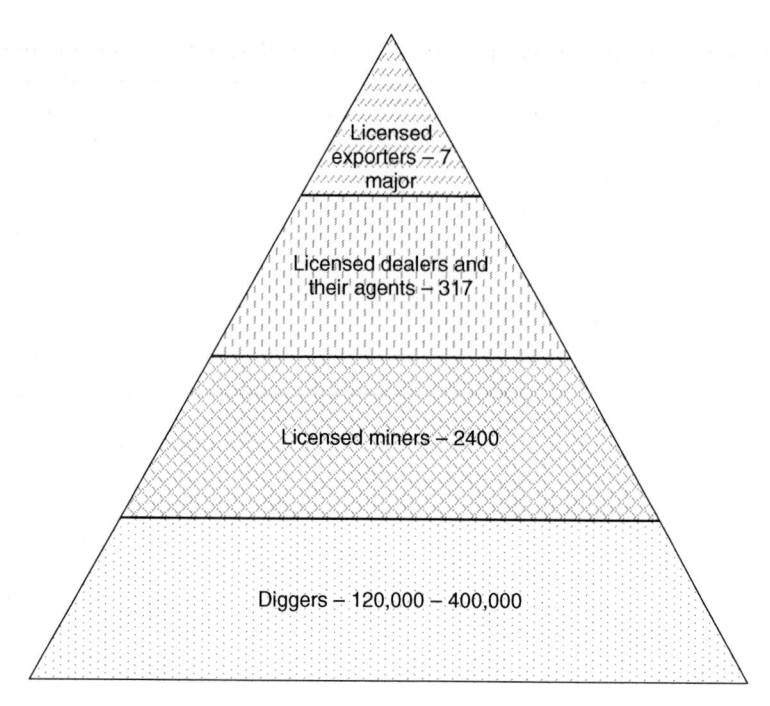

```
                    /\
                   /  \
                  /Licensed\
                 /exporters – 7\
                /    major      \
               /------------------\
              /                    \
             / Licensed dealers and \
            /   their agents – 317   \
           /--------------------------\
          /                            \
         /                              \
        /    Licensed miners – 2400      \
       /----------------------------------\
      /                                    \
     /                                      \
    /                                        \
   /        Diggers – 120,000 – 400,000       \
  /--------------------------------------------\
```

*Figure 6.2* The diamond pyramid in Sierra Leone
Source: Levin and Gberie, 2006: 30.

pyramid (Figure 6.2). At the base there are thousands of diggers, estimated at 120,000–400,000. Next up the pyramid are those who organise and manage the mining of diamonds. Officially, they require a licence from the Ministry of Mines and are often referred to as licence holders or miners, although many who mine plots may not actually hold a licence. Licensed miners will often be funded or 'supported' by those further up the pyramid. These include dealers and their agents who purchase diamonds and sell them on to exporters who are the only actors in the industry officially authorised to export Sierra Leone's diamonds (Temple et al., 2005).

It should be noted that the rewards for diggers in terms of income, financial stability and access to powerful contacts are attractive compared to available alternative income sources (Temple et al., 2005). Nevertheless, the diamond pyramid is highly exploitative. Working conditions for diggers are generally poor with one report listing malaria, diarrhoea, respiratory diseases and schistosomiasis among the prevalent illnesses suffered, and noting that drowning or suffocation after a mine has collapsed is not uncommon (DFID, 2006: 2). Traditionally, most diggers have not been employed as wage labourers but work under one of various profit-sharing agreements with the licence holder.

It is unclear, therefore, exactly how much diggers earn, but there is general agreement that it is very little (PAC and NMJD, 2006: 2; Temple *et al.*, 2005; World Bank, 2005b: 12). This is perhaps best reflected in the model contract promoted by the United Mineworkers Union (UMU) for those working as wage labourers. This stipulates a payment of LE 6000 per day (roughly £1 in 2008) plus the provision of food (costing roughly LE 3000). In the event of death the licence holder is required to provide compensation amounting to LE 350,000 (£56), plus a funeral and two bags of rice (UMU, undated; personal interview, 2007). Given that the vast majority of workers in the alluvial sector are not unionised, the model contract is perhaps best regarded as an aspiration. As a diamond is traded up the pyramid, its value increases substantially with one estimate suggesting prices rise over 800 per cent from mine to exporter (Levin and Gbeire, 2006: 29). In 2005 the three leading exporters, who account for the majority of artisanal diamond exports, officially exported diamonds amounting to US$105 million (ibid.: 28).

As noted above, donors have funded initiatives aimed at redressing the exploitation of the diggers, three being of particular note. The first promotes cooperative mining, supported by USAID's Integrated Diamond Management Program (IDMP) run by the consultancy firm Management Systems International (MSI) and the local Peace Diamonds Alliance (PDA) (also initiated under the IDMP programme). However, while some 50 cooperatives were registered with the government, only 5 actually began operations in 2005. Private investment for them had to be sought when expected funding from USAID did not materialise (Global Witness, 2006: 10). Under the terms of this arrangement, investors would recoup their original loan, plus a commission on the sale of the diamonds. Crucially, the fixing of prices to 10 per cent below the Antwerp market price guaranteed the cooperatives a higher price for their diamonds, and the model aimed to bypass the dealer layer of the pyramid where most of the local profit on diamonds is made (Levin and Gberie, 2006: 9). Unfortunately, all the cooperatives made a loss in their first year and there have also been allegations of corruption involving the diversion of funds provided by the financiers (ibid.). Consequently, the experiment stalled, although this is also partly a function of USAID's review of its own activities in Sierra Leone more generally. However, with roughly 100 people in each cooperative (personal interview, 2007) the programme was never implemented on a scale that could have made a meaningful difference to the majority of diggers and miners in the industry anyway.

The second major project was an initiative implemented under the auspices of the PDA to provide training in the valuation of diamonds so as to better equip diggers and miners with the knowledge necessary to negotiate a fairer return from local dealers. However, while an estimated 1000 diggers have been trained, like the cooperative experiment, the project has ceased (personal interview, 2007). Moreover, the main players in the diamond market operate rather like a cartel. Consequently, the fact that sellers know they are being offered an unfair price for diamonds does not alter the fact they are unlikely to get a better one elsewhere.

The third key initiative has been DFID support for the UMU. This has certainly been an important innovation, the union being involved in negotiating wages and conditions with major mining companies such as Koidu Holdings. However, as noted above, very few alluvial diggers are actually members of the union. This seems unlikely to change unless union recognition is made a condition of granting licences to engage in alluvial mining. It should also be noted that (as of mid-2007) DFID was widely perceived in Sierra Leone to be preparing to reduce its diamond sector activities (personal interviews, 2007).

Thus at the global level, the DDI has produced little in the way of concrete initiatives to improve the lot of diggers across the world, while low funding levels and an absence of long-term commitment for programmes introduced in Sierra Leone have left them essentially looking tokenistic.

### Raising government revenue from the mining sector

While Kimberley is purely designed to prevent the trade in conflict diamonds, it is argued that the regime can also help to strengthen governments by increasing the volume of official diamond exports to provide much needed revenue from licensing fees and income and export taxes (PAC, 2006: 4). This argument has particular resonance for Sierra Leone, where diamonds accounted for 94 per cent of exports in 2005 (World Bank, 2006: 7). However, the permeability of borders means that, like all alluvial diamond exporters, the government is limited in the taxes it can impose on the diamond sector for fear of stimulating the unofficial trade into neighbouring countries. Consequently, the export tax is set at just 3 per cent, and revenue from this and licensing fees was an estimated $5.2 million in 2004 (PAC, 2006: 7). This is a marked improvement compared with levels prior to, and during, the conflict. Moreover, a proportion of the export tax has been specifically allocated to a Diamond Area Community Development Fund which distributed some $850,000 in 2004 – although proposals for donors to provide seed money/match funding do not appear to have materialised (Temple, 2005). Nevertheless, this is hardly the kind of return that would permit the government to kick start development. The situation is even worse in neighbouring Liberia where government revenue from the now sanction-free diamond sector is predicted to be just $500,000–750,000, enough to cover the costs of implementing the regulation required for membership of Kimberley but little else (PAC, 2007: 5).

In theory, the same concerns about smuggling do not arise in the case of larger mining companies such as Koidu Holdings. However, commentators have highlighted the lack of transparency over government decisions on mining and other concessions, fuelling suspicions of corruption (ICG, 2001: 11). Arguably of even more relevance though is the fact that the government is constrained in its ability to impose taxes on such companies because its reputation as a post-conflict state located in an area marked by regional instability already makes it an unattractive investment (personal interviews, 2007). Ironically, the campaign around the issue of conflict diamonds has also made major diamond companies wary of the reputational risks involved in investing in the country while its relatively small share of the global market means companies do not feel compelled to have a stake in Sierra Leone.

Consequently, Koidu Holdings has been granted tax concessions, including duty free facilities for equipment and other mining-related imported goods as well as waivers for the residential permits of its foreign employees. Outside of the diamond sector, one government review has estimated revenue losses from concessions granted to the titanium operations of the company Sierra Rutile would amount to $98 million from 2004 to 2016 (PAC, 2006: 8).

Regional harmonisation of tax and other policies within the Mano River Union (MRU: Sierra Leone, Liberia and Guinea) would arguably provide some limited scope to increase tax rates but while efforts have been made in this direction, progress has been limited by the persistence of regional security concerns and the under-resourcing of the MRU Secretariat. However, for Kimberley to deliver significant returns for the government from the diamond sector, it would have to be radically restructured in ways that seem unlikely to eventuate (see below).

Furthermore, the 'conflict' motif attached to Sierra Leone's diamond sector has meant that donors have prioritised action on this sector whereas other sectors, most notably gold, have been relatively neglected in terms of both Kimberley-type anti-smuggling initiatives and the promotion of DDI development initiatives. Consequently, the vast majority of gold production is assumed to be smuggled across the border via Guinea (personal interview, 2007).

## Capital flight

Even if the government is unable to raise taxes on the diamond sector, the economy should be able to benefit more generally from the profits made by actors in both the formal and the informal diamond sectors. However, the legal diamond sector is dominated by the Lebanese community while nationals from other Economic Community of West African States such as Guinea, Gambia, Senegal and Mali are heavily represented in the dealer/supporter category. Both groups, and particularly the Lebanese community, retain substantial personal and business interests outside the country, often selling to affiliates in diamond centres such as Antwerp (Levin and Gberie, 2006: 37–8). Some of the funds from diamond sales do return, as many individuals use the profits to support enterprises in other sectors of the economy such as construction and the import of rice, permitting them to dominate these sectors too. Nevertheless, much of the value added inside Sierra Leone's diamond pyramid is only realised outside the country, leading one report to conclude that 'hardly any of the profits generated by the diamond sector are reinvested in Sierra Leone' (Zohar, 2003: 7). From this perspective, Sierra Leone's main problem is not so much the scale of smuggling but the phenomenon of capital flight, an issue that is widely recognised but one on which little substantive action has been taken, either in the context of Kimberley or the wider reforms of the diamond sector in Sierra Leone.

## Conclusion

In conclusion, the security dimension of the security–development nexus has been pursued relatively successfully in Sierra Leone – order has been restored, the police and army are now among the more effective institutions and Charles Taylor has been removed from neighbouring Liberia. In the diamond sector, while smuggling levels are significant and the local buy-in to certification is highly contingent on a range of other factors, the conflict and policing approach inherent in Kimberley probably has made a contribution to the steep rise in official exports. Thus, Hanlon's suggestion that external intervention has produced a restoration of the *status quo ante* is not quite accurate.

However, the pursuit of 'development as security' in the broader economy has been either encroached by security or 'neoliberalised'. Within the diamond sector the security framework has meant that action on 'conflict diamonds' has been aggressively pursued while other sectors such as gold have been relatively neglected. The pay and conditions of the diggers have mainly been addressed via laudable but mainly tokenistic initiatives. Similarly, the ability of the government to raise revenue through taxes and to prevent capital flight is limited by the local, regional and global structure of the industry, while Kimberley does not have a formal remit to promote development, raise government revenue or address capital flight. Nor does current global and local action on the diamond sector more generally offer solutions – at best it is aimed at marginally ameliorating the devastating human consequences arising from Sierra Leone's position in the global market, rather than transforming global market structures to benefit-producing countries.

There are potential reforms that might make a difference to diggers, government and the economy. These include, for example, reforming Kimberley so that it includes an explicit remit to promote development, and so that it acts as a global income redistribution scheme with a Kimberley tax on jewellery sales used to properly fund social protection and development initiatives in the diamond sectors of producing states. It might also include a greater role for the state in the production and marketing of diamonds and the provision of state/donor subsidies to finance the establishment of a niche cutting and polishing industry designed to add value within Sierra Leone. However, such initiatives seem unlikely to occur in the short term at least given the securitisation and 'neoliberalisation' of approaches to Sierra Leone in general and the diamond sector in particular. Thus, on the development side of the security–development equation Hanlon's analysis appears more accurate. Indeed, international policy on Sierra Leone is best described as an example of relatively successful (short-term) 'liddism'. If Sierra Leone is a model of liberal peacebuilding, then it rather begs the question 'Is this really as good as it gets?'

## Notes

1. See UN Integrated Office in Sierra Leone (at: www.uniosil.org/content.asp?catid=1& navid=14).
2. See Department of Peacekeeping Operations (at: www.un.org/Depts/dpko/missions/unamsil/facts.html).

## References

Balogun, Paul and Lansana Gberie, 2005, *Assessing the Performance of the Long-Term Partnership Agreement Between the Governments of Sierra Leone and the UK*, London: DFID.
Castañada, Carla, 2006, 'Trickle Down Peace: Security and Political Economy Discourse in Sierra Leone', unpublished MPhil thesis, University of Bradford.
Chan, Steve, 1985, 'The Impact of Defense Spending on Economic Performance: A Survey of Evidence and Problems', *Orbis*, Vol. 29, No. 2, pp. 403–34.
Collier, Paul, Lani Elliott, Harvard Hegre, Anke Hoeffler, Marta Reynol-Querol and Nick Sambanis, 2003, *Breaking the Conflict Trap: Civil War and Development Policy*, Oxford: World Bank/Oxford University Press.
Collier, Paul and Anke Hoeffler, 2004, 'Military Expenditures in Post-Conflict Societies', Centre for the Study of African Economics Working Paper Series, No. 213 (at: www.bepress.com/csae/paper213).
Cooper, Neil, 2006, 'Chimeric Governance and the Extension of Resource Regulation', *Conflict, Security and Development*, Vol. 6, No. 3, pp. 315–35.
DACO (Development Assistance Coordination Office), 2006, 'Development Assistance to Sierra Leone 2006' (at: www.daco-sl.org/reports/Dev_ass_rep06.pdf).
DFID (Department for International Development), 2006, *Livelihood Report*, London.
Duffield, Mark, 2001, *Global Governance and the New Wars: The Merging of Development and Security*, London: Zed Books.
Duffield, Mark, 2005, 'Getting Savages to Fight Barbarians: Development, Security and the Colonial Present', *Conflict Security and Development*, Vol. 5, No. 2, pp. 141–59.
Gberie, Lansana, 2005, *A Dirty War in West Africa: The RUF and the Destruction of Sierra Leone*, London: Hurst.
Global Witness, 2005, 'Making It Work: Why the Kimberley Process Must Do More to Stop Conflict Diamonds' (at: www.globalwitness.org).
Global Witness, 2006, 'Experiences and Lessons Learned: Monitoring the Integrated Diamond Management Program's Diamond Tracking System in Sierra Leone' (at: www.globalwitness.org).

Goodhand, Jonathan, 2006, *Aiding Peace? The Role of NGOs in Armed Conflict*, Boulder, CO: Lynne Rienner.
Hanlon, Joseph, 2005, 'Is the International Community Helping to Recreate the Preconditions for War in Sierra Leone?', *The Round Table*, Vol. 94, No. 381, pp. 459–72.
Hehir, Aidan, 2007, 'The Myth of the Failed State and the War on Terror: A Challenge to the Conventional Wisdom', *Journal of Intervention and Statebuilding*, Vol. 1, No. 3, pp. 307–32.
ICG (International Crisis Group), 2001, *Sierra Leone: Managing Uncertainty*, ICG Africa Report No. 35, Freetown/Brussels.
ICG, 2007, *Sierra Leone: The Election Opportunity*, Africa Report, No. 129, Dakar/Brussels.
IMF, 2001, *Joint Staff Assessment and the Interim Poverty Reduction Strategy Paper*, July 16 (at: www.imf.org/external/np/jsa/2001/sle/eng/071601.pdf).
IMF, 2005, 'Sierra Leone: Sixth Review Under the Poverty Reduction and Growth Facility Arrangement, Requests for Waiver of Performance Criteria and Additional Interim Assistance Under the Enhanced Initiative for Heavily Indebted Poor Countries, Review of Financing Assurances and Ex Post Assessment of Longer Term Program Engagement', IMF Country Report No. 05/194, June, Washington, DC.
IMF, 2007, *Annual Progress Report. Sierrra Leone: Poverty Reduction Strategy Paper*, September 2006, IMF Country Report No. 07/17, January, Washington, DC.
Kamara, Siapha with John Nkaw, 2006, *Poverty Reduction Strategy Paper Sensitization and Budget Advocacy Project* (at: www.nmjd.org/Governance%20and%20Accountability.htm).
Keen, David, 2005, *Conflict and Collusion in Sierra Leone*, Oxford: James Curry.
Lancaster, Carol, 2007, '"We Fall Down and Get Up" State Failure, Democracy and Development in Sierra Leone', Centre for Global Development, Washington, DC (at: www.cgdev.org/content/publications/detail/14314).
Levin, Estelle A. and Lansana Gberie, 2006, *Dealing for Development? A Study of Diamond Marketing and Pricing in Sierra Leone*, Diamond Development Initiative, Ottawa: Partnership Africa–Canada.
PAC (Partnership Africa–Canada), 2006, *Killing Kimberley? Conflict Diamonds and Paper Tigers*, Occasional Paper No. 15, rev. edn, Ottawa.
PAC, 2007, *Land Grabbing and Land Reform: Diamonds, Rubber and Forests in the New Liberia*, Occasional Paper No. 17, Ottawa.
PAC and NMJD (Network Movement for Justice and Development), 2004, *Diamond Industry Annual Review: Sierra Leone 2004*, Freetown/Ottawa.
PAC and NMJD, 2006, *Diamond Industry Annual Review: Sierra Leone 2006*, Freetown/Ottawa.
PricewaterhouseCoopers (for DFID), 2007, 'Technical Assistance to the National Commission for Privatisation, Sierra Leone', Inception Report, January (at: www.dfid.gov.uk/pubs/files/sierra-leone-inception report.pdf).
Richards, Paul, 1996, *Fighting for the Rainforest: War, Youth and Resources in Sierra Leone*, London: James Curry.
Richmond, Oliver P., 2005, *The Transformation of Peace*, London: Palgrave.
Rogers, Paul, 2000, *Losing Control: Global Security in the Twenty-first Century*, London: Pluto.
Sandler, Todd and Keith Hartley, 1995, *The Economics of Defence*, Cambridge: Cambridge University Press.
Temple, Helen, Estelle, Levin, Anusmana Babar Turay and M. Renzie, 2005, 'Mining the "Chaos" in Sierra Leone's Diamond Fields: Policy and Program Implications of the Structure of the Artisanal Mining Sector in Sierra Leone',

Management Systems International for USAID (at Peace Diamonds Alliance: www.resourcebeneficiation.org/publications.asp?ID=06&RID=27).

Temple, Paul, 2005, 'Improving the Effective Use of the Diamond Area Community Development Fund (DACDF): Report for Submission to the Government of Sierra Leone High Level Diamond Steering Committee', Washington DC: Management Systems International for USAID, December.

Thomson, Brian, 2007, *Sierra Leone: Reform or Relapse? Conflict and Governance Reform*, London: Chatham House, June.

Turner, Mandy, 2006, 'Taming Mammon: Corporate Social Responsibility and the Global Regulation of Conflict Trade', *Conflict, Security and Development*, Vol. 6, No. 3, pp. 365–87.

UMU-SL (United Mineworkers Union Sierra Leone), 'Terms and Conditions of Work for Grass Root Diggers and Miners Engaged in Diamond and Gold Mining Activities in Sierra Leone', Freetown, undated.

United Nations, 2005, *A More Secure World: Our Shared Responsibility. Report of the High Level Panel on Threats, Challenges and Change*, New York: United Nations.

UNDP, 2007, *Human Development Report 2007/2008. Fighting Climate Change: Human Solidarity in a Divided World*, Basingstoke: Palgrave Macmillan.

United Nations Peacebuilding Commission, 2007, 'Informal Thematic Discussion: Sierra Leone Energy Sector Development', 13 November, Chair's Summary Note, New York: United Nations.

USAID/Management Systems International (MSI), 2004, 'Potential Diamond Anti-Smuggling Activities for Consideration in Sierra Leone', Freetown/Washington.

World Bank, 2003, 'Sierra Leone: Strategic Options for Public Sector Reform', Report No. 255110-SL, 5 August, Washington, DC.

World Bank, 2005a, 'Republic of Sierra Leone Joint IDA-IMF Staff Advisory Note on the Poverty Reduction Strategy Paper', 13 April, Washington, DC.

World Bank, 2005b, 'Sierra Leone: Tapping the Mineral Wealth for Human Progress – A Break With the Past', 25 July, Report No. 26141-SL, Washington, DC.

World Bank, 2006, 'Sierra Leone: Adding Value Through Trade for Poverty Reduction. A Diagnostic Trade Integration Study', 27 October (at: http://siteresources.worldbank.org/SIERRALEONEEXTN/Resources/DTIS_Final.pdf).

World Bank, 2007, *Africa Development Indicators 2007*, Washington, DC.

Zohar, Chaim Evan, 2003, 'Sierra Leone Diamond Sector Financial Policy Constraints', MSI for Peace Diamonds Alliance and USAID (at: www.resourcebeneficiation.org/home.asp?id=12).

# Part III
# Employment

# 7
# From Waging War to Peace Work: Labour and Labour Markets

*Christopher Cramer*

## A developmental astigmatism

Gary Fields has argued (2007: 5) that

> The status of labor market analysis and labor market policy in the development economics community now is similar to the status of poverty analysis and anti-poverty policy two or three decades ago. At the time, the profession knew that it wanted to take on poverty more fully but most in it didn't know how.

Others might agree that there has indeed been a striking neglect of labour markets within development economics, development studies more broadly, and certainly the policy advice and 'models' of poverty reduction among development agencies. His argument implies a turning tide, scope for a much needed expansion of empirical and theoretical work in this field. Sure enough, there has been some activity, much of it reflecting common trends in the intellectual shifts within development economics of late.

If there is a general weakness in understanding labour markets (and little effort to overcome this weakness) in developing countries, this applies *a fortiori* to labour markets in contexts of war and in 'transitions' from war to peace. The liberal interpretation of war – particularly of the 'war retards development and development retards war' or 'war is development in reverse' variety – cannot conceive of violent conflict as a source of class formation (especially not of capitalist classes). Mainstream economic analyses of war in contemporary developing countries tend to envisage a shrinking, if anything, of labour markets. Rural people, for example, are assumed to 'retreat into subsistence'. This is just one feature of the way that war wipes slates clean. And labour markets barely feature as a policy focus in the programmes for economic recovery after wars that are encouraged by international development agencies. The post-war peace is about liberalising markets and importing the institutions of capable states and good governance. Displaced people and demobilised soldiers, it is hoped, will drift back to their villages and take up where neo-populist pipe-dreams of development are most comfortable imagining them, taking up again activities of self-employment.

Thus, the combination of the imaginings of the liberal interpretation of peace with those of mainstream development economics produces a developmental astigmatism. This is remarkable. It ignores the history of major conflicts within and between countries, in which the destructive activities of warfare are as much produced as they are exchanged and in which there have been dramatic impacts of conflict on labour (and vice versa). Yet the economics of war in recent years has emphasised the grinding out of an equilibrium between two parties to a transaction and a choice made between cooperation/exchange of goods and conflict/exchange of fire (Hirshleifer, 1994).[1]

Beyond the production of the *means* of violence, there is the mobilisation of labour power by various institutional mechanisms to produce violence: people have to be recruited and organised to fight and to provide logistical support, cooking, porterage, and other services that may be central to the reproduction of the labour force of war or that may be incentive goods (including a supply of sources of sexual 'favours').[2] The current astigmatic vision is also blind to the way the organisational tasks of raising and reproducing an effective military force may be easier where membership of an army or militia confers the benefits of social bonds that might not be available from other sources. In this sense, Fithen and Richards's (2005) emphasis on a Durkheimian perspective on the division of labour, stressing the bonds of solidarity (rather than Adam Smith's more technical analysis of the division of labour), is relevant and will be discussed below. The blind spot blots out the way that war might create new entrants to the labour force outside of direct fighting forces, by 'displacing them from the means of production'. Thus, war might create supplies to a wage labour market within countries (e.g., southern Sudanese displaced by war and feeding the demand for cheap labour in the Khartoum construction industry) and in neighbouring countries ('hosts' to refugees; e.g., illegal female immigrants/refugees from the war in Mozambique working, in the early 1990s, in the export horticulture businesses of Mpumalanga, South Africa). Further, the relevance of institutions for the mobilisation of labour and extraction of surplus from labour power to the processes generating violent conflict and to the viability, participation in, and distributional consequences of conflict are rarely acknowledged in the recent economics or even political economy of war.

From this perspective one distinction might be between the study of labour and labour markets under conditions of conflict and the study of the way in which conflict is a mechanism engaged by other mechanisms that reproduce processes of capitalist accumulation and development globally. From the first perspective the relevant questions are about the effect of conflict on the quality and quantity of labour supplies, the terms of engagement of labour in conflict-related activities and in activities happening in spite of or under the regulatory umbrella of conflict, and the socialisation of wartime labour. From the second perspective, the relevant questions are about the way conflict produces intra-national, regional, and international migrants who often provide a source of cheap labour for 'normal', peacetime production; and about the way conflict involves the production of internationally traded commodities whose production finances conflict and is itself often internationalised – as is clear, to take one example, from the multiple interests in the production and trade of coltan during Congolese wars. This particular example links wartime labour conditions in Congo with technologically advanced manufacturing in which coltan is an input. Further, the astigmatism renders benighted observers incapable of seeing more than the faintest blur of the social significance of the effects of war on the labour force that last into and are affected in different ways by a post-war political settlement. War economies shape peace. War economies involve the mobilisation and control of labour under conditions regulated by force. It is, therefore, worth asking how wartime labour relations persist or are subject to change and different forms of regulation during peacetime. *A priori*, this can go two clear ways: on the one hand, war economy relations may carry over into and shape peacetime labour relations, to the detriment of the conditions of labour but possibly to the advantage of particular forms of linkage into the world economy; on the other hand, participation in conflict may generate social ties and 'voice' that presses for improved or changed labour relations in peacetime (see, e.g., Chapter 8, this volume). Furthermore, conflicts may generate new experiences of labour force participation for women, which may or may not be sustained in post-war economic and political settlements.[3]

Mozambique provides examples of this astigmatism affecting policy and research in the context of conflict. For in much research work on Mozambique there has been precisely this development blind spot, combined with a conflict 'lazy eye'. First, a range of economists and sociologists have noted how visions of, and policy ideas about, rural Mozambique have imagined a homogeneous and homeostatic peasant population (Cramer and Pontara, 1998; Duffield, 2007; O'Laughlin, 1996; Sender *et al.*, 2006; Wuyts, 2003). These visions have sustained fantasies of rural self-reliance and are thus instances of what some argue is a far more widespread ideology of 'neo-populist pipe dreams' (Byres, 1979). Second, there is evidence that war, far from representing simply 'development in reverse', actually accelerated processes of socio-economic differentiation and class formation, including pitching people into wage labour – processes that historically have been part and unpleasant parcel of 'development' (Cramer, 2006; Chingono, 1996; Wuyts, 2003).

There are, however, different ways of seeing the links between war, peace, and development in which labour and labour markets play a far more important role. To explore these and to trace some elements of a necessary research agenda, this chapter first discusses contrasting theories of labour markets in developing countries, emphasising their applicability to rural areas. Next it points to the common ailment of empirically blurred vision, whereby rural labour markets especially are regarded as barely existing, let alone relevant to poverty reduction, and it contrasts this with a clearer view offered by some evidence from sub-Saharan Africa. Then the chapter outlines how a clearer theoretical and empirical vision of labour markets, and indeed of the political economy of war, helps to identify a series of connections between labour, labour markets, and war and peace. The point is to identify fields for policy design and research.

## Labour market theories

There is a stark contrast between orthodox, neo-classical economic theories of labour market behaviour and political economy theories influenced by Marxism. Where neo-classical economics treats labour as a commodity like any other, whose exchange is settled by the interplay of supply and demand until an equilibrium (at a market clearing price) is found, Marxist political economy highlights the special characteristics of a commodity inseparable from human labour power and the fact that people selling their own labour power are complex creatures of class, habit, and diversity. Political economy stresses the labour relation, that is the relation between providers of labour power and those who mobilise and hire that labour power, rather than an arms-length exchange. Where neo-classical economics stresses the mutual benefit from the voluntary labour market transaction, political economy may accept the principle of mutual benefit but at the same time stresses the essentially exploitative feature of the relationship between buyer and seller of labour power in a capitalist economy. This exploitation – even where there are gains to the seller of labour power – is what allows the capitalist to derive surplus value from production involving labour and other inputs. Because labour is, by dint of being inseparable from the human beings supplying labour power, different from other commodities and because capitalists too are human and diverse in their needs and reactions (and because of diverse conditions of production in their sectors), political economy is more likely to acknowledge a huge diversity in plural labour markets. Neo-classical economics, traditionally, conceives of a single labour market. Finally, political economy analysis is more attuned to the fuzzy categorical boundaries involved in the distinction between 'free' and 'forced' labour and, indeed, to the continuing relevance of various forms of 'non-economic' compulsion to participate in labour markets (including the interlinkage of labour and other markets in contexts of power), while neo-classical economics by dint of its axiomatic foundations is drawn more to analysing free choice.

There have, however, been developments in orthodox labour market economics, reflecting broader trends in economics. After initially rejecting the arguments by non-orthodox economists and others, neo-classical economists increasingly acknowledged the copious evidence that labour markets did not clear (i.e., that prices, or wages, often do not effectively reconcile supply and demand) and that different labour market outcomes could be observed among populations with, for example, similar human capital 'endowments'; some neo-classical economists came to embrace what has become known as 'segmented labour markets' theory. This involved explanations – from the precepts of methodological individualism but now combined with models of market failure and information issues – of why wages could differ in different parts of an economy for workers with similar attributes (human capital). Others, meanwhile, sought to enhance orthodox economic approaches to labour markets by adopting additional assumptions that might allow models to predict, still from orthodox foundations, that minimum wages can be non-distorting interventions (Basu et al., 2005), or adopting new insights such as those of 'information theoretics' or the acknowledgement that market participants have asymmetric information that can result in sub-optimal outcomes from market transactions. From this latter perspective, for example, Bruce Kaufman (2007) argues that there cannot logically ever be a frictionless labour market.

These developments partly account for the fact that a mainstream economist like Fields (2007) can share very similar views, superficially at least, with a heterodox political economist like Ben Fine (1998). Thus, Fields (2007: 55) argues that 'Developing countries' labour markets are marked by distinct labour market sectors that work in different ways from one another and by complicated interrelationships among the sectors.' Meanwhile, Fine (1998) argues that 'labour markets are not only structurally differentiated from one another in the limited sense of being separate or divided, but that they are internally structured in different ways'. The implication is that 'there is no single generally applicable labour market theory' (ibid.: 5).

Behind this similarity there remain fundamental differences, only partly hinted at by Fields' assumption that the issue of labour market plurality and complexity is particular to developing countries, implying that in developed countries none of this is relevant. Rather, in developed as well as in developing countries, 'underlying socioeconomic determinants endow particular labour markets with particular labour market structures, relations and processes attached to their reproduction and/or transformation' (Fine, 1998: 251). These differences need not be explored in detail here. What matters is to draw out the simple implications for the political economy of war from neo-classical and heterodox labour market economics.

Against the background of competing explanations of labour markets, the following issues are important: how is labour mobilised; what determines labour force participation (labour supply quantity); how do labour relations vary within and between countries; what affects the quality of the labour supply; and how are these issues affected by violent conflict? So little has been written or studied on these questions in the context of wars that there is barely any framework for analysing them. Thus, much of what might be known or recorded in research is fragmented and nudged to the sidelines even where it is relevant.

The theoretical neglect is matched by the typical fragility of empirical knowledge on labour markets, even in terms of the most basic forms of information. International Labour Organisation (ILO) data on employment and unemployment in sub-Saharan Africa, for example, suggests continent-wide trends but draws on a remarkably uneven and weak foundation in national labour force surveys. For example, the most recent official labour market survey in Nigeria is for 1995 and this covers only Lagos state.[4] The ILO's main database on labour has data only on youth unemployment for seven sub-Saharan African countries. 'In the case of Africa...lack of adequate and reliable data makes it difficult to properly assess youth labour force participation, youth unemployment and even more so youth underemployment' (Cling et al., 2007: 8). Further, established practices in household surveys (counting non-kin residents as 'unpaid family workers' rather than as domestic servants; random sampling techniques that neglect the non-random distribution of labour activities; 'main activity' questions; etc.) typically reproduce images of very thin labour market activity in many parts of rural Africa, especially. Yet the ILO (2003) stresses the lack of reliable statistics on waged agricultural labour, which is often 'invisible'. And other studies highlight the neglect of rural non-farm employment in national datasets and the growth of non-agricultural rural employment in many areas (Adams, 1991; Bryceson, 1999; Elbers et al., 2003; Kevane, 1994; Reardon, 1997; Sender et al., 2006). There is also evidence showing precisely how localised the variation and specificity of labour market institutions and relations can be (Cramer et al., 2008). Finally, echoing Fields' hunch that labour markets are stirring in the minds of the 'development economics community', the World Bank's *World Development Report 2008* (chapter 9) for the first time acknowledged the probable significance of (and lack of sufficient knowledge about) rural labour markets in the lives of the poor and as a transmission mechanism between trade, growth and poverty reduction.

## Waging war: labour and conflict

If the analysis of violent conflicts is to incorporate a sharper focus and fuller view of the links between conflict and labour (labour force participation, labour market institutions, labour relations, the quality of the labour force), then it must engage from the outset with two related matters: the need for data and the appreciation of diversity. Rather than imposing a model developed from axiomatic first principles, which typically confers uniformity of expectations and diverts attention from empirical niceties, development economists and others studying violent conflicts need to draw on the insights of labour market theory. It will then come as no surprise and should be emphasised that there is a diversity of labour market institutions and experiences in (before, during and after) conflict contexts that cannot be contained by simplistic (single, dualistic, or even segmented) labour market models. There is work to be done, it follows, in mapping some of this diversity in conflict contexts. It also follows that policy in and towards countries emerging from large-scale organised violent conflict will need to be sensitive to this variation rather than projecting policies derived either from overly abstract models or from 'lessons learned' from elsewhere.[5]

Above all, donors and funding agencies should commit resources to support governments in developing countries and independent researchers in collecting more and better data on labour force characteristics and activities in conflict-affected countries. There are substantial challenges to this endeavour. Collecting data in the midst of conflict is never easy but it is not always impossible, especially in this case, given the extremely low base for evidence of labour experiences. But this kind of data needs to be made a priority in 'post-conflict' phases, during which to some extent it is also possible to reconstruct labour market evidence from the conflict itself. Even if large, well-designed random sample surveys might be some form of benchmark; they are likely to be neither possible nor entirely desirable in these conditions. Therefore, a range of complementary research methods need to be employed. These include purposive sampling, often more capable than random sampling of picking up diversity and change in socio-economic contexts, and various qualitative methods such as key informant interviews, focus groups and life histories. Life histories or labour relation biographies need to be collected both for those with labour force experiences (before, during and after conflict) and for those with experience in mobilising and employing labour. Further, these methods need to be applied not just in obvious economic sectors such as agriculture or trade but also in military and insurgent groups. This might begin to counter the silly assumptions sometimes made that in a given post-conflict region there 'are no labour markets', assumptions derived from the intellectual astigmatism noted above and from failing to ask empirical questions. These assumptions also chime with the cliché of the post-conflict blank slate (Cramer, 2006).

The data required and the type of diversity that matters will involve, but cannot be reduced to, quantitative outcome data (on the quantity of labour supplies, wages, the correlation of these variables with others such as educational attainment, gender, and so on). For the significance and diversity of labour experiences will only make sense (and be useful for policy design and resource allocation) in the context of the socio-economic characteristics that shape diverse labour market structures, relations and processes. And these socio-economic characteristics will typically involve interwoven factors such as geography, historical institutional developments, policy interventions, histories of political struggle and violent conflict itself.

If there can be no single labour market theory (Fine, 1998) and if there can be no single theory of war (Cramer, 2006), it will not be straightforward to set up a common framework for analysing the interaction of labour and conflict. Nonetheless, the core questions revolve around the mobilisation of labour (securing labour force participation), distinguishing between labour mobilisation before, during and after war; the related issue of the relations between employers of and suppliers of labour power; and the quality of labour and the impact of conflict on that quality. Many of these issues – though in varying ways – are regional and global as well as national/provincial/local. A further distinction is between the mobilisation of labour before conflicts and the ways this may help make possible and/or then shape violent conflict, on the one hand, and the mobilisation of labour for and during conflict, on the other hand. The latter involves both the mobilisation of labour power for the production of violent conflict (for military groups, territorial control, production to pay for the war) and the mobilisation of labour for economic activities springing up in or responding to the conditions of a war economy. War economy conditions involve not only supply and demand but also regulatory issues.

Nicely tractable models of the causes of wars have not proven hugely effective. It is, accordingly, unlikely that much is to be gained by proposing that labour issues are direct and discrete causes of violent conflicts. However, labour issues, themselves often inseparable from other issues like access to and use of land, are certainly often part of the 'explanatory mix' (Chauveau and Richards, forthcoming, 2008) in the processes that generate such conflicts. They make for mechanisms that can be engaged by other mechanisms, where the combined effects are what produce political conflict: thus, for example, strains in rural institutions that regulate labour relations and relations between youth and elders may interact with political developments and with political mobilisation in cities or other rural areas to make insurgent collective action less organisationally challenging.[6] But the salience of labour market mechanisms within larger processes will, of course, vary. This may be illustrated by examples from, among others, the American Civil War, El Salvador, Angola, South Africa and West Africa (Sierra Leone and Côte d'Ivoire).

The institutions for mobilising labour and for controlling the terms of its use and the extraction of value from labour power were very different in each of these places, yet were closely bound up in each with the origins and then character and trajectory of violent conflict. If Northerners did not at first view the American Civil War as 'about' or caused by slavery, clearly the institution of slavery in the South was central to issues at the heart of the constitutional conflict between states that generated the war. Further, the slavery question became more and more explicitly central to the war aims of both sides. For example, in 1862 Lincoln said that his objective was to save the Union and neither to save nor destroy slavery; but in his second inaugural speech of 4 March 1865, he said, 'One-eighth of the whole population were colored slaves, not distributed generally over the Union, but localized in the southern part of it. These slaves constituted a peculiar and powerful interest. All knew that this interest was somehow the cause of the war.'

In El Salvador, labour relations in the countryside were, along with land inequality and tenancy terms, a powerful source of the norms and ideals that had come over a protracted period of political mobilisation to represent the basis for support for the Faribundo Martí National Liberation Front insurgency (Wood, 2003). At issue – again alongside, indeed inseparable from, land relations and institutions – was the fierce control of poorly remunerated labour on the plantations, where in some instances plantation owners employed private armies partly to manage farm labourers. In Angola, one of the sparks for the anti-colonial armed struggle was the uprising in the northern coffee growing regions: a complex conflict pitting Angolans from the area against Portuguese settlers and against thousands of migrant workers from the Angolan central highlands who had been contracted out to private coffee farmers by the colonial state. In South Africa, obviously, the institutions of apartheid were organised around the mobilisation and control of cheap labour for agriculture and other sectors, notably mining. The successful development of South African capitalism meant that labour relations and, especially, trades unions became central to the interests of the major protagonists in the trajectory of the conflict over apartheid and, indeed, in the drawn-out process of ending that conflict.

Comparing interlinked but different conflicts in the Upper Guinea Forest region of West Africa, particularly those in Sierra Leone and Côte d'Ivoire, shows particularly well how different socio-economic histories shape different labour relations and processes and, in turn, different linkages between war and labour. Chauveau and Richards (forthcoming, 2008) make this comparison, situating the differences in the political economy of violent conflict in the two countries in the context of the geographical and agro-climatic variations in the region and their different histories of institutional and economic development, partly turning on varying degrees of incorporation into Muslim mercantile networks over the *longue durée*. These histories have influenced social structures such that, to simplify, in parts of rural Sierra Leone a highly exploitative and restrictive institution of chieftaincy increasingly generated grievances among youth (youth being an age and social class category), while in parts of Côte d'Ivoire a more egalitarian social structure persisted that has led to a different political dynamic to youth enrolment in armed conflict, whereby the youth are less focused on changing the institution and more focused on the particular policies of elders who, they argue, have violated the 'rules of the game'. Thus, historically, Ivoirian youth have been able to expect more inclusion in the benefits of farming over time, often migrating to the cities and later returning to take up land. But the failure of migratory experiences in a context of economic crisis combined with high levels of inward migration by 'strangers' into rural areas has generated tension between the returning youth and the elders. It might be difficult or pointless in either case to emphasise labour institutions and relations as a 'cause of war' but neither can war be explained without understanding these differences in labour relations and the long-run socio-economic structures and histories that have affected them.

Rather less is known about the mobilisation and relations of labour in the midst of conflict. One source of variation may well be the relative availability of different kinds of resources – economic and social – for organising warfare. As Jeremy Weinstein (2007) argues, where insurgents have access to, or have to have recourse to, social resources (norms, ideals, collective identity) in order to pursue the challenges of logistics, recruitment and organisation involved in insurgency, and especially where they do not have access to external aid or domestic economic resources, they are likely to form social contracts with local populations and they are less likely to commit atrocities. Arguably, this might extend to the treatment of those whose labour is central to the success of the insurgent project. Meanwhile, those groups with easier access to external finance or to resource rents may take organisational short cuts: they may be more prone to recruiting through direct material rewards than appeals to solidarity and shared grievance; consequently, they may be more likely to hire people with weak commitment, whose loyalty is more fragile. The consequence, argues Weinstein, is a greater organisational fragmentation and decentralisation, and a greater propensity for atrocity. Again, however, not enough has been done to assess the working conditions of those in armed forces and insurgent groups in the light of varying contexts such as these. We know rather more about recruitment – through voluntary means and coercion – than about the conditions of those recruited, though there have often been oddments of evidence, for example, pointing to widespread 'slave labour conditions' in areas controlled by groups like the *União Nacional para a Independência Total de Angola* (UNITA) in Angola, *Renamo* in Mozambique, and the Revolutionary United Front in Sierra Leone. Human Rights Watch (1999), among other sources, pointed to the commonplace abduction by UNITA of civilians, in which women were taken and forced into sexual labour and men and boys were drafted into combat or porterage roles.

Meanwhile, there is not only a demand for labour, from warring groups, during armed conflicts, but also a demand for labour from others with varying connections to the war effort. The characteristics of a war economy (including, often, high risk and high returns, underpinned by violence, shortage and uneven formal regulation, as well as the uneven application and implementation of international regulations such as sanctions or embargoes) make for economic opportunities, in parallel with the equally significant constraints and loss of opportunities faced by many during war. Militaries need supplying. Civilians need supplying with goods too. There are often possibilities for cross-border arbitrage. Meanwhile, some producers simply make do and survive, within the constraints of war but also by responding to the particular incentive sets of wartime. The war economy is often a site of what Mark Chingono (1996) aptly termed a 'vicious market fundamentalism', which is typically anything but a free or perfectly competitive market economy.

For employers are not bound by ILO standards or by national labour laws. And employers often have no difficulty recruiting – they may deploy or adapt labour practices established before the war (e.g., the 'two pile' system used by the RUF in Sierra Leonean diamond mining) or they may reproduce in new activities historically entrenched norms such as the forms of *corvée* labour common in colonial Mozambique before the war. As Bridget O'Laughlin (1996) put it of wartime employers in Mozambique's war economy, the war 'resolved their labour recruitment' problem.

Central to war economies is the mechanism, as explained elsewhere (Cramer, 2006), of primitive accumulation. Primitive accumulation occurs where there is a forcible, 'non-economic' appropriation of land and other assets, which then has the dual effect of first accelerating accumulation by one group of people, and second, displacing people from their own source of livelihoods, rendering them incapable of self-sufficiency. Therefore, they have the 'options' of becoming alms-dependent destitutes or making 'distress sales' of their labour power. In wartime this happens in various ways. First, people whose peasant livelihoods have been undermined by violence may search for labour opportunities in rural areas, on farms, with traders, with military groups. Second, they may flee to cities in search of greater security and employment opportunities. Third, they may join flows of refugees to neighbouring countries, moving to formal camps or living illegally. Refugee camps are often sources of labour for host country employers. Fourth, some war refugees may join larger flows of migration/trafficking internationally, often then joining labour markets with commonly poor conditions.

Thus, institutions, relations and processes before an armed conflict have powerful effects on the origin, form and trajectory of that conflict. Given the variations in these prior conditions, clearly the labour dimensions of conflict will themselves vary greatly, especially given the additional diversity of dynamics of conflicts themselves. If anything, this should reinforce rather than detract from acknowledgement that wars require immense efforts of labour. Conflict should not be seen – as it is in much neo-classical economics of conflict – as primarily akin to exchange and transaction but as something whose violent encounters are produced and reproduced. This production of violence rests on institutions, technologies, and relations that are unlikely simply to evaporate at the signing of a formal peace agreement.

## Peace work: working through the war to peace 'transition'

Contemporary economic policies for post-conflict societies have usually been a far cry from the concerns of economists – such as Nicholas Kaldor and J.M. Keynes during the Second World War in the UK, envisaging and seeking to influence the post-war economy, for both of whom the pursuit of full employment after the war was central (King, 2007). Obviously, the Second World War was fought in utterly different circumstances, by an advanced capitalist country producing most of its own technologically sophisticated war effort – an example of Jacques Sapir's (1990) *'l'économie mobilisée'*. But, first, it is as much a sign of the shift in economic priorities that economists nowadays are less interested in progressive labour market developments. And, second, as argued in this chapter, the sharp differences between a war economy in a late twentieth or early twenty-first century low-income country and an advanced capitalist war economy during an inter-state conflict have diverted attention from the extent to which developing country, 'intra-state' armed conflicts are themselves domestically produced by labour power.

Yet here, again, the liberal imagination kicks in. War is assumed to have wiped clean the labour market slate, packing rural people especially off in developmental reverse gear, into subsistence. And, for example, in demobilisation and reintegration programmes, the end of war is assumed to release the naturally peaceable character of human societies.[7] As one evaluator put it, quoted by Stephanie Hanson (2007), 'As soon as you get guns out of their hands, they are suddenly innocuous human beings again, but that is not the case at all.' Hence, little attention is typically paid to labour institutions, markets and relations, other than through fairly blanket prescriptions by multilateral agencies for market liberalisation, combined with some training projects. As with recommendations for productive sectors and enterprises (and often also for non-productive sectors, including, e.g., health provision in Afghanistan), the common ideal is for liberalisation without regulation. Of course, there have been modifications to the Washington consensus that have edged their way onto major donors' agendas in recent years. Part of this has involved a greater focus on labour relations and even, in some circumstances, the provision of direct support to unions, in Sierra Leone, for example (see Chapter 6, this volume). Nevertheless, it is still the case that the level of attention given to labour issues is generally inadequate and to the extent that they have been considered, it is even less common to find awareness translated into new policy models. At best one finds a simulation of concern about labour issues rather than serious policy engagement with the challenges they present for post-conflict societies.

The lessons of accumulating studies of recent and ongoing armed conflicts show, however, not only that labour is likely to be more salient economically and socially than is acknowledged but also that the war economy (itself shaped by specific pre-war processes and structures) will shape the peace. The second life of the war economy, during peace, may be all the more significant where it is largely ignored. Indeed, this is one of the many ways in which the very notion of a neat transition from war to peace is often questionable. For it is not just the post-war violence – common from the American South (during the reconstruction era) to El Salvador and Afghanistan – but also many of the relations and practices of a wartime political economy that carry over. And labour is often a key feature of this. The risk is that the *faux* liberalisation emerging in the economic version of Michael Barnett and Christoph Zuercher's (2008) 'peacebuilder's contract' will allow for the perpetuation of extremely exploitative labour relations, hidden by the liberal view of war, blotted out by the developmental astigmatism discussed above, and traded off against the anxieties of neo-classical economists about the inefficiencies of labour market intervention (such as minimum wage legislation).

If the Oslo peace process for Israel and Palestine was one that perpetuated the terms and relations of conflict (Turner, 2006) – making it in a different way an example of what Horne (1977, 2006) calls in Algeria a 'savage war of peace' – labour relations between the two continued to be central to the trajectory of political relations. Thus, one effect of the intricately forceful array of border closures and the nearly complete security wall, fence or barrier has been to stifle labour flows that had been an economic lifeline for large numbers of Palestinians working in Israel. Meanwhile, Israel has pursued its war/peace aims by hiring huge numbers of Asian immigrants to replace Palestinians. Thus, the non-economic regulation of Palestinian labour supply is at the heart of the conflict and the prospects for peace.

Indeed, the political salience of labour relations in an armed conflict is no guarantee of progressive post-war outcomes. A renowned historical example is the aftermath of the American Civil War, when, following the thirteenth and fourteenth amendments to the constitution, the aims of the Radical Republicans were scuppered by white Southerners, 'redemptionists', who succeeded by violent and other means to reverse civil rights gains for black Americans and to secure access to labour – through the Black Codes – on terms as close to those of slavery as possible (Foner, 1988; Lemann, 2006).

Labour relations continue to be not so much the site of political conflict but the locus of the war economy's shaping of peacetime society in other contexts too. These include Angola, where, since the end of war in 2002 there has been a form of 'resource peace' in the diamondiferous Lunda region. The primitive accumulation that was enabled by, and that sustained, the war persists in the organisation of diamond mining. Rafael Marques (2006) documents how diamond concession companies and their associated private security firms – which typically have close ties to the state – claim a monopoly over legitimate economic activity. No economic activity is allowed at all – including farming or fishing – that is not sanctioned by these enterprises. Anyone living there cannot, therefore, subsist without either migrating elsewhere or trying to mine for diamonds. Small-scale diamond miners, *garimpeiros*, are also technically illegal, but are tolerated so that the companies can buy the diamonds produced by *garimpeiro* labourers at extremely cheap prices. There is evidence too of high levels of physical violence and human rights abuses of workers in this area. Further, '[f]orced labour at the installations and the working areas of the aforementioned diamond extraction companies has become a routine part of life for the *garimpeiros*. It is used as a form of punishment which is administered by these companies' (Marques, 2006: 5). Marques further alleges that many abuses are carried out by a private security company, Alfa-5, that was originally set up in 1993 to protect diamond mining areas during the civil war.

One further, more commonly acknowledged issue with labour market implications in war to peace transitions is the fate of demobilised combatants. As is often recognised, demobilisation spews large numbers of people with particular training, skills and know-how, that is 'specialists in violence', into the wider economy. They may or may not be the 'innocuous human beings' that one evaluator claimed they are imagined to be. However, what is clear is that much too little is actually known in any systematic way about the economic fate and labour market experiences of demobilised combatants.[8] An exception is Norma Kriger's (2003) analysis of the politics of 'veteran' status in post-liberation Zimbabwe.

## Conclusion

This chapter has argued that labour markets and associated institutions, labour relations and labour power itself have been woefully neglected in the abundant and multidisciplinary study of violent conflict in recent years. The chapter has argued for the development of a more labour-sensitive conflict analysis. This neglect applies also, and perhaps most importantly, to the work of economists. This weak spot in the political economy of recent wars is a function of a quirk of much development economics, it flows from the reflexes of the liberal interpretation of war, and it reproduces an analysis of war as a transaction rather than as produced.

If this imbalance in the literature (and in policy design) is to be corrected, greater understanding of the way that labour markets work and of their roles in violent conflict and its aftermath needs to be developed. Above all, this requires an investment of resources in the collection of new evidence by different methods. But while a rough framework of questions to pursue is useful, the temptation to design models for labour market analysis in conflict contexts ought to be avoided. For this chapter has also argued that a single labour market theory, a single theory of violent conflict, or indeed a single model of labour markets in/and conflict is likely to miss the point. The challenge, nonetheless, is to acknowledge the diversity and specificity of labour markets in violent conflicts without tripping into the pit of *ad hoc* analysis or an inconsistent eclecticism.

In spite of the fragility of knowledge in this field, there may yet be a case for a more direct focus on labour relations and institutions in the design of foreign aid programmes, support for government policy and the activities of private companies and NGOs in conflict-affected or post-conflict societies. Where other initiatives in peacetime economies have targeted 'fair trade' standards or other certification schemes for primary commodity exports (e.g., *Utz Kappeh* for coffee), there is no equivalent initiative to encourage the payment of peace dividends to workers with experience of the often-dreadful conditions of war economy labour markets. Perhaps a 'peace work' label would help reward enterprises – both domestic enterprises in Afghanistan, Mozambique, Sri Lanka, and multinational corporations engaged in post-war economies, whether or not they have been implicated in the global economic circuitry of war – that showed signs of making their own transition from war to peace by respecting labour rights and providing progressive working conditions. Finally, post-war 'governance' and 'capacity building' initiatives should focus as much on trade unions as on ministries of finance and electoral commissions. In itself though, focusing on labour relations may be insufficient – to the extent that these issues have been incorporated into an emerging post-Washington consensus (albeit at the margins) the record to date is not particularly good. Instead, there has been something of a *simulation* of concern about reforming labour relations, particularly when the production of meaningful reforms would challenge the macroeconomic assumptions of donors and the international financial institutions. Thus, if the first challenge is simply to focus on the issue of labour relations, the second may be to translate analysis of these issues into policy shifts – an even more difficult enterprise in the current environment.

## Notes

1. Employing that view of economics as principally a science of choice, Hirshleifer (1994) argued that economists had neglected 'the dark side of the force'. Recognising this nastier side, an economist could deploy the tool kit of microeconomic analysis (opportunity cost, preferences, opportunities, etc.) to predict under what conditions individual agents would 'choose' cooperation rather than conflict. Cooperation as an option derives from Ronald Coase's maxim that no two rational economic agents would willingly pass up the opportunity for mutually beneficial exchange. Reintroducing the dark side suggested economists also needed to bear in mind a Machiavellian insight that no two parties would ever pass up the opportunity to extort or get the better of one another.
2. See Weinstein (2007) on recruitment as a major challenge of insurgencies, one whose resolution, varying with the available types of economic and social resources, affects the type of insurgency and level of violence.

3. On the way in which localised agendas are rolled into and help to sustain the headline political agendas of armed conflicts, and in particular on the way in which rural women provided support to guerrillas in Zimbabwe's liberation war partly in order to pursue their own conflict agenda against patriarchal institutional norms, see Kriger (1991).
4. Thus, 'the ILO's *Global Employment Trends 2003* presents labour market indicators for 19 African countries, but data for employment growth covering the period 1995–1999 are only given for three of these countries, while data for the whole period 1990–2000 are available for four countries. Unemployment rates are given for 14 countries in 1999, but only for two countries in 1990. Nevertheless, labour force *growth* estimates are presented for all 19 countries, simply as estimated projections from general population data' (ILO, 2004: 138–45, cited in Sender *et al.*, 2005: 73).
5. This might be called the 'Dominica fallacy', after the consultancy team leader I met at Maputo airport, Mozambique, who had never been to Mozambique (or, indeed, sub-Saharan Africa) but who said this would not matter as we could apply the 'Dominican model'.
6. Here I follow Charles Tilly's (2000) definition of a process as a set of mechanisms: a mechanism is an event that changes relations 'among specified sets of elements in identical or closely similar ways over a variety of situations'; a process is a frequently occurring combination or sequence of mechanisms.
7. See Michael Howard (1978) for the long history of this underlying theme in the liberal interpretation of war.
8. One of the more empirically careful analyses of disarmament, demobilisation and reintegration programmes (Humphreys and Weinstein, 2007) does include employment variables in its survey questionnaire, though it does not collect information on labour market institutions, conditions or relations.

# References

Adams, Jennifer, 1991, 'The Rural Labour Market in Zimbabwe', *Development and Change*, Vol. 22, No. 2, pp. 297–320.
Barnett, Michael and Christoph Zuercher, 2008, 'The Peacebuilder's Contract: How External Statebuilding Reinforces Weak Statehood', in Roland Paris and Timothy Sisk (eds), *The Dilemmas of Statebuilding: Confronting the Contradictions of Postwar Peace Operations*, London: Routledge.
Basu, Arnab K., Nancy H. Chau and Ravi Kanbur, 2005, 'Turning a Blind Eye: Costly Enforcement, Credible Commitment, and Minimum Wage Laws', Working Paper 205–13, Department of Applied Economics and Management, Ithaca, NY: Cornell University.
Bryceson, Deborah, 1999, 'African Rural Labour, Income Diversification and Livelihood Approaches: A Long-Term Development Perspective', Working Paper 35, Leiden: African Studies Centre.
Byres, Terence J., 1979, 'Of Neo-Populist Pipe Dreams: Daedalus in the Third World and the Myth of Urban Bias', *Journal of Peasant Studies*, Vol. 6, No. 2, pp. 210–44.
Chauveau, Jean-Pierre and Paul Richards, 2008, 'West African Insurgencies in Agrarian Perspective: Côte d'Ivoire and Sierra Leone Compared', *Journal of Agrarian Change*, Vol. 18, No. 4.
Chingono, Mark, 1996, *The State, Violence, and Development: The Political Economy of War in Mozambique, 1975–92*, Aldershot: Avebury.

Cling, Jean-Pierre, Flore Gubert, Christophe J. Nordman and Anne-Sophie Robilliard, 2007, 'Youth and Labour Markets in Africa: A Critical Review of the Literature', Working Paper 49, Paris: *Agence Française de Développement*.

Cramer, Christopher, 2006, *Civil War is Not a Stupid Thing: Accounting for Violence in Developing Countries*, London: Hurst.

Cramer, Christopher and Nicola Pontara, 1998, 'Rural poverty and Poverty Alleviation in Mozambique: What's Missing from the Debate?', *Journal of Modern African Studies*, Vol. 36, No. 1, pp. 101–38.

Cramer, Christopher, Carlos Oya and John Sender, 2008, 'Lifting the Blinkers: A New View of Power, Diversity and Poverty in Mozambican Rural Labour Markets', Development Studies Working Paper, London, School of African Studies.

Duffield, Mark, 2007, *Development, Security and Unending War: Governing the World of Peoples*, London: Polity.

Elbers, Chris, Peter Lanjouw, Johan Mistaien, Berk Özler and Ken Simler, 2003, 'Are Neighbours Equal? Estimating Local Inequality in Three Developing Countries', Discussion Paper 2003/52, World Institute for Development Economics Research, Helsinki.

Fields, Gary, 2007, 'Labor Market Policy in Developing Countries: A Selective Review of the Literature and Needs for the Future', Policy Research Working Paper No. 4362, Washington: World Bank.

Fine, Ben, 1998, *Labour Market Theory: A Constructive Reassessment*, London: Routledge.

Fithen, Caspar and Paul Richards, 2005, 'Making War, Crafting Peace: Militia Solidarities and Demobilisation in Sierra Leone', in Paul Richards (ed.), *No Peace, No War: An Anthropology of Contemporary Armed Conflicts*, Oxford: James Currey, pp. 117–36.

Foner, Eric, 1988, *Reconstruction: America's Unfinished Revolution, 1863–1877*, New York: Harper & Row.

Hanson, Stephanie, 2007, 'Disarmament, Demobilisation, and Reintegration (DDR) in Africa', backgrounder, Council of Foreign Relations, Washington, DC (at: www.cfr.org/publication/12650/).

Hirshleifer, Jack, 1994, 'The Dark Side of the Force', *Economic Inquiry*, Vol. 32, pp. 1–10.

Horne, Alistair, 1977, *A Savage War of Peace: Algeria, 1954–62*, London: Macmillan.

Horne, Alistair, 2006, *A Savage War of Peace: Algeria 1954–1962*, New York: New York Review of Books.

Howard, Michael, 1978, *War and the Liberal Conscience*, New Brunswick: Rutgers University Press (also 2008 edn, London: Hurst).

Human Rights Watch, 1999, *Angola Unravels: The Rise and Fall of the Lusaka Peace Process*, New York: Human Rights Watch.

Humphreys, Macartan and Jeremy Weinstein, 2007, 'Demobilization and Reintegration', *Journal of Conflict Resolution*, Vol. 51, No. 4, pp. 531–67.

ILO, 2003, *Decent Work in Agriculture*. International Workers' Symposium on Decent Work in Agriculture (ILO). Background Paper.

Kaufman, Bruce, 2007, 'The Impossibility of a Perfectly Competitive Labour Market', *Cambridge Journal of Economics*, Vol. 31, pp. 775–87.

Kevane, Michael, 1994, 'Village Labor Markets in Sheikhan District, Sudan', *World Development*, Vol. 22, No. 6, pp. 839–57.

King, John E., 2007, 'Kaldor's War', Discussion Paper 25/07, Department of Economics, La Trobe University.

Kriger, Norma, 1991, *Zimbabwe's Guerrilla War: Peasant Voices*, Cambridge: Cambridge University Press.

Kriger, Norma, 2003, *Guerrilla Veterans in Post-War Zimbabwe*, Cambridge: Cambridge University Press.
Lemann, Nicholas, 2006, *Redemption: The Last Battle of the Civil War*, New York: Farrar, Strous & Giroux.
Marques, Rafael, 2006, 'Operation Kissonde: The Diamonds of Humiliation and Misery', Cuango, Lunda-Norte, Angola (at: www.cuango.net/kissonde/texto/Kissonde ING.pdf).
O'Laughlin, Bridget, 1996, 'Through a Divided Glass: Dualism, Class, and the Agrarian Question in Mozambique', *Journal of Peasant Studies*, Vol. 23, No. 4, pp. 1–39.
Reardon, Thomas, 1997, 'Using Evidence of Household Income Diversification to Inform Study of the Rural Nonfarm Labor Market in Africa', *World Development*, Vol. 25, No. 5, pp. 735–47.
Sapir, Jacques, 1990, *L'Économie Mobilisée: Essai sur les économies de type Soviètique*, Paris: La Découverte.
Sender, John, Christopher Cramer and Carlos Oya, 2005, 'Unequal Prospects: Disparities in the Quantity and Quality of Labour Supply in sub-Saharan Africa', World Bank Social Protection Discussion Paper No. 0525, Washington, DC.
Sender, John, Carlos Oya and Christopher Cramer, 2006, 'Women Working for Wages: Putting some Flesh on the Bones of a Rural Labour Market Survey in Mozambique', *Journal of Southern African Studies*, Vol. 32, No. 2, pp. 313–33.
Tilly, Charles, 2000, 'Mechanisms in Political Processes', Columbia University, NY (at: www.asu.edu/clas/polisci/cqrm/papers/Tilly/TillyMechs.pdf).
Turner, Mandy, 2006, 'Building Democracy in Palestine: Liberal Peace Theory and the Election of Hamas', *Democratization*, Vol. 13, No. 5, pp. 739–55.
Weinstein, Jeremy, 2007, *Inside Rebellion: The Politics of Insurgent Violence*, New York, Cambridge: Cambridge University Press.
Wood, Elizabeth J., 2003, *Insurgent Collective Action and Civil War in El Salvador*, Cambridge: Cambridge University Press.
World Bank, 2007, *World Development Report, 2008: Agriculture for Development*, Washington, DC.
Wuyts, Marc, 2003, 'The Agrarian Question in Mozambique's Transition and Reconstruction', in Tony Addison (ed.), *From Conflict to Recovery in Africa*, Oxford: Oxford University Press, pp. 141–54.

# 8
# Employment, Labour Rights and Social Resistance

*Michael Pugh*

> *Livelihoods and Employment Generation – finished*
> *No documents found in this section*
>                     Webpage: Joint Needs Assessment for Iraq
>                                              Reconstruction[1]

Employment and rights in work, in common with other subjects investigated in this book, have barely registered in the academic literature on peacebuilding. Moreover, agencies and practitioners have only recognised the relevance of employment issues because of the social damage caused by the neoliberal economy of peacebuilding, not least in Iraq where the Coalition Provisional Authority under Paul Bremer deformed the economic order contrary to the laws of occupation, and half the labour force was thrown out of work. The epigraph quoted above (on the otherwise completely blank webpage of the international Iraq reconstruction programme) testifies to a pervasive prejudice.

As a touchstone of the neoliberal political economy of war-torn societies, the equivocal attention of international actors to income generation also exposes the prejudicial policies of interveners. Their priorities have favoured macroeconomic stability, economic liberalisation, controlling the resource dimensions of conflict, curbing corruption and informal economic activity, establishing rule of law for predictable commercial relations, and relying heavily on small business energy and microcredit as growth generators. To the extent that economic rights have received attention, it has been in the realm of property rights: the restitution of property to returnees, and property transfers in relation to the privatisation of public assets, so essential to economic reform programmes. According to surveys of dispossessed communities, property restitution has been a high priority for them, but so also has income generation, employment and purchasing power issues (e.g., UNDP, 2005: 33–5).

This chapter discusses whether labour rights are meaningful in war-torn societies or whether they are necessarily traded for security and survival. For millions of the world's workers, and for many more with no secure means of support, employment rights may appear to be a remote aspiration at best. Huge disparities in labour rights exist and unions are suppressed in many areas (outlawed, for example, in wartime Herceg–Bosna, though they had performed important social functions in former Yugoslavia). For the 400,000 Palestinian workers expelled from Saudi Arabia during the 1991 Gulf War, for the non-unionised alluvial diamond workers in Sierra Leone and for textile workers of South Asia earning less than a living wage, esoteric debates about rights may have little meaning relative to physiological needs. High levels of unemployment make securing a registered job a dim prospect rather than an attainable right, and only rudimentary safety measures, if any, may protect workers in hazardous work. In Chechnya and Ingushetia (the latter economically affected by the Chechen conflict), the estimated unemployment rates reached well over 50 per cent of the active populations in 2004, and was as high as 70 per cent among young males in some parts of the north Caucasus (Sagramoso, 2007: 691–70). In war-torn societies from Kosovo to Sierra Leone the typical norms are high unemployment levels, significant long-term unemployment, desertion of the formal labour market and resort to employment in the informal sector.

The central contention of this chapter is that the employment policies of interveners exhibit a competitive market-led approach that international and local entrepreneurs exploit. In neoliberal programmes of transformation, both employment generation and formal rights in work are frequently treated as dispensable hindrances to modernisation by capital, and as secondary to survival by the economically vulnerable population. Moreover, labour rights are not just employment/unemployment issues. The apparent abnegation of rights (or *faute de mieux* submission to economic exploitation) by people for survival can be construed as a form of social resistance in a broader engagement with the impact of peacebuilding. Alternatives to registered work not only act as welfare safety nets but as alternative sources of authority and social power. As Neil Stammers argues (1999), rights are constructed in specific contexts through challenges by social movements to the forms of power embedded in social relations.

The first section of the chapter problematises the issue of labour rights and highlights the varied discourses that leave room for a political economy approach. The second section shows that, while rights are highly politicised in relation to globalising capitalism generally, conflict and post-conflict environments accentuate the abuse of employment rights. The third section critically examines the norm-setting strategies and projects of the International Labour Organisation (ILO) and its capitulation to flexible working ('flexicurity'). The fourth section suggests that the dominant model of peacebuilding leads not to labour passivity but to social resistance through informal economies. The chapter concludes that the political economy of 'peace' requires a strategic re-configuration in which labour rights are fully represented.

## Problematising employment and labour rights

Contemporary rights discourses have been pervaded by the Lockean tradition of prior liberties for the individual and the individual's property. The tradition is reinforced by two presumptions. First, civil–political rights are said to merely require abstention from physical abuse, whereas economic rights require resources that are unavailable to many governments. Henry Shue (1980) and Jack Donnelly (2002) demolish this mantra, showing that civil–political rights entail costly measures of state protection while economic rights require employers to desist from causing harm; and that dictatorships have trouble with political rights but less often with welfare rights. Besides, property is an economic right (Donnelly, 2002: 27) and, as Tony Evans observes, resistance to aggressive capitalism results in human rights violations (2000: 422; 2001: 62). Dismissal of such consequences on the grounds that they represent collateral damage in a pre-ordained economic order etherealises socio-economic rights beyond human responsibility. Second, the traditional construction of rights can disempower 'beneficiaries' by excluding them from decisions (Sanghera, 2009), and it ignores the importance of collective struggles, not only for individual survival but also to uphold values that define and shape a community (Fierke, 2007: 14). Evidence that individuals and collectives demand empowerment in such contexts is provided by Edward Said who recalled that from the late 1960s Palestinian rights were tools to repossess land and history through a critique of Arab nationalism 'at a grass-roots level – and not because a colonel or king commanded us' (Said, 1995: xv).

It is beyond the scope of this chapter to provide an exhaustive account of thinking about rights, but a brief survey of dominant ethical, legal and institutional discourses indicates the need for a political economy approach.

### Ethics discourse

Socio-economic rights have traditionally been subordinated by the privileging of civil and political liberties. Although developing states have secured a formal place for socio-economic rights, in practice these are regarded as secondary, aspirational rights. Obligations inscribed in the 188 ILO conventions fall into a category of 'soft law', reliant on norms and moral influence for their implementation.

From a consequentialist perspective, however, the global order is not only ethically indefensible; without social protection the conflict and poverty arising from self-interest in the international system would be limitless (Pogge, 1989: 218–22; 2002). But the discourse on socio-economic rights also has a deontological pedigree and imprimatur in the anti-utilitarian liberalism of John Rawls. Three aspects of Rawlsian distributive justice, in which the most disadvantaged should have confidence in improvement (Rawls, 1967; 1971 [1972]: 61), are contravened in liberal peacebuilding.

First, although Rawls firmly privileged liberty over welfare, his standpoint is contradicted by the neoclassical philosophy that has informed contemporary peacebuilding, notably the primacy accorded to assets and 'stakeholding' which is protected by self-interested groups of entrepreneurs and the monopoly of force commanded by a minimal state (see Nozick, 1974). Second, Rawls' emphasis on a social contract in which participants have a say in how they are governed is contradicted by the operations of contemporary international interventions and administrations – and sharply criticised on this score (see Chapter 19, this volume). Moreover, in the distribution of resources in civil war, entrepreneurs acquire power unhindered by social contracts. Third, Rawls does not presume that one kind of arrangement is preferable to another – though as Raymond Geuss points out (2002: 330), his analysis yields an ideal polity suspiciously similar to the US constitution. In contrast, peacebuilders have claimed superiority for neoliberalism on account of its subscription to supposedly objective economic laws. But what is uniformly expected of transition societies, such as deregulation, is not necessarily applicable to the interveners who protect themselves from competition. If not in propaganda and donor conditionality, neoliberalism is essentially anti-universalist in practice, though in cosmopolitan readings, globalisation also presents opportunities for a global ethics of rights (e.g., McGrew, 1998).

The ethics of choice has nevertheless influenced peacebuilding discourses, particularly through the work of the economist Amartya Sen (1999) who champions the freedom to interact economically without impediment as a universal right with intrinsic value. Rejecting a utilitarian approach that privileges self-interested maximisation of welfare but recognising that social development is a precursor of economic transition, Sen proposes empowerment of people to seek entitlements. These include the freedom to adopt values that are not measured by economic outcomes as instituted in the UN Development Programme (UNDP) *Human Development Index*. This may mean that the harmful impacts of globalisation need to be addressed. But Sen's approach reinforces the neoliberal framework of rights in several respects: heavy reliance on individual rather than collective agency; silence about social struggles manifest in informal economies; and the contention, vigorously disputed by critics, that democracy and economic globalisation are compatible (see Chua, 2004; Falk, 2000; Gray, 1998 [2002]; Saul, 2005).

## Legal discourse

Critical law commentators admit the role of politics and social struggle. For example, Rama Mani's study of post-war justice (2002) dissects the inequities that lie behind the demands for distributive justice and illuminates the role of peacebuilding in worsening these inequities. But, as a Gramscian analysis suggests, quests for justice cannot rely on the self-reform of international peacebuilders but has to be located in counter-hegemonic strategies and has to articulate with common elements of social practice as well as appeals to law. Social movements can gain a capacity to create norms, which might, for instance, encompass property protection for all and eliminate trade union gender discrimination (Hunt, 1990: 312–16, 324–5).

Legal optimists demonstrate that corporate interests do try to provide worker benefits and have adopted codes, for example in sports goods manufacture. This occurs partly in obedience to national legislation, partly for competitive advantage through 'rights branding' and partly under consumer and investor pressure, such as the UK campaign since 2006 to get companies and shops to end sweated labour in the fashion industry (Labour Behind the Label, 2007). Some analysts praise the European social model in generating a convergence of norms and regulations on employment rights that should be demanded of competitors on economic and ethical grounds (Moreau, 2005: 373). They note that employment measures feature strongly in the indicators of social progress adopted at the Laeken (Belgium) summit in 2001. Others identify a 'steady accumulation of heightened expectations' and an emerging equivalent of medieval merchant law, a voluntary *lex mercatoria* of the marketplace that paves the way for legislation (Steinhardt, 2005: 210–24).

Nevertheless, the contrary evidence is substantial. In practice transnational corporations have a high degree of impunity, their obligations to abide by human rights standards dependent on the spread of norms, local resistance and consumer pressure (De Schutter, 2005: 227; Steinhardt, 2005: 177). Against the power of state-backed corporate interests, international trade unions and rights NGOs failed to get core labour standards adopted by the World Trade Organisation in 1996 (He and Murphy, 2007: 714–17; Wells and Elias, 2005: 171–2). Labour rights have been under siege from the International Financial Institutions (IFIs), capitalist cadres that shape globalisation, and political elites everywhere who cultivate influential global investors. Governments in the OECD are reluctant to intervene to remove competitive advantage from corporations that migrate to sites of low rights compliance (Alston, 2005: 3–4). The EU avoids the language of rights in labour matters for 'fear of giving strong legal recognition and priority to particular social values in the face of competing economic interests' (De Búrca, 2005: 13–14). At the same time, the EU and the United States have demanded labour rights from producers in war-torn and other countries, while failing to enforce ILO core standards themselves (Moreau, 2005: 378; Novitz, 2005: 241). The United States boycotts unfair competition from labour rights abusers but also refuses to ratify the 1966 Covenant on Economic, Social and Cultural Rights because it conflicts with US constitutional liberties. This politicisation of labour rights in conditions of neoliberalism prompts scholars to conclude that the 'free market' will prevent such rights from shifting beyond unenforceable codes and standards unless neoliberalism is resisted by social movements (Alston, 2005; Evans, 2001: 78; Thomas, 1998: 181–3). As discussed below, adaptability in post-conflict conditions of high unemployment invariably fuels exploitation and resort by labour to informal economic sectors.

### Agency discourse

Abundant and long-standing household and livelihood surveys in war-torn societies have been undertaken by the International Committee of the Red Cross, NGOs, military units and national authorities. CARE International (1997), for example, assessed household needs over five-year periods, with the objective of empowering at least one breadwinner per family so that each unit gradually becomes self supporting. But such surveys and strategies are conducted in the context of assisting individuals to become independent of relief aid, not in a quest to establish socio-economic rights for entire classes of people.

Indeed, when broader employment issues receive attention by institutions that explore post-conflict economic strategies, a market-led approach dominates. A typical agenda highlights the need to 'nurture back into life a *market economy*' by setting up mobile phone systems and facilitating credit for trade, transport and export promotion (UNDP–USAID, 2007, original italics). None of it would contribute significantly to a long-term employment strategy or to establishing socio-economic rights. Emergency job creation schemes are securitised and seen as essential for absorbing ex-combatants and unemployed youth – both inscribed by the World Bank and its partners in the Balkans as potentially dangerous (World Bank, EC and EBRD, 1996). However, industry and value-added production get dismissed as employing few people. More opportunities are said to lie in construction, the retail sector, services and agriculture. Apart from the relatively strong focus on agriculture as a destination for workers in many war-torn countries, emphasis lies on the market power of the tertiary sector: services, retailing and construction. The last of these can stimulate building booms, for private housing for example, but – as in Kosovo, where only about half of the diaspora remittances used for construction is spent locally – this can cause a surge in the import of specialist materials, such as fixtures and fittings, rather than invigorating local supply (Priština, 2006).

To summarise, ethical, legal and agency discourses reveal the political, hierarchical and contingent aspect of rights, but do not mesh rights struggles in conflict contexts with critiques of neoliberal political economy. The next section brings conflict more centrally into the picture.

## Globalisation, war and rights in neoliberal peacebuilding

The social construction of rights may be specific to contexts of struggle, exacerbated in war, but they also interact at a global level with the imperatives of finance capital and neoliberalism. The dispensation of surplus capital requires 'reliance on the market to guide economic priorities, the minimization of the social role of government, and the encouragement of maximum privatization of economic life' (Falk, 2000: 47; also Harvey, 2003). As Richard Falk notes (ibid.), the repudiation of other approaches to well-being, such as cooperatives or public enterprises, displaces rights relevant to people without access to wealth and entitlements, including 'the right to just and favourable remuneration... supplemented, if necessary, by other means of social protection' (Universal Declaration, 1948, article 23.3).

In the construction of rights it has been axiomatic that conflict disrupts development and damages human rights, whereas globalisation supports rights, using state revenues to finance entrepreneurship, protect property and secure 'freedoms' (Collier et al., 2004). Moreover, peacebuilding presents opportunities to reify the equation that globalisation equals rights through economically determined policies of global integration. Consequently, neoliberal peacebuilding severely accentuates the weakening of socio-economic rights.

First, interveners assume that an absence of democracy and civil–political rights was closely linked to the outbreak of conflict, and so privilege the introduction of new 'freedoms' under the rubric of 'democratisation' as a crucial aspect of transition. There is less concern, indeed denial, that the powerful advance of finance capitalism and its institutions may have played a part in creating the conditions for conflict. Gross abuses before and during conflict foster a moral imperative to restore or establish civil–political rights. Moreover, in the absence of functioning legal systems, protecting the rights of the person from the killing, rape and abduction that persists after ceasefires is clearly an essential element in intervention agendas.

Second, flight from conflict and the forced removal of people (amounting to an estimated 20 million people worldwide) creates another dimension to rights as a peacebuilding instrument. Displaced persons and refugees have special needs because they experience most difficulty accessing sites of employment and the bureaucratic structures required for formal work (citizenship, address and communication facilities). The scale of exploitation (wage cuts, dismissals, extended working hours and absence of social protection) is such that exploitation is also a norm for those who flee to other countries, including those in the global North who may not be entitled to work legally (see Lawrence, 2007). Since the 1980s the ILO has tailored income generation for the displaced and refugees, for example with handicrafts and farming in Somalia (Date-Bah and Hall, 2003: 172). In the Balkans, institutions were established to assist returnees gain compensation and restitution of land and property, over 100,000 property cases raised in Kosovo alone (von Carlowitz, 2005).

Third, other sectors of the population have particular needs as a consequence of conflict. Peace is often uncomfortable for former combatants in terms of status and well-being. Although demobilisation programmes include provision for re-training and job-seeking, these are not necessarily followed up and, as in Mozambique, soldiers are tipped back into poverty and unemployment (McMullin, 2006). The gender dimension of socio-economic rights has been discussed elsewhere (Chapter 2, this volume). A survey of ILO support for women's income generation in Mozambique, Lebanon, Guatemala and Bosnia and Herzegovina (BiH) highlights training programmes, small enterprises, microcredit, cooperatives and business support services (Date-Bah, 2003: 148). These may provide a degree of relief but many are insecure, reinforce womens' reliance on low-paid and long-hour working, and do little to redress the loss of jobs in public sector employment, agriculture or industry. Youth is also neglected in peace processes and excluded from decision-making in spite of sometimes taking on new responsibilities during conflict (Kosovo, 2006a: 8–9). Security and income generation were a preoccupation, prominent among young rioters in Timor-Leste in 2002 and Kosovo in 2004. In Kosovo, 70 per cent of the population is under 30 years old, there were 25,000–30,000 new entrants annually to a labour market that in 2007 could only absorb 7000. In 2004 over 40 per cent of unemployed youth had been job searching for over a year (Priština, 2006; Kosovo, 2006b). The young employed are also often the first to get laid off work during and after conflict, and a breakdown in education and training opportunities affects them disproportionately. As in Colombia, they are then liable to avail themselves of opportunities provided by gangs and informal economic sectors (Achio and Specht, 2003: 154–6). The ILO and other donors sponsor enterprise start-ups, training, internship and apprenticeship projects (such as a market-driven programme in Timor-Leste). But without strategic employment creation such tinkering contributes to frustration and efforts to migrate.

Fourth, the orthodox view of the impact of conflict stresses the destruction and reallocation of material capital stock, but disruption to labour markets and mass displacement of work forces also alters social capital. In theory, huge opportunities for employment exist because of the labour requirements in rebuilding assets, a dynamic adopted throughout Europe after the Second World War. However, in the liberal peace framework, fragmentation, regrouping and material impoverishment of social capital makes labour vulnerable to post-conflict exploitation. A weakening or prohibition of labour organisation also occurs in conflict. In BiH, for example, the syndicalists split into three ethnic unions that were as dedicated to rewarding heroic veterans and discriminating against women and non-nationalists as in protecting jobs (Pugh, 2003: 60). Locally, the loss of rights can be catastrophic. The largest mining and metallurgical complex in Europe employed about 20,000 at Trepca in Kosovo in the late 1980s. It employed a mere 200 in 2007, partly as a consequence of asset stripping and discrimination against Kosovar Albanians under Slobodan Milošević, but mainly because of NATO's subsequent occupation, expropriation and virtual closure of the complex. Conflict transitions certainly provide new opportunities for privileging businesses, such as the DynCorps and Blackwater transnational security firms that pay risk wages to employees who suspend control over rights (Klein, 2007). But much social capital is diverted into coping and survival in the informal economies (Pugh et al., 2004: 8–9).

Fifth, to the extent that transnational corporations change the role of the state 'to a passive unit of administration' (Evans, 2001: 117), public influence in setting socio-economic rights agendas declines, state authorities lose capacity to foster these, and politicians can deny responsibility for corporate trimming of rights (Craig and Lynk, 2006; Wells and Elias, 2005: 143–6). In post-conflict settings liberal participatory processes are introduced by donors and international agencies, to provide new opportunities for pursuing civil rights through national forums and elections. But the power to set and implement a rights agenda may also be more severely limited in war-torn societies on account of conditionalities imposed by external agencies and the administrative 'capacity building' that replaces organic politics (Chapter 19, this volume). In conjunction with the priorities of a neoliberal economic order, the opportunities for agenda setting for socio-economic rights through the state are severely denied to war-torn societies. War-torn societies are also fertile ground for economic experiments by external agencies. Humanitarian relief, state fiscal discipline, privatisation and financing small-and-medium enterprises (SMEs) are priorities (the last because SMEs spread the ideology of entrepreneurialism without challenging the monopolistic tendencies of capital), whereas employment is relegated to the status of deferred gratification. A turnaround appeared to be marked by the provision of 'thousands of jobs' for 'quick effect' in the West Bank and Gaza to bolster peace talks in 2007. But unless Israel's grip on the Palestinian economy is reversed, the new industrial zone initiatives, funded by Japan and Turkey, will replicate the costly white elephants of past projects (Butcher, 2007). In general, livelihood and employment strategies are a variation on structural adjustment policies and conditional on private sector development (see, e.g., Mendelson-Forman and Mashatt, 2007).

## Rights in Bosnia and Herzegovina (BiH)

For example, the absence of an employment strategy in BiH was mirrored in the Office of the High Representative's 'Jobs and Justice programme, 2002–05', which relied heavily on indirect effects in the operation of market forces, rather than direct employment policy. Its authors even denied that the state could create jobs, conveniently forgetting that their own salaries were paid by states or intergovernmental institutions. Claiming the initiative would provide 60,000 jobs, officially registered unemployment (in a country where about 50 per cent of the employed work in the informal sector) rose steadily from 39 per cent in 1999 to an estimated 46 per cent by 2006. True, the SME sector was the most important in creating *new* jobs, hardly surprising considering the funds poured into it, but it still experienced an *overall* fall in employees. In 2006 the mission statement of the Prime Minister's Economic Transition Unit (ETU) in Sarajevo, in which the World Bank was represented, made no mention at all of jobs, unemployment or poverty. It stressed improvement to Bosnia's fiscal architecture and making the business environment more attractive to international and domestic investors.[2]

Yet unemployment is repeatedly a major political issue for voters (reflected in a countrywide social movement, the 2006 *Gradjanska Platforma* (Citizens' Platform)). Indices of unemployment are fed into political discourses and huge variations in the rate are cited, partly because of the difficulty of defining unemployment in a war-affected context, but partly to support political objectives. However, in both the registered and unregistered markets, abuse of labour rights has been a settled norm. The author's survey in 2005 revealed that 14.1 per cent of 92 respondents had experienced failure by employers to pay wages; 57.6 per cent experienced failure to be paid on time; 26.1 per cent had experience of only being paid part of their money; 72.8 per cent had been required to work longer hours than contracted; 23.9 per cent had been dismissed without notice or valid reason; 21.7 per cent had been harassed or asked to do something illegal. It made little difference whether the employer was in the formal or informal sector, but more respondents had experienced abuse in private companies than the public sector; over a third who had experienced denial of labour rights believed that an international donor had subsidised an abusive employer.

## The ILO and norm-setting

If global corporations, local entrepreneurs and the international community of donors and IFIs do not press employment rights, where is the locus of power and norms to critique and overcome contemporary models? Can supranational organisations be empowered to regulate 'free markets' as Stammers (1999: 1003) proposes? The most appropriate institution would seem to be the ILO, which was promoted by pre-1914 international labour movements and NGOs. But the ILO can be construed as a conservative body, founded to counteract social unrest after the First World War. It had some impact in the interwar years in bringing labour standards to newly industrialising countries such as Japan (Murphy, 2005: 95). As part of the post-1945 UN family it set minimum standards through the Tripartite Declaration of Principles Concerning Multinational Enterprises and Social Policy (1978) and Fundamental Principles of Rights at Work (1998). It has also promoted labour-intensive projects in war-torn societies (discussed below). UN norms and the non-binding 'Global Compact' (formally launched in 2000) are also designed to promote respect for labour rights that were long disregarded by multinationals, the World Bank and the IMF (Steinhardt, 2005: 207–8).

The ILO is also a unique example of sub-state multilateral governance. But the 14 'labour' members on the executive are counterbalanced by 14 'employer' and 28 state representatives. The governing body, like those of the IFIs, also has disproportionate Western representation because Article 7(2) of its constitution privileges states of 'chief industrial importance'. Like the global trade and financial institutions it has limited public accountability. Unlike them, however, it has no great enforcement capacity (used only once against Myanamar/Burma). In the view of the pre-eminent labour rights lawyer, Philip Alston, the organisation is increasingly marginalised as other agencies favour voluntary codes that are written and administered by employers with limited inspection provisions (2005: 21).

In its norm-setting role, the ILO has been influenced by the imperatives of global capitalism and the accompanying reduction in collective bargaining power. The ILO-sponsored 'World Commission on the Social Dimension of Globalisation' (2004), whose membership included the advocate of property rights for the poor, Hernando de Soto, and the Nobel Prize winner Joseph Stiglitz, adopted a restricted, if essential, view of rights: freedom of association, non-discrimination in the work place, freedom from child labour, and health and safety conditions. The right to paid work, the minimum wage, redress for abuse of contracts and benefit rights (including benefits for women) were marginalised. Together with standard setting in the 1989 UN Convention on the Rights of the Child, the ILO can claim success on the child labour issue. The proportion of working children declined markedly between 2000 and 2004, through there were still 74.4 million aged 5 to 14 engaged in hazardous work (Hagemann *et al.*, 2006: 2).

Equally significant, however, has been the ILO's adoption of 'flexicurity', in line with the EU's social and labour market agenda (ILO, 2006). Retraining and labour inflexibility can be a major problem for employers and workers after conflict. Flexicurity aims to increase productivity and mobility by rejecting job security. It endorses the demands of business and the World Bank to deregulate employment protection to make it easier to hire and fire people for short-term needs. It intersects with the notion of comparative advantage in seeking the least economically onerous labour supply through, for example, shaking out over-staffing, switching to individual, temporary or fixed-term contracts rather than collective bargaining, and the removal of ancillary benefits such as housing (Zenica and Sarajevo, 2006). Disregarded are the costs of redundancy payments (where applicable), of training new personnel and correcting shoddy work arising from inexperience. Labour's willingness to adjust is to be complemented by a cushion of individual security through various stages of employment. But social protection threatens to contradict the market – by taxing capital and labour or by requiring an accommodating state budget for the security that flexicurity implies. Damage to social capital is likely to occur because the strategy means increased instability in labour relations, inferior pensions for the retired and reductions in long-term consumption horizons. In war-torn societies the premium placed on retraining, adequate institutional support for job-seeking such as job centres, geographical and skill mobility and access to information and communications is non-existent or inadequate. With such large constituencies of the needy in war-torn societies, weak institutional provision and reliance on the market rather than an active state in the economy is not likely to be a substitute for job creation. Flexibility entails shrinkage in labour rights, with employers in the registered market free-riding on the absence of labour rights in the unregistered market. In trying to marry labour rights with market libertarianism the ILO endorses a framework that diverts transition costs onto labour and shifts from a rights-based approach towards codes and guidelines.

## Resistance

In the aftermath of conflict, populations are scripted parts by interveners as exhausted victims or unruly, often irrational, militants to be rendered governable. But this is to underestimate the vigour of survivors in which resistance to liberal peacebuilding plays a role. As Chris Cramer demonstrates, violent conflict has developmental as well as destructive attributes, facilitating capital accumulation and releasing popular energies (Cramer, 2006). Remarkably, given its apparent weakness, labour is not passive even in unpropitious circumstances.

In Guatemala, employers simply tyrannise unionists, who were debilitated by the 1996 peace accords because employers no longer faced the threat of retaliation for abusive conduct by the revolutionary guerrilla movement. Nevertheless, as in Colombia where death squads routinely murder labour protestors, unionism is kept alive by subventions from Europe (Acevedo et al., 2007). In Cambodia, a trade agreement with the United States in 1999 led to rapid expansion of the garment industry, employing over 300,000, of whom 80 per cent are young women, many from poor rural backgrounds. But this export boom was possible because the Cambodian government was obliged by US unions to adopt labour standards, enabling a women's social movement to form the Free Trade Union, the country's first consolidated union. It grew in spite of continuing employer abuse of the Labour Law, violence (including assassinations) and police brutality (Hall, 2000). In BiH, industrial protests and strikes have been rife since the war in spite of the risks to workers and the queues of replacements. Typical of hundreds of examples are: workers at a Kakanj company who had not received salaries for nine months and were then told they had no jobs (OBN, 19 November 1999); the Brcko fire brigade went on strike in early May 2000 over non-payment of salaries and dangerous equipment (OBN, 2 May 2000); and teachers in Herzeg.–Neretva Canton striking for a 30 per cent salary increase and a collective contract (*Večernji List*, 2006: 9).

Some social and political movements have adopted partial alternatives to neoliberalism in association with 'non-Western' models of post-conflict assistance. In Lebanon, for example, after Israel's invasion of 2006 the government adopted a liberal peace model, shored up by funds from the Arab Gulf states. But the latter also deviated from the model by adopting villages, handing out cash payments and directing repairs. In the south, Hezbollah supplemented its support for private entrepreneurship with unofficial, sectarian-based welfare that met the socio-economic needs of its followers without having to kowtow to the IFIs (Mac Ginty, 2007: 470, 476).

Reliance on informal income sources is a more widespread form of resistance. It signals not merely a struggle to survive and cope but a rejection of official authority and its auditing procedures, sometimes, as in former Yugoslavia, drawing on traditional evasion techniques. By 2007 an estimated 57 per cent of the active labour force in BiH had withdrawn from the formal market (UNDP, 2007: 75). The World Bank (2002) estimated that 36 per cent of the employable population were in unregistered work. Some depended on illegal activities. Rights as such are unrecognised and it is essential not to romanticise this form of resistance. But informality undermines the very concept of the social contract with the state and signifies retaliation by what Mark Duffield calls the 'uninsured surplus' population that is expected to manage (actually to circulate) poverty on the basis of self-reliance. And since self-reliance pushes people into anti-state, often clientilistic, alternatives, external agencies have ameliorated market imperatives so as to support localised, still largely self-reliant, risk management initiatives, rather than contemplating universal social protection (Duffield, 2007: 118, 228). Thus rights struggles in unprotected economies are marked by resistance through desertion of the state.

## Conclusion

Efforts in peacebuilding to provide a right to work are generally secondary to market-led opportunism, to subsidies for 'free' enterprise (notably in trade and service sectors) and to counter-terrorism strategies intended to reduce unrest. Alternative political economies tend to be excluded: protectionism, universal public goods and industrial and agricultural employment strategies. For instance, several Indian states make employment a constitutional right and guarantee days of work on community assets (ODI, 2007: 3). Such schemes exclude groups, such as the elderly, with no, or limited, labour to offer. A focus on the relief element can also lead to 'make-work' schemes and an over-emphasis on the short-term costs to public budgets. Economists tend to regard public works as a form of outdoor relief to provide wages or 'in-kind' payments in times of shock (McCord, 2006: 484–7). Such a relief perspective in war-torn societies can be justified as a safety net. But there can also be benefits in terms of infrastructure development, improved labour skills and social cohesion through the provision of common public goods and services. Indeed, the ILO has sponsored various labour-intensive projects in Uganda, Mozambique and Cambodia, sometimes with World Bank support (Shone, 2003). However, without *dirigiste* long-term employment strategies, such projects may have only short-term relevance and delay economic transformation.

In the absence of strategies for agriculture and industry, and in the absence of increased purchasing power, neoliberal policies are liable to contradict the quest for rights. While some see a convergence of socio-economic and civil–political rights (e.g., Steinhardt, 2005), others see 'little reason to expect that labour rights will be accorded anything near the sort of priority which is inherent in the very notion of a human right' (Alston, 2005: 23). In truth, an end to the constructed dichotomy between sets of rights would undermine 'the whole purpose of the post-war human-rights regime, which is to gain legitimation for free market, laissez-faire practices and the expansion of the neoliberal economy on a global scale' (Evans, 2000: 58–61, 431). In this case structural causes of violations would have to be addressed, including radical revision of supranational institutions and heavier regulation of transnational corporations.

Even so, the consolidation of fully legitimate un-imposed norms, as Robert Cox argues, 'would have to be gained through struggle within each civilization or culture' (Cox, 2002: 63). The political economy of rights – from the alienation of labour in production and exchange to 'casino capitalism' and the disintegration of the social functions of markets – entails a universal striving for economic justice, evidenced in ethical, legal and institutional discourses, even though struggles for labour rights in war-torn societies are manifested in different ways and in specific contexts.

## Notes

1. UN Development Group/World Bank (at: http://iraq.undg.org/index.cfm?Module=Document&Page=Document&Category=31&Type=finished).
2. The ETU website is at www.ohr.int/ohr-dept/econ (accessed 20 March 2006).

## References

Acevedo, Sariah, Jørn Holm-Hansen and Henrik Wiig, 2007, 'Report on Unistragua', GuaNGO, Oslo, draft report, 5 November.

Achio, Francoise and Irma Specht, 2003, 'Youth in Conflict', in Eugenia Date-Bah (ed.), *Jobs After War: A Critical Challenge in the Peace and Reconstruction Puzzle*, Geneva: ILO, pp. 153–66.

Alston, Philip (ed.), 2005, 'Labour Rights as Human Rights: The Not So Happy State of the Art', *Labour Rights as Human Rights*, Oxford: Oxford University Press, pp. 1–24.

Butcher, Tim, 2007, 'Tony Blair's Plan for Palestinian Jobs', *Daily Telegraph* (London), 21 November.

CARE International, 1997, 'Household Livelihood Security – An Overview', unpublished commentary by Timothy R. Frankenberg (interviewed by author, Brussels).
Chua, Amy, 2004, *World on Fire: How Exporting Free Market Democracy Breeds Ethnic Hatred and Global Instability*, New York: Anchor.
Collier, Paul, V. L. Elliott, Håvard Hegre, Anke Hoeffler, Marta Reynal-Querol and Nicholas Sambanis, 2004, *Breaking the Conflict Trap*, Oxford: Oxford University Press.
Cox, Robert W. with Michael G. Schechter, 2002, *The Political Economy of a Plural World: Critical Reflections on Power, Morals and Civilization*, London: Routledge.
Craig, John D. R. and S. Michael Lynk (eds), 2006, *Globalization and the Future of Labour Law*, Cambridge: Cambridge University Press.
Cramer, Christopher, 2006, *Civil War is Not a Stupid Thing: Accounting for Violence in Developing Countries*, London: Hurst.
Date-Bah, Eugenia, 2003, 'Women and Other Gender Concerns in Post-Conflict Reconstruction and Job Promotion Efforts', in Eugenia Date-Bah (ed.), *Jobs After War: A Critical Challenge in the Peace and Reconstruction Puzzle*, Geneva: ILO, pp. 111–48.
Date-Bah, Eugenia and Eve Hall, 2003, 'Promoting Income-Generating Activities among Refugees: A Case Study', in Eugenia Date-Bah (ed.), *Jobs After War: A Critical Challenge in the Peace and Reconstruction Puzzle*, Geneva: ILO, pp. 167–90.
De Búrca, Gráinne, 2005, 'The Future of Social Rights Protection in Europe', in de Búrca and Bruno de Witte (eds), *Social Rights in Europe*, Oxford: Oxford University Press, pp. 3–14.
De Schutter, Olivier, 2005, 'The Accountability of Multinationals for Human Rights Violations in European Law', in Philip Alston (ed.), *Non-State Actors and Human Rights*, Oxford: Oxford University Press, pp. 227–314.
Donnelly, Jack, 2002, *International Human Rights*, 3rd edn, Boulder, CO: Westview.
Duffield, Mark, 2007, *Development Security and Unending War: Governing the World of Peoples*, Cambridge: Polity.
Evans, Tony, 2000, 'Citizenship and Human Rights in the Age of Globalization', *Alternatives*, Vol. 25, No. 4, pp. 415–38.
Evans, Tony, 2001, *The Politics of Human Rights: A Global Perspective*, London: Pluto.
Falk, Richard A., 2000, *Human Rights Horizons: The Pursuit of Justice in a Globalizing World*, New York: Routledge.
Fierke, Karin M., 2007, *Critical Approaches to International Security*, Cambridge: Polity.
Geuss, Raymond, 2002, 'Liberalism and its Discontents', *Political Theory*, Vol. 30, No. 3, pp. 320–38.
Gray, John, 1998, *False Dawn: The Delusions of Global Capitalism*, London: Granta, 2002 edn.
Hagemann, Frank, Yacouba Diallo, Alex Etienne and Farhad Mehran, 2006, *Global Child Labour Trends 2002–2004*, Geneva: ILO International Programme on the Elimination of Child Labour, April.
Hall, John, 2000, 'Human Rights and the Garment Industry in Contemporary Cambodia', *Stanford Journal of International Law*, Vol. 36, pp. 119–74.
Harvey, David, 2003, *The New Imperialism*, Oxford: Oxford University Press.
He, Baogang and Hannah Murphy, 2007, 'Global Social Justice at the WTO? The Role of NGOs in Constructing Global Social Contracts', *International Affairs*, Vol. 83, No. 4, pp. 707–27.
Hunt, Alan, 1990, 'Rights and Social Movements: Counter-Hegemonic Strategies', *Journal of Law and Society*, Vol. 17, No. 3, pp. 309–28.

ILO (International Labour Organisation), 2004, *A Fair Globalization: Creating Opportunities for All*, Report of the World Commission on the Social Dimension of Globalisation, Geneva: ILO.

ILO, 2006, 'Combining Labour Market Flexibility and Security in the West Balkans', 95th session of the International Labour Conference, ILO, Geneva, Dept of Communications (at: www.ilo.org/public/english/bureau/inf/features/06/ilc06balkans.htm).

Klein, Naomi, 2007, *The Shock Doctrine: The Rise of Disaster Capitalism*, London: Allen Lane.

Kosovo, 2006a, Ministry of Youth, Culture and Sport, 'Kosovo Youth Policy', public draft prepared by Artan Duraku, Secretariat, Kosovo Youth Action Plan, Priština, 27 October.

Kosovo, 2006b, Ministry of Labour and Social Welfare, 'Action Plan for Kosovo Youth Employment, a mid-term policy framework 2006–2008', October.

Labour Behind the Label and War on Want, 2007, 'Let's Clean up Fashion, Update' (at: www.labourbehindthelabel.org/images/pdf/lcuf2007.pdf).

Lawrence, Felicity, 2007, 'Underpaid, Easy to Sack: UK's Second Class Workforce', *The Guardian* (London), 24 September, pp. 20–21.

McCord, Anna, 2006, 'Public Works', in David Alexander Clark (ed.), *The Elgar Companion to Development Studies*, Cheltenham: Edward Elgar.

Mac Ginty, Roger, 2007, 'Reconstructing Post-War Lebanon: A Challenge to the Liberal Peace?', *Conflict, Security & Development*, Vol. 7, No. 3, pp. 457–82.

McGrew, Anthony G., 1998, 'Human Rights in a Global Age: Coming to Terms with Globalization', in Tony Evans (ed.), *Human Rights Fifty Years On*, Manchester: Manchester University Press, 1998, pp. 188–210.

McMullin, Jaremey R., 2006, 'The Soldier and the Post-Conflict State: Assessing Ex-Combatant Reintegration in Namibia, Mozambique and Sierra Leone', unpublished PhD, University of Oxford.

Mani, Rama, 2002, *Beyond Retribution: Seeking Justice in the Shadows of War*, Cambridge: Polity.

Mendelson-Forman, Johanna and Merriam Mashatt, 2007, 'Stabilization and Reconstruction', United States Institute for Peace, Stabilization and Reconstruction Series No. 6, March.

Moreau, Marie-Ange, 2005, 'European Fundamental Social Rights in the Context of Economic Globalization', in Gráinne de Búrca and Bruno de Witte (eds), *Social Rights in Europe*, Oxford: Oxford University Press, pp. 367–82.

Murphy, Craig N., 2005, *Global Institutions, Marginalization, and Development*, London: Routledge.

Novitz, Tonia, 2005, 'The European Union and International Labour Standards: The Dynamics of Dialogue between the EU and the ILO', in Philip Alston (ed.), *Labour Rights as Human Rights*, Oxford: Oxford University Press, pp. 214–41.

Nozick, Robert, 1974, *Anarchy, State and Utopia*, New York: Basic Books.

OBN (Open Broadcast Network), Sarajevo.

ODI (Overseas Development Institute), 2007, *Rural employment and migration: in search of decent work*, briefing paper, No. 27, London, October.

Pogge, Thomas W., 1989, *Realizing Rawls*, Ithaca: Cornell University Press.

Pogge, Thomas W., 2002, *World Poverty and Human Rights*, Cambridge: Polity.

Priština, 2006, Author's Interview with Professor Muhamet Mustafa, Riinvest Institute, 13 September.

Pugh, Michael, 2003, 'Protectorates and Spoils of Peace: Intermestic Manipulations of Political Economy in South-East Europe', in Dietrich Jung (ed.), *Shadow Globalisation: Ethnic Conflicts, and New Wars. A political economy of Intra-State Wars*, London: Routledge, pp. 47–69.

Pugh, Michael and Neil Cooper with Jonathan Goodhand, 2004, *War Economies in a Regional Context*, Boulder CO: Lynne Rienner.

Rawls, John, 1967, 'Distributive Justice', in Peter Laslett and W. Garry Runciman (eds), *Philosophy, Politics and Society*, Oxford: Blackwell, pp. 58–82.

Rawls, John, 1971, *A Theory of Justice*, Oxford: Oxford University Press, 1972 edn.

Sagramoso, Domitilla, 2007, 'Violence and Conflict in the Russian North Caucasus', *International Affairs*, Vol. 83, No. 4, pp. 681–705.

Said, Edward W., 1995, *The Politics of Dispossession: The Struggle for Palestinian Self-Determination, 1969–1994*, London: Vintage.

Sanghera, Gurchathen S., 2009, 'The "Politics" of Children's Rights and Child Labour in India: A Social Constructionist Perspective', *International Journal of Human Rights*, Vol. 13, No. 1 (forthcoming).

Saul, John Ralston, 2005, *The Collapse of Globalism and the Reinvention of the World*, London: Atlantic Books.

Sen, Armatya, 1999, *Development as Freedom*, Oxford: Oxford University Press.

Shone, Mike, 2003, 'Labour-based Infrastructure Rebuilding', in Eugenia Date-Bah (ed.), *Jobs After War: A Critical Challenge in the Peace and Reconstruction Puzzle*, Geneva: ILO, pp. 243–57.

Shue, Henry, 1980, *Basic Rights: Subsistence, Affluence, and U.S. Foreign Policy*, Princeton, NJ: Princeton University Press.

Stammers, Neil, 1999, 'Social Movements and the Social Construction of Human Rights', *Human Rights Quarterly*, Vol. 21, No. 4, pp. 980–1008.

Steinhardt, Ralph G., 2005, 'Corporate Responsibility and the International Law of Human Rights: The New *Lex Mercatoria*', in Philip Alston (ed.), *Non-State Actors and Human Rights*, Oxford: Oxford University Press, pp. 177–226.

Thomas, Caroline, 1998, 'International Financial Institutions and Social and Economic Human Rights: An Exploration', in Tony Evans (ed.), *Human Rights Fifty Years On*, Manchester: Manchester University Press, 1998, pp. 161–85.

UN, 1966, 'International Covenant on Economic, Social and Cultural Rights', UN Doc. A/6316.

UNDP, 2005, *BiH Early Warning System III Quarterly report*, July–September, Sarajevo.

UNDP, 2007, *Social Inclusion in Bosnia and Herzegovina*, National Human Development Report, 2007, Sarajevo.

UNDP–USAID, 2007, 'First steps in Post-conflict Statebuilding: A UNDP–USAID Study, Final Report', by Management Systems International and Katarina Ammitzbøll (UNDP), Washington, DC: UNDP, February.

Večernji Lis (Zagreb), 2006, 'Professors surrounded Schwarz-Schilling in Mostar', 17 February.

von Carlowitz, Leopold, 2005, 'Resolution of Property Disputes in Bosnia and Kosovo: The Contribution to Peacebuilding', *International Peacekeeping*, Vol. 12, No. 4, pp. 547–61.

Wells, Celia and Juanita Elias, 2005, 'Catching the Conscience of the King: Corporate Players on the International Stage', in Philip Alston (ed.), *Non-State Actors and Human Rights*, Oxford: Oxford University Press, pp. 141–75.

World Bank, 2002, 'Bosnia and Herzegovina. Labor Market in Postwar Bosnia and Herzegovina: How to Encourage Businesses to Create Jobs and Increase Worker

Mobility', Human Development Unit, South-East Europe Country Unit, Europe and Central Asia region, World Bank Report no. 24889-BIH, 4 November.

World Bank, EC (European Commission) and EBRD (European Bank for Reconstruction and Development), 1996, 'Bosnia and Herzegovina: Towards Economic Recovery', Discussion Paper for Second Donors' Conference.

Zenica and Sarajevo, 2006, author interviews in Bosnia, July–September.

# 9
# Securitising the Economy of Reintegration in Liberia

*Kathleen M. Jennings*

Disarmament, demobilisation and reintegration (DDR) programmes are now standard features of post-conflict peacebuilding interventions. The aim of such programmes is straightforward: to take away the guns, disperse the fighters and facilitate their transformation into socially and economically productive citizens. The two DD components are essentially exercises in field management and crowd control. They are quantifiable – by number of weapons collected or average stay in cantonment camps – and amenable to technical approaches. Defined as 'the process by which ex-combatants acquire civilian status and gain sustainable employment and income... a social and economic process... primarily taking place in communities at the local level.... part of the general development of a country [that] often necessitates long-term external assistance' (UN, 2006: 19), reintegration is more ambiguous than DD. In Liberia, it comprised provision of education or vocational training, a small monthly stipend and a set of tools upon course completion. Although reintegration programming tends to vary little from place to place, there is no such uniformity on what reintegration actually means and implies. In the absence of critical thinking on the social, economic and political project that the reintegration concept seems to promote, reintegration in Liberia essentially meant the temporary removal of idleness. This reflected a securitised approach. As elsewhere, reintegration devolved from the 'soft' development counterpart to the 'hard' security DD components, into a primarily security-driven and security-justified activity. The implications of this shift in Liberia, the assumption underpinning it and the functions it serves, are the focus of this chapter.

The removal of idleness from a particular adult population is not itself an unworthy goal. Nor is the presumed connection between idleness and instability always ill-conceived. However, in Liberia the removal of idleness seemingly bore only an accidental relation to actual employment, income generation or wider development. Keeping the ex-combatants busy was an end in itself: yet not a particularly productive one for ex-combatants, or one that could be realistically sustained beyond the life of the programming. As a strategy for development – the original and still supposed justification for reintegration – this was clearly flawed. As a strategy for conflict prevention, it was at best temporary, and at worst counterproductive.

This chapter focuses on the reintegration programme implemented from 2004 in Liberia by the Joint Implementation Unit, comprising representatives from the National Commission on Disarmament, Demobilisation, Rehabilitation and Reintegration, the UN Mission in Liberia and the UN Development Programme. I argue that the development goals of reintegration were instrumentalised in favour of a security agenda built on a conflation of insecurity and ex-combatant idleness. After examining the functions of this securitising act, the chapter concludes that, as a practical matter, an inability to deliver promised outcomes meant that the securitisation of reintegration compromised both development and security goals. Future attempts at reintegration should be preceded by proper conceptualisation of the reintegration project itself, with due regard to the affected population and society and the resources available to national and international actors. Such conceptual work may point to more minimalist approaches to reintegration than the highly interventionist training-and-education paradigm currently in favour. This could include delinking reintegration from disarmament and demobilisation, focusing reintegration resources instead on open-access employment programmes, which could be complemented by incentives for local and international business to hire ex-combatants. Nevertheless, the importance of this work would be to ensure that minimalism in approach and implementation would occur by design, not by default.

## Preliminary impacts of DDR in Liberia

The Liberian DDR process has been examined at some length elsewhere (Jennings, 2007, 2008; Nichols, 2005; Paes, 2005). This brief overview focuses on the process beginning after the signing of the peace agreement in 2003, which formally comprised disarmament, demobilisation, rehabilitation and reintegration (though rehabilitation had little impact on programming and is omitted here).[1] Although this chapter focuses more on DDR's preliminary impacts than on the intricate details of its implementation, some basic background is nevertheless required.

DDR was mandated in the August 2003 Comprehensive Peace Agreement (CPA), signed shortly after former president Charles Taylor went into exile. The process began – and temporarily ended – in December 2003, after riots in the cantonment camp at Camp Schieffelin spread to nearby Monrovia, resulting in nine civilian deaths. DDR was suspended pending further deployment of UN peacekeepers and the establishment of more cantonment sites; during this period, the entry requirements for DDR were also downgraded, requiring only the submission of 150 rounds of ammunition in lieu of a weapon. Significantly, this move to expand participation in DDR overlooked two important points. The resources available for reintegration remained the same; and training more people in the same trades did not ensure more employment afterwards. Indeed, training was likely to produce the opposite result, with labour supply vastly outstripping demand in a context where the return of refugees and internally displaced persons added to a labour glut.

DDR formally resumed in April 2004 in Gbarnga, proceeding at cantonment sites nationwide until the formal conclusion of the DD components on 31 October 2004. Reintegration programmes continue as of mid-2007.[2] Disarmed ex-combatants were briefly housed in the cantonment sites, and received two cash reinsertion payments of US$150 each and a DDR identification card (necessary for access to reintegration programming). This programming consisted of subsidised access to three years of formal education or to shorter vocational courses, including training in auto mechanics, plumbing, carpentry, masonry and computers; public works training; and agricultural, livestock and fishing programmes. Those actively enrolled in reintegration programmes also received a small monthly stipend (decreasing from $30 per month in year one, to $15 per month in year two, to nothing in year three) and, if relevant, a set of tools upon course completion.

Particularly striking was the gap between the number of ex-combatants and the number of weapons collected: over 101,000 people registered as disarmed and demobilised, whereas just over 28,000 weapons and 6.5 million rounds of ammunition were turned in.[3] Two questions immediately arise. Were there really 101,000 fighters and camp followers in Liberia? And where were the rest of the weapons? The enfeeblement of the entry requirements means that the two issues are linked. The number of ex-combatants was undoubtedly inflated, bolstered by non-combatants taking advantage of the low entry criteria in order to access the cash and other benefits they would otherwise be denied. A mutually beneficial transaction, in which a percentage of the first cash payout was pledged in return for access to a gun or ammunition, seems to have been commonplace (Jennings, 2007; Nichols, 2005; Paes, 2005). Conversely, ex-combatants with access to weapons could either sell them or hold them in reserve, disarming with ammunition instead. The weakening of the entry criteria thus directly undermined the security goal of disarmament, by enabling more guns to be kept in circulation. It is impossible to know with any certainty how many 'real' ex-combatants there are in Liberia; in any case, the question is hardly relevant. What is certain, however, is that there were (and remain) more guns in circulation than were handed in, and that many of the DDR participants were never combatants.

It is difficult to condemn those who disarmed without fighting: initiative and entrepreneurialism are, after all, characteristics typically extolled as vital to post-conflict rebuilding, even if in this case they were channelled in ways inconvenient to the programmers. Nevertheless, the explosion in DDR enrolment (exceeding original estimates of approximately 40,000 ex-combatants) did have a detrimental impact on the DDR participants. The reintegration components were grossly over-subscribed and under-resourced, resulting in a long gap between demobilisation and entry into reintegration programming. By November 2006, two years after the DD components formally ended, over 40,000 registered ex-combatants still had no access to reintegration programmes.[4] Popular courses had long backlogs and, in interviews, some ex-combatants in Monrovia complained that they were only offered agricultural training, despite having no intentions to leave the capital. Perhaps unsurprisingly, corruption was common, both as a means of gaining access to reintegration programmes and in relation to the stipends participants received: many complained that their stipends were often delayed and, when eventually received, less than they were supposed to be. Crucially, those who did enrol in training courses found there were no jobs waiting for them afterwards – despite the common belief that they were promised employment.[5]

I have argued elsewhere (Jennings, 2007, 2008) that the DDR programme was compromised by an inability to live up to its promises (whether real or imagined), resulting in little change in ex-combatants' social and economic situations, disappointing their expectations and potentially feeding their dissatisfaction. Moreover, the dilution of the entry requirements, combined with relatively generous cash benefits, seems to have exacerbated the problem by creating a market for ex-combatants. That not all claimants were genuine is to some degree incidental: upon accepting the label and participating in the process, they 'became' ex-combatants, subject to the same assumptions, prejudices and expectations as their genuine counterparts. Insofar as ex-combatants are presumed to be a major problem in post-conflict environments, then expanding their ranks seems a counterproductive strategy. Moreover, privileging them above their equally impoverished countrymen (through the provision of DDR benefits) arguably helped harden the divisions between former fighters and civilian society, thus undermining reintegration's rationale (see, e.g., IRIN, 2005).

Finally, although national and international actors in Liberia can rightly claim an absence of large-scale organised violence since 2003 – notwithstanding an urban violent crime problem so troubling that the Ministry of Justice urged the formation of community vigilante groups (IRIN, 2006) – establishing a causal link with DDR is extremely difficult (see Humphreys and Weinstein, 2005). As of May 2007, the country still hosted over 15,000 UN peacekeepers and civilian police, and progress on the reconstitution of the armed forces and the development of a national security strategy was sluggish.

The impact of reintegration is, of course, integrally connected to the programme's conceptualisation (or lack thereof) and subsequent implementation. Central to these are the assumptions upon which the programme was based, and how these were translated into action.

## Idle hands are the devil's workshop

The Liberian DDR programme was predicated on a number of assumptions, reflecting a particular notion of the constitution and organisation of armed groups and societies affected by conflict. Of primary interest here is the assumption that, among ex-combatants, idleness equates to instability. This is different from merely recognising the economic dimensions of the conflict. Noting that fighters and commanders profited from the 'rule of the gun' is one thing; assuming that violent conflict is the default position of idle ex-combatants, quite another, but assumed in the literature (Aboagye and Bah, 2004; Collier and Hoeffler, 1998; Spear, 2006; UN, 2006).

As Cramer (2006 and Chapter 7, this volume) points out, we still know little about the role of labour markets in conflict or post-conflict scenarios, including whether unemployment is causally related to instability. Interestingly, with respect to Liberia, Bøås and Hatløy (2008) argue that idleness has been overstated as a motivation for youths to join armed groups, thus leading them to question why idleness should be presumed to be a determinant of insecurity after conflict ends. Nevertheless, the idleness = instability equation persists, probably because it *seems* so fundamentally sensible. After all, troublemaking, especially of an organised variety, is presumably easier to instigate in the absence of other demands on one's time. Those with a job to lose are also probably less likely to foment disorder than those with no such stake. The priority is thus to keep rank-and-file ex-combatants – excluded from anti-spoiler strategies targeted at elites – satisfied and occupied. The cash reinsertion payments in the disarmament and demobilisation processes are a means of providing immediate satisfaction to ex-combatants looking for concrete benefits from peace (Jennings, 2007). Keeping them occupied falls to the process of reintegration.

Throughout the 1990s reintegration was generally perceived and represented more as a development than as a security imperative – a long-term activity focusing on the economic and social adaptation of ex-combatants to 'productive' civilian life (UN, 2000: 2) as part of a newly cohesive and rehabilitated society. The vision was ambitious and transformative. Technically, the vision has not changed: the UN's definition (2006, 1.2: 19) states that reintegration 'is essentially a social and economic process with an open time frame... part of the general development of a country'. However, reintegration's presumed benefits to security have also become more explicit and extravagantly expressed: 'Failure to successfully implement such [reintegration and rehabilitation] programs will result in youth unemployment and fuel the development of criminal gangs and violence and ultimately a relapse into conflict' (High-Level Panel, 2004: 72). Such claims suggest that reintegration is the main barrier preventing relapse into organised armed conflict – a task against which mere development goals pale. The dual function accorded to reintegration is illustrated by the UN's (2006) framework for Integrated DDR Standards, which invokes both sustainable development and basic security provision as the principal goals of reintegration. Where reintegration's development potential is emphasised, its security benefits are also stressed; yet the reverse is less often the case.

In Liberia this tension over reintegration's role resolved in favour of security. Because idleness was conflated with instability, it had to be confronted less as a social or economic problem than a security one. The content of programming was thus secondary to the action itself. So long as ex-combatants were busy, they would be mollified and thus neutralised. If positive developmental impacts should happen as well, then so much the better.[6] The upshot was a massive job training and education programme, presumably predicated on future large-scale entry into wage labour. Yet the country had a mostly informal, commodity-based economy; a staggeringly high unemployment rate in the formal economy according to World Bank estimates; a high degree of capital flight; and a small (largely destroyed) manufacturing base. Informal economies are not jobless economies, but they are characterised by high degrees of worker vulnerability, job instability, and low and irregular incomes (see ILO, 2002). Training thousands of people for nonexistent formal jobs would be putting the cart before the horse, were it not for the fact that the development aspect of reintegration was not the key consideration driving reintegration programming. Instead, the point was to buy time for the transitional and newly elected governments[7] – seemingly ignoring the predicament that without jobs the protection provided by training lasted only as long as the programming. The practical outcomes of this approach will be further examined after considering its mechanics.

## The function of securitisation

The co-option of development programming by a security agenda is not new (Duffield, 2001, 2002; Pugh, 2006). Nor is it necessarily one-sided: development policymakers and practitioners may adopt the priorities and rhetoric of security in order to increase their own indispensability, or because they believe the argument that security and development are inextricably linked, and that what is good for one is good for the other (DFID, 2005). Yet in Liberia the development component seemed strikingly incidental. Expansion of DDR participation expanded the size of the 'problem' to be handled, thus diminishing the extent to which an overstressed reintegration component could improve the socio-economic conditions and prospects of ex-combatants – thereby increasing the sense of its irrelevance. Moreover, the project had been securitised at the outset, before the size of the DDR programme became evident.

Securitisation does not refer simply to policies or programming enacted or justified according to security imperatives. Securitisation is described as

> the move that takes politics beyond the established rules of the game and frames the issue either as a special kind of politics or as above politics.... [to do so] the issue is presented as an existential threat, requiring emergency measures and justifying actions outside the normal bounds of political procedures.
>
> (Buzan *et al.*, 1998: 23–4)

At the same time, security is 'a self-referential practice, because it is in this practice that the issue becomes a security issue – not necessarily because a real existential threat exists but because the issue is presented as such a threat' (Buzan *et al.*, 1998: 24). In Liberia, accordingly, the masses of ex-combatants posed an existential threat from within, specifically to the governing authority of both the national and international administrations. This provided the justification for a reintegration policy that privileged the perpetrators of armed conflict over its victims, in a conflict where the 'rule of the gun' enabled many fighters to live significantly better than civilians. What would otherwise seem politically and ethically indefensible – the special treatment of ex-combatants – could be justified by the existential threat they presented.

Yet this securitising act created a problem and a paradox. The problem was in situating reintegration 'above' or 'outside' the normal bounds of politics in a post-conflict polity where political rules were evolving in response to changed internal and external circumstances and relationships. This is problematic precisely because of the reintegration project's nature and implications. Reintegration is inherently political in its target population; its professed end of transformative change at a group and, implicitly, societal level; and its assumption that this process can be engineered by national or international actors. It involves questions of resource distribution, preferential status for particular groups, economic and labour policy, access to education and prioritisation. But strangely (because reintegration has such political goals and impacts that it would seem that its form should vary greatly between countries), reintegration also has a relatively set form and content from country to country. This effectively means that the securitising act that makes DDR a necessity also entails the imposition, by outside actors, of a specific process with manifold political implications, thus reducing the political space in which local actors can manoeuvre and have an impact. Securitising reintegration essentially limits the scope for political action on the issues reintegration affects.

This leads to the paradox. Taking reintegration outside the normal rules of politics does not just make its necessity self-evident; it also seems to privilege the use of extraordinary measures to address it. But as seen in Liberia (and elsewhere), this was not the case, either in terms of funding or programming innovation. Instead, the securitisation of reintegration merely led to the paring down of the concept, from a positive act (becoming a social and economic asset to one's community) to a negative one (refraining from the use of organised violence). This resulted in an undifferentiated, technocratic approach, in which the provision of training and education was both the pre-requisite and guarantor of reintegration. Such an approach to reintegration entails a downgrading from the transformative to the technical. Yet ease of implementation did not translate into satisfactory outcomes. This demonstrates the fundamental limitations of a technical approach to a project that – like other elements of peacebuilding – is essentially predicated on constraining and changing the incentive structures, activities and modes and drivers of behaviour that prevailed during conflict.

Because the securitisation of reintegration comprises a contraction rather than an expansion, it obscures the structural issues that might impede social and economic development among ex-combatants or, indeed, within society as a whole. It shifts attention from the wider political, economic and social space to specific individuals or groups (Jennings, 2007). This allows for both segmentation and scapegoating, insofar as emphasis is placed on the 'refusal' (rather than inability) of ex-combatants to reintegrate. The obscuring of the structural issues also helps explain the contradiction that reintegration comprised a large job training programme in a country acutely lacking jobs, including in the informal sector. This is not to say that training is always a useless exercise; merely that training people in these circumstances is not an efficient use of resources, particularly when the potential for dissatisfaction among those being trained is heightened by the assumption that training will lead to a job.

Further, the focus on educating or training ex-combatants for wage labour was undercut by the reliance of international agencies on the private sector to provide employment and spur economic growth (see, e.g., IMF, 2007: 37–60, 77–86; Governance and Economic Management Assistance Program Agreement Document [GEMAP], 2005).[8] In post-conflict Liberia, the private sector was simply unable to shoulder this burden. The economy was predominantly informal, operating in an inadequate and inconsistent legal environment that discriminated against foreign investors and engendered unpredictable (but often steep) operating costs. Land tenure and land use policies were unclear and occasionally contradictory, and there was extremely low capacity in both the public and private sectors, especially in agri-business (FIAS, 2006). Without precluding the possibility of future development, formalisation and growth in the private sector, it is nevertheless the case that in the immediate post-war period dependence on the private sector to provide employment was grossly misguided.

Finally, it is notable that the securitised approach to reintegration seemingly depended on the homogenisation of ex-combatants, as if to remove unpredictability from the context. This is evident in the fact that the vast majority of ex-combatants – at both foot soldier and commander levels – were treated as an undifferentiated mass with the same interests, resources, circumstances, networks and opportunities. Yet this was clearly no more the case in Liberia than earlier in Mozambique, where ex-officers, offended at being treated the same as foot soldiers, chose to orient their organisational skills and networks towards criminal rather than licit enterprises (Alden, 2002).

The homogenising process that securitised DDR seemed to compel was also evident in the relatively low percentage of female ex-combatants or camp followers in the Liberian DDR programme. Despite a great deal of attention and concern, DDR programmes here and elsewhere consistently under-represent women. The extent to which this represents women 'spontaneously' reintegrating out of neglect or choice remains an open question. However, as MacKenzie (2007) argues with respect to the Sierra Leonean DDR programme, the focus on security rather than development in DDR facilitated women's exclusion. The reluctance to label women 'combatants' is one important factor in denying women access to 'the immediate attention of post-conflict programs' (MacKenzie, 2007: 6). She further contends that

> While there is concern that idle men will become violent, the greatest concern regarding idle women and girls seems to be their participation in prostitution.... First, males were identified as the primary beneficiary of most programs designed to meet the needs of former soldiers. Second, the reintegration process for women and girls was largely seen as a social process that aimed to return females back to their communities and back into more 'traditional' roles.
>
> (MacKenzie, 2007: 10)

This analysis can usefully be extended to the Liberian case, where the weakening of the entry criteria seems to have been driven in part by the desire to increase women's participation. This in turn seems predicated on the assumption that women could not be 'real' combatants, and therefore would not have access to weapons.

## Undermining security through unfulfilled promises

Ultimately, the securitisation of reintegration would be more comprehensible if it was effective, if the response met the need. The Liberian experience indicates the contrary: that the problematic impacts of reintegration were integrally related to its securitisation. The crux of the problem with the Liberian programme was the disconnect between expectations and reality, prompted by the (intentional or unintentional) promises of employment, a vocation or a better life through the DDR programme. This disconnect is evident in Pugel's (2007) finding that, in terms of income, ex-combatant non-participants in DDR do at least as well as those that complete reintegration training: whereas 26 per cent of non-participants in Liberia earned US$5 or more per day, only 21 per cent of former participants did so. The reintegration programme thus generated expectations that it was not properly resourced or equipped to fulfil. Nor was it necessarily designed to, its 'real' remit being the temporary busying of a fractious population. Even according to this degraded standard, however, the fact that 40,000 ex-combatants were still awaiting reintegration programming in November 2006 indicates severe shortcomings. Interestingly, in the absence of evidence that this group poses a more acute security threat to society than other demobilised ex-combatants, this long waiting period may lend credence to Bøås and Hatløy's claim that the idleness = insecurity link is overstated. Indeed, although Pugel (2007) finds that demobilised ex-combatants who do not access reintegration profess to be socially and economically worse off than participants, he does not link this to actual differences in the security situation posed by these groups. Ironically, from a security perspective the unfulfilled promises may be especially problematic, because they add resentment to the existing stew of unemployment or under-employment, perceived victimisation, loss of power (the inability to live by the gun) and poverty (Jennings, 2007). Furthermore, as noted above, the security benefits of DDR as a whole were compromised by the dilution of the entry criteria to the programme, which resulted in fewer weapons than anticipated being collected.

Finally, it is notable that the unexpectedly large number of participants seems to have amplified the reliance by national and international actors on more physical forms of control, centred on deterrence and containment, rather than normative or social (positive) control (Baaré, 2004). Informants in Monrovia described regular, sometimes violent, confrontations between DDR programme participants and programme administrators, mostly locals. Confrontations often resulted from failure to pay the monthly stipend, or were precipitated by ex-combatants claiming they were not respected by the administrators. Indeed, many informants, especially those enrolled in education programmes, claimed they were singled out for harsh or unfair treatment by programme administrators, but could not complain for fear of expulsion from the programme. Meanwhile, some peacekeeping contingents had a more aggressive approach towards ex-combatants than others, wading into neighbourhoods to break up fights or other small-scale conflicts, sometimes with brutal results.[9] Yet to the extent that DDR administrators sought recourse to these peacekeepers in the event of disorder, the potential for escalation was evident.[10] Reliance on physical forms of control could backfire, with the likely result being further cycles of confrontation and violence. In other words, a securitised approach does not seem the best way to reduce the levels of conflict in society.

## Alternatives: rethinking reintegration

Could reintegration have succeeded in Liberia if it had been conceived and implemented differently? A more effective approach could have been to focus less on training and education and more on actual employment, by delinking disarmament and demobilisation from reintegration, and channelling reintegration resources into open-access job programmes (prioritising infrastructure rehabilitation) with discrete, complementary, bilateral or multilateral education or support programmes for particularly vulnerable groups, including ex-combatants. Although the focus would still be to some extent the occupation of ex-combatants, the implementation would shift from prioritising unproductive to productive activity. In Liberia, delinking would have mitigated the unintended consequence of creating a market for ex-combatants, while at the same time bringing about broader developmental and income-generating impacts within communities. Moreover, because the reinsertion payments for disarming would remain intact, the DD components would retain the capacity to provide immediate 'satisfaction' to ex-combatants. Although these payments would likely have continued to attract non-combatants hoping for an easy payout, this would not have had the same deleterious knock-on effects on subsequent programming. A key feature to this approach would be expectations management, so as to prevent ex-combatants from feeling cheated or wronged. Yet to some extent, delinking would make managing expectations easier, its straightforwardness removing the element of misunderstood or unrealisable promises.

An alternative approach is suggested by Braud (2004), who proposes connecting DDR to the private sector by giving businesses incentives to hire ex-combatants. Incentives could include access to low-interest credit for businesses that link with the DDR programme. The employment of ex-combatants could also be made a pre-requisite for receiving infrastructure-related contracts. Such incentives could also complement a delinked DDR programme, as both would prioritise employment rather than training or education. Creating formal links between the DDR programme and the private sector could also provide crucial assistance to rehabilitating the latter.

Yet alternative approaches to reintegration, whether through delinking or otherwise, will not be implemented without proper conceptualisation of the reintegration project itself. Reintegration has become a catch-all policy, with little connection to identifiable or achievable ends. As suggested above, the reintegration goal of transforming ex-combatants into socially and economically productive citizens, if taken seriously, would imply social engineering through affirmative action policies; the channelling of resources into large-scale employment activities; far-reaching security sector reform; and monetary or in-kind incentives to encourage migration or return. It would likely overlap with land reform and tenure issues, and require the development or support of local mechanisms of conflict resolution. This idea of the reintegration project is clearly not being translated into practice. Yet nor are other ideas being developed, thus allowing the ascendance by default of the securitised, generic reintegration programme seen in Liberia.

First-order questions must be asked. Given the needs of society, and the place of ex-combatants in that society, is reintegration really needed in addition to disarmament and demobilisation? What kind of reintegration is reasonably possible – transformative and maximalist, or 'keep them busy' minimalist? What is the minimum outcome desired? What are the potential implications of both more maximalist and more minimalist approaches? If a maximalist approach is implemented, to what extent does this further close off the political space available to local actors, and how does this impact on sovereignty – already diminished by the presence of an international mission and aid apparatus? And what resources can be brought to bear? Asking these questions – and taking reintegration seriously – may in fact point to more minimalist approaches, such as delinking. If so, at least this would be a deliberate strategy, rather than one driven by an inability to deliver on promises.

## Notes

1. Fieldwork was conducted in Monrovia (Red Light and Duala Market), 4–21 November 2005, with the Liberian Institute for Statistics and Geo-Information Services. Some 490 informants were interviewed for the quantitative component (see Bøås and Hatløy, 2008). The qualitative component comprised over 40 open-ended interviews and nearly 20 focus group discussions, ranging from 2 to 8 participants per discussion. Informal conversations with ex-combatants at the field sites were used for background.
2. See www.unddr.org/countryprogrammes.php?c=52.
3. In addition to the small arms ammunition, other types of munitions were also collected, totalling an additional 33,604 pieces. Heavy weapons were surrendered by military or armed group commanders (see ibid.).
4. Ibid.
5. The belief that employment was promised as part of DDR participation may have resulted from misunderstandings on the part of programme participants. However, many informants claimed that they were told that they would get a job at the end of it. Another researcher has confirmed that some DDR practitioners were incorrectly informing participants that they would get or be given jobs after their training (author conversation with James Pugel, 29 January 2007, Oslo).
6. Private correspondence between the author and a UN official with experience from three DDR programmes, December 2006.
7. Ibid.
8. The GEMAP Agreement Document is available at www.gempaliberia.org.

9. The author witnessed confrontations between a contingent of peacekeepers and local residents, which seemed to constitute harassment and physical intimidation. She also heard from several informants that it was common for these peacekeepers to 'beat down' anyone giving them trouble, especially ex-combatants. This accusation was obliquely confirmed by the peacekeepers themselves, who promised to 'take care of any troublemakers' that our fieldwork might attract (response paraphrased). We did not take advantage of this. At another site, conversely, the peacekeepers essentially stayed at the perimeter and did not seem to have regular engagement with residents.
10. The author experienced threatening behaviour towards researchers and a group of informants by a group of youths (not participating in the research), and the informants made it clear that the worst course of action would be to involve the peacekeepers quartered nearby because this would escalate the situation and ensure a violent response.

## References

Aboagye, Festus and Alhaji M.S. Bah, 2004, *Liberia at a Crossroads: A Preliminary Look at the United Nations Mission in Liberia (UNMIL) and the Protection of Civilians*, Pretoria: Institute for Security Studies.

Alden, Chris, 2002, 'Making Old Soldiers Fade Away: Lessons from the Reintegration of Demobilized Soldiers in Mozambique', *Security Dialogue*, Vol. 33, No. 3, pp. 341–56.

Baaré, Anton, 2004, *An Analysis of Transitional Economic Reintegration*, Stockholm: Swedish Initiative for Disarmament, Demobilization and Reintegration.

Bøås, Morten and Anne Hatløy, 2008, ' "Getting In, Getting Out": Militia Membership and Prospects for Reintegration in Liberia', *Journal of Modern Africa Studies*, Vol. 46, pp. 33–55.

Braud, Pierre-Antoine, 2004, 'DDR and the local private sector: A forgotten player', background paper for the Government of Sweden's Stockholm Initiative on Disarmament, Demobilization and Reintegration, First Meeting, Stockholm, pp. 10–12, November.

Buzan, Barry, Øle Wæver and Jaap de Wilde, 1998, *Security: A New Framework for Analysis*, Boulder, CO: Lynne Rienner.

Collier, Paul and Anke Hoeffler, 1998, 'On Economic Causes of Civil War', *Oxford Economic Papers*, Vol. 50, No. 4, pp. 563–73.

Cramer, Christopher, 2006, 'Labour Markets, Employment, and the Transformation of War Economies', *Conflict, Security and Development*, Vol. 6, No. 3, pp. 389–410.

Department for International Development, 2005, *Fighting Poverty to Build a Safer World: A Strategy for Security and Development*, London.

Duffield, Mark, 2001, *Global Governance and the New Wars: The Merging of Development and Security*, London: Zed Books.

Duffield, Mark, 2002, 'Social Reconstruction and the Radicalization of Development: Aid as a Relation of Global Liberal Governance', *Development and Change*, Vol. 33, No. 5, pp. 1049–71.

FIAS (Foreign Investment Advisory Service), 2006, *Liberia: Mini-Diagnostic Analysis of the Investment Climate*, Washington, DC.

GEMAP, 2005, Governance and Economic Management Assistance Program Agreement (at: www.gemapliberia.org/).

High-level Panel on Threats, Challenges and Change, 2004, *A More Secure World: Our Shared Responsibility*, New York: United Nations.

Humphreys, Macartan and Jeremy M. Weinstein, 2005, 'Disentangling the Determinants of Successful Disarmament, Demobilization, and Reintegration', unpublished MSS.
ILO (International Labour Office), 2002, 'Decent Work and the Informal Economy', International Labour Conference 90th Session, Geneva.
IMF, 2007, *Liberia: Interim Poverty Reduction Strategy Paper*, Washington, DC.
IRIN (Integrated Regional Information Networks), 2006, *Urban Crime Wave Beating Police*, (at: www.irinnews.org/Report.aspx?ReportId=61057).
IRIN, 2005, 'What About us?' Ask Those Liberians Who Didn't Fight or Flee (at: www.irinnews.org/Report.aspx?ReportId=55115).
Jennings, Kathleen M., 2007, 'The Struggle to Satisfy: DDR Through the Eyes of Ex-Combatants in Liberia', *International Peacekeeping*, Vol. 14, No. 2, pp. 204–18.
Jennings, Kathleen M., 2008, 'Unclear Ends, Unclear Means: Reintegration in Postwar Societies – The Case of Liberia', *Global Governance*, Vol. 14, No. 3, pp, 327–45.
MacKenzie, Megan, 2007, 'Reconstructing Women? Post-conflict Security and the Return to "Normal" in Sierra Leone', paper at Canadian Political Science Association Annual Conference, Saskatchewan, 30 May–1 June.
Nichols, Ryan, 2005, 'Disarming Liberia: Progress and Pitfalls', in Nicolas Florquin and Eric G. Berman (eds), *Armed and Aimless: Armed Groups, Guns and Human Security in the ECOWAS Region*, Small Arms Survey, Geneva.
Paes, Wolf-Christian, 2005, 'Eyewitness: The Challenges of Disarmament, Demobilization and Reintegration in Liberia', *International Peacekeeping*, Vol. 12, No. 2, pp. 253–61.
Pugel, James, 2007, *What the Fighters Say: A Survey of Ex-combatants in Liberia*, Monrovia: UN Development Programme.
Pugh, Michael, 2006, 'Post-war Economies and the New York Dissensus', *Conflict, Security and Development*, Vol. 6, No. 3, pp. 269–89.
Spear, Joanna, 2006, 'From Political Economies of War to Political Economies of Peace: The Contribution of DDR after Wars of Predation', *Contemporary Security Policy*, Vol. 27, No. 1, pp. 168–89.
UN, 2000, *Disarmament, Demobilization and Reintegration of Ex-Combatants in a Peacekeeping Environment: Principles and Guidelines*, New York: Department of Peacekeeping Operations.
UN, 2006, *Integrated Disarmament, Demobilization and Reintegration Standards (IDDRS) Framework*, New York.

# Part IV
# Diasporas

# 10
## Three Discourses on Diasporas and Peacebuilding

*Mandy Turner*

Over the past decade academics and policymakers have increasingly recognised the growing importance of diasporas. While diasporas have been variously defined, an important common element is continued identity with the 'home' country even when many years have been spent in the 'host' country (Lyons, 2004b: 3). Some may even not have visited their 'home country' but offer valuable political support. For example, even though many of the Jewish diaspora in the United States have never been to Israel, let alone been born there, they nevertheless mobilise support for the Jewish 'homeland' (Mearsheimer and Walt, 2006). For the academic community, diasporas thus offer a challenge to the traditional 'inside/outside' conception of social life whereby socio-political activities are defined as either purely 'domestic' or purely 'international' (Al-Ali and Koser, 2002). Diasporas are, at one and the same time, both and neither. As suggested by Shain (2002), diasporas form a distinct 'third level' between interstate and domestic politics – a type of transnational actor that is becoming increasingly important due to the globalisation of markets, politics and culture. How, through what mechanisms and with what impact diasporas express themselves as 'transnational actors', therefore, is currently a matter of intense research. While there is an expanding literature in this area, there has been less research on diasporas in the field of conflict and peace studies. Here research has tended to emphasise the role of diasporas as 'peace-wreckers', though work has emerged emphasising the role of diasporas as 'peace-makers' (Smith and Stares, 2007).

When this academic research is translated into the policy arena, it feeds into a number of complex and contradictory discourses emerging around diasporas: first, as 'positive development actors' through remittances; second, as 'negative security risks' both to their homeland and their host country thus feeding into a political climate hostile to diaspora groups and the tightening of civil liberties through anti-terror legislation; and third, as potential partners in post-conflict peacebuilding conversant with and sympathetic to Western interests and sensibilities. These discourses, explored below, underpin the variety of ways in which peacebuilding processes and policies have attempted to co-opt diasporas in the context of promoting a liberal peace agenda, often with unanticipated and highly contradictory results.

This chapter has four sections. The first three explore the discourses outlined above, as well as potential contradictions between them. The fourth and final section examines key issues surrounding diasporic ability to contribute to a political economy of peace. It concludes that while diasporas can play both conflict-creating and peacebuilding roles, these are ascribed *and* proscribed within the agenda set by liberal peace policies and processes.

### Discourse 1: Diasporas as development actors

One of the key discourses surrounding diasporas is their role as development actors. Recent research has captured this shift in opinion, reflected even in the change of language from 'migrants' to 'diasporas'. While traditional approaches focused on the motivations for migration and saw refugees as victims, new approaches see diasporas as being important transnational actors with widely varying relationships with host and home countries (Koser in Al-Ali and Koser, 2002). Lyons (2004b: 3) distinguishes between migrants and diasporas – the latter, he argues, are a 'particular subset of migrants and are characterised by their networks that link the migrants in the host country to their brethren in the homeland'. It is this active engagement, he argues, that is important.

The activities that connect the diaspora with 'home' include economic (e.g., remittances and investment), political (e.g., linking with civil society, taking part in political parties and elections), social (e.g., the transmission of ideas and values) and cultural (e.g., preserving and passing on language traditions and promoting arts activities). These 'solidarity networks' and 'informal economic systems' create what Radtke (2005: 12–14) refers to as the 'moral economy of the diaspora', which is motivated by an intense obligation to help family and friends. This moral economy also often extends to a more generalised sense of obligation to, and affinity with, those ethnic kin that are not part of the immediate circle of family and friends. Solidarity networks form an important part of securing livelihoods in difficult circumstances, particularly in war-torn societies. While social capital within the homeland may have been severely stretched through the experience of conflict, diasporas may, on occasion, be able to partially fill that gap through creating transnational solidarity networks with friends and relatives in the homeland. These connections show, as argued by Mohan and Zack-Williams (2002: 233), that 'diasporas represent a form of "globalisation from below" in which "small" players, as opposed to mega-corporations, make use of the opportunities afforded by globalisation'.

And it is this final observation that has provoked the interest of policymakers. International financial institutions such as the World Bank and major donors such as the UK have reported the enormous annual rise of diaspora remittances. 'Remittances are generally defined as that portion of a migrant's earnings sent from the migration destination to the place of origin. Although remittances also can be sent in-kind, the term "remittances" usually refers to monetary transfers only' (Sørenson, 2005: 4). Figures from a World Bank study (2006a: 88) show that in 2005, remittances to developing countries reached US$199 billion, dwarfing official development assistance of US$79 billion in 2004. Unrecorded flows through informal channels could add as much as 50 per cent or more to these recorded flows (Savage and Harvey, 2007: 3). Furthermore, the World Bank (2006a: 120) predicts that a 10 per cent increase in remittances translates into a 3.5 per cent reduction in global poverty. In recognition of this potentially huge developmental role, the African Union (AU) in 2003 recognised the diaspora as the sixth 'region' of the AU's organisation structure alongside the Southern, Central, West, East and Saharan regions (Davies, 2007). Remittances are thus now recognised as a key tool in economic development – as a major source of foreign exchange and as a more stable flow of capital than other sources.

The World Bank (2006a) suggests that, at the macroeconomic level, remittances could help to increase the creditworthiness of countries and raise long-term financing. At the national level, they may help to compensate for decreases in other financial flows, such as foreign direct investment and government investment, that accompany conflict. Remittances are also seen as an inventive way of bypassing corrupt elites and political structures, thus ensuring that resources go directly to those in need. This is an important part of the discourse and represents what Duffield (2002) refers to as a process of representing the poor as allies of the liberal peace. The 'diasporas as development actors' discourse thus promotes diasporas as potential partners with development agencies and NGOs against corrupt regimes.

There is little doubt that in war-torn societies, where there is often a slow recovery of livelihoods, a lack of international investment and persistent violence and repression, remittances play a key role in helping families and communities afford basic needs and provide a crucial safety net in the absence of a social welfare system and a reduction in social capital. Remittances can be both individual and collective, and are often channelled through charities and community organisations. Research on the Eritrean diaspora by Koser (2007) shows how central remittances were for both local communities (the rebuilding of schools and other community projects) and the government (probably uniquely to the Eritrean experience, the diaspora were asked to voluntarily contribute 2 per cent of their monthly income directly to the government). The Eritrean government devised several innovative ways to encourage diaspora contributions, including issuing government bonds, which by August 1999 had brought in US$30 million from the United States, US$20 million from Europe and US$15–20 million from the Middle East (Koser, 2007: 245–6).

The 'moral economy' of the diaspora can thus help to provide much-needed assistance during conflict, in the immediate post-conflict phase and often for many years after. The Croatian diaspora, often portrayed as an example of peace-wreckers, gave regular and significant contributions of humanitarian aid, medicine, clothes and food during the conflict in Croatia and Bosnia–Herzegovina, much of it through an organisation headed by Franjo Tudjman's wife (Skrbis, 2007: 233). The Palestinian diaspora has contributed to the economy of the West Bank and Gaza, through investment and philanthropy, as much as all other sources of foreign aid (Bamyeh, 2007: 101). Remittances may also play a central role in supporting refugee populations struggling in countries neighbouring the homeland. For example, remittances from the Liberian diaspora in the United States were crucial for many Liberian refugees in Ghana (Savage and Harvey, 2007: 11). And the 200,000 Somali refugees who arrived in Europe and the Gulf States after the beginning of the war in the Horn of Africa sent home an estimated US$140 million in 1996 (Radtke, 2005: 14). In one city alone – Hargeisa, Somaliland – an estimated 40 per cent of the city's residents received remittances in 2000, for a quarter of whom it was the main source of income (Savage and Harvey, 2007: 32). This income is particularly important for Somaliland, given that it is not recognised as a state (although it has political contact with many countries) and is thus generally unable to take advantage of access to international development finance (although the EU approved a €4.5 million redevelopment project in 2003 (Global Policy Forum, 2003)).

Conflict, however, can also have severe direct and indirect effects on labour migration and thus remittance flows. Research on Darfur, for instance, shows that since the conflict began in 2003, it has been more difficult for people to leave or send back remittances. Migration has been hindered by insecurity as young Darfurians (a traditional source of remittances) have been conscripted by the rebels or the *janjaweed*, or ended up in camps for displaced people; and transfer mechanisms (either hand-carried or through *hawala* systems)[1] have been disrupted (Savage and Harvey, 2007: 27–30). However, patterns of labour migration and transfer mechanisms do adapt to fit this environment, and are often the first aspects to recover when the situation stabilises as people strive to rebuild livelihoods and support families (Savage and Harvey, 2007: 30).

Remittances are thus key lifelines for families and communities. But remittance flows can also be strongly partisan and therefore divisive and exclusionary. Diasporas, of course, largely remit to family and friends (although they also often remit on a community/village level also), and research suggests that it is the poorest and vulnerable (often rural and uneducated people) who are least likely to benefit (Savage and Harvey, 2007: 35). Zunzer (2004: 30) shows Afghani remitting may only be felt in Kabul, thus reinforcing the long-entrenched division between the capital and the rest of the country. And in Somalia, most remittances are received in urban areas, despite the fact that only a third of the population live in urban areas. Of those who received remittances in Somaliland, a higher proportion lived in brick or stone houses, indicating a higher socio-economic status (Savage and Harvey, 2007: 32–3). Furthermore, community activists in both the diaspora and the home country tend to be elites and male (Al-Ali, 2007). This lack of wider community representation is particularly problematic in war-torn societies where there has often been an increase in the number of female-headed households who are locked out of access to property and livelihoods due to patriarchal structures. Al-Ali (2007: 50) also indicates that while voluntary migration has traditionally been a predominantly male phenomenon (although this is changing, see Sørenson, 2005), a high percentage of international refugees are women, thus making it imperative to examine the issue through a 'gender lens', particularly to address the key issues facing the political mobilisation of diaspora women and the type of jobs they are able to access in the host country and thus their ability to remit. Research is still needed to answer key questions such as the following: how does the growing feminisation of migration affect remittance flows; how can remittances contribute to the achievement of gender equality; and how can remittances achieve sustainable development that includes women?

Researchers have also started to raise doubts about the development potential of remittances, which tend to assist immediate poverty alleviation rather than productive investment. Of remittances to Morocco and Somaliland, most are used for subsistence and daily living expenses and only a small proportion for 'productive investment' – setting up businesses and improving agricultural practices (Ramirez, 2005; Savage and Harvey, 2007: 33). Thus, while diaspora remittances certainly fill an aid gap, it is important not to overemphasise the developmental impact. One consequence of such a focus is that the excitement generated by policymakers around remittances reduces the pressure on political actors (particularly the state) to provide social welfare by relinquishing responsibility for the provision of social welfare to 'civil society'. The risk is that remittances may well be seen as a substitute for government policy and action (Zamora, 2006). Statistical analysis of remittances from 114 countries from 1992 to 2002 provides strong support for the hypothesis that increases in remittances lead to a corresponding decrease in government spending in developing countries (Kapur and Singer, 2006).

## Discourse 2: Diasporas as security risks

While some research on remittances has promoted a positive image of diasporas as 'development actors', there is another strand of research which has painted an extremely negative picture of their involvement in homeland conflict. Anderson (1998) refers to diasporas as unaccountable and irresponsible 'long-distance nationalists'. Kaldor *et al.* (2003) dismiss them as 'regressive globalisers' promoting nationalism, through transnational means, rather than cosmopolitanism. Ignatieff (2001) argues that 'diaspora nationalism is a dangerous phenomenon because it is easier to hate from a distance: You don't have to live with the consequences – or the reprisals'. Lyons (2004b: 1) offers an explanation for this negative role: 'diaspora groups created by conflict and sustained by memories of the trauma tend to be less willing to compromise and therefore reinforce and exacerbate the protractedness of conflict'.

Collier and Hoeffler (2001) gave econometric weight to this negative image by arguing that, statistically speaking, countries with large diaspora populations living abroad were six times more likely to experience a recurrence of violence. This was, they argued, because a major source of rebel finance was provided by diaspora donations, though one might conclude to the contrary that large diaspora populations were merely an indication of continuing poverty and repression in the homeland that produced instability and recurrent conflict. In fact, Collier et al. (2006: 12) later revised their conclusion, arguing instead that 'diasporas significantly reduce post-conflict risks'. Nevertheless, the discourse of 'diasporas as a source of conflict finance' prompted a plethora of studies into these links, including a 2001 report from the Rand Corporation tracing diaspora support for insurgent movements (Byman et al., 2001), as well as studies of the huge diaspora resources received by groups such as the Liberation Tigers of Tamil Eelam (Gunaratna, 2003) and the Kurdish Workers' Party (PKK) (Østergaard-Nielsen, 2006). There is no doubt that diasporas give money to insurgent groups. However, remittances provide a tiny amount of the funding for international criminal and insurgent activities (Fagen and Bump, 2005). The '9/11 Commission', for instance, found that those terrorist attacks were funded through formal banking and money wiring systems, not informal transfers (Savage and Harvey, 2007: 8). And in the case of Sri Lanka, which is normally regarded as providing clear proof of the channelling of remittances to insurgents, the largest share of remittances is sent by Sinhalese guest workers to the poorest region of the south of the island (Zunzer, 2004: 26). But if diasporas are *seen* to be a key source of rebel and criminal finance, as originally posited by Collier et al. (2003), one needs to close this avenue down. Policymakers have thus duly obliged with wide-ranging financial regulations imposed through anti-terror legislation. But the groups most negatively affected by the increase in financial regulation are those trying to transfer funds to countries where governments are weak and institutions do not function or are unreliable as in war-torn Afghanistan and Somalia (Fagen and Bump, 2005). Much has been written about how the *hawala* informal remittance transfer system has fallen victim to this (Fagen and Bump, 2005; Zunzer, 2004). The World Bank and the UN Development Programme have urged the United States and other governments to review regulations so that legitimate businesses, families and individuals do not lose an important source of income (Fagen, 2006).

A sub-strand of this 'diasporas as a security risk' discourse conceptualises diasporas as influencing their host country's foreign policy towards their homeland (Cochrane, 2007; Lyons, 2004a; Mearsheimer and Walt, 2006; Shain, 2002; Shain and Barth, 2003). While some of the research suggests that diasporas are a potential 'fifth column' negatively interfering with foreign policy, which should be based on the national interest, it is difficult to discern how much of an impact they actually have. Shain (2002) argues that Armenia and Israel are the largest recipients of US foreign aid partly as a result of the political weight of the Armenian-American and the Jewish-American lobbies. In the case of Jewish diaspora groups in the United States, those who opposed the Oslo Accords campaigned to obstruct improved US relations with the Palestine Liberation Organisation (PLO), and for the government to move its embassy from Tel Aviv to Jerusalem (Shain, 2002). Jewish lobby groups such as the American–Israel Political Affairs Committee are highly influential in the US Congress and can make or break political careers (see Dumke, 2006). However, others emphasise that there are other factors at work, including the influence of Christian Zionist groups and US strategic interests (Pappe, 2007). Indeed, Østergaard-Nielsen (2006) argues that diaspora mobilisation will only affect host state policy if it fits in with the host state's foreign policy agenda.

Diasporas caused by forced migration often experience an intense feeling of alienation and insulation from both home *and* host countries (Cheran, 2003: 4–5). This alienation from host country has been the subject of intense debate in the West about 'home-grown terrorists' responsible for suicide attacks in the name of Islam attending *jihadi* training camps in Pakistan and Afghanistan. This has accelerated since the terrorist attacks of 9/11, 2001, prompting governments across Europe and North America to strengthen border controls as well as internal controls over non-citizens. The US Patriot Act, enacted in the months immediately after 9/11, massively extended the definition of 'terrorist activity' so that even an immigrant giving money to an organisation active in support of Palestinian children could be detained and deported, or prosecuted and imprisoned (Tirman, 2004).

Within this discourse, therefore, diaspora individuals and groups are represented as constituting a security risk to the West by giving financial support to insurgents back home and campaigning for specific foreign policy responses which are perceived as against the host state's national interest. The 'diasporas as development actors' discourse thus rubs up against another (highly negative) discourse that characterises them as bellicose and thus a security risk. This is not to suggest that the 'moral economy' of the diaspora will not, on occasion, encompass criminal activities as well as insurgent networks. After all, transnational criminal networks and smuggling rings are often facilitated, enhanced and expanded by diasporas, creating networks in the global economy (Duffield, 2002). They may not be the type of linkages that the development and peacebuilding community would like to see, but constitute a form of 'globalisation from below'. Yet shadow economies are not merely occupied by insurgents and powerful criminals, but are also often the only source of livelihood for the poorest and most vulnerable sectors of society. Attempts to clamp down on the former can have devastating consequences for the latter (Pugh *et al.*, 2004). The political economy of war-torn societies thus offers a highly complex developmental jigsaw – and the networks that support war cannot be easily separated from the networks that support peace (Duffield, 2002). Diasporas can be both peace-wreckers and peace-makers, as presented by Smith (2007).

If this is so, it is important to ask why the 'diasporas as security threat' discourse is what appears to be guiding current Western immigration and security policy. Terrorist attacks have had a huge influence in providing a veil of respectability to political forces trying to tighten up immigration and integration policies. For example, in Germany, the passage of a new immigration law was delayed because agreement could not be reached on tighter checks upon applicants for citizenship (Faist, 2002: 8). The dominance of this discourse has important consequences. First, it will have major repercussions on the potential for diasporas to play their 'positive development' role by tightening restrictions around asylum and thus reducing the ability to migrate and settle in Western countries. The second consequence of this discourse is that it justifies increased state surveillance and control of diaspora and immigrants in their host countries and the co-option of other institutions for these tasks, as exemplified by calls for UK universities to vet overseas students for potential terrorist activities. The third consequence of this discourse is that it helps to further alienate diaspora communities from their host country and creates a climate of suspicion and fear. As Faist (2002: 12) argues, 'it helps to make culture even more important as a marker between natives and migrants, and firmly establish dichotomies of "us" versus "them"'.

All of this sustains the security–development discourse, where underdevelopment and civil war (and thus conflict-generated migration) have been refashioned as a security risk for the West (see Cooper, 2006). As Faist (2002) notes, this has contributed to a new policy context where sovereign states have begun to view security as the collective management of subnational or transnational threats resulting in both the policing of borders and immigrant communities. One consequence has been to give a new twist to Samuel Huntington's 'clash of civilisations' thesis by extending his idea of divisions *between* civilisations with different values and culture (geographically based) to divisions increasingly *within* states. While the battle between the two discourses is a continuous one, the 'security threat' discourse has, for the time being, achieved primacy over the 'development actor' discourse, creating contradictory policy responses towards diasporas in host states.

## Discourse 3: Diasporas as partners in post-conflict peacebuilding

The main goal of the host of activities central to peacebuilding is 'to bring war-shattered states into conformity with the international system's prevailing forms of governance' (Paris, 2002: 638). Post-conflict peacebuilding is thus not a neutral 'technicist' process, assessing conditions on the ground and working out the best policy options for a particular society (although I am not suggesting there is no nuancing), but an ambitious project attempting to reshape war-torn societies into the end-product found in the West; that is, a market economy and a liberal state. This is a highly ambitious goal representing a major attempt to redistribute political, economic and social power – in highly unstable and violent circumstances (Krause and Jütersonke, 2005: 449). It is into this complex environment that the role and activities of diasporas must slot. A new discourse has thus begun to emerge in the context of peacebuilding: 'diasporas as partners'. Diasporas have come to play two main peacebuilding roles in war-torn societies: as 'external' promoters of post-conflict peacebuilding through economic, political and social support (the 'moral economy of the diaspora'); and as 'internal' promoters of post-conflict peacebuilding through their recruitment to help address the shortage of personnel and kick-start development and governance programmes (as 'agents of the liberal peace'). Obviously, given the transnational activities of diasporas, the terms 'external' and 'internal' are not meant to imply a sharp division between the domestic and the international, but to indicate the main base from which they operate: outside the country or inside as returnees.

The 'moral economy' of the diaspora is a key source of support in post-conflict environments. In addition to the role of remittances (as outlined earlier), much enthusiasm has been generated about harnessing the potential for diaspora business people to invest in their countries of origin (see Mills and Fann, 2006; Feil, 2007; International Alert, 2006), Business networks are common among diasporas, often operating as transnational chambers of commerce. This makes it relatively easy to woo them, and leading members are invited to participate in conferences and round-table discussions. In 2006, for instance, the Sierra Leone Investment Fund held a forum, opened by President Ahmad Tejan Kabbah, which brought together diaspora business people with the government of Sierra Leone, and senior representatives of business sectors (SLIP, 2006). These strategies often produce positive results. In Afghanistan about US$75 million was invested in the new Afghan Wireless Communication Company, which is 80 per cent owned by Telecommunications Systems International, a company founded by a US-based Afghan diaspora entrepreneur (International Alert, 2006). Diaspora business people and groups are thus increasingly being seen as a key resource for promoting private sector development in war-torn societies as true allies of the liberal peace.

When one turns to the political arena, diasporas have been involved in campaigning from their host countries, often for the right to vote in home contests. They have been involved in drafting new constitutions, advising political parties and, on occasion, have taken key positions in post-conflict governments. The Eritrean diaspora, for example, organised peace demonstrations in their host countries, and representatives were involved in drafting a new constitution in 1993 (Koser, 2007: 245–6). The new government rewarded them with voting rights, thus ensuring their continued importance in Eritrean politics. Studies emphasising the peacebuilding role of diasporas have highlighted *inter alia* the roles of the Irish-American diasporas in the Good Friday Agreement which led to the resolution of the Northern Ireland conflict (Cochrane, 2007); the Sudanese diaspora (Mohamoud, 2006); and the Somalian diaspora (Sørenson, 2004). Some studies have also shown that while some diaspora groups may be belligerent, others help to promote human rights and democratic ideals (Brinkerhoff, 2006; Mohamoud, 2006).

This political involvement, however, becomes much more pronounced, and contradictory, when diaspora returnees take up key roles in government, as the examples of Afghanistan and Iraq show. In Afghanistan, for instance, President Hamid Kharzai and three-quarters of the cabinet of the transitional government were from the diaspora. The international community's desire to quickly reshape war-torn societies has meant greater external intervention, often under extremely fragile political and social conditions, which on frequent occasion caused friction with local stakeholders (Chesterman, 2004; Krause and Jütersonke, 2005; Paris, 2004; Turner and Pugh, 2006). Utilising individuals within the diaspora has thus been seen as a good way to avoid this friction. Yet this has sometimes sparked resentment from the local population, particularly when diaspora members have been 'parachuted in' to take key positions in post-conflict governments and are supported because they are sympathetic and friendly to Western interests.

In the case of Iraq, Ahmed Chalabi and the Iraqi National Congress were the diasporic 'government-in-waiting', but were hardly welcomed in Iraq with open arms. In mid-April 2003, Chalabi and between 400 and 600 American-trained militia of the Free Iraq Forces were flown into Iraq by the US government. According to US officials, Chalabi 'was jeered more than cheered. Iraqis were shouting him down. It was embarrassing...We had to help bail him out' (cited in Manning, 2006: 278). That these elites were hand-picked by the US administration was a grievance that fed into the insurgency which continues to engulf Iraq (Herring and Rangwala, 2006; Manning, 2006). Diaspora returnees who have been away from the homeland for many years are often ignorant of the political economy which has emerged during conflict, and often dependent on external agencies for support. Yet they are far from being completely co-opted by major donors as they also have to win domestic support. In the run-up to the January 2005 elections in Iraq, for instance, Ahmed Chalabi tried to reinvent himself as a critic of the occupation.

The shortage of skilled personnel to fill posts in public institutions is a key problem for many war-torn societies. One stark example is the estimate that in 2004, southern Sudan had only 30–40 lawyers in a territory as large as Germany and France combined, a shortage adding to the country's governance problems (NSCSE and UNICEF, 2004). In order to help fill the skills-gap, some governments and donors have created expatriate programmes, such as the Afghanistan Expatriate Programme (AEP) and the Palestinian Expatriate Professional Project (PEPP), to recruit suitably qualified diaspora individuals (World Bank, 2006b). The AEP was launched in 2002 at the beginning of the reconstruction process and recruited 60 highly qualified expatriate Afghans for between six months and two years as advisers in government ministries and agencies to help address the shortage of skilled personnel. The PEPP was set up in 1997 to address the shortage of suitably qualified individuals to staff the new public institutions of the Palestinian Authority in the West Bank and Gaza over a three-year period (World Bank, 2006b). While these programmes help to address short-term needs, mainstreaming these skills and ensuring that local people feel they have ownership over the process is a critical issue. Utilising diaspora individuals often allows donors to claim they have 'ticked the box' for local engagement and support. However, this can cause resentment among locally-recruited employees as expatriates are often considered 'outsiders' enjoying preferential treatment and who are usually paid much more than the local salary.

A major contradiction arising from attempts to impose the liberal peace in war-torn societies is in creating a state rooted in civil society (an essential requirement for a social contract to emerge and thus local support), but one which is also sympathetic to the goals and values of the West (an essential requirement for donors and IFIs and thus international support). Diasporas have been seen as offering one solution to this problem – and thus the 'diaspora as partners' discourse encourages their co-option to bridge this contradiction.

## Towards a political economy of diasporas and peacebuilding

While there has been limited direct research on diasporas and peacebuilding, it is possible to discern a triple discourse emerging around this relationship: 'diasporas as development actors', 'diasporas as security risks' and 'diasporas as liberal peace partners'. While these different discourses play themselves out in a myriad of ways, two major contradictions have emerged that will affect the ability of diasporas to contribute to a political economy of peace.

The first contradiction is the problematic relationship between utilising diaspora individuals and building local capacity and thus a sustainable peace. These problems are compounded (or indeed created) by the current international statebuilding agenda which redefines sovereignty as state capacity rather than independence (see Chapter 19, this volume). And yet the circle has still not been squared. How can one create a state and its political elites with support in civil society which also promotes Western development and political agendas? When these interests clash, political elites have been undermined or removed, as the example of Bosnia shows (see Manning, 2006).

The second contradiction emerges from recognition that diasporas can promote economic and political development in their homeland, while denying them the legal or economic status in their host country which would allow them to do so (Zunzer, 2004). People fleeing from conflict have varying degrees of success in making a livelihood, but their ability to contribute to peacebuilding in the homeland depends on three key factors: first, the capacity to contribute; second, the opportunity to contribute; and third, the desire to contribute (Koser, 2007). Employment was the single most important factor in the Eritrean diaspora's capacity to contribute (Koser, 2007). Ability to gain employment is dependent upon a number of factors including a secure legal status, market conditions in the host country, educational and language skills and access to training. The anti-immigration climate in many Western countries makes it increasingly difficult for exiles to acquire a clear legal status and thus access to training and jobs. Furthermore, exiles are likely to be reluctant to get involved in any political activities that might jeopardise their legal status. It is also clear that the host country's attitude and tolerance towards diaspora political activism is extremely important. For instance, Eritreans were able to campaign openly in Germany as their cause was seen as a just (Radtke, 2005), whereas the ban on the PKK in Germany restricted Kurdish political and lobbying activities. However, when key organisations in the Kurdish diaspora in Germany dropped their commitment to communism/socialism and reformulated their goals in terms of human rights and democracy, German policymakers and NGOs were more sympathetic (Østergaard-Nielsen, 2006: 12–13). When diasporas learn to speak the language of the liberal peace, they are rewarded with recognition and support.

The 'political opportunity structure' in both host and home countries is thus a key factor in diaspora peacebuilding capacity. Investigation into the involvement of the Kurdish diaspora in the Iraq conflict points to the differentiated opportunities arising from the different political systems that Kurdish diaspora communities faced both in their homelands (Iraq, Turkey, Iran and Syria) and in their host countries (Natali, 2007). Political attitudes among diaspora communities towards post-conflict governments back home also influence their willingness to participate. Hostility to those in power or opposition to particular government policies, while not reducing the desire to send remittances to family and friends, will affect enthusiasm for offering political capital to the government. For instance, Jewish and Palestinian diaspora groups play a key role in the potential for peace between Israel and the Palestinian people. The highly influential Jewish-American lobby, the American–Israel Public Affairs Committee, comprises hardline Likudites who are against the creation of a Palestinian state and have consistently opposed Oslo and other peace initiatives (Dumke, 2006; Mearsheimer and Walt, 2006; Pappe, 2007). But while the right of return for Palestinian refugees created by the Naqba in 1948 and after the occupation of the West Bank and Gaza in 1967 is completely rejected by Israel, this is a key aspiration for the Palestinian diaspora, particularly those in refugee camps in the region. All Palestinian political parties have had to show a commitment to this goal (Lavie, 2007). The support of some diaspora groups and organisations is thus dependent on their home state or political organisation following policies which may not be conducive to ensuring a 'negative peace' (i.e., the absence of direct violence) but which they may feel are necessary for 'positive peace' (i.e., the presence of social justice and thus a sustainable peace). While it is usually assumed that negative peace is a precursor to positive peace, in many circumstances it is a denial of justice, often entrenched in peace agreements themselves (see Chapter 1, this volume), that makes a return to violence highly likely. This is evident in the case of the Oslo Accords which sidestepped the issues of territory, borders and Jewish settlements, the status of Jerusalem, and the fate of the Palestinian refugees in neighbouring countries – thus dooming it to failure. Indeed, Bamyeh (2007) argues that the right to return to property lost in 1948 and 1967 is seen, by Palestinian refugees and the diasporas, as an 'ethical' rather than a 'practical' issue.

Divisions within the diaspora itself in the host country, on the basis of religion or ethnicity, for example, will also affect peacebuilding participation. For instance, Eritrean Muslims perceived the diaspora community structures in the UK as being dominated by Christians and this limited their desire to participate in activities ranging from charitable collections to festivals (Koser, 2007: 250). Making it easier to remit or offering other forms of support, as well as providing a range of economic incentives to do so such as tax breaks and the issuing of bonds (as well as publicising them widely amongst the diaspora), is also a significant factor in the desire to contribute (Koser, 2007: 250). Many countries have now recognised the potential rewards in courting their diaspora populations. A number of Sierra Leonean political parties, for instance, have offices in both the United States and the UK. Some countries offer dual citizenship or a special status such as the Non-Resident Indian or Persons of Indian Origin categories of Indians living abroad. Smith (2007) suggests that an analysis of the political opportunities available in the host country as well as the international normative environment that supports or condemns diaspora activity in a particular conflict could help to build a model of 'diaspora opportunity'. Their capacity, opportunity and desire to contribute is highly dependent on factors within the host country, within the homeland, and within the structure and make-up of the diaspora itself. It is also important to bear in mind that diasporas are not unitary actors – they are highly heterogeneous reflecting different life experiences influenced by class, gender, age, ethnicity, religion and so on. There is always a plurality of voices in the diaspora, especially when different 'waves' of displacement are taken into account. That diaspora individuals and groups reflect a multitude of voices is confirmed by the observation that the Somali diaspora were used by all factions at the 2003 peace talks but were nevertheless a very important bridge to international actors (Zunzer, 2004: 33). There are, therefore, a variety of elements that influence diaspora activity, and context is all important. It is necessary, as Smith (2007) points out, to trace both the 'capacities of diaspora' (agency) as well as the 'transnational opportunities available to it' (structure).

An approach that thus tries to stack up the evidence either for or against diasporas is therefore misguided. Diasporas can be both 'peace-makers' and 'peace-wreckers'; they can be both at different periods and at the same time, and in order to assess their role it is necessary to understand the historical context, as well as their interests, aspirations, institutions and objectives (Smith, 2007). This is the conclusion one draws from the emerging research on the subject. However, what is also interesting, and what this chapter has begun to explore, is how certain discourses around diasporas have emerged – and the contradictions inherent in these clashing against each other. The moral economy of the diaspora is likely to continue (and perhaps increase) in importance in our highly globalised world, but their resources and skills should be regarded as a useful addition – not a substitute – to the development of a *nationwide* socio-economic and political strategy aimed at building an equitable economy and inclusive political structures.

## Note

1. The *hawala* system allows parties to transfer funds outside of banks or formal money exchange operations. Although it is an 'informal' exchange mechanism, it operates according to well-established rules based on trust. A person who wants to send money home pays a *hawaladar*, who makes contact with a counterpart in the destination country who pays the designated individual.

## References

Al-Ali, Nadje, 2007, 'Gender, Diasporas and Post–Cold War Conflict', in Hazel Smith and Paul Stares (eds), *Diasporas in Conflict: Peace-makers or Peace-wreckers?* Tokyo: UN University Press.
Al-Ali, Nadje and Khalid Koser, 2002, *New Approaches to Migration? Transnational Communities and the Transformation of Home*, London: Routledge.

Anderson, Benedict, 1998, 'Long Distance Nationalism', in Anderson (ed.), *The Spectre of Comparisons: Nationalism, Southeast Asia and the World*, London: Verso.
Bamyeh, Mohammed A., 2007, 'The Palestinian Diaspora', in Smith, Hazel and Paul Stares (eds), *Diasporas in conflict: Peace-makers or Peace-Wreckers?* Tokyo: UN University Press.
Brinkerhoff, Jennifer M., 2006, 'Digital Diasporas and Conflict Prevention: The Case of Somalinet.com', *Review of International Studies*, Vol. 32, No. 1 pp. 25–47.
Byman, Daniel, Peter Chalk, Bruce Hoffman, William Rosenau, David Brannan, 2001, *Trends in Outside Support for Insurgent Movements*, Santa Monica, CA: RAND.
Cheran, Rudrhramoorthy, 2003, 'Diaspora Circulation and Transnationalism as Agents for Change in the Post-Conflict Zones of Sri Lanka', policy paper for the Berghof Foundation for Conflict Management, Berlin, (at: www.berghof-foundation.lk/scripts/diasporaCirc.pdf).
Chesterman, Simon, 2004, *You, The People: The United Nations, Transitional Administration, and State-Building*, Oxford: Oxford University Press.
Cochrane, Feargall, 2007, 'Irish-America, the End of the IRA's Armed Struggle and the Utility of "Soft Power"', *Journal of Peace Research*, Vol. 44, No. 2, pp. 215–31.
Collier, Paul and Anke Hoeffler, 2001, 'Greed and Grievance in Civil War', October (at: www.worldbank.org/research/conflict/papers/greedgrievance_.23oct.pdf).
Collier, Paul, Lani Elliott, Havard Hegre, Anke Hoeffler, Marta Reynal-Querol and Nicholas Sambanis, 2003, *Breaking the Conflict Trap: Civil War & Development Policy*, Oxford: Oxford University Press/World Bank.
Collier, Paul, Anke Hoeffler and Mans Söderbom, 2006, 'Post-conflict Risks', Centre for the Study of African Economics Working Paper Series 2006/12 (at: www.csae.ox.ac.uk/workingpapers/pdfs/2006-12text.pdf).
Cooper, Neil, 2006, 'Chimeric Governance and the Extension of Resource Regulation', *Conflict, Security and Development*, Vol. 6, No. 3, pp. 315–35.
Davies, Rebecca, 2007, 'Reconceptualising the Migration-Development Nexus: Diasporas, Globalisation and the Politics of Exclusion', *Third World Quarterly*, Vol. 28, No. 1, pp. 59–76.
Duffield, Mark, 2002, *Global Governance and the New Wars*, London: Zed Books.
Dumke, David, 2006, 'A View from the Inside: Congressional Decision making and Arab-Israeli Policy', Center for Contemporary Arab Studies, Georgetown University, Washington, DC.
Fagen, Patricia Weiss, 2006, 'Remittances in Conflict and Crises: How Remittances Sustain Livelihoods in War, Crises and Transitions to Peace', *Access Finance*, No. 11, May, World Bank Group.
Fagen, Patricia Weiss and Micah N. Bump, 2005, 'Remittances in Conflict and Crisis: How Remittances Sustain Livelihoods in War, Crises, and Transitions to Peace', policy paper International Peace Academy, New York.
Faist, Thomas, 2002, ' " *Extension du domaine de la lutte* ": International Migration und Security before and after September 11, 2001', *International Migration Review*, Vol. 36, No. 1, pp. 7–14.
Feil, Moira, 2007, 'Investing in Peace: Spurring Private Involvement in Post-conflict Peace-building', Wilton Park Conference report WP848 (at: www.wiltonpark.org/documents/conferences/WP848/pdfs/WP848.pdf).

Global Policy Forum, 2003, 'EU Breaks Ice on Financing Somaliland', 11 February (at: www.globalpolicy.org/nations/sovereign/sover/emerg/2003/0211euaid.htm).
Gunaratna, Rohan, 2003, 'Sri Lanka: Feeding the Tamil Tigers', in Karen Ballentine and Jake Sherman, *The Political Economy of Armed Conflict*, Boulder, CO: Lynne Rienner.
Herring, Eric and Glen Rangwala, 2006, *Iraq in Fragments: The Occupation and Its Legacy*, London: Hurst.
Ignatieff, Michael, 2001, 'The Hate Stops Here', *Toronto Globe and Mail*, 25 October.
International Alert, 2006, 'Local Business, Local Peace: the Peacebuilding Potential of the Domestic Private Sector' (at: www.international-alert.org/our_work/themes/LBLP.php#download).
Kaldor Mary, Helmut Anheier and Marlies Glasius, 2003, 'Global Civil Society in an Era of Regressive Globalisation', in Helmut Aheier, Marlies Glasius, and Mary Kaldor (eds), *Global Civil Society 2003*, Oxford: Oxford University Press.
Kapur, Devish and David Singer, 2006, 'Remittances, Government Spending and the Global Economy', paper at the International Studies Association Annual Convention, San Diego, 22–25 March.
Koser, Khalid, 2002, 'From Refugees to Transnational Communities', in Nadje Al-Ali and Koser (eds), *New Approaches to Migration: Transnational Communities and the Transformation of Home*, London: Routledge.
Koser, Khalid, 2007, 'African diasporas and post-conflict reconstruction: An Eritrean case study', in Hazel, Smith and Paul Stares (eds), *Diasporas in Conflict: Peace-makers or Peace-wreckers?* Tokyo: UN University Press.
Krause, Keith and Oliver Jütersonke, 2005, 'Peace, Security and Development in Post-Conflict Environments', *Security Dialogue*, Vol. 36, No. 4, pp. 447–62.
Lavie, Ephraim, 2007, 'Hamas and the Palestinian Unity Government: Between the Exigencies of Government and Ideological Principles', *Tel Aviv Notes*, Moshe Dayan Center for Middle Eastern and African Affairs, Tel Aviv University (at: www.dayan.org/Lavie%20-%20Hamas%20and%20the%20Palestinian%20Unity%20Government-23.pdf).
Lyons, Terrence, 2004a, 'Diasporas and Homeland Conflict', paper DC Area Workshop on Contentious Politics, Institute for Conflict Analysis and Resolution, George Mason University, March.
Lyons, Terrence, 2004b, 'Engaging Diasporas to Promote Conflict Resolution: Transforming Hawks into Doves', Institute for Conflict Analysis and Resolution, George Mason University, April (at: www.tamilnation.org/.conflictresolution/lyons.htm).
Manning, Carrie, 2006, 'Political Elites and Democratic State-building Efforts in Bosnia and Iraq', *Democratization*, Vol. 13, No. 5, pp. 724–38.
Mearsheimer, John J. and Stephen M. Walt, 2006, 'The Israel Lobby and US Foreign Policy', Working Paper RWP06-011, Kennedy School of Government, Harvard University, 13 March.
Mills, Rob and Quimiao Fan, 2006, 'The Investment Climate in Post-conflict Situations', Washington, DC: World Bank (at: http://info.worldbank.org/etools/docs/library/235864/postconflict_paper.pdf).
Mohamoud, Abdullah A., 2006, 'African Diaspora and Post-Conflict Reconstruction in Africa', Brief, Danish Institute for International Studies.
Mohan, Giles and Alfred B. Zack-Williams, 2002, 'Globalisation from Below: Conceptualising the Role of African Diasporas in Africa's Development', *Review of African Political Economy*, Vol. 92, pp. 211–36.

Natali, Denise, 2007, 'Kurdish interventions in the Iraq war', in Hazel Smith and Paul Stares (eds), *Diasporas in Conflict: Peace-makers or Peace-wreckers?* Tokyo: UN University Press.

NSCSE (New Sudan Centre for Statistics and Evaluation) and UNICEF, 2004, 'Towards a Baseline: Best Estimates of Social Indicators for Southern Sudan', May.

Østergaard-Nielsen, Eva, 2006, 'Diasporas and Conflict Resolution – Part of the Problem or Part of the Solution?' Paper at seminar on Diaspora and Conflict, Peace Builders or Peace Wreckers? Danish Institute for International Studies, 8 December.

Pappe, Ilan, 2007, 'Clusters of History: US Involvement in the Palestine Question', *Race & Class*, Vol. 48, No. 3, pp. 1–28.

Paris, Roland, 2002, 'International Peacebuilding and the *"Mission Civilisatrice"*', *Review of International Studies*, Vol. 28, No. 4, pp. 637–56.

Paris, Roland, 2004, *At War's End*, Cambridge: Cambridge University Press.

Pugh, Michael and Neil Cooper with Jonathan Goodhand, 2004, *War Economies in a Regional Context*, Boulder, CO: Lynne Rienner.

Radtke, Katrin, 2005, 'From Gifts to Taxes: The mobilisation of Tamil and Eritrean diaspora in intrastate warfare', Working Papers Micropolitics 2/2005, Humboldt-University, Berlin.

Ramírez, Carlota, Mar García Domínguez and Julia Míguez Morais, 2005, 'Crossing Borders: Remittances, Gender and Development', Working Paper, UN International Research and Training Institute for the Advancement of Women, Santo Domingo, Dominican Republic.

Savage, Kevin and Paul Harvey, 2007, 'Remittances During Crisis: Implications for Humanitarian Response', Humanitarian Practice Group, Report No. 25, Overseas Development Institute, London.

Shain, Yossi, 2002, 'The Role of Diasporas in Conflict Perpetuation or Resolution', *SAIS Review*, Vol. 22, No. 2, pp. 115–44.

Shain, Yossi and Aharon Barth, 2003, 'Diasporas and International Relations Theory', *International Organization*, Vol. 57, No. 3, pp. 449–79.

Skrbis, Zlatko, 2007, 'The Mobilized Croatian Diaspora: Its Role in Homeland Politics and War', in Smith, Hazel and Paul Stares (eds), *Diasporas in Conflict: Peace-makers or Peace-wreckers?* Tokyo: UN University Press.

SLIP, 2006, 'Sierra Leone Investment Forum 2006' (at: www.africarecruit.com/.sierra/the forum.htm).

Smith, Hazel, 2007, 'Diasporas in International Conflict', in Hazel Smith and Paul Stares (eds), *Diasporas in Conflict: Peace-makers or Peace-wreckers?* Tokyo: UN University Press.

Sørenson, Ninna Nyberg, 2004, 'Opportunities and Pitfalls in the Migration-Development Nexus: Somaliland and Beyond', Working Paper 2004/21, Danish Institute for International Studies.

Sørenson, Ninna Nyberg, 2005, 'Migrant Remittances, Gender and Development', Brief, Danish Institute for International Studies, July.

Tirman, John, 2004, 'The Movement of People and the Security of States', in Tirman (ed.), *The Maze of Fear: Security and Migration After 9/11*, New York: The New Press.

Turner, Mandy and Michael Pugh, 2006, 'Towards a New Agenda for Transforming War Economies', *Conflict, Security & Development*, Vol. 6, No. 3, pp. 471–9.

World Bank, 2006a, *Global Economic Prospects: The Economic Implications of Remittances and Migration*, Washington, DC.

World Bank, 2006b, 'What Role for Diaspora Expertise in Post-Conflict Reconstruction? Lessons from Afghanistan, and West Bank and Gaza', Social Development Notes, Conflict Prevention and Reconstruction, Washington, DC, July.

Zamora, Radolfo Garcia, 2006, 'A Better Quality of Life?', *ID21 Insights* No. 60, Institute of Development Studies, Sussex, January.

Zunzer, Wolfram, 2004, 'Diaspora Communities and Civil Conflict Transformation', Berghof Occasional Paper No. 26, September.

# 11
# Diaspora Engagement in Peacebuilding: Empirical and Theoretical Challenges

*Kenneth Bush*

> *'How dare you compare the Jewish diaspora to those Congolese, Sudanese, and Rwandans that are shunned and spit upon in the streets of Europe. How can you compare the most powerful political lobby in the world – with bottomless financial, intellectual, political resources – to groups that come from the margins of the margins of margins. If, with all those resources, it took the Jewish lobby over 50 years to win back what was stolen from them by banks and businesses in Switzerland, what chance do you really think a bunch of scattered, poor, and black groups have to repatriate the stolen gains of the Western-backed dictators and kleptocrats – which, by the way, are sitting in banks in the rich North guarded by secrecy rules, government complicity, and self-interested fois-gras-eating bankers?'*
>
> *'You can't say that.'*
>
> *'Why not?'*

This private exchange at a conference on 'Diaspora and Peacebuilding' in Toronto in October 2006 highlights the issues central to this chapter – the interconnections between power and methodology. In the study of the role of diasporas in peacebuilding it is increasingly recognised that the activities of subgroups within diaspora communities have contributed to both the continuation and the reduction of violent conflict in the land they call their original home (Fagen, 2006; Smith, 2007; see also Chapter 10, this volume). Current research on diasporas tend to be driven by case studies of specific groups: the Irish, Palestinians, Armenians, Kurds, Tamils, Ethiopians, Eritreans, Jews, Somalis and others. The challenge is to collect these rich, complex and unique stories into shared understandings of common or comparable structures and processes. It is necessary to move towards more systematic comparative case studies that are critical in their analytical stance, and that allow identification and examination of the similarities and differences in patterns of experience. In short, it is important to move from the idiographic (individualising, particularising and interpretive) to the nomothetic (generalising, rule-seeking and integrative). While several diaspora and peace/conflict projects have been initiated, there remains a substantial need for solid, empirically grounded comparative research. This chapter offers a critical discussion of some of the central theoretical and empirical questions in the study of diaspora and peacebuilding. The analysis is intended to encourage thinking about the generalisable patterns of dynamics and relationships within and between transnational communities, so that lessons for peacebuilding may be drawn across cases. It begins with a discussion of contextual and conceptual issues, before turning to a consideration of the way academics and policymakers understand, and therefore approach and support, the peacebuilding capacities of diaspora communities.

## The politics of context

The heavily politicised environment within which diaspora research takes place cannot be over-emphasised – whether it is associated with the increasing parochialism of immigration practices in the global North, or whether it is associated with the intellectually stifling 'war on terror'. The consequence of the former is the legitimation and reinforcement of mean-spirited and unjust policies that subsidise and normalise xenophobic and racist practices. A consequence of the 'war on terror', on the other hand, is a metastasising securitisation of research: that is, research comes to be strained through the pin-hole aperture of national security. In this context, 'security' is understood in its most narrow, atavistic, sense – despite vigorous debates in the 1990s which expanded security studies to include a panoply of threats such as environmental degradation, economic competition and epidemiological crises (Buzan, 1993; Intriligator, 1991; Klare and Thomas, 1991; Mathews, 1989). Despite the institutionalisation of the consequent concept of 'human security' within academic and policy networks, the 'war on terror' quickly eclipsed these developments.

In keeping with 'the Law of the Instrument',[1] problems defined as security issues, in part or in whole, need to be addressed with the blunt instruments of the increasingly securitised state. The field of diaspora research, and migration studies more broadly, has become tethered to the war on terror/security problematique – evident, most conspicuously, in the analytic and policy focus on the conflict-generating, rather than peace-nurturing, impacts of migrant groups (e.g., Faist, 2004; Léonard, 2004; Tirman, 2004). However, if the channels through which diaspora groups subsidise conflict are the same as those through which they contribute to development and peacebuilding

(Fagen, 2006; Savage and Harvey, 2007; Chapter 10, this volume), then even conflict-focused research may be subverted and harnessed to an interest in the promotion of peacebuilding.

## The politics of labels

There is considerable debate over the definition of 'diaspora' some of which is addressed briefly below. Here it is important to note the debate over the question of whether 'birth connection' is the *sine qua non* of the diaspora experience. If so, then this definition would exclude groups such as Jews born outside of Israel, but who, nonetheless, possess a strong sense of attachment to the country (*contra* Mearsheimer and Walt, 2006). Such groups might be more accurately identified as lobby groups or interest groups, or simply as anomalies when compared to the experiences of diasporic groups within more tightly defined limits. More problematic, analytically, are the children and grandchildren of the first wave of diaspora to arrive in a place outside the land of their birth. Intuitively, and empirically, there are important intergeneration differences between first, second and third generation diaspora that require more systematic examination than is possible here. For the purposes of this chapter, the term diaspora includes different generations, with the caveat that one needs to be attentive to inter-generational differences in the nature, intensity and frequency of contact between and within 'homeland' and 'hostland'. The timing of a wave of migration – within the context of changing political, economic and security conditions within the homeland – may also affect a diasporic subgroup's relations to, and conceptions of, home.

The definition of the term 'diaspora' is not simply a technical or analytical exercise involving the parsing of words to describe and demarcate a particular group of people. According to the International Organisation for Migration, over 175 million people, or roughly 3 per cent of the global population, live outside their countries of birth (IOM, 2005a). A wide range of labels have been pasted onto people who are members of diverse transnational communities: 'refugees', 'asylum seekers', 'guest workers', 'development displacees', 'economic migrants', 'immigrants', 'illegal immigrants', '*sans papiers*', 'first generation nationals', 'hyphenated nationals' and so on. It is important to emphasise that such labelling is, first and foremost, a political exercise because it serves, for instance, to include or exclude; impute and frame relationships within and between groups; focus and direct the allocation of social, political and economic resources; confer legal and political rights and obligations; create expectations; and shape life opportunities. Further, the choice of label is a process imbued with value-laden assertions about those who are being labelled. Each carries normative connotations of being legitimate/illegitimate, legal/illegal, desirable/undesirable and giver/taker. The choice of label always says more about who is using it (and their interests), than the group to which it is being applied (and their needs and aspirations).

In the most general sense, the term 'diaspora' refers to a collection of heterogeneous subgroups which share one thing in common: a complex set of attachments to a perceived place of origin in which it is not resident. This, as Lyons (2006) notes, is what distinguishes diaspora from migrants whose principal political, social and economic points of reference lie more conspicuously within the hostland than the homeland. The anthropologist, James Clifford (1994), attempts to illuminate the character of this attachment when he asserts that each individual is 'part of an on-going transnational network that includes the homeland, not as something simply left behind, but as a place of attachment in a contrapuntal modernity'. The utility of this analysis is the emphasis on: first, the coexistence of homeland and hostland in the psychological and lived experiences of individuals; and second, the need for a 'transnational network' to nurture and sustain attachments (broadly defined) to the homeland.

Forces of globalisation have accentuated these two features of contemporary diaspora experience – in particular, mass electronic communication and ease of intercontinental travel. Thus, in a less globalised past, attachments to homeland would gradually attenuate and allow for the growth of more localised forms of attachment within the hostland – ultimately opening the possibility for a sociological (usually inter-generational) reconfiguration in which 'hostland' becomes 'homeland'. If the arguments concerning the impacts of globalisation are valid, then we should expect diaspora self-consciousness (or 'diasporisation') to increase with globalisation. To the extent that normal processes of migration are politicised – whether due to an adherence to a narrow securitised world view, or through protectionist or xenophobic-tinged policies – it is reasonable to expect increased political sensitivities around issues of diaspora relationships within the global North and global South.

What needs to be added, or emphasised, in Clifford's discussion is the heterogeneity *within* diaspora populations. That is, there may be multiple, and often competing, conceptions of homeland between diasporic subgroups. Consider, for example, the different possible conceptions of homeland within the Sri Lankan diaspora between Sinhalese and Tamil subgroups – particularly the hard line between conceptions tied to a 'unitary' Sri Lankan state and those premised upon a separate territorial entity of Tamil Eelam. Yet, also *within* Sinhalese and Tamil populations there are numerous subgroups and possible variations on the idea of homeland according to political, paramilitary, regional, caste and social affinities. Even this, more nuanced, appreciation of the differences between and within Tamil and Sinhalese populations overlooks other significant diasporic subgroups such as the Sri Lanka Muslim communities, Burghers and the neglected plantation Tamil community with its notable presence in south India (Bush, 2003).

Two points should be highlighted: first is the need for analysis to focus on specific diasporic subgroups rather than undifferentiated and artificially homogenised constructs of 'diaspora-writ-large'. This will enable a better understanding of the internal dynamics of diaspora politics and to identify where, how, when and with whom to work in order to support peacebuilding initiatives. The level of anthropological detail and trust required for this exercise is considerable. The second point to be highlighted, discussed below, is that mapping and examining diasporic subgroups reveals the crucial roles played by diasporic organisations – structured entities that develop within diaspora communities to articulate interests and needs.

## Diasporic organisations

A 'diasporic organisation' is similar to the concept of 'social movement organisation' developed in the social movement literature (cf. Morris and Mueller, 1992; Tarrow, 1989). In both cases, the term 'organisation' does not necessarily imply 'formal organisation' (Tilly, 1978). The more integrated the sense of common identity and internal network of a group, the more organised it is. Thus, diasporic organisations may be understood as complex, formal, informal or semi-formal organisations that articulate and pursue goals *that are asserted to be* representative of the interests and aspirations of 'the diaspora' as a whole. The level of support for these entities, as well as their internal structure, objectives, tactics and efficacy vary from case to case. Nonetheless, these organisations constitute pools of aggregated interests and agency that should be a central referent in the work of researchers and policymakers since they suggest potential allies and access points for peacebuilding initiatives – with one important caveat: while every diasporic organisation will present itself as being both legitimate and representative of the diaspora writ large, such claims need critical assessment before working relationships are initiated. Diasporic organisations serve as conduits between homeland and hostland – the impacts of which may be either positive or negative for peacebuilding. Examples of such organisations include cultural centres and associations, lobby groups, diaspora-created NGOs, 'friendship societies', religious bodies, support groups, community and lobby groups.

The term 'diasporic organisation' may be used to identify those organisations which attempt to mobilise individuals along selected axes of collective identity: 'Mobilisation processes do not have to start from scratch. They can build on pre-existing networks of informal relations as well as on pre-existing networks of formal organisations, political and otherwise' (Kriesi, 1988: 362). In this process, they not only mobilise individuals into self-conscious groups, but also mobilise and politicise the very identity boundaries according to which groups define themselves. Thus, the choice of which diasporic organisation to support, or work with, unavoidably entails tacit endorsement for its political, economic and social goals, as well as its particular definition of group boundaries.

While electronic communication extends and deepens the existing ability of mobilisers to gain access to mobilisable members, it also allows unmobilised individuals to maintain an extensive network of contacts with the homeland and other diasporic members independently of mobilisers or diasporic organisations. From a policy perspective, this opens the possibility of developing two-pronged approaches that work carefully with selected diasporic organisations as well as with those mechanisms that facilitate constructive person-to-person linkages within diaspora networks. A diasporic organisation-focused initiative might include efforts to work through temples and churches to encourage members to contact authorities if they are extorted by paramilitary fundraisers in their hostlands – the difficulty of which is illustrated in a report by Human Rights Watch on fundraising by the Liberation Tigers of Tamil Eelam (LTTE) in Canada and Britain (HRW, 2006). An example of an approach that focuses on the latter is the legislation or practices that affect the ability of individual members of diaspora to send remittances back to war-affected homes (whether such remittances have peacebuilding or conflict-exacerbating impacts remains to be determined on a case-by-case basis). Although such an initiative does not work directly with diaspora organisations, it will have profound and immediate impacts.

## Diaspora impacts on peacebuilding and conflict maintenance

Without clear and consistent understanding of the term 'peacebuilding', discussions of the various roles of diaspora in conflict situations are conceptually loose. In this chapter, 'peacebuilding' is used in a broad sense to refer to those initiatives that foster and support sustainable structures and processes which strengthen the prospects for peaceful coexistence and decrease the likelihood of the outbreak, recurrence, or continuation, of violent conflict. This process entails both short- and long-term objectives, for example short-term humanitarian operations and longer-term developmental, political, economic and social objectives.

There are very clear implications: efforts to support the peacebuilding capacities of diaspora groups need to be conceptualised and operationalised in tandem with efforts to defuse the conflict-sustaining activities of some diasporic organisations. Peacebuilding is not about the imposition of 'solutions', but about the creation of opportunities. The challenge is to identify and nurture the political, economic and social space within which indigenous actors and diasporas can identify, develop and employ the resources necessary to build a peaceful, prosperous and just society. If peacebuilding is understood as an impact, then it is necessary to delineate the 'peacebuilding impact' of an initiative, from its developmental, economic, environmental, gender and other impacts. What are the implications of understanding 'peacebuilding-as-impact' for supporting the peacebuilding capacity of diasporas? In practical terms, it means not limiting our focus to the obviously labelled (though rarely evaluated) peacebuilding projects – dialogue project, community-based conflict resolution and so on. Any and all diaspora-based initiatives focusing on violence-prone regions should be seen to possess the potential to either build peace or exacerbate violent and non-violent conflict. The discussion next identifies some of the ways that diaspora communities have contributed to peace or conflict in their homelands – as well as their hostlands.

## Political impacts

There are many ways in which the activities of diaspora subgroups may affect political decision-making that contribute directly and indirectly to conflict. In a particularly interesting example, the Canadian Federal Minister of Finance (subsequently Prime Minister), Paul Martin, and the Minister for International Cooperation, Maria Minna, attended a dinner organised by a fundraising organisation for the LTTE, a proscribed terrorist organisation – despite warnings from advisers and public doubts expressed in the media (*The National Post*, 2001). Five years later, Danny Davis, a US Congressman, who enjoyed an LTTE-funded trip to Sri Lanka, was accused of accepting bribes to buy his assistance in having the LTTE removed from the US list of terrorist organisations (*Chicago Tribune*, 2006). Other examples of political impacts include the manipulation or lobbying of the hostland public and politicians by extremist diaspora organisations (i.e., using or endorsing indiscriminate or disproportionate violence for political goals); and the use of the hostland as a means of funding and channelling weapons and war-related equipment to warriors in their homeland, for example the cases of Croatia, Sri Lanka (*The Sunday Times*, 2006), Armenia and Kurdistan (Skrbis, 2007: 128, 233).

But there are contrasting occasions where the activities of a diaspora have had positive impacts in the political sphere. This is illustrated in the role of immigrants in public life and all levels of electoral politics. In the Canadian context, this includes the election of Ujal Dosanjh as provincial première in British Colombia in 2000, the first from an ethnic minority. Indeed, the last two Governors-General of Canada were members of diaspora communities (Haitian-born, Michaelle Jean, 2005; and Hong Kong-born, Adrienne Clarkson, 1999). In these cases, the values of tolerance and multiculturalism are promoted within both homeland and hostland.

Other activities include human rights advocacy and consciousness-raising among the hostland public and decision-makers; direct political support for pro-peace actors in the homeland; participation of members of the diaspora on homeland advisory councils, negotiation teams and other war-to-peace transition mechanisms; the return of progressive pro-peace diaspora leaders to take up political leadership positions in their homeland; and the ways in which well-placed members of the diaspora may serve to facilitate pro-peace contacts and communications between critical decision-makers in the homeland and allies in the hostland (see Abd-El-Aziz *et al.*, 2006; Lyons, 2006; Orjuela, 2006).

### Economic impacts

Conflict-sustaining activities of diasporic subgroups in the economic sphere include direct funding for pro-war political parties, organisations and campaigns, as well as for armed groups in their homelands. Within the hostland, this might include the ways in which some criminalised diasporic groups contribute to local, national and global criminalised economies (linking local crime like extortion, drugs, people smuggling and prostitution to global criminal networks). In Toronto – whose Tamil population is larger than that in the Jaffna peninsula – the LTTE typically demands between Cdn$2500 and Cdn$5000 from Tamil families, with some being asked for as much as Cdn$10,000. Business owners were asked for Cdn$25,000–50,000. Similar sums were demanded in the UK, France and Norway (HRW, 2006: 25). Other examples of diaspora funding of armed conflicts are found in Aceh, Somalia, Afghanistan, Kashmir, Palestine and the Balkans (Newland and Patrick, 2004). This might also include the provision of black and grey market labour (increasing vulnerability, economic insecurity and exploitative relationships).

More positively, members of the diaspora have volunteered their professional skills back in the homeland for humanitarian, development or peacebuilding initiatives. This is especially important for university-trained diasporic youths who have the skills, knowledge and desire to contribute something to their homeland. Diaspora actors have also provided economic support for moderate, pro-peace political parties, organisations and campaigns in their homelands, and for pro-peace organisations and initiatives within the diaspora in their own and other hostlands.

In 2005, the cash remittances that migrants sent home 'exceeded $232 billion...of that about $166.9 billion goes to poor countries, nearly double the amount in 2000' (IMF, 2005). Dilip Ratha, a senior World Bank economist, estimates the figure as being closer to US$350 billion, 'since migrants are estimated to send one-third of their money using unofficial methods, including carrying it. That money is never reported to tax officials, and appears on no records (Cheran and Aiken, 2005; *Guardian Weekly*, 9–15 December 2005: 16). Also noteworthy is the finding that 'Despite the prominence given to remittances from developed countries, South–South remittance flows make up between 30 and 45 per cent of total remittances received by developing countries, reflecting the fact that over half of migrants from developing countries migrate to other developing countries' (World Bank, 2006: 9). The sums remitted by members of the diaspora dwarf official Overseas Development Assistance. Furthermore, the benefits of migrants to hostland economies and society are well established, if not sufficiently extolled. An International Organisation for Migration study (IOM, 2005a) finds that 'Northern' fears about the negative effects of migration on jobs and social services are largely unfounded. According to Brunson McKinley, head of the IOM, 'If managed properly, migration can bring more benefits than costs' (IOM, 2005b). Indeed, between 1999 and 2000, migrants in the UK contributed £2.5 billion more in taxes than they received in benefits (Gott and Johnston, 2002: 5). Similar findings have been reported in other studies (see Iregui, 2002; Moses and Letnes, 2002).

Remittances have received much attention as a double-edged sword that can help or hinder peacebuilding (see Fagen, 2006; Savage and Harvey, 2007). As Camilla Orjuela (2006) points out, diaspora remittances and development projects can provide alternatives to the war economy. Diaspora engagement in development/reconstruction can also address grievances that are at the roots of armed conflicts, such as lack of opportunities, unequal development and a sense of discrimination along ethnic, class, geographical or other lines. Alternatively, remittances may exacerbate tensions and inequalities if they create or sharpen the sense of inequality or difference. And, finally, development/reconstruction can help create trust in a peace process, peace agreement and the actors that support it. Seeing concrete benefits of peace – a 'peace dividend' – can give people hope for the future, encourage their support for peace efforts and lend legitimacy to new leaders and structures.

### Social impacts

The social activities of diaspora groups can have a range of negative impacts, such as the maintenance and perpetuation within the diaspora of a demonising and militarised mindset of divided communities in the homeland. And they can serve to replicate the conflict patterns from homeland in the hostland. The positive peacebuilding impacts of social activities include the creation of neutral space; the importance of which, within hyper-politicised environments, cannot be over-estimated because it opens up the possibility of reintegrating communities segregated by violent conflict. This may be done within the context of professional associations that enable oppositional diaspora to engage in work-related activity on purely professional levels (Bush, 2004). It might take the form of meeting spaces around shared interests or formal or informal gatherings over dinner – an approach used by 'Potlucks for Peace' in Canada, which simply brings together men and women from the Jewish and Arab diasporas to share the food each has brought for the occasion. Cultural contributions to peace include diaspora-generated art in all forms which may play an important role in (re)framing peace and conflict issues (Abd-El-Aziz et al., 2006). Again, this may be a double-edged sword depending on whether the ultimate impact is (intentionally or unintentionally) integrative or disintegrative within and between diasporic communities.

The informal 'influencing people back home' contribution consists of the transmission of pro-peace ideas through social networks and in the homeland as a means of influencing decisions (e.g., on voting), attitudes (e.g., stereotypes) and behaviour (treatment of 'the other'). Relatedly, diaspora-run media are important and widely used mechanisms for introducing and elaborating pro-peace ideas back in the homeland, thus contributing to shaping opinions and framing understandings of conflict and peace issues. In some cases, this creates the space for the discussions and debates that are too dangerous or difficult to engage in the homeland. A prime example is Shireen Ebadi, the Nobel Peace Prize winner, representative of a subgroup of Iranians who are struggling to create and expand the democratic space and respect for human rights through a truly transnational diasporic network. Iranian exiled writers, film makers and academics are part of this network, who use their specialised sets of skills for the same ends (Abd-El-Aziz et al., 2006). These processes are sometimes lumped within the category of 'social remittances', described by Peggy Levitt as the 'ideas, behaviour, identities, and social capital that flow from receiving countries to sending country communities' (1996: 2).

## Conclusions

The heterogeneity and anthropological complexity of diaspora groups quickly becomes apparent in any rigorous case study. A number of implications follow from this. First, one cannot adequately analyse, understand, or respond to challenges and opportunities if diaspora groups are treated in a one-dimensional way. Second, as noted above, it is important to distinguish between person-to-person relationships between diaspora and those in the homeland, and those relationships that are mobilised and mediated through 'diasporic organisations'. This is not to imply that diasporic organisations are necessarily separate from the larger diasporic community, but it does indicate the need to establish the legitimacy of diasporic organisations, the level of public support for them and their representativeness before investing political and financial resources. Otherwise, there is a considerable risk that hostland support for unrepresentative authoritarian diasporic organisations will prevent potential peace-nurturing initiatives, and support conflict-sustaining structures and processes – as noted above in the example of support by the Canadian Ministries of Finance and of International Cooperation for the Federation of Associations of Canadian Tamils in 2000 – a group widely identified as a fundraising front for the LTTE (Bell, 2000; Chalk, 2000). Finally, it suggests the utility of pursuing a two-prong approach to supporting and cultivating diaspora peacebuilding capacity. One approach works with and through diasporic organisations while a second, complementary approach, works to cultivate person-to-person peacebuilding relationships. Consider, for example, the idea of a carefully and sensitively constructed, implemented and monitored cultural exchange programme for second- and third-wave diaspora youths such as those supported by the American Friends Service Committee, including the Africa Initiative Youth Exchange Program. Typically diaspora-run development initiatives in the homeland are organisations established by individuals who are drawn back to their homelands to work for peace and development – often having been initially displaced by the militarised conflict. In Sri Lanka, this includes Paikiasothy Saravanamuttu who returned from an academic post in the UK to successfully establish the Centre for Policy Alternatives and Kumar Rupasinghe who returned to establish the Foundation for Coexistence.

The considerable international mobility and connectivity of current diasporic groups sets them apart from earlier waves of migrants. When combined with electronic communication – particularly the internet and specialised media access – the sense of common diasporic identity may be mobilised and harnessed despite geographic separation from the homeland and from other members of the diaspora. This is a form of 'imagined community', in which, according to Benedict Anderson, a nation 'is imagined because the members of even the smallest nation will never know most of their fellow-members, meet them, or even hear of them, yet in the minds of each lives the image of their communion' (Anderson, 1991: 6). Mass communication allows for the mediation not just of time and space, but of the anomie which would otherwise develop between separated and compartmentalised social groupings. A diasporic identity is enacted and reinforced digitally within virtual time that transects global time zones so that identity maintenance occurs across state boundaries. This is a process that nurtures a collective sense of community through a shared attachment to a memory of a geographical entity which has, in essence, become de-territorialised – in the sense that personal attachment to a physical place is not dependent upon physical presence.

Indeed, it is this very de-territorialisation that enables the political mobilisation of geographical attachment to, and desire for, the homeland. This creates conditions in which important facets of individual and collective identity of diaspora are more closely associated with the homeland rather than the hostland. However, this is not, or need not, always be the case. Indeed, in order to understand and respond adequately to this phenomenon, we need to simultaneously examine cases where constructive attachment to homelands evolves in tandem with on-going positive relations with the hostland.

The degree to which the analysis of diaspora in an 'Age of Terror' takes its reference point from the destruction of the twin towers in New York (9/11) rather than the commencement of allied bombing of Afghanistan (10/7) suggests a narrow westernised conception of the world which hinders the development of constructive peacebuilding initiatives with diaspora communities. It is therefore rational for diaspora groups to initially distrust Western initiatives to support their peacebuilding activities. It should not be assumed that diaspora communities will perceive external initiatives of Western governments or actors in the same way as their initiators. Obviously, neither should researchers uncritically accept the rationale and motives of diaspora initiatives related to migration and/or peacebuilding in light of the 9/11 and 10/7 hypersensitivities surrounding both areas of activities.

There is no question that diaspora groups contribute substantially to the economy and society of the homeland. Research for the World Bank receives considerable attention – not least because of the benefits it represents for countries of the North who have been reducing their commitment to international development (and its anaemic twin brother, poverty reduction) over the past decade. This form of research is particularly exercised with calculating the volume and channels of such flows. While this is a necessary starting point for understanding this phenomenon, the implicit and explicit politics of this exercise ought not to be obscured. Aside from the dimension of overseas aid flows, there is the obvious connection between this research and interests in choking off international financial support for international criminal and terrorist actors – or at least those actors which fell on the wrong side of the 'for us-against us' dichotomisation of US foreign policy under the Bush regime.

The current approach to the assessment of remittances is problematic if it ignores or hides the benefits the North gains through the maintenance of the financial and political infrastructure which siphons resources out of the global South, whether by predatory dictators of kleptocratic regimes or neoliberal economic regimes. Likewise, the study of remittances is problematic if it is part of an 'anti-immigrant project' that increases the political, social and economic pressures on already vulnerable diasporas, which include 'illegal' workers living and working under exploitative conditions separated for years from children, family and community – all to send a small portion of their earnings back home each month. As long as remittance research is in the hands of researchers directed by the interests of the global North, then the ability to nurture and cultivate genuine peacebuilding capacities of diasporas will be less than what it could be. More broadly, there is a clear need – and opportunity – to support diaspora-driven research on peace and conflict dimensions of diasporas that will improve understanding of how to support and nurture peacebuilding capacities while avoiding or limiting conflict-maintaining impacts.

## Note

1. Attributed to Abraham Kaplan, a Ukrainian-born American philosopher: 'Give a small boy a hammer, and he will find that everything he encounters needs pounding.'

## References

Abd-El-Aziz, Alaa, Lloyd Axworthy, Parvin Ghorayshi, Claire Reid, Benita Kliewer and Charlotte Kudadirgwa, 2006, 'Scoping the Role of Canadian Diaspora in Global Diplomacy and Policy Making', paper at the Expert Forum on 'Capacity Building for Peace and Development: Roles of Diaspora', Toronto, Canada, 19–20 October 2006.

Anderson, Benedict R., 1991, *Imagined Communities: Reflections on the Origins and Spread of Nationalism*, London: Verso.

Bell, Stewart, 2000, 'Sri Lanka's Civil War and the Canadian Connection', *The National Post* (Toronto), 3 June.

Bush, Kenneth D., 2003, *The Intra-group Dimensions of Ethnic Conflict in Sri Lanka: Learning Reading Between the Lines*, Basingstoke: Palgrave Macmillan.

Bush, Kenneth D., 2004, 'Building Capacity for Peace and Unity: The Role of Local Government in Peace Building', Ottawa: International Centre for Municipal Development Federation of Canadian Municipalities, January (at: www.fcm.ca).

Buzan, Barry, 1993, *People, States and Fear: An Agenda for International Security*, Boulder, CO: Lynne Rienner.

Chalk, Peter, 2000, *Liberation Tigers of Tamil Eelam's (LTTE) International Organisation and Operations pp A Preliminary Analysis*, Commentary No. 77, Canadian Security Intelligence Service, Ottawa.

Cheran, Rudrhramoorthy and Sharryn Aiken, 2005, 'The Impact Of International Informal Banking On Canada: A Case Study Of Tamil Transnational Money Transfer Networks (UNDIYAL), Canada/Sri Lanka', working paper, Law Commission of Canada and Nathanson Centre for the Study of Organized Crime and Corruption, York University.

*Chicago Tribune*, 'Rebel Group Funded Congressman's Trip to Sri Lanka, Sources Say'; '2 more Canadians arrested in Tamil Tigers investigation', 23 August 2006 (at: www.cbc.ca/story/world/national/2006/08/23/tamil-weapons-bust.html).

Clifford, James, 1994, 'Diasporas', *Cultural Anthropology*, Vol. 9, No. 3, pp. 302–38.

Fagen, Patricia Weiss, 2006, 'Remittances in Conflict and Crises: How Remittances Sustain Livelihoods in War, Crises and Transitions to Peace', Access Finance, No. 11, May, World Bank Group (at: www.ipacademy.org/Programs/Research/ProgReseSec Dev_Pub.htm).

Faist, Thomas, 2004, 'The Migration-Security Nexus. International Migration and Security Before and After 9/11', Willy Brandt working paper, Malmö University School of International Migration and Ethnic Relations, Sweden.

*Guardian Weekly* (London), 9–15 December 2005.

Gott, Ceri and Karl Johnston, 2002, *The Migrant Population in the UK: Fiscal Effects*, study by the UK Home Office Research, Development and Statistics Directorate, the Performance and Innovation Unit and the Institute for Public Policy Research, London.

HRW (Human Rights Watch), 2006, *Funding the Final War: LTTE Intimidation and Extortion Among the Tamil Diaspora*, Vol. 18, No. 1.

Intriligator, Michael, 1991, 'Defining Global Security', *Disarmament*, Vol. 14, pp. 59–72.

IOM (International Office for Migration), 2005a, *World Migration 2005: Costs and Benefits of International Migration*, Geneva.

IOM, 2005b, *World Migration: Costs and Benefits of International Migration* (at: www.unesco.org).

Iregui, Anna María, 2002, 'Efficiency Gains from the Elimination of Global Restrictions on Labour Mobility: An Analysis using a Multiregional CGE Model', paper at UNU–WIDER conference on 'Poverty, International Migration and Asylum', Helsinki, 27–28 September.

Klare, Michael and Daniel Thomas, 1991, *World Security*, New York: St. Martin's Press.

Kriesi, Hanspeter, 1988, 'The Interdependence of Structure and Action: Some Reflections of the State of the Art', in Bert Klandermans, Hanspeter Kriesi and Sidney Tarrow (eds), *From Structure to Action; Comparing Social Movements Across Cultures*, London: JAI Press, pp. 349–68.

Léonard, Sarah, 2004, 'Studying Migration as a Security Issue: Conceptual and Methodological Challenges', paper for Standing Group on International Relations, 5th Pan-European International Relations Conference, The Hague.

Levitt, Peggy, 1996, 'A Conceptual Tool for Understanding Migration and Development', working paper series No. 96.04, Harvard Center for Population and Development Studies, Cambridge, MA, October.

Lyons, Terrence, 2006, 'Conflict-Generated Diasporas and Peacebuilding: A Conceptual Overview and Ethiopian Case Study', background paper for expert forum on 'Capacity Building for Peace and Development: Roles of Diaspora', Toronto, 19–20 October.

Mathews, Jessica Tuchman, 1989, 'Redefining Security', *Foreign Affairs*, Vol. 68, No. 2, pp. 168–71.

Mearsheimer, John J. and Stephen M. Walt, 2006, 'The Israel Lobby and US Foreign Policy', working paper RWP06-011, Kennedy School of Government, Harvard University, 13 March.

Morris, Aldon D. and Carol McClurg Mueller, 1992 (eds), *Frontiers in Social Movement Theory*, New Haven, CN: Yale University Press.

Moses, Jonathan and Björn Letnes, 2002, 'The Economic Costs of International Labour Restrictions', paper at UNU–WIDER conference, Helsinki, September.

*National Post*, 2000, 'Sri Lanka's Civil War and the Canadian Connection' (Toronto), 3 June.

Newland, Kathleen and Erin Patrick, 2004, *Beyond Remittances: The Role of Diaspora in Poverty Reduction in their Countries of Origin*, Washington DC: Migration Policy Institute.

Orjuela, Camilla, 2006, 'Distant Warriors, Distant Peace Workers? Multiple Diaspora Roles in Sri Lanka's Violent Conflict', background paper, Expert Forum on 'Capacity Building for Peace and Development: Roles of Diaspora', Toronto, Canada, 19–20 October.

Ratha, Dilip, 2005, 'Sending Money Home: Trends in Migrant Remittances', *Finance and Development*, Vol. 42, No. 4, December (at: www.imf.org/external/pubs/ft/fandd/2005/12/picture.htm).

Savage, Kevin and Paul Harvey, 2007, 'Remittances During Crisis: Implications for Humanitarian Response', report No. 25, Humanitarian Practice Group, Overseas Development Institute, London.

Skrbis, Slatco, 2007, 'The Mobilized Croatian Diaspora: Its Role in Homeland Politics and War', in Hazel Smith and Paul Stares (eds), *Diasporas in Conflict: Peace-makers or Peace-wreckers?* Tokyo: UN University Press, pp. 218–38.

Smith, Hazel, 2007, 'Diasporas in International Conflict', in Smith and Paul Stares (eds), *Diasporas in Conflict: Peace-makers or Peace-wreckers?* Tokyo: UN University Press, pp. 3–16.

*Sunday Times*, 2006, 'British [Physician] charged over rocket sales' (London), 27 August.

Tarrow, Sidney, 1989, 'Struggle, Politics, and Reform: Collective Action, Social Movements, and Cycles of Protest', occasional paper No. 21, Western Societies Program, Center for International Studies, Cornell University.

Tilly, Charles, 1978, *From Mobilisation to Revolution*, Englewood Cliffs, NJ: Prentice-Hall.

Tirman, John, 2004, *The Maze of Fear: Migration and Security after September 11th*, New York: The New Press.

World Bank, 2006, *Global Economic Outlook – Overview and Global Outlook*, Washington, DC: World Bank (at: http://siteresources.worldbank.org/INTGEP2006/Resources/GEP_i-xii.pdf).

# 12
# Rwandese Diasporas and the Reconstruction of a Fragile Peace

*Rebecca Davies*

Once regarded as a major test of the emerging post-conflict agenda (Uvin, 2001: 177), post-genocide Rwanda has become accepted by the international donor community as a politically stable and relatively successful state. However, there is growing disquiet at the country's slide into oppression, exclusion and dictatorship (International Crisis Group, 2002; Reyntjens, 2004, 2006), its activities in neighbouring states (Marysse, 2003), and the collusion of the ruling class and their allies in criminal activities (Hintjens, 2006; Reyntjens, 2005). This chapter explores the political economy of peace in Rwanda since 1994 by examining in particular the role of the diaspora and returnees in reconstruction and development processes more broadly. This reconstruction has, to a large extent, been circumscribed both within the parameters of the liberal peace and by the sustained involvement of key diaspora actors.

Perhaps uniquely in sub-Saharan Africa, the Rwandan diaspora has been highly significant in both the conflict itself and post-conflict reconstruction. The Tutsi-dominated government came to power after the Rwandan Patriotic Front's (RPF) military victory during 1994 and is led by and largely comprised of returnees. These returnees form the core of the new *akazu*;[1] returned 'old caseload' refugees are at the centre of land reform disputes (Pottier, 2006: 511); formal and informal remittances whilst low are increasing, as is investment by local and diaspora companies; and, the country's development plan Vision 2020 aimed to draw heavily on the skills, investment and networks of the diaspora. Indeed, President Paul Kagame devoted much of his presidency to engaging with diaspora communities worldwide to mobilise 'this very important resource' in order to realise this developmental vision (Kagame, 2006). Yet to date, the nature of this unprecedented political, economic and social engagement by elements of a predominantly Tutsi diaspora remains an important but overlooked aspect of the study of this post-conflict society.

Alongside the usual range of development actors in Rwanda, then, various diasporic groupings are integral to building a sustainable peace. The relevance of the diaspora's contribution to development outcomes on the African continent is increasingly acknowledged (Davies, 2007; De Haas, 2005), but less so its significance in post-conflict reconstructions. Whilst it is recognised that building a sustainable peace requires an understanding of how 'local, micro-economic practices interlink with state, regional and global aspects of war economies' (Turner and Pugh, 2006: 472), there is considerable ambiguity about the role that diasporas play in the transformation of war-torn societies. However, it is clear that 'the impact of diaspora and migrant remittances on conflict is highly context-specific: it can fuel conflict but it can also act as a brake on violence and mitigate destabilising socioeconomic tensions and divisions within a society' (Berdal, 2005: 694).

Thus, while engaging in a country-specific analysis which recognises the complexity of this dimension, the chapter will evaluate its role *vis-à-vis* a number of common themes which include state consolidation and the rise of new elites, development processes and the renewal of the nation. The analysis will assist in overcoming the empirical and analytical omissions which characterise this element of post-conflict reconstruction. Typically, it is the impact of remittances in terms of achieving both developmental and security outcomes which has been the main focus of scholarly and policy attention. In Rwanda the diasporic focus has been narrow: certain communities have been integral to building the liberal peace, while others, most notably the Hutu diaspora, have been excluded. The nature of the post-1994 transformation can best be defined in terms of a 'striking continuity' between the pre- and post-genocide regimes which is evident both in the 'exercise of power [and] also in the nature of the state' (Reyntjens, 2004: 209). With this in mind, the role of the diaspora and returnees in the reconstruction project will now be examined.

## The diaspora as an agent of reconstruction in post-conflict Rwanda

From the 1972 genocide in Burundi to the Tutsi-dominated RPF invasion of Rwanda during 1990, from Museveni's military victory in Uganda during 1986 assisted by 'warrior refugees' (Pottier, 2002: 24), to fighting in the eastern Democratic Republic of Congo (DRC) from 1996 onwards, Rwandese diaspora groups have been central not only to the political trajectory of Rwanda but to the Great Lakes region more widely. Indeed, the 'systematic re-imagining of Rwanda' since the 1994 genocide has been directed by a government comprised of returnees telling the simplified 'story of a Rwanda imagined by diaspora-scholars who have finally made the long trek home' (Pottier, 2002: 7, 207). Yet it took over 30 years for the approximately 150,000 Tutsi refugees – in the exodus resulting from the 'social revolution' of the late 1950s when the monarchy was replaced with a presidential republic – to return to their homeland and assume political power. Any account of how power is exercised in post-conflict Rwanda needs to acknowledge not merely how 'state and non-state, local and external forces interact to produce order and authority' (Callaghy et al., 2001: 4), but crucially the constitutive effect of the diaspora, its complexity and the impact of exile conditions on the political economy context of diaspora connections.

Prior to the end of colonial rule, Rwanda's population was relatively mobile in response to various environmental, economic and political upheavals. The imposition of fixed state boundaries began to take its toll on these movements during this same period (Newbury, 2005), as political rather than economic migrations became more common. The most significant migrations, both in terms of identity formation and ethnic polarisation as well as political organisation and alliances, began with the 1959 exodus of Rwandan Tutsis. It is the refugee diaspora which developed in the aftermath of this movement in the neighbouring countries of Burundi, Tanzania, the DRC and Uganda that forms the empirical focus of this chapter. A series of similar and internal migrations followed, including a second wave of approximately 100,000 Tutsi refugees during 1963–1964 and the later relocation of communities and individuals facing severe land shortages (Pottier, 2002: 11).

Each of these displacements was overtly political, but a number of factors distinguished the so-called '59-ers' or 'old caseload' refugees from earlier population flows:

> They originated from within the state; they often had formerly held close ties to the centres of dynastic power; they were forced to leave Rwanda for political reasons; and they strongly maintained their identity as Rwandans – they saw themselves as distinct from the host community, and ardently sought to return 'home'.
>
> (Newbury, 2005: 270)

While a wide range of refugees were included in this exodus, by and large this was a privileged group, albeit one which perceived itself not so much as 'the Tutsi' but as a victim 'of colonial policy in the struggle for political power' (Van der Meeren, 1996: 256). The second wave was more overtly ethnic in nature with a broader range of Tutsi affected (Newbury, 2005: 272), although many Tutsi did remain in Rwanda becoming prominent in due course in business if not formal politics.

The tensions within this refugee diaspora have never entirely faded. From the start, economic, entrepreneurial and educational opportunities and experience ensured that the elite sector among the '59-ers' and their descendants succeeded in business and government positions across the region (Newbury, 2005: 273). But the levels of integration differed considerably depending upon both these opportunities and the host country. The most successful resettlement occurred in Tanzania where they were in the main welcomed as settlers. In Uganda which absorbed the bulk of refugees (approximately 200,000), the DRC and Burundi, they gradually became entangled and victimised in domestic political struggles and even civil war (Van der Meeren, 1996: 259–64). Despite the long history of population mobility and connections in the Great Lakes region, the foundations of distinctive diasporic identities were laid during these decades as the sheer scale of these cross-border movements raised considerable tensions over citizenship issues, land shortages and other resources.

Over the course of the post-genocide era, the significance of these Tutsi diaspora has become increasingly apparent. In the first government of 1994, the majority of ministerial and high-ranking military positions were held by a small component of the Ugandan diaspora. Indeed, Kagame is himself a member of this Ugandan network. Although some transformation has occurred since the end of the post-war transition period 2003, the post-genocide ruling elite is largely a product of the networks established in exile during the 1980s. These were based on three parameters: their refugee camp in Uganda, places of education and family ties (Dorsey in: Doom and Gorus, 2000: 328). During exile a particular ethnic angle of this diasporic identity, beyond class and regional interests, hardened to the extent that the fluidity which once characterised social relations disappeared almost entirely. In fact, 'over time some of these refugees came to construct an idealised vision of "home" which diverged from the experiences of those who had stayed behind.... It was a vision that applied essentialist and rigid concepts of an unchanging "home" community in a fluid and changing social world' (Newbury, 2005: 270). Under Kagame's presidency, the vision became institutionalised around issues of entitlement, in particular regarding land and other resources, and belonging.

The link between diaspora activities and the dynamics of reconstruction in post-conflict Rwanda then is inevitably a complex one. While certain diaspora groupings retain a strong grip on the main political, military and economic networks of power, following the elections in 2003 there were signs of a broadening of this elite (Musahara and Huggins, 2005: 280). Generally, however, the returnee-dominated RPF government continued to consolidate and centralise their political ascendancy after coming to power. Certainly, diaspora actors and income may have the potential to assist reconstruction, playing an important role in achieving the variant of political stability and economic development envisaged by the liberal peace. But the complexity of these elements in Rwanda means that a more careful exploration of its involvement in reconstruction processes, as well as the restructuring of relations between key social forces and the state-society formation, is required.

Indeed, the terms of the liberal peace indicate no obvious role for the diaspora in reconstruction processes. Arguably, there is little historical precedent on the African continent for the singular role currently pursued by various Rwandese diasporas. Somalia is an exception, with an economy more dependent on remittances than any other in the world (Maimbo, 2006). This has meant that there is a tendency to either exaggerate or underestimate the capacity of the diaspora. Thus it has been argued that on the one hand diasporas pose a high risk in terms of conflict persistence (Collier *et al.*, 2003: 85), and on the other offer considerable potential for post-conflict reconstruction on all of the macroeconomic, household, community and regional levels (IOM, 2002: 30, 2006a: 11–14; Koser, 2003). Local dynamics and political interests are all too rarely addressed, even while studies have confirmed the usefulness of adopting a country-specific approach to the study of development, security and migration (IOM, 2005: 11).

After 2002 migration became increasingly acknowledged as an important solution to Africa's security problems. A wide range of actors, including states, NGOs, regional, pan-continental and international organisations are involved in strategies to tap the potential of migration flows. These range from the safe transfer of remittances to achieving the Millennium Development Goals (MDGs), from harnessing skills for innovation to promoting political stability and reducing intra-state conflict and insecurity. In each of these arenas, mobilising diasporas offers significant developmental and security outcomes, and it is acknowledged that 'better management of migration' is required if it is to contribute to Africa's development (UNECA, 2006: 107). Even so, there is little grasp of the realities of power in African politics, and the 'ability or otherwise of governance and development initiatives... to successfully operate in the context of neo-patrimonialism and Big Men politics' (Taylor, 2005: 158) in these policy frameworks. While diaspora actors and income can contribute to a political economy of peace in Rwanda, the migration-security nexus needs to be expanded to explain their impact in different political economy and governance contexts.

## Rebuilding the post-conflict state

The implications of this contextual deficit are compelling when considering the challenges of building a sustainable peace in Rwanda. Diasporas straddle both the local and the global levels and can be conceptualised as 'transboundary formations' which: 'link global, regional, national and local forces through structures, networks and discourses that have a wide ranging impact [playing] a major role in creating, transforming, and destroying forms of order and authority' (Callaghy *et al.*, 2001: 5). In this interpretation, it is the 'structures and relations' that emerge from the intersection of these social phenomena that matter. However, the continuity evident in the exercise of power and nature of the state which characterises the post-genocide political economy is perhaps the most overlooked aspect of the transformation project. The difficulties of peacebuilding are myriad. Understanding the changing interests of key local actors is critical in determining what new political orders and economies of peace emerge. Peacebuilding interventions in post-1994 Rwanda are in large part being shaped at the local level by elites and a government, led and composed of exiles, which demonstrate clear continuities with the pre-genocide era. Closer scrutiny of these continuities is essential if the possibility of a sustainable peace in Rwanda is to be properly evaluated.

One of the virtues of this analysis is that it illuminates how the nature of African politics, combined with the unprecedented centrality of the Tutsi-dominated refugee diaspora, has propelled various elites from this diaspora to the forefront of Rwandese politics. The hegemony of neo-patrimonial systems of governance across the continent has received considerable scholarly attention, even as its implications *vis-à-vis* the migration-security nexus and diasporas in particular are more or less wholly unexplored (Blundo and Olivier de Sardan, 2006; Chabal and Daloz, 1999; Van de Walle, 2001). In particular, there have been few attempts to address the issue of state capacity, the 'adjustment' of the central mechanisms of neo-patrimonial rule, and the consequent displacement of 'patrimonial dynamics to new arenas' (Van de Walle, 2001: 157) – all of which will now be considered briefly.

Fundamentally, little has changed in terms of the organisation of power and authority since the 1994 genocide. Neither the wider international community nor the government itself has supported any genuine transformation of the working of the state or the social relations of power. The so-called 'genocide credit' has precluded genuine reform (Melvern, 2000), and the pronounced centralisation of power which has characterised the modern Rwandan state has deepened. In this respect, the power-sharing logic behind the liberal political regime agreed in Arusha has been 'profoundly modified' (Reyntjens, 2004: 178). A series of ministerial and judicial departures began in 1995 and peaked in 2000 as high-profile Hutus left the government to be replaced by Tutsis (Pottier, 2006: 510; Reyntjens, 2006: 1110). The presidential and parliamentary elections of 2003 were tainted by irregularities and a 'general suppression' of the political opposition which has continued and broadened to include civil society groups, the press and NGOs (Buckley-Zistel, 2006: 111; Jordaan, 2006: 347–8). The post-genocide state has even been labelled a 'national security state' which believes that 'the precondition for Tutsi survival is Tutsi power' (Mamdani, 2002: 501). Taken together, each of these actions has served to consolidate the RPF's monopoly of political power and state control.

Nor is Rwanda typical of the majority of post-colonial African states which are distinguished by high levels of autonomy and low institutional capacity. Following independence, successive regimes have pursued a state-building mandate intended both to define and strengthen the state as an institution, and to legitimate this control (Uvin, 1997: 97). Consequently, the country enjoys relatively strong public authority structures built on the continued centrality of state power and supported by external agents including the World Bank and International Monetary Fund (IMF) (Storey, 2001: 366). Structural adjustment and continued international financial institution (IFI) engagement may have succeeded to some extent in 'rationalising' governance in line with liberal economic prescriptions, but it has also dramatically increased financial support and afforded legitimacy to state structures. Indeed, according to the World Bank's 2005 Country Policy and Institutional Assessment ratings which measure the robustness of policies and institutions in terms of economic management and structural and social inclusion policies, Rwanda exceeds the regional average in sub-Saharan Africa. Thus even as concerns mount about the post-genocide state, the IFIs continue to support it 'as a benevolent actor committed to national development albeit in difficult circumstances' (Williams, 2004: 109).

At the apex of this state apparatus rest political networks managed by a new elite or *akazu* which functions through neo-patrimonial relations. In this respect, Rwanda is not dissimilar to the vast majority of African countries where neo-patrimonial systems of governance are dominant and political authority is 'based on the giving and granting of favours, in an endless series of dyadic exchanges that go from the village level to the highest reaches of the central state' (Van de Walle, 2001: 51). In the Rwandese political tradition, the *akazu* are intimately tied to the regime operating as its 'ears and eyes' (Prunier, 1995: 85–7). A new *akazu* has expanded steadily under a resurgent Tutsi elite. Indeed, the extreme version of neo-patrimonialism which characterises this post-conflict state is marked by the manipulation of ethnicity, widespread violence and the concealment of human rights abuses aimed at securing access to power, wealth and knowledge for Tutsi (Reyntjens, 2004: 187–8).

The accumulation of wealth and resources under this patrimonial system may have bolstered political stability, but it has also widened the gap between the rural majority and the new elites. The next section examines the implications of this rising inequality, but it is clear that the patrimonial order has been redrawn. Certainly, prior to the genocide, and faced with threats to their grasp on power and dwindling resources, formal adjustment measures likely encouraged the *akazu* to 'reject power-sharing and protect their control over what external resources remained available' (Williams, 2004: 112). Scholars have contended that the genocide should be represented as a strategy by this beleaguered elite attempting to respond to 'the combined assault of economic crisis and demands for democratisation' (Abrahamsen, 2001: 88; Prunier, 1995: 227). Political and economic liberalisation and its associated development agenda have likewise progressed unevenly in post-conflict Rwanda.

Here too the restructuring process has come up against the persistence of clientelistic networks whereby the state continues to 'protect key areas of discretion which continue to generate important rents for state elites' (Van de Walle, 2001: 186–7).

Following Bayart (2000), the politics of the Rwandan diaspora is currently best understood as the continued exercise of the strategy of 'extraversion' which has enabled the new *akazu* to guarantee the transfer of external resources, typically from rent-seeking activities, in order to maintain power. While Rwanda's post-war economic growth path has been remarkable, the new elite has continued to rely upon patrimonial networks for the maintenance of cohesion. In particular, the enforced reduction in military spending as a precondition for IFI financing has been a significant contributing factor in an increased reliance on these networks (Marysse, 2003: 89). Thus military-commercial networks have been heavily implicated in the spread of conflict into the resource-rich DRC – to the extent that the UN has called it 'militarised patrimonialism' (UN, 2002). Extensive predation has enabled the Rwandan government not only to disguise illicit increases in the military budget, but also to obtain 'much needed domestic loyalty' and consolidate the regime (Reyntjens, 2005: 599). If there are signs of a new political order and sustainable peace emerging, set against these continuities in the organisation of power and authority, they are fragile indeed.

## Development and security challenges for the diaspora

Given that development is considered one of the most important components of the liberal peace, the lack of substantial poverty reduction and growing economic disparity in post-genocide Rwanda raises questions about the sustainability of this peace. Pugh contends that whether or not peacebuilding can transform 'depends a great deal on what kind of economy of peace is introduced – and its rationale' (Pugh, 2006: 279). Attempts to renovate Rwanda's governance structures were begun through the ill-fated 1993 Arusha Accords whose terms were adopted in July 1994 by the new government. These laid the groundwork for a liberal approach towards a stable peace categorised as a 'conservative model', associated with top-down approaches to peacebuilding and development which typically use force or conditionality and dependency creation (Richmond, 2006: 300–6). Indeed, with neo-liberal ideology dominant in the development agenda of a pre-genocide Rwanda, which was considered a 'model developmental citizen' (Williams, 2004: 109), the RPF's orthodox manifesto for the country has effected only a limited societal transformation.

Prior to the genocide, Rwandan society was defined by 'structural violence', as inequality, exclusion and poverty grew during the economic and political crises of the 1980s and early 1990s, and were in turn aggravated by the official development regime (Uvin, 1998: 7). In its aftermath, Rwanda remains a society circumscribed by these same dynamics despite a post-conflict growth path portrayed as nothing short of exceptional (Ansoms, 2005: 498). The restructuring process is underpinned by key policy instruments including the national development programme, Vision 2020,[2] and the MDGs which were adopted by the government during 2000. The country also formally entered the IFI's Poverty Reduction Strategy Programme (PRSP) from 2002 until 2005, with the prospect of a second PRSP known as the Economic Development and Poverty Reduction Strategy to follow in 2007. Building a sustainable peace requires remedying all forms of structural violence. In fact, the achievements of the economic recovery are disappointing in terms of sustainability, poverty reduction, inequality and pro-poor growth more generally. This vulnerability can be explained not merely by a dependence on aid inflows far above the regional average, but also by the economy's structural limitations, which include overpopulation, resource scarcity and a restricted potential for diversification away from subsistence agriculture (Ansoms, 2005: 499).

Thus, Rwanda's development challenges remain more or less unchanged in terms of translating economic growth into poverty reduction. Rural development is a key issue in this respect, and land reform and resettlement initiatives are a vital part of a wider process of post-conflict reconstruction. While there is no single explanation for the 1994 genocide, an important structural factor was the restrictive land tenure arrangements which contributed to poverty (Huggins and Pottier, 2005: 383). After country-wide consultations, the National Unity and Reconciliation Council (NURC) concluded that land disputes are the 'greatest factor hindering sustainable peace' (Government of Rwanda, 2001). The 2005 Land Law was intended to overcome both land scarcity and the inequitable distribution of land by facilitating land consolidation and security of tenure. Other objectives include raising land productivity and thereafter establishing the conditions for the commercialisation of agriculture which may well prejudice subsistence agriculture.

Unsurprisingly, the government has focused on allocating land to 'old-caseload' returnees from the Tutsi-dominated diaspora who had been out of the country for more than ten years, excluding other categories of landless persons such as women (Musahara and Huggins, 2005: 317). There is evidence that the new *akazu* are 'acquiring land for the purpose of speculation rather than agricultural production' (Pottier, 2006: 511). Far less attention has been given to the worsening inequalities which even now characterise land access and tenure. The forced villagisation programme (*imidugudu*) has likewise proven problematic and unpopular, not least because of its questionable agenda which ostensibly favours Tutsi survivors and repatriates (Pottier, 2002: 196). Land disputes have increased and it is by no means clear that this new regime will reinforce a sustainable peace as long as policies continue to fuel social and ethnic polarisation.

Access to land remains at the heart of social development in this post-conflict setting. Redistributive policies are important for reconstruction but rising levels of inequality in Rwanda suggest that the gap between the elites and the wider population is growing, most markedly between the rural majority and the urban population (Ansoms and Marysse, 2005: 71–100; Government of Rwanda, 2002a). It has been suggested that a worrying 'indifference' among the new *akazu* to local production and rural poverty has grown (Hintjens, 2006: 606). Coupled with the RPF-led government's assertions of ethnic equality, these policies have produced a framework which runs the risk of reconstructing identity along ethnic lines. Indeed, the 'ethnicisation of landlessness', illicit land acquisitions by the Tutsi-dominated *akazu*, and moves towards commercialisation run the risk of a rejuvenated version of neo-patrimonialism dominating the post-genocide political economy (Pottier, 2006: 533). It is a bleak outlook.

The prospect of renewed structural violence is likewise to be found in the attempts to 'renew the nation'. Liberal peace processes have placed emphasis on social justice, nation-building, reconciliation and discourses of citizenship and identity as key dimensions of any sustainable peace. This new agenda is being pushed both by external actors and by the government, NGOs and civil society organisations. Here too the distinct involvement of diaspora elites in the peacebuilding consensus has subverted this aspect of the liberal agenda. Consolidating the regime relies upon a pro-RPF revisionist version of Rwanda's history, which glosses over 'significant social complexities' and is used to 'intellectually justify a system of leadership by Tutsi minority rule' (Pottier, 2002: 111). In keeping with the country's conservative version of the liberal peace, this historical narrative and the nation-building efforts which flow from it remains an elite-driven process. The nature of 'being Rwandan' and 'Rwandan-ness' beyond ethnic uniformity has barely been considered. Consequently, highly charged issues of reconciliation and formal justice in the transformation project have suffered greatly.

In the immediate aftermath of the RPF victory, the transitional government promoted a project of national unity headed by the NURC in order to build a sustainable peace (NURC, 2004: 12). The promotion of an 'all-Rwandan citizenship' is at the heart of this project (Buckley-Zistel, 2006: 112). With an emphasis firmly on this version of citizenship, common values and community cohesion, the likelihood of constructing an inclusive national identity is slight. Instead, a deeply flawed reconciliation process has emerged, whereby 'the current policy of national unity is potentially counter-productive since it denies a space for difference and silences criticism and legitimate grievances. The government fabricates unity without reconciliation' (Buckley-Zistel, 2006: 102).

In terms of social justice those forms of violence and injustice related to the genocide have been the focus of the rebuilt justice system. This has left the human rights abuses committed by the RPF army during the civil war and 'as a matter of general routine against opponents of the regime' wholly unanswered (Uvin, 2001: 183). It was only after 2002 that the international donor community began very slowly to acknowledge these warning signs of continuing abuses (Human Rights Watch, 2002). In the short term this politicisation of ethnicity and identity is ominous, but in the longer term it prefigures a divided Rwanda and the prospects for renewed violence.

The unprecedented involvement of the diaspora-dominated government in the transformation project in post-genocide Rwanda cannot be overstated. More typical diaspora activities and their peacebuilding roles are discussed in preceding chapters. Evidently, the impact of diaspora networks is not clear-cut. There is evidence that migration can strengthen pre-existing inequalities, form new social hierarchies, and may not even be 'developmental for the whole, or even the majority' (Bracking, 2003: 641). Context matters but so too does an understanding of the complexity of the diaspora linked to a range of power relations, interests and political agendas as well as factors including class, ethnicity, race, generation, political affiliation and gender (Davies, 2007: 72). Certainly, the migration-security nexus is not uniform in its outcomes.

However, there is little accurate data and very few studies on the size of the Rwandan diaspora worldwide, or the impact of remittances on the home country (IOM, 2006: 59). A series of often forced displacements arising from episodic conflict and resource scarcity have created a sizeable diaspora concentrated in neighbouring countries, and to a lesser extent in Europe (in Belgium the Rwandan diaspora is approximately 6000), the United States and South Africa. During 2004 individual remittances outweighed collective remittances, although total formal remittances were estimated at only US$16 million, which is low even within the sub-Saharan region (IOM, 2006: 71). There are only a very small number of either governmental or non-governmental initiatives which aim to facilitate their distribution (IOM, 2006: 59–65).

After 2000 the government attempted to generate economic development by mobilising the diaspora. The aim was to contribute to development, albeit indirectly by building upon the skills, capital and trade connections of the new elite. Rwanda's development programme Vision 2020 was launched during 2000 with a strong emphasis on human resource development and capacity building, proposing a major role for its expatriate population. Strong political direction by Kagame was reflected in the establishment of a Department for the Diaspora within the Ministry of Foreign Affairs and Cooperation during 2001. Three Rwandan Diaspora Global Conventions were held between 2001 and 2006. Other initiatives included the establishment of a dedicated investment and export promotion agency which handles a variety of investment issues, including that from the diaspora. Record investment receipts and company registrations for 2006 demonstrate considerable interest from the diaspora, which in some sectors surpasses that of foreign investors (African Research Bulletin, 2007: 17254). Similarly, the creation of a knowledge-based economy comprises a cornerstone of Vision 2020 and the MDGs, and Rwanda's flourishing information technology sector has benefited greatly from the skills of returnees (Mwangi, 2006). By 2007, however, their role in building a political economy of peace had been far less influential than that of the returnee-dominated government and there were few indications that this would change.

## Conclusion

By examining the specific challenges posed in rebuilding Rwanda, this chapter has evaluated the contribution of a predominantly Tutsi diaspora in addressing a wide range of reconstruction challenges. Alongside existing accounts of the mechanisms dedicated to achieving a sustainable peace, the impact of this complex set of actors has been obscured. The new regime is headed by a government comprising essentially of Tutsi returnees that has shown a readiness to adopt key tenets of the liberal peace project and associated peacebuilding tasks. Nonetheless, the continuity which defines the pre- and post-genocide regimes has meant that thus far this post-conflict transformation has proven inadequate. Despite impressive annual average economic growth between 1996 and 2001 of 8.56 per cent, falling to 4.6 per cent between 2001 and 2006, there has also been an increase of inequality levels as the benefits of this growth have been concentrated in the hands of a narrow clientelistic elite, the so-called *akazu* (Ansoms, 2007: 372). Indeed, over the period 2001–2006 the Gini coefficient reached 0.51 (Ansoms, 2007: 374). As both social and ethnic polarisation have resurfaced under this regime alongside the rising inequality, the likelihood of renewed structural violence has risen.

The potential for diaspora networks and income to sustain a political economy, where 'short-term economic gain is paramount [and] political leaders find that their legitimacy as Big Men is conditional upon their ability to obtain resources – by all means' (Chabal, 2002: 453), should not be overlooked. Post-conflict transformation in Rwanda has led to a political economy caught between complex sub-economies defined by predation, criminality and newer economic opportunities so that a new political order is emerging only slowly. It is a political economy of peace increasingly dominated not merely by international actors but by an elite, narrowly drawn from the ranks of the Tutsi refugee diaspora, who, given their ethnic background, are not best placed to address certain key political and economic issues.

A more fundamental cultural and political transformation is required. If the Tutsi elites remain wedded to externally imposed liberal reconstruction policies, they will continue to ignore crucial features of the organisation of power and authority and the nature of the Rwandan state. The constitutive effect of the diaspora in Rwanda raises important questions about the extent to which there needs to be a far better understanding of the complex issues related to peacebuilding. These issues might include how conflict dynamics, local political interests, structural constraints and the development paradigm itself inhibit the effectiveness of the liberal peacebuilding consensus and interventions. For while its impact remains very much context-specific, the diaspora can represent only one part of any solution to Rwanda's regeneration.

## Notes

1. The term (literally 'little house') initially referred to former President Habyarimana's inner circle with a 'strongly critical connotation of power abuses and illicit enrichment' (Prunier, 1995: 401). It is used more broadly here to refer to the clientelistic networks which expanded under President Kagame's regime.
2. Vision 2020 comprises seven goals: good political and economic governance; rural economic transformation; development of services, manufacturing and mining; human resource development; lowering risks and costs of doing business in Rwanda and development of the private sector; regional and international economic integration; and poverty reduction (Government of Rwanda, 2000).

## References

Abrahamsen, Rita, 2001, 'Development Policy and the Democratic Peace in Sub-Saharan Africa', *Conflict, Security & Development*, Vol. 1, No. 3, pp. 79–103.

Ansoms, An, 2005, 'Resurrection after Civil War and Genocide: Growth, Poverty and Inequality in Post-conflict Rwanda', *European Journal of Development Research*, Vol. 17, No. 3, pp. 495–508.

Ansoms, An, 2007, 'How Successful is the Rwandan PRSP? Growth, Poverty and Inequality', *Review of African Political Economy*, Vol. 34, No. 112, pp. 371–9.

Ansoms, An and Stefaan Marysse, 2005, 'The Evolution and Characteristics of Poverty and Inequality in Rwanda', in Marysse and Filip Reyntjens (eds), *Political Economy of the Great Lakes Region in Africa*, Basingstoke: Palgrave, pp. 71–100.

Bayart, Jean-François, 2000, 'Africa in the World: A History of Extraversion', *African Affairs*, No. 99, pp. 217–67.

Berdal, Mats, 2005, 'Beyond Greed and Grievance – and Not Too Soon', *Review of International Studies*, Vol. 31, No. 4, pp. 687–98.

Blundo, Giorgio and Jean-Pierre Olivier de Sardan, 2006, *Everyday Corruption and the State: Citizens and Public Officials in Africa*, London: Zed Books.

Bracking, Sarah, 2003, 'Sending Money Home: Are Remittances Always Beneficial to Those Who Stay Behind?', *Journal of International Development*, Vol. 15, No. 5, pp. 633–44.

Buckley-Zistel, Susanne, 2006, 'Dividing and Uniting: The Use of Citizenship Discourses in Conflict and Reconciliation in Rwanda', *Global Society*, Vol. 20, No. 1, pp. 101–13.

Callaghy, Thomas, Ronald Kassimir and Robert Latham (eds), 2001, *Intervention and Transnationalism in Africa: Global-Local Networks of Power*, Cambridge: Cambridge University Press.

Chabal, Patrick, 2002, 'The Quest for Good Government and Development in Africa: Is NEPAD the answer?' *International Affairs*, Vol. 78, No. 3, pp. 447–62.

Chabal, Patrick and Jean-Pascal Daloz, 1999, *Africa Works: Disorder as a Political Instrument*, Oxford: James Currey.

Collier, Paul, Lani Elliott, Havard Hegre, Anke Hoeffler, Marta Reynal-Querol and Nicholas Sambanis, 2003, *Breaking the Conflict Trap: Civil War and Development Policy*, Washington, DC: World Bank.

Davies, Rebecca, 2007, 'Reconceptualising the Migration-Development Nexus: Diasporas, Globalisation and the Politics of Exclusion', *Third World Quarterly*, Vol. 28, No. 1, pp. 59–76.

De Haas, Hein, 2005, 'International Migration, Remittances and Development: Myths and Facts', *Third World Quarterly*, Vol. 26, No. 8, pp. 1269–84.

Doom, Ruddy and Jan Gorus (eds), 2000, *Politics of Identity and Economics of Conflict in the Great Lakes Region*, Brussels: VUB University Press.

Dorsey, Michael, 2000, 'Violence and Power-Building in Post-Genocide Rwanda', in Ruddy Doom and Jon Gorus (eds), *Politics of Identity and Economics of Conflict in the Great Lakes Region*, Brussels: VUB University Press, pp. 311–48.

Government of Rwanda, 2000, *Rwanda Vision 2020*, Ministry of Finance and Economic Planning, Kigali.

Government of Rwanda, 2001, *Brookings Initiative in Rwanda*, Ministry of Lands, Environment, Forestry, Water and Natural Resources, Kigali.

Government of Rwanda, 2002a, *A Profile of Poverty in Rwanda*, Ministry of Finance, Kigali.

Government of Rwanda, 2002b, *Poverty Reduction Strategy Paper*, Ministry of Finance and Economic Planning, Kigali.

Hintjens, Helen, 2006, 'Conflict and Resources in Post-Genocide Rwanda and the Great Lakes region', *International Journal of Environmental Studies*, Vol. 63, No. 5, pp. 599–615.

Huggins, Chris and Jenny Clover (eds), 2005, *From the Ground Up: Land Rights, Conflict and Peace in Sub-Saharan Africa*, Pretoria: Institute for Security Studies.

Huggins, Chris and Johan Pottier, 2005, 'Land Tenure, Land Reform and Conflict in Sub-Saharan Africa: Towards a Research Agenda', in Huggins and Jenny Clover (eds), *From the Ground Up*, Pretoria: Institute for Security Studies, pp. 383–92.

Human Rights Watch (HRW), 2002, *Human Rights Watch World Report 2002: Africa*, New York.

International Crisis Group (ICG), 2002, *Rwanda At The End of The Transition: A Necessary Political Liberalisation*, Africa Report No. 53, Brussels.

IOM, (International Organisation for Migration) 2002, *The Migration-Development Nexus: Evidence and Policy Options*, Geneva.

IOM, 2005, *Migration and Development: New Strategic Outlooks and Practical Ways Forward: The Cases of Angola and Zambia*, Geneva.

IOM, 2006, *Remittances in the Great Lakes Region*, Geneva.

Jordaan, Eduard, 2006, 'Inadequately Self-critical: Rwanda's Self-Assessment for the African Peer Review Mechanism', *African Affairs*, Vol. 105, 333–51.

Kagame, Paul, 2006, *Address of the President of Rwanda at the third Rwanda Diaspora Convention*, New York, 28 September.

Koser, Khalid (ed.), 2003, *New African Diasporas*, London: Routledge.

Maimbo, Samuel M. (ed.), 2006, *Remittances and Economic Development in Somalia*, Social Development Paper No. 38, Washington, DC: World Bank Conflict Prevention & Reconstruction.

Mamdani, Mahmood, 2002, 'African States, Citizenship and War: A Case-study', *International Affairs*, Vol. 78, No. 3, pp. 493–506.

Marysse, Stefaan, 2003, 'Regress and War: The Case of the DRCongo', *European Journal of Development Research*, Vol. 15, No. 1, pp. 73–98.

Marysse, Stefaan and Filip Reyntjens, (eds), 2005, *Political Economy of the Great Lakes Region in Africa: The Pitfalls of Enforced Democracy and Globalisation*, Basingstoke: Palgrave.

Melvern, Linda, 2000, *A People Betrayed: The Role of the West in Genocide in Rwanda*, London: Zed Books.

Musahara, Herman and Chris Huggins, 2005, 'Land Reform, Land Scarcity and Post-conflict Reconstruction: A Case Study of Rwanda', in Huggins and Jenny Clover (eds), *From the Ground Up*, Pretoria: Institute for Security Studies, pp. 269–346.

Mwangi, Wagaki, 2006, 'The Social Relations of e-Government Diffusion in Developing Countries: The Case of Rwanda', paper at International Conference on Digital Government Research, San Diego, CA.

Newbury, David, 2005, 'Returning Refugees: Four Historical Patterns of "Coming Home" to Rwanda', *Comparative Studies in Society and History*, Vol. 47, No. 2, pp. 252–85.

NURC (National Unity and Reconciliation Council), 2004, 'The Road towards Unity and Reconciliation: Ten Years After (1994–2004)', Kigali.

Pottier, Johan, 2002, *Re-Imagining Rwanda: Conflict, Survival and Disinformation in the Late Twentieth Century*, Cambridge: Cambridge University Press.

Pottier, Johan, 2006, 'Land Reform for Peace? Rwanda's 2005 Land Law in Context', *Journal of Agrarian Change*, Vol. 6, No. 4, pp. 509–37.

Prunier, Gerard, 1995, *The Rwanda Crisis: History of a Genocide,* London: Hurst & Company.

Pugh, Michael, 2006, 'Post-war Economies and the New York Dissensus', *Conflict, Security & Development*, Vol. 6, No. 3, pp. 269–89.

Reyntjens, Filip, 2004, 'Rwanda, Ten Years On: From Genocide to Dictatorship', *African Affairs*, Vol. 103, pp. 177–210.

Reyntjens, Filip, 2005, 'The Privatization and Criminalization of Public Space in the Geopolitics of the Great Lakes Region', *Journal of Modern African Studies*, Vol. 43, No. 4, pp. 587–607.

Reyntjens, Filip, 2006, 'Post-1994 Politics in Rwanda: Problematising "Liberation" and "Democratisation"', *Third World Quarterly*, Vol. 27, No. 6, pp. 1103–17.

Richmond, Oliver P., 2006, 'The problem of peace: understanding the "liberal peace"' *Conflict, Security and Development*, Vol. 6, No. 3, 291–314.

Storey, Andy, 2001, 'Structural Adjustment, State Power & Genocide: the World Bank & Rwanda', *Review of African Political Economy*, Vol. 28, No. 89, pp. 365–85.

Taylor, Ian, 2005, *NEPAD: Towards Africa's Development or Another False Start?*, Boulder, CO: Lynne Rienner.

Turner, Mandy and Michael Pugh, 2006. 'Towards a new agenda for transforming war economies', *Conflict, Security & Development*, Vol. 6, No. 3, pp. 471–9.

UN, 2002, 'Report of the Panel of Experts on the Illegal Extraction of Natural Resources and Other Forms of Wealth of the Democratic Republic of Congo', UN doc., S/2002/1146, 16.10.2002.

UNECA (UN Economic Commission for Africa), 2006, *International Migration and Development: Implications for Africa*, Addis Ababa.

Uvin, Peter, 1997, 'Prejudice, Crisis and Genocide in Rwanda', *African Studies Review*, Vol. 40, No. 2, pp. 91–115.

Uvin, Peter, 1998, *Aiding Violence: The Development Enterprise in Rwanda*, West Hartford, CT: Kumarian.

Uvin, Peter, 2001, 'Difficult Choices in the New Post-conflict Agenda: The International Community in Rwanda after the Genocide', *Third World Quarterly*, Vol. 22, No. 2, pp. 177–89.

Van der Meeren, Rachel, 1996, 'Three Decades in Exile: Rwanda Refugees 1960–1990', *Journal of Refugee Studies*, Vol. 9, No. 3, pp. 252–67.

Van de Walle, Nicolas, 2001, *African Economies and the Politics of Permanent Crisis, 1979–1999*, Cambridge: Cambridge University Press.

Williams, Paul, 2004, 'Peace Operations and the International Financial Institutions: Insights from Rwanda and Sierra Leone', *International Peacekeeping*, Vol. 11, No. 1, pp. 103–23.

# Part V

# Borderlands and the Cartography of Violent Economies

# 13
# War, Peace and the Places in Between: Why Borderlands are Central

*Jonathan Goodhand*

> *Boundaries prevent people from stepping on things accidentally. And they're the first thing you point out when someone steps on something intentionally.*
>
> Atom Egoyan, 2006

Wherever there is violent conflict, boundaries and borders are taken seriously. As the quote above implies, boundaries play an ambiguous role, acting simultaneously as source of security and antagonism, inclusion and exclusion. Which boundaries become salient and on which side of the boundary one stands may make the difference between life and death. Both war fighting and peacebuilding are in essence collective action problems involving processes of 'debordering' and 'rebordering'. Because they are perceived to be so important, the transition from war to peace involves complex and always conflictual bargaining about the nature of physical and social boundaries. Peace processes that are insensitive to boundary politics risk re-igniting conflict rather than consolidating the peace. In Sri Lanka, for instance, a bipolar model of negotiations, based on the assumption that there were two coherent conflicting parties – the Sri Lankan government and Liberation Tigers of Tamil Ealam (LTTE) controlling contiguous 'real estate' in the south and northeast respectively – failed to accommodate the complex intra-group divisions which ultimately tore the peace process apart.

This chapter, focusing primarily, but not exclusively, on spatial-territorial boundaries in areas affected by, or recovering from, violent conflict, explores how borders and borderlands are influenced by, and in turn play a role in shaping, the transition from war to peace (or conversely a return to violence). It is argued that a borderland perspective is almost completely missing in the literature and policy debates on peacebuilding, due largely to the way that social scientists and policymakers have tended to stand in awe of the state. We consequently know more about how states deal with borderlands than about how borderlands deal with states (van Schendel, 2005). However, if the analytical starting point is the border, one can question the idea that statebuilding and 'post-conflict' peacebuilding involve the gradual diffusion of power outwards from the centre. Mainstream accounts do not merely leave out the periphery; they ignore a set of boundary conditions and exchanges that make the centre what it is (Scott, 2007: 16).

## Boundaries, frontiers and borderlands

Borders and borderlands are frequently viewed as staging posts, which are crossed over but not treated as entities in their own right. This chapter places the analytical centre of gravity on the so-called margins, while recognising that 'central' or 'peripheral' areas are social and political constructs and subject to renegotiation (Ron, 2003: xii). In the following section, key terms are defined, before examining how they are relevant to debates on civil wars and war-to-peace transitions.

### Boundaries

Boundaries signify the point at which something changes, at which 'we' end and 'they' begin, at which certain rules for behaviour no longer obtain and others take hold (Migdal, 2004: 5). People act according to a code of laws on one side of the boundary; others act according to another code across this boundary. Boundaries have various functions including delimiting ownership, delimiting authority, establishing defensive lines and marking the difference between 'us' and 'them'. They are mental constructs that become social and physical realities. Although they may be abstract and 'artificial' as in the case of many state borders they always have material effects.

Migdal (2004) usefully distinguishes between the 'mental maps' through which people divide home from alien territory and the 'checkpoints' or sites and practices that are deployed to differentiate members from others. The 'ability to identify boundaries of social groups is tremendously important for people simply to make out the lay of the land – where they believe that threats lurk and where safety resides' (ibid.: 10). Contradictory mental maps and checkpoints can tear people in different directions (ibid.: 23) and they may be forced to choose which boundaries to submit to. Therefore boundaries can simultaneously be zones of uncertainty and security (Newman and Paasi, 1998: 188). 'Successful' conflict (and peace) entrepreneurs understand well the dynamics of antagonism, skilfully infusing some boundaries with greater meaning than others. Those who promote war have the job of rendering the enemy 'not like us' (Richards, 2005: 17). As Charles Tilly (2003) notes, conflict is all about 'boundary activation', which involves hardening some boundaries and repressing others. For instance, the LTTE mobilises supporters through an ethno-nationalist discourse based on the notion of a 'Tamil homeland' whilst downplaying caste-based and regional divisions within the Tamil polity. Which boundaries become salient is clearly determined by underlying power relations.

Battlefields are arenas in which psychological as well as physical boundaries must be crossed. Organised killing involves the transgression of 'normal' practices and constraints. The military invest heavily in training recruits so as to normalise the crossing of this boundary – though 'high tech' weaponry makes it relatively easy to do so, when mass killing increasingly resembles a computer game. As argued later, in frontiers and borderlands, warfare is frequently more brutal and barbarised. Conversely, war-to-peace transitions may involve the redrawing of some boundaries (for instance, between murder and 'legitimate' killing) and the 'de-activation' of others.

## Frontiers

Romans adopted the Greek term *oikoumen* ('the known world'; see Colas, 2006) to denote the zone where the settled and unsettled, the civilised world and the wilderness met. The purpose of imperial frontiers was to keep the barbarian tribes at bay (Hirst, 2005: 77). Frontiers are seen to pre-date the modern state period, belonging to a world of empires – for instance, the Roman marches – in which there are jagged edges or zones of transition between competing centres of power. Empires have been unwilling or unable to close their frontiers and they have claimed to be, and often succeeded in being, literally boundless (Colas, 2006: 19). In the early twentieth century frontiers were seen as a necessary safety valve, belt of separation or 'moving periphery' between expanding states. And frontier societies are frequently seen as exemplars of nature, barbarity, rudeness, disorder and irreligion (Geiger, 2002) – influenced by the Turnerian frontier thesis and the idea that frontiers were to be tamed, settled and civilised (Newman and Passi, 1998: 189). It is assumed that frontiers will wither away or be swallowed up as a single political authority establishes hegemony over a region – ultimately frontiers harden into state boundaries as part of a linear and irreversible process (Geiger, 2002).

## Borders and borderlands

> States as territorially demarcated institutions have always imposed barriers, whether to deter armies, tax trade, protect domestic producers or keep out 'undesirables'.
>
> (Andreas, 2003: 78)

States were no longer satisfied with 'rough edges' and they saw a need to define sharper boundaries between citizens with rights and duties and aliens. Whereas empires sought to control people, states sought to control territory (Colas, 2006). State borders are understood to be fixed, legal, geopolitical entities. They establish fences between sovereignties, mediating exchanges between states, between states and non-state actors and between actors in the centre and periphery (Blanchard, 2005: 691). Legal and political sovereignty was confirmed cartographically (Hirst, 2005), codified in treaties and sanctioned in law. Borders were mapped onto pre-existing socio-cultural boundaries and frequently did not coincide with them. Most states are 'younger' than the societies they purport to administer and the demarcation of borders preceded nation building. States in many developing countries continue to pursue the same processes of political and administrative pacification as their colonial predecessors – which Scott (2007) refers to as the 'last great enclosure'. Modern borderlands mark the sovereign frontiers of the state and they mimic classical frontiers in the sense of being 'non-state spaces', characterised by fuzzy, mobile and permeable boundaries between the 'civilised' centre and the 'unruly' periphery. As discussed below, wars (and the transition from war to peace) involve a redrawing of these boundaries and a re-calibration of the power relationships underpinning them.

Rather than use the term 'borderland' as a 'catch all' phrase for marginal regions, a tentative typology is proposed here to give the term more analytical 'bite' and to further theorise about the relationships between borderlands and peacebuilding.

*Classical borderlands*: regions situated on the edges of states which straddle an international border. Borders separate people and the separating qualities of these borders influence interactions between them (Baud and van Schendel, 1997). Where the borderland periphery ends and the state-controlled centre begins may be conceptualised as a mobile, semi-permeable, internal frontier – a zone of transition from low to high administrative intensity and where the 'border effect' has become less significant than the 'state effect'.[1] As Baud and van Schendel (1997) argue, rather than conceptualising the zones on each side of the border as separate regions, they might be more usefully conceptualised and studied as a single spatial unit. The openness of the border and regional development patterns influence the level of inter-dependence and integration between the two territories – which may vary along a continuum from alienated to integrated borderlands (Martinez, 1994).

*Internal borderlands*: regions which do not straddle an international border, but remain non-state spaces because of weak state penetration or (re)emerge as semi-autonomous zones because of state breakdown. Some regions may have certain physical characteristics which lend themselves to 'illegibility' and resistance, including mountains, forests, marshes and deserts (Scott, 2000). Such areas represent unpromising sites for statebuilding because of low population density, extensive forms of agriculture and frequently an insurrectionary tradition (ibid.). The Federally Administered Tribal Areas of Pakistan (FATA) constitute both an internal borderland, which is subject to different laws from the rest of Pakistan, and also a classical borderland, straddling the 'Durrand Line' that divides Afghanistan and Pakistan. Arguably in peacetime, internal administrative boundaries have more impact on daily life for most individuals than national and international boundaries (Newman and Paasi, 1998: 197). And in wartime the same applies to the often mutating and moving boundaries of internal borderlands (see Chapter 15, this volume). It is in these dangerous liminal spaces, on the edges of competing politico-military regimes where the most extreme forms of violence and predation are enacted.

If we understand internal borderlands as non-state spaces, then they are not the exclusive preserve of developing or war-affected countries. They exist wherever state rules are suspended, within the territory of a state. For instance, at a micro level, internal borderlands exist within urban environments as territory is carved up by street gangs and certain zones become virtually no-go areas for state officials. Gated communities, off-shore tax havens and US detention centres, though very different in most respects, all are bounded spaces created to evade state rules and regulations – they fall outside or 'below' the law, enabling state or private actors to side step responsibilities, duties and restraints normally associated with states.

*Frontier states and global borderlands*: in many respects these mimic classical imperial frontiers, situated on the edge of politically and militarily controlled imperial space; a zone of transition of low administrative intensity outside the centres of empire (Moraya, 2003: 271). Mark Duffield (2001) uses the term 'borderlands' to denote the unruly regions on the edges of the 'liberal peace'. Entire regions may become non-state spaces, when states collapse and borders dissolve (or become privatised) as occurred during the 1990s in Afghanistan and Somalia. These 'bad neighbourhoods' (or regional conflict systems) are commonly perceived to be pathologies of the margins – excluded from, or failing to integrate into, the globalised economy.

But there is plenty of evidence to suggest the opposite: that war and shadow economies are highly integrated into global structures and processes. Borderland populations and wartime entrepreneurs have learned to cope or profit from the high degrees of political and economic extroversion associated with state collapse. War in Afghanistan, for instance, has led to greater integration, not less, as shown by the growth of the drugs industry. This has involved the transformation of the rural economy, which has shifted from predominantly subsistence agriculture to the production of a cash-based export crop. Therefore, borderlands are far from being disconnected or marginal, as the events of 9/11 confirmed. The new political economy of danger, as defined by the 'global war on terror', means that 'everywhere' becomes strategically critical. The global borderlands are too dangerous to be left alone. Liberal wars, a boundless, limitless form of warfare, have dismantled traditional conceptions of state boundaries. According to Vivienne Jabri, they aim at 'the transformation of the international from a location subject to the restrictions of sovereignty to one that is primarily defined in terms of humanity as a whole' (Jabri, 2007: 8). As Duffield (2005) argues, the new interventionary logic of the liberal peace signifies a shift from geopolitics to biopolitics, as a means of regulating the lives of borderland populations. In this paradigm development becomes an instrument to pacify and regulate unruly borderland zones by promoting forms of self reliance.

To summarise, borderlands are not isolated peripheries, but places located in an orbit of national and transnational networks of travel, trade, migration, knowledge exchanges, political alliances and conflicts (Aggarwal, 2004: 14). Each borderland has its own historic trajectory and specificities. The typology of borderlands advanced here denotes different zones or spaces, characterised by various levels or scales (global, national and local). These spaces are simultaneously inter-connected horizontally through the movement of people, ideas and commodities, while being separated vertically by borders and boundaries, underpinned and reinforced by power relations.[2] These boundaries delineate different forms of sovereignty, citizenship and regulatory regimes and far from being fixed and unchanging they are continually negotiated and contested – and as explored in the next section, these negotiations are likely to be at their most intense during periods of rapid transition.

## Peace-to-war transitions: borders, borderlands and civil wars

> The history of humanity is the history of wars and most wars have boundary change as at least one objective.
> 
> (Kolossov, 2005: 607)

Drawing on Richard's (2005) notion of a peace–war–peace bell curve or continuum, in order to understand the 'debordering' and 'rebordering' associated with war-to-peace transitions, the following section explores some of the connections linking borderlands with the emergence or sustenance of civil wars.

### A history of violence: where the Leviathan is a stranger[3]

The Kivus in the Democratic Republic of Congo (DRC) and FATA in Pakistan did not become borderlands with the advent of colonialism as they long constituted frontier zones (Jackson, 2006; Nichols, 2001). But colonialism left a violent legacy. FATA is a heavily militarised, oppressively policed borderland. The colonial regime invested in elaborate surveillance and intelligence networks and exercised brutality in protecting this strategic border. Even today the population possesses fewer civil liberties and democratic concessions than the rest of the country (Banerjee, 2001). Frontier crises led to transfrontier campaigns and a troubled frontier served as a convenient metaphor justifying imperial domination (ibid.). Therefore, for imperial powers, frontiers represented both a means of control of population and a source of threat (Hirst, 2005).

Rather than 'withering away', the frontier remained a zone of insecurity on the margins of the state. Many borderlands retain an insurrectionary tradition, as the sites of secessionist movements, indigenous rights struggles, millennial rebellions, regionalist agitation and armed opposition to lowland states (Scott, 2007: 12). States deal with troublesome borderlands in various ways. One is to resettle borderlanders elsewhere – Stalin's mass relocation of Chechens – or to settle loyal groups in borderland regions – Sinhalese settlers as frontiersmen of the Sri Lankan state in Tamil-speaking regions (Thangarajah, 2003). Another strategy is to rule indirectly through 'men of violence' on the frontier. As McCoy (1999: 130) notes, Burmese drug lords such as Khun Sa are manifestations of an ongoing and incomplete process of state formation: 'In these mountain and maritime fringes, weak state control can provide an opening for men of prowess – pirates, bandits, warlords or ethnic chiefs – to mediate between the centre and its margins.' And instability on the margins has played a catalytic role in state formation – what Gallant (1999) calls a 'border effect' – by forcing the Rangoon government to impose control over its frontier. Frontier wars may be the driving force for military innovation – a moving frontier was crucial to the formation of the Ottoman empire, which in the fifteenth and sixteenth centuries developed an effective state machine and army commissariat and became a society organised for war (Hirst, 2005: 104).

'Low capacity regimes' (Tilly, 2003), which have limited penetration of society, tend to unleash violence as a tool of governance. As Reno (2000) argues, shadow state rulers like Zaire's Sese Mobutu sought to make life *less* secure for their populations. Borderland elites may play a crucial mediating role, acting as power brokers with the capacity to extend the influence of the state or make the borderlands ungovernable. Because of their history of violence, borderlands are frequently militarised zones. Political authority resides in the barracks and police headquarters (Geiger, 2002: 8), and the border landscape may be dominated by forts, barbed wire, settlements and internment camps. Frequently, the Leviathan is a stranger, as borderlands are usually administered by outsiders who are distant from the border. Some borders have higher salience, remain harder and are more militarised than others because of a perception of external threats. The 'performance' of security at borders works to conjure the authorial power of the state (Taussig cited in Bornstein, 2002: 213). As Bornstein argues, West Bank–Israel border closures work against terror, but not terrorism in the sense that they reassure the Israeli public of their security, whilst having little impact on the objective threat of terrorism (ibid.: 214).

Imperial frontiers were managed and monitored but rarely passively defended (Hirst, 2005). Modern states similarly intervene in other people's borderlands in order to secure their own borders. Israel uses settlements across its borders as an antidote to uncontrolled Palestinian population growth and as part of a defensive system which begins with placing civilians on the front line and ends in layer upon layer of security in order to secure 'security' (Mendel, 2007: 13). James Ron usefully distinguishes between 'ghettoes', which are marginal spaces within states, and 'frontiers', which are borderlands in neighbouring states. The crucial difference is the extent to which the state controls these arenas and feels a bureaucratic, moral and political sense of responsibility for their fate (Ron, 2003: 9). According to Ron, states police ghettoes, but deploy despotic violence in frontiers, illustrated by the differential treatment meted out by the Serbian state to Muslims living inside and outside its borders. The territorial border thus marks a boundary between legality and violence. Borders shape state violence in dramatic ways, shifting the state's coercive repertoire from ethnic cleansing to policing and vice versa (ibid.).

However, the norm of territorial integrity means that military violations of sovereignty can be costly for states. To some extent, government agents are 'caged' by international borders: 'sovereignty grants states an advantage in the domestic use of force, but it also confines that force to a given geographic area' (Salehyan, 2007: 224). Because they are less constrained by national boundaries, states often work through non-state proxies in order to influence events across their borders. For example, Pakistan funded, trained and provided a safe haven for rebel groups in order to pursue strategic objectives in Kashmir and Afghanistan. In civil wars and insurgencies, the existence of sanctuaries in neighbouring states provides an opportunity for rebel mobilisation, gives the rebels bargaining power and reduces the probability of government victory (ibid.). Military technology and tactics also influence these bargaining processes. For instance, in Afghanistan, technological innovations have historically had the effect of re-calibrating power relations between the centre and the periphery – from the introduction of matchlock rifles in the nineteenth century (Barfield, 2004) to stinger missiles during the Cold War conflict and the use of improvised explosive devices and suicide bombing in the current neo-Taliban insurgency.

War interacts with, and shapes, space and boundaries in complex ways (Hirst, 2005: 52). Prolonged conflict may forge new connections between unstable borderlands – linking, for example, Kashmir, FATA, southern Afghanistan and the Ferghana valley – which become 'neuralgia points' in a wider regional conflict system (Pugh and Cooper, 2004). Notions of core and periphery may change – for radicalised Islamists, the Afghan–Pakistan borderlands, far from being peripheral constitute a centre and a training ground for global jihad. Transnational terrorism, according to Appadurai, has created a new geography of anger, blurring the boundary between military and civilian space and divorcing war from the idea of nation (2006: 92).

## Borders, belonging and purification

As Migdal notes, people live in a 'world of multiple types of boundaries overlapping one another. Those boundaries produce numerous mental maps, and they generate many different forms of belonging' (2004: 23). States aim to harden certain boundaries and dissolve others. Citizenship explicitly ties populations to unique, territorially defined polities. Citizens undergo a lifelong process of 'territorial socialization' (Duchacek in Newman and Passi, 1998), involving boundary-related narratives which manifest themselves in social and cultural practices and legislation, as well as in films, novels, memorials, ceremonies and public events (Newman and Paasi, 1998: 196). The state as an 'imagined community' is conjured up through the production of its flip side, the 'margin' (Das and Poole, 2004). The idea of a purposive centre is produced through various forms of marginalization of groups, regions and concerns (Lund, 2006; Migdal, 2004). The production of in-groups and out-groups is fundamental to the building of nationhood. Statecraft involves processes of 'othering' or the creation of dangerous populations, and hostility to out-groups increases in-group cohesiveness (Migdal, 2004a).

Violence is a way of redrawing boundaries, of producing certainty – Appadurai's 'vivisectionist violence' that seeks to eliminate difference. According to Appadurai, the sense of social uncertainty which drives projects of ethnic cleansing is heightened by globalisation, which simultaneously blurs boundaries and creates new incentives for cultural purification: 'The virtually complete loss of even the fiction of a national economy... now leaves the cultural field as the main one in which fantasies of purity, authenticity, borders and security can be enacted' (Appadurai, 2006: 23).

It is at borders where the nation is experienced most intimately in the daily dramas of chauvinism that monitor identity and citizenship and where extremism frequently flourishes (Aggarwal, 2004; Ron, 2003: 14). Sinhala nationalism, for example, emerged from Sri Lanka's southern periphery, as a critique of the political elites at the centre. A study of practices and performance at the Uzbekistan border highlights its central role in the dynamics of identity formation: 'the border whilst at the skin of the state literally, rhetorically is at its heart' (Megoran et al., 2005: 735).

But rulers' efforts to draw an unbroken line between state power, sovereignty and territory do not go uncontested. State 'simplifications', including attempts to purify and unmix populations, are works in progress and invariably meet resistance from above and below. Borderlands are hybrid zones, where identity is constantly negotiated, thus contaminating notions of purity and unsettling orderliness (Aggarwal, 2004). The political loyalty of borderland populations cannot be guaranteed. Borderland elites use cross-border political networks to give them leverage with regard to the state, and their authority may be weakened if they are seen to be agents of the state rather than protectors of local rights and concerns.

Borders are both containers of nationalism and conduits of transnationalism. People, ideas and commodities cross and challenge the border. Migrants unsettle the glue that attaches persons to ideologies of soil and territory (Appadurai, 2006: 19). Diasporic communities may challenge the notion of a unitary, territorially defined national entity (Adamson, 2006: 183). Globalisation processes, it has been argued, threaten the particularity of places, borders and territoriality (Mlinar, 1992, cited in Newman and Paasi, 1998: 193). But Andreas (2003: 78) convincingly argues that geopolitics has been transformed, but not transcended. States far from losing control of their borders are retooling and reconfiguring their border regulatory apparatus to prioritise policing. The EU border control strategy, for example, has involved turning immediate eastern neighbours into law enforcement buffer zones. Borders can therefore be seen as 'enactments of power.... diagnostics of how the apparatus of rule unfolds in the global landscape' (Cunningham, 2004: 345).

As the EU example shows borders are never static – they emerge, exist and disappear (Newman and Passi, 1998). Wars may accelerate and intensify processes of rebordering and debordering. Borders do not disappear, they multiply, as public space becomes privatised and a logic of plunder prevails. The borders may be extremely fluid, in many respects replicating pre-state forms of 'itinerant territoriality' (Abraham and Van Schendel, 2005: 11). Conflict entrepreneurs, may mimic the efforts of the state to unmix and 'purify' populations, by extruding unwanted groups – for example the LTTE forcing out Muslims from the Jaffna peninsular – and the targeting of individuals who aim to soften or transgress boundaries.

## Borderland economies

As already noted, marginal frontier regions on the edges of imperial space frequently became marginal borderlands on the edges of states. In Southeast Asia, people have historically moved to the margins, usually the hills, to escape the civilisational project of the valleys. Their modes of production were alien, or illegible, to the intruding state (Scott, 2007). Extensive forms of agriculture can be understood as a form of 'escape agriculture' designed to thwart state-appropriation. In Afghanistan to this day Pashtun tribes that remained in the hills and deserts continue to draw a sharp distinction between themselves with their tax-free way of life (*nang*) and those Pashtuns who live under state control and pay taxes (*qalang*) (Barfield, 2004: 26). Borderlands can be understood as 'spaces of avoidance', where much that goes on is less than fully legal – in fact, they have a comparative advantage in illegality, with the allure of high economic windfalls attracting 'adventure entrepreneurs', settlers and criminal groups (Geiger, 2002: 11). Logging companies in the Amazon basin or mining contractors in the DRC are attracted by the high opportunity–high risk environment, in which there is limited government regulation.

But few borderland groups entirely resist state incorporation. David Turton (2005) describes how Ethiopian agro-pastoralists were drawn into the spatial practices of the state, by becoming dependent on values, norms and technologies which lay beyond their own means of production and control. Insecurity on the periphery may be the catalyst for government-supported development programmes. For example in Afghanistan, the Helmand Valley Authority, a government-implemented and US-funded dam project during the 1950s and 1960s, constituted an (unsuccessful) attempt to sedentarise and incorporate the unruly tribes in the southern and eastern borderlands of the country (Cullather, 2002).

Not all borderlands are economically marginal. The Jaffna peninsular on the northern margins of the Sri Lankan state and the heartland of the Tamil insurgency was historically an advanced region – due in large part to the legacy of missionary education, which meant that Jaffna Tamils tended to be over-represented in the public sector and professional classes. In Moldova, the breakaway republic of Transdniestria is more industrially advanced than the rest of the country and benefited from close political and economic ties to Russia. In both cases, secessionist conflicts were associated with a sudden shift in centre–periphery relations, as a result of new state policies in the areas of education, language and employment, which threatened the privileged positions of borderland elites.

Borders fence wealth (van Houtum, 2002: 39) and are a means of protection for a territorialised economy. They define who will pay taxes and where taxes are collected. Conversely, an open frontier operates as an automatic brake on what the state can extract. Hard borders may embody extreme economic divides. Ports of entry – airports, seaports, border roads and bridge crossings – act as the checkpoints that selectively deny or allow entry to people and commodities. The dramatic images of dehydrated, illegal African immigrants landing on European beaches in the Canary Islands illustrate extreme difference across a slender border. For such immigrants, the world far from being a borderless, open terrain is a 'jigsaw puzzle of socially unequal spaces with check-points or passage ways between them' (Heyman, 2004: 304).

Value steps up or down at borders, for example when heroin crosses the Afghan–Iranian border the price increases four-fold. For economists, borders are above all the site for the establishment of relations of difference which give rise to exchange. Difference, not homogeneity, is what makes for the richness of exchange, connecting economic systems, in which, typically, two or more currencies circulate. Therefore borders create opportunities and they are not simply zones of separation or obstacle points.

Borderland communities learn to reconcile arbitrary state policy with economic rationality: 'A frontier dweller's loyalty to his own country may ... be emphatically modified by his economic self interest in illegal dealings with the foreigners across the border' (Lattimore, cited by Donnan and Wilson, 1999: 87). Borders therefore create incentives for transgression and for borderland populations they constitute a resource, an opportunity to profit. At a microlevel gatekeeper livelihoods emerge around borders – from soldiers extracting bribes at checkpoints to customs officials skimming off a percentage of goods and materials. At a macrolevel entire regions may depend on economic activities generated by the border – for example, the arbitrage economy of the Afghan–Pakistan borderlands is a product of long-standing differences in regulatory regimes and cross-border social ties.[4] The hardening of this border would likely lead to a social explosion, given the lack of alternative economic opportunities on both sides. Paradoxically, the securitisation of a border may increase the incentives for transgression, since the more heavily policed the border, the higher the associated risk premium and consequently the profits both for gatekeepers and smugglers.

The dynamics of cross-border trade are never static – they are susceptible to fluctuations in the wider market economy, social and political events and the changing institutional arrangements at the border. On the Afghan–Tajik border the drugs trade underwent significant changes after the emergence of the Karzai regime in 2002. During the 1990s the trade was highly decentralised, reflecting the fragmented nature of power structures, both at the border and at a national level. Relatively small shipments – usually raw opium – crossed a poorly policed border through multiple crossing points along the Amu Darya river. With 'post-conflict' statebuilding on both sides of the border, there has been a level of political consolidation, growing efforts to police the border and an increased centralisation of the drugs trade. The pattern of flows has consequently changed from a 'capillary action' of multiple crossing points to a 'funnel action' pattern involving larger shipments, mostly in the form of heroin, and fewer crossing points controlled by a smaller number of state and non-state players.

Cross-border smugglers attempt to 'outwit' the state, but paradoxically they reaffirm the very borders which they seek to subvert, as without borders these activities would simply cease to exist (Wilson and Donnan, 1998). Therefore, because smugglers depend upon the existences of states and borders they are rarely revolutionaries. Shadow economies are part of the 'subversive but integral underbelly of the state, undermining it at the same time as they constitute it' (ibid.: 106). And frequently state agents collude in its perpetration. However, there is a constant tension between the centripetal thrust of statebuilding and the centrifugal dynamic of borderland economies. Historically, contrabanders have actively contested the expansion of states, refusing to relinquish older trading patterns, or establishing new ones (Tagliacozza, 2005). Smuggling was a mode of resistance to geographic and political changes brought about by growing states. It was also a means by which local people tilted these changes to their advantage (ibid.). Smuggling and other illicit practices structured relationships between border people and the state and imposed limits on the exercise of power.

Borderland economies may become entwined with organised crime, armed rebel organisations and terrorist networks. Andreas (2003), for example, highlights the role played by transnational criminal networks in providing the material basis for the Bosnian conflict. Similarly, the Kurdistan Workers Party is reported to be heavily involved in human trafficking in order to raise money for the conflict with Turkey and to smuggle in supporters engaged in political activities in Europe (Adamson, 2006: 193). During wartime there may be a reversal of pre-war economic and political relations with the political centre of gravity shifting to the border regions, which also become the areas where economic surplus is generated. The centre may increasingly become dependent on economic activities in the hinterland. Neighbouring states also use and profit from the instability of an open frontier. For example, Rwanda treats the Kivus as both a zone of demographic expansion and a source of wealth (Reyntjens, 2005: 602).

## War-to-peace transitions: redrawing boundaries with blood?[5]

With the end of civil war, as David Keen notes, there is 'unlikely to be a clean break from violence to consent, from theft to production, from repression to democracy, or from impunity to accountability' (2000: 10). Just as outbreaks of war are usually preceded by other forms of violence, so war-to-peace transitions are inherently conflictual and involve strong continuities between wartime and peacetime conditions. They may be as much about the *reproduction* as the transformation of political and economic relations – for instance, the 'sell game' tactics of warring factions may be reproduced in peacetime patterns of corruption as has occurred in Sierra Leone and Afghanistan. Therefore, war and peace may be better understood as concurrent and competing modes of existence, rather than alternating phases in the ordering of social relations (Richards, 2005: 12).

Although they rarely represent a clean break with the past, successful war-to-peace transitions do involve new forms of political order and hegemony and the redrawing of boundaries (between state and non-state, legal and illegal, in-group and out-group), the re-establishment (and re-imagining) of state borders and the re-calibration of relations between centre and periphery. Peace settlements have involved the mutual recognition of borders or boundaries. The three major phases of rebordering in the twentieth century followed two world wars and the end of the Cold War – the Soviet Union's collapse alone creating more than 20 new boundaries (Newman and Passi, 1998: 190). Historically, conquest and annexation in war were common. However, since the Second World War, the norm of fixed borders has grown stronger (Atzili, 2007) and after 1950 there have been only ten cases of foreign military conquest of homeland territory. Perhaps because borders were historically 'redrawn with blood', borderlands and political borders 'have largely been studied in the context of conflict, separation, partition and barriers as contrasted with peace, contact, unification and bridges' (Newman and Passi, 1998: 190). This mirrors a gap in the wider policy literature, in the sense that more is known about the political economy of war than how a political economy of peace emerges from the ashes of war (see Chapter 1, this volume).

In the mainstream policy discourse, peacebuilding and statebuilding have become synonymous. Statebuilding is viewed as the antidote for failing, fragile or collapsed states. Although the spatial dimensions of peacebuilding are rarely dealt with explicitly in the literature, statebuilding is understood to involve the diffusion of power outwards – by mobilising coercion, capital and legitimacy – in order to tame the unruly borderlands. In this centripetal approach, statebuilding involves various forms of 'enclosure'.

Re-establishing control over external borders is one of the most basic requirements of statehood – this includes border recognition by external powers and the creation of institutions able to secure and police the borders. Concentrating the means of coercion and establishing the regulatory regime to control flows of commodities and people across the border may be an early priority for 'post-conflict' states – since the border areas often become the primary sites of accumulation during wartime, and a war-to-peace transition can involve competition for control of key points of entry and the revenue flows generated through trade and customs. New institutional arrangements around the border lead to changes in its permeability for particular groups and commodities – border 'hardening' for drugs (which increases the risk premium and therefore profits for traffickers) may be accompanied by border 'softening' to facilitate legitimate trade in an attempt to squeeze the illicit and grow the licit economy.

Although borders may not shift as a result of war, it is people who give meaning to borders, and relations across the border as well as within it may be subjected to repeated re-definition (Wilson and Donnan, 1998). For certain groups, the legitimacy of the border may be called into question as peoples' 'mental maps' and 'checkpoints' change. War may empower borderland groups to challenge the border, as appears to have happened with the Kurds in post-invasion Iraq and Turkey.

War-to-peace transitions may also involve processes of internal 'de-bordering', with the state attempting to re-establish control over internal borderlands and extend its reach to the periphery. State 'simplifications' range from, at the most basic level, removing road blocks and disarming private militias, to more sophisticated strategies that aim to make society more legible (e.g., re-establishing the capacity for census making) as well as undercutting internal boundary activation dynamics (e.g., constitutional reform relating to language policies and/or minority rights). International peacekeeping missions may inadvertently have the effect of freezing internal boundaries as has been the case, for example, in Moldova/Transdniestria and Nagorno–Karabakh. They may also override the complex bargaining processes between core and periphery as did the CIA's arming of regional strongmen in Afghanistan.

Central to the peacebuilding problematic is the re-forging of the relationship between the central state and its margins. This centripetal approach to statebuilding was exemplified in post Bonn Afghanistan's 'shock therapy' centralisation. The country's new constitution made Afghanistan one of the most centralised states in the world on paper, though power in practice was highly fragmented. Historically, state formation in Afghanistan involved complex bargaining processes between central state and borderland elites, and the emergence of political order depended upon the creation of complex inter-dependencies and jointly controlled institutions giving both groups access to revenue streams derived from trade, aid and agricultural production.

These bargaining processes between state and borderlands, which it is argued here are central to war-to-peace transitions, can be conceptualised as a 'double diamond' model.[6] In the case of Afghanistan and Pakistan it involves a common border (the 'Durrand Line') and four sets of actors (at each point of the diamond) in each country: international/transnational players, central elites, borderland elites, and borderland populations. The different points of the diamond interact with each other, both within a country and with other players across the border. In addition, the model is complicated further by the fact that central elites have to simultaneously engage with and/or manage other borderlands, in this case on the borders with Tajikistan, Uzbekistan, Turkmenistan and Iran. The 'post-conflict' transition has involved a complex renegotiation and rebalancing of this matrix of vertical and horizontal relationships, as illustrated by interactions following the Bonn Agreement of December 2001.

- International policy on Afghanistan does not happen in isolation to the (often contradictory) policies pursued in relation to Pakistan. And a highly internationalised (and militarised) presence in Afghanistan has had a destabilising impact on the political dynamics in Pakistan's borderlands.
- Borderland populations move freely across the border and so influence one another. For example, *madrassas* in Pakistan have exported their radical Islamic doctrine across the border. Similarly, fighters move backwards and forwards across the border with Pakistan's tribal areas having become sanctuaries for the Taliban.
- Central state elites in Pakistan build alliances with, and support, borderland elites and populations in Afghanistan in order to pursue a strategy of asymmetric warfare. Similarly, central elites in Afghanistan have stirred up irredentist sentiments among the Pashtun population in Pakistan.
- Peripheral elites are able to circumvent the centre and build their autonomy *vis-à-vis* the state through links to international (e.g., CIA funding of regional strongmen, Pakistan's support for the Taliban) and transnational actors (e.g., religious networks, the international drugs mafia).

Evidently, the reality is far more complex than this model implies. One needs to disaggregate players at each point of the diamond since none of them can be treated as unitary actors – for example, international players have multiple and conflicting interests in Afghanistan which is reflected in competing and contradictory policies.

## Conclusion

Borderlands are central to the dimensions of war and peace, yet they tend to be peripheral to policy discourse and practice. In war-to-peace transitions these reflect several factors.

First, the 'grand bargain' of the peace settlement has a crucial impact on the balance of power in the post-conflict moment. In the case of Afghanistan, the Bonn Agreement prioritised the interests of borderland elites from the north of the country (notably Tajiks from the Panshir) but marginalised Pashtuns and the interests of Pakistan, thus leading to disaffected borderland groups unwilling to support the new political dispensation.

Second, at the risk of oversimplifying there is a constant tension between the centripetal thrust of the state policy of enclosure and control versus the centrifugal tendency of borderland elites who prioritise autonomy and mobility. The analysis in this chapter has placed borderlands, and particularly peripheral elites, at the centre of peacebuilding processes. In Afghanistan they act as both the connective tissue between the state and the borderlands and a constant source of friction. They have the capacity to either extend the control of the state or make the borderland ungovernable. Their ability to leverage patronage and resources, because of their proximity to the border gives them a great deal of autonomy. Institutional arrangements on the border are therefore not only reflective of, but constitutive of power relations. For instance, an open or semi-porous border gives borderland elites greater leverage and acts as a brake on the state's ability to mobilise capital, coercion and legitimacy.

Third, neighbouring countries act differently in other people's borderlands than they do in their own. Both countries have acted with less restraint and responsibility when operating through proxies across the border, thus suggesting the critical importance of regional approaches to peacebuilding.

Fourth, in high-profile peace operations, statebuilding takes on a highly extroverted form. International actors clearly have an important influence on the bargaining processes between domestic players. But their impacts are often contradictory and perverse. For instance, there is a major contradiction between the centripetal thrust of statebuilding and the centrifugal effects of economic policies which emphasise open trade regimes, limited state control and open borders.

Fifth, liberal wars as already mentioned signify a new border politics, and have important implications for the domestic politics of intervening countries. The war on terror with its focus on pre-emptive action, surveillance and policing, is leading to the deeper penetration of Western societies by eroding the boundary between the public and the private sphere.

Thus a range of factors influence the nature of the war-to-peace transition including the pre-conflict state and the configuration of centre–periphery relations; the nature and legacies of the conflict; the inclusiveness and perceived legitimacy of the peace settlement; the role of international actors during and after the war; specific policy choices by domestic and international players; and the regional environment, particularly the role of neighbouring states. While borderlands may be neuralgia points in civil wars, they may also have the potential to be strategic nodes in peacebuilding processes. There is plenty of scope, and a need for further comparative research which explores the precise nature of the linkages between borders, borderlands and particular war-to-peace transitions.

## Notes

1. Baud and van Schendel (1997) divide the zones within borderlands into a border heartland (which abuts the border and is dominated by its existence), an intermediate borderland and an outer border.
2. I am grateful to Paolo Novak for this idea of the 'horizontal' and 'vertical' aspects of boundaries.
3. This term is borrowed from Geiger (2002: 1).
4. The Afghan Transit Trade Agreement allows Afghanistan, as a land locked country, to import from Pakistan via Karrachi port various items tax free. Legally imported goods into Afghanistan are then smuggled back across the border into Pakistan, thus undercutting local markets.
5. Taken from a comment by Bill Clinton that 'The current era does not reward people who struggle in vain to redraw borders with blood' (cited in Atzili, 2007: 144).
6. This draws upon Baud and van Schendel (1997), but they use a double triangular model which misses out the critical role of international actors.

## References

Abraham, Itty and Willem van Schendel, 2005, 'Introduction. The Making of Illicitness', in van Schendel and Abraham (eds), *Illicit Flows and Criminal Things*, Bloomington, IN: Indiana University Press.

Adamson, Fiona, 2006, 'Crossing Borders. International Migration and National Security', *International Security*, Vol. 31, No. 1, pp. 165–99.

Aggarwal, Ravina, 2004, *Beyond Lines of Control. Performance and Politics on the Disputed Borders of Lakakh, India*, Durham, NC: Duke University Press.

Andreas, Peter, 2003, 'Redrawing the Line: Borders and Security in the Twenty-first Century', *International Security*, Vol. 28, No. 2, pp. 78–111.

Appadurai, Arjun, 2006, *Fear of Small Numbers. An essay on the Geography of Anger*, Durham, NC: Duke University Press.

Atzili, Boaz, 2007, 'When Good Fences Make Bad Neighbours. Fixed Borders, State Weakness, and International Conflict', *International Security*, Vol. 31, No. 3, pp. 139–73.

Banerjee, Mukulika, 2001, *Pathan Unarmed*, Oxford: James Currey.

Barfield, Thomas, 2004, 'Problems in Establishing Legitimacy in Afghanistan', *Iranian Studies*, Vol. 37, No. 2, pp. 263–93.

Baud, Michiel and Willem van Schendel, 1997, 'Towards a Comparative History of Borderlands', *Journal of World History*, Vol. 8, No. 2, pp. 211–42.

Blanchard, Jean-Marc F., 2005, 'Linking Borders Disputes and War: An Institutional-Statist Theory', *Geopolitics*, Vol. 10, pp. 688–711.

Bornstein, Avram S., 2002, 'Borders and the Utility of Violence. State Effects on the "Superexploitation" of West Bank Palestinians', *Critique of Anthropology*, Vol. 22, No. 2, pp. 201–20.

Colas, Alexandro, 2006, *Empire*, Cambridge: Polity.

Cullather, Nick, 2002, 'Damming Afghanistan: Modernization in a Buffer State', *The Journal of American History*, Vol. 89, No. 3, pp. 512–37.

Cunningham, Hilary, 2004, 'Nations Rebound? Crossing Borders in a Gated Globe', *Identities: Global Studies in Culture and Power*, Vol. 11, No. 3, pp. 329–50.

Das, Veena and Deborah Poole (eds), 2004, *Anthropology in the Margins of the State*, Oxford: James Currey.

Donnan, Hastings and Wilson Thomas (1999), *Borders: Frontiers of Identity, Nation and State*, Oxford Berg.

Duffield, Mark, 2001, *Global Governance and the New Wars: The Merging of Development and Security*, London: Zed Books.

Duffield, Mark, 2005, 'Getting Savages to Fight Barbarians: Development, Security and the Colonial Present', *Conflict, Security & Development*, Vol. 5, No. 2, pp. 141–160.

Gallant, Thomas, 1999, 'Brigandage, Piracy, Capitalism and State-Formation: Transnational Crime from a Historical World System Perspective', in Josiah McC. Heyman (ed.), *States and Illegal Practices*, Oxford: Berg.

Geiger, Jeffrey and Danilo Petrović, 2002, 'Turner in the Tropics: The Frontier Concept Revisited', paper at the workshop on 'Dimensions, Dynamics and Transformation of Resource Conflicts between Indigenous Peoples and Settlers in Frontier Regions in South and Southeast Asia', Mt.-Soleil St. Imier, Switzerland, 25–29 Sept.

Heyman, Josiah, 2004, 'Ports of Entry as Nodes in the World System', *Identities: Global Studies in Culture and Power*, Vol. 11, pp. 303–27.

Hirst, Paul, 2005, *Space and Power: Politics, War and Architecture*, Cambridge: Polity.

Jabri, Vivienne, 2007, *War and the Transformation of Global Politics*, Basingstoke: Palgrave Macmillan.

Jackson, Stephen, 2006, 'Borderlands and the Transformation of War Economies: Lessons from the DRC', *Conflict, Security & Development*, Vol. 6, No. 6, pp. 425–48.

Keen, David, 2000, 'War and Peace: What's the Difference?', *International Peacekeeping*, Vol. 7, No. 4, pp. 1–22.

Kolossov, Vladimir, 2005, 'Theorizing Borders. Border Studies: Changing Perspectives and Theoretical Approaches', *Geopolitics*, Vol. 10, No. 4, pp. 606–32.

Lund, Christian, 2006, 'Twilight Institutions: An Introduction', *Development and Change*, Vol. 37, No. 4, pp. 673–84.

Martinez, Oscar, 1994, *Border People: Life and Society in the U.S.-Mexico Borderlands*, Tucson: University of Arizona Press.

McCoy, Alfred, 1999, 'Requiem for a Drug Lord: State and Commodity in the Career of Khun Sa', in Josiah Heyman (ed.), *States and Illegal Practices*, Oxford: Berg, pp. 129–67.

Megoran, Nick, Gael Raballand and Jerome Bouyou, 2005, 'Performance, Representation and the Economics of Border Control in Uzbekistan', *Geopolitics*, Vol. 10, No. 4, pp. 712–40.

Mendel, Yonatan, 2007, 'Imagined Territories', *London Review of Books*, Vol. 29, No. 15, 2 August, pp. 13–14.

Migdal, Joel, 2004, *Boundaries and Belonging. States and Societies in the Struggle to Shape Identities and Local Practices*, Cambridge: Cambridge University Press.

Migdal, Joel, 2004a, 'Statebuilding and the Non-Nation State', *Journal of International Affairs*, Vol. 58, No. 1, pp. 17–46.

Moraya, A., 2003, 'Rethinking the State from the Frontier', *Millennium: Journal of International, Studies*, Vol. 3, No. 2, pp. 267–92.

Newman, David and Anssi Paasi, 1998, 'Fences and Neighbours in the Post Modern World: Boundary Narratives in Political Geography', *Progress in Human Geography*, Vol. 22, No. 2, pp. 186–207.

Nichols, Robert, 2001, *Settling the Frontier. Land, Law and Society in the Peshawar Valley, 1500–1900*, Oxford: Oxford University Press.

Pugh, Michael and Neil Cooper with Jonathan Goodhand, 2004, *War Economies in a Regional Context: The Challenge of Transformation*, Boulder, CO: Lynne Rienner.

Reno, William, 2000, 'Shadow States and the Political Economy of Civil Wars', in Mats Berdal and David Malone (eds), *Greed and Grievance: Economic Agendas in Civil Wars*, Boulder, CO: Lynne Rienner, pp. 43–68.

Reyntjens, Filip, 2005, 'The Privatization and Criminalization of Public Space in the Geopolitics of the Great Lakes Region', *Journal of Modern African Studies*, Vol. 43, pp. 587–607.

Richards, Paul, 2005, 'New War and Ethnographic Approach', in Richards (ed.), *No Peace No War. An Anthropology of Contemporary Armed Conflicts*, Oxford: James Currey, pp. 1–21.

Ron, James, 2003, *Frontiers and Ghettos. State Violence in Serbia and Israel*, Berkeley, CA: University of California Press.

Salehyan, Idean, 2007, 'Transnational Rebels: Neighbouring States as a Sanctuary for Rebel Groups', *World Politics*, Vol. 59, No. 2, pp. 217–42.

Scott, James C., 2000, 'Hill and Valley in Southeast Asia...or Why the State is the Enemy of People who Move Around...or...Why Civilizations Can't Climb Hills', paper at symposium on 'Development and the Nation State', Washington University, St. Louis, Feb.

Scott, James C., 2007, 'Introduction', in *The Moral Economy of the Peasant: Subsistence and Rebellion in Southeast Asia* (orig. 1976), New Haven: CT, Yale University Press.

Tagliacozza, Eric, 2005, *Secret Trades, Porous Borders. Smuggling and States Along a Southeast Asian Frontier, 1865–1915*, New Haven, CT: Yale University Press.

Thangarajah, Yuvi, 2003, 'Ethnicization of the Devolution Debate and the Militarization of Civil Society in North-Eastern Sri Lanka', in Markus Mayer, Dirini Rajasingham-Senanayake and Yuvi Thangarajah (eds), *Building Local Capacities for Peace: Rethinking Conflict and Development in Sri Lanka*, New Delhi: Macmillan.

Tilly, Charles, 2003, *The Politics of Collective Violence*, Cambridge: Cambridge University Press.

Turton, David, 2005, 'The Meaning of Place in a World of Movement: Lessons from Long-term Field Research in Southern Ethiopia', *Journal of Refugee Studies*, Vol. 18, No. 3, pp. 258–80.

van Houtum, Henk, 2002, 'Borders of Comfort: Spatial Economic Bordering Processes in the European Union', *Regional and Federal Studies*, Vol. 12, No. 4, pp. 35–58.

van Schendel, Willem, 2005, 'Spaces of Engagement: How Borderlands, Illegal Flows, and Territorial States Interlock', in van Schendel and Itty Abraham (eds), *Illicit Flows and Criminal Things*, Bloomington, IN: Indiana University Press.

# 14
## Microfinance and Borderlands: Impacts of 'Local Neoliberalism'

*Milford Bateman*

The October 2006 award of the Nobel Peace Prize jointly to Bangladesh's Grameen Bank and to Mohammad Yunus, Grameen's founder, crowned over a decade of unprecedented attention and media hype surrounding the concept of microfinance. The Grameen Bank's microfinance model was 'discovered' by the international development community in the 1980s. Thereafter it was quickly and extensively deployed as poverty reduction and local development policy within developing countries and, from 1990 onwards, in the newly designated transition economies too. The messy collapse of the former Yugoslavia from 1990 onwards provided the international development community with its first major test of the microfinance model in post-communist Eastern Europe, and it was subsequently operationalised in the Southeast Europe region as part of post-conflict reconstruction and development support.

The concept of 'borderlands' is particularly relevant in the economic and political geography of Southeast Europe. Historically, the Balkans region (bordered by Slovenia, Albania and Bulgaria) has been a rich *macedoine* of religions, ethnicities and cultures on the peripheries of Christian and Ottoman empires, the formal borders of communities and polities continually contested. With the collapse of Yugoslavia, Republic boundaries and border crossings were established, creating new external 'borders' and borderlands. Customs duties were imposed between new states and traditional markets made more difficult to access, in turn depleting hinterland cohesion and fostering smuggling. In some cases, notably in Bosnia and Herzegovina (BiH) and Kosovo, borders with neighbours were porous to unregulated trade (such as the Herzegovinian border with Croatia), or new ones were erected to control war assets and exact trade taxes (as around Bihać). In Tito's Yugoslavia extractive industries, the military-industrial complex and hydroelectric power had been important motors of development in rural areas, and a pattern of 'decentralised concentration' of heavy industry and agricultural processing arose, notably in Bosnian cities such as Bihać, Mostar, Banja Luka, Travnik, Zenica and Tuzla. This ensured a degree of economic balance between all parts of the country and avoided 'hot-spots' of marginalisation and severe poverty as might have been the case had the market been the primary determinant of industrial location and economic activity. But the decline and abandonment of industry since the early 1990s and the cultivation of cantonal, entity and state economic boundaries after the Dayton Peace Accords have increased dependency on cross-boundary illicit activities and the informal economy, a trajectory significantly extended by the arrival of microfinance. In some borderland areas, such as in eastern Slavonia and Knin county in Croatia and in western Macedonia, the collapse of large-scale industry was inevitable once it was clear that there was no real financial support other than microfinance.

This chapter examines the rationale, progress and sustainable impact of the microfinance model in the region. After a summary of the core objectives of microfinance as 'local neoliberalism', the main part of the chapter explores the factors affecting the likely longer-run economic and social impacts of microfinance, with a particular spatial focus upon impacts made within borderland regions. While the microfinance model has generated some quick economic and social impacts just about everywhere, in the medium to longer term many of these quick poverty reduction gains have been reversed and, more seriously, it has manifestly helped establish a local institutional framework that is almost wholly antagonistic to sustainable post-conflict development and growth. Both in general terms and particularly with regard to borderlands, the microfinance model has worked to frustrate the post-conflict reconstruction and development effort underway in Southeast Europe since 1995, ultimately working against the establishment of a sustainable peace.

## Microfinance as 'local neoliberalism'

The fascination with microfinance has its genesis in Bangladesh in the 1970s and the pioneering work of Mohammad Yunus, who formally established the Grameen Bank in 1976 to provide small-scale working capital inputs that would allow the poor – primarily women – to begin or expand income-generating activities. By the mid-1980s, the international development community and the international financial institutions (IFIs) had begun to notice the rapid rise of microfinance institutions (MFIs), including Grameen-style 'clones' (e.g., BRAC also in Bangladesh, PRODEM in Bolivia), and to accept claims that these were successfully reducing poverty and promoting local economic and social development. The IFIs quickly adopted the view that, with their help, there was enormous scope for the model to be replicated and the presumed benefits introduced elsewhere.

An equally attractive aspect of the Grameen concept for the IFIs, however, was the fact that the practice and ideology of microfinance were almost perfectly in tune with the core imperatives of neoliberalism (on the last, see Harvey, 2006). Largely because of its pioneering method of securing joint guarantees by groups of borrowers to repay the microloan of any defaulter among them (known as 'solidarity circles'), the Grameen Bank was able to achieve high repayment rates. In an era when the IFIs were imposing fiscal austerity upon all developing countries, and because many previous attempts to deal with poverty through state-subsidised, small-scale finance programmes were seen as expensive failures (Adams et al., 1984), an independent seemingly financially self-sustaining finance institution for the poor was an extremely attractive proposition. Here, according to Robinson (2001), was a radically new poverty reduction model that could be supported by the IFIs and international community, delivering financial services to the disadvantaged on a large scale through commercially oriented, independent and financially self-sustaining MFIs.

Neoliberals were also quick to see the usefulness of microfinance in furthering another core objective – to embed 'further down' in society the notion that development is a process exclusively involving individual entrepreneurial activity necessarily animated by the prospect of unlimited personal enrichment (see Friedman and Friedman, 1980). Realising this goal would also help to delegitimise and dismantle all 'bottom-up' attempts to propose, both through the democratic process and by popular pressure, alternative strategies that might primarily and directly benefit the majority, but which would circumscribe the power and freedom of established elites. To the extent that microentrepreneurship backed up by MFIs became universally embedded as the *sole* legitimate exit route out of poverty for both the individual and the community, especially with regard to women (see Feiner and Barker, 2007), demands for state intervention, robust social welfare programmes, income and wealth redistribution, and all forms of state, collective and cooperative ownership could be progressively blocked. Instead, microfinance would supposedly give the poor the 'freedom' to 'pull themselves up by their own bootstraps' and become 'empowered' through ownership of microenterprises.

Microfinance, as Weber (2002) argues, also became an important aspect of the IFIs' drive towards financial sector liberalisation. MFIs that have achieved financial self-sufficiency provide working examples to governments of 'efficient', subsidy-free, financial institutions. Other financial institutions would have to follow suit. Enormous effort has also been invested by the IFIs into ensuring that all MFIs, institutions, advisers and policymakers abide by 'market-driven' operating rules. In the same vein, microfinance has also been used to support privatisation by, for example, being deployed to temporarily maintain consumer demand and public support for privatised services in the face of price increases, such as in the water supply industry (see Shiva, 2002). Similarly, in India, Harper (2007: 258) reports that government officials deflect community demands for basic education and health services on the grounds that 'they now have microfinance' and can purchase such services (albeit at high prices) from the private sector.

Perhaps the most important factor of all, however, is that microfinance has been allocated a major 'containment' role within the globalisation project. It is widely argued by neoliberals that globalisation has the potential to provide a major reduction in poverty. Yet it is hardly coincidence that globalisation is being determinedly driven by a handful of the wealthiest of the developed countries – by the US government most of all (Gowan, 1999) – which clearly expect to be, and are by far, its major beneficiaries (Chang, 2003; Stiglitz, 2002). As globalisation increasingly concentrates wealth and power in the hands of a small number of countries, regions and corporate elites, the flip side, as Faux and Mishel (2000) explain, is a growing worldwide population of the unemployed, powerless, marginalised, hyper-exploited and insecure. And the rub here is that these 'losers' are beginning to reject both the outcome assigned to them and, most dangerous of all for neoliberals, the globalisation process itself. Symptomatic of this rejection is rising social unrest, increased social and gang violence, an explosion in substance abuse, increasing crime and illegal business activities, the huge rise in pseudo-religions and cults, collapsing levels of social capital in the community, and associated violent conflict (see Burbach *et al.*, 1997; Chua, 2003; Collier, 2007; Putnam, 2000; Sennett, 2003). In this potentially explosive situation microfinance provides a crucial 'safety valve'. With universal social welfare systems being dismantled under international financial institution (IFI) guidance, secure public employment opportunities disappearing, and formal sector employment an increasing rarity too, the microenterprise sector is projected as the 'better than nothing' option.

All told, the microfinance model has reached its huge popularity for two basic inter-related reasons. First, microfinance is seen as a beneficial and relatively low-cost poverty reduction instrument, with particular application in marginalised and 'at-risk' regions, localities and borderlands. Second, and probably more important, microfinance has an unrivalled serviceability to the goals and imperatives of neoliberalism: it is, in fact, 'local neoliberalism'. Let us now consider the specific situation of microfinance in the borderlands of post-conflict Southeast Europe.

## The sustainable impact of microfinance in post-conflict Southeast Europe

Following nearly a decade of economic decline, institutional fragmentation, aggressive nationalism, political chaos and social disintegration, the reconstruction of post-communist Southeast Europe effectively began in 1987 (see Woodward, 1995). When the Yugoslav Civil War was finally brought to an end in late 1995, the international community returned to provide a package of policy advice, technical support and financial aid that outstripped the Marshall Plan in real per capita financial value (CFER, 2000). In early 1999, NATO's campaign against Serbia meant that another round of international aid and support for regional reconstruction was required.

As in other post-conflict countries and regions, the IFIs and international development agencies pushed for the rapid establishment of microfinance programmes. While many government officials and policy elites in the region were initially sceptical of a system that implied comparability with poor non-industrialised countries, the IFIs converted them with aid conditionality, generously funded study tours and research contracts, and by encouraging local microfinance activists (often with promises of financial support for future microfinance activities) to lobby their governments. The IFIs also blocked the establishment of other possible local financial institutions, such as development banks and financial cooperatives (Bateman, 2003).

The first microfinance programmes were established after 1991, when Slovenia obtained EU support for its declining industrial and mining regions. Other Yugoslav successor states also began to acquire support for microfinance to help manage the decline of heavy industry and collapsing state factories. From late 1995 onwards the microfinance model took off, being quickly identified as having enormous relevance to the most hard-pressed post-conflict localities and borderlands. Microfinance was conjectured as an intervention that could, among other things, quickly create urgently needed income-generation opportunities, support household reconstruction, promote the revival of local asset accumulation and restart important intra- and inter-community social capital accumulation processes (World Bank *et al.*, 1996).

The narrative supporting the model in Southeast Europe, as everywhere else, has been simple and straightforward: escape from poverty was facilitated for many tens of thousands of the 'entrepreneurial poor' because they were able to access microfinance and start a new, or expand an existing, microenterprise (Dunn, 2005; Matthäus-Maier and von Pischke, 2004; Matul and Tsilikounas, 2004). Such was the presumed success in BiH that the IFIs almost immediately classified it as one of the most important international examples of 'best practice'. As Nancy Barry of Women's World Banking put it, 'Any war-torn country should look to Bosnia as a role model' (cited by Dolan, 2005).

However, the evidence was weak (as elsewhere – see Dichter and Harper, 2007). In fact, the high profile of microfinance has been largely constructed on mere assumption (e.g., 'outreach is an impact'), the disingenuous use of 'outlier' individual case studies, unwarranted extrapolations derived from short-run outcomes, the deployment of increasingly discredited 'client versus non-client' impact evaluation methodologies (see Ellerman, 2007), and even, at a more mundane level, intense IFI pressure on evaluation experts simply to 'come up with good things to say'. Reflecting on the many self-serving impact evaluations undertaken in Southeast Europe, the internationally respected microfinance analyst Dale Adams (2003: 6) candidly concluded:

> Consultants aren't asked to do additional studies if they report the 'emperor is naked'.... Likewise, donor employees who are assigned evaluation duties have difficulties finding lunch companions in the agency, or getting promoted, if they report that a finance project accomplished far less than designers anticipated. I suspect this helps explain why there is so much tolerance, even enthusiasm, for badly flawed impact studies that can be adjusted to find positive results.

A more balanced assessment of the genuine *sustainable* impact of microfinance in post-conflict Southeast Europe must take into account local dynamics and wider structural trends that have received almost no attention to date.

### Accounting for 'saturation' and 'displacement effects' in the informal sector

The informal sector everywhere serves as the final destination of almost all microfinance-induced enterprises. However, this does not mean that the informal sector has the unlimited power to simply expand and absorb without difficulty an unlimited number of poverty-push microenterprises. Other things being equal, new informal sector microenterprises increasingly do not raise the total volume of business so much as redistribute or subdivide the prevailing volume of business between new and existing microenterprises. Globalisation-driven conditions of an unlimited labour supply and dramatically reduced formal sector (especially public sector) employment opportunities combine to result in the unemployed and poor turning to microenterprises in order to survive. The local economy quickly becomes 'saturated' with informal sector microenterprises, which in turn imparts significant downward pressure on the local price level, negatively affecting both new and long-established microenterprises via reduced margins, wages and profits, as well as worsening working conditions.

'Saturation' has been reached in some countries of Latin America, sub-Saharan Africa and Southeast Asia, where microfinance expanded dramatically over 20 years and just about all who want a microloan can now access one. High-profile reports (e.g., UN Human Settlements Programme, 2003) testify that the steady inflow of millions of new poverty-push microenterprises has not generally led to a reduction in poverty. Instead, largely thanks to 'saturation' effects, there has been a broad *decline* in incomes, wages and working/life conditions within the increasingly dominant urban slums. Even worse, the ever expanding informalisation trajectory is intimately associated with increased violence and urban conflict, as unregulated informal sector competition inevitably ends up being regulated instead by those with power, connections and muscle. As Davis (2006: 185) puts it:

> Those engaged in informal sector competition under conditions of infinite labour supply usually stop short of a total war of all against all: conflict, instead, is usually transmuted into ethnoreligious or racial violence... the informal sector, in the absence of enforced labour rights, is a semi-feudal realm of kickbacks, bribes, tribal loyalties, and ethnic exclusion... the rise of the unprotected informal sector has too frequently gone hand in hand with exacerbated ethnoreligious differentiation and sectarian violence.

Since 'saturation' and displacement effects can dramatically reduce the imputed net employment and local income gains, accounting for their longer-run impact is crucial to any meaningful evaluation of microfinance impact.

These 'saturation' and displacement phenomena are now becoming the norm in Southeast Europe as well. A long list of local market sectors are increasingly under severe pressure from the continual influx of new entrants, all desperate to survive in conditions of flat demand. Obvious examples include the retail sector (especially food and clothes), cross-border trade, simple services, prepared food outlets and local transport. This phenomenon is particularly critical in borderland areas that do not enjoy the concentration of public sector jobs, fiscal strength, tourism or a large international presence to be found in regional capitals. In fact, 'saturation' occurred almost immediately after the war ended in BiH, partly because 'survivalist' microenterprises active during the conflict were able to ramp up their activities. Matul and Tsilikounas (2004: 458) reported that markets were flooded:

> many people were producing bread, [raising] cows or chickens but did not know where to sell their goods given the large level of available supply and market saturation. Many refugees were selling clothes that had been imported from Hungary and had to sell them for very small margins due to high competition.

It was therefore inevitable that most of the microfinance programmes would register major displacement-related negative impacts. The only question was: to what extent?

Consider the case of the dairy sector in BiH, where thousands of poor individuals were encouraged to access microfinance in order to purchase one or two cows and generate a little additional income from the sale of raw milk. While this was widely seen as a very favourable intervention by the MFIs, most agricultural specialists thought otherwise. They feared that important structural barriers preventing the sustainable development of the dairy sector were being *raised*, rather than *reduced*, thanks to the widespread proliferation of microfinance. First, the local over-supply of raw milk arising from the vast increase in small-scale producers precipitated a general price decline, which in turn was undercutting the day-to-day operations of potentially sustainable dairy farms; and second, the proliferation of small-scale producers desperate for a 'spot-sale' at any price had made it more difficult for local commercial farmers to establish a regular demand for their output (Agripolicy, 2006). The most potentially efficient commercial dairy farms were gradually being 'crowded out' of the local market. Under such artificial microfinance-induced conditions, therefore, many agricultural advisers argued that BiH was effectively being held back from establishing a modern, competitive dairy industry which would likely generate a far larger number of sustainable positive impacts within the community than the mass of inefficient small-scale 'one-cow' farms. These could have included well-paid formal sector jobs, exports, local taxation (some of which could be directed towards helping local 'at-risk' individuals who might otherwise think about buying a cow), a reduction in imports (legal and illegal), reduced environmental footprint (less use of transport) and cheaper and better quality locally processed milk for local consumption.

In other sectors, displacement effects simply meant that most of the original microenterprises did not survive. Those that did were elevated by the MFIs and their IFI sponsors into 'role model' status. However, the 'failures' were numerous and plunged people into long-term poverty. For example, the massive post-war expansion of small-scale retail and kiosk operations in Southeast Europe encountered demand-side problems from the outset, even more so when large retail sector investments later came on-stream. In Croatia, for instance, small shops have traditionally dominated food retailing and many new poverty-push entrants were registered after 1996. But as widely predicted by retail analysts, the situation began to change quite rapidly in the late 1990s, and by 2002 the share of small shops in retail trade had fallen from 70 per cent of the market to 45 per cent, in the process leading to a major shake-out. In 2002 alone, more than 4500 small shops were forced to close (Reardon et al., 2003), many of them MFI clients, leading to even deeper poverty and insecurity than before for a large proportion of them.

The pattern was replicated in BiH. Many of the small retail enterprises in the immediate aftermath of the war quickly ran into the sand, especially when large retail ventures finally began to operate in 1999–2000. The survivors meanwhile had to cope with steadily falling margins and profits, and often took to working extremely long hours in order to avoid losing their initial investment in property and stock, as well as their jobs. A lot of these failures and survivors were the very first clients of the MFIs, which now could do little to help. In an evaluation of the World Bank's Local Initiatives Project (LIP) that started in 1996, evaluation experts Dunn and Tvrtković (2004: 28) admitted to the severe difficulties faced by all small shops and kiosks and the extent of 'the damage done to their businesses by the advent of large shopping centres and department stores. Even though they have the desire to develop their business activities and improve their incomes, they have largely been unable to adapt to the increased competition'. One of the obvious reflections of the high level of 'saturation' is the high rate of exit. The evaluation of LIP in 2005 indicated that 30 per cent of the microenterprises supported since 2001 had failed after just two years of operation (Dunn, 2005). Using panel household survey data in BiH for 2001–2004, World Bank researchers estimated that around half of all individuals starting a new microenterprise in 2002 and 2003 were forced to close their new business within just one year of its establishment (Demirgüç-Kunt et al., 2007).

Borderlands in Southeast Europe fared the worst. In the borderlands of Croatia, for example, the expansion of the microenterprise sector appears to have achieved little because 'saturation' occurred quickly. A survey by Bateman and Sinković (2007) of 30 randomly selected recent clients of DEMOS, an MFI operating in the war-affected region of south-central Croatia, uncovered a quite widespread and damaging microfinance-driven downward dynamic. Of those interviewed, 20 were involved in simple dairy farming and used the microcredit to purchase an additional cow or, at most, two (the other 10 clients used their microcredit mainly for consumption purposes). But with many new such microfinance-induced suppliers coming on-stream in the locality, thanks to the activities of DEMOS, a local over-supply of raw milk quickly arose. This led on to declining farm-gate prices, and declining margins for all small producers. The situation was not helped when the two local dairy processors predictably took advantage of the over-supply and began to more vigorously 'cherry-pick' their suppliers, weeding out the smallest and most inefficient producers from their supply chain, a high proportion of which were DEMOS clients. Of the 20 DEMOS clients involved in the dairy sector, the interviews revealed that half of them had 'failed' and were in the process of selling off the additional cow(s) bought with their microcredit. They were also left with additional debts, had lost long-held assets and had encountered other problems, so that their overall situation was now appreciably worse than before. The other 10 DEMOS clients reported that they were just about surviving, but only because, on DEMOS's advice, they had immediately entered into the Croatian government's dairy subsidy programme. Pointedly, all but 2 of the 20 in the dairy sector reported that they had only been able to survive and repay their microloan (with half eventually 'failing', as just noted), because they enjoyed the government subsidy.

In Kosovo, 'saturation-driven' dynamics are equally in evidence. A 2004 survey found that microenterprises – now representing nearly 98 per cent of the total enterprise population – were reporting excess competition as by far the main obstacle to their survival and development. This was why, for instance, even though Kosovo experienced a 17 per cent growth in GDP in 2001, nearly all the microenterprises they interviewed 'complained of a decline in their business' (Addai and Nienborg, 2004: 188). The number of kiosks expanded massively after 1999, far outstripping the demand for the simple items they sell. This reduced average turnover and earnings per kiosk, forcing owners to sell up and become employees, with lower wages and additional duties (sometimes illegal). Other unprofitable kiosks came under the control of criminal gangs who supply them entirely with smuggled items, many of which are damaged or past their 'sell-by' dates and rejected for sale in EU countries.

While there is as yet no study in Southeast Europe to assess the consequences for those unfortunate individuals – now the majority – who within just a couple of years predictably succumb in their attempt to establish a viable microenterprise, the emerging evidence, as elsewhere, points to the fact that the long-term negative effect on poverty may be considerable (for Bangladesh, see Davis, 2007: 8). One should just note that other programme mechanisms exist that can also offer immediate financial support to groups 'at-risk' in post-conflict conditions but without the serious longer-run downside risks associated with widespread microenterprise failures, such as community-driven public works schemes and Brazilian-style *bolsa familia* programmes.

### Microfinance 'crowds out' the industrial sector and technology

Entrepreneurship theory and studies in institutional economics both hold that it is new, creative, technically innovative ideas and institutions that are the key catalysing factors in economic development (Drucker, 1985; North, 1990). To develop in a sustainable fashion and to reduce poverty, both developing and transition countries need to master key technologies, better understand 'state of the art' industrial products and processes, develop and manufacture at least some of their own innovations, and establish a tissue of pro-active development-focused institutions (see Amsden, 2007; Chang, 2007). Economies that emerged from the collapse of Yugoslavia (particularly Slovenia, BiH and Croatia) already possessed many of these development preconditions, including a significant endowment of advanced technologies, world-class companies operating at or near the technology frontier, a highly skilled and entrepreneurial population, high quality R&D institutions and an advanced educational system. And although the ravages of civil war undermined much of the not inconsiderable legacy of the former Yugoslavia, it was not destroyed by any means.

Among other things, such an endowment provided the obvious, if not ideal, 'entry point' for sustainable 'bottom-up' development and growth through rafts of relatively sophisticated microenterprises and small and medium-sized enterprises (SMEs) (see Ellerman, 2005). However, rather than work to support – or at least not hinder – the transformation of a major industrial inheritance into as many relatively sophisticated, technology-intensive microenterprises as possible, the microfinance model effectively undermined the chances of this scenario emerging. This was because the microfinance model contains an 'adverse selection' bias. Put simply, entrepreneurs wishing to work on relatively sophisticated projects are generally unable to service the onerous terms and conditions offered by local MFIs, whereas the simplest of microenterprises are generally offered as much support by their local MFI as they can handle.

The consequences of 'adverse selection' are compounded by an additional dynamic prevalent in borderland areas. Cross-border trade has been the mainstay of many borderlands, and it is well known that extensive concentrations of trading activity help to 'crowd out' local investment in sustainable productive activities. This is mainly because a higher local cost of capital arises to reflect the local opportunity cost of capital, which is represented by the temporarily high profits made by traders, importers and smugglers. In many borderlands, local financial institutions, including MFIs, were keen to capture 'their share' of the high returns being generated in the trading sector. They generally did this by inflating their interest rates as much as possible, imposing 'one-off' charges and demanding management fees. These restrictive conditions then applied to *all* other local clients, including potential and existing local industrial enterprises. The local industrial sector in many borderlands was thus presented with an even *more* restrictive local financial sector at *precisely* the time when it urgently required an accommodating local financial system in order to have a chance of restructuring, reinvesting and surviving. The long-run outcome of such a short-run financial bonanza in many borderlands was thus the 'crowding out' of local industrial operations, many with the potential to survive given a reasonable amount of support.

Consider the situation in BiH, with its significant military-industrial complex as the obvious entry point for many microenterprises. The country had enormous potential to draw upon technology, innovation, international markets and high skills. Why this potential was largely wasted can be illustrated by the experience of the Energoinvest network, once one of Bosnia's most technically advanced, innovative and R&D-driven companies (see Bateman, 2007a). Seeking ways to drastically reduce its workforce after 1996, Energoinvest offered its employees additional support to move into self-employment. Such a company represented an almost ideal practical 'breeding ground' for new and spin-off ventures based on reasonably sophisticated and innovative product and process ideas. Potential entrepreneurs had prepared business plans based upon achieving 'break-even' in a couple of years, or where profitability would be quite modest. But with microfinance virtually the only local financial structure geared up to working with new small ventures, most potential entrepreneurs quickly realised that they would not be able to meet the strict conditions required in their early years of operation. The result was that virtually all of the potential new small business ideas arising from Energoinvest employees were aborted. Some individuals were forced to substantially 'downgrade' their plans into something that the MFI sector would be willing to finance, such as a shop or a simple trading venture. Comically, a number of potential entrepreneurs took advantage of a German government scheme offering support to set up a new technology-intensive business – but in Germany.

Other countries experienced similar negative outcomes. For example, the restructuring, from the mid-1900s onwards, of the internationally reputable EMO electronics company in Ohrid, Macedonia, created significant potential for high-value spin-offs. A UK government-funded local technical support project (the Enterprise Support Agency) was available to facilitate the process. But very few ideas came to fruition over the following decade because of the local absence of capital on appropriate terms and maturities. Meanwhile, Ohrid saw an initial expansion of its microenterprise sector, before hitting the 'saturation' barrier and stagnating. The same situation prevails in Pelagonia, around Prilep and Bitola, a southern borderland with Greece, where many ideas to develop sustainable business projects involving successful local companies, such as plans for wind power generation, remain stillborn while no-growth retail/kiosk microenterprise ventures with easy access to microfinance increasingly dominate (Bateman, 2006).

At the same time as developing countries are being strongly recommended to move up manufacturing, technology and innovation-based value chains in order to escape their poverty and under-development (UNCTAD, 2003), the formerly sophisticated, institutionally rich and largely industry-based systems of Southeast Europe have effectively been ignored as the source of renewed 'bottom-up' industry-led growth and development. The microfinance model's 'adverse selection' bias wilfully ignored the region's industrial inheritance and potential, thereby actively contributing to the establishment of a 'shallow' and ultimately unsustainable local enterprise structure.

### The importance of scale and scope economies

For all enterprise sectors, there is an accepted minimum efficient scale of production, below which it becomes increasingly difficult to be competitive. Very often this involves simply the necessary use of a modicum of technology to ensure low unit costs. It might mean that a particular machine is required, rather than a more labour-intensive technology, in order to ensure both low unit costs and reaching a minimum quality threshold. However, the structure of microfinance generally ensures that supported microenterprises are well below the minimum efficient scale for their particular sector. MFIs promoting the entry of large numbers of tiny and basic microenterprises largely refuse to register the crucial importance of scale *within sector*. The result is that each microenterprise has very little chance of becoming competitive within their particular activity or market, and so many end up failing simply because of the *scale* of their operations. Many developing countries are experiencing adverse results, thanks to the structural bias arising from the contemporary focus on microenterprises. As Karnarni (2007) reports,

'The average firm size in India is less than one-tenth the size of comparable firms in other emerging economies. The emphasis on microcredit and the creation of microenterprises will only make this problem worse.'

Scale issues are particularly evident in the agricultural sector in Southeast Europe, particularly in the borderland regions. Most of the international donor programmes established in Croatia's borderlands of western Slavonia and Knin county have under-performed because of a critical misunderstanding of the importance of scale. One international evaluation points out that the small amounts of capital disbursed to returnees and refugees as 'start-up' packages generated almost no sustainable development impact whatsoever (WM Global Partners, 2003). None of the recipients could use this financial support to establish any sort of sustainable enterprise. The crux of the problem was that individual recipients were able to undertake only simple activities commensurate with the tiny sums of money allocated to them. In farming communities this just 'committed the village to remaining at a level of subsistence and denied the opportunity of building a farming community with complementarity between the farming activities' (ibid.: 45). The credits were 'too small, with too short repayment periods, and thus inadequate for longer term investment in farm businesses and buildings' (ibid.: 46).

Of course, a handful of very small-scale microfinance-assisted microenterprises have survived in Southeast Europe, but these are exceptional 'outliers'. Otherwise, it is widely recognised that the proliferation of tiny production-based and subsistence farming units is not a sensible foundation upon which to build a sustainable industrial or agricultural sector. Material support for the perpetuation and extension of such ultimately unsustainable structures, as opposed to their conversion, has therefore served only to add to the huge structural problems already weighing down the region.

### A lack of 'connectability'

It is now well understood that the tissue of inter-enterprise connections within the local enterprise sector is a crucial determinant of a local economy's ultimate sustainability and progress. With a variety of enterprises engaged in demanding areas of technology, innovation, skills, coordination and planning, managerial competences, and so on, it is possible for a local economy to gradually advance and prosper in a sustainable manner. This insight is pretty conclusively underpinned by academic and research traditions encompassing the new economic geography, industrial districts, social capital theory, cluster and network theory, value chain analysis, the role of technology and innovation. As Weiss (1988) concludes in reflecting particularly on the successes of both the Italian and the Japanese microenterprise sectors since 1945, 'the core of modern micro-capitalism is not competitive individualism but collective endeavour'.

However, as widely predicted, such beneficial grassroots dynamics have largely failed to materialise 'spontaneously' in Southeast Europe. Several factors are responsible, not least the region's paucity of genuinely pro-active local economic development, including SME development and institutions (see Bateman, 2000). But the microfinance model has contributed to the difficulties. While succeeding in terms of producing large *numbers* of new (albeit largely temporary) microenterprises, the overwhelming majority of these new entrants had no need, wish or ability to meaningfully cooperate in order to begin to forge the required efficiency-enhancing horizontal ('proto-industrial districts') and vertical (sub-contracting) connections. The basic 'raw material' required for 'connectability' is simply not being produced.

The result has been little movement towards a more 'connected' economy. A lack of potential sub-contracting partners has dissuaded some large international companies from relocating their operations to Southeast Europe. At the same time, cluster building programmes find it hard to identify sufficient local enterprises with the technology, market and scale requirements to benefit from cooperation with their counterparts. Governments in the region risk losing valuable resources establishing technology-upgrading programmes because there are no enterprises with any technology to upgrade. For example, the Croatian government's attempts to establish a 'knowledge-based economy' are blocked by an absence of sufficient enterprises with the basic technical, innovative and human capital capacities and potential to provide the necessary foundations (Bartlett and Čućković, 2007).

### Establishing an unsustainable trade-based and import-dependent local economic structure

One of the most damaging features of the neoliberal programmes that developing countries were forced into during the 1970s and 1980s was the collapse in local manufacturing and agricultural production brought about by instant trade liberalisation and an ensuing flood of (often subsidised) imports. Thanks to the basic operations of 'quick and easy to enter' small importing ventures, import dependence was quickly embedded into the system. The debilitating longer-run impact of import dependency ultimately destroyed any short-term poverty reduction gains made during the initial phase of microenterprise expansion in trading. An expert review of structural adjustment concluded that the initial uncontrolled surge of imports needlessly contributes to 'The failure of many local manufacturing firms, particularly innovative small and medium sized ones that generate a great deal of employment.' Furthermore, the import displacement of local production 'has been exacerbated by the absence of an industrial policy to support domestic firms in dealing with new conditions or with shocks in international markets' (SAPRIN, 2001: 5).

Given that simple trading ventures are cheap and easy to enter and require little in the way of special skills, they were understandably the first destination of many individuals in Southeast Europe seeking a route out of poverty. MFIs in the region were willing to deal with such business propositions, because the initial profitability was usually enough to deal with their high interest rates and short repayment periods. Accordingly, the small-scale trading sector quickly began to grow, particularly cross-border trading ventures, suggesting some employment and wealth creation. But the immediate result of the flood of imports was the collapse of many small-scale local manufacturing ventures.

A proliferation of simple trade-based – 'buying cheap and selling dear' – microenterprises has many drawbacks. In BiH, the majority of MFI clients, at least initially, have been simple trade-based microenterprises. But this simple trade-based foundation made it extremely difficult for the country to evolve into higher value-added areas involving manufacturing and technology, not least because the continuing flood of illegal or 'black' goods coming into the country undermined local production capacities (Bateman, 2007a).

The situation is probably even more disturbing in Kosovo. Consider the case of Pro-Credit, one of the most celebrated microfinance banks established with the technical and financial support of the international donor community. Praised by *The Economist* (4 September 2002) for its strong financial performance which, among other things, led to it becoming the most profitable bank in Eastern Europe, Pro-Credit is the largest and most profitable financial institution in Kosovo. However, it operates in an unstable borderland where genuine economic opportunities are rare. Most large-scale industries in Kosovo are effectively dead, while the petty services sector (shops, kiosks, shuttle trading) is over-populated with poverty-push ventures most realising increasingly minimal returns (European Stability Initiative, 2002). Virtually the only potential for sustainable growth in Kosovo are the many small-scale commercial farms and intermediate agricultural institutions (e.g., agricultural cooperatives) with the potential to service the local market, and to replace the now unsustainable level of food imports (80–90 per cent of food items were imported in 2004 compared to 10–20 per cent before the conflict). However, Pro-Credit Bank has deliberately had few dealings with this particular sector (representing less than 2 per cent of its loan portfolio in 2002), preferring to generate higher and safer returns by focusing on the local trade sector (66 per cent of its loan portfolio). But this commercially driven preference results in Pro-Credit using its initial financial endowment, as well as increasingly monopolising local savings, to add to a 'bazaar economy' of quite impressive proportions, but which contains almost no inherent sustainable development potential whatsoever. As a tiny island of spectacular commercial success operating in a sea of trade-related businesses, Pro-Credit is actually doing very little to help secure the long-term future of this poor and undeveloped borderland – if indeed it is not manifestly *destroying* the very development outcome it was originally established by the international donor community to pursue.

## The importance of social capital accumulation

By recasting individual survival as a function of individual entrepreneurial success facilitated through microfinance, the bonds of solidarity, shared experience and trust that exist within poor communities are undermined. This is a truism. More specifically, recasting community development and support activities as commercial and strict cost-recovery operations – a central operating principle of the 'local neoliberal' microfinance model (Drake and Rhyne, 2002) – dramatically increases the likelihood of a reduction in local solidarity, interpersonal communication, volunteerism, trust-based interaction and goodwill.

The rapid rise of the commercialised microfinance model has everywhere been associated with declining social capital levels, especially where private shareholder capital has gained entry into the MFI and where local government involvement and oversight are deliberately prohibited. By first engaging with poor communities and their most pressing problems under the watchful eye of the IFIs and international donors, and generally receiving financial support in order that they can 'help the community', but then abandoning these same communities in order to grow and to expand the financial rewards accruing to shareholders and senior staff, many MFIs are looked upon with cynicism and mistrust. Unlike in credit unions or financial cooperatives, where community ownership and control largely ensures that the institution remains true to its founding principles of community development and intergenerational solidarity (see Bateman, 2007b), MFIs are deliberately structured to eventually become private profit-making institutions, with often nothing more than 'wishful thinking' backing up the routine declaration that they will remain permanently answerable to their poor clients and to the community. It is therefore unsurprising that many MFIs established with IFI and international donor support right across the developing and transition economies have already been hijacked by their senior employees and private shareholders and converted into profit-making vehicles serving their own financial interests, most spectacularly in the 2007 case of *Compartamos*, Mexico's largest microfinance bank (see *Microcredit E-News*, Vol. 5, Issue 1, 2007).

Southeast Europe has not been exempt from this destabilising and unethical global trend. Many, if not most, MFIs in the region began to shift their strategic and operational foci quickly after they were established, and particularly after international donor support ended. To become self-sustainable/profitable, they have edged away from their original development mandate to support poor clients and have moved to increasingly work with the not-so-poor and new elites. Many MFIs are increasingly working in the more profitable and lower risk, but negligible development impact, area of consumption credit. Typically, in most MFIs senior staff remuneration levels and benefits have gradually moved from the NGO average towards those of the commercial banking sector. Many senior managers have taken advantage of the loose institutional format and lack of local government engagement to quietly manoeuvre their way into important shareholding positions as well. Many of the earliest MFIs in BiH moved into collateralised SME loans, property mortgages and consumer credit. Many are increasingly receiving injections of new finance from private financial institutions and the IFIs, moving them further towards becoming wealthy, fully private financial institutions with private shareholder satisfaction and profit-maximisation now being the operative goals. Perhaps most cynical of all, commercial imperatives have encouraged many MFIs to support rafts of microenterprises that will predictably collapse, but generally *after* they have repaid their microloan, or where clients are actually encouraged to sign up for government subsidies in order to survive (at least temporarily) and repay their microloan (as in the above example of DEMOS in Croatia).

In most parts of Southeast Europe, the commercialisation inherent in the MFI model has largely precluded popular legitimacy and voluntary support from the community. Particularly in the most remote and poverty-stricken borderlands, where most MFIs initially received a warm welcome, the atmosphere changed considerably when it later transpired that 'they were just businesses all along'. These negative developments stand in sharp contrast to the pre-communist and even communist-era community-based MFIs (e.g., financial cooperatives) that evinced significant popular support, community involvement and the construction of social capital. Unless major changes are made to the microfinance model, the inevitable fate in store for poor communities in the region is the transfer of potentially crucial community development institutions into the hands of private shareholders and senior MFI employees. The effects on local social capital can only be negative. And with international donor and government-funded local financial institutions increasingly turning inwards and away from their original mandate, the local community is effectively dispossessed of a local financial institution with real potential to underpin sustainable and equitable enterprise development. There are, of course, many local alternatives to the microfinance model, including the local financial cooperative model, that demonstrate a dramatically better post-conflict record than the microfinance model in terms of promoting sustainable enterprise development, sustainable poverty reduction and high levels of social capital (Bateman, 2007b).

## Conclusion

Microfinance has been one of the most high-profile local development interventions in Southeast Europe since the end of the Yugoslav Civil War in late 1995. It is routinely portrayed as a success story. The analysis of general trends and developments presented here, however, provides an alternative plotline: microfinance has played a role in *undermining* the hoped-for sustainable and equitable development of the region. While some short-run benefits of microfinance are visible in many cases, principally some quickly created income-generation opportunities involving 'at-risk' groups, in the longer run significant reversals, negative knock-on effects and important opportunity costs have to be factored into any assessment. The overall impact of the microfinance model has thus been a limited, if not an entirely negative, intervention. In terms of the effects on borderlands, this conclusion is only amplified.

Put simply, the microfinance model has generated a set of 'initial conditions' that because of path dependency have given rise to an increasingly backward local economic and social foundation. In Southeast Europe, MFIs were encouraged to reach high levels of efficiency as increasingly commercially focused institutions in their own right, but the objectives they followed were seriously at odds with the sustainable development goals and objectives of the local economy and society. The neoliberal institutional framework has simply reproduced across the region a set of negative local incentive structures typical of Third World countries, ensuring that 'The organizations that develop in this institutional framework will become more efficient – but more efficient at making the society even more unproductive and the basic institutional structure even less conducive to productive activity' (North, 1990: 9). Moreover, these negative local incentives become ever more powerful and destructive in Southeast Europe because MFIs are increasingly expanding their operations through the mobilisation of local savings. In effect, more of a community's valuable surplus resources will end up being locked into a sub-optimal, MFI-mediated 'local savings and investment cycle'. All told, the microfinance model can best be likened to a case of 'bad medicine' – it has created temporary feel-good effects for both 'patients' (communities, countries) and 'doctors' (IFIs, MFIs, international development agencies), but over the longer term we begin to realise that it has actually been killing, not curing, the 'patient'.

## References

Adams, Dale, 2003, 'Comments by Dale Adams on the Matthäus-Maier and von Pischke book', *Devfinance* (Annex to the *Quarterly Review* October–December).

Adams, Dale, Douglas Graham and J.D. von Pischke, 1984, *Undermining Rural Development with Cheap Credit*, Boulder, CO: Westview.

Addai, Abenaa and Kristine Nienborg, 2004, 'Enterprise Level Impacts of Financial Sector Projects in Southeast Europe', in Ingrid Matthäus-Maier and J.D. von Pischke (eds), *The Development of the Financial Sector in Southeast Europe: Innovative Approaches in Volatile Environments*, Berlin: Springer.

Agripolicy, 2006, 'Structure and Competitiveness of the Milk and Dairy Supply Chain in Bosnia and Herzegovina', country report prepared for the CEEC Agripolicy project (513705).

Amsden, Alice, 2007, *Escape from Empire: The Developing World's Journey Through Heaven and Hell*, Cambridge, MA: MIT Press.

Bartlett, Will and Nevenka Čućković, 2007, 'SME Policy and the Emerging Knowledge Economy in Croatia: Competitive Pressures and Employee Skills', paper at 7th International Conference 'Enterprise in Transition', Bol, Croatia, 24–26 May.

Bateman, Milford, 2000, 'Small Enterprise Development in the Yugoslav Successor States: Institutions and Institutional Development in a Post-War Environment', *MOCT-MOST*, Vol. 10, No. 2.

Bateman, Milford, 2003, ' "New Wave" Micro-Finance Institutions in South-East Europe: Towards a More Realistic Assessment of Impact', *Small Enterprise Development*, Vol. 14, No. 3, pp. 56–65.

Bateman, Milford, 2006, 'Mission Report', Final Report to Swiss Development Corporation on situation and recommendations for Prilep Region Enterprise Development Agency programmes in Pelagonia region, Prilep, Macedonia.

Bateman, Milford, 2007a, 'Deindustrialisation and Social Disintegration in Bosnia', in Thomas Dichter and Malcolm Harper (eds), *What's Wrong with Microfinance?* London: Practical Action Publishers.

Bateman, Milford, 2007b, 'Financial Co-operatives for Sustainable Local Economic and Social Development', *Small Enterprise Development*, Vol. 18, No. 1, pp. 37–49.

Bateman, Milford and Dean Sinković, 2007, 'Assessing the Sustainable Impact of Microfinance in Croatia: A New Approach and Some New Tools of Analysis', paper at European Association for Comparative Economics Studies seminar 'The Role of Microfinance in Promoting Sustainable Development in Southeast Europe', Great Brioni Island, Croatia, 5 July.

Burbach, Roger, Oscar Nunez and Boris Kagarlitsky, 1997, *Globalization and its Discontents: The Rise of Postmodern Socialisms*, London: Pluto Press.

CFER (Council on Foreign Economic Relations), 2000, 'Promoting Sustainable Economies in the Balkans: Report of an Independent Task Force Sponsored by the Council on Foreign Economic Relations', Washington, DC.

Chang, Ha-Joon, 2003, *Globalisation, Economic Development and the Role of the State*, London: Zed Books.

Chang, Ha-Joon, 2007, *Bad Samaritans: Rich Nations, Poor Policies and the Threat to the Developing World*, London: Random House.

Chua, Amy, 2003, *World on Fire: How Exporting Free-Market Democracy Breeds Ethnic Hatred and Global Instability*, London: Heinemann.

Collier, Paul, 2007, *The Bottom Billion: Why the Poorest Countries Are Failing and What Can Be Done About It*, Oxford: Oxford University Press.

Davis, Mike, 2006, *Planet of Slums*, London: Verso.

Davis, Peter, 2007, 'Discussions Among the Poor: Exploring Poverty Dynamics with Focus Groups in Bangladesh', Chronic Poverty Research Centre Working Paper 84, February, Institute for Development Policy and Management, University of Manchester.

Demirgüç-Kunt, Asli, Leora Klapper and Georgios A. Panos, 2007, *The Origins of Self-Employment*, World Bank Development Research Group, Washington, DC, February.

Dichter, Thomas and Malcolm Harper (eds), 2007, *What's Wrong with Microfinance?* London: Practical Action Publishers.

Dolan, Kerry, 2005, 'Up from the Rubble; Can $2,000 Loans help Revive a War-Torn Economy? Entrepreneurs in Bosnia and Herzegovina are Putting Microfinance to the Test', *Forbes*, 18 April.

Drake, Deborah and Elisabeth Rhyne (eds), 2002, *The Commercialisation of Microfinance: Balancing Business and Development*, Bloomfield, CT: Kumarian.

Drucker, Peter, 1985, *Innovation and Entrepreneurship*, London: Pan.

Dunn, Elizabeth, 2005, *Impact of Microcredit on Clients in Bosnia and Herzegovina*, Washington, DC: Impact LLC.

Dunn, Elizabeth and Josip Tvrtković, 2004, 'Case Study Report: "Then I Learned I Could get a Loan"', Sarajevo: Local Initiatives (Microfinance) Project II, Impact Assessment/Research Development Component.

Ellerman, David, 2005, *Helping People Help Themselves: From the World Bank to an Alternative Philosophy of Development Assistance*, Ann Arbor, MI: University of Michigan Press.

Ellerman, David, 2007, 'Microfinance: Some Conceptual and Methodological Problems', in Thomas Dichter and Malcolm Harper (eds), *What's Wrong with Microfinance?* London: Practical Action Publishers.

European Stability Initiative, 2002, *De-Industrialisation and its Consequences: A Kosovo Story*, Lessons Learned and Analysis Unit of the EU Pillar of UNMIK, Prishtina and Berlin: European Stability Initiative.

Faux, Jeff and Larry Mishel, 2000, 'Inequality and the Global Economy', in Will Hutton and Anthony Giddens (eds), *On the Edge: Living with Global Capitalism*, London: Jonathan Cape, pp. 93–111.

Feiner, Susan, and Drucilla Barker, 2007, 'Microcredit and Women's Poverty – Granting this year's Nobel Peace Prize to Microcredit Guru Muhammad Yunus Affirms Neoliberalism', *The Dominion*, Issue 42, 17 January.

Friedman, Milton and Rose Friedman, 1980, *Free to Choose*, London: Penguin.

Gowan, Peter, 1999, *The Global Gamble: Washington's Faustian Bid for World Dominance*, London: Verso.

Harper, Malcolm, 2007, 'Some Final Thoughts', in Thomas Dichter and Malcolm Harper (eds), *What's Wrong with Microfinance?* London: Practical Action Publishers.

Harvey, David, 2006, *A Brief History of Neoliberalism*, Oxford: Oxford University Press.

Karnarni, Aneel, 2007, 'Microfinance Misses its Mark', *Stanford Social Innovation Review*, Summer.

Matthäus-Maier, Ingrid and J.D. von Pischke (eds), 2004, *The Development of the Financial Sector in Southeast Europe: Innovative Approaches in Volatile Environments*, Berlin: Springer.

Matul, Michal and Caroline Tsilikounas, 2004, 'Microfinance in the Household Reconstruction in BiH', *Journal of International Development*, Vol. 16, No. 3, pp. 429–66.

North, Douglass, 1990, *Institutions, Institutional Change and Economic Performance*, Cambridge: Cambridge University Press.

Putnam, Robert, 2000, *Bowling Alone: The Collapse and Revival of American Community*, New York: Simon & Schuster.

Reardon, Thomas, Goran Vrabec, Damir Karakas and Conrad Fritsch, 2003, *The Rapid Rise of Supermarkets in Croatia: Implications for Farm Sector Development and Agribusiness Competitiveness Programs*, Zagreb: Development Alternatives Incorporated, September.

Robinson, Marguerite, 2001, *The Microfinance Revolution: Sustainable Finance for the Poor*, Washington, DC: World Bank.

SAPRIN (Structural Adjustment Participatory Reviews International Network), 2001, *The Policy Roots of Economic Crisis and Poverty*, Washington, DC.

Sennett, Richard, 2003, *Respect: The Formation of Character in an Age of Inequality*, London: Penguin.

Shiva, Vandana, 2002, *Water Wars: Privatisation, Pollution, and Profit*, London: Pluto.
Stiglitz, Joseph, 2002, *Globalisation and its Discontents*, London: Allen Lane.
UN Human Settlements Programme, 2003, *The Challenge of Slums: Global Report on Human Settlements*, London: Earthscan.
UNCTAD, 2003, *Annual Report 2003*, Geneva.
Weber, Heloise, 2002, 'The Imposition of a Global Development Architecture: The Case of Microcredit', *Review of International Studies*, Vol. 28, No.3, pp. 537–55.
Weiss, Linda, 1988, *Creating Capitalism: The State and Small Business Since 1945*, Oxford: Blackwell.
WM Global Partners, 2003, 'Evaluation of the programme for the return of refugees and internally displaced persons in Croatia: Final Report', Birmingham: WM Global Partners, February.
Woodward, Susan, 1995, *Balkan Tragedy: Chaos and Dissolution After the Cold War*, Washington. DC: The Brookings Institution.
World Bank, European Commission and EBRD, 1996, 'Bosnia and Herzegovina: Towards Economic Recovery', discussion paper 1, for Second Donors' Conference.

# 15
# Potential Difference: Internal Borderlands in Africa

*Stephen Jackson*

> *Congo now appears to be a large open space that includes several boundaries, none of which corresponds to its official place on the map... Against a background of armed violence and a severe depreciation of currencies, alliances are constantly made and unmade. Ephemeral coalitions are formed on the regional scale. But no force accumulates sufficient power to dominate all the others in an enduring way. Everywhere, lines emerge and vanish. Structural instability makes Congo–Kinshasa the perfect example of a process of the delocalization of boundaries.*
>
> Mbembe, 2000: 282

Borderlands, those undefined and ambiguous 'grey zones' that straddle the territorial boundaries between contiguous states, have increasingly been highlighted in literature as both a pivotal locus in the emergence of violent political economies and a vital area in which to focus attempts to construct a post-conflict peace (Chapter 13, this volume; Bouvier, 1972; Donnan and Wilson, 1999; Goodhand, 2005; Jackson, 2006a; Mbembe, 2000; Nugent and Asiwaju, 1996; Richards, 1996).

Drawing largely on case materials from the Democratic Republic of Congo (DRC, formerly Zaire), this chapter extends that analysis to a less examined phenomenon: the proliferation in countries afflicted by violence or instability of internal borderlands. These are interstices within national boundaries which have grown to share some of the same ambiguous features of the zones across national frontiers and which similarly play strong roles in the political economies of war and peace. The chapter begins by proposing a somewhat abstract model of how borderlands in general engender 'potential difference' – energies and opportunities arising from the contrasts and discontinuities that they both create and then police. Contending, then, that 'potential differences' have come to operate equally across borders emerging within national territories, the chapter proposes and explores a typology of such internal borderlands: (historical) borderlands of inter-ethnic blurring or interpenetration; politico-administrative internal borderlands; economic internal borderlands; and enclaves violently dominated by privatised force. A particular point of attention is the relationship between each of these and the production of conflict. The chapter closes with thoughts about how the *problématique* of internal borderlands might be addressed within the broader compass of efforts at post-conflict reconstruction.

## 'How can they demand a visa?'

In March 1999, the rebel *Rassemblement Congolais pour la Démocratie* (RCD) began to fracture. Six months earlier, it had launched a rebellion from the DRC's eastern extreme aimed at toppling President Laurent-Désiré Kabila, who had come to power only the year before. The RCD had been strongly backed by Rwanda and Uganda – the DRC's militarily powerful neighbours – but now, the RCD's split made manifest those neighbours' divergent interests as well as the movement's lack of a coherent internal ideology.

The then RCD leader, Ernest Wamba dia Wamba, decamped with his advisers from Goma (North Kivu) to Kisangani (in Orientale Province), saying 'there is no coup d'etat but there is some malaise in Goma' (International Crisis Group, 2000: 22). By May 1999, there were now two RCDs – the RCD–Goma, led by Emile Ilunga, and Wamba's RCD–Kisangani (soon the RCD-*Mouvement de Libération* or RCD–ML). A year or so later, splits had proliferated. Jokes circulated in the Congo at the RCD's expense: 'You know that *orchestre* [Congolese dance music group], Wenge Musica, who have split into all these different *"ailes"* [wings], Wenge Musica Aile Paris and so on? Well, it is just like that... Not the RCD, but the RCDs, plural – from wings to feathers.'

Now, RCD–Goma, RCD–ML, RCD–*National*, RCD–*Originel*, RCD–Congo and the RCD (plain and simple) vied for supremacy. Each sub-faction fought with the others to claim the dwindling symbolic capital attaching to the initials RCD. Organisational mimesis was the order of the day: devising emblems, letterhead, cabinets, spokesmen, imitating the impedimenta of governmentality (Foucault, 1991), political style trumping substance. This variety of Congolese 'schismogenesis' (Bateson, 1958) was accompanied by greatly elevated violence. Indeed, it goes some way to explaining how a war which, after 1999, rarely witnessed major pitched battles between principal belligerents but nonetheless claimed almost four million lives in five short years, becoming the 'deadliest crisis in the world' (International Rescue Committee, 2004). Indeed, a rough rule of thumb emerged: the smaller the movement, the less its dwindling legitimacy in Congolese eyes, the stronger its repression and its determination to wring what profit it could from the ever smaller portions of territory it controlled. This dynamic produced a shifting and unstable honeycomb of paramilitary control – mineral-rich centres dominated through brute force surrounded by 'no-man's lands' where control remained contested, often also mineral rich and emptied of their populations, violent interstices across which profit could be leveraged.

One effect of this territorial carve-up was the establishment of 'internal borders' with immediate opportunities for profit. Travelling back to Europe via Uganda in 1999, the 12-seater plane in which I was travelling from Goma made a scheduled stop in Butembo, northern North Kivu, long the unofficial capital of the 'Grand Nord' and of the Nande ethnic group, noted traders (Bayart *et al.*, 1999; Vwakyanakazi, 1991). Now under the control of the RCD–ML, that movement's 'immigration officials' demanded passports from all those on board and a payment of US$30 to receive a 'visa stamp' – even from those remaining on the plane. Similar fees were levied on those making the dangerous journey by road. Traders additionally found 'customs duties' applied to their wares for what was, by any normal definition, simply a commercial movement within the internationally established boundaries of the DRC. For *Kivutiens* travelling across the 'internal border' to Butembo, the outrage was as much existential as economic – 'how can they demand a visa from me to travel within my own country?'

## 'Potential difference' or the 'across variable'

The violent carving out of these interstices within a supposedly integral and sovereign state represents just one example of the proliferation of 'internal borderlands'. To explore how such borderlands within states can become integral to the political economy of violent conflict, it is necessary first to make a formal model of the political economy of borderlands, drawing centrally on the experience of the DRC but also looking elsewhere in Africa.

National borders are, first and foremost, 'sites and symbols of power' (Donnan and Wilson, 1999: 1). Marking the bounds of states, they are an attempt to make a clear demarcation and delimitation of the potencies and powers of sovereign actors. Symbolising the extent of the state's remit, border posts – with their barriers, customs points, immigration procedures and special police forces – literally and metaphorically 'beat the bounds', inscribing power politics onto geography and territory. The symbolic magnitude of international boundaries invests them with a high degree of sensitivity and sanctity. Conversely, the persistence of their symbolic power depends crucially on that sanctity (hence the pervasive nervousness about photographing them).

Borders – and border posts in particular – also serve a regulatory function, governing, moderating and taxing flows between sovereign units, shutting down those that are not permitted, enabling those that are permitted (for a fee). Traditionally, such flows have included categories of people – migrants, refugees, armed forces, diplomats, commercial actors and so on – and material goods.

But if the material presence of state power at borders stages an image of potency and permanency by now, it is also 'something of a truism that... their existence as barriers to movement can simultaneously create reasons to cross them' (Donnan and Wilson, 1999: 87) – to traverse or transgress them. Borders, in fact, are emblematic of the very uncertainty, ambiguity and ambivalence that is at the heart of the 'national order of things' (Malkki, 1995). They are not a permanence but merely a staged claim to permanence. To borrow from Clifford Geertz, borders remain an attempt 'to view culture, geography, politics, and self in the blocked-out spaces of the absolute map, as a matter of countries, lead[ing] to the conception of the past as prologue and the future as dénouement – history with a permanent subject' (1995: 21–2). Even where borders coincide with apparently natural obstacles – such as rivers, lakes or mountain ranges – these manifest themselves less as absolute boundaries than as *marches*, semi-permeable zones that restrict certain flows and incentivise others.

Thus, if borders stage themselves as concrete delimitations, they also give rise to borderlands which work against their efforts. These are, as Zygmunt Bauman suggests, 'leftover places which remain after the job of structuration has been performed on such spaces as really matter' (Bauman, 2000: 103). Resurrecting the core/periphery distinction, this perspective suggests a remainder left behind – historically, (develop)mentally. In the conventional romance of the distant metropole, borderlands are imagined as either impossibly remote and boring hinterlands or wild and untamable frontiers (Jackson, 2006a). They are areas set apart, akin to Marc Augé's notion of 'non places' (Augé, 1995), 'no-man's lands': no men own the border, non-men live there. Yet a border-zone is neither exactly *terra nullis* nor *terra incognita*, but merely a partially successful attempt at establishing the necessary limits of continuous national integrity and identity. Accordingly, in social science, there has been increased interest in the porosity of borders and its impact on both politico-cultural identity and politico-economic activity (e.g., Behar, 1993; De Boeck, 1996; Donnan and Wilson, 1996; Flynn, 1997; Long and Villareal, 1999; Nugent and Asiwaju, 1996; Richards, 1996; Vila, 1999). We can no longer be surprised, then, that border zones are areas of contest, ambiguity, transgression and flux. So much attention has been devoted to the porosity of borders in anthropology, that they are verging on clichés as objects of analytical attention.

In the abstract, 'the DRC' and 'Rwanda' are two opposed poles interrupted by a strict discontinuity. But the border zone that comprises North and South Kivu provinces completes the circuit between them. To borrow a metaphor from physics, borderlands are the sites of 'potential difference' (also known more colloquially in physics as the 'across variable'). In technical terms, potential difference is a quantity related to the amount of energy that would be required to move an object from one place to another against various types of forces. Inherent in the notion is a sense of differences both potential (realisable) and potent (powerful). In a battery, the difference in tension between two electrical poles, positive and negative, galvanises electrical current to flow between them once the circuit is completed. In a similar fashion, while borders purport to exist in order to bring predictability and governability to the flows across them, paradoxically their very existence sets up a 'potential difference' which provides just the incentives to try to transgress them through illicit trans-border circuits and flows. The potential for profit – not just economic, but in other senses too – arises precisely because some people are in a powerful position to 'complete the circuit' while others are not. In short, borders establish differences that can be leveraged to individual or collective advantage, and borderlands, unsurprisingly, tend to be where this leveraging is at its most frenzied, particularly under conditions of conflict. Bluntly put, without borders there would be no point to smuggling (and, to some extent, vice versa). Some such smuggling is on a massive, commercial scale, such as the trade in tantalum ore ('coltan') in the Kivus. But many Congolese also eke out tiny survival livelihoods through small-scale smuggling of items as innocent as milk (Jackson, 2003b).

Borders exert potential differences across a variety of sectors, waiting to be actualised by those with the power and determination. Potential differences across the Rwandan/Congolese border excite currents of violence, switch on or off population flows, induce or resist commodity flows, attract or repel aid, and electrify rumour – all with their impact on the political economy of conflict. As next investigated, beyond their activity across national borders, potential differences have come to operate in very much the same fashion across proliferating *internal* borderlands. Indeed, the creation of potential difference that can be harnessed to profit is one reason why internal borders come into existence at all.

## Internal borderlands

Four kinds of internal borderland are identified here: those that emerged out of inter-ethnic penetration or blurring in the precolonial period; those left as remainders after the imposition of colonial political geographies of administration and control; those bequeathed by post-colonial urbanisation, followed by economic and infrastructural decline under neoliberalism; and those that emerged through the fissiparous rebel dynamics within recent wars in several African states.

Achille Mbembe paints a vivid picture of the later kind, the atrophying of the post-colonial African state's ability to extend authority across vast and logistically challenging national territories, leading to internal borderlands: intermediate, liminal areas wholly contained within the territory of a single state, but caught suspended between two or more zones more comprehensively controlled by either state or non-state actors:

> Borders... no longer simply separate states from one another but are becoming 'internal' to states themselves (as with some regions of the Congo, the countries around the Great Lakes, Uganda and southern Sudan).... whole areas... are effectively left to their own devices, with pockets of territory more or less emptied of inhabitants and abandoned, and gaps and intermediate spaces where no writ runs are appearing within a single state.
>
> (Mbembe, 2001: 87)

At one level there is little new in this. As a multitude of historians and anthropologists have noted, the precolonial history of African state formation was characterised by the shifting dynamics along frontiers. Igor Kopytoff (1989) – perhaps the leading exponent of this reading of African history – emphasises that cycles of advance and retreat of 'internal African frontiers' formed the leading edge of interaction between competing, comparatively centralised polities and statelets. This process regularly involved mergers, dissolutions, discontinuities, the composition and decomposition of competing political entities – kingdoms, clans, tribes and more amorphous groupings. New and centralising political identities were constantly coalescing around temporarily fixed centres of power and influence. The by-product was the continual generation of new frontier regions. On the one hand, these frontiers were often romanticised from the centre as energetic domains where the collective identity of the new statelet was being forged in adversity. On the other hand, identity was also, precisely, most 'up for grabs' there. Population groups continued to intermix, alternately battling and blurring, taxing and trading. As Mbembe (2000: 263) suggests,

> It might be said that operating by thrusts, detachments, and scissions, precolonial territoriality was an itinerant territoriality. In other cases, mastery over spaces was based on controlling people or localities, and sometimes both together. Vast areas might lie between distinct polities, veritable buffer zones not subject to direct control, exclusive domination, or close supervision.

Despite colonialism, the relics of this kind of 'itinerant territoriality' can be detected today as the first element in a tentative taxonomy of internal borderlands – *borderlands of inter-ethnic blurring or interpenetration*. In numerous parts of Africa one finds configurations similar to that in the highlands of North Kivu province, on the border between Masisi and Walikale *territoires*, where it becomes hard, even by local people's own admission, to distinguish between members of ethnic groups, the Nyanga and Hunde, elsewhere considered quite distinct. These are two ethnic groups who consider themselves to be 'related': very close linguistically, and claiming descent from two brother chieftains (Biebuyck, 1978). The portion of land that exists at the intersection of their separate domains of influence is effectively a borderland in which the language spoken is a (re?)-blending of the two main languages and customary authority is diffuse, competitive and bi-directional; their territories interpenetrate – or perhaps more accurately, form a continuum of belonging, two relatively centralised groups have emerged over time. The populations represent the remnant of an earlier and more hybrid identity, and loyalties are confused and sometimes cantankerous.

Both Hunde and Nyanga are sedentary agriculturalist groups; a parallel, but different kind of borderland exists where agriculturalist populations mix with nomadic or semi-nomadic pastoralist communities. This is the case, for example, around the Tana River area in Kenya, where pastoralist Boran, Somali and Waaldai peoples range widely without great regard for the settlement of land by the agriculturalist Pokomo and Malakote peoples (Weiss, 2004), or in the northern DRC, where Mbororo cattle herders migrate seasonally into agriculturalist areas, in both cases with often incendiary consequences (Marks, 2007).

It is often suggested that colonialism drew African boundaries at the whim of European rulers gathered around a conference table in Berlin in 1885, artificially incising difference across African polities (e.g., Pakenham, 1991). The truth turns out to be more complex, with 'European' boundaries across some of the continent bearing some resemblance to the political and/or geographic demarcations already in place at the moment of colonisation (Katzenellenbogen, 1996; Mbembe, 2000). However, through policy instruments such as censuses, cartography, settlement (or resettlement) and the political co-option of chieftaincies, colonialism did begin reifying and dichotomising what had previously been fluid and overlapping categories of identity and belonging (Anderson, 1991). The exact details varied by context, colonial power and mode of colonialism (e.g., direct or indirect rule: Mamdani, 1996; Willame, 1997). But the underlying schema was broadly similar across much of the continent. Driven by a desire to impose order on a perceived confusion of identities, loyalties and political affinities, a new colonial political and administrative geography attempted to engineer largely mono-ethnic homelands. In South Africa these were dubbed 'Bantustans'. In the DRC, they were provinces and territories. So closely were these designed to police an equation between identity and area that in many parts of the country there was no pretence at bestowing a toponym – the territories were simply given ethnonyms: *territoire des wanyanga* (territory of the Nyanga people), *territoire des bahunde* and so on. Again, the carving up of territory into such supposedly discrete and homogeneous zones delimited by administrative boundaries left lacunae, intermediate spaces – *politico-administrative internal borderlands*.

As is well known, the newly independent states largely agreed to respect *uti possedetis*, the international legal principle that decolonised states continue to respect the colonial administrative borders they held at independence. To some extent, they applied this principle to borders established within their territories too: 'this colonial structuring of economic spaces was not abolished by post-colonial regimes. The latter have often prolonged it; sometimes, they have radicalised the logic of creation of internal boundaries that was inherent in it, particularly in rural zones' (Mbembe, 2000: 267). The internal borders and borderlands created under colonialism have, in many instances, survived to the present. In a self-fulfilling prophecy, they have had a profound impact in reifying both cultural politics and political economy. For while in origin, the Bantustans, provinces or other forms of colonially established territorial units were only inexact efforts at carving out mono-ethnic spaces, over time, processes of political and economic integration within them and disengagement with the outside, through either deliberate policy or the atrophy of infrastructural and other connections, have led to the emergence of often extremely powerful sentiments of belonging and exclusion, expressed through a rising language of provincial 'indigenousness', 'locality' or 'autochthony', leading to 'identity closure' and even ethnic cleansing and/or genocide (see Geschiere and Ceuppens, 2005; Geschiere and Nyamnjoh, 2001; Geschiere and Jackson, 2006; Jackson, 2003a,b; Mbembe, 2001: 87).

In the first, enthusiastic nation- and statebuilding period after independence, there were sincere and energetic attempts to connect the several (and severed) parts of the new national territories. Grand infrastructural projects – attempts to complete railway or highway networks, construct hydroelectric dams and pursue rural electrification – became all but synonymous with development in its 'high authoritarian' mode (Scott, 1998). But these efforts remained only partially successful and were, moreover, often undercut by the drawing in of populations from the rural hinterlands, either through villagisation (another hallmark of 'high authoritarianism') or urbanisation, leading to the semi-evacuation of certain rural areas.

By the neoliberal 1980s, amidst structural adjustment and privatisation and starved of resources and attention, the grand, half-finished infrastructure of state interconnectedness began to decay. Contrary to stereotypes of 'state failure', this did not produce a universal absence of the state from the hinterlands. Just as interconnecting the state remained patchwork, so the decline of its infrastructure has also been uneven, leading to a honeycomb pattern of enclaves, internally connected, but disconnected from each other. Importantly, the pattern of connection versus disconnection left behind was not identical to previous patterns of organisation. Instead, the new patchwork lay inexactly over older ones, leading to circumstances where circuits of effective economic exchange were not coterminous with areas of common politico-cultural identity. As Mbembe (2000: 279) notes for Nigeria,

> within a process of consolidating a federal state, a set of embedded forms of control and regulation that were encouraged by colonial indirect rule are still dominant. Localities and internal divisions, some historical and

others institutional or even cultural and territorial, are superimposed on the space of the state. Each locality is subject to several jurisdictions: state jurisdiction, traditional jurisdiction, religious jurisdiction. Different orders coexist within an interlacing of 'homelands' and 'communities'.

The engendering of these new enclaves produced a new variety of margins across which exchange was rendered difficult, but not impossible, by the decline in economic infrastructure. As with the other varieties, these *economic internal borderlands* could be leveraged for profit by entrepreneurs of all stripes willing to assume the effort, risk and cost in trading across them.

This uneven retreat of centralised state power from the rural hinterlands brings us full circle to the point where this chapter began – the emergence in the new wave of warfare in the 1990s of *enclaves violently dominated by privatised force*. The forces at play are too complex to offer more than a summary here. The end of the Cold War removed an ideological polarisation that had previously imposed a bipolar logic of a kind, on violent challenges to state power. Experiments with decentralisation, devolution, multipartyism and other modes of democratisation that followed in many states in the 1990s were accompanied by a sharp rise in localist politics under the sign of 'authocthony' (a radical discourse about authentic belonging, anchored in claims on territory – see Jackson, 2006b), as was the opening up of the continent to new forms of neoliberal globalisation (Geschiere and Nyamnjoh, 2001; Meyer and Geschiere, 1999).

At the same time, the privatisation – or the simple collapse – of state dominance of natural resource exploitation (see, e.g., Vwakyanakazi, 1991) provided new rebel movements in resource-rich parts of the continent with a means and an end to pursue violence (Le Billon, 2001). This is not to indulge in a reductionist explanation of African conflicts in the 1990s that would boil them down to a simple 'greed' versus 'grievance' formulation (cf. Berdal and Malone, 2000). Nor is it to assert that Africa alone suffered this kind of violent enclavisation in the 1990s (for the Latin American case, see, e.g., Richani, 2002; for the Central Asian case, Goodhand, 2004). Indeed, one might rather argue that these factors, notable in the emergence of regional war complexes in West Africa, Central Africa, and the Horn, as well as elsewhere in the global South, were but the extreme examples of processes generally at work across the globe during the 1990s. In any event, they engendered localised rebel and militia movements which quickly splintered and fractured, furthering the production of 'rebel enclaves', consisting of a 'series of complex transboundary formations between local elites, regional armed actors and global forces' (Vlassenroot and Raeymaekers, 2005: 13).

Regional actors played a key role in these processes too. Interventions by neighbours (e.g., Rwanda and Uganda's in the DRC, Ugandan and Sudan's mutual support for each other's insurgencies, see Prunier, 2004) were a central element in the dynamics driving the carving out of violent enclaves and, thus, the creation of internal borderlands. As Vlassenroot and Raeymaekers also note, in some cases, emerging (and unstable) alliances between rural armed actors, economic entrepreneurs, local administrations and regional 'godfathers' created a degree of continuity and security within these enclaves. In others, ongoing struggles for control generalised insecurity. The spaces between the enclaves formed borderlands across which potential difference operated and an opportunity for leverage and influence was afforded – symbolised by the ubiquitous roadblock, perhaps the example *par excellence* of potential difference exerted across an internal borderland.

A concrete illustration of the effects may be helpful. As the violent enclavisation of North Kivu, DRC, continued apace during the late 1990s, large areas were emptied of their populations and turned over to the exploitation of the province's mineral wealth. As I have discussed elsewhere (Jackson, 2001, 2002, 2003a,b), this period (roughly 1999–2001) coincided with a ten-fold increase in the spot price of tantalum – known as 'coltan' – on international metal markets (a vital metal in microelectronics, including in mobile phone technologies). The Kivus are enormously rich in coltan, which can be mined artisanally. A 'coltan fever' erupted. Some exploitation was deep in equatorial forests. But much took place on land formerly agriculturally productive, from which populations had been cleared. Food insecurity rose dramatically as areas that had been net food-exporting were driven to importing ('everything that is consumed comes from elsewhere', one interviewee told me in Goma in July 2001). These enclaves were violently severed from each other and from those markets still able to furnish supplies, compounding food insecurity. The comparatively large sums of cash (Congolese francs and dollars) being earned by the coltan miners and intermediaries further fuelled inflation. In a two-year period, the prices for basic commodities such as beans or manioc ('cassava' – the local staple) increased as much as 9000 per cent in Congolese franc terms in key coltan areas; even in dollar terms, they increased 300–400 per cent. Just as striking was the price reversal in food staples when, in August–September 2000, prices in the rural market of Sake overtook those in the urban market of Goma. Normally, Goma consumers were supplied from Sake and paid higher prices because of transport and other overheads; but coltan prices had reached an all-time high (Jackson, 2003b). Such price differentials provided a potential difference across what had now become internal borderlands between urban centres and violent enclaves of mineral extraction. Entrepreneurs of all stripes took advantage, swarming around the mineral camps selling everything from beer to batteries, weapons and sex.

To recap, the emergence of internal borderlands has been a multi-layered and overlapping historical process. The advent of colonialism advanced a process of overlaying fixed state boundaries on an often-fluid pre-existing set of polities and ethnic identities. Within those boundaries, it drew politico-administrative boundaries that engendered further internal borderlands across those polities and identities. Post-colonial attempts to connect or reconnect the severed parts of the national territories were left moribund by fiscal retrenchment and the retreat of the state in the 1980s and by the widespread rural–urban exodus. Finally, a wave of armed conflict in the 1990s further accelerated a process of violent enclavisation.

The four categories defined above are not intended to appear mutually exclusive, but rather represent succeeding waves of phenomena that interfere with each other in complex and locally specific ways. The internal borderlands that emerged as a result of violent splits within proliferating militias in the late 1990s in the eastern DRC, for example, traced inexactly the contours laid down both by both physical geography (rivers, valleys), ethnic authority (chieftainships) and local administration (*territoires*). While to some extent the militias were ethnically organised, the shifting territories over which they exerted control did not precisely coincide with the homelands they purported to protect. This imprecision increased further the ambiguity of power and control that is at the heart of 'potential difference', offering further gaps and spaces in the structure of authority that could be exploited for profit on an opportunistic basis.

Before discussing what might be done to address the issue of proliferating internal borderlands in Africa, it is worth noting that the regional, transfrontier dimensions of the wars in the 1990s also accelerated a process through which national boundaries began more and more to resemble internal ones. Scholars have long noted that national boundaries in Africa and elsewhere were, from the beginning, far more porous – to population flows, to the licit and illicit movement of commodities – than governments contended. Thus, illicit export of the DRC's rich mineral wealth through regional trading routes was already alive and well at independence in 1960 (Vwakyanakazi, 1991). But just as the regional war complexes of the 1990s hardened internal demarcations and carved out violent interstices within state boundaries, so they also straddled those state boundaries and further softened their efficacy. Arguably, therefore, for periods in the late 1990s, the effective boundary between Rwanda and the DRC was no longer the internationally recognised one running North/South up the middle of Lake Kivu, but was rather the internal one reflected by the East/West partition of Congolese territory between forces loyal to the Kinshasa government and those of the RCD. Across the international border, people, arms and goods flowed with relative abandon; across the internal partition, almost everything had come to a deadly standstill.

## Internal borderlands and post-conflict reconstruction

Several points relevant for reconstruction become immediately apparent. First, internal borderlands are numerous and diverse in contemporary Africa, particularly in the aftermath of violent conflict. Second, one should assume neither that such borderlands are uniformly new, contingent products of recent violence, nor that they are primordially and unfathomably old. Each borderland, rather, must be understood within its own particular historical context. Third, the existence of a border of any kind, including an internal one, creates a potential difference: an inducement to leverage a profit across it, and an incentive, therefore, to preserve it, experienced both by powerful conflict entrepreneurs and those realising only survival livelihoods. Measures to redress the effects of enclavisation may, thus, expect to meet some resistance, not only from the powerful but also, more surprisingly, from the weak (Jackson, 2005).

Before continuing, however, it should be stressed that this chapter takes as an operating assumption that the re-knitting together of enclavised states would represent, on balance, a net good for both the inhabitants of those states and for global welfare too. Post-conflict state reconstruction is, of course, never the entirely neutral endeavour that it pretends to be – its theory and practice cannot be insulated from the embedded interests of political elites at the global, regional, national or local levels. Whether those engaged in 'liberal peace interventions' are best understood as 'coercive external powers' rather than 'facilitating partners in a shared project' of reconstruction – as Chandler (Chapter 19, this volume) suggests – disenclavisation represents, even after the most bleak mode of political economy analysis, the choice of the lesser of two evils. Bluntly put, the majority of civilians caught in the paramilitary crossfire along the frontlines of the war economy that internal borderlands have come to represent are likely to be better off (and, in all likelihood, to understand themselves as better off), on balance, if their territory can be reclaimed from the violent control of fragmentary militias and re-joined politically, economically and socially to the national territory. It might be argued that statebuilding's primary goal is to reinsert post-conflict territories back into a globalised economy on unfavourable terms (Chapter 3, this volume). But the point about war economics, at least in the DRC, is that enclavisation never severed these internal borderlands from the global, or from global forms of, economic predation. Rather, the paramilitary control of artisanal mining of commodities such as coltan during the years of war ensured that mineral-rich parts of the DRC were bound into global relations of production more tightly than ever. In short, enclavisation severed the DRC from itself, never from the global. As first principles of political economy suggest, any prescription for reform should take careful account of that reform's likely redistributive impact (in terms of both economic and political power) and, thus, of the likelihood of attempts from both 'above' and 'below' (Jackson, 2006a) to undermine, divert or co-opt it. But to recognise this danger is not to concede that all efforts at reform are inexorably doomed to failure; nor that all such reforms are, in reality, Trojan horses for special interests.

What measures, then, can be taken to reverse the trend towards enclavisation and the proliferation of internal borderlands? The first and most obvious priority is assisting the state to gain or regain its Weberian monopoly of the legitimate means of coercive violence within the national territory. Extending authority is easier to state than to effect in a continent awash with light arms and where rampant rates of unemployment leave large numbers of youths with little visible alternative to making survival livelihoods with an AK-47. But concerted efforts at disarmament, demobilisation and reintegration (DDR) following peace processes have paid dividends in countries such as the DRC, Liberia and Sierra Leone, reducing – if not eliminating – violent enclaves beyond the state's reach. These efforts must be followed up with thoroughgoing endeavours at reform of the security sector (SSR) in order to consolidate the state's monopoly of legitimate force, balanced by the development of mechanisms of democratic oversight.

Even during the phase of ongoing conflict, some efforts at disenclavisation can begin. The establishment of humanitarian corridors or the basic rehabilitation and reopening of trunk roads can have a considerable and immediate impact. In March 2001 (during the phase of active conflict in the DRC), an independent study of the socio-economic impact of road rehabilitation noted that after the reopening of the road between Sake, Mweso and Kanyabayonga, North Kivu, food prices in local markets dropped by 30–50 per cent, returning towards prevailing prices in the provincial capital, Goma (Endanda, 2001). Similarly, throughout 2002 and 2003 long negotiations with multiple belligerents by the UN Mission in the DRC, MONUC, resulted in the gradual reopening of the Congo River to commercial traffic – still the primary and essential means for the transport of basic goods through the gigantic territory that forms the DRC – symbolically and actually beginning to suture a country that had been severed by five years of war (UN, 2003).

In the immediate post-conflict phase, further efforts in these directions become possible. After the conclusion of the Sun City Peace Accords and with the 2003 transition to a Chapter VII peace enforcement mandate for MONUC, it became possible for blue helmets to deploy to secure and reopen principal trunk roads, clearing away roadblocks, carrying out minor rehabilitation and patrolling primary commercial axes in the eastern part of the country (a process that is still far from complete).

Finally, as the post-peace-settlement context begins slowly and unevenly to consolidate and the major bilateral and multilateral aid donors re-engage, further and large-scale reconstruction of the physical infrastructure reconnecting enclaves becomes imaginable. In March 2007, with Belgian government assistance, the newly elected Congolese government celebrated the reopening of a key railway bridge at Nyemba, in Katanga province, at a cost of some €2.5 million, with the intention of reopening trade routes across Lake Tanganyika and (explicitly) disenclavising the eastern DRC (Belgian Development Cooperation, 2007). And in May 2007, the World

Bank announced a US$297 million financing of turbine rehabilitation at the DRC's massive Inga Dam, as well as for transmission lines and a distribution network, promising to reconnect much of the DRC as well as providing electricity for export to South Africa (Wachter, 2007). While such efforts are expensive, their symbolic impact is likely to be as large as their economic effect, with the potential to reconnect a country and provide the first signs of the all-important but elusive peace dividend.

Turning from economic infrastructure to political structures, the proliferation of multiple armed actors in Africa's wars of the 1990s engendered peace agreements that responded by visualising new, rearranged and often decentralised political dispensations. Thus, to turn to a Sudan example, the so-far unsuccessful attempts to negotiate a political peace for Darfur have suggested rebalancing the powers of Khartoum with a substantial measure of devolution to the provincial level. Similarly, the DRC's post-conflict constitution envisages both a vertical de-concentration of powers to the provinces and a redrawing of their boundaries, increasing their number from the present 11 to 26 within the first three years after elections. The explicit logic of this multiplication is to try to form an administrative geography that more closely matches the territorial distribution of ethnic groups.

A number of dangers are inherent in the Congolese urge to decentralise, not least in the aftermath of such a divisive armed conflict. First, it is by no means clear that is either feasible or desirable to try to delineate administrative territories on the basis of monoethnicity (indeed, containing several hundred ethnic groups, the DRC could not realistically do so). Rather, the 26 provinces are more likely to constrain the space within which either single majority ethnic groups dominate politics at the expense of much smaller minorities or contests for power take place between several such groups. Such contests are likely to be strongly marked by a rise in the incendiary language of ethnic authenticity ('autochthony' once more).

Second, in the DRC, the decentralisation of political power is to be accompanied by fiscal autonomy: provinces are to be entitled to 40 per cent of the revenues generated from their territories. This raises several concerns. There will be a strong incentive for elites within resource-rich provinces that are to be split up – such as the mineral-rich Katanga, known for its history of secessionism and ethnic cleansing (Bakajika Bankajikila, 1997) – to ensure that whatever rump territory they continue to dominate includes the areas where natural resources lie. One can therefore expect serious disputes over how the new internal borders are to be drawn, with the language of authenticity instrumentalised to drive the arguments. Equally, once new borders are in place, disparities between 'rich' and 'poor' provinces will be strongly felt in the new internal borderlands created between them, concerning everything from contrasts in social provision to the state of infrastructure.

These concerns collectively raise the question of how well the logic of decentralisation is thought through in post-conflict contexts. The DRC may be an extreme case, but it is hardly untypical. It may not be wise to attempt to decentralise (or at least, to do so too rapidly) in contexts which, arguably, have never been adequately centralised and disenclavised to begin with. As an alternative to 'federalism' after war, Réné Lemarchand, following the work of Arendt Lijphart, has pointed out that institutionalised forms of power-sharing and consociationalism (in which 'incorporation rather than exclusion is seen as the key to conflict resolution') may have more to offer, provided that the underlying dynamic of peace-making is conducive (Lemarchand, 2007).

## Conclusions: an uneven development?

As Mbembe suggests (2000: 286), colonisation and its post-colonial aftermath witnessed forms of development that impacted with distinct unevenness across terrains that were transformed, over the same period, into states. The confident promise of the nation-building regimes that took power after independence has been thwarted in many post-colonial African states by varieties of political, economic and cultural enclavisation. This chapter has suggested a typology of internal borderlands that resulted through a variety of processes. But all forms of internal borderland share a common feature: their ability to present 'potential difference', an incentive to use political power or violent force to leverage profit across them.

While some unevenness will always remain in any society – and may indeed be desirable – post-conflict reconstruction strategies, as well as those of longer-term development, must ensure that they directly address the need to suture war-torn countries back together again, consigning internal borderlands largely to history.

## References

Anderson, Benedict, 1991, *Imagined Communities: Reflections on the Origins and Spread of Nationalism*, London: Verso.

Augé, Marc, 1995, *Non Places: Introduction to an Anthropology of Supermodernity*, London: Verso.

Bakajika Bankajikila, Thomas, 1997, *Epuration Ethnique en Afrique: Les Kasaïens (Katanga 1961 – Shaba 1992)* [Ethnic Cleansing in Africa: the Kasaiens (Katanga 1961 – Shaba 1992)], Paris: L'Harmattan.

Bateson, Gregory, 1958, *Naven: A Survey of the Problems Suggested by a Composite Picture of the Culture of a New Guinea Tribe Drawn from Three Points of View*, Stanford, CA: Stanford University Press.

Bauman, Zygmunt, 2000, *Liquid Modernity*, Cambridge: Polity.

Bayart, Jean-François, Stephen Ellis and Béatrice Hibou, 1999, 'From Kleptocracy to the Felonious State?', in Jean-François Bayart, Stephen Ellis and Béatrice Hibou (eds), *The Criminalization of the State in Africa*, Oxford: James Currey, pp. 1–31.

Behar, Ruth, 1993, *Translated Woman: Crossing the Border with Esperanza's Story*, Boston, MA: Beacon.

Belgian Development Cooperation, 2007, 'Cooperation between Belgium and Congo Officially Resumed', press release, 9 March (at: www.dgcd.be/EN/the_minister/press_releases/20070309.html).
Berdal, Mats and David M. Malone (eds), 2000, *Greed and Grievance: Economic Agendas in Civil Wars*, Boulder, CO: Lynne Rienner.
Biebuyck, Daniel, 1978, *Hero and Chief: Epic Literature from the Banyanga (Zaire Republic)*, Berkeley, CA: University of California Press.
Bouvier, Pierre, 1972, 'Un Problème de Sociologie Politique: Les Frontières des Etats Africains' [A Problem of Political Sociology: The Frontiers of African States], *Revue de l'Institut de Sociologie*, No. 4, pp. 685–720.
De Boeck, Filip, 1996, 'Postcolonialism, Power and Identity: Local and Global Perspectives from Zaire', in Richard Werbner and Terence Ranger (eds), *Postcolonial Identities in Africa*, London: Zed Books, pp. 75–106.
Donnan, Hastings and Thomas M. Wilson, 1996, 'An Anthropology of Frontiers', in Donnan and Wilson (eds), *Border Approaches: Anthropological Perspectives on Frontiers*, New York: University Press of America, pp. 1–14.
Donnan, Hastings and Thomas M. Wilson, 1999, *Borders: Frontiers of Identity, Nation and State*, Oxford: Berg.
Endanda, Samuel K., 2001, 'Evaluation Socio-Économique des Travaux de Réhabilitation de la Route Sake–Mweso–Kanyabayonga Réalisés par Agro Action Allemande' [Socio-economic Evaluation of the Reconstruction of the Sake–Mweso–Kanyabayonga Route Undertaken by German Agro Action], Goma: Université Libre des Pays des Grands Lacs.
Flynn, Donna K., 1997, 'We Are the Border: Identity, Exchange, and the State Along the Bénin-Nigeria Border', *American Ethnologist*, Vol. 24, No. 2, pp. 311–30.
Foucault, Michel, 1991, 'Governmentality', in Graham Burchell, Colin Gordon and Peter Miller (eds), *The Foucault Effect: Studies in Governmentality*, Chicago: University of Chicago Press, pp. 87–104.
Geschiere, Peter and Bambi Ceuppens, 2005, 'Autochthony: Global or Local?', *Annual Review of Anthropology*, Vol. 34, pp. 385–407.
Geschiere, Peter and Stephen Jackson, 2006, 'Autochthony and the Crisis of Citizenship: Democratization, Decentralization, and the Politics of Belonging', *African Studies Review*, Vol. 49, No. 2, pp. 1–14.
Geschiere, Peter and Francis Nyamnjoh, 2001, 'Capitalism and Autochthony: The Seesaw of Mobility and Belonging', in Jean Comaroff and John Comaroff (eds), *Millennial Capitalism and the Culture of Neoliberalism*, Durham, NC: Duke University Press.
Goodhand, Jonathan, 2004, 'Afghanistan in Central Asia', in Michael Pugh and Neil Cooper with Jonathan Goodhand (eds), *War Economies in a Regional Context: Challenges of Transformation*, Boulder, CO: Lynne Rienner, pp. 45–89.
Goodhand, Jonathan, 2005, 'Frontiers and Wars: The Opium Economy in Afghanistan', *Journal of Agrarian Change*, Vol. 5, No. 2, pp. 191–216.
International Crisis Group, 2000, *Scramble for the Congo: Anatomy of an Ugly War*, Africa Report No. 26, 20 December.
International Rescue Committee (IRC), 2004, 'Mortality in the Democratic Republic of Congo: Results from a Nationwide Survey (Conducted April–July 2004)', Bukavu and New York: IRC.
Jackson, Stephen, 2001, 'Nos Richesses Sont Pillées: Economies de Guerre et Rumeurs de Crime dans les Kivus, République Démocratique du Congo' [Our Wealth Pillaged: War Economies and Rumours of Crime in the Kivus, DRC], *Politique Africaine*, No. 84, December.

Jackson, Stephen, 2002, 'Making a Killing: Criminality and Coping in the Kivu War Economy', *Review of African Political Economy*, Vol. 29 (93/94), pp. 21–36.

Jackson, Stephen, 2003a, 'War Making: Uncertainty, Improvisation & Involution in the Kivu Provinces, DR Congo, 1997–2002', unpublished PhD thesis, Princeton University.

Jackson, Stephen, 2003b, 'Fortunes of War: The Coltan Trade in the Kivus', in Sarah Collinson (ed.), *Power, Livelihoods and Conflict: Case Studies in Political Economy Analysis for Humanitarian Action*, Humanitarian Policy Group report No. 13, Overseas Development Institute, London.

Jackson, Stephen, 2005, 'Protecting Livelihoods in Violent Economies', in Karen Ballentine (ed.), *Peaceful Profits: Approaches to Managing the Resource Dimensions of Armed Conflict*, Boulder, CO: Lynne Rienner, pp. 153–84.

Jackson, Stephen, 2006a, 'Borderlands and the Transformation of War Economies: Lessons from the DR Congo', *Conflict, Security & Development*, Vol. 6, No. 3, pp. 425–47.

Jackson, Stephen, 2006b, 'Sons of Which Soil? The Language and Politics of Autochthony in Eastern D.R. Congo', *African Studies Review*, Vol. 49, No. 2, pp. 95–123.

Katzenellenbogen, Simon, 1996, 'It Didn't Happen at Berlin: Politics, Economics and Ignorance in the Setting of Africa's Colonial Boundaries', in Paul Nugent and Anthony I. Asiwaju (eds), *African Boundaries: Barriers, Conduits and Opportunities*, London: Pinter, pp. 21–34.

Kopytoff, Igor, 1989, *The African Frontier: The Reproduction of Traditional African Societies*, Bloomington, IN: Indiana University Press.

Le Billon, Philippe, 2001, 'The Political Ecology of War: Natural Resources and Armed Conflicts', *Political Geography*, Vol. 20, No. 5, pp. 561–84.

Lemarchand, Réné, 2007, 'Consociationalism and Power Sharing in Africa: Rwanda, Burundi and the Democratic Republic of the Congo (DRC)', *African Affairs*, Vol. 106, No. 422, pp. 1–20.

Long, Norman and Magdalena Villareal, 1999, 'Small Product, Big Issues: Value Contestations and Cultural Identities in Cross-Border Commodity Networks', in Birgit Meyer and Peter Geschiere (eds), *Globalization and Identity: Dialectics of Flow and Closure*, Oxford: Blackwell, pp. 125–50.

Malkki, Liisa, 1995, *Purity and Exile: Violence, Memory, and National Cosmology among Hutu Refugees in Tanzania*, Chicago: University of Chicago Press.

Mamdani, Mahmood, 1996, *Citizen and Subject: Contemporary African and the Legacy of Late Colonialism*, London: James Currey.

Marks, Joshua, 2007, *Border in Name Only: Arms Trafficking and Armed Groups At the DRC–Sudan Border*, Geneva: Small Arms Survey.

Mbembe, Achille, 2000, 'At the Edge of the World: Boundaries, Territoriality, and Sovereignty in Africa', *Public Culture*, Vol. 12, No. 1, pp. 259–84.

Mbembe, Achille, 2001, *On the Postcolony*, Berkeley, CA: University of California Press.

Meyer, Birgit and Peter Geschiere (eds), 1999, *Globalization and Identity: Dialectics of Flow and Closure*, Oxford: Blackwell.

Nugent, Paul and Anthony I. Asiwaju (eds), 1996, *The Future of African Boundaries*, London: Pinter.

Pakenham, Thomas, 1991, *The Scramble for Africa: White Man's Conquest of the Dark Continent from 1876 to 1912*, New York: Avon Books.

Prunier, Gerard, 2004, 'Rebel Movements and Proxy Warfare: Uganda, Sudan and the Congo (1986–1999)', *African Affairs*, Vol. 103, No. 412, pp. 359–83.

Richani, Nazih, 2002, *Systems of Violence: The Political Economy of War and Peace in Colombia*, Albany, NY: State University of New York Press.

Richards, Paul, 1996, 'The Sierra Leone – Liberia Boundary Wilderness: Rain Forests, Diamonds and War', in Paul Nugent and Anthony I. Asiwaju (eds), *African Boundaries: Barriers, Conduits and Opportunities*, London: Pinter.

Scott, James, 1998, *Seeing Like a State: How Certain Schemes to Improve the Human Condition Have Failed*, New Haven, CT: Yale University Press.

UN, 2003, 'Second Special Report of the Secretary-General on the United Nations Organization Mission in the Democratic Republic of the Congo', UN doc., S/2003/566.

Vila, Pablo, 1999, 'Constructing Social Identities in Transnational Contexts: The Case of the Mexico–US Border', *International Social Science Journal*, Vol. 51, No. 159, pp. 75–88.

Vlassenroot, Koen and Tim Raeymaekers, 2005, 'The Formation of Centres of Profit, Power and Protection: Conflict and Social Transformation in Eastern DR Congo', occasional paper, Centre of African Studies, University of Copenhagen.

Vwakyanakazi, Mukohya, 1991, 'Import and Export in the Second Economy in North Kivu', in Janet MacGaffey (ed.), *The Real Economy of Zaire: The Contribution of Smuggling and Other Unofficial Activities to National Wealth*, Philadelphia, PA: University of Pennsylvania Press, pp. 43–71.

Wachter, Sarah, 2007, 'Giant Dam Projects Aim to Transform African Power Supplies', *International Herald Tribune*, 19 June.

Weiss, Thomas G., 2004, 'Guns in the Borderlands: Reducing the Demand for Small Arms', monograph No. 95, Institute for Security Studies, Pretoria.

Willame, Jean-Claude 1997, *Banyarwanda et Banyamulenge: Violences Ethniques et Gestion de L'identitaire au Kivu [Banyarwanda and Banyamulenge: Ethnic Violence and the Emergence of the Kivu Identity]*, Paris: L'Harmattan.

# Part VI
# Civil Society

# 16
# Welfare and the Civil Peace: Poverty with Rights?

*Oliver P. Richmond*

> *Everyone, as a member of society, has the right to social security and is entitled to realization, through national effort and international cooperation and in accordance with the organization and resources of each State, of the economic, social and cultural rights indispensable for his dignity and the free development of his personality.*
>
> Article 22

> *Everyone has the right to a standard of living adequate for the health and well-being of himself and of his family, including food, clothing, housing and medical care and necessary social services, and the right to security in the event of unemployment, sickness, disability, widowhood, old age or other lack of livelihood in circumstances beyond his control.*
>
> Article 25

> *Everyone has the right freely to participate in the cultural life of the community, to enjoy the arts and to share in scientific advancement and its benefits.*
>
> Article 27
> UN Universal Declaration of Human Rights, 1948

Though the importance of a social contract and civil peace has long been recognised, peacebuilding approaches have increasingly been co-opted by a statebuilding agenda that reflects a predatory, neoliberal, ideological perspective aiming to justify and enhance the governance of unruly others. Lockean liberalism, which aimed at the social contract between subjects and rulers over the preservation of life, liberty and property is heavily reflected in the intellectual discourses of conflict resolution and liberal peacebuilding. Yet, societies, groups, identities, cultures and welfare are often only rhetorically part of this discourse, even though the problem of the civil peace has come to preoccupy the Western-dominated peacebuilding consensus.

Peacebuilding is supposed to both create and promote a vibrant civil society. It receives much of its support and legitimacy in war-torn situations from civil society and local actors, meaning that the notion of a civil society acts as a validation of peacebuilding strategies and objectives. While this might be taken to denote the indigenous nature of peace, 'civil society' represents a Western view of non-governmental actors, citizens, subjects, workers, consumers and institutions. These are claimed to be empowered from above in order to represent themselves, exercise their own agency, lobby and advocate. It often conflates welfare and cultural rights in similar, but secondary, rhetorical categories. Empowerment must be carried out in the shadow of 'security' and within the dominant neoliberal ethic, and must comprise individual rights, economic freedom and independence and access to politically representative institutions. An indigenous civil peace and civil society represents a dichotomy much noted by critical thinkers, and also by indigenous actors in conflict zones, who often point to the gulf between them and the socially engineered and artificially promoted civil society imagined by international actors (Sylvester, 2006).

While culture has received some attention in the literature, the question of social welfare is rarely mentioned. For example, a consultation paper for the UK's Department for International Development conflict policy (2006) recognised the close relationship between conflict and development, and the importance of 'culture', but omitted social welfare. Yet, welfare is integral to the Declaration of Human Rights (Articles 22, 23 and 25) and the International Covenant on Economic, Social and Cultural Rights (Articles 6, 9, 11 and 13). Indeed, the post-Second World War Marshall Plan provided an early example, in a Keynesian context, of provision for employment and assistance. It is particularly perplexing that welfare has been ignored, when it might be expected to have been seen as a way of empowering and co-opting civil society and 'culture' for the purposes of the liberal peace. Instead, it has been displaced by neoliberalism.

This chapter argues that the key feature of the dominant liberal approach to peacebuilding represents a neoliberal marketisation of peace, rather than engagement with the agents and subjects of this peace. This is a particularly Western and Enlightenment-derived discourse of peace, which is far from culturally and socially sensitive, and has little chance of establishing a locally self-sustaining peace. The following section examines welfare theories. This is followed by a discussion of peacebuilding and neoliberalism. The chapter then turns to the importance of incorporating welfare in peacebuilding strategies if a viable social contract and self-sustaining peace are to be achieved in post-conflict environments.

## Theories of welfare

The need for welfare strategies was powerfully established by Thomas Paine in his *Rights of Man* (1791–1792). He argued that welfare was needed to provide both justice and stability. Subsequently, welfare was not necessarily about empowering the individual (as indicated by Bismarck's reforms) but designed to prevent workers from rebelling, and in its modern, post-William Beveridge form this was a key assumption. Asa Briggs made the case in more modernist terms: the welfare state emerged to moderate the market by guaranteeing a minimum wage, dealing with economic insecurity and vulnerability, and providing universal access to key services (Briggs, 1961). Richard Titmuss outlined the questions that arose. These included: whether entitlement is determined by legal, contractual, contributory, financial, discretionary or professional calculations; who is entitled and why; and what methods are used to determine the above, allocate and make payments (Titmuss, 1968). The task of the welfare state was to redistribute or compensate, but in both senses to provide for social justice, economic stability and efficiency (Barr, 1998).

The welfare state has been described as the 'peace formula of advanced capitalist democracies... following the Second World War' (Offe, 1982). This consisted of the state's obligation to provide welfare where the market could not oblige, in order to overcome societal contradictions between capital and labour. Such systems often emerged as a result of conflict or crisis (Offe, 1982: 8). They may offer universal or minimalist solutions to welfare issues. In the Keynesian environment, welfare was seen as an economic method to stabilise the political system. Indeed the Marshall Plan, an early experience of the sort of reconstruction that this indicated, has been widely lauded. Some, however, saw it as indicative of a US superiority syndrome, of a totalitarian form of liberalism (Jennings, 2003). Others abstracted from this experience the need to make the development of social capital a key part of peacebuilding/statebuilding, which would have the effect of making reconstruction as local as possible so that local participants, own, define, control and develop their own social capital. This would lead, it was suggested, to much great sustainability (Coyne, 2005: 22). Tellingly, Christopher Coyne argued that indigenous institutions should reflect reconstruction efforts rather than the other way around, meaning that the indigenous is a rubber stamp, for the reconstruction effort (Coyne, 2005: 24), but the key is that without an engagement with indigenous welfare needs, peacebuilding will not lead to a sustainable outcome.

In poor societies, the state is less likely than in wealthy societies to be stable or able to develop (Przeworski *et al.*, 2000: 269–70). Because of this, Anthony Giddens has argued for what he calls 'positive welfare' which goes beyond wealth creation and includes psychological welfare that avoids creating situations of moral hazard, provides for individual behaviour to follow a dependent pattern and focuses on the development of civil society (Giddens, 1998: 114–17). Guiliano Bonoli argues that welfare systems are crucial in sustaining successful political mobilisation through the creation of labour movements and social democratic parties, which lead to the adoption of market regulations, social insurance and welfare services (Bonoli, 2005: 434).

Despite the experience of liberal states that stability is easily undermined for individuals by direct economic difficulties (from the Weimar Republic to East Timor in 2006), welfare support is institutionally absent in most conflict zones, often only supplied in a patchy manner by a smattering of NGOs. Indeed, land ownership is often thought of as the social insurance system in developing, post-conflict countries, especially where land is owned and worked on a small scale by peasant farmers. Yet it is generally accepted that development is necessary for, and parallel to, democratisation, and that a strong economy will lead to a representative politics that will undercut and replace both violence and unrepresentative political processes. These are reciprocal conditions in that democratisation allows for a fairer distribution of economic resources, and development provides resources to distribute and coordination of their distribution (Kotze, 2004: 70–1). Thus, this provides navigation points for policymakers involved in peacebuilding processes in post-conflict environments who work to establish a sustainable and self-sustaining peace. Local partners amongst the elites and civil society are expected to accept this framework, and the relationship this develops is structured around political and economic conditionalities established by the World Bank, IMF, and other organisations they cooperate with. Yet the development model articulated by these conditional relationships does not meet the expectations of the vast bulk of the populations.

Adam Przeworski has argued that development requires structural transformation and ethical change, *growth* and increases in income, productivity, consumption, investment, education, life expectancy, employment, childbirth survival and other quality of life factors in a liberal state setting (Przeworski *et al.*, 2000: 1–3). However, economic growth may not be linked to democracy in poor states, especially where sufficient income replacement is unlikely or absent. Indeed, egalitarian income distribution is a necessary condition for the development of democratic stability, which may be dependent to a large degree on income replacement (Przeworski *et al.*, 2000: 73). However, because most peacebuilding takes place in low development contexts, local cultures are often defined as subsistence-based, patronage-based, corrupt and nepotistic, in order to absolve international actors of welfare responsibility and to indicate that societies are incapable of developing without external direction. Yet, these are often substitution strategies in the absence of a buoyant economy. Because there is no interim welfare substitution, local culture is deemed unsuited for development, rather than neoliberal strategies being deemed unsuited to the local environment. In targeting these deficiencies, neoliberal policies fail to provide welfare, undermine what little substitution strategies there are and infantilise local culture, while proponents remain unaware of or, even worse, unconcerned with their own cultural assumptions and deficiencies.

But why is welfare not generally taken to be part of the short-term attempt to consolidate transitions from war to processes of peace? After all, given strong evidence that democratisation requires individuals to be able to count on economic survival, given that neoliberal strategies cannot provide this immediately, and given that aid agencies and NGOs often struggle even to provide emergency assistance on a scale needed, it would seem obvious that an international agency tasked with the provision of income replacement and welfare is required. Furthermore, because peace processes often occur in developing countries where incomes are low, the costs of such a process would not necessarily be exorbitant. The obvious benefit – beyond a humanitarian contribution – would be to prevent further marginalisation of individuals, their radicalisation and their co-option into grey or black markets or into militias.

Yet arguments such as Charles Murray's that welfare states produce underclasses or Lawrence Mead's that they produce new forms of poverty and dependency (Pierson and Castles, 2000) tend to dominate. Neoliberals argue that welfare is a disincentive to investment and work, and create dependence (Offe, 1982: 9). Similarly, some have argued that government welfare enables it to claim rights and exercise powers over individuals that it would not otherwise be able to (Hayek, 1959). As has been comprehensively shown (Goldman, 2005; McEwan, 1999) – to the extent that 'Marshall Plans' and basic welfare proposals are now mentioned in the context of conflict environments such as Iraq or parts of sub-Saharan Africa – these are weak and ideological, rather than substantive criticisms, especially if an *everyday peace* is to be achieved.

## The neoliberal culture of peacebuilding

In the context of peacebuilding, welfare policies would, if supported through outside means in the short term, support the creation of stable polities. Individuals, knowing that peacebuilding entails welfare, might be more predisposed towards the development of a long-term peace process. This would necessitate the engagement of an international institution capable of communicating directly with locals about their everyday needs, free of neoliberal prescriptions. This would enable an open discussion about what requirements might enable the construction of a social contract and prevent a reversion to violence. This would require that international actors and donors had linguistic and cultural competency, and could engage with the local context. On this basis, it might engender a locally led discussion about what constitutes the welfare policies necessary to stabilise everyday life and lead to democratic politics. This might include pensions, child benefit, unemployment benefit, food subsidies, free schooling, free healthcare, other public services and infrastructure, as well as an international discussion about how these services can be funded with immediate effect.

Though the liberal peace does not discount the need for such institutions, the gradual insertion of neoliberal strategies into peacebuilding (for ideological reasons, or following US and Western national interests) has undermined the crucial link between welfare and politics in a way which undermines the liberal project. The current proscription of welfare ties in very closely with the positivist emphasis on the state and with the subjugation of the individual and her subjective constitution through emotional, cultural, material resources and connections. The fatal error of institutionalised liberal peacebuilding has been its willingness to be co-opted within the positivist, problem-solving methods and epistemology, which have effectively led to its failure as a practice in various parts of the world. Why, then, have such a set of insights, based upon the experience of post-war reconstruction, and the development of the Western liberal state, been ignored, particularly in the context of the now common assertion that a stable and dynamic civil society (at least as it is understood in the eyes of the peacebuilding community) is required, and that local cultural dynamics should be respected by external interveners?

Much hope is placed upon the assumed 'natural' desire of civil society for peace, as a collective will. As Vivienne Jabri has argued, some see this as a product of a new cosmopolitan order. Such an order allows for cultural difference and rests on an emancipatory global governance, but where: 'The local is in these circumstances the exotic, the private, the traditional, the parochial, the non-democratic, the non-political. Culture... [constitutes] that which is associated with the other of the modern, the progressive, the universal' (Jabri, 2007: 267).

This cosmopolitan process, which is effectively constituted by the construction of the liberal peace in post-conflict peacebuilding environments, is also the cause and target of resistance, often from the local for identity and cultural reasons (Jabri, 2007: 267). The local, however, is also connected transnationally within the context of a broader civil society and conceptualisation of peace, endeavouring to articulate its own cosmopolitan values. But this connection between a local and international civil society reifies a particular notion of local and international activism and its associated civil society, concerned with the pillars of the liberal peace – democratisation, human rights, rule of law, and neoliberal marketisation and development. This leads to a notion of the individual as a producer/worker/consumer, rather than as someone located within social and cultural networks, which interact evenly with their material needs and capacities. Thus, the way that liberal peacebuilding has projected the concept of civil society reflects the marketised and neoliberal ideology of the 'developed' states (where political and social rights take precedence over all human capacity). This dynamic is obscured by positivist problem-solving assumptions so that when local recipients of peacebuilding practice react negatively, it looks to the 'neutral' eye of the peacebuilder as if they are somehow dysfunctional, rather than being a problem caused by a failure of peacebuilding. Significantly, however, modernisation and liberalisation through peacebuilding practices lead to the reassertion of local identities as a reaction (Castells, 2003).

Michael Doyle offers a nuanced critique of liberalism and its claims to 'pacific' qualities (Doyle, 1997). He argues that the three main traditions – liberal pacifism, liberal imperialism and liberal internationalism – all propose democracy as an essential component of peace, but make underlying normative assumptions about liberalism's universality. When confronted, these assumptions lead to conflict between liberal supporters and those who reject its internal value system. Liberal states are prone to war with non-liberal states, make a separate peace amongst themselves and have 'discovered liberal reasons for aggression' (Doyle, 1997: 1). Doyle points to Machiavelli and Thucydides as supporters of this thesis, which is aimed at glory through expansion to meet the needs of the population (Doyle, 1997: 2). This indicates that the liberal peace argument is strongly focused on an international peace between states rather than economic welfare, and makes little room for the subjects of the social contract or cultural considerations. In a liberal context the civil peace is viewed from above, from the perspective of elites strongly influenced by neoliberalism as part of the overall liberal peace. It is rarely considered from the perspective of the actual subject. The idea that the subject might be an agent, not just in material terms, is another distant leap.

The liberal–realist discourse in academic International Relations has a similar tendency towards reductionism with particular effects on human life and culture through its neoliberal bias. Doyle's problematisation of liberalism only goes part way to uncovering this. Liberal–realism's reduction and abstraction of human life and culture, symbolised by 'actors, anarchy, interdependencies, threats, rationality', power and interests, lead to dangerous rational calculations that ultimately sacrifice human life and the chance of peace (Sylvester, 2001: 540). International Relations, of course, represents its knowledge systems as universal, when they are actually local to the West/North (Harding, 1998; Sylvester, 2001: 541). Liberal–realism has the advantage of maintaining sovereign control, through a liberal biopolitics of 'peace as governance' (Richmond, 2005) but only through the marginalisation of welfare among those deemed 'backward' in culture or development.

There is, of course, a long geneaology critiquing such thinking. For example, Joseph Schumpeter argued that the success of capitalism would lead to a counter response in which democracy would lead to the election of social democratic parties in order to introduce welfare states. Capitalism would therefore collapse as democratic majorities demanded the creation of a welfare state, as in many cases appeared to happen as civil society voiced grassroots concerns about their access to resources in a capitalist system (Schumpeter, 1943: 63–71). This would indicate that neoliberal systems are merely the extension of elite interests and unsuited to democratic situations, even if they promote the most economic growth over the long term. In this context the state is developed, but not the society, which continues to be marked by inequality. This is debatable in the context of the already developed states, but in a post-conflict development context, the paradox is much more exaggerated. It indicates that peacebuilding does not respond to societal needs, but instead promotes a top-down culture of neoliberal wealth creation in a situation where such institutions are likely to be co-opted by the very elites that conducted conflict in the first place. The conduct of liberal peacebuilding exacerbates the marginalisation of grassroots grievances because of its culture of top-down institutionalism and neoliberalism.

Another body of work extends such a critique into a development context. Development studies aims to improve living standards and prosperity in the developing world, using Western knowledge and technology rather than indigenous approaches. Development work therefore focuses on material gain as conceptualised by Western governance. This has been heavily criticised, not just from the point of view of being counter-productive, but also for its inherent violence and for monopolising the 'developing' body and mind in order to homogenise polities within the broader liberal community of states (Briggs and Sharp, 2004; Duffield, 2002; Sylvester, 2006). This neocolonial/imperial critique therefore requires that local knowledge and culture be reconfigured within a democratic, neoliberal statebuilding process entirely controlled by liberal peacebuilders. As Sylvester has argued, this risks the creation of 'bare life' for those being 'developed' (Sylvester, 2006: 67; also Agamben, 1998). Their inter-subjective existence is not valued unless it corresponds to the objective liberal project. As Agamben writes, bare life comes about because of the Western political habit of exclusion that simultaneously claims to be inclusive (Agamben, 1998: 7). Thus bodies are managed and governed and resistance is not tolerated. Resistance is described as terrorism or corruption, and those who then police the liberal system are counter-described as fascists (Patel and McMichael, 2004). Even if society aspires to the liberal project, however, neoliberalism means bare life for many who suffer from poverty despite their aspirations for a liberal state. What appears to be emerging is open to Franz Fanon's critique of the postcolonial state. For example, in Algeria, which he argued was economically defunct, the state could not support social relations, and resorted to coercion to control unfulfilled citizens (Fanon, 1967). Similarly, liberal peacebuilders create capacity-less, virtually liberal, post-conflict states and governments in the expectation that society will respond positively and follow. By implication, liberal peacebuilding identifies local politics as deviant and therefore constructs democratic processes with almost immediate effect. But though they mark local economies as corrupt, they fail to provide welfare for local communities. Local communities are consigned to a bare life of political rights without economic opportunities, and deaths are put down to poverty rather than inadequate economic provision by liberal peacebuilders. There is no local culture worth intervening to preserve as the preceding conflict is often taken to demonstrate. The focus must be on democratic and market institutions as the precursor of societal and cultural well-being.

This ties in with post-colonial debates, which see Western liberalism constantly juxtaposing itself with other systems, which are identified as 'barbaric' and contrary to the liberal norm (Chan *et al.*, 2001). Barbarians are noted only for their violence, whereas those not engaged in violent acts of resistance or terrorism are essentially the pupils of liberalism and are invisible (Spivak, 1999: 277) until they have graduated into the school of mature liberal societies and states. For Edward Said the cultural implications of this denoted 'orientalism', in which liberals discursively dominate and dehumanise the non-liberal, non-Western subject (Said, 1978: 291), this means death through conflict, humanitarian intervention, preventive war, torture, genocide, human rights abuse, with little direct concern from the liberal international community. But disturbingly, those for whom this means poverty-with-rights (civil, political and human) are nevertheless insecure. These subjects are politically enabled but economically vulnerable. The cultural assumption is that these two fundamental components of liberalism, connected in most Western states by long agreement on a set of welfare-oriented policies, can be disconnected in under-developed (read primitive) polities in which civil society is minimal. Indeed, following Polanyi some argue that capitalism and its inculcation into multilateral development institutions promotes a disciplinary approach in which social relations are dismembered if they impede neoliberalism (cited in Patel and McMichael, 2004: 235). Karl Polanyi argued that fascism was the outcome of liberalism's failure, leading to civil society's resistance being disciplined by the capitalist state (ibid., 2004: 239). On a larger scale, this sort of disciplining became part of global governance whereby international financial institutions (IFIs) impose strategies that would lead to bare life, and cause civil resistance that requires states to take on a disciplinary role. Thus, neoliberal development strategies do not support the liberal peace, or at least its civil component, but instead betray a cultural blindness on the part of peacebuilders who do not see contradictions between replicating liberal states in post-conflict settings, while treating locals as voiceless, unempowered and sacrificeable. Indeed, neoliberalism entails the active elimination of any existing welfare entitlements and social safety nets that are often rooted in cultural practices.[1]

## The social contract and the neoliberal denial of welfare

A pioneering study by Michael Pugh *et al.* (2004) has investigated the impacts of these sorts of strategies in the context of war economies and attempts to develop a political economy of peace. Pugh is clear about the dangers of a lack of social welfare in peacebuilding, and the futility of leaving it to the market, thereby reproducing the empty shell of the state. Agencies need to be focused on income generation and poverty reduction and so distributive justice, avoiding doing this in a neocolonial fashion. Peacebuilding approaches therefore need to establish meaningful forms of participation for local actors and civil society (Turner and Pugh, 2006), a clear implication of engaging with welfare.

While liberal peacebuilding is based upon claimed universal norms, and eschews relativist accounts of peace, when it comes to the problem of transitional social welfare, peacebuilding donors and policymakers are content to adopt a relativist position without developing a centralised policy and leave such issues to the *ad hoc* ministrations of NGOs and agencies. It reflects how liberal states treat their own citizens who are unable to be productive or are unemployed. Indeed liberal peacebuilding itself, though conducted by many social democracies, tends to follow the neoliberal state model. Intellectually, this induces a relativism between existing liberal states and others, indicating that supposed cultural sensitivities at the grassroots level among international actors mask their relative lack of interest in the lives of individuals beyond their political and human rights. Yet it is a fundamental truism that economic expectations and rights need to be resolved early if the state itself is to be protected from political and social instability. Also apparent, however, is that local actors are, if not materially, then discursively, able to resist the implications of such peacebuilding strategies, through vocal and physical resistance, discursive deconstruction and through a process of negotiation over the nature of the liberal peace being laid down. Indeed, such resistance often results in a subtle co-option of the liberal peacebuilding process by the local actors who are assumed to be its subjects, as has occurred, for example, in Kosovo (Richmond and Franks, 2008). In this sense the newly emerging social contract, a reaction to neoliberal versions of peacebuilding, represents a reassertion of the local (though not the absent or romanticised local of neoliberalism), and will connect decisively not just with discussions of governance, power and institutions, but basic needs and cultural empowerment.

Some of these issues are now being investigated in the context of an emerging literature on culture, conflict resolution and peacebuilding, on local ownership, custodianship and participation, and on indigenous methodologies and ontologies of peace. However, there is very little work on the question of how peacebuilders see or ignore the indigenous by focusing on basic human rights and political representation and identity, which is constituted according to the interveners' own normative frameworks and social or political expectations. This biases peacemaking efforts towards the replication of life via top-down governance in post-conflict zones as a parallel to that in developed liberal states. The major omissions this causes relate in particular to a general belief that a social contract appears in parallel to institutions of governance.

There is an obvious inconsistency, or at least an obvious assumption, here relating to the relative value ascribed to political, economic, social and cultural practices, the need for normalisation within the liberal model, and a relative devaluing of the economic and welfare rights of individuals in post-conflict zones. Symptomatic is the emergence of the predatory liberal state and the undermining of a social contract. This represents an unexplained institutional framework that implicitly argues for top-down building of political, economic and social structures, at the same time accepting that these make an impact on post-conflict societies at different speeds. Democratisation is experienced as soon as elections are held, and in the interim period beforehand it provides an expectation of political rights soon to be established. Social intervention by agencies is longer term, though this is generally accepted as something that may take years or even generations. Votes and social change effectively represent abstract reforms for the individual in this interim period. Yet, after security, the most basic attribute of a liberal society is the ability to be productive and therefore independent, offering individuals the capacity to support themselves and their families as political and social reform develops. Yet, for all the trumpeting of aid and development (the role of the World Bank and the IMF), this aspect often lags far behind other reform projects. Individuals are left to fend for themselves in an economic environment where opportunities are generally absent. It appears that international actors reflect upon this as a separate problem, relating to local culture and to long-standing and traditional power hierarchies in which economic resources have always been extremely scarce for the masses. Where there is a concern about local culture, and an indigenous, civil peace, this is also associated with identifying local cultural psychoses, ethnic entrepreneurs and their motivations, or with attempts to co-opt the potential of indigenous peacemaking.

What emerges from all of this is the massive emphasis on top-down institution building, external trusteeship and administration, and the importation of liberal values, political, social, economic and development models, by an epistemic community of peacebuilders who focus on blueprint institutions over individual needs and the social contract. These actors profess to 'do no harm', and often turn to local cultural practices in order to assimilate them into the top-down construction of the liberal peace, in order to give this project a sheen of legitimacy and grassroots consent. But this turn normally does not occur until after a top-down institutionalist approach has been tried and has begun to show signs of failure. This reflects the mindset of neoliberalism exactly, however, in that a blueprint based upon a set of assumptions about institutions and economic development establishes a situation where privileged or wealthy actors are enabled in order to drag along the rest of society.

The civil peace is often said to be the most significant component of the liberal peacebuilding project. After all, what good are institutions if the general population of a state does not take part in them, or they do not represent a contract between individuals, representatives and the state? This requires a consistent and long-term welfare component, not just to the peace process but to the polity that emerges from that process. Yet critical thinkers have pointed out that the civil peace is often virtual, a charade, referred to by international actors only to legitimate the new institutional reforms they sponsor, and at best is recognised only as a dependent entity in a relationship of conditionality with international actors, who purport to act benevolently, do so according to their own interests and norms. It has been argued that the civil peace, and indeed the notion of a civil society, is predicated on the notion of NGOs taking responsibility for civil society and providing its requirements for a helpless, hapless and deficient society. It is a Western cultural conception, predicated on social and political rights, which are divorced through a neoliberal sleight of hand from an economic construction of needs that would require the provision of financial support to the individual through the institutionalisation of social welfare programmes. Neoliberal aspects of peacebuilding create a predatory framework of empty governance structures which prevent a social contract from forming, or a stable everyday form of peace.

## Conclusion

Clearly, welfare considerations need to be built into peacebuilding and into the resultant polity that emerges from a successful peace process. Does the general oversight of welfare in contemporary peacebuilding mean that there are cultural reasons for a lack of consideration on this score? The Western and liberal focus on political rights as separate and superior to economic rights betrays a certain Orientalism towards the inhabitants of post-conflict states, whose populations value political rights but might well give economic rights and opportunities a higher priority.

Interestingly, the failures in Iraq have led to more concrete policies being devised for job creation (Pilkington, 2007). Apparently, the foreign occupiers have realised that the responsibilities they took on include not just security, political reform and marketisation, but also building a social contract by engaging with the everyday life of ordinary Iraqis.[2] Indeed, one could interpret the shift towards a military disengagement in Iraq as an attempt to evade the full responsibilities that liberal peacebuilding implies in terms of everyday life and as confirmation of the failures of neoliberalism. Similarly, in Afghanistan the toleration by internationals of the opium trade, corruption and poor governance might also be read as an abrogation of the responsibilities that even liberal peacebuilding implies, and evasion of this implied critique of neoliberalism.

This may well reflect developed states' post-Cold War experience and their over-emphasis on security and institutions in peacebuilding. But parallel development of these strategies, both from a theoretical and institutional perspective, has not caught up with the increasingly obvious needs *in situ*, nor with the notion that such a reorientation would necessitate a broader engagement with local cultural norms and with the high interventionary aspects of liberal peacebuilding. After all, it is probable that such a realisation necessitates either a change in focus for the World Bank (personal interview, Ian Bannon, World Bank, February 2007) and IMF or a new international architecture to take on this role. Of course, even engaging with more welfare-oriented strategies still runs the serious risk of leading to even more conditionalities imposed by welfare strategies, effectively using them to buy local cooperation rather than to open channels of communication with the local. This is a particular problem when peacebuilding is heavily top-down and fails to engage equally with local voices and bottom-up processes.

Is there also a danger that such an approach would lead to even more interventionary strategies by international sponsors of peacebuilding who would now be able to exert further influence and conditionality? This has already occurred to some degree. Where it has been taken up at all, welfare has been generally treated as a tool of neoliberal conditionality rather than a right. This is clear from the policy evolution that has occurred from Somalia to East Timor, and extending into intervention in Afghanistan and Iraq. Yet internationals fail to see that they are offering frameworks that do not provide welfare, and often actively intervene to prevent indigenous welfare institutions from supporting populations. Local cultures often engender a social and economic system that is an expression of mutual responsibility despite limited resources and lack of market infrastructure. Liberal peacebuilding often interferes with this.

This was recognised to some degree in an UNCTAD report on Africa, which reflected on the lessons of the Marshall Plan in the context of contemporary liberal peacebuilding (UNCTAD, 2006). It calls for generous, predictable long-term aid, without outside conditionalities or shock treatment. Furthermore, it is increasingly recognised that 'social peace' (or civil peace in my terminology) depends upon social welfare programmes and is a vital component of the overall liberal peace project. It is only through such provision that social justice, growth and economic stability can be achieved in a balanced manner. Moreover, this is not simply a choice to be made by peacebuilders, but is integral to the standards that are held to be binding in international agreements. Peacebuilding, particularly in its neoliberal incarnation, is institutionally attuned, but not culturally attuned, and therefore, to its cost, discounts welfare.

The claims developed in this chapter indicate the need for the hegemonic liberal peacebuilding agenda to accept that it has taken on a predatory neoliberal character that strips out culture and society by assuming that these are exogenous to the key priorities of statebuilding. A radical rethinking of this agenda is needed, led by its recipients, that would not be resisted for reasons of expediency, efficiency, cost or interest. This seemingly major task is essential if peacebuilding is to become self-sustaining and materially and culturally relevant to the lives of its 'subjects'.

## Acknowledgements

I would like to thank the editors for their very useful comments; errors are, of course, my own.

## Notes

1. Thanks to Neil Cooper for this important point.
2. Thanks to Neil Cooper for this point.

## References

Agamben, Giorgio, 1998, *Homo Sacer: Sovereign Power and Bare Life*, Stanford: Stanford University Press.
Barr, Nicholas, 1998, *The Economics of the Welfare State*, Oxford: Oxford University Press.
Bonoli, Guliano, 2005, 'The Politics of the New Social Policies', *Policy and Politics*, Vol. 33, No. 3, pp. 431–49.
Briggs, Asa, 1961, 'The Welfare State in Historical Perspective', *European Journal of Sociology*, Vol. 11, No. 2, pp. 221–58.
Briggs, John and Joanne Sharp, 2004, 'Indigenous Knowledge and Development', *Third World Quarterly*, Vol. 25, No. 4, pp. 661–76.
Castells, Manuel, 2003, *The Power of Identity*, Oxford: Blackwell.
Chan, Steve, Peter Mandaville and Roland Bleiker, 2001, *The Zen of IR*, London: Palgrave Macmillan.
Coyne, Christopher, 2005, 'After War: Understanding Post-War Reconstruction', Global Prosperity Initiative Working Paper, No. 40, Mercatus Center, George Mason University, Washington, DC.
Doyle, Michael, 1997, *Ways of War and Peace*, New York: Norton.
Duffield, Mark, 2002, 'Social Reconstruction and the Radicalisation of Development', *Development and Change*, Vol. 33, pp. 1049–71.
Fanon, Franz, 1967, *The Wretched of the Earth*, London: Penguin.
Giddens, Anthony, 1998, *Positive Welfare, The Third Way*, Cambridge: Polity.
Goldman, Michael, 2005, *Imperial Nature: The World Bank and the Struggle for Social Justice in an Age of Globalisation*, New Haven, CT: Yale University Press.
Harding, Sandra, 1998, *Is Science Multicultural?* Bloomington, IN: Indiana University Press.
Hayek, Friederich von, 1959, 'The Meaning of the Welfare State', in *The Constitution of Liberty*, London: Routledge.

Jabri, Vivienne, 2007, *War and the Transformation of Global Politics*, London: Palgrave.
Kotze, Dirk, 2004, 'Implications of the Democracy–Development Relationship for Conflict Resolution', *African Journal on Conflict Resolution*, Vol. 4, No. 2, pp. 119–43.
McEwan, Arthur, 1999, *Neo-Liberalism or Democracy*, London: Zed Books.
Offe, Claus, 1982, 'Some Contradictions of the Modern Welfare State', *Critical Social Policy*, Vol. 2, No. 2, pp. 7–16.
Patel, Rajeev and Philip McMichael, 2004, 'Third Worldism and the Lineages of Global Fascism', *Third World Quarterly*, Vol. 25, pp. 231–54.
Pierson, Christopher and Francis Castles, 2000, *The Welfare State Reader*, Cambridge: Polity.
Pilkington, Ed, 2007, 'Bush $1bn Jobs Plan to Draw Iraqis into Fold', *The Guardian*, 8 January.
Przeworski, Adam, Michael Alvarez, J.A. Cheibub and Fernando Limongi, 2000, *Democracy and Development*, Cambridge: Cambridge University Press.
Pugh, Michael, 2007, 'Limited Sovereignty and Economic Security', Working Paper (at: www.st-andrews.ac.uk/intrel/cpcs/papers.htm).
Pugh, Michael and Neil Cooper with Jonathan Goodhand, 2004, *War Economies in a Regional Context: Challenges of Transformation*, Boulder, CO: Lynne Rienner.
Richmond, Oliver P., 2005, *The Transformation of Peace*, London: Palgrave.
Richmond, Oliver P. and Jason Franks, 2008, 'Co-opting the Liberal Peace: Untying the Gordian Knot in Kosovo', *Cooperation and Conflict*, Vol. 43, No. 1, pp. 81–103.
Said, Edward, 1978, *Orientalism*, London: Penguin.
Schumpeter, Joseph, 1943, *Capitalism, Socialism and Democracy*, London: George, Allen & Unwin.
Spivak, Gayatri C., 1999, *A Critique of Post-Colonial Reason*, Cambridge, MA: Harvard University Press.
Sylvester, Christine, 2001, 'Art, Abstraction, and IR', *Millennium*, Vol. 30, No. 3, pp. 535–54.
Sylvester, Christine, 2006, 'Bare Life as Development/Post-Colonial Problematic', *The Geographical Journal*, Vol. 172, No. 1, pp. 66–77.
Titmuss, Richard, 1968, *Universalism versus Selection, Commitment to Welfare*, London: Allen & Unwin.
Turner, Mandy and Michael Pugh, 2006, 'Towards a New Agenda for Transforming War Economies', *Conflict, Security & Development*, Vol. 6, No. 3, pp. 471–9.
UNCTAD, 2006, 'Doubling Aid: Making the *Big Push* Work', Report on Economic Development in Africa (at: www.unctad.org).
Utley, Freda, cited in Ray Salvatore Jennings, 2003, 'The Road Ahead', *Peaceworks*, No. 49, April, pp. 1–40.

# 17
# Peace Constituencies in Peacebuilding: The *Mesas de Concertación* in Guatemala

Cécile Mouly

How do people build peace in the midst of armed confrontation or during post-conflict periods marked by outbreaks of violence? Many scholars argue that a peacebuilding process is sustainable only if it is owned by the population (e.g., Jeong, 2006: 33). This is why it is essential to study the role of local actors in this process. In practice, however, local peace initiatives are often overlooked because they do not fit into the agendas of international agencies. As Prendergast and Plumb (2002: 346–7) argue, 'The potential contributions of local civil society organisations (CSOs) are often ignored or unrecognised by academics and policy makers, who look principally at larger strategic issues and do not view these actors working on "softer" issues such as people-to-people reconciliation as relevant to the larger picture of peace implementation.'

This chapter examines how, despite their limitations, local CSOs can contribute to peacebuilding significantly by broadening the ownership of the process. It does this by drawing on the concept of 'peace constituency', which refers to a network of people from different social sectors, who act in concert in order to build sustainable peace (for extensive analysis, see Mouly, 2004). It is divided into seven sections. The first briefly outlines the concept of 'peace constituency'. The second advocates a critical conflict studies perspective for the understanding of violence and peace. This feeds into the third section, which examines how to build sustainable peace through a 'transformative peacebuilding approach'. The fourth section critically explores the concept of 'peace constituencies', drawing on critiques of approaches to civil society. The fifth section uses insights from social movement theory to further and deepen our understanding of peace constituencies. The sixth section illustrates these points with the Guatemalan *mesas de concertación y seguimiento de los Acuerdos de Paz* (*mesas de concertación* or *mesas* in short), a concept difficult to translate, but which might be conveyed as 'forums for consultation and follow-up of the peace process'. The final section concludes that while peace constituencies are a useful vehicle for ensuring people's ownership over peacebuilding, they are not a panacea and thus their role in peacebuilding must be subjected to critical examination in each context.

## Peace constituencies in civil society

The concept of 'peace constituency' was introduced in the 1990s by John Paul Lederach (1995a, 1997) and has since been used with different nuances by several academics and peace organisations (e.g., Fischer, 2006: 25; International Alert, 1998: 29; Paffenholz, 2002: 9). The concept is attractive since it conveys ideas of comprehensiveness and sustainability. As such, peace constituencies may hold the key to the societal ownership advocated by peacebuilding scholars, their main role being to sustain a peacebuilding process over time and build broad support for it. Defined here as networks of people from different social sectors who act in concert to build sustainable peace, peace constituencies are multisectoral and can include any social actor working for peace.

They can overall be considered as part of civil society since their prevailing interest in building peace and their multisectoral character make them unlikely to be strictly commercial or entirely subordinated to a government. Accordingly, their study can be approached from a social theory perspective and build on theoretical discussions of civil society (see the fourth section). 'Civil society' is defined here as a 'collective of formal and informal associations that are not strictly familial, commercial, or on behalf of government' (see Biekart, 1999: 30). As such, it encompasses a broad range of associations, including, for example, local NGOs, trade unions, women's organisations, human rights groups and peace movements. This definition allows for overlaps between civil society, state and market. Thus it can include popular organisations controlled by the state, or, in the case of some *mesas*, representatives of various sectors, including members of state institutions. The *mesa* of Jutiapa, for example, included representatives of state institutions, women's organisations, peasant organisations, indigenous people, trade unions, the academic and cultural sector, and the media. Civil society is also shaped according to the forms of social organisations, cultural and political traditions proper to each society, as well as state and market structures (Barnes, 2005).

## A critical review of approaches to violence and peacebuilding

Direct, structural and cultural violence are so inter-linked that they cannot be overcome independently from one another. In Guatemala, for instance, the armed conflict was rooted in a history of socio-economic and political exclusion, as well as racism. The report of the Guatemalan truth commission concluded that political violence was a direct expression of structural violence (*Comisión de Esclarecimiento Histórico*, 1999: 18). Yet, not all situations of structural violence lead to direct violence. As Ho-Won Jeong (2000) explains, for violent conflict to arise, subordinate groups must become aware of the unjust power relations that maintain them in a situation of oppression, and mobilise around this issue. Conversely, direct violence in Guatemala reinforced existing patterns of exclusion and racism and came to be perceived as a legitimate way of addressing oppression. While a comprehensive series of peace agreements were signed, culminating in 1996 with the Agreement on a Firm and Lasting Peace, the three types of violence continued to pervade life in Guatemala. Criminal violence and lynching, in particular, have been among the most enduring types of direct violence in post-conflict Guatemala and have reflected high levels of social polarisation and acceptance of violence as a means to address certain social problems.

Cultural violence, the violence embedded in discourses, both stems from and produces other types of violence (Galtung, 1990). Discourses, as shared meanings and practices, result from a process of socialisation, and provide a framework for people to understand their environment and decide a course of action. On the one hand, the cultural norms shared by a group are altered by direct and structural violence. As the Brazilian popular educator Paulo Freire (1998: 40) argues, 'Once a situation of violence and oppression has been established, it engenders an entire way of life and behaviour for those caught up in it.' On the other hand, cultural violence reinforces structural and direct violence. Culture is indeed 'the preserver of the very structures by which it was formed' (Freire, 1998: 161), and it encourages resort to direct violence to address conflict by preventing conflicting parties from perceiving other alternatives (Nagler, 1999). Given that one form of violence breeds other forms, it is necessary to deal with all types of violence to break the vicious circle. Moreover, in the case of an internal armed conflict, one has to address not only the violence at its origin but also the various forms of violence engendered in its course because violent conflict sparks off destructive processes that feed back into it (Ryan, 1995: 226). Armed conflicts indeed do not have clear-cut beginnings or endings and are often followed by other forms of violence (Goodhand, 2006: 10).

Further, agency and structure interact either to foment violence or to build peace (Goodhand, 2006; Goodhand and Hulme, 1999). It is therefore necessary to use different levels of analysis to study the role of peace constituencies in peacebuilding and take into account the influence of their wider context and organisational structure, as well as the values and preferences articulated by peace constituencies as a whole and those of their members. The duality of structure both enables and constrains actors (Giddens, 1984). Actors can contest structures, yet they are often blinded by dominant discourses and cannot see unjust structures around them. The only way to address violent conflict is to progressively replace dominant discourses of war by transformative discourses that enable the various voices in society to be heard and to interact constructively through dialogue (Jabri, 1996). A transformative peacebuilding process requires the free participation of large segments of the population, at the local level, in a collective process of redefining the surrounding conflict situation and establishing bases for peaceful coexistence. This requires opening up 'critical space, where the very foundations of social meaning and practice are examined' and a normative base constructed among local actors (Fetherston, 2000b: 213).

Critical conflict studies have stressed the importance of taking into account cultural violence, present not only in the localities of violence, but also in the 'external' environment. Although several authors have shown, for example, how the neoliberal restructuring imposed by the global multilateral establishment can strongly undermine peacebuilding processes (see, e.g., Boyce and Pastor Jr, 1997), there has been a lack of debate on the impact of international paradigms on local peacebuilding. Moreover, on the whole, peace and conflict researchers have foreclosed discussion of their own participation in discourses of violence (Fetherston, 2000a: 12). Alejandro Bendaña (1996: 75) hence warns that peace and conflict researchers from industrialised countries may propose models and techniques that perpetuate structures and cultures of domination by not paying sufficient attention to the discourses that they bring in.

In addition, it is important to acknowledge, as anthropologists do, that violence is socially constructed and is not experienced in the same way across cultures (see, e.g., Nordstrom, 1997; Robben and Nordstrom, 1995). Thus, what appears as direct violence for some people may not have the same significance for people who do not share the same cultural norms, on the issue of genital mutilation, for instance. Since there is no unanimity as to which acts constitute violence, it is difficult to give an unambiguous definition of the term. Yet, it is possible to observe common patterns empirically, such as the condemnation by many legal systems of rape and homicide. This is why it can still be meaningful to use the term 'violence' while bearing in mind its limitations.

According to Nancy Scheper-Hughes and Philippe Bourgeois (2004a), the social and cultural construction of violence provides interconnections between its different forms. Violence operates 'along a continuum from direct physical assault to symbolic violence and routinised everyday violence, including the chronic, historically embedded structural violence whose visibility is obscured by globalised hegemonies' (Scheper-Hughes and Bourgeois, 2004b: 318).

The fact that conflict and peace researchers work on the basis of a generally accepted notion of peace is also problematic. We can observe empirically that peace, like violence, is socially constructed and is not conceived in the same way by different social actors. This means that researchers risk imposing their own definition of 'peace' without paying due attention to the various meanings of the notion articulated by different social actors. Further, there is a tendency to overlook the contributions to peace by actors who do not frame their main interest in terms of 'peace', as can be seen in the case of human rights or women's groups.

A 'transformative peacebuilding approach', by contrast, requires a questioning of assumptions and discourses (Fetherston, 2000a, b). The concept of 'conflict resolution', for instance, suggests that conflict needs to be eliminated; yet conflict is an essential mechanism for social change (Lederach, 1995b). This concept is consistent with discourses characteristic of modernity, which assume that 'we can "know" – objectify, make rational, understand – violent conflict to such an extent that we can have *power over* it – solve the problem of it' (Fetherston, 2000b: 197). By contrast, the concept of 'conflict transformation' does not suggest a need to put an end to conflict, only a need for it to be transformed so as to reduce its violent manifestations. It is therefore an open-ended and dynamic process, closely related to 'peacebuilding' (Rupesinghe, 1995). While conflict transformation focuses on the transformation of conflict *per se* to overcome contradictions and eliminate its violent expressions, peacebuilding is concerned with building peaceful alternatives to the violence surrounding conflict (Lederach, 1995b: 17). However, in practice, peacebuilding often refers to this dual endeavour, as both processes are intrinsically linked.

## Key elements of a transformative peacebuilding approach

Peacebuilding is thus a long-term process that seeks to address the roots of violent conflict and promote social change by challenging structural inequalities and discourses of violence. Yet people are embedded in discourses which may prevent them from contesting power structures. A crucial means for peace constituencies to influence dominant discourses and structures, therefore, is to raise awareness and empower people. 'Empowerment' is the process by which people acquire the means to overcome their subordination, while awareness-raising is usually understood in the sense of Freire's concept of 'conscientisation', which refers to the process by which people learn to 'perceive social, political, and economic contradictions, and to take actions against the oppressive elements of reality' (Freire, 1998: 17). Awareness-raising is thus 'empowering', but there are other means of empowerment, such as training, for example.

Peacebuilding overall encompasses four interdependent levels of transformation – personal, relational, structural and cultural (Lederach, 1997). At a personal level, it aims at individual transformations, such as the recovery of self-esteem, or changes in perceptions and behaviours. At a relational level, peacebuilding is concerned with the (re)building of social relationships. At a structural level, it intends to produce structural changes with a view to reducing structural violence; and at a cultural level, it corresponds to the transformation of the cultural patterns that contributed to violence into more peaceful ones (Lederach, 1997: 82–3).

According to Lederach (1997: 39), peacebuilding should ideally create bridges between top, intermediate and grassroots levels of leadership, while reaching out to broad sectors of the population. While this model is useful for overemphasising the role of local actors in peacebuilding, thus breaking with the tendency to regard peacebuilding as an external endeavour, it can also be criticised for overemphasising local matters to the detriment of broader issues. Such an approach can divert us from addressing the global structures and discourses that hamper the building of sustainable peace. Hence, according to Bendaña (1996), any strategy to address violent conflict that does not challenge the dominant neoliberal discourse will not build peace, but reinforce structural inequalities. Depending on the context, peace constituencies may not have enough leverage to influence dominant transnational discourses; yet they can usually find ways to challenge some of their local manifestations, as we shall see in the example of the *mesas* below.

## Civil society and social change

There are many approaches to civil society and its role in social change. It is impossible to review all of them here, but it is important to point out the practical implications of these conceptualisations on peace constituencies at a time when strengthening national CSOs has become an essential part of the strategy of the international community to address both 'authoritarianism' and 'underdevelopment' (see Eade, 2000; Howell and Pearce, 2001; Van Rooy, 1998).

At the extremes, civil society can be regarded as either a benign realm separate from the state and the market or a space penetrated by the forces of the state and the market. The first approach, with some nuances, currently underpins the practice of mainstream international donor agencies, which tend to regard civil society as inherently good and support it as a means to foster or strengthen democracy. This view, however, fails to recognise the existence of civil society organisations that promote violence rather than peace (Hermann, 2006) and does not take into account the power relations that pervade civil society and prevent marginalised social sectors from being equally represented in it. Consequently, strengthening civil society may foster a model of democracy that reproduces the unequal power structures of society. Such a view is inconsistent with the objectives of peacebuilding, which include a gradual reduction of structural inequalities. In addition, the tendency to romanticise civil society in opposition to an authoritarian and inefficient state may lead to a further weakening of the state in countries, such as Guatemala, where the state has been weak and absent from large swathes of the countryside. Rather than contributing to peace, this could create further inequalities between the communities that benefit from civil society assistance and those that do not (Pugh, 2000).

While focusing on the democratic potential of civil society, this approach often leaves the market outside the debate. The liberal view, in particular, tends to restrict the role of civil society to the political sphere, and see the market as an independent realm. Such premises have led some scholars and mainstream international organisations to equate peacebuilding with democratisation, or 'peacebuilding as politics' (Cousens et al., 2001). According to this perspective, a society governed by efficient political institutions will be able to not only channel conflict peacefully but also address the roots of violent conflict by political means. This assumption, however, forgets that many violent conflicts are rooted in deep socio-economic inequalities. Such recognition is implicit in the Guatemalan peace agreements, which contemplate several reforms to reduce socio-economic disparities; and a number of CSOs have pushed for the implementation of these reforms in the name of 'peace'. In Guatemala the so-called 'peace agenda' included agrarian, labour and fiscal reforms, alongside the promotion of indigenous rights, democratisation and demilitarisation, among other issues. Considering civil society's role in peacebuilding purely in terms of democratising the state and ensuring that its institutions can channel conflict peacefully therefore disregards the need to address the structural violence rooted in unjust economic systems, and overlooks the fact that many CSOs contest the logic of the free market in countries riven by deep socio-economic cleavages.

Another common tendency is to consider 'civil society' as an instrument to promote not only democracy but also development, and help reduce the social costs of structural adjustment programmes. This view, like the preceding one, is problematic insofar as it does not allow civil society to foster peace outside of democratisation and development activities. In Guatemala, however, many CSOs have conceived their role in building peace in broader terms and considered the struggle to reduce socio-economic inequalities as a key aspect of their endeavour. Thus the *mesa de concertación de Occidente*, one of the most prominent *mesas* in Guatemala, once launched a protest against an increase in value-added tax because it unfairly burdened the poor and was contradictory to the spirit of the peace agreements.

If we now regard civil society as penetrated by the forces of the state and the market, a view held by Marxists, civil society can no longer be idealised. It is, as much as the state, embedded in structures and discourses of domination. Although the prospects for building peace might seem bleak according to this perspective, Marxist theory suggests that social change is possible, but it must be brought about by marginalised social sectors, which need to mobilise to challenge dominant structures and discourses. From this perspective, peace constituencies, like civil society in general, are not inherently good, but reflect power relations in society. In order to build peace, they must involve marginalised social sectors and enable them to express their views in the public sphere. The only way to build peace is to foster counter-hegemonic discourses that will gradually replace dominant ones. Peace constituencies should intend to reform the state, as well as change the norms that dominate civil society.

If we adopt such a view, a crucial issue remains unresolved: how can we ensure that peace constituencies contribute to an emancipatory or transformative peacebuilding project? How can they bring about radical change in society and gradually replace (or transform) dominant structures and cultures into just (and peaceful) ones? Cohen and Arato (1992) have reflected on this dilemma and suggest that civil society should engage in a process of communicative action to establish common norms. Accordingly, peace constituencies can only build peace if they involve a broad spectrum of society in a consensus-building process to challenge dominant structures and discourses, and to agree on norms for peaceful coexistence.

## Insights from social movement theory

Social movement theory offers insights into peace constituencies, which, like peace movements, are the product of collective action. In particular, both 'resource-mobilisation' and 'new social movements' theory can shed light on the formation and development of peace constituencies in specific socio-political contexts.

Resource-mobilisation theory helps us understand the formation and development of peace constituencies in relation to political opportunities, forms of organisation and framing processes. It is argued, for example, that the educated middle classes have more resources to mobilise around systemic issues while popular classes tend to mobilise out of immediate concerns such as wages, housing or food (Foweraker, 1995: 31). Resource-mobilisation theorists also stress the role and influence of external actors in helping social actors to mobilise for peace by making resources available to them.

For new social movement theorists, social actors mobilise for peace with a view to integrating previously marginalised groups in the public sphere and contesting the discourses 'which have held them in a subordinate position through a dense web of discrimination and exclusion' (Paoli and da Silva Telles, 1998: 66). They describe mobilisation as a process in which social actors construct a collective identity to articulate their demands according to the socio-political context in which they are embedded (Foweraker, 1995: 13). Thus in countries affected by internal armed conflict, social actors may decide to act collectively to achieve a broad range of objectives coming under the umbrella of 'peace'. What might otherwise be termed 'human rights', 'development' or 'democratisation' will be defined as 'peace' at that particular moment. This means that peace constituencies encompass social actors with different views of 'peace' in accordance with their social background, and that their success will depend on their capacity to embrace these different views of 'peace' and bring them onto the public agenda, as we shall see in the study of the *mesas*.

From this perspective, peace constituencies can generate social change through two chief means: bringing new issues into the public sphere and promoting state reforms. Yet their members, as any social actors, may unconsciously reproduce the structures of the political or economic systems that they seek to challenge (Camacho, 1994; Cohen and Arato, 1992; Jelin, 1998). The *mesas* are no exception. Their members often reproduced patterns of discrimination, for instance, by using Spanish instead of local indigenous languages or by organising most meetings in departmental capitals, thereby hindering the participation of the rural population. Nevertheless, insofar as social actors foster counter-hegemonic discourses to struggle against exclusion, they can help broaden the public sphere and enable marginalised social sectors to make themselves heard (Alvarez *et al.*, 1998). Here too, the *mesas* are a point in case. For example, the *mesa* of Sololá became an important space for indigenous people to voice their concerns and a platform to push for the implementation of the Agreement on Identity and Rights of Indigenous Peoples.

In sum, social movement theory, and social theory more generally, shows that peace constituencies are embedded in particular social structures and cultures, which they necessarily reproduce to a certain extent. They emerge, define their objectives and play different roles in peacebuilding, depending on their socio-political context and the resources available to them. They also adopt different views of peace in different settings and at different times. Social theory also points to the different notions of 'peace' articulated by the members of peace constituencies, and shows the importance of involving as broad a range of people as possible in order to give voice to previously marginalised social sectors and challenge unjust structures and discourses. It enables us to analyse the role of peace constituencies not simply in terms of the concrete actions that they carry out to build peace, but also in terms of promoting state reforms and expanding the public sphere. 'Building peace' is thus seen as an emancipatory project in which dominant discourses and structures are gradually challenged and replaced by more inclusive ones. Peace movements, as mass-based mobilisations for peace, are a key element in this process, but peace constituencies can also play a crucial role by involving large segments of society in the process. While peace movements do not occur in all contexts of armed conflict, it is often possible to observe the emergence of peace constituencies. Let us now turn to a concrete example of peace constituency in Guatemala and examine its role in peacebuilding.

## The *mesas de concertación y seguimiento de los Acuerdos de Paz*

The *mesas* appeared in Guatemala towards the end of the 1990s as a means to decentralise the peacebuilding process (for an in-depth study of the *mesas*, see Mouly, 2004). The first were forums made up of representatives of various sectors of society, which emerged in the administrative departments most affected by the armed conflict in the immediate aftermath of the signing of the peace agreements. The peace agreements emphasised the need for decentralisation, and called for public participation in their implementation. The *mesas* emerged in response to this call, out of the will of various departmental organisations, most of which had not participated in the peace negotiations but were eager to play a role in this new context. According to their statutes, each *mesa* is

> A space of dialogue, *concertación* and consensus within civil society, which is autonomous and democratic; which fosters the public participation of all social sectors, respecting multiethnic, pluricultural, multilinguistic, gender, political and socio-economic diversity; and which makes proposals regarding the issues of peace and development at community, municipal, departmental and national levels.
> (*Mesa de Jutiapa et al.*, 2003)

The *mesas* gradually expanded to include a national coordinating body, as well as municipal forums. Their objectives included the dissemination of information about the peace agreements and the status of their implementation; the promotion of public participation of all social sectors in the implementation of the agreements; the peaceful transformation of local conflicts; and the formulation of public policy proposals to address key problems and consolidate peace. In order to achieve these objectives, the *mesas* used various strategies, including advocacy, participation in policymaking, capacity-building, mediation and organisation of public events to disseminate the peace agreements and discuss key aspects of peacebuilding.

In general, all CSOs based in the departments, as well as state representatives and the private sector, were invited to join departmental *mesas*. A few *mesas*, however, rejected the participation of state agents out of distrust. According to the degree of participation of state actors, the *mesas* played different roles and used different strategies to have an impact. The choice between a strategy of opposition to the state and one of engagement with it depended on how the *mesas*, and local inhabitants in general, perceived the willingness of the government to implement public policies in accordance with the demands of the population. In cases of distrust, public protests, press releases and such strategies were deemed more useful, as they could influence public opinion and have a symbolic impact sufficient to oblige the government to change its policies. On the other hand, when the *mesas* believed that the state apparatus was open to the demands of the population, they were more likely to participate in institutional forums to design public policies and formulate new laws that could generate structural change.

While political parties were usually not represented as such – except the *Unidad Revolucionaria Nacional Guatemalteca* (URNG) a former rebel group represented in a few *mesas* – they often had an influence on the *mesas* through civil society or state representatives. Hence, at one point, five out of seven members of the steering committee of the *mesa de concertación de Occidente* were linked to the URNG. During elections politicisation was even stronger with some *mesa* members running as candidates.

The composition of the *mesas* mirrored the characteristics of each department. In departments where the population was predominantly Mayan, traditional indigenous authorities exerted a strong leadership. Indeed, 'peace' did not mean the same in the department of Sololá, where 94 per cent of the population was indigenous, as in El Progreso, which had only 2 per cent of indigenous population. The *mesa* of Sololá therefore conceived 'peace' as an important vehicle for the recognition of indigenous identity and rights, while the *mesa* of El Progreso almost did not tackle the issue.

Context created both opportunities and limits for the development of the *mesas*. In Quiché, for example, the fact that the population had greatly suffered from the armed conflict cut two ways. While it motivated people to consolidate peace and join the *mesa*, it also made people afraid to participate, all the more when the military was involved. The pace of the implementation of the peace agreements at the national level also impinged on the development of the *mesas*. In times of setback, for example when the 1999 referendum on constitutional reforms failed, several *mesas* slackened off. By contrast, they gained strength as a consequence of conditionalities imposed by international donors on the Guatemalan government in 2002.

The *mesas* appeared in a globalised context where the state is shrinking and CSOs have to compete for external funding. By tapping into external resources in order to increase their impact on society and the state, they became subject to the influence of external actors. The support of organisations, such as the UN Verification Mission in Guatemala (MINUGUA), proved critical, and the subsequent closure of some MINUGUA regional offices undermined the work of local *mesas*. Two other key entities played a pivotal role in supporting, and encouraging the establishment of, the *mesas*: the Guatemalan Peace Secretariat, a state entity, and the Commission of Follow-up to the Peace Agreements. Both initially saw the *mesas* as a means to extend their influence outside the capital and fostered the institutionalisation of the *mesas* on the same footing as the peace institutions envisaged in the peace agreements. However, while both entities provided financial and logistical support to the *mesas* and enabled them to channel their demands to the state, they also tried to put forward their views. This prompted strong reactions from some of the *mesas*, two of which decided to renounce their full participation in national assemblies and adopt instead the status of observers. For the latter, such interference was associated with past authoritarianism, and broke with the participatory spirit of the *mesas*.

Other problems included microfactors, such as financial difficulties or disputes between members, which are underestimated in most academic work on peacebuilding organisations. The internal dynamics of the *mesas* had a strong influence on their role in peacebuilding, particularly given that diverse conceptions of 'peace' – sometimes mutually reinforcing, sometimes clashing – coexisted within the *mesas*. For instance, peasant organisations considered the *mesas* as an important space to push for land reforms, while women's organisations made sure that gender issues were high on the agendas. The presence of respected leaders was often crucial to ensure cohesion.

While the role of each *mesa* depended on the socio-political context, local involvement and resources, they all shared a common goal: to promote people's participation in the peacebuilding process and press for the implementation of the peace agreements. As a *mesa* leader told the villagers of San Antonio La Paz, 'the peace process is only viable through *your* participation'.[1] *Mesas* thus helped to bridge gaps between social sectors, expand spaces of dialogue and build consensus. By bringing together a variety of social sectors, they fostered reconciliation and horizontal integration; that is, equal opportunities for all sectors to participate in the peacebuilding process. They also helped to reduce structural violence by opposing the historical marginalisation of administrative departments, offering excluded social sectors a chance to participate in public affairs and promoting reforms to diminish structural inequalities.

Guatemala has been marked by cultures of violence and authoritarianism, embodied in the violent handling of conflict, top-down decision-making processes and the exclusion of broad segments of the population. The *mesas* broke with these patterns by fostering cultures of non-violence, dialogue and inclusiveness. They did so by setting examples of alternative social practices, promoting counter-hegemonic discourses and encouraging people to participate. While the closure of the political space to popular demands was a root cause of the armed conflict, the *mesas* offered a space for citizens to express themselves.

While some *mesas* continued to play an active role at the departmental level years after the signing of the peace agreements, others gradually collapsed as a result of combined factors, including a diminishing interest in the peace agenda, a reduction in funding, the departure of MINUGUA and the restructuring of the peace institutions, as well as a lack of popular base for some *mesas*. But despite this and their shortcomings, the *mesas* undoubtedly contributed to broadening the public debate about the implementation of the peace agreements and represented a significant attempt to make the peacebuilding process in post-conflict Guatemala more inclusive.

## Conclusion

This chapter has proposed a conceptual framework to maximise the transformative potential of peacebuilding and critically examine the role of peace constituencies in this process. Drawing on the concepts of 'peace constituency', 'peace' as an end to 'direct', 'structural' and 'cultural' violence, and 'civil society', it has identified peacebuilding as a long-term process to reduce the three forms of violence and build peaceful alternatives. Building peace is a process of personal, relational, structural and cultural transformation, which requires challenging discourses of violence and engaging in a process of communicative action to establish norms of peaceful coexistence. Local actors, with different levels of leadership, can make important contributions to this process, for example by raising awareness and empowering people. Yet it is equally important to address the unjust structures and discourses of violence that exist at a global level.

Peace constituencies, as any group in civil society, are far from being a panacea. They simultaneously reproduce and aim at challenging structural and cultural violence. Their formation and development are shaped by the socio-political context. The support of external organisations can also be critical, but can subject them to the agendas of external actors. The members of peace constituencies influence, and are influenced by, surrounding structures. Depending on their social background and the socio-political context, they articulate different views of 'peace' at different times, playing a crucial role in peacebuilding by bringing different views of 'peace' into the public sphere.

The *mesas*, for example, enabled various social actors to contribute to the debate about the implementation of the peace agreements with their various conceptions of 'peace'. Their evolution reflected the interactions between agency and structure, and their composition and strategies revealed the complex relationships between civil society and the state. Some *mesas* included state representatives; others refused to do so; and they used different strategies to have an impact on the state. The most active *mesas* tended to reject the interference of the state and political parties, while others were sometimes co-opted by them. Likewise, the *mesas* were caught between the need to abide by the rules of external organisations in order to increase their impact on the peacebuilding process and the need to conform to certain normative standards. While some barely opposed the imposition of outsiders' criteria, others strongly resisted it.

The *mesas* also demonstrated that in spite of good intentions, peace constituencies may unconsciously reproduce the unfair structures that they seek to challenge, as some of the *mesas* did when conducting public events only in Spanish. Nevertheless, they concomitantly aspired to fight against exclusion and enable marginalised social sectors to have their voice heard. Their endeavour helped to widen public debate and encouraged the discussion, by a variety of social sectors, of important aspects of peacebuilding, which were not necessarily on the public agenda. They played a critical role in that regard, enhancing Guatemalan people's ownership of the peacebuilding process and fostering the establishment of local capacities for sustaining peace.

## Note

1. Words of a leader of the *mesa* of El Progreso during a peace forum in San Antonio La Paz, 3 May 2002.

## References

Alvarez, Sonia E., Arturo Escobar and Evelina Dagnino, 1998, 'Introduction: The Cultural and the Political in Latin American Social Movements', in Sonia E. Alvarez, Arturo Escobar and Evelina Dagnino (eds), *Culture of Politics/Politics of Cultures: Re-visioning Latin American Social Movements*, Boulder, CO: Westview, pp. 1–29.

Barnes, Catherine, 2005, 'Weaving the Web: Civil-Society Roles in Working with Conflict and Building Peace', in Paul van Tongeren, Malin Brenk, Marte Hellema and Juliette Verhoeven (eds), *People Building Peace II: Successful Stories of Civil Society*, Boulder, CO: Lynne Rienner, pp. 7–24.

Bendaña, Alejandro, 1996, 'Conflict Resolution: Empowerment and Disempowerment', *Peace and Change*, Vol. 21, No. 1, pp. 68–77.

Biekart, Kees, 1999, *The Politics of Civil Society Building: European Private Aid Agencies and Democratic Transitions in Central America*, Utrecht: International Books.

Boyce, James K. and Manuel Pastor Jr, 1997, 'Macroeconomic Policy and Peace Building in El Salvador', in Krishna Kumar (ed.), *Rebuilding Societies after Civil War: Critical Roles for International Assistance*, Boulder, CO: Lynne Rienner, pp. 287–314.

Camacho, Daniel, 1994, 'Movimientos populares y partidos políticos en Centroamérica', in Günther Maihold and Manuel Carballo Quintana (eds), *¿'Qué será de Centroamérica?: Gobernabilidad, legitimidad electoral y sociedad civil*, San José: Fundación Friederich Ebert, pp. 191–8.

Comisión de Esclarecimiento Histórico, 1999, 'Guatemala: Memoria del Silencio. Conclusiones y recomendaciones del Informe de la Comisión para el Esclarecimiento Histórico', Guatemala City.

Cohen, Jean L. and Andrew Arato, 1992, *Civil Society and Political Theory*, Cambridge, MA: MIT Press.

Cousens, Elizabeth M., Chetan Kumar and Karin Wermester (eds), 2001, *Peacebuilding as Politics: Cultivating Peace in Fragile Societies*, Boulder, CO: Lynne Rienner.

Eade, Deborah (ed.), 2000, *Development, NGOs, and Civil Society*, Oxford: Oxfam.

Fetherston, A. Betts, 2000a, 'From Conflict Resolution to Transformative Peacebuilding: Reflections from Croatia', Working Paper 4, Department of Peace Studies, University of Bradford.
Fetherston, A. Betts, 2000b, 'Peacekeeping, Conflict Resolution and Peacebuilding: A Reconsideration of Theoretical Frameworks', *International Peacekeeping*, Vol. 7, No. 1, pp. 190–218.
Fischer, Martina, 2006, 'Civil Society in Conflict Transformation: Ambivalence, Potentials and Challenges', Berlin: Berghof Research Center for Constructive Conflict Management.
Foweraker, Joe, 1995, *Theorizing Social Movements*, London: Pluto Press.
Freire, Paulo, 1998, *Pedagogy of the Oppressed*, New York: Continuum.
Galtung, Johan, 1990, 'Cultural Violence', *Journal of Peace Research*. Vol. 27, No. 3, pp. 291–305.
Giddens, Anthony, 1984, *The Constitution of Society: Outline of the Theory of Structuration*, Cambridge: Polity Press.
Goodhand, Jonathan, 2006, *Aiding Peace? The Role of NGOs in Armed Conflict*, Boulder, CO: Lynne Rienner.
Goodhand, Jonathan and David Hulme, 1999, 'From Wars to Complex Political Emergencies: Understanding Conflict and Peace-Building in the New World Disorder', *Third World Quarterly*, Vol. 20, No. 1, pp. 13–26.
Hermann, Tamar, 2006, 'Civil Society and NGOs: Building Peace in Israel', in Edy Kaufman, Walid Salem and Juliette Verhoeven (eds), *Bridging the Divide: Peacebuilding in the Israeli–Palestinian Conflict*, Boulder, CO: Lynne Rienner, pp. 39–58.
Howell, Jude and Jenny Pearce, 2001, *Civil Society and Development: A Critical Exploration*, Boulder, CO: Lynne Rienner.
International Alert, 1998, *Code of Conduct for Conflict Transformation Work*, London: International Alert.
Jabri, Vivienne, 1996, *Discourses on Violence: Conflict Analysis Reconsidered*, Manchester: Manchester University Press.
Jelin, Elizabeth, 1998, 'Toward a Culture of Participation and Citizenship: Challenges for a More Equitable World', in Sonia E. Alvarez, Arturo Escobar and Evelina Dagnino (eds), *Culture of Politics/Politics of Cultures: Re-visioning Latin American Social Movements*, Boulder, CO: Westview, pp. 405–14.
Jeong, Ho-Won, 2000, *Peace and Conflict Studies: An Introduction*, Aldershot: Ashgate.
Jeong, Ho-Won, 2006, *Peacebuilding in Postconflict Societies: Strategy and Process*, Boulder, CO: Lynne Rienner.
Lederach, John Paul, 1995a, 'Conflict Transformation in Protracted Internal Conflicts: The Case for a Comprehensive Framework', in Kumar Rupesinghe (ed.), *Conflict Transformation*, Basingstoke: Macmillan, pp. 201–22.
Lederach, John Paul, 1995b, *Preparing for Peace: Conflict Transformation Across Cultures*, New York: Syracuse University Press.
Lederach, John Paul, 1997, *Building Peace: Sustainable Reconciliation in Divided Societies*, Washington, DC: US Institute of Peace Press.
*Mesa departamental de concertación de Jutiapa, et al.*, 2003, 'Estatutos de la Asamblea Nacional de Mesas de Concertación, ANAMEC; Coordinadora Nacional de Mesas de Concertación, CONAMEC y Mesas Departamentales de Concertación, MDC y Seguimiento de los Acuerdos de Paz', Puerto Barrios, Guatemala.
Mouly, Cécile, 2004, 'The Role of Peace Constituencies in Building Peace in Nicaragua and Guatemala', unpublished PhD thesis, University of Cambridge.

Nagler, Michael N., 1999, 'What is Peace Culture?', in Ho-Won Jeong (ed.), *The New Agenda for Peace Research*, Aldershot: Ashgate, pp. 233–58.

Nordstrom, Carolyn, 1997, *A Different Kind of War Story*, Philadelphia: University of Pennsylvania Press.

Paffenholz, Thania, 2002, *Strengthening Peace Constituencies*, Eschborn: Deutsche Gesellschaft für Technische Zusammenarbeit (GTZ).

Paoli, Maria Celia and Vera da Silva Telles, 1998, 'Social Rights: Conflicts and Negotiations in Contemporary Brazil', in Sonia E. Alvarez, Arturo Escobar and Evelina Dagnino (eds), *Culture of Politics/Politics of Cultures: Re-visioning Latin American Social Movements*, Boulder, CO: Westview, pp. 64–92.

Prendergast, John and Emily Plumb, 2002, 'Building Local Capacity: From Implementation to Peacebuilding', in Stephen J. Stedman, Donald Rothchild and Elizabeth M. Cousens (eds), *Ending Civil Wars: The Implementation of Peace Agreements*, Boulder, CO: Lynne Rienner, pp. 327–49.

Pugh, Michael (ed.), 2000, 'The Social–Civil Dimension', *Regeneration of War-Torn Societies*, Basingstoke: Macmillan, pp. 112–33.

Robben, Antonius C. G. M. and Carolyn Nordstrom (eds), 1995, 'The Anthropology and Ethnography of Violence and Sociopolitical Conflict', *Fieldwork Under Fire: Contemporary Studies of Violence and Survival*, Berkeley, CA: University of California Press, pp. 1–23.

Rupesinghe, Kumar, 1995, 'Conflict Transformation', in Kumar Rupesinghe (ed.), *Conflict Transformation*, Basingstoke: Macmillan, pp. 65–92.

Ryan, Stephen, 1995, 'Transforming Violent Intercommunal Conflict', in Kumar Rupesinghe (ed.), *Conflict Transformation*, Basingstoke: Macmillan, pp. 223–65.

Scheper-Hughes, Nancy and Philippe Bourgeois (eds), 2004a, 'Introduction: Making Sense of Violence', *Violence in War and Peace: An Anthology*, Oxford: Blackwell, pp. 1–27.

Scheper-Hughes, Nancy and Philippe Bourgeois, 2004b, 'Comments', in Paul Farmer, 'An Anthropology of Structural Violence', *Current Anthropology*, Vol. 45, No. 3, pp. 305–25.

Van Rooy, Alison, 1998, *Civil Society and the Aid Industry: The Politics and Promise*, London: Earthscan.

# 18
# El Salvador: The Limits of a Violent Peace

*Mo Hume*

> *Maybe the country failed because at the time of the demobilisation, there were no opportunities for work made available. The creation of jobs would have been the most essential thing to do to mobilise people and see where they could work. Many people were left [when the war was over] and when they had no money, they resorted to crime.*
> Interview with prisoner in Salvadoran prison, 2002

There has been a growing emphasis in conflict scholarship on critically assessing the long-term impacts of political conflict, the limitations of peace-building initiatives and the role of domestic and international actors in building civil society following sustained conflict (Debiel, 2002; Pearce, 1998; Richmond, 2006). In particular, empirical evidence from post-conflict situations increasingly demonstrates that the political economies of war spill onto and constrict the development of peace (Pugh, 2006). Matters of political economy in post-conflict contexts create particular points of 'vulnerability' and one area in which these vulnerabilities are most brutally manifest is in continuing and even rising rates of violence and crime *after* the cessation of hostilities (AVPI, 2004). This has led to broader interrogation on the relationship between transition and violence (Kooning and Kruijt, 1999; Pereira and Davis, 2000; Rotker, 2002). The nature of this relationship has sparked debates on the 'newness' of the violence to emerge in fledgling democratic and post-war contexts, particularly in Latin America where levels of interpersonal violence are among the highest in the world (Kooning and Kruijt, 2004). Violence in Latin America has certainly undergone a transformation, and moves towards democratic governance have been marked and undermined by the continued 'ubiquity' of violent actors (Torres-Rivas, 1999: 287).

One of the most violent countries in the region – indeed, the world – is El Salvador, the Central American Republic which was the site of a brutal civil war between 1980 and 1992. The conflict claimed over 75,000 lives and led to the displacement of more than a million men, women and children in the region (Ardón, 1998). El Salvador's conflict was complex. More than a civil war between the rightist state and the leftist guerrilla movement, Farabundo Martí National Liberation Front (FMLN), it constituted an important ideological battleground in the politics of the Cold War, attracting international attention and economic investment in the military campaign at all its stages. For example, the United States sent an estimated US$6 billion in aid during the war years, much of it in the form of direct military assistance to the state, and arguably prolonging the war (Murray, 1997). Following a military stalemate by the end of the 1980s the reduction of military aid, and increased pressure from the international community, the UN brokered the January 1992 Chapultepec Peace Accords, signed by the FMLN's high command and government members. The Accords brought Salvadoran citizens the hope of replacing violence with meaningful peace. For the international community, principally the UN, this marked a historic innovation for its role in peacebuilding initiatives and 'set an important precedent for international promotion of human rights principles and democratic institutions' (Burgerman, 2000: 63).

Nonetheless, the reality of this 'transformation' remains contested. As well as being a period of reform and democratic opening, the 1990s and 2000s have seen the emergence of new challenges that threaten not only the quality of reforms but also their sustainability. During the 1990s in El Salvador there were more violent deaths than during the war (Ramos, 2000). In the years following the signing of the Peace Accords (1994–1997), there was an annual minimum of 80 murders per 100,000 citizens and rising concern among citizens (Cruz, 2003a: 18; 2003b: 8). From 1998 to 2002, the number decreased, but in 2000, there were 2341 murders, falling to 2161 in 2002 (PNC register). In 2005 there were 55.5 murders per 100,000 citizens, ranking El Salvador as the most violent country in the region (FESPAD, 2006: 55). Such 'new' violence is also manifest in a sharp rise in street crime, gang activities and gender-based violence.

Popkin (1999: 162) argues that El Salvador offers 'an example to be avoided', labelling the process a 'peace without justice'. Pearce (1998: 589–90) states that 'while Central America has ceased to be "at war", it remains anything but peaceful'. Examining the state of the country ten years after the Accords, the Central American Human Rights Institute comments that there is little discernible difference between the 'point of departure and the point of arrival; the issues are the same: the majority of the population is excluded and vulnerable' (IDHUCA, 2002: 2). These ongoing high levels of violence raise serious questions about the limited nature of peace in the country.

Against this critical backdrop, this chapter exposes the limits of El Salvador's 'peace'. In particular, it analyses the development of post-conflict violence, exposing both 'continuities' with and 'discontinuities' from historical processes. I emphasise that more than a debate between 'old' and 'new' violence, it is important to explore how the political and economic imperatives of neoliberalism reinforce and indeed exacerbate historic structural conditions of inequality and exclusion. Moreover, exclusionary and polarised political attitudes still shape the ways in which violence is understood and legislated against in the post-war period. First, the discussion introduces the limited political context of peacebuilding, emphasising the 'narrowness' of the process, both in terms of the actors involved and in terms of the scope of the agreement for mandating reform. I then examine the changing panorama of violent actors, paying particular attention to the issue of youth gangs, who are arguably the most symbolic representation of 'new' violence in the post-war context. The emergence of violent non-state actors is now seen as one of the greatest threats to democratic governance in the region (McCoy, 2006). Less attention is paid to the role of the state and civil society in perpetuating this violence: the final sections of the chapter therefore explore the emergence of gangs and offers a critical analysis of both the state's and society's response to the issue of violence. A key premise of this chapter is that violence in El Salvador has not emerged in a political or economic vacuum. It is a product of uneven development and political choices as well as being reliant on the active engagement of civil society for its reproduction. For this reason, the following discussion is structured around three key themes which are reflective of certain continuities along historic axes of conflict: violence, exclusion and polarisation.

## Violence: El Salvador's 'narrow' peace

The 1990s marked a process of transition on multiple levels for El Salvador, though this has been very much a double-edged process for its citizens. Indeed, Pearce (1998: 589) argues that 'the idea that the region's conflicts have been "resolved" may be true at the formal level of peace accords between armies and insurgents, but is less so at the level of people's everyday lives'. The Chapultepec Peace Agreement is widely recognised as an important political settlement. Nonetheless, it has been accused of failing in its mission to build a new and more equal society. The agreement was the result of a 'narrow' process of negotiation conducted between elites from both the left and the right, with little input from broader civil society representatives (Burgerman, 2000). As Juhn remarks (1998: 9), 'The goal of the talks was to end a war. The key to ending the war lay not in economic restructuring or power-sharing arrangements, but in a total overhaul of civil–military relations.' This notable disregard of key cornerstones of the civil conflict – structural inequalities, polarisation and exclusion – has framed citizens' experience of the post-war context. Arguably, this glaring omission set the tone for liberal peacebuilding in the country: 'the minimum accepted by Salvadoran society and the international community' (ECA, 1999: 963).

To compound this limited process, the government aggressively followed a neoliberal economic model, which has merely exacerbated historic social and political cleavages since the formal ending of the armed conflict in 1992. Pugh (2006) reminds us that the neoliberal project is not benign and in El Salvador, the economic interests of the country's elite have consistently dictated the limits of any meaningful reform. Livelihood opportunities for the majority of El Salvador's population remain severely constrained in the post-war period. The country is one of the most unequal in the region, ranking 0.54 on the GINI index (against the global average of 0.4 and Latin American average of 0.47), and over 40 per cent of its population live in poverty (UNDOC, 2007). Employment strategies have focused on attracting low-paid and unstable job opportunities in the form of *maquilas* (export-processing zones) and exporting large sections of its workforce to the United States. Mass migration to the United States has become an important survival strategy on both macro- and microlevels: remittances reached over $2.5 billion in 2004 and accounted for an estimated 16 per cent of the GDP. This is more than double the annual budget for social spending in the same year (IDHES, 2005). Approximately 1.5 million Salvadorans live in the United States, equivalent to 25 per cent of Salvadorans living in El Salvador (Towers, 2004: 31), and an estimated 39.5 per cent of Salvadorans with a university degree live outside the country (IDHES, 2005: 4).

In 2001, the national currency, the *colon*, was replaced by the US dollar, much to the advantage of the country's financial elite, but with detrimental effects for the poor (Towers, 2004). Many state resources such as the pensions system, telecommunications and electrical services underwent a process of privatisation. Attempts to privatise water services were met with widespread protest by civil society actors. These protests have been brutally quashed by state agents and, in a 'misuse' of counterterrorism legislation, 13 civil society activists were imprisoned on charges of 'terrorism' (HRW, 2007). This highlights the limited space available to articulate alternatives to the neoliberal project and indicates the endurance of a particularly violent hegemonic politics in the country that quashes opposition, albeit within the new context of liberal democratic governance. Predictably, this 'minimalist' approach to peacebuilding failed to translate into real structural reform of Salvadoran society and the limited advances that have been made are fragile and challenged by ongoing fault lines. The most striking characteristic of El Salvador's 'peace' is the continued high level of violence. Salvadoran historian, Miguel Huezo Mixco (2000: 124), states that the great 'paradox' of El Salvador's efforts to achieve peace is that they have only succeeded in increasing violence and crime.

Scholars have called for a need to distinguish current manifestations from past violences, often making a distinction between 'political' violence during conflict and more 'social' or 'economic' violence in its wake (Moser and McIlwaine, 2004; Pereira and Davis, 2000). Nonetheless, there are important historical axes of conflict that predate the neoliberal peace and continue to facilitate violence in current times. Arguably, certain manifestations of current violence are also 'political' in tone because they are rooted in structures of uneven development and the sustained failure of governments to address structural problems (see, e.g., Hume, 2007b; Rodgers, 2007; Tedesco, 2000).

Contemporary violence, like the politically ideological violence of previous decades, is rooted in the material reality, outlined above, of inequality, power and exclusion (Savenije and Van der Borgh, 2004). Unlike the politically motivated violence of previous decades, it is not rooted in an ideological battle over competing worldviews, but it is very much a struggle against structural constraints and limited opportunity. This debate between 'old' and 'new' forms of violence has echoes of similar discussions on the changing nature of warfare (Kaldor, 2006). The distinction between 'old' and 'new' is certainly useful to frame the increasing civilianisation and criminalisation of war and also the de-ideologisation of modern conflict. These distinctions resonate with the changing dynamics of violence in contemporary El Salvador. However, these distinctions are also reductive in that they fail to capture important historic and political continuities in both the dynamic of war and the structural bases of violence. Importantly, the distinction between old and new fails to capture the complexities of historic forms of violence, citizens' threshold for tolerating certain types of brutality and, specifically, risks silencing and sidelining certain types of violence that affect particular groups in society such as women, young people and the poor. Political conflict may have overshadowed everyday life for decades and it continues to dominate both popular memories and official accounts of this period. Nevertheless, it is also important to analyse what is recognised as 'violence', particularly in conflict areas. Ramos (2000) reminds us that political conflict co-existed alongside other expressions of violence throughout the war in El Salvador. Tombs (2004) notes that gender-based crimes were not recognised in the report of the Truth Commission and gendered abuses are still minimised in comparison to other crimes. This particular construction of violence has led some citizens to believe that life 'is worse now, because before, if you did not get involved in politics, you did not get killed, now it is different: you could be at home and you could be killed there' (Cruz et al., 1998: 3, citing IUDOP, 1996: 240).

To understand the nature of the changing theatre of violence in El Salvador, it is necessary to cast a brief glance at the country's brutal history. An examination of the historical processes at play uncovers a country where politics, violence and economics have been entwined since independence from Spain in 1821. The cornerstones of political life in El Salvador have been exclusion, polarisation and violence and these characteristics continue to impinge on the post-war context. Throughout its history, the Salvadoran state used widespread repression and terror in order to ensure the continued political and economic hegemony of a small, but powerful elite (Dunkerley, 1982). This same elite continues to hold political and economic power (ECA, 1999). The intensity of state brutality together with acute social and economic inequalities and the impossibility of democratic struggle ultimately proved decisive factors in FMLN's decision to resort to violence in 1980. The role of the state and elite groups in embedding violence into Salvadoran political, social and economic life should not be underestimated. The state was the key protagonist in the campaign of brutality against the Salvadoran population. Holden (1996) reminds us, however, that the success of this hegemonic project was made possible only through the active collaboration of ordinary citizens. Political violence may have provided a backdrop of terror to everyday life for decades, but it co-existed alongside other expressions such as institutionalised corruption, gender-based abuse and violent crime (Ramos, 2000).

> Salvadorans already had a serious problem of violence. In this sense, the problem is not new and was not created by the war. However, the war did contribute greatly to the institutionalisation of violence in the system of values and norms that regulate social behaviour in a tacit way as a part of personal interaction. When violence ceased to have a meaning in the socio-political order, the space for it was reinforced in interpersonal relations.
>
> (Cruz and Beltrán, 2000: 40)

The de-ideologisation of violence in the post-war period and the growing protagonism of non-state violent actors are seen as key developments in the changing theatre of conflict in the country. Bourgois (2001: 8) grounds these 'everyday peacetime crimes' securely in matters of political economy, regarding these as a 'neoliberal version of peace time', in which violence fills the vacuum left by unemployment, underemployment and social disinvestment. In this context, it is often the urban poor who are deemed responsible for high rates of crime, yet they are rarely the ones to benefit from it in any meaningful way. The post-conflict political economy certainly provides particular 'opportunities' for crime; it also restricts spaces that provide alternatives to violence. The final sections of this chapter will explore the emergence of new violence in the post-war context with special reference to youth gangs, arguably the most 'emblematic' manifestation of 'new' violence to emerge in the post-war conflict (De Cesare, 1998). These *maras*, as they are widely known, are also its most 'misunderstood' and politicised expression of post-war violence (Hume, 2007b). I locate youth gangs within a discussion of exclusion and polarisation, in terms of both economic inequality and the broader responses to the problem of gangs, which are characterised by a 'heavy handedness'.

## Exclusion and the political economy of 'opportunity': youth gangs

El Salvador combines historic structures of violence together with widespread availability of arms and a dispossessed workforce 'skilled' in their use. The destruction of human and material resources closed down opportunities for large parts of the workforce and this has been exacerbated by the exclusionary economic policies followed by the state since the cessation of conflict. The 'combination of peace, democracy and free markets' has not yielded positive dividends for El Salvador's poor (Richmond, 2006: 292). Certain demobilised groups have been accused of becoming involved in organised crime, especially ex-army personnel who have formed criminal groups. These groups bring together both the skills acquired during armed conflict and relatively easy access to weaponry. Lax laws and a high level of illegal firearms in circulation (dating from the war but also coming into the country since then) mean that, at a conservative estimate, there are some 400,000–450,000 arms in the hands of civilians, or 2 for every 10 adults, only about 36 per cent of which are held legally (Cruz and Beltrán, 2000).

It would be simplistic, however, to suggest that all of those who are now involved in criminality participated directly in the war.[1] This is particularly noteworthy given the growing attention to the emerging problem of youth crime and, in particular, youth gangs. There are two main gangs in operation: *Mara Salvatrucha* (MS 13) and *Mara 18* (MS 18), both with transnational links throughout Central America and the United States. These gangs are now so highly regarded as a major threat to hemispheric security that the Federal Bureau of Investigation (FBI) set up a special task force to combat gang activity in the region in 2004, using El Salvador as its centre of operations (FESPAD, 2006). Community research carried out in Greater San Salvador in 2001 and 2002 indicated that gangs were the biggest issues facing these low-income neighbourhoods (Hume, 2007a).

One of the most striking characteristics of the *Mara* phenomenon is its visibility. Gang presence in communities is marked not just by physical presence on street corners, but also by ubiquitous graffiti, which are used to demarcate territorial boundaries between rival gangs. Another characteristic is the general confusion and misinformation about gang-related violence (UNDOC, 2007). In a December 2005 address, President Tony Saca contended that gangs were responsible for 50 per cent of murders and 'disorder in the streets' (Saca, 2005). Press reports have agreed, and attributed 60 per cent of all criminal activities to them, yet offer few sources of evidence as to how this estimate was reached (FESPAD, 2006: 22). An interview with a high-ranking officer in September 2004 revealed that police sources estimate that gangs are responsible for no more than 30 per cent of crime. The state Forensic Unit (*Instituto de Medicina Legal*) calculates that the causes of around 59 per cent of murders are unknown, 23.3 per cent are attributable to 'common crime' and 13.4 per cent are gang-related, mostly involving rival *pandilleros* (gang members) (cited in FESPAD, 2006: 22). FESPAD (2006: 23–4) estimates that 51.6 per cent of homicide victims are between the ages of 18 and 30, a sizeable majority being young men. The average homicide rate for people aged 20 to 24 is estimated at 114 per 100,000 of the population in that cohort (Santacruz Giralt, 2005: 1089).

Estimates suggest that there were around 10,500 active gang members in El Salvador in 2007 (UNDOC, 2007). *Maras* are predominantly made up of young people (particularly, but not exclusively, young men) from low-income sectors. Young gang members can be understood as products of a changing 'political economy of brutality' both in terms of embodying broader issues of exclusion and in terms of illuminating the contemporary 'ordering' of the problem (Rodgers, 2007). These young people may not have been directly involved in the war, but they have experienced its broader repercussions. They have first-hand experience of limited opportunities for education and employment. Indeed, many have been forced to make the journey to the United States in search of a future and subsequently have been deported back to El Salvador where they implement gang practices learned on the streets of Los Angeles and Washington, DC (De Cesare, 1998; Santacruz Giralt, 2005). In this situation, a minority of young people have learned to survive and assert their identity by reproducing violence (Cárdia, 2002). In the words of one gang member, 'you could say that their sport is killing, robbing, raping women, all sorts' (interview with member of *Mara Salvatrucha*, 2002).

Local level studies indicate that citizens live in fear of the *mara* and see their presence in communities as negative, although many of the young people have grown up in these communities and their families still live there. Gangs have been linked to localised drug provision and consumption, extortion and sexual violence. In some cases, residents have stated that individuals employ gang members as *sicarios* (contract killers). In neighbourhoods where gangs are present, there is often a tacit agreement that they will not attack local residents, though evidence from Greater San Salvador demonstrates that this is not necessarily the case (Hume, 2007a). Aguilar and Miranda (2006) point to a change in the internal norms and values of gangs since the introduction of tough anti-gang legislation in 2003. Since then, they have become increasingly criminalised and better organised. Most notably, they are involved in extortion in the transport sector. Instead of being motivated to join the gangs for friendship and a sense of belonging, young people are now attracted by the lure of alcohol, drugs and economic gain.

Within debates on public security, much emphasis has been placed on the protagonism of the *maras* in the broader local and global political economy of violence. In particular, the widespread availability of firearms and the strategic location of El Salvador on an international drugs route are seen to have a bearing on the types of activities gangs undertake. Some studies, however, have suggested that these international links are overestimated (Aguilar and Miranda, 2006; Manwaring, 2006; Sullivan, 2006). Furthermore, given the material conditions of many of these young people, such allegations are likely unfounded. Rather than based on actual data, these allegations are used to justify narrow and repressive policies that target gangs. State response to ongoing problems of crime and violence has not been informed by reliable data and is characterised by its inconsistency and reactionary tone (UNDP, 2007: 34). The next section deals with responses to the problem.

## Polarisation: prioritising repression over development

The only articulate governmental response to high levels of violence in recent years has been to target gangs, through repressive and reactionary policing. Little attention has been given to preventive measures and generating more sources of employment. Even less attention has been given to how this state and broader civil society response to the growing pandemic of violence also serves to undermine nascent democratic structures. The ways in which the state and 'good citizens' facilitate violence are complex and neglected in research. Such responses reflect historic patterns of governance that rely on the logic of repression so as to privilege order and control (Hume, 2007b). The rise in violence has coincided with widespread security and justice reforms throughout the country and the region more generally (Call, 2001). The National Civil Police (PNC) was formed in El Salvador after the signing of the Peace Accords in 1992. The numbers of security agents were reduced drastically from 75,000 (including the army, the guerrilla, civil defence and the old police forces) to 6000 (Stanley, 1996). Initially, this severely reduced force enjoyed the support of the population though its credibility has been detrimentally affected since the late 1990s by its ineffectiveness in dealing with the crime wave as well as a series of high-profile cases, implicating agents in criminal activities. The former security apparatus was considered responsible for some 95 per cent of the serious human rights violations that occurred between 1980 and 1992 (Truth Commission, 1993). The replacement comprised 20 per cent of those old, criminal, security forces, 20 per cent of FMLN combatants and 60 per cent civilians. The new force became increasingly politicised – the former Director Rodrigo Avila has been a member of parliament for the ruling ARENA party and has been nominated as their candidate for the 2009 presidential elections. Furthermore, the radical reform of the police was not accompanied by a similar reform of judicial bodies, compromising the very foundations of the peace process and contributing to a situation of widespread impunity (Popkin, 1999). There is also a widespread perception that the new police force does not represent the interests of the poor. One interviewee revealed,

People don't report [crimes] mainly because the reports are filed away. You might report something but it is rare that it is followed up. I think that it's because they only work for certain sections of the population. The middle class and the poor have no influence there. When the powerful men in government or those who have economic power report a crime, it appears in the press straight away. Reporting is like me going to the sea and throwing salt in.

(interview with community resident, Greater San Salvador, 2002)

Citizens – or at least those who can afford it – respond to the weakness in public security provision by turning to private security firms to insulate them against the excesses of everyday crimes. High levels of fear among the citizenry have material costs and consequences, generating important sources of profit and employment. Public spaces are increasingly abandoned and there has been a growth of gated communities and private security firms (Cruz, 2000; IUDOP/FUNDAUNGO, 2002). In 2001, there were an estimated 70,000 private security agents in operation in the country, compared to the PNC, which has an active force of approximately 20,000 officers (Melara, 2001). Links have been identified between private security agents and organised criminality. In particular, these groups are involved in the illegal ownership and distribution of arms, the state lacking the capacity to effectively control them (Godnick *et al.*, 2002). This vacuum in the provision of public security serves to further exacerbate tensions and conflict among certain groups, revealing the 'uncivil' elements or the 'dark' side of civil society (see Keane, 1997: 63–4). According to a community activist in Greater San Salvador, 'when you know the facts, you can act [in response to crime]. Perhaps not through the attorney general's office or the justice system, which quite frankly do not help society, that's not protection, it's not protection for citizens.' Citizens 'manage' their fear of violence by demanding greater security and heavy-handed policies that directly contradict and undermine the spirit of democratisation and peacebuilding (Hume, 2007b).

This is evidenced in public policy responses at national and international levels, in the series of heavy-handed anti-gang measures adopted in Central America since 2003, in Honduras and Guatemala particularly. El Salvador's *Mano Dura* (Iron Fist) policy has led the way on many of these initiatives and throughout the country, specialised military anti-gang units (*Grupos Territoriales Antipandilleros* – territorial anti-gang groups) have been deployed and extradition treaties have been signed with neighbouring countries. The re-employment of the military in matters of public security directly contravenes peace accords which sought to remove them from this function (Call, 2003; Williams and Walter, 1997).

The legislation allows for the immediate imprisonment of gang members, who can be arrested 'simply for having gang-related tattoos or flashing signs' (Boraz and Bruneau, 2006: 38). Thousands of young people have been detained, almost 20,000 being arrested in the first year of its operation – though there was a conviction rate of less than 5 per cent on account of lack of evidence and the initial law being declared unconstitutional (FESPAD, 2004). Allegations of human rights abuses of gang members in custody have been widespread (FESPAD, 2004). The *Mano Dura* response represents the systematic failure of government crime strategies (ECA, 2003). In the longer term, repressive measures fail to address the roots of the problem and serve to displace attention from other urgent priorities, such as the strengthening of local democratic institutions and historic problems of political polarisation and corruption (Arana, 2005). Elsewhere, I emphasise the links between the identity and behaviour of male *pandilleros* and aggressive notions of maleness or 'hegemonic masculinity' through the use of violence (Hume, 2007b). In particular, gender-based violence within the gang is common, both as a form of 'punishment' for women members and as a rite of passage into the gang for some young women (Hume, 2004). This series of values that award importance to violence and aggressive masculinity have not emerged in a vacuum; rather they indicate the continued presence of violence in Salvadoran social relations (Hume, 2006; Alvarenga, 1996). Gangs may produce an alternative social space for a minority of young people, but it is a space that is reliant on the use of violence and the dominance of certain groups over others.

In spite of this – or perhaps because of it – these measures met widespread and strong support in the population. Indeed, the *Mano Dura* initiative was originally floated in time for the 2004 presidential elections, where it became a popular rallying issue for ARENA. Support for ARENA increased dramatically, overtaking that for the FLMN (Artiga González, 2004: 21). Three years after its introduction, a majority of citizens continue to express support for the policy despite rising murder rates and a consensus that the policy has been ineffective (IUDOP, 2006). By the end of 2006, about 40 per cent agreed and 26 per cent disagreed with the policy, though 32.6 per cent affirmed that it had not reduced gang violence whilst another 31 per cent of respondents considered it had reduced violence only a little (IUDOP, 2006: 3). Although such support for repressive policies may not be an uncommon reaction to high levels of violence, it has broader implications for civil society in El Salvador, given the historic context where violence and repression have been prioritised and legitimised as tools of governance. It reinforces mistrust and polarisation, particularly between those perceived as 'upstanding citizens' and those perceived as 'criminals'. Furthermore, it is constitutive of a wider context of historic polarisation in which the logic of the state as an agent of repression – albeit updated to a democratic context – has not been displaced (Hume, 2007b). Thus 'violence itself is ignored, justified and, sometimes, stimulated by those who see themselves as upstanding and exemplary citizens, against those they consider the scum of society' (Cruz and Beltrán, 2000: 5).

Figures from 2003 indicate that 55 per cent of respondents would approve of the killing of a criminal who terrorises the community and 40.5 per cent would approve of lynching the criminal (UNDP, 2003: 142). In this context, order is recognised as more important than civil liberties and human rights in the face of high levels of criminality (Cruz, 2000: 518). In 2003, there were several incidences of decapitated corpses found in San Salvador reflecting tactics used by the death squads in the late 1970s and 1980s. These dismembered corpses of young women were found dumped in different locations. The deaths were blamed on gangs, but studies have pointed to the emergence of new generations of death squads, and allegations have been made of official involvement in these initiatives (Aguilar and Miranda, 2006: 56). One such group is the *Mano Blanco* operating in the San Miguel area with the stated aim of cleansing communities of gang members and murdering *todo aquel tatuado* (all who have tattoos). *Mano Blanco* is also the name given to a death squad responsible for the murder of thousands of peasants, workers and leftist sympathisers in the 1970s and 1980s, indicating important continuities in the mobilisation of certain polarised rhetoric and practices in the post-war period. Sources estimate that such bodies may be responsible for as many as 96 extrajudicial killings of young people (FESPAD, 2006). Although it might seem an extreme indicator, survey data found that 46.6 per cent of respondents would 'understand' another person/group killing 'undesirables'; 15.4 per cent would condone it, while only 38 per cent would not approve, some 58. 2 per cent of respondents declared themselves in favour of the death penalty (IUDOP/ACTIVA, 1998: 42, 51). Such figures indicate a degree of 'complicity', or at least a conspiratorial silence, regarding the use of social cleansing mechanisms, reflecting a tolerance, if not overt respect, for authoritarian measures. While these examples may be extreme, they indicate an endpoint to which citizens may resort. The limited peace in El Salvador has facilitated few alternatives for resolving conflict in a non-violent manner. Citizens use and applaud violence to attack criminality and violence. Polarisation and the construction of an 'other' based on grounds of class, and often age, are fundamental to this logic. This polarised logic, where the 'other' is seen as an enemy of the state and 'good' citizens, has been used to justify historic patterns of coercion in El Salvador and continues to mark its peace (Martín-Baró, 1983). In this context, order continues to be privileged over civil liberties. Thus, rather than the emergence of an entirely 'new' violence, we can see the reworking of historic patterns of control, complicity and coercion within a limited democratic framework.

## Conclusion

This chapter has attempted to draw out the key continuities in the changing political economy of violence in El Salvador. It has addressed the ways in which the historic fault lines of violence, exclusion and polarisation continue to undermine the achievement of peace. A new generation of violent actors – youth gangs – can be located within a broader critique of neoliberal governance in order to illuminate how historic forms of violence are understood, practised and updated to the democratic context. Knowledge about violence in El Salvador (and in post-war societies generally) remains fragmented and the rhetorical focus on youth gangs detracts attention from other powerful violent actors who perhaps 'gain' more from crime economies. At an extreme, the fixation on youth also provides a platform for 'good' citizens to engage in and legitimise certain behaviours such as social cleansing.

To say that the process in El Salvador has been entirely negative would be misleading. Spaces for political participation have opened up, allowing the FMLN to emerge as a major political party. Civil society has also been strengthened with the emergence of new forces, such as the women's movement and environmental organisations. The military and old security apparatus have undergone a transformation and no longer wield the same level of control over Salvadoran society, particularly in the area of human rights abuses. Nonetheless, for peace to mean more than the 'absence of war' for the citizens, structural reform is necessary. The neo-liberal peace has not been a 'benign' process for Salvadoran citizens. It has not fostered real alternatives to violence and continues to generate winners and losers. Without dedicated reform, the factors that facilitate the continued pervasiveness of violence will not simply disappear.

## Note

1. In the late 1990s, a study of the prison system found that 3 in every 10 prisoners played an active role during the war, a relatively high proportion given that no more than 6 per cent of the population participated in conditions of combat (Cruz et al., 2000: 71).

## References

Aguilar, Jeanette and Lisette Miranda, 2006, 'Entre la articulación y la competencia: las respuestas de la sociedad civil organizada a las pandillas en El Salvador', in José M. Cruz (ed.), *Maras y pandillas en Centroamérica, las respuestas de la sociedad civil organizada*, Vol. IV, San Salvador: UCA Editores.

Alvarenga, Patricia, 1996, *Cultura y Etica de la Violencia: El Salvador 1880–1932*, San José, Costa Rica: EDUCA.

Arana, Ana, 2005, 'How the Street Gangs Took Central America', *Foreign Affairs*, Vol. 84, No. 3, pp. 98–110.

Ardón, Patricia, 1998, *Los Conflictos y el Proceso de Paz en Centroamérica*, Oxford: Oxfam UK and Ireland.

Artiga González, Álvaro, 2004, 'El Salvador. Maremoto Electoral en 2004', *Nueva Sociedad*, No. 192, pp. 12–22.

AVPI (Armed Violence and Poverty Initiative), 2004, 'The Impact of Armed Violence on Poverty and Development', Centre for International Cooperation and

Security, University of Bradford (at: www.bradford.ac.uk/acad/cics/publications/AVPI/poverty/AVPI_Synthesis_Report.pdf).
Boraz, Steven and Thomas Bruneau, 2006, 'Are the *maras* Overwhelming Central America?', *Military Review*, November–December, pp. 36–40.
Bourgois, Pierre, 2001, 'The Power of Violence in War and Peace: Post-Cold War Lessons from El Salvador', *Ethnography*, Vol. 2, No. 1, pp. 5–34.
Burgerman, Susan, 2000, 'Building the Peace by Mandating Reform: United Nations-Mediated Human Rights Agreements in El Salvador and Guatemala', *Latin American Perspectives*, Issue 12, Vol. 27, No. 3, pp. 63–87.
Call, Charles T., 2001, 'Sustainable Development in Central America: The Challenges of Violence, Injustice and Insecurity', CA 2020: Working Paper 8 (at: http://ca2020.fiu.edu/Themes/Charles_Call/Call.pdf).
Call, Charles T., 2003, 'Democratisation, War and State-Building: Constructing the Rule of Law in El Salvador', *Journal of Latin American Studies*, Vol. 35, pp. 827–62.
Cárdia, Nancy, 2002, 'The Impact of Exposure to Violence in Sao Paolo: Accepting Violence or Continuing Horror?', in Susan Rotker (ed.) *Citizens of Fear: Urban Violence in Latin America*, New Brunswick: Rutgers University Press, pp. 152–86.
Cruz, José Miguel, 2000, 'Violencia, Democracia y Cultura Política en América Latina', *ECA*, San Salvador: UCA, May–June, pp. 619–20.
Cruz, José Miguel, 2003a, 'Violence, Insecurity and Legitimacy in Post-War Central American Countries', unpublished MSc dissertation, St Antony's College, Oxford.
Cruz, José Miguel, 2003b, 'Violence, Citizen Insecurity and Elite Maneuvering: Dynamics of Police Reform in El Salvador', unpublished paper, St Antony's College, Oxford.
Cruz, José Miguel and María Antonieta Beltrán, 2000, *Las Armas de Fuego en El Salvador: Situación e Impacto sobre la Violencia*, San Salvador: UCA.
Cruz, José Miguel, Luis Armando González, Luis Ernesto Romano and Elvio Sisti, 1998, *La Violencia en El Salvador en los Años Noventa: Magnitud, Costos y Factores Posibilitadores*, San Salvador: Inter-American Development Bank and IUDOP.
De Cesare, Donna, 1998, 'The Children of War Street Gangs in El Salvador', *NACLA Report on the Americas*, Vol. 32, pp. 21–9.
Debiel, Tobias with Axel Klein (eds), 2002, *Fragile Peace: State Failure, Violence and Development in Crisis Regions*, London: Zed Books.
Dunkerley, James, 1982, *The Long War: Dictatorship and Revolution in El Salvador*, London: Junction Books.
ECA, 1999, 'Editorial: Valoración del Siglo XX desde los Mártires', *Estudios Centroamericanos*, November–December, pp. 957–74.
ECA, 2003, 'Editorial: La campana electoral de ARENA: populismo punitivo', *Estudios Centroamericanos*, pp. 657–58 (at www.uca.edu.sv/publica/ued/eca-proceso/ecas_anter/eca657.html) 26 June 2007.
FESPAD (Foundation for Studies on the Application of Rights), 2004, *Informe Anual Sobre Justicia Penal Juvenil*.
FESPAD, 2006, *Informe Anual Sobre Justicia Penal Juvenil*, 2005 (at: http://fespad.org.sv/portal/html/Archivos/Descargas/ESPyJPES2005.pdf).
Godnick, William, Robert Muggah and Camilla Waszink, 2002, *Stray Bullets: The Impact of Small Arms Misuse in Central America*, Geneva: Small Arms Survey.
Holden, Robert H.,1996, 'Constructing the Limits of State Violence in Central America: Towards a New Research Agenda', *Journal of Latin American Studies*, Vol. 28, No. 2, pp. 435–59.

HRW (Human Rights Watch), 2007, 'El Salvador: Terrorism Law Misused Against Protesters' (at: http://hrw.org/english/docs/2007/07/31/elsalv16545.htm).

Huezo Mixco, Miguel, 2000, 'Cultura y Violencia en El Salvador', in PNUD *Violencia en una Sociedad en Transición: Ensayo*, San Salvador: PNUD, pp. 115–38.

Hume, Mo, 2004, *Armed Violence and Poverty in El Salvador*, Centre for International Cooperation and Security, University of Bradford, pp. 1–40 (at http://www.bradford.ac.uk/acad/cics/publications/AVPI/poverty/AVPI_El_Salvadors.pdf).

Hume, Mo, 2006, 'Contesting Imagined Communities: Gender, Nation and Violence in El Salvador', in Will Fowler and Peter Lambert (eds), *Political Violence and the Construction of National Identity in Latin America*, London: Palgrave Macmillan, pp: 73–90.

Hume, Mo, 2007a, '(Young) Men with Big Guns: Reflexive Encounters with Violence and Youth in El Salvador', *Bulletin of Latin American Research*, Vol. 26, No. 4, pp. 480–96.

Hume, Mo, 2007b, '*Mano Dura*: El Salvador Responds to Gangs', *Development in Practice*, Vol. 17, No. 6, pp. 739–51.

IDHES (Information of Human Development in El Salvador), 2005, *Human Development Report for El Salvador: A Look at the New 'Us': The Impact of Migration*, San Salvador: UNDP.

IDHUCA, 2002, 'La agenda pendiente, diez años después (de la esperanza inicial a lasresponsabilidades compartidas)' (at: http://www.uca.edu.sv/publica/idhuca/agendapendiente.pdf), May 8, 2008.

IUDOP, 1996, 'La violencia en El Salvador'. *Estudios Centroamericanos (ECA)*. LI (569): 240–49. San Salvador, El Salvador: UCA.

IUDOP, 2006, 'Evaluación del país a finales del 2006 y perspectivas para 2007', *Boletín de prensa* XXI, No.3 (at: www.uca.edu.sv/publica/iudop/Web/2006/bolet306.pdf).

IUDOP/FUNDAUNGO, 2002, *Encuesta Sobre la Percepción de la Seguridad Ciudadana a Nivel Navional, Municipal y Zonal*, San Salvador: Misiterio de Justicia and Consejo Nacional de Seguridad Pública, January.

Juhn, Tricia, 1998, *Negotiating Peace in El Salvador: Civil Military Relations and the Conspiracy to End the War*, London: Macmillan.

Kaldor, Mary, 2006, *New and Old Wars: Organised Violence in a Global Era*, 2nd edn, Cambridge: Polity.

Keane, John, 1997, *Reflections on Violence*, London: Verso.

Kooning, Kees and Dirk Kruijt (eds), 1999, *Societies of Fear: The Legacy of Civil War, Violence and Terror in Latin America*, London: Zed Books.

Kooning, Kees and Dirk Kruijt (eds), 2004, *Armed Actors: Organised Violence and State Failure in Latin America*, London: Zed Books.

Manwaring, Max, 2006, 'Gangs and Coups D' Streets in the New World Disorder: Protean Insurgents in Postmodern War', *Global Crime*, Vol. 7, No. 3, pp. 505–43.

Martín-Baró, Ignacio (1983), *Acción e Ideología: Psicología Social desde Centroamérica*, San Salvador: UCA.

McCoy, Jennifer (2006), 'International Response to Democratic Crisis in the Americas, 1990–2005', *Democratization*, Vol. 13, No. 5, pp. 756–75.

Melara Minero, Michelle, 2001, 'Los servicios de seguridad privada en El Salvador', Estudios Centroamericanos, 636 October pp. 907–32.

Moser, Caroline and Cathy McIlwaine, 2004, *Encounters with Violence in Latin America: Urban Poor Perceptions from Colombia and Guatemala*, London: Routledge.

Murray, Kevin, 1997, *El Salvador: A Peace on Trial?* Oxford: Oxfam UK/Ireland.

Pearce, Jenny, 1998, 'From Civil War to "Civil Society": Has the End of the Cold War Brought Peace to Central America?', *International Affairs*, Vol. 74, No. 3, pp. 587–615.

Pereira, Anthony and Diane Davis, 2000, 'New Patterns of Militarized Violence and Coercion in the Americas', *Latin American Perspectives*, Vol. 27, No. 2, pp. 3–18.

Popkin, Margaret, 1999, *Peace without Justice: Obstacles to Building the Rule of Law in El Salvador*, Philadelphia, PA: Pennsylvania State University Press.

Pugh, Michael, 2006, 'Post-war Economies and the New York Dissensus', *Conflict, Security & Development*, Vol. 6, No. 3, pp. 269–89.

Ramos, Carlos Guillermo, 2000, 'Marginación, Exclusión Social y Violencia', in PNUD [UNDP], *Violencia en una Sociedad en Transición: Ensayos*, San Salvador: UNDP, pp. 7–48.

Richmond, Oliver P., 2006, 'The Problem of Peace: Understanding the "Liberal Peace"', *Conflict, Security & Development*, Vol. 6, No. 3, pp. 291–314.

Rodgers, Dennis, 2007, 'Slum Wars of the 21st Century: the new geography of conflict in Central America', Crisis States Programme Working Papers No. 10, London School of Economics and Political Science.

Rotker, Susan (ed.), 2002, *Citizens of Fear: Urban Violence in Latin America*, New Brunswick, NJ: Rutgers University Press.

Saca, Tony, 2005, press conference, 27 December (at: www.casapres.gob.sv/presidente/declaraciones/2005/12/dec2701.html).

Santacruz Giralt, Maria, 2005, 'Creciendo en El Salvador: una mirada a la situación de la adolescencia y juventud en el país', *Estudios Centroamericanos*, No. 685–6, pp. 1079–99.

Savenije, Wim and Chris Van der Borgh, 2004, 'Youth Gangs, Social Exclusion and the Transformation of Violence in El Salvador', in Kooning and Kruijt (eds), *Armed Actors: Organised Violence and State Failure in Latin America*, London: Zed Books, pp. 155–71.

Stanley, William, 1996, *The Protection Racket State: Elite Politics, Military Extortion and Civil War in El Salvador*, Philadelphia, PA: Temple University Press.

Sullivan, John, 2006, 'Maras Morphing: Revisiting Third Generation Gangs', *Global Crime*, Vol. 7, pp. 3–4.

Tedesco, Laura, 2000, 'La Ñata contra el Vidrio: Urban Violence and Democratic Governability in Argentina', *BLAR*, Vol. 19, No. 4, pp. 527–45.

Tombs, David, 2004, 'Unspeakable Violence: The Truth Commissions in El Salvador and Guatemala', paper at Society for Latin American Studies Annual Conference, Leiden, 2 April.

Torres-Rivas, Edelberto, 1999, 'Epilogue: Notes on Terror, Violence, Fear and Democracy', in Kooning and Kruijit (eds), *Societies of Fear: The Legacy of Civil War, Violence and Terror in Latin America*, London: Zed Books, pp. 285–300.

Towers, Marcia, 2004, 'The Socioeconomic Implications of Dollarization in El Salvador', *Latin American Politics & Society*, Vol. 46, No. 3, pp. 29–54.

Truth Commission, 1993, 'From Madness to Hope: the 12 year war in El Salvador' (at: www.usip.org/library/tc/doc/reports/el_salvador/tc_es_03151993_toc.html).

UN, 1995, 'The United Nations and El Salvador, 1990–1995', *United Nations Blue Books Series*, Vol. 4, New York: UN.

UNDOC, 2007, 'Crime and Development in Central America: Caught in the Crossfire' (at: www.unodc.org/pdf/Central%20America%20Study.pdf).

UNDP, 2003, *Armas de Fuego y Violencia*, San Salvador.

UNDP, 2007, 'Seguridad y paz: Un reto de país. Recomendaciones para una política de seguridad ciudadana en El Salvador', San Salvador.

Williams, Philip J. and Knut Walter, 1997, *Militarization and Demilitarization in El Salvador's Transition to Democracy*, Pittsburgh: University of Pittsburgh Press.

# Part VII
# Global Governance

# 19
## Post-Conflict Statebuilding: Governance Without Government

*David Chandler*

Statebuilding, the development of international regulatory mechanisms aimed at addressing cases of intra-state conflict and state 'collapse', or at shoring up 'failing states', is commonly held to be the most pressing problem of global security, on ethical, humanitarian, and, in the wake of 9/11, realist security grounds. It is not unusual for leading commentators to argue that 'statebuilding is one of the most important issues for the world community' and to note that the issue has rapidly 'risen to the top of the global agenda' (Fukuyama, 2004: ix–xi). As the 2002 US National Security Strategy stated, 'America is now threatened less by conquering states than we are by failing ones' (US Government, 2002: section 1). It seems that no international policy or strategy document is complete without the focus on statebuilding as a key objective. Since the 1990s, the United States, the UK and other major Western governments have established new statebuilding departments and policy units, while international institutions, from the UN down to more specialised international bodies engaged in economic development, democracy or human rights promotion, have seen statebuilding as a key policy focus. International aid is increasingly channelled directly into strengthening governing capacity rather than used to support discrete projects concerned with sectoral improvements in areas such as health and social welfare, economic sustainability or security reforms; more than a quarter of bilateral aid to Africa, for example, is channelled directly into state capacity-building (Commission for Africa, 2005: 136).

The focus on state capacities and institutions seems to herald a shift away from the 1990s when new, more interventionist, norms were heralded, which challenged the post-colonial codification of the rights of state sovereignty. These rights – of self-government and non-intervention – took their clearest institutional form in the UN Charter framework of international law which emphasised the rights of peoples to self-government (Article 1.2), the sovereign equality of member states (Article 2.1) and the principle of non-intervention – outlawing the threat or use of force

(Article 2.4). Throughout the Cold War, successive judgments of the International Court of Justice upheld these rights to self-government and denied the existence of any legitimate grounds for external intervention, even on the basis of 'humanitarian' or 'human rights' justifications (Chandler, 2002: 157–66).

After the end of the Cold War, the focus appeared to shift to an emphasis on the rights of individuals. States were no longer seen to be the primary security referent and state sovereignty was not considered to be an absolute barrier to external intervention. Following extended intervention in Iraq to protect the Kurds and Marsh Arabs after the 1991 Gulf War, and external military intervention for humanitarian purposes in Somalia in 1992–1993 and Bosnia and Herzegovina (BiH) in 1993–1995, the high point of this new focus on individuals rather than states was the NATO-led international intervention over Kosovo in 1999. Much of the debate in the 1990s posed the human rights of individuals as counter to, and as undermining of, the rights of state sovereignty and as necessitating new rights of intervention for international institutions.

Rather than international intervention being posed in terms of the undermining of non-Western state sovereignty, international discourse now constructs international intervention as necessary to support and enhance the sovereignty of the non-Western state. This shift in international policy discourse demonstrates the socially constructed nature of 'sovereignty' and its conceptual opposite 'intervention' (see, e.g., Weber, 1995). However, the focus of this chapter is not so much on the 'simulation' of sovereignty, its lack of fixed representational meaning at the level of discourse, but how the changing discursive construction of sovereignty reflects changing material relations and practices. In particular, it seeks to demonstrate that the sovereignty of non-Western states – their capacity for self-government – is being transformed through the liberal political economy of international intervention.

Thus the non-Western state appears at the centre of security concerns, whether couched in terms of realist national interest or liberal and cosmopolitan frameworks of human security. However, the non-Western state is perceived less as a threat than as a potential ally or partner, in need of support and assistance. It now appears that states, particularly those that have been marginalised by the world economy or weakened by conflict, can no longer be ignored or isolated. In the aftermath of 9/11 – where the failure of the Afghan state to control its borders and the activities of its citizens was held to have opened the way for Al Qaeda's operations – the state is no longer viewed from a mainly negative perspective. Non-Western states now appear less obviously as objects of opprobrium and are more likely to be fêted by international institutions and leading Western states that offer programmes of poverty reduction, capacity-building, democratisation and good governance.

This chapter questions the vision of the state which is being placed at the centre of the policies and programmes associated with the political economy of liberal peace. The following section puts the statebuilding discussion in the context of current problems in conceptualising the role of states and in response to the 1990s decade of humanitarian intervention. Further sections then lay out specific problems, which highlight the corrosive nature of current policy practices in this area. I show how the redefinition of sovereignty, central to this statebuilding framework, facilitates the erosion of ties linking power and accountability, enabling international interveners, acting under the programmes of liberal peace, to distance themselves from the consequences of the political and economic policies they promote.

## From the 'right to intervene' to statebuilding

The discussion of statebuilding – of international mechanisms to capacity-build weak states – seems, at face value, to herald a return to traditional pluralist frameworks of international relations. But this focus on a familiar political form should not obscure what is, in effect, a radical transformation of the mechanisms of international regulation. All observers seem to agree that states are not what they used to be. As Francis Fukuyama notes, 'for well over a generation, the trend in world politics has been to weaken stateness', a trend particularly marked since the end of the Cold War (Fukuyama, 2004: 161). It is only in the context of current uncertainties over the role and purpose of the state that we can understand the novel processes at the heart of liberal peace statebuilding policy and practice.

It would seem that states are losing their capacities rather than gaining them. For many commentators this is clearly a positive shift (Archibugi et al., 1998; Linklater, 1998; Rosenau and Czempiel, 1992). Across the board of social theory, from historical sociology to postmodern international relations, states have been increasingly cast as problems rather than solutions. Charles Tilly's work is regularly drawn on to argue that states are merely government-run 'protection rackets' based on the repression and exploitation of their citizens in the interest of criminal or self-interested elites (Tilly, 1985). Postmodernists draw on the work of Foucault to argue that Clausewitz's famous dictum should be inverted to reveal the illegitimacy of the liberal democratic state and understand 'politics as the continuation of war by other means' (Foucault, 2003). David Campbell et al. argue that it was the state-orientated perspective of the international community – the view that the problems of nationalist conflict could be solved, rather than just reproduced, by the creation of new totalising unitary states – that encouraged many post-Cold War conflicts, such as the Bosnian war (Campbell, 1998; Kaldor, 1998).

In this context, the focus on the state rather than on alternative forms of international governance might seem to be an unexpected development.

Some commentators have explained this by suggesting that the new focus on state capacity is a reaction against the 'humanitarian intervention' policies of the 1990s which were held to have underestimated the importance of states for maintaining international stability (Malone, 2005: xv). One example of interventionist policies, often held to have been counterproductive in this context, is that of international aid provision which bypassed state institutions establishing parallel bureaucracies and encouraging a brain drain from the underpaid state sector (Ghani *et al.*, 2005: 10). The UK's Commission for Africa report argues that statebuilding policies should

> stand in marked contrast to the approach in the 1980s and much of the 1990s, when aid was often used to try to compensate for poor governance, simply ignored governance issues, tried to force policies on reluctant countries, or aimed primarily at advancing the economic or political interests of the donor.
>
> (Commission for Africa, 2005: 94)

Several commentators have stressed that the result of the 1990s humanitarian and human rights interventions has been the 'sucking out' of state capacity – as core state functions have been taken over by the UN agencies, international institutions and international NGOs – thereby undermining the legitimacy and authority of non-Western states (European Stability Initiative, 2005: 10; Fukuyama, 2004: 139; Ignatieff, 2003).

With the end of the Cold War, there rapidly developed increasingly interventionist regimes of international regulation, clearly exposing claims of international sovereign equality and in the process forcing Western powers and international institutions to account for the outcomes of these regulatory practices. Once relations of sovereign equality were openly brought into question through aid conditionality and human rights intervention, the question of Western responsibility was sharply posed. This was most strikingly raised in the Balkans, where individual Western states and the EU, UN and other international institutions played a major role in overseeing the fragmentation of the Yugoslav state, making key decisions on state recognition and boundaries. The result of this process of being drawn directly into conflict prevention was the unwieldy international protectorates of BiH, since 1995, and Kosovo, since 1999, which have left intervening institutions overstretched and exposed to criticism (so much so that the UN was opposed to assuming responsibilities in Afghanistan). Since 9/11, with the likelihood that new Western responsibilities would be acquired through 'regime change', there was even greater pressure to develop new approaches which could help distance the West from the consequences of interventionist policies.

There is little doubt that international policy intervention in the 1980s and 1990s tended to bypass or reduce the non-Western state's administrative and political institutional capacity. They gave coercive powers of conditionality to international financial institutions (IFIs) which imposed fiscal regimes cutting the state's role in the economy and service provision; implemented discrete projects run independently by international agencies and NGOs; and dictated policy outcomes through tying aid to donor goods and services. However, the key element common to these various interventions was their overtly external and coercive nature. The relations of authority were transparent; nowhere more so than in aid conditionality where the IFIs specified detailed policies which the recipient countries had to accept. It was clear that, in these cases, non-Western governments, particularly those in Africa, were more accountable to international donors than to their own people (Commission for Africa, 2005: 92).

Bearing this context in mind, the argument here is that the new focus on the non-Western state has less to do with the desire for strong non-Western states, or a new-found confidence in non-Western governing elites, than a desire on the behalf of Western advocates of the programmes of liberal peace to avoid direct accountability for policy interventions, which have thrown up as many problems as they have answered. The fact that statebuilding is not driven by the need to strengthen non-Western states is highlighted by the strong consensus, among those engaged in the field, that 'strong' states are deeply problematic; that state capacities should not include the traditional 'right to do what they will within their own borders'.

For example, I. William Zartman argues that 'weak/soft' states are no worse than 'hard/brittle' states – while weak states cannot exercise adequate authority over the domestic arena, 'strong/hard/brittle' states exercise too much authority and tend to marginalise other voices in civil society (Zartman, 2005). Robert I. Rotberg agrees that there is a 'special category of weak state: the seemingly strong one' and that the number of states in this category has grown rapidly in recent times (Rotberg, 2004: 5). States that are resistant to external engagement in their affairs, which cling to traditional ideas of 'Westphalian sovereignty, referring to the exclusion of external actors from domestic authority configurations', are seen to be problematic (Fearon and Laitin, 2004; Keohane, 2002, 2003; Krasner, 1999: 9, 2004). In fact, the more one investigates the capacity-building literature, the more difficult it is to isolate exactly what is meant by claims that states are being 'capacity-built' by external interveners. It is patently clear that the aim is not to create states as classically understood: self-governing, independent and autonomous political subjects.

The contemporary thrust for 'bringing the state back in', in the policy discussions of state failure and statebuilding, can be better understood as a radical extension of the practices of the 1980s and 1990s which internationalised the domestic policymaking sphere of non-Western states (Straw, 2002). The key difference with the overtly 'interventionist' approach of the 1990s is that the emphasis is now on the non-Western states rather than on those states and institutions doing the intervening. The transition away from justifying and holding intervening powers to account was presaged by the International Commission on Intervention and State Sovereignty (ICISS) *Responsibility to Protect* report of December 2001, and formulated prior to 9/11.

The Commission proposed a shift in language away from the 'human-centred' framework of a 'right to intervention' and towards a 'state-centred' framework of the 'responsibility to protect'. Whereas the 'right of intervention' put the emphasis on the international interveners to justify and legitimise their actions, the 'responsibility to protect' sought to avoid this 'attention on the claims, rights and prerogatives of the potentially intervening states' (ICISS, 2001: 16). The 'responsibility to protect' seeks to off-load responsibility onto the non-Western states at the same time as these states increasingly lose their policymaking authority.

The ICISS report successfully set out to 'shift the terms of the debate' and facilitated the evasion of any clarification of the competing rights of state sovereignty and of those of intervening powers by arguing that state rights of sovereignty can coexist with external intervention and statebuilding. The report contends that 'sovereignty then means accountability to two separate constituencies: internally, to one's own population; and internationally, to the community of responsible states' (ICISS, 2001: 11). As the Commission co-chairs noted, this shift changes 'the essence of sovereignty, from control to responsibility' (Evans and Sahnoun, 2002: 101). The major implications that this would have for accountability (a power which is accountable to another, external, body clearly lacks sovereign authority – the capacity for self-government) have been consistently played down by the report's authors and academic commentators. Robert Keohane, for example, disingenuously argues that the ICISS report is not at all 'devaluing' sovereignty, merely that it is 'reinterpreting' it, to bring the concept more into line with the modern world (Keohane, 2003: 276).

Rather than the 1990s debate, where international intervention was posed as a clash of competing rights – the 'right of intervention' against the 'right of state sovereignty' – today the language is one of 'shared responsibilities' and 'new partnerships'. Where the non-Western state was the subject of overtly coercive external intervention, it is now more likely to be the focus of supportive, empowering and capacity-building practices and new modalities of surveillance. The product of this change has been the enthronement of the statebuilding discourse as the framework for discussing Western regulation of and intervention in non-Western states.

This shift in the language of the Western projection of power reflects both the new relations of subordination with the end of the bipolar world and at the same time the desire of Western institutions to reject direct accountability and distance themselves from the direct management of 'zones of instability'. The statebuilding framework seeks to obfuscate and confuse relations of power and accountability which stood clearly exposed in the 1990s as a fundamental clash of rights. The *Responsibility to Protect* report, in emphasising the responsibilities of the non-Western states, heralded the shift towards statebuilding as a policy of both intervention and avoidance. The contradictions involved in this process are highlighted in the irony that states are alleged to be 'built' at the same time as they increasingly lose the traditional attribute of sovereignty: self-government.

## States without sovereignty

Sovereignty in international relations signifies political and legal autonomy: constitutional independence. It is a legal concept which is unconditional and indivisible. As Robert Jackson summarises,

> [It is] legal in that a sovereign state is not subordinate to another sovereign but is necessarily equal to it by international law.... Absolute [unconditional] in that sovereignty is either present or absent. When a country is sovereign it is independent categorically: there is no intermediate condition. Unitary [indivisible] in that a sovereign state is a supreme authority within its jurisdiction.
>
> (Jackson, 1990: 32)

Prior to decolonisation in the last century, the sovereign state form was only one of several kinds of international status. Under European colonialism territorial entities took the form of 'colonies', 'protectorates', 'mandates', 'trust territories' or 'dominions' (ibid.: 33). These various forms had in common a formal legal subordination to a foreign power; they were a denial of sovereignty. There is nothing inevitable or natural about the sovereign state form or about its universalisation in the twentieth century, in the wake of the First and Second World Wars (Morgenthau, 1970: 258–61; Wight, 1979: 23).

Few people engaged in the field would argue that international statebuilding in post-conflict situations is a framework for the creation or support of traditional sovereign entities. This can be seen clearly in practice in the cases of international engagement in BiH, Afghanistan, the handing over of 'sovereignty' in Iraq, and moves to make Kosovo an independent state and more broadly in the UN and G8 proposals for state capacity-building in Africa. The sovereign state forms are held up but sovereignty is being redefined (or 'unbundled' in Stephen Krasner's phraseology), emphasising the importance of the legal shell of the state form while abandoning its political content of self-government and autonomy (Krasner, 1999).

This is done in three ways. First, sovereignty is redefined as a variable 'capacity' rather than an indivisible right, thereby legitimising a new hierarchy of variable sovereignty and undermining the UN Charter principle of sovereign equality. Second, sovereignty is redefined as a duty or responsibility rather than a freedom; legitimising external mechanisms of regulation, held to enhance 'sovereignty' despite undermining the traditional right of self-government or autonomy. Third, the formal importance of international legal sovereignty is exaggerated; this formal shell then facilitates the repackaging of external domination as 'partnership' or 'country ownership' and the voluntary contract of formally equal partners.

### Sovereignty as capacity?

The most important challenge to traditional conceptions of sovereignty has been the conflation of the formal political and legal right to self-government (an absolute quality) with the question of state capacity (a variable quantity), usually formulated in terms of 'good governance'. The conception of sovereignty as a capacity, rather than as a formal legal right to self-government and international legal equality, creates a 'continuum' of sovereignty or a hierarchical structure of sovereignty, in which some states are considered to be more sovereign than others. This approach was famously developed by Robert Jackson, with his conception of 'quasi-states' (Jackson, 1990). For Jackson, the sovereignty granted to post-colonial states was artificial: not because they were often still under the influence of their former colonial rulers, but because many of these states did not have the capacity to regulate and control their societies to the same extent as states in the West. For Jackson, these states possessed *de jure* sovereignty, formal international legal rights, but lacked *de facto* sovereignty, the capacity to govern domestically.

This idea of the 'unbundling' of sovereignty into its different attributes was popularised by Stephen Krasner in *Sovereignty: Organized Hypocrisy* (1999). In later work, he has focused on sovereignty as a 'bundle' of three separate attributes: 'domestic sovereignty', the capacity of domestic governance structures; 'Westphalian/Vattelian sovereignty', that is self-government or political autonomy; and international legal sovereignty, formal juridical independence (Krasner, 2004: 87–8). Krasner uses the problem of weak capacity to argue that self-government should not be a barrier to international intervention. Whereas in the 1990s intervention would have been posed as a conflict between human rights (or the right of intervention) and the right of state sovereignty (self-government and autonomy), in Krasner's terminology there is no conflict with sovereignty because human rights would be protected if governments possessed adequate governing capacity ('domestic sovereignty'): 'Honoring Westphalian/Vattelian sovereignty...makes it impossible to secure decent and effective domestic sovereignty.... To secure decent domestic governance in failed, failing, and occupied states, new institutional forms are needed that compromise Westphalian/Vattellian sovereignty for an indefinite period' (ibid.: 89).

The discovery that the equality of sovereignty hides the inequality of state capacities was not a new one. The same problem, although to a lesser extent, is present in domestic politics, where equality at the ballot box or under the law in liberal democracies does not necessarily ameliorate social and economic inequalities between individuals. In the domestic context, of course, relatively few people would argue that these inequalities should mean that formal political and legal equalities should be abandoned. In the international sphere, the existence of vast inequalities of power was one of the reasons why state sovereignty, held to be unconditional and indivisible, was the founding principle of international society. It was only on this basis, of formally upholding the equality and autonomy of states and the sovereign rights of non-intervention, that post-colonial societies could be guaranteed the rights to self-government. UN General Assembly declarations during the Cold War regularly asserted that differences in state capacity could never be grounds for undermining the rights of state sovereignty.

The affirmation that differences in capacity were no justification for the unequal treatment of sovereign equals was confirmed most notably in the UN General Assembly Declaration on the Granting of Independence to Colonial Countries and Peoples of 14 December 1960 (Resolution 1514 (XV)) which proclaimed that 'all peoples have the right to self-determination; by virtue of that right they freely determine their political status and freely pursue their economic, social and cultural development' and that 'inadequacy of political, economic, social or educational preparedness should never serve as a pretext for delaying independence' (Declaration, 1960). This was passed in the General Assembly by a vote of 89 to 0, with 9 abstentions. Even the colonial powers were unwilling to reject it (Jackson, 1990: 77). This was followed by the Declaration on the Inadmissibility of Intervention in the Domestic Affairs of States and Protection of their Independence and Sovereignty of 21 December 1965 (Resolution 2131 (XX)) and the Declaration on Principles of International Law Concerning Friendly Relations and Co-operation among States in Accordance with the Charter of the United Nations of 24 October 1970 (Resolution 2625 (XXV)). The latter declaration makes it clear that 'All States enjoy sovereign equality. They have equal rights and duties and are equal members of the international community, notwithstanding differences of an economic, social, political or other nature' (Declaration, 1970).

By associating sovereignty with a sliding scale of 'capacities', rather than political and legal rights of equality, not only is a new international hierarchy legitimised but intervention can be framed as supporting 'sovereignty' at the same time as it is undermining the rights of self-government. This inversion of the concept of 'sovereignty' is formulated in the clearest terms in the UK Overseas Development Institute (ODI) working paper report 'Closing the Sovereignty Gap'. In this report, sovereignty is understood in functional rather than political or legal terms:

> The consensus now emerging from global economic, military and political institutions signals that this gap between *de jure* sovereignty and *de facto* sovereignty is the key obstacle to ensuring global security and prosperity. The challenge is to harness the international system behind the goal of enhancing the sovereignty of states – that is, enhancing the capacity of these states to perform the functions that define them as states. Long-term partnerships must be created to prepare and then implement strategies to close this sovereignty gap.
> 
> (Ghani *et al.*, 2005: 4)

Here sovereignty is no longer conceived as a right to self-government. Sovereignty is merely a capacity which can be 'enhanced' or, presumably, 'weakened'. The conflation of external intervention for the purposes of 'capacity-building' with enhancing state sovereignty and independence is central to the statebuilding discourse. In Africa, where state capacity is held to be a fundamental concern for external powers engaged in supporting a multitude of empowering projects, headlined by the UN Millennium Development Goals (MDG), these governance interventions have gone furthest (Commission for Africa, 2005: ch. 4; UN Millennium Project, 2005).

If sovereignty is defined as the capacity of non-Western states for 'good governance', there would seem to be little wrong in external institutions implementing strategies for long-term engagement in these societies in order to enhance their 'sovereignty'. In fact, governments which resisted this external assistance could, in the Orwellian language of international statebuilders, be accused of undermining their own sovereignty. The key to the success of this conceptual conflation is not in its legitimisation of external intervention (already accepted in the 1990s) but in its portrayal of external regulation as somehow empowering or strengthening non-Western states. Here is the virtuous circle for the new political economy of liberal intervention, one that was not possible in the post-conflict interventions of the 1990s: the more intervention there is, the more the target state is held to be responsible and accountable for the consequences of these practices.

### Sovereignty as responsibility?

The second shift articulated by the advocates of statebuilding as empowerment is the assertion that non-Western states have the 'responsibilities' of sovereignty rather than the rights of sovereignty. The constitution of these 'responsibilities' is not held to be a decision made solely by the citizens of a state or their representatives, but in 'partnership' with external bodies. Rather than being a barrier to external interference, sovereignty becomes a medium through which non-Western states and societies become integrated into networks of external regulation. International regulatory mechanisms of intervention are legitimised, first, through the role of international institutions in deciding the content of the 'responsibilities' of sovereignty, and second, through holding states to external account for 'failings' in the exercise of sovereignty (now discussed in the language of responsibility/capacity).

Sovereignty as 'responsibility' enables a new consensual or 'partnership' approach to statebuilding. Non-Western states are in a poor position to resist new international mechanisms of regulation which come replete with carrots of international aid, trade privileges, debt forgiveness or integration into international organisations, in return for external support for governance reforms and institutional capacity-building. Statebuilding or 'sovereignty-building' involves non-Western states being firmly embedded in international institutional frameworks, over whose decision-making processes they have little influence. For the UK's ODI, the focus on strengthening sovereignty entails a much more interventionist role by external institutions:

> We define a sovereignty or statebuilding strategy as... the alignment of the internal and external stakeholders.... In order to design and implement statebuilding strategies, the operation of the current international system must be reorientated towards a model where partnership and co-production of sovereignty becomes the aim of both national leaders and international partners.
>
> (Ghani et al., 2005: 13)

This 'co-production of sovereignty' has involved opening up all aspects of domestic governance to external regimes of liberal political economy. This is highlighted in the strategies adopted by the EU towards Balkan states from 2000 onwards where international partnerships enmeshing applicant states in a network of international institutional processes were coordinated through the Stability Pact, the Stabilisation and Association Process, the Community Assistance for Reconstruction, Development and Stabilisation Programme, and the 'European Partnership' process. The prospect of future EU membership was explicitly offered to Albania, BiH, Croatia, Macedonia and the Federal Republic of Yugoslavia at the Feira European Council in June 2000. At this point the EU shifted away from external conditionality and towards statebuilding in the Balkan region, initiating a project of 'reforming and reinventing the state in South Eastern Europe' (EastWest Institute, 2001: 18).

This shift from external relations of aid and trade conditionality to 'partnership' in domestic governance is symbolised by the dropping of the term 'Balkans' by international institutions, as too 'negative' and 'hegemonic', and its replacement by 'South Eastern Europe' symbolising that this is a joint project of partnership, addressing 'European problems' with 'European solutions' (see, e.g., *Balkanologie*, 1999; Hatzopoulos, 2005). The EU argued that it was well placed to assist these states in developing governance capacity which was identified as not just their main barrier to progress but also an area where the EU held a vital 'comparative advantage' and could 'provide real added value' (European Commission, 2001: 9). This engagement in domestic policymaking is held to have 'both pedagogical and political' benefits for the target states (EU, 2001). Although talking up the partnership between international institutions, the EU and target states, the statebuilding process has been directed by close cooperation between the EU and the IFIs. Together they provided 'an effective means of focusing authorities' minds on essential reforms and of engaging with them in a sustained way to secure implementation' (ibid.: section 111c).

Since 2000, the concept of statebuilding through international partnerships to enhance governance capacities has increasingly replaced external pressures. Where the incentive of European membership is not available, a wide range of other governance partnerships have been established around acceptance that the core problem of non-Western states is that of state capacity and that the solution lies with the shared 'responsibilities' of both the non-Western states and international institutions. The general rule of thumb appears to be that the greater the inequalities at play in the relationship between non-Western states and international institutions, the more grandiose the language of partnership. As would be expected, it is in relation to Africa that the rhetoric and reality are most out of step. Here the language is of 'African leadership' and an entirely 'new kind of partnership' not based on inequality and hierarchy but based on 'mutual respect and solidarity' (Commission for Africa, 2005: 17). The UN MDG project, following and extending the 'country ownership' approach of the interventionist Poverty Reduction Strategies, requires that states engage in far-reaching governance reform and open up every area of domestic policymaking to international scrutiny and involvement. The 'responsibilities' or 'leadership' or 'ownership' lie with the domestic state but their partners (or joint 'stakeholders', in the language of the ODI authors) decide the policies:

> The host country should lead and own the effort to design the MDG strategy, drawing in civil society organizations; bilateral donors; the UN specialized agencies, programs, and funds; and the international financial institutions, including the IMF, the World Bank, and the appropriate regional development bank. The contributions of the UN specialized agencies, programs and funds should be coordinated through the UN Country Team, and the UN Country Team should work closely with the international financial institutions.
>
> (UN Millennium Project, 2005: 53)

The 'host country' books the meeting rooms but the 'guests' come along with the policy frameworks. These external policy prescriptions closely tie international aid to new institutional frameworks of regulation and monitoring. In effect, this transforms external assistance from being a subject of international relations, between states, to one of domestic politics, of management and administration. This radical transformation in the relationship between non-Western states and international institutions is highlighted forcefully by the UK's Commission for Africa report (2005), which stresses that it is 'not simply recommending throwing money at the problems' but a 'fundamental change in the way in which aid works' (Commission for Africa, 2005: 94).

Once IFIs have a more direct role in the *internal* governance mechanisms of non-Western states, aid is much less likely to be based on overt external regulation in the form of *external* conditionality. Graham Harrison usefully highlights the 'post-conditionality' regimes of IFIs in states such as Tanzania and Uganda, where the influence of external donors is better conceived not as a 'strong external force' but as 'part of the state itself', through direct involvement in policymaking committees (Harrison, 2001: 669; 2004). The undermining of sovereign autonomy and the enmeshing of subject states in international institutional frameworks fundamentally blur the lines of accountability and control and the relationships of power behind these mechanisms. The relationship between Western institutions and non-Western states is a highly coercive one which forces these states to cede their sovereign powers to external institutions; the fiction of 'partnership' then relies heavily on an exaggeration of the importance of international legal sovereignty.

## International legal sovereignty?

Despite the new interventionist consensus and the international attention given to 'failing' states and the lack of governance capacities in 'zones of instability', there is surprisingly little support for the return of international protectorates and direct external administrations. Few commentators argue that states should be 'allowed to fail' and more capable neighbours allowed to directly govern these territories (e.g., Herbst, 2003), or that the UN Security Council should establish new international trusteeships (Helman and Ratner, 1993).

Intervening powers and international institutions seem to have a particularly strong desire to preserve the formal trappings of sovereignty. The contradictory desire to intervene but also to avoid responsibility is most sharply posed in questions of military intervention, such as post-9/11 'regime change' in Afghanistan and Iraq. Few acts are as fundamentally undermining of sovereignty as the external removal of a state's government. Yet, no sooner have intervening actors destroyed sovereignty than they are talking up its fundamental importance and pledging to restore authority to local actors at the soonest possible moment. Statebuilding is the process of negotiating these contradictory drives towards intervention and away from responsibility for outcomes.

Leading US policy advisers and international think-tanks are increasingly singing from the same hymn sheet, suggesting that international regulation should no longer be seen in the old ways. Today's policy context means that the old restrictions on international intrusion no longer exist. In the absence of Cold War rivalries between competing great powers, external intervention no longer needs to be overtly recognised in the undermining of sovereignty and open return to trusteeships and protectorates. In fact, the maintenance of formal sovereignty is at the heart of new approaches to 'neotrusteeship' (Fearon and Latin, 2004), 'pooled sovereignty' (Keohane, 2002) or 'shared sovereignty' (Krasner, 2004). In Krasner's words,

> Shared sovereignty would involve the engagement of external actors in some of the domestic authority structures of the target state for an indefinite period of time. Such arrangements would be legitimated by agreements signed by recognized national authorities. National actors would use their international legal sovereignty to enter into agreements that would compromise their Westphalian/Vattellian sovereignty [self-government/autonomy] with the goal of improving domestic sovereignty [governing capacity]. One core element of sovereignty – voluntary agreements – would be preserved, while another core element – the principle of autonomy – would be violated.
>
> (Ibid.: 108)

The key difference between new forms of liberal governance – 'neo-trusteeship' or, even more user-friendly, 'shared sovereignty' – and traditional notions of a trust or protectorate is that, today, the subordinated territory will formally be a contracting legal equal. International legal sovereignty is maintained while political autonomy – self-government – is given up. The Bosnian Peace Agreement at Dayton in 1995 is the epitome of the voluntary surrender of sovereignty; the 'neo-trusteeship' was legitimised not through war and intervention or through international legal agreement (the UN Security Council's blessing was bestowed retrospectively) but through the signature of the Bosnian parties (Chandler, 2005).

Law and reality no longer coincide when considering the location of sovereign power and authority (Yannis, 2002: 1049). Kosovo, for example, is, in mid-2007, still formally part of the state of Serbia, but again the lack of fit between the formal location of sovereignty and external mechanisms of regulation makes discussions of final status hard to resolve. Decision-making authority lies with neither the elected Kosovo government in Pristina nor the government in Belgrade. Afghanistan and Iraq have the juridical status of independent states despite their dependence on the political and security role of the United States. The artificial nature of these regimes is highlighted by the fact that their governments' writs seldom extend outside the protected security zones of the capitals. The restrictions on the Iraqi interim government's authority have meant that the formal transfer of Iraqi sovereignty from the US-led Coalition Provisional Authority to an Iraqi government in June 2004 did not reflect any change in the real relations of authority (Klein, 2005).

Here we have states without sovereignty. States exist on paper, in terms of juridical status, for example, as members of the United Nations, with national flags, and maybe their own currencies, but not as independent political subjects capable of self-government. As Keohane argues,

> We somehow have to reconceptualize the state as a political unit that can maintain internal order while being able to engage in international cooperation, without claiming the exclusive rights ... traditionally associated with sovereignty.... The same institutional arrangements may help both to reconstruct troubled countries that are in danger of becoming 'failed states', and to constrain the autonomy of those states.
>
> (2003: 277)

He suggests that statebuilding can establish the 'institutional arrangements' which are capable of taking responsibility for maintaining order ('domestic sovereignty') but without giving rise to rights of self-government ('Westphalian sovereignty'). He recommends an exit strategy for Kosovo, for example, where there is a shift from existing trusteeship status, which could be called 'nominal sovereignty' to 'limited sovereignty', with external powers able to override domestic authorities, to a final stage of 'integrated sovereignty' where the state is locked into international institutions able to override domestic authorities (ibid.: 296–7). This would resolve the problem of Kosovo's independence as it would never achieve independence beyond the purely formal trappings of statehood: 'Westphalian sovereignty ... is simply bypassed in the movement from limited to integrated sovereignty' (ibid.: 297).

His proposals are strikingly similar to those subsequently advocated by the International Commission on the Balkans. The commission's report, *The Balkans in Europe's Future* (2005), discussed Kosovo's 'independence without full sovereignty', to be followed by 'guided sovereignty' with 'reserve powers' for the EU and a final stage of 'full and shared sovereignty' (International Commission on the Balkans, 2005: 18–23). Here statebuilding refers to technical success in securing the regulatory controls of liberal regimes of political economy, rather than to any change in social and political relations. The new state, which will have formal 'sovereignty' (UN membership, a national flag and a national anthem) will be essentially in the same position to determine its own policies as it was when it was formally a protectorate. The difference is that formal accountability has been shifted away from the international policy managers and back to the non-Western state.

James Fearon and David Laitin suggest a similar approach arguing that a return to traditional forms of sovereignty is not the solution, but instead that the transfer of power in cases of post-conflict intervention and regime change should be 'not to full sovereignty but rather as a state embedded in and monitored by international institutions' (Fearon and Laitin, 2004: 42). Krasner argues the point even more openly in his support for the concept of 'shared' sovereignty, which similarly uses 'sovereignty' as a means of enabling external regulation. Here, international legal sovereignty allows post-conflict states to enter into 'partnerships' which informally violate their sovereign rights:

> For policy purposes, it would be best to refer to shared sovereignty as 'partnerships'. This would more easily let policymakers engage in organized hypocrisy, that is, saying one thing and doing another. Shared sovereignty or partnerships would allow political leaders to embrace sovereignty, because these arrangements would be legitimated by the target state's international legal sovereignty, even though they violate the core principle of Westphalian/Vattellian sovereignty: autonomy.... Shared sovereignty or partnerships would make no claim to being an explicit alternative to conventional sovereignty. It would allow actors to obfuscate the fact that their behaviour would be inconsistent with their principles.
> 
> (Krasner, 2004: 108)

## Conclusion

It is this 'obfuscation' of the maintenance of international legal sovereignty that enables the new forms taken by the political economy of liberal peace interventions to present intervening states and international institutions as facilitating partners in a shared project rather than as coercive external powers. Robert Cooper, focusing particularly on the enlargement policies of the EU, describes this as a new conflict-free 'postmodern' or 'voluntary' form of imperialism (Cooper, 2003). Mark Leonard argues that unlike the old imperialism based on conflict and overt subordination, the EU is completely transforming states from the inside, rather than ruling them from above, for example, 'Europe is changing all of Polish society, from its economic policies and property laws to its treatment of minorities and what gets served on the nation's tables' (Leonard, 2005: 6).

The more 'sovereignty' is voluntarily shared between target states and intervening institutions upholding the liberal peace, the more coercive external conditionality is exchanged for internal forms of 'enhanced surveillance' through the reporting mechanisms generated by the good governance requisites of openness and transparency enforced by international institutions (Commission for Africa, 2005: 376). Policy advisers can no doubt see the gains to be made in enabling liberal interventionist powers to talk about sovereignty and accountability in non-Western states, while avoiding policy responsibility and political accountability for their actions and policy prescriptions.

## References

Archibugi, Daniel, David Held and Martin Kohler (eds), 1998, *Re-imagining Political Community: Studies in Cosmopolitan Democracy*, Cambridge: Polity.

*Balkanologie*, 1999, Special issue, 'South-Eastern Europe: History, Concepts, Boundaries', Vol. 3, No. 2, pp. 47–127.

Campbell, David, 1998, *National Deconstruction: Violence, Identity and Justice in Bosnia*, Minneapolis, MN: University of Minnesota Press.

Chandler, David, 2002, *From Kosovo to Kabul: Human Rights and International Intervention*, London: Pluto.

Chandler, David, 2005, 'From Dayton to Europe', *International Peacekeeping*, Vol. 12, No. 3, pp. 336–49.

Commission for Africa, 2005, *Our Common Interest* (at: www.commissionforafrica.org/english/report/introduction.html).

Cooper, Robert, 2003, *The Breaking of Nations: Order and Chaos in the Twenty-first Century*, London: Atlantic Books.

Declaration on the Granting of Independence to Colonial Countries and Peoples, 1960 (at: www.unhchr.ch/html/menu3/b/c_coloni.htm).

Declaration on Principles of International Law Concerning Friendly Relations and Co-Operation among States in Accordance with the Charter of the United Nations, 1970 (at: www.hku.edu/law/conlawhk/conlaw/outline/Outline4/2625.htm).

EastWest Institute and European Stability Initiative, 2001, 'Democracy, Security and the Future of the Stability Pact for South Eastern Europe: A Framework for Debate', April (at: www.esiweb.org/docs/printdocument.php?document_ID=15).

EU, 2001, 'Review of the Stabilisation and Association Process', General Affairs Council Report (at: www.seerecon.org/Calendar/2001/Events/2536GA-Annex.pdf).

European Commission, 2001, 'The Stabilisation and Association Process and CARDS Assistance 2000 to 2006', paper for the Second Regional Conference for South East Europe (at: www.seerecon.org/Calendar/2001/Events/src/ec_sap_cards_2000_2006.pdf).

European Stability Initiative, 2005, *The Helsinki Moment: European Member State Building in the Balkans*, 1 February (at: www.esiweb.org/pdf/esi_document_id_65.pdf).

Evans, Gareth and Mohamed Sahnoun, 2002, 'The Responsibility to Protect', *Foreign Affairs*, Vol. 81, No. 6, pp. 99–110.

Fearon, James D. and David D. Laitin, 2004, 'Neotrusteeship and the Problem of Weak States', *International Security*, Vol. 28, No. 4, pp. 5–43.

Foucault, Michel, 2003, *Society must be Defended: Lectures at the Collège de France 1975–1976* (trans. David Macey), London: Allen Lane/Penguin.

Fukuyama, Francis, 2004, *Statebuilding: Governance and World Order in the Twenty-First Century*, London: Profile Books.

Ghani, Ashraf, Clare Lockhart and Michael Carnahan, 2005, 'Closing the Sovereignty Gap: An Approach to Statebuilding', Overseas Development Institute Working Paper No. 253, September (at: www.odi.org.uk/publications/working_papers/wp253.pdf).

Harrison, Graham, 2001, 'Post-Conditionality Politics and Administrative Reform: Reflections on the Cases of Uganda and Tanzania', *Development and Change*, Vol. 32, No. 4, pp. 634–65.

Harrison, Graham, 2004, *The World Bank and Africa: The Construction of Governance States*, London: Routledge.

Hatzopoulos, Paul, 2005, 'Non-Nationalist Ideologies in the Balkans: The Interwar Years', unpublished thesis, London School of Economics.

Helman, Gerald B. and Stephen R. Ratner, 1993, 'Saving Failed States', *Foreign Policy*, No. 89, pp. 3–21.

Herbst, Jeffrey, 2003, 'Let Them Fail: State Failure in Theory and Practice: Implications for Policy', in Robert Rotberg (ed.), *When States Fail: Causes and Consequences*, Princeton, NJ: Princeton University Press, pp. 302–18.

ICISS (International Commission on Intervention and State Sovereignty), 2001, *Responsibility to Protect*, Ottawa: International Development Research Centre.

Ignatieff, Michael, 2003, *Empire Lite: Nation-Building in Bosnia, Kosovo and Afghanistan*, London: Vintage.

International Commission on the Balkans, 2005, *The Balkans in Europe's Future* (at: www.balkan-commission.org/activities/Report.pdf).

Jackson, Robert, 1990, *Quasi-states: Sovereignty, International Relations and the Third World*, Cambridge: Cambridge University Press.

Kaldor, Mary, 1998, *New and Old Wars: Organized Violence in a Global Era*, Cambridge: Polity.

Keohane, Robert O., 2002, 'Ironies of Sovereignty: The European Union and the United States', *Journal of Common Market Studies*, Vol. 40, No. 4, pp. 743–65.

Keohane, Robert O., 2003, 'Political Authority after Intervention: Gradations in Sovereignty', in Jeff L. Holzgrefe and Keohane (eds), *Humanitarian Intervention: Ethical, Legal and Political Dilemmas*, Cambridge: Cambridge University Press, pp. 275–98.

Klein, Naomi, 2005, 'Baghdad Year Zero', in Klein *et al.*, *No War: America's Real Business in Iraq*, London: Gibson Square Books.

Krasner, Stephen, 1999, *Sovereignty: Organized Hypocrisy*, Princeton, NJ: Princeton University Press.

Krasner, Stephen, 2004, 'Sharing Sovereignty: New Institutions for Collapsing and Failing States', *International Security*, Vol. 29, No. 2, pp. 85–120.

Leonard, Mark, 2005, *Why Europe Will Run the 21st Century*, London: Fourth Estate.

Linklater, Andrew, 1998, *The Transformation of Political Community*, Cambridge: Polity.

Malone, David M., 2005, 'Foreword', in Simon Chesterman, Michael Ignatieff and Ramesh Thakur (eds), *Making States Work: State Failure and the Crisis of Governance*, Tokyo: UN University Press.

Morgenthau, Hans, 1970, *Truth and Power: Essays of a Decade, 1960–1970*, New York: Praeger.

Rosenau, James N. and Ernst-Otto Czempiel (eds), 1992, *Governance Without Government: Order and Change in World Politics*, Cambridge: Cambridge University Press.

Rotberg, Robert I., 2004, 'The Failure and Collapse of Nation-States: Breakdown, Prevention and Repair', in Robert I. Rotberg (ed.), *When States Fail: Causes and Consequences*, Princeton, NJ: Princeton University Press, pp. 1–45.

Straw, Jack, 2002, 'Order out of Chaos: The Challenge of Failed States', in Mark Leonard (ed.), *Reordering the World*, London: Foreign Policy Centre, pp. 59–61.
Tilly, Charles, 1985, 'War Making and State Making as Organized Crime', in Peter B. Evans, Dietrich Rueschemeyer and Theda Skocpol (eds), *Bringing the State Back In*, Cambridge: Cambridge University Press, pp. 169–91.
UN Millennium Project, 2005, *Investing in Development: A Practical Plan to Achieve the Millennium Development Goals* (at: www.unmillenniumproject.org/reports/index_overview.htm).
US Government, 2002, *The National Security Strategy of the United States of America* (at: www.whitehouse.gov/nsc/nssall.html).
Weber, Cynthia, 1995, *Simulating Sovereignty; Intervention, the State and Symbolic Exchange*, Cambridge: Cambridge University Press.
Wight, Martin, 1979, *Power Politics* (ed. by Hedley Bull and Carsten Holbraad), Harmondsworth: Penguin.
Yannis, Alexandros, 2002, 'The Concept of Suspended Sovereignty in International Law and its Implications in International Politics', *European Journal of International Law*, Vol. 13, No. 5, pp. 1037–52.
Zartman, I. William, 2005, 'Early and "Early Late" Prevention', in Simon Chesterman, Michael Ignatieff and Ramesh Thakur (eds), *Making States Work: State Failure and the Crisis of Governance*, Tokyo: UN University Press, pp. 273–95.

# 20
## The UN Peacebuilding Commission: The Rise and Fall of a Good Idea

*Mats Berdal*

When Kofi Annan, as the UN Secretary-General, initiated his ambitious reform process with a speech to the General Assembly in September 2003, he saw it as a necessary response to the tensions and fault lines running through the UN membership which the US-led invasion of Iraq had sharply exposed and exacerbated. Those very tensions, however, were always going to frustrate and complicate the reform drive itself, especially one as radical and wide-ranging as envisaged by Annan. In particular, given the climate of open mistrust and ill-concealed bitterness that had come to characterise politics at the UN by mid-2003, his insistence on substantive reform of inter-governmental bodies, notably of the Security Council, was bound only to fuel political tensions among member states. It was hardly surprising, therefore, that the so-called World Summit of September 2005 – a grand meeting of heads of state and government designed as the culminating event in Annan's reform drive – should have come so close to complete failure, with agreement on a 'Final Outcome Document' reached only at the very last minute (UNGA, 2005; see Traub, 2006: 381–95). One consequence of this 'near-failure' was that only a few of the more innovative proposals developed over the previous two years survived the deeply politicised process of pre-Summit negotiations among member states. One of those was the idea for a Peacebuilding Commission (PBC) and an associated Peacebuilding Fund (PBF), originally proposed by the 'High Level Panel on Threats, Challenges and Change' (HLP) commissioned by the Secretary-General at the outset of his reform drive in 2003.[1]

Established as an 'intergovernmental advisory body', uniquely by *concurrent* resolutions of the Security Council and the General Assembly in December 2005, the PBC was formally inaugurated in June 2006 and presented its first annual report in July 2007.[2] Its Organising Committee, a kind of steering committee with representation from 31 member states, will also meet in country-specific configurations or committees. By mid-2007 one each had been created for Sierra Leone and Burundi (see ActionAid *et al.*,

2007). The work of the PBC is supported, as originally envisaged in the HLP report by a new Peacebuilding Support Office (PBSO) in the Secretariat whose tasks are also to advise the Secretary-General on 'effective strategies of peacebuilding' and to 'oversee the operation of the Peacebuilding Fund' (PBC, 2007, annex V).

The PBC's establishment attracted much attention and received strong support, albeit expressed in vague and general terms, by the membership as a whole. This was not merely because it was one of the few concrete achievements to emerge from the 2003–2005 reform drive. It was also widely accepted that the challenge which the PBC was intended to meet was real and urgent: to provide a 'dedicated institutional mechanism to address the special needs of countries emerging from conflict towards recovery, reintegration and reconstruction and to assist them in laying the foundation for sustainable development' (UNGA, 2005: para. 97). Beyond this, however, member states remained deeply divided about the PBC's precise role and function. These divisions account for the extensive period spent since its creation on discussion of 'organizational, procedural and methodological' issues (PBC, 2007). Dressed up in bureaucratic language and 'UN-speak', these discussions have had, in truth, everything to do with politics and little to do with any genuine attempt to translate the vague and easily agreed upon statements of intent contained in constitutive resolutions into workable arrangements at headquarters or in the field. The 'solutions' and compromises arrived at – including the size, composition and ill-defined focus and institutional status of the Organising Committee itself – are hardly encouraging as far as the overall aim of bringing 'more coherence and impact to the international community's approach to peacebuilding' is concerned (PBC, 2007: para. 32).

## Focus and argument

This chapter does not seek to provide a preliminary assessment of the PBC's record, nor does it consider in any detail its potential as an institutional mechanism or focal point for coordinating the disparate efforts of actors to consolidate peace in war-torn societies. A small industry devoted to this important subject has already emerged. The focus here is on the origins and evolution of the idea of a PBC from its initial articulation in the HLP report to its final incarnation in the 'Outcome Document'. In particular, the chapter examines the contrast between original conception and final product. The PBC was conceived as a body with decision-making powers, institutionally aligned to the Security Council and with the ability, in theory at any rate, to provide 'proactive assistance' to countries 'under stress' or at risk from 'state collapse' (HLP, 2004: para. 264). The outcome was an 'advisory subsidiary organ' of *both* the General Assembly and the Security Council.[3] It has no operational capacity of its own and the post-Summit discussions regarding rules of procedures, working methods and reporting lines to intergovernmental organs are indelibly marked by the political tensions and fault lines within the organisation as a whole. This move from what on paper was a robust and focused body to something altogether more woolly and vague was not only to be expected; it also tells us a great deal about the obstacles inherent in UN reform generally about the highly charged political atmosphere in which reform has been played out since 2003 and, by extension, about the prospects for a more systematic and coordinated approach to UN post-conflict activities. The argument advanced is not meant as a counsel of despair and, indeed, the creation of the PBC, the PBF and the PBSO is significant for providing a three-way institutional 'peacebuilding architecture' on which to build. Any assessment of precisely what can be built, however, must start with an appreciation of the political and bureaucratic forces that shaped the outcome of an initiative designed to improve on a record of international 'peacebuilding' performance that has too often been blighted by a lack of overall strategic direction, the absence of coordination among a wide range of actors and a lack of funds at critical moments and stages of an operation.

To this end, the chapter is structured around three sets of questions. First, what was, and indeed, what remains, the rationale for the establishment of a peacebuilding commission? Second, how did the early ideas and plans for a peacebuilding commission evolve and, in particular, what have been the underlying political and bureaucratic forces shaping its evolution? Third, has the effort to establish a commission been in vain?

## Origins and rationale

The history of UN operational activity since the early 1990s is distinguished by a dramatic expansion of the organisation's role in efforts to consolidate or build peace in societies ravaged by war and violent conflict. The level and intensity of UN involvement has varied greatly, from small-scale electoral and human rights monitoring missions to comprehensive trusteeship functions (Berdal and Economides, 2007). But for a brief period of retrenchment between late 1995 and 1999, following the traumatic experience of UN-mandated forces in Bosnia and Rwanda, the trend has been one of growth and increased complexity in the size and mandate of missions. By mid-2007, the number of civilian and military personnel deployed worldwide under UN auspices had risen to record levels. Nearly all of the operations launched since the 1990s have had some 'peacebuilding' dimension to their mandates. The growth and scope of UN involvement in this area, then, provided an important stimulus to the Commission's creation. That involvement, however, had also highlighted some recurring deficiencies in the UN's peacebuilding and recovery efforts. As originally conceived, the PBC may be viewed as an attempt to address five, partly overlapping, needs as identified of governments, whether NGOs or other civil society representatives, whose activities require harnessing and coordination. Both these factors place a premium on engagement with civil society and the creation of mechanisms with which to foster such engagement. The acknowledgement of this requirement was a further motivation for creating the PBC.

### Predictability of funding and speed of disbursement

An issue that has long bedevilled UN field operations – whether those of the traditional peacekeeping kind or the more complex assignments taken on by the UN over the past decade and a half – has been the lack of available funds in the early and critical start-up phase of a mission (see Brahimi, 2001: paras 151–69). A major part of the problem has been the UN's byzantine procurement system whose rules and regulations are only intelligible once their deep roots in political power struggles between member states are factored in, something which also explains why, over the years, they have proved nearly impervious to reform. In the meantime, the problems relating to the predictability and rate of disbursement of funds have remained. Funding for UN peacebuilding, as opposed to traditional peacekeeping or more conventional development activities, has faced the additional problem of falling into a 'grey area' with funding gaps often arising in areas considered, for obvious reasons, politically sensitive by donor countries, including, most notably, reform of the Security Sector (Wilton Park, 2006: 2). To address this deficiency the HLP proposed a standing fund for peacebuilding of at least US$250 million to allow for greater predictability, more rapid disbursement and more flexibility in the use of funds in the early phase of a mission (HLP, 2004: para. 228). In addition to addressing emergency needs to mitigate the slow, complex and politicised process of budgetary approval in New York, such a fund was also 'meant to catalyse and encourage longer term engagement' by other agencies and donors (PBC, 2007: para. 29).

For the UN to begin to address all five of these overlapping needs effectively, the HLP envisaged the PBC as a subsidiary organ of the Security Council. This was partly because of the political significance which such a direct link signalled but also because of the Council's greater authority and comparative effectiveness as an inter-governmental organ. An additional reason was the perceived need for peacekeeping *and* peacebuilding operations, which in practice always overlap as activities in the field, to be brought together on the Council's agenda (CIC, 2005: 3). Although the HLP did not suggest a figure, it was clearly envisaged that the PBC would not be unwieldy, but 'reasonably small', with its standing body, the Organising Committee, comprising no more than 12–15 member states (see CIC, 2005: 8). Its precise powers, in terms of decision-making and executive functions, were not laid down, though the rationale and logic of the Panel's thinking pointed to something more than just a grand forum for consultation.

## A death by many cuts

The process whereby these original ideas were transformed into present arrangements may be seen as having gone through three phases. In the course of that process, the assertion of competing political and bureaucratic interests – among member states but also within the UN system itself – gradually, though surely and predictably, combined to denude the boldness of the HLP's original conception. The first phase ran from the presentation of the initial proposal through to Annan's announcement of his own reform package in late March 2005, contained in the report entitled 'In Larger Freedom'. The second phase covered the period between Annan's presentation and the World Summit in September 2005, which formally decided on the creation of the PBC. The final stage covers the subsequent period which in theory should have been devoted to fleshing out and giving real substance to the PBC 'idea' (Wilton Park, 2006: para. 8). In practice, the period has been overshadowed by a further polarisation of the membership between a large group of developing countries – an ill-defined category but given some substance through the G77 – and a group of mostly Western countries, though again with shades of opinion running through it.

### From the HLP to 'In Larger Freedom'

'In Larger Freedom', presented by Annan to the General Assembly on 21 March 2005, endorsed the HLP's analysis regarding the need for a body that would fill a 'gaping hole in the UN's institutional machinery' and called on member states to 'create an intergovernmental Peacebuilding Commission, as well as a Peacebuilding Support Office' (Annan, 2005: para. 114). It emphatically ruled out, however, one of the key functions envisaged by the HLP: an early warning and monitoring role in relation to countries 'under stress' (Annan, 2005: para. 115). That aspect of the original proposal was always likely to provoke a strong and negative reaction from developing countries, voicing their collective opinion on UN reform through the platform of Non-Aligned Movement (NAM) and G77, bodies that, while defunct in other respects, have since 2003 been revived for negotiating and 'blocking' purposes in UN fora. What explains the negative reaction?

In early 2005, at one of many academic gatherings convened to discuss the HLP and its recommendations, Muchkund Dubey, former Foreign Minister of India, spoke specifically about the PBC proposal. If implemented, he maintained, its establishment would have

> the effect of institutionalising continuing interventions in the domestic affairs of the developing-country members of the UN. The mandate of identifying countries that are under stress and risk sliding towards state collapse is a very wide one, under which any developing member state can be kept under surveillance. The identification of such states will be

highly subjective and political factors, particularly the strategic and other interests of major powers, would play a decisive role. This recommendation amounts to creating a new trusteeship system in the UN – not to assist the emergence of colonial countries into independence, as was the mandate of the Trusteeship Council, but as a means to bring independent sovereign states from the developing world under a new form of colonization.

(Dubey, 2005: 65)

While such views are difficult to reconcile with the spirit in which the HLP broached the idea of a PBC – that is, a justifiable concern for improving the UN's operational effectiveness in the field of peacebuilding – it would be wrong to dismiss them altogether. Although expressed in more diplomatic terms, it quickly became clear that developing countries were deeply unhappy with a role for the PBC in any other than a 'post-conflict' capacity, and especially concerned about a body 'empowered to monitor and pay close attention to countries at risk' (HLP, 2994: para. 225). The reasons for this were twofold.

First, through the G77, they had all along insisted that the PBC should focus on 'development' issues in countries emerging from conflict.[4] The practical implications of this insistence, however, have never been spelt out in any detail beyond a generally expressed desire to establish a 'close link' between the PBC and the Economic and Social Council (ECOSOC), however dysfunctional and lacking in operational capacity that body has long proved to be. It needs to be seen, therefore, as part of a more general concern that 'the Report [of the HLP as a whole] does not adequately address many issues of concern to the South'.[5]

Second, and more fundamentally, as Dubey's comments make clear, it was feared that a monitoring and prevention role for the PBC would pose yet another threat to the principle of non-intervention in the internal affairs of member states, a principle already perceived to be under assault from two other directions: by the US 'doctrine of pre-emption', promulgated in the aftermath of 9/11 and laid out in its National Security Strategy of 2002, and by the growing tendency, exemplified by NATO's Kosovo campaign in 1999, for Western countries or Western-led coalitions to justify military intervention on humanitarian grounds. Whether or not these fears were justified – and Dubey's attempt to encapsulate them in the statement above is plainly much too crude and simplistic – in the context of the HLP's proposal for a PBC and the political climate of 2004, this did not matter much.[6] The notion of an early warning and monitoring role, leading to preventive action, only reinforced a long-standing and strongly held conviction among the G77 that Western powers, especially the United States, were actively seeking to mould multilateral mechanisms and institutions, if they did not bypass them altogether, to serve the 'strategic and other interests of major powers' (Dubey, 2005: 65).

The strength of this conviction also helps to explain another source of concern among the G77, which Annan's 'In Larger Freedom' sought to address: the relationship between the PBC and the Security Council. Whereas the HLP saw the PBC as a subsidiary organ under the Council, 'In Larger Freedom' recognised more clearly the need, for reasons of legitimacy and probably also to pre-empt likely objections, to involve other intergovernmental bodies, notably ECOSOC. Still, the Secretary-General accepted that muddled reporting lines and unclear institutional status would likely affect the efficiency of any proposed body. Accordingly, he suggested that the PBC 'would best combine efficiency with legitimacy if it were to report to the Security Council and the Economic and Social Council in *sequence*, depending on the phase of the conflict.... Simultaneous reporting lines should be avoided because they will create duplication and confusion' (my emphasis, Annan, 2005: para. 116). Even so, several countries expressed concerns early on, and continued to do so before and after the Summit, about the PBC being too closely tied to the Security Council. This was in line with a more general and long-standing concern, voiced by the G-77, that the

> location of development issues within the confines of security threats and prevention strategies would lead to an undesirable alteration in the balance of responsibilities between the various organs of the system. It would contribute to increased concentration of power in the hands of the Security Council and further undermine the role of the Economic and Social Council.[7]

Given this and the political divisions and bitterness that engulfed the UN after the crisis over the UN Special Commission's inspections in Iraq in 2003 and the subsequent invasion, those concerns were only reinforced by the US preference, expressed by John Bolton (and thus much like waving a red flag to a bull), for the PBC to be a subsidiary organ of the Council, to 'take its direction [only] from that body' and for its work to be limited to 'post conflict stabilization and reconstruction, not development'.[8]

Beyond these concessions to political realities, in particular ruling out prevention as a statutory role for the PBC, the Secretary-General did not go into further details about the planned commission, promising instead a 'more fully developed proposal' in advance of the Summit later in the year. This, however, did not happen.

### The World Summit and after

At the Summit in September 2005, member states agreed in their Outcome Document to establish the PBC as an 'inter-governmental advisory body'. But, apart from inserting the word 'advisory', thus signalling its non-operational role, and providing some more detail on its broad remit and constituent parts, key issues were left for later. These included: the precise role and institutional location of the PBC within the UN system; its size, composition and the internal relationship between the standing body and country-specific configurations of the commission; its reporting lines and relationship to the (yet-to-be-created) PBSO. Indeed, the only other significant addition in the Outcome Document in terms of the PBC's *modus operandi* was a clear statement that 'the Commission should act in all matters on the basis of consensus of its members', potentially a recipe for paralysis (UNGA, 2005: para. 98).

At one level, the failure to reach detailed agreement on these issues is hardly unexpected. Viewed as a whole, the period since mid-2003 to the September 2005 Summit corresponds closely to what Edward Luck has perceptively identified as a familiar 'cycle of UN reform' (Luck, 2004a: 407). The cycle has nearly always started with a 'demand for sweeping renovations' and ended with incremental reform which governments and UN officials have then found 'reasons to paint...in glowing colours', all the while issuing new 'declarations about unfinished work and renewed dedication' (Luck, 2004a: 408). An intermediate stage of this cycle – in this case evident in Annan's modifications to the HLP's original proposal – consists of the Secretary-General translating 'ideas into digestible policy steps for consideration by the membership' (Luck, 2004a: 408). What accounts for this predictable trajectory is the fact that governments tend only to 'become fully engaged as decision points approach and the implications for their national interests become clear' (Luck, 2004a: 408). At that point, different perspectives and genuine conflicts of interest among member states emerge more sharply. These invariably place limits on the scope for substantive agreement and force compromises around, at best, piecemeal though *potentially* useful change, or, at worst, bland and empty statements.

The only way in which the 2003–2005 reform drive appears to have departed from the cycle sketched by Luck is, discouragingly, in its final stage. Historically, as Luck notes, the tendency has been for 'business as usual' to resume after every bout of UN reform activity, and 'culminating events', such as the World Summit of 2005, have served to 'provide an impetus for the next round of UN reform' (Luck, 2004a: 409). This time around the reform process coincided with a particularly inauspicious political setting and, by the time of the September 2005 Summit, as Mark Malloch Brown, Annan's *chef de cabinet*, later put it, the UN had become 'a political bog. Almost nothing moved' (Malloch Brown, 2007). This state of affairs did not improve with the Summit:

> as soon as the Presidents were gone, battle was joined again. Impassioned divisions between North and South reopened: the North wanted more on security, including an unambiguous definition of terrorism; the South wanted more on development, choosing to treat the huge aid pledges made at Gleneagles in preparation for the Summit as old news and less

important than having a few extra officials to service UN meetings on development. On management reform, even more damagingly, developing countries chose to view a stronger Secretary-General with greater authority but also greater accountability as a plot to increase American and Western control over the organization.

(Malloch Brown, 2007)

In large part, this development, which inevitably influenced subsequent efforts to operationalise the PBC and its associated bodies, was a function of the wider political crisis at the UN. More specifically, it was tied to the role played by John Bolton, US permanent representative to the UN in the run-up to the Summit, though his presence in New York was simply emblematic of an unusually fraught relationship between this particular Republican administration and the UN (Traub, 2006: 294–5). Paradoxically, the US permanent representative had, at one point, to be reined in by the US State Department, and his actual behaviour in pre-Summit negotiations – with few concrete ideas of his own and unsure of his brief – left UN officials unclear as to his deeper purpose, whether 'to reform or wreck the UN' (Malloch Brown, 2007). His record and known hostility to the UN as an institution, however, was never in doubt (see Bolton, 1997), and this, coupled with his links to prominent 'neo-cons' in the Bush administration (notably Vice-President Dick Cheney), was bound to fuel distrust and suspicion. At the same time many developing countries did not (before or after the Summit) shy away from engaging in their own form of hypocrisy and grand-standing, professing commitment to reform but firmly opposing proposals that would unquestionably have improved the day-to-day workings of the organisation both in the field and at headquarters. This became clear when, in May 2006, Annan's proposals for perfectly rational, long-overdue management reforms – addressing, *inter alia*, disabling features of the UN's personnel and budget practices – were voted down by the General Assembly which chose to view the proposals as a 'power grab by the developed world' (Trevelyan, 2006). The divide and suspicion was expressed a year later, in March 2007, when three weeks of negotiations within the Peacekeeping Committee (or Committee of 34) broke down without agreement and the NAM caucus, led by Morocco, stormed out amidst accusations of a US attempt to force through unacceptable changes to the final text. For a committee with a record of producing fairly anodyne and uncontroversial reports, it was an unusual end to its annual session.

The intensification of political infighting among key member states, while reflecting the international politics of the time, was also stimulated by the manner in which the reform process was conceived, specifically by the importance Annan attached to Security Council reform. This, one may suppose, ought not to have prevented progress in other areas. The difficulty was that the Secretary-General and his closest advisers, throughout the process, urged member states not to disaggregate his set of proposals, but to treat them 'as a single package'.[9] Indeed, when 'In Larger Freedom' was launched Malloch Brown spoke of 'a very well-prepared gamble', stressing that member states should 'not go for à la carte shopping' on the package presented.[10] This approach to UN reform was consistent with Annan's belief in the need for radical reform, discussed above. As a strategy for achieving results, however, it was plainly ill-advised and ran counter to the historical experience of UN reform efforts (Luck, 2004a: 409). Its chief consequence was to encourage long-standing aspirants to permanent Security Council membership – Germany, India, Japan and Brazil (G4) – to concentrate their diplomatic attention, not on the day-to-day operations of the organisation (to which Germany, Japan and India, in particular, were such key contributors) but on their campaign for Council membership – campaigns which stood very little chance of success except in generating, as widely predicted, 'further disharmony among states' (Sutterlin, 2005: 180).

The third phase, since the PBC's formal establishment in December 2005 has inevitably been coloured by this political backdrop. Most fundamentally, as India's representative to the UN told the General Assembly in February 2007, and repeated in October, the PBC had found it difficult to define precisely what it 'would do and how it would go about achieving its goals'. The Indian statement, albeit diplomatic, reveals the frustrations that have attended the early life of the PBC, with the permanent representative euphemistically calling for a 'more result oriented discourse', 'a more forward-looking frame of mind' and 'a larger sense of overarching purpose' to the meetings of the Organisational Committee.[11]

The fact that the PBC was created by a concurrent resolution of the Security Council and the General Assembly, and is now also uneasily linked to ECOSOC, is testimony to deeper tensions among member states – as is the size of the Organising Committee (seven Security Council members including the P-5, seven elected by ECOSOC, seven elected by the General Assembly, five top providers of assessed and voluntary contributions to UN funding and five top providers of civilian and military personnel to UN missions). It is, of course, possible to view the co-equal status given to the General Assembly and Security Council in the creation and, presumably also the workings, of the PBC as giving it greater 'democratic legitimacy' (Quaker UN Office, 2007). Jayantha Dhanapala, former Under Secretary-General, has suggested that the PBC 'represents a synthesis of several bodies in the UN system and augurs well for concrete, coordinated action' among them (Dhanapala, 2006). However, there is little historical evidence to support this view; indeed, if there is any 'rule' to be inferred from the history of UN reform, it is rather that 'inter-governmental bodies tend to be enlarged until they become dysfunctional' (Luck, 2004b: 10). In this respect, one is bound to be concerned with the General Assembly's role. As the HLP noted with a welcome dose of candour in its final report, the relevance and potential of the Assembly have long been undermined by its failure 'to reach closure on issues', by its 'unwieldy and static agenda', resulting in resolutions that are 'repetitive, obscure or inapplicable, thus diminishing the credibility of the body'. It correctly added, however, that there are no 'procedural fixes' to this state of affairs, and 'making the General Assembly a more effective instrument than it is now... can only be achieved if its Members show a sustained determination to put behind them the approach which they have applied hitherto' (HLP, 2004: para. 241). There is at present very little evidence to nourish that hope.

In addition to the uncertainty surrounding reporting lines and the coordination of inter-governmental bodies, the country-specific meetings on Sierra Leone and Burundi have also highlighted continuing conceptual confusion 'regarding the PBC's role at the practical level'.[12] In terms of the original purposes for the PBC discussed above, country-specific activities have also shown that the modalities and terms of participation for civil-society actors in the work of the PBC, and exactly how these should be identified, have still to be clarified and that doing so involves complex political choices of its own (see ActionAid *et al.*, 2007).

It would be wrong to attribute the difficulties encountered in working out acceptable arrangements entirely to the internecine politics of member states. The UN Secretariat and its wider bureaucracy of agencies and bodies clearly also have an interest in the new creation, something which in particular will affect the PBSO whose precise role is shrouded in uncertainty. According to the Secretary-General, the PBSO 'will need to act as a hinge between the UN system on the one hand and the PBC on the other, working to ensure maximum coordination between UN departments, agencies, funds' while also representing the Secretary-General.[13] Whilst careful to stress that the new office will not duplicate existing capacities, the history of earlier management reforms leaves room for scepticism about the ability of the PBSO to secure the 'necessary cooperation from UN agencies and departments, including offices in the field' (UNSC, 2006). Specifically, like other entities created outside the larger, more operationally oriented departments of peacekeeping and political affairs, the peacebuilding office is likely to be viewed with suspicion by those very departments. Indeed, it may well suffer a fate similar to the Strategic Planning Unit, also created within the Executive Office of the Secretary-General, which has never been able to develop the role that its champions had envisaged. Specialised agencies, such as the UN Development Programme, answerable to their boards on which, of course, sit donor countries, are also bound to want to protect their accumulated powers and freedom of action within the system.

## Conclusion: All in vain?

It is possible to be deeply pessimistic about the prospects for the Peace Building Commission, a body whose creation was so widely welcomed and in which a great deal of faith was evidently reposed. Indeed, it may well be argued that the intensely political process of translating a broad commitment into specific institutions and mechanisms has, by providing new arenas for conflict and political in-fighting, only served to reinforce wider divisions and tensions within the UN's body-politic. Worse still, given that the UN has a dismal record of shutting down inefficient and moribund parts of its sprawling system, a dysfunctional and irredeemably politicised PBC may work against the original objective of greater 'system wide coherence' by providing new blocking mechanisms for effective action in the field.

To leave this as an unqualified conclusion may, however, be too harsh. There is, in the first instance, nothing unusual about bold and ambitious ideas for UN reform to undergo modifications, often of a drastic kind, in response to political realities. Indeed, there is often a profound sense of unreality to much of the writings that bemoan the failure of statesmen to implement imaginative, far-reaching and idealistic blueprints for UN reform. That sense of unreality was plainly evident in much of the commentary surrounding the outcome of the World Summit in 2005. What is arguably *unusual* in the story of the PBC is the fact that the political circumstances in which the proposal was launched, and during which its details have been negotiated by member states, have been particularly inauspicious, and were not helped by the 'big bang' approach to UN reform adopted by the Secretariat. Against such a backdrop, the establishment and limited achievements of the PSB and of the PSBO are themselves noteworthy.

Beyond this, any grounds for optimism must start with the oft-forgotten recognition that away from the delegates' lounge, from summit meetings and grandstanding in New York, the UN still goes about its core day-to-day business and that this includes an unprecedented number of civilian and military personnel, now over 100,000, deployed in a 'peacebuilding' capacity. The way in which the creation of the PBC may still assist their deployment is two-fold.

The first is to encourage within the organisation the habit of thinking in strategic terms. There is a subtle but important difference between this and actually acting strategically. The PBC, even as conceived by the HLP, seeks to address what in military terminology is known as the 'operational level of war', that is, what the US Department of Defense defines as the level at 'which campaigns and major operations are planned, conducted, and sustained to accomplish strategic objectives'. Setting those strategic objectives, however, which involves defining the political end state of operations, is done at a higher level. In the UN context, strategy is, or should in theory be, set in the Security Council and this is precisely what explains why proper strategic direction is always bound to be a weakness in UN operations. Thinking in strategic terms, even if it only means harmonising disparate activities and directing them towards some common objective, is still enormously important for a 'system' as fragmented and disjointed as that of the UN, where key parts, such as the Bretton Woods institutions, are unaccustomed or resistant to consultation across bureaucratic boundaries. If the PBC can assist in that process of conditioning – something which the development of so-called 'integrated peacebuilding strategies' for individual countries is meant to encourage – its establishment may yet prove valuable (PBC, 2007: paras 40–50).

The second, more prosaic, reason to welcome the establishment of this 'peacebuilding architecture' relates to funding and the marshalling of resources. For reasons alluded to above, the UN has long suffered from a lack of flexible funding mechanisms for peacebuilding activities (see Fafo, 1999: 42–5). The size of the fund is small but pledges of nearly US$230,000 by more than 30 donors were met surprisingly quickly and the rules governing disbursement should improve the responsiveness of missions to developments on the ground and enable so-called 'catalytic' funding. Small and incremental improvements these may well be, but that does not diminish their *potential* importance, especially, lest one forgets, where they matter most: in the field and in the actual countries emerging from violence and conflict.

## Acknowledgement

I am grateful for the comments and the research support provided by David Ucko in the preparation of this chapter.

## Notes

1. Report of the High-level Panel, UN doc. A/59/565, 2 December 2004.
2. See UNSC resolution 1645, 20 December 2005, S/Res/1645; 'Report of the Peacebuilding Commission on its first session', UN doc., A/62/137–S/2007/458, 25 July 2007.
3. UNSC resolution 1645, 20 December 2005, S/Res/1645, para.2(a).
4. David Ucko's interviews with PBSO staff, New York, August 2007. In the Non-Aligned Movement's formal statement responding to the first annual report of the PBC, it 'continues to emphasize that the development aspects of any strategy geared towards extricating countries emerging from conflict cannot be over emphasized'. See 'Statement on behalf of the Caucus of the Non-Aligned Movement in the Peacebuilding Commission', 10 October 2007 (at: www.cubanoal.cu/ingles/index.html).
5. Statement of Ambassador Stafford Neil (Jamaica), Chairman of G-77, informal GA meeting on Recommendations of HLP, New York, 27 January 2005 (at: www.g77.org/Speeches/012705.htm), p. 2.
6. Dubey's caricature would certainly not have been recognised by countries that have pushed for a properly functioning committee, including the Netherlands, Norway, Canada, Denmark and Sweden, some of which are represented on the PBC by virtue of their status as top contributors to various UN funds, programmes and agencies.
7. See Statement of Ambassador Neil (n. 5 above).

8. 'Letter from Ambassador John Bolton on Peace Building Commission', 29 August 2005 (at: www.reformtheun.org/index.php/issues/105?theme=alt4).
9. UN press release, SG/SM9770, 21 March 2003.
10. Quoted in 'Annan Charts New Course for UN', CBS News, 21 March 2005 (at: www.cbsnews.com/stories/2005/03/21/world/main681998.shtml); see also UN press release, SG/SM 9770, 21 March 2005.
11. Statement by H. R. Nirupam Sen to UN General Assembly on Agenda Item 149, Permanent Mission of India to the UN, New York, February 2007. The sense of drift and limited progress on substance was confirmed by author interviews and communications with UN staff.
12. Update Report No. 5, PBC, Security Council Report, 25 January 2007 (at: www.securitycouncilreport.org).
13. Secretary-General's Note on the Peacebuilding Support Office, ND 9 (at: www.peacewomen.org/un/women_reform/PBC/PBSO_SG_note.pdf).

## References

ActionAid, CAFOD and CARE International, 2007, 'Consolidating the Peace? Views from Sierra Leone and Burundi on the UN PBC'.
Annan, Kofi, 2005, 'In Larger Freedom: towards development, security and human rights for all', Report of the Secretary-General, UN doc. A/59/2005, 21 March.
Berdal, Mats and Spyros Economides (eds), 2007, *United Nations Interventionism, 1991–2004*, Cambridge: Cambridge University Press.
Bolton, John, 1997, 'The Creation, Fall, Rise, and Fall of the United Nations', in Ted Galen Carpenter (ed.), *Delusions of Grandeur: The UN and Global Intervention*, Washington DC: CATO Institute, pp. 45–9.
Brahimi, 2001, 'Report of the Panel on UN Peace Operations' (Brahimi Report), UN doc. A/55/305–S/2000/809, 21 August.
CIC (Center on International Cooperation), 2005, 'Discussion Paper on HLP Recommendation to Establish a PBC', prepared for meeting hosted by Governments of Denmark and Tanzania, 17 January
Cousens, Elizabeth M., 2001, 'Introduction', in Elizabeth M. Cousens and Chetan Kumar (eds), *Peace-building as Politics: Cultivating Peace in Fragile Societies*, Boulder, CO: Lynne Rienner.
Dhanapala, Jayantha, 2006, *Changing the United Nations*, Address at the Royal Institute of International Affairs, Chatham House, London, 17 July.
Dubey, Muchkund, 2005, 'Comments on the HLP', Reforming the UN for Peace and Security (at: www.ycsg.edu/core/froms/Reforming_un.pdf).
Fafo (Norwegian Institute of Applied Social Science), 1999, 'Command from the Saddle: Managing UN Peacebuilding Missions', Recommendations Report of the Forum on the Special Representative of the Secretary-General: Shaping the UN's Role in Peace Implementation, Oslo, January, Peace Implementation Network, Fafo Programme for International Co-operation and Conflict Resolution.
HLP (High-level Panel), 2004, UN doc. A/59/565, 2 December.
HLP, 2006, 'Delivering as One', Secretary-General's High-level Panel on UN System-wide Coherence, 9 November.
Luck, Edward, 2004a, 'How Not to Reform the UN', *Global Governance*, Vol. 11, No. 4, pp.407–14.
Luck, Edward, 2004b, 'Power, Reform, and the Future of the UN', MS in author's possession, p. 10.

Malloch Brown, Mark, 2007, 'Can the UN be Reformed?', speech to Annual Meeting of the Academic Council on the UN System, 7 June (at: www.maximsnews.com/107mnunjune18markmallochbrownunitednationsreform.htm).

PBC (Peacebuilding Commission), 2007, 'Report of the Peacebuilding Commission on its first session', UN doc. A/62/137–S/2007/458, 25 July.

Pouligny, Béatrice, 2005, 'Civil Society and Post-Conflict Peacebuilding: Ambiguities of International Programmes Aimed at Building "New" Societies', *Security Dialogue*, Vol. 36, No. 4, pp. 495–510.

Quaker UN Office, 2007, 'The UN Peacebuilding Commission: Getting Down to Work', Briefing Paper, Vol. 26, No. 3, May–July, Geneva.

Sriram, Chandra Lekha and Karin Wermester (eds), 2003, *From Promise to Practice: Strengthening UN Capacities for the Prevention of Violent Conflict*, Boulder, CO: Lynne Rienner.

Sutterlin, James S., 2005, 'Some Thoughts – Mostly Cautionary – on the Recommendations of the HLP', in *Reforming the UN for Peace and Security* (at: www.ycsg.edu/core/froms/Reforming_un.pdf).

Traub, James, 2006, *The Best Intentions: Kofi Annan and the UN in the Ear of American Power*, London: Bloomsbury.

Trevelyan, Laura, 2006, 'The UN's Management Crisis', 4 May (at: www.news.bbc.co.uk/1/hi/programmes/from_our_own_correspondent/4972490.stm).

UN, 1998, Report of the Secretary-General on the Work of the Organization – 1998, UN doc. A/53/1.

UNGA (UN General Assembly), 2005, '2005 World Summit Outcome', UN doc. A/60/L.1,15 September.

UNSC (Security Council), 2006, 'Peacebuilding Commission', Special Research Report, No. 3, 23 June (at: www.securitycouncilreport.org).

Wilton Park, 2006, 'Putting Decisions into Practice: How Will the UN Peacebuilding Commission fulfil its Mandate?', Report of Wilton Park Conference, WPS06/2, 9–10 February.

# 21
# Material Reproduction and Stateness in Bosnia and Herzegovina

*Berit Bliesemann de Guevara*

A state's capacity to govern, that is to guarantee universal rights to its citizens, to provide public goods, and to implement coherent decisions despite potential competing interests, depends on different factors, of which a basic one is the state's extraction capacity. Its fundraising determines the scope of the state's room for manoeuvre, its governance possibilities and thereby, ultimately, its potential to peacefully regulate social conflict. Historically, the monopolisation of extraction was both a necessary condition for establishing the state's monopoly of violence as well as its effect. Later, state monopolies were gradually depersonalised, subjected to procedural principles and, finally, democratised (Elias, 1976: 279–311). In the Western welfare states of the twentieth century, (re-)distributive functions became core state tasks and a foundation for the potentially pacifying force of bourgeois-capitalist modernity (Siegelberg, 1994: 79–101). In the ideal-type nationally bounded state, state capacity and fiscality are mutually dependent: sufficient finances shape governance capacity, while state capacity, in turn, is essential for the efficient extraction of resources from society (Bönker, 2003).

Where the state's material reproduction is at least partly based on internationally derived resources like political or economic rents, development aid or loans, this has implications for the relations between state and society: the ideal-type 'fiscal bond' between them is loose (Schlichte, 2005: 182–221). In internationalised contexts, a viable system of revenue extraction and redistribution does not depend solely on national conditions but also on international ones. In cases of external peace- and statebuilding, international interference is quite intense, and global governance concepts are a possible way of shaping these international conditions. As a political counter-model to neoliberal globalisation, the ideal-type 'governance without government' is a multi-level system consisting of states and non-state actors, which are overseen by inter- and supra-national institutions possessing certain powers to ensure policy implementation. Global governance is based on a global legal system and a minimum of democratic legitimation, and aims at solving interdependent global problems, bringing about peace and common welfare worldwide. The envisaged role of the state is that of a manager or hinge between different governance levels in a net of actors (Behrens, 2004; Hauchler et al., 2001: 18–21).

Whether today's international peacebuilding interventions are part of an emerging global governance structure is highly disputed. With regard to the global governance potential of international financial institutions (IFIs), which form the core of economic interventions, critics argue that the IFIs are at most engaged in global public policy, the technocratic variant of global governance, that they are dominated by specific interests of the world's leading industrial countries, and that what they term 'global governance' is just a complementary concept to deal with the shortcomings of neoliberalism rather than an alternative model (Behrens, 2004: 119–21; Müller, 2002: 130–44). Their defenders, by contrast, point to changes, highlighting the substitution of neoliberal priorities – strict budget discipline, public sector privatisation, restrictive social reforms, labour market liberalisation and market incentives for economic growth – by concerns for poverty reduction, development and social justice, accompanied by ownership, empowerment and participation (Müller, 2002: 126–9). Such a paradigm shift would imply visible changes in priorities and measures. At least in their documents, the IFIs now acknowledge a general link between economic, financial and governance issues, and pay more attention to an active – rather than retreating – state role, highlighting state capacity as an important precondition for economic reforms and development (e.g., IMF, 2001a; World Bank, 1997). This is also reflected in the World Bank's current instrument, the poverty reduction strategy papers (PRSPs), which are prepared by national governments with the participation of civil society representatives and overseen by the IFIs.

Yet, are these revised international governance concepts suitable for post-conflict statebuilding, and do they actually strengthen the state, enabling it to contribute to social justice and peace? Drawing on the specific case of statebuilding in Bosnia and Herzegovina (BiH), this chapter explores the contradictory dynamics of stateness and fiscality under the conditions of international intervention. The next section elaborates on state-strengthening practices, that is, practices which are consistent with the ideal-type modern state in that they favour the institutionalisation of power and promote the expansion of state rule (Migdal and Schlichte, 2005: 18–19, 22–4). In the Bosnian case, the dismantling of para-state structures, the creation of central-state institutions, governance rationalisation, and EU pre-accession processes have all shown state-strengthening effects. There are, however, limits to these positive tendencies because of simultaneous state-weakening dynamics outlined in the subsequent section of the chapter. State-weakening practices hinder state institutionalisation and legitimacy and favour practices which escape, resist or bend the rules of the state (Migdal and Schlichte, 2005: 19,

24–6). International practices of bypassing and downsizing the state, local practices of informalisation, the resistance-provoking effects of technocratic statebuilding strategies and the persistent internationalisation of BiH fall into this category.

In sum, the case study reveals that the current economic intervention approach is limited in that it undermines the recreation of state capacity and legitimacy by constricting the state into a close internationally determined reform corset without providing for the leeway to include local social interests. Instead of concentrating on BiH's biggest challenge – the creation of a vibrant labour market – economic growth and budget discipline have remained the predominant concerns with adverse consequences for the statebuilding project. The global governance approach is thus questionable because the findings neither hint at a strategic change on the part of the interveners nor hint at goal attainment regarding state capacity and legitimacy.

## State-strengthening dynamics

After the signing of the Dayton Peace Agreement (DPA) in 1995, a plethora of international agencies rushed into BiH to (re-)build the country and flank the peace process. These statebuilding agents' strategies have shown some important state-strengthening effects which have hindered the decay of the statebuilding project and are to be judged as major qualitative improvements from the immediate post-war situation.

### Negative statebuilding

The Bosnian war's structural legacy was a division of the political, economic and social spheres into three systems of rule, basically separated along ethnically defined lines (see Bojičić-Dželilović and Kaldor, 1997; Bougarel, 1999; Calic, 1996). Therefore, one of the most important strategies pursued by the interveners in their aim to build a Bosnian state was the dismantling of the military, political and financing structures of the Bosnian-Serb, Bosnian-Croat and Bosniak para-states. The practices of breaking ethno-nationalist control over revenue sources can be characterised as 'negative statebuilding', defined as the absence of antagonistic projects of rule.

The most visible symbol of success in narrowing the ethno-nationalists' powers by drying up their war chests was that former state antagonists started channelling their claims through formal state institutions. A demonstrative example is the Croat war veterans' association HVIDRA, a reservoir for war veterans, demobilised soldiers and hardcore nationalists, which until 2001 was the Croat nationalists' most important source of public mobilisation and violence. When the Croat nationalist party lost much of its revenue sources through a mixture of external changes in neighbouring Croatia and the interveners' political and military measures, HVIDRA started to process its economic claims through formal channels, for example, by submitting its own draft laws about state expenditures on war veterans (Bojičić-Dželilović, 2006; see also Grandits, 2007).

The dismantling of parallel revenue systems resembles historical processes of political expropriation and state monopolisation of extraction competences. Yet, although it created conducive conditions for 'positive statebuilding', such an effect failed to appear immediately. The successes in taking away revenue sources and thereby power from anti-state actors were based on the military, political and legal powers of the interveners and primarily strengthened their position. Therefore, though weakening state antagonists, negative statebuilding did not directly provide the Bosnian central state with more power or legitimacy.

### Institutional statebuilding

According to the BiH constitution inserted in the DPA, the right to extract revenues falls into the jurisdiction of the two Bosnian entities – the Federation of Bosnia and Herzegovina (FBiH) and Republika Srpska (RS) – and sub-entity levels of government, that is the 10 cantons of the FBiH and municipalities in both FBiH and RS (see Čaušević, 2001; EC Delegation to BiH, 2003; Fox and Wallich, 2003). Until the end of 2004, the central state did not have any revenue sources of its own apart from its few agencies' administrative fees used to cover operating costs (e.g., passport issuing fees) and occasional extraordinary revenues. The main part of its income, averaging about 85 per cent of total revenues between 1998 and 2004, consisted of transfers from the entities which were mainly to service external debts and, secondarily, to cover the operational costs of central state institutions (IMF, 2001b: 28; 2003: 35; 2004: 45; 2005b: 51). While the proportional share of transfers was fixed to one-third from the RS and two-thirds from the FBiH, the total amount of transfers depended on negotiations between the state and the entities. This created a strong dependency of central state institutions on the entity governments, prolonging the Bosnian entities' quasi-state qualities. The fact that less than 5 per cent of GDP went towards central state functions and that these functions did not comprise any redistributive or developmental tasks demonstrates the marginal role of the Bosnian state in the political and economic process.

Since 2004, the situation has gradually changed. The share of international debt service in total state expenditures decreased from an annual average of 65 per cent in 1997–2003 to 47 in 2004 and 42 per cent in 2005. In parallel, the state experienced an internationally forced phase of statebuilding with the creation of new state ministries and agencies. In 2005, 42 per cent of the central state's expenditures were spent on BiH ministries and institutions. An additional 16 per cent went on new central state institutions: the War Crimes Chamber of the State Court, the State Investigation and Protection Agency, the Ministries of Justice, Civil Affairs, Security and Defence, and the

Intelligence and Security Agency. Furthermore, BiH was required by the EU to establish more than 25 regulatory agencies by the end of 2005 as prerequisite for a Stabilisation and Association Agreement (IMF, 2005a: 96).

With the internationally promoted creation of the Indirect Tax Agency (ITA) in January 2005, the Bosnian state had secure revenues at its disposal for the first time. From the indirect taxes, now administered centrally, international debts and central state institutions are paid first. The rest is transferred to the entities, whereby the ITA is more a 'State cum Entity hybrid' (IMF, 2005a: 88) than a fully fledged central state agency. Nevertheless, the ITA is judged as a major breakthrough. These instances of internationally promoted institutional statebuilding have contributed to an expansion of the central state's realm and thereby to a strengthening of Bosnian stateness.

### Rational statebuilding

Many technical statebuilding projects in BiH aim at formalising, documenting, registering, regulating and controlling state–society relations. The construction sites of this rationalisation are manifold, and efforts to modernise the administration of direct taxes beginning in 2001 are but one example. Under the guidance of the US Treasury, the US Agency for International Development (USAID), the German Technical Assistance Corporation, the EU and the IMF, centralised taxpayer registries and computerised forms of processing and sharing tax information countrywide were introduced. The international agencies also assisted in staff training and developing service-oriented approaches to dealing with taxpayers.

According to the international agencies, these rationalisations have already shown an impact on indirect tax revenues: the taxpayer base has expanded, tax declarations are processed with greater efficiency, and errors in taxpayer assessments are found more easily – all leading to an increase in government revenues. Additionally, efforts were made to improve the tax agencies' enforcement capabilities which resulted in an improved taxpayer discipline and, again, in revenue increases (interview at USAID Tax Modernization Project, Sarajevo, Sept. 2005; Nguyen-Thanh and Rose, 2004; Rozner, Šahinagić and Marjanović, 2005). International efforts in rationalising and modernising the bureaucracy have broadened the state's realm *vis-à-vis* society and led to better outputs, more transparency and predictability in state–society relations and can therefore be assessed as state-strengthening.

### Member-state building

Since 2000, the international intervention in BiH has subordinated the course of reforms to the requirements for EU accession. The High Representative has assumed the parallel function of EU Special Representative to BiH and is supposed to abandon his political powers in the further course of peace consolidation. The EU approach to statebuilding is more technocratic than previous ones, which will have implications for the form of further intervention. The effects of institutional and rational statebuilding will probably be more pronounced with growing technical support in the context of the accession process. The minimum requirements for EU membership negotiations, for example, demand more than ten agencies to be established between 2006 and 2010 (IMF, 2005a: 96). Additionally, revenues provided by EU programmes will play an increasingly important role in state funding.

Notwithstanding the EU's constitutional crisis, which revealed its citizens' scepticism about the deepening and further enlargement of the Union, BiH's as yet unclear future status within the EU architecture (full membership or 'backyard associate'), and the uncertainty about the timeframe for accession, with dates as remote as 2020, all have the potential to disappoint local expectations and to slow down possible state-strengthening dynamics accruing from an EU accession process.

## State-weakening dynamics

While the state-strengthening dynamics have obviously narrowed state antagonists' room for manoeuvre, it is questionable whether they have contributed considerably to the strengthening of all-Bosnian stateness. Reforms have so far depended on interventions by international agencies in the political process. The Bosnian state, by contrast, has not gained much governance competence. In its room for manoeuvre it is almost as constricted as it was in the first post-war years, due to the comprehensive economic and fiscal control of international agencies. The change that has taken place hints at a shift from local to international dependency of the Bosnian state.

### Bypassing the state

Between 1996 and 2000, international intervention in BiH was marked by the practice of bypassing the central state, leaving it weak and even opening up possibilities for appropriation by local actors. Money flows controlled by the international agencies *de facto* addressed the entity, cantonal and municipal levels, while the functions of the Bosnian state in managing international aid were reduced to formally signing for grants and loans, an accountancy procedure required by the internationals, which in practice did not mean any central state control over money flows and which only ceased completely in 2004 (interview at World Bank, Sarajevo, September 2005). The rationale behind bypassing the state was that an efficient and effective process in physical and social reconstruction was more certainly expected from powerful local actors than from powerless and chronically blocked central state institutions. However, large amounts of aid money, the interveners' often inconsistent ways of aid management and distribution, and the prominent role given to sub-state levels enabled local wartime elites to siphon off significant sums which they used to maintain state antagonist power structures and to manipulate economic intervention strategies in their favour. The stalled privatisation process, that is, the often criminal appropriation of state-owned assets by networks of nationalist politicians, war profiteers and tycoons, demonstrates this (see Donais, 2002; Pugh, 2006). Yet, more subtle forms of state appropriation also took place prolonging the ethnic division of state administrations. Control over subsidised housing and land allocations, for example, were forms of cementing ethnic majorities in 'ethnically-cleansed' municipalities (Ó'Tuathail and Dahlman, 2004: 455–6).

After the first four-year aid commitment framework, the quantity and quality of international money flows and the practices of bypassing the state changed. Insights into the dysfunctional strategies of the first phase and the international agencies' need for an exit strategy – now seen to depend on having a capable Bosnian state to transfer the political process to – led to a more extensive use of the interveners' powers against local resisters, lower levels of aid and a stronger link between international revenues and conditionality (Suhrke and Buckmaster, 2005: 740–1). The international agencies also tried to mould the material reproduction of the Bosnian state increasingly through institution-building at central state level.

In parallel, the scope of state appropriation decreased. Growing international control over finances, for example, through special audits of state-owned enterprises and party financing, and the effects of rational state-building contributed to reducing opportunities to make use of the state. Yet, some features have remained in place. Local resisters still use state assets and bureaucracies, especially the issuing of licences and building permits, as political instruments and personal income sources. Moreover, bribery has flourished and become institutionalised in many public sectors, including the universities – a development in close relation to low wages and public arrears (Transparency International BiH, 2004: 114–27). Such phenomena are indicators of the still limited scope and weakness of central state rule.

### Downsizing the state

Despite the alleged 'post-Washington turn' in economic interventionism, the downsizing of public expenditures by reforming social welfare systems, lowering levels of public wages and salaries, and reducing the number of public servants has remained a core measure of international interventions in to the material reproduction of states, and BiH is no exception (World Bank, 2002). Regarding BiH's public expenditures, the international agencies especially criticised high public spending on wages and salaries which amounted to 20 per cent of GDP in 2000 (World Bank, 2002: 35–8). They recommended reducing public sector employment and containing wages and salaries, which are seen to be relatively high as compared to the private sector. The actual reduction of public expenditures on wages and salaries since 2000 was due mainly to demobilisation processes in the military sector. In the FBiH, for example, the share of administrative wages and salaries in all expenditures remained relatively stable at around 11 per cent, while the share of military expenditures was reduced from 32 per cent in 2000 to 18 per cent in 2005. Although demobilisation and restricted public employment have unburdened the entities' budgets, the wider economic and social results of these processes are at least mixed in view of the tense employment situation in the private sector (see Pietz, 2004). Without job alternatives, the reduction of public sector employment potentially contributes to unemployment, informal sector growth and the likelihood of social conflict.

Another recommendation for reducing public sector employment is to abandon sub-state administrative levels. It is a popular belief among internationals and locals in the RS that the FBiH cantonal structure creates the highest budget burden (World Bank, 2002: 38). However, critics, as well as Bosnian Croats who rely on canton control to secure their interests, argue that the vast majority of cantonal and municipal administrators actually work in the health, education and police sectors – posts that would persist even after structural administration reforms. A strong budgetary effect of such reforms can thus be doubted. Nevertheless, some international financial experts keep hoping that fiscal instabilities, evolving from the burden of further institutional statebuilding, paired with the burden of domestic claims and foreign debts, will pressure local actors to downsize the number of administrative levels. Perversely, strong growth would not create the necessary budgetary pressure to achieve this (interview, World Bank Sarajevo, August 2005).

The second, heavily criticised, expenditure is transfers to disabled war veterans which in 2004 amounted to 66 per cent of total welfare spending (UNDP BiH, 2007: 125). According to the World Bank (2002: vi), these transfers 'constitute the single major social transfer channelled by the Entity budgets contributing not only to fiscal pressures but also to budget constraints for other social programs'. Although this welfare is used to reinforce power structures, particular interests and discrimination (see UNDP BiH, 2007: 121–31; World Bank, 2002: 42–4), the small sum of each single transfer contradicts the idea of war invalids as post-war profiteers. In a 2004 survey of war veterans, invalids and survivor families in the FBiH, 64 per cent named finances and housing as their main problems (Bieber, 2007: 289). On average, 43 per cent of the invalids said they had just enough money to live on and 46 per cent responded that their economic situation was insufficient for decent living (Bieber, 2007: 307). At the same time, 74 per cent of veterans and 40 per cent of invalids said they had difficulty finding a job (Bieber, 2007: 289). In this situation, government transfers, though small and often irregular, are a momentary cushion against worse circumstances (Bougarel 2007: 185). In the long run, however, due to the mixture of the distorting budgetary impact of welfare spending, the narrow financial frame set by the IFIs and social exclusion, the deficient Bosnian welfare system is more likely to foment social conflict potential than to channel it (Pugh, 2006: 149), especially because there is more at stake than material losses. For war veterans, state interest in their socioeconomic situation and identity issues are interwoven, as exemplified in 2001 when the FBiH drafted a new law on war pensions which 'reversed the relationship of indebtedness linking veterans to society as a whole and exposed their difficulties in earning a legitimate income, caring for their families and building a new social status under post-war circumstances. In short, it turned war heroes into social misfits and powerless family heads' (Bougarel, 2007: 187–8). In order to be socially accepted and sustainable, any reform of transfers to war veterans, disabled and survivor families has to be accompanied by better labour market conditions.

## Informalising the state

Taxation in BiH is based on the derivation principle. Revenues are entitlements of the territory where they were collected, which means that cantons and municipalities with a weaker tax base are also weak in raising the revenue levels needed to match their expenditures (Fox and Wallich, 2003: 473–5). In contrast to the entity governments which may finance budget deficits by foreign concessional loans, sub-entity levels are not allowed to borrow internationally or domestically. In view of tight budgets and under the pressure of local demands, some state agencies have therefore used informal sources to secure their functioning within the narrow framework determined by the interveners. Unable to match their expenditures on education, health, social protection and culture, some FBiH cantons, for example, resorted to the informal practice of accumulating arrears by suspending the payment of public wages, pensions and social contributions. Others adjusted expenditures downwards, resulting in an inappropriate provision of basic services to the population (IMF, 2005a: 97–107). Furthermore, in attempting to clear the accumulated arrears, some cantons handed out privatisation vouchers. State-owned assets were transferred into private hands, but without it generating investment capital needed to modernise the ailing enterprises.

In 2003, BiH's internal public debt, including public arrears and claims on the basis of foreign currency savings and war damages, amounted to 67 per cent of GDP (Council of Ministers of BiH *et al.*, 2004: 48; OHR, 2004). The IFIs suggest that statebuilding without domestic claims would not be problematic. Statebuilding and clearance of arrears at once, however, will lead to fiscal instabilities (IMF, 2005a: 63–73). These, in turn, are most likely to provoke even stronger international interference and adjustment demands. Although in the long run the mixture of tight budgets, informal coping strategies and international demands might trigger reforms to improve the situation, in the short run it bears social and economic costs which predominantly affect economically and socially weak groups in Bosnian society.

## Technocratic statebuilding

Some dilemmas of statebuilding in BiH can be traced back to technocratic intervention strategies. The IMF's reaction to the costs of new central state agencies is a telling example. Concerned with the budgetary burden arising from the increasing number of central state institutions from 17 to 40 between 2000 and 2004, the IMF proposed sequencing EU requirements in a hierarchical way to slow down the statebuilding process and lower its annual costs (IMF, 2005a: 87–96). The proposal subordinated political requirements and processes to fiscal concerns about the sustainability of budgets, demonstrating the predominantly technical nature of statebuilding and underlining the IMF's self-image as a non-political agency (interview at IMF, Sarajevo, August 2005) – in sharp contrast to the deeply political impacts of its policies. The already discussed adjustments in sub-state spending and lower state-level remuneration rates were other deeply technocratic proposals that would thwart a political initiative to pay central state agents better than their entity counterparts in order to promote loyalty and reduce corruption. Despite the IMF's declared commitment to governance issues, fiscal sustainability has remained its top priority while the Bosnian political context plays only a subordinate role. The notorious lack of finance, personnel, buildings, training and equipment from which Bosnian central state institutions suffer (Working Group Political Analysis, 2005: 12–16) is at least partly rooted in the half-hearted international financial commitment to statebuilding, thereby limiting existing state-strengthening dynamics.

Value-added tax (VAT) reform is another example of problems accruing from technocratic intervention approaches. The international agencies in charge of the reforms – the IMF, the Delegation of the European Commission to BiH, and the Customs and Fiscal Assistance Office – opted for the introduction of a single-rate consumption tax of 17 per cent to reduce the alleged administrative complexities of a multiple-rate structure, taking efficiency criteria as their guiding principle. The Bosnian state parliament, by contrast, argued for a two-rate system following the example of other European states because it was feared that a single-rate tax would adversely affect the poor (Martens, 2004). This local concern was dismissed, the EU arguing that a single rate would help police combat corruption. Despite dissent among the international agencies regarding the expected effects of a unitary VAT on the economy (interview, World Bank, Sarajevo, August 2005), they defended the reforms jointly against local opposition and pressed for the reform.

It is not surprising that Bosnians complain of double standards. It is widely believed that technocratic internationals use BiH as a laboratory for their ideal-type reform models. There is reason for scepticism regarding the potential for such technocratic experiments to produce sustainable outcomes. The way in which reforms are imposed by international agencies evokes resistance among local actors, hindering the governance capacity, social acceptance and legitimacy of Bosnian state institutions and regulations (interview, Transparency International BiH, Banja Luka, August 2005).

## Internationalising the state

In the immediate post-war years, BiH depended heavily on foreign aid for its physical, social and institutional reconstruction, the alleviation of the humanitarian situation and the restoration of basic services. This situation has gradually changed. The share of budgetary grants and loans plus foreign-financed investment projects which amounted to nearly 28 per cent of total revenues in 1998 decreased steadily to about 10 per cent in 2005. Yet, although the strong aid dependency ceased, the material reproduction of the Bosnian state remains highly internationalised. Because BiH lacks creditworthiness, it depends on conditional grants and loans to balance budget deficits. Conditioning has become the international agencies' strongest long-term tool in reforming Bosnia's economy and fiscal system.

Due to limited domestic revenues, the Bosnian state cannot escape from its international dependency. Like most transforming and developing countries, BiH relies heavily on indirect taxes, whereas direct taxes only amount to a small percentage of total domestic revenues (IMF, 2005b: 44; 2006: 27). Although tax revenue levels have partly been optimised with the rationalisation of tax collection, administration and enforcement, domestic revenues are insufficient to finance future budget deficits. Indirect taxes have inherent limitations because their growth depends on significant expansions of trade and consumption which are not to be expected in the near future. Also, the progression of income taxes, the most important form of direct revenues, has been limited so far. The international agencies have insisted on a reduction in income tax rates and social contributions as an incentive for economic growth. In 2007, the RS introduced a progressive three-rate income tax of 0, 10 and 15 per cent according to income thresholds (Hadžiabdić, 2007) which substitutes the previous flat-rate system of 10 per cent effective since 2001 that, in turn, had reformed a socially incompatible regressive system. While it is too early to assess the reform's impact on direct tax revenue, it has stimulated growth which, in turn, is hoped to reduce the second constraint on direct taxes: the scope of the informal economy.

The World Bank (2005a: 108–11; cf. 2005b) notes an increase in informal economic activities from 37 to nearly 40 per cent of the employed between 2001 and 2002. Of all jobs created in this period, 87 per cent were informal. Shadow-economic activities contribute to low state revenue levels because informal workers do not pay taxes or social contributions. Additionally, some informally employed remain registered unemployed and continue calling upon the meagre welfare provisions attached to this status, predominantly to obtain health insurance. It is estimated that this over-registration applies to about 12 per cent of the registered unemployed (UNDP BiH, 2006: 46–8).

Informal sector activities in BiH – 43 per cent of which are in the agricultural, 30 per cent in the industrial and 27 per cent in the service sectors – were more volatile than formal jobs, often short term, of lower quality and less well paid (Krstić and Sanfey, 2006: 7–8, 20). Moreover, although the informal sector momentarily ameliorates poverty, informal workers were also less likely to escape from poor living conditions (Krstić and Sanfey, 2006: 13–19). Interestingly, the violation of labour rights – such as non-compliance or delay of payments, exploitation, unlawful dismissals or harassment – was not a specific feature of the informal sector but also common among formal employers unblushingly taking advantage of a labour situation that does not offer job alternatives to employees (Pugh, 2007: 12). In sum, the effects of the thriving informal sector on the state are overtly negative. The state is deprived of revenues while social distress and discontent continue – and are projected onto the state.

In view of limited domestic revenues, international sources are the only alternative. In return for financing budget imbalances and investment projects, international agencies have determined the shape of BiH's fiscal system, prescribed reforms and adjustments, and interfered with the economic transition. Budgets are prepared by the entity and central governments but need the IFIs' approval. The legislative function of approving budgets has been reduced to a mere formality (interview, RS Ministry of Economic Affairs and Coordination, Banja Luka, August 2005). Furthermore, the IFIs exert influence on BiH's economic policies by advising the Bosnian Council of Ministers' Economic Policy Planning and Implementation Unit (EPPU), later the Directorate for Economic Planning (DEP). BiH's PRSP – which is formulated and further developed under the responsibility of the EPPU/DEP – shows differences between the first document of 2004 and the revised 2006 version which can be traced back to international influence (cf. Council of Ministers of BiH *et al.*, 2004; EPPU, 2006). The international exigencies and priorities subject BiH to trade liberalisation, EU harmonisation and regional economic integration. This ignores local policy suggestions such as interim tariff protection of the precarious agricultural sector which is an important part of the Bosnian labour market, absorbing especially unskilled workers. Here again, the Bosnian state's room for manoeuvre is narrowly limited. The result of this interference is a persistent internationalisation of the Bosnian state, which with a stronger EU role might change in form but is unlikely to change significantly in substance.

## Conclusion

Regarding the questions raised in the introduction – whether current international governance concepts are suitable for post-conflict statebuilding, and whether they actually strengthen the state, enabling it to contribute to social justice and peace – the case study of Bosnian fiscality shows two main findings.

First, the economic intervention in BiH has not achieved a sustained strengthening of extraction and state capacity. The Bosnian state is trapped in a vicious circle of limited domestic revenue sources, a costly welfare system in need of reform, disappointed expectations by its population, and a tight financial and political framework determined by the internationals. The key to break this vicious circle is as banal as it is basic: job creation. Active labour market policies by the Bosnian state – for which it would need the international agencies' permission and money – are an instrument to expand the labour market, reduce informal sector activities and unemployment, enhance the taxpayer basis, and lift consumption and thereby indirect tax levels. This would not only augment domestic state revenues, but also reduce the pressure on budgets posed by welfare transfers, bolster reforms of transfers to war invalids, and help reintegrate discharged public servants into the economy. Of course, job creation is not decoupled from economic growth. Yet, economic growth *per se* – hitherto an international core priority realised by relying almost entirely on creating a business environment – has proved to be insufficient to expand the labour market (Pugh, 2007: 9, 11). While GDP growth rates have been in line with plans, the transition process has not been distribution neutral, with (formal) job creation and poverty reduction lagging behind (UNDP BiH, 2007: 69–87). The interveners' top priority against which to measure reform projects and spending should be labour market expansion, not fiscal stability which is definitely important for sustainable stateness, but in the long rather than in the short run.

Second, although the international intervention has contributed to the stabilisation of a modern state façade by enframing the Bosnian state in formal, internationally supported institutions, the ideal-type ties between state and society created by locally generated state funding, distributive and redistributive functions, democratic participation and adherent legitimacy have not been established. The determination of economic and fiscal policies by international agencies, the stress on strict budget constraints and the ways chosen to introduce reforms by overriding local concerns and initiatives have left the Bosnian state with little leeway in negotiating local interests, considering social demands, or developing alternative economic strategies. The latter, however, would be necessary steps in providing the still fragile Bosnian state with output legitimacy. There is definitely a strong need for structural fiscal reforms, especially regarding the Bosnian welfare system. Still, reforms which deeply affect parts of society always bear social conflict potential. While a consolidated state can usually cope with this, a nascent and still politically and socially contested state like BiH is in danger of destabilisation. To make reforms socially acceptable, there need to be transitional solutions preceding new arrangements. Yet, these are cost-intensive and may only be implemented with the help of international donors – who have opted for other priorities. Thus, the current economic intervention approach applied to BiH not only limits the strengthening of state capacity, but also is unsuitable to generate the state's much-needed legitimacy after a war which put the very existence of a Bosnian state into question.

These predominantly negative findings are all the more worrying in view of the fact that BiH has relatively good premises for the success of sustainable peacebuilding. As a European country with a manageable size, prospects of EU membership, and a direct (geographical) significance to West European security interests, there has been a much stronger international commitment to statebuilding than in most other cases (perhaps excluding Kosovo). Furthermore, the number and power of state antagonists putting the Bosnian state and its territorial integrity into question have decreased substantially. And lastly, unlike some Third World countries, BiH has a long history of functioning public administration, legal apparatus and tax system providing a good basis from which to start. Still, the statebuilding experience has been startlingly deficient.

Finally, the Bosnian case also allows for some more general conclusions about the limits of current economic interventions as instruments of global governance. Neither the inclusive multi-level character nor the goals of the normative global governance approach are reflected in current economic interventions. First, the international priorities regarding the state – budget sustainability, reduction of public expenditures and little active market interventions – are very similar to neoliberal concepts, contradicting the idea of a significant paradigm shift. Second, instruments like the PRSP do not possess a substantially new quality because formally including local actors does not equal local ownership as long as strong international interference persists. And finally, the assumption that reintroducing the state into international strategies would help to overcome the negative effects of neoliberal reforms has proven to be false unless state–society relations are taken into consideration. In fact, the Bosnian example confirms that a fundamentally new paradigm with the basic needs of the people at its centre is indispensable.

## References

Behrens, Maria, 2004, 'Global Governance', in Arthur Benz (ed.), *Governance – Regieren in komplexen Regelsystemen. Eine Einführung*, Wiesbaden: VS Verlag für Sozialwissenschaften, pp. 103–24.

Bieber, Benjamin, 2007, *Die Hypothek des Krieges. Eine soziologische Studie zu den sozialen Effekten von Kriegen und zur Reintegration von Veteranen, Kriegsinvaliden und Hinterbliebenen in Bosnien-Herzegowina*, Hamburg: Dr Kovač.

Bojičić-Dželilović, Vesna, 2006, 'Peace on Whose Terms? War Veterans' Associations in Bosnia and Herzegovina', in Edward Newman and Oliver P. Richmond (eds), *Challenges to Peacebuilding: Managing Spoilers During Conflict Resolution*, Tokyo: UN University Press, pp. 200–18.

Bojičić-Dželilović, Vesna and Mary Kaldor, 1997, 'The Political Economy of the War in Bosnia-Herzegovina', in Mary Kaldor and Basker Vashee (eds), *Restructuring the Global Military Sector. Volume I: New Wars*, London: Pinter, pp. 137–76.

Bönker, Frank, 2003, 'Staatseinnahmen und staatliche Handlungsfähigkeit: Das Beispiel der osteuropäischen Transformationsländer', in Petra Bendel, Aurel Croissant and Friedbert W. Rüb (eds), *Demokratie und Staatlichkeit. Systemwechsel zwischen Staatsreform und Staatskollaps*, Opladen: Leske und Budrich, pp. 81–98.

Bougarel, Xavier, 1999, 'Zur Ökonomie des Bosnien-Konflikts: zwischen Raub und Produktion', in François Jean and Jean-Christophe Rufin (eds), *Ökonomie der Bürgerkriege*, Hamburg: Hamburger Edition, pp. 191–218.

Bougarel, Xavier, 2007, 'Death and the Nationalist: Martyrdom, War Memory and Veteran Identity Among Bosnian Muslims', in Xavier Bougarel, Elissa Helms and Ger Duijzings (eds), *The New Bosnian Mosaic. Identities, Memories and Moral Claims in a Post-War Society*, Aldershot: Ashgate, pp. 167–91.

Calic, Marie-Janine, 1996, *Krieg und Frieden in Bosnien-Hercegovina*, Frankfurt-a-M: Suhrkamp.

Čaušević, Fikret, 2001, 'The Fiscal Structure in B-H and the Problems it Generates', in Žarko Papić (ed.), *International Support Policies in South-East European Countries: Lessons (Not) Learned in B-H*, Sarajevo: Müller, pp. 101–13.

Council of Ministers of BiH, 2004, *Mid-term Development Strategy of Bosnia and Herzegovina (PRSP) 2004–2007*, Sarajevo: BiH Council of Ministers of BiH.

Donais, Timothy, 2002, 'The Politics of Privatization in Post-Dayton Bosnia', *Southeast European Politics*, Vol. 3, No. 1, pp. 3–19.

EC Delegation to BiH, 2003, *Study on Potential Revenue Sources for the Institutions of Bosnia and Herzegovina*, Sarajevo: European Commission Delegation to BiH.

Elias, Norbert, 1976, *Über den Prozeß der Zivilisation. Zweiter Band: Wandlungen der Gesellschaft. Entwurf zu einer Theorie der Zivilisation*, Frankfurt-a-M: Suhrkamp.

EPPU, 2006, *The Medium-term Development Strategy BiH 2004–2007 (PRSP). Revised Document*, Sarajevo: EPPU – Office for Monitoring and Implementation of BiH MTDS.

Fox, William and Christine Wallich, 2003, 'Fiscal Federalism in Bosnia–Herzegovina: Subsidiarity and Solidarity in a Three-Nation State', *Public Finance and Management*, Vol. 3, No. 4, pp. 460–504.

Grandits, Hannes, 2007, 'The Power of "Armchair Politicians": Ethnic Loyalty and Political Factionalism Among Herzegovinian Croats, in Xavier Bougarel, Elissa Helms and Ger Duijzings (eds), *The New Bosnian Mosaic. Identities, Memories and Moral Claims in a Post-War Society*, Aldershot: Ashgate, pp. 101–22.

Hadžiabdić, Alma, 2007, 'Republic Srpska Introduces Personal Income Tax Changes', *International Executive Alert*, KPMG B-H, 2007–087, 19 April.

Hauchler, Ingomar, Dirk Messner and Franz Nuscheler, 2001, 'Global Governance. Notwendigkeit – Bedingungen – Barrieren', *Globale Trends 2002*, Frankfurt-a-M: Fischer, pp. 11–37.

IMF, 2001a, *Review of the Fund's Experience in Governance Issues*, Washington, DC: IMF Policy Development and Review Department.

IMF, 2001b, 'Bosnia and Herzegovina: Fourth and Fifth Reviews Under the Stand-By Arrangement and Requests for Extension and Rephasing of the Arrangement – Staff Report and Press Release on the Executive Board Discussion', IMF Country Report, 01/08, January.

IMF, 2003, 'Bosnia and Herzegovina: Second and Third Reviews Under the Stand-By Arrangement – Staff Report; Staff Supplement; Press Release on the Executive Board Discussion; and Statement by the Executive Director for Bosnia and Herzegovina', IMF Country Report, 03/204, July.

IMF, 2004, 'Bosnia and Herzegovina: 2004 Article IV Consultation – Staff Report; Fourth Review Under the Stand-by Arrangement and Request for Waiver of Nonobservance of a Structural Performance Criterion – Staff Report; Staff Supplement; and Public Information Notice and Press Release on the Executive Board Discussion', IMF Country Report, 04/67, March.

IMF, 2005a, 'Bosnia and Herzegovina: Selected Economic Issues', IMF Country Report, 05/198, June.

IMF, 2005b, 'Bosnia and Herzegovina: 2005 Article IV Consultation – Staff Report; Staff Supplement; Public Information Notice on the Executive Board Discussion; and Statement by the Executive Director for Bosnia and Herzegovina', IMF Country Report, 05/199, June.

IMF, 2006, 'Bosnia and Herzegovina: 2006 Article IV Consultation – Staff Report; Public Information Notice on the Executive Board Discussion; and Statement by the Executive Director for Bosnia', IMF Country Report, 06/371, October.

Krstić, Gorana and Peter Sanfey, 2006, *Mobility, Poverty and Well-being Among the Informally Employed in Bosnia and Herzegovina*, London: EBRD.

Martens, Michael, 2004, 'Teures Experiment mit Milch und Brot. Die bosnische Regierung stürzt über die Mehrwertsteuer', *Frankfurter Allgemeine Zeitung*, 8 November, p. 8.

Migdal, Joel S. and Klaus Schlichte, 2005, 'Rethinking the State', in Klaus Schlichte (ed.), *The Dynamics of States. The Formation and Crises of State Domination*, Aldershot: Ashgate, pp. 1–40.

Müller, Klaus, 2002, *Globalisierung*, Bonn: Bundeszentrale für politische Bildung.

Nguyen-Thanh, David and Manfred Rose, 2004, 'Reforming Income and Profit Taxation: The Case of Bosnia-Herzegovina', *Bulletin for International Fiscal Documentation*, Vol. 58, No. 7, pp. 297–303.

Ó'Tuathail, Gearóid and Carl Dahlman, 2004, 'The Effort to Reverse Ethnic Cleansing in Bosnia-Herzegovina. The Limits of Return', *Eurasian Geography and Economics*, Vol. 45, No. 6, pp. 439–64.

OHR (Office of the High Representative), 2004, 'What BiH's decision on internal debt means for you', Sarajevo (at: www.ohr.int/ohr-dept/presso/pic/econ-campaigns/internal-dept/).

Pietz, Tobias, 2004, *Demobilization and Reintegration of Former Soldiers in Post-war Bosnia and Herzegovina. An Assessment of External Assistance*, Hamburg: Institut für Friedensforschung und Sicherheitspolitik.

Pugh, Michael, 2006, 'Transformation in the Political Economy of Bosnia Since Dayton', in David Chandler (ed.), *Peace Without Politics? Ten Years of International State-Building in Bosnia*, London: Routledge, pp. 142–56.

Pugh, Michael, 2007, 'Limited Sovereignty and Economic Security: Survival in Southeast Europe', paper at the Harriman Institute, Columbia University, NY, 1 March.

Rozner, Steve, Dželila Šahinagić and Sandra Marjanović, 2005, *Revenue Performance and Tax Administration Modernization in Bosnia and Herzegovina 2001–2004*, Sarajevo/Banja Luka: Tax Modernization Project.

Schlichte, Klaus, 2005, *Der Staat in der Weltgesellschaft. Politische Herrschaft in Asien, Afrika und Lateinamerika*, Frankfurt: Campus.

Siegelberg, Jens, 1994, *Kapitalismus und Krieg. Eine Theorie des Krieges in der Weltgesellschaft*, Münster/Hamburg: Lit.

Suhrke, Astri and Julia Buckmaster, 2005, 'Post-War Aid – Patterns and Purposes', *Development in Practice*, Vol. 15, No. 6, pp. 737–46.

Transparency International BiH, 2004, *Corruption Perception Study 2004: Bosnia and Herzegovina*, Banja Luka/Sarajevo.
UNDP BiH, 2006, *Jobs and... more jobs (special web edition)*. Early Warning System Special Report 2006, Sarajevo.
UNDP BiH, 2007, *Social Inclusion in Bosnia and Herzegovina*. National Human Development Report 2007, Sarajevo.
Working Group Political Analysis, 2005, *Arithmetic of Irresponsibility. When and How to Make a Functional Transition of Responsibilities from the International Community to the Local Authorities*, Sarajevo: Friedrich Ebert Foundation.
World Bank, 1997, *The State in a Changing World*. World Development Report 1997, New York: Oxford University Press.
World Bank, 2002, 'Bosnia and Herzegovina – from Aid Dependency to Fiscal Self-Reliance. A Public Expenditure and Institutional Review', World Bank Report No. 24297-BiH.
World Bank, 2005a, 'Bosnia and Herzegovina. Country Economic Memorandum', World Bank Report No. 29500-BA.
World Bank, 2005b, 'Bosnia and Herzegovina. Labor Market Update: The Role of Industrial Relations', World Bank Report No. 32650-BA.

# Conclusion: The Political Economy of Peacebuilding – Whose Peace? Where Next?

*Michael Pugh, Neil Cooper and Mandy Turner*

The contributions to this book have critically examined the construction of political economies of peace processes and peacebuilding, with a focus not just on the inside of war-torn societies but also on the broader influences of the global economy and shifts in the discursive constructions of security and development. They have concentrated particularly on those aspects of political economy that tend to be neglected in the literature on interventions in war-torn societies: from gender and trade liberalisation to employment and diaspora engagement, and from borderlands to the welfare of citizens. In particular, a key issue has been to identify the modes of negotiation (or lack of it) between the external and internal interlocutors and the impacts of global and dominant international norms on the 'recipient' populations. Answers to the question, 'whose peace?', are clearly related to asymmetries of power that help determine the normative project of liberal peacebuilding, the securitisation of welfare and local responses that involve incorporation of external values but also resistances.

The interpretations that follow in this conclusion represent the editors' views and not necessarily those of the other contributors, and it was never the intention of the book to produce a consensus. But there are several conclusions to be drawn from the empirical findings of these studies, which may have wider acceptance, including indicative directions for policymakers, practitioners and researchers. They may be briefly summarised as seven points, signalling the need for peace agendas that can also facilitate consideration of a paradigmatic shift in the negotiation of political economies of peace:

1. Peace processes and peacebuilding practices need political roots in local societies, and political communities should have the freedom to set their economic priorities including protection of economic activities from negative effects of global integration.

2. Accordingly, a new 'geometry of power' should be assembled with its roots in local community structures which enables a constant feedback of local needs to decision-making.
3. Gender relations should be renegotiated to examine ways of eliminating the post-conflict backlash against women.
4. A rights agenda should be open to the inclusion of socioeconomic rights such as programmes of welfare, redistribution and democracy in the workplace.
5. The concept of 'property' should be broadened to include public, socially owned and community property that is protected from dispossession by private accumulation.
6. An ethic of economic regulation should aim to reconstitute global economic regimes away from silent complicity in 'conflict trade' and freedom for capital, towards moral responsibility and discrimination in favour of the uninsured poor.
7. The 'subaltern geographies of political economy' – informal economies, borderlands and transnational networks such as diasporas – need to be 'de-securitised' and their potential roles in peacebuilding realised.

Together, these critiques imply the need for a fundamental change in the approach to the analyses of war economies and the political economy of peace. The political economy of post-conflict peace and statebuilding in a liberal peace framework has involved a simulacra of empowerment where peacebuilders transfer responsibility to societies without transferring power. Moreover, populations have been subjected to calculated techniques of discipline under liberal agendas requiring individual self-reliance, a loss of public goods and unequal integration into the world economy (Duffield, 2007). Creating an uninsured 'surplus' population may not be an overt goal, but it is a function of 'accumulation by dispossession and the predatory forms of capitalism associated with it' (Harvey, 2003: 210). Critics tend to offer two kinds of alternative – here characterised as problem solving and paradigm shifting.

## Problem solving

In problem-solving constructions the existing conceptual frameworks are broadly taken as given (see Call and Wyeth, 2008) and indeed sometimes it is posited that there are no alternatives to the liberal peace. The chief purpose of investigation is to 'learn lessons', avoid mistakes and improve the planning and implementation of peacebuilding in war-torn contexts. Positive interactions with the 'subjects' of political-economy transitions are also anticipated. The assumption is that economic systems and economic behaviour can be changed by external agency to suit a securitised model of development, and that interventions can be nuanced to achieve this.

Examples of problem-solving reforms include the UN's Inter-Agency Consolidated Appeals system, created in 1993 for humanitarian relief, and the donor conferences (usually under World Bank auspices) that have been held since 1995 to provide aid for post-conflict and post-disaster reconstruction. Such measures have been accompanied by the formation of 'integrated missions' by the UN and partner agencies, with the Special Representative of the UN Secretary-General responsible for coordination. First attempted for the humanitarian response in Sierra Leone, integrated missions have aimed for cohesion between all agencies in the reconstruction and state-building efforts of war-torn societies (sometimes attempting to coordinate military and civil components, as in Liberia). In practice, coherence and coordination have proved highly problematic, as evidenced in Sudan with a hybrid UN–African Union operation and considerable disagreement over whether 'integration' constitutes the merger of policies and programmes, a coordinating mechanism or an 'enabling framework' for planning and prioritisation (Muggah, 2007). As Mats Berdal points out in this volume, the establishment of the Peacebuilding Commission has the potential to cut across bureaucratic divides in the UN system but has been hampered by political wrangling and a limited mandate and configuration. The UN resolution establishing the Commission encompasses political economy perspectives in peacebuilding by, for example, providing participation of the international financial institutions (IFIs) in the Commission's meetings. Significantly, however, such incorporation is divorced from any reform of the World Bank, and other international economic institutions. Consequently, the Commission, and the incentive to establish integrated missions, is essentially designed to make the liberal peace more efficient, and inevitably more intrusive.

This is not to deny that war-torn societies have queued up to get reconstruction aid, help with running elections and de-mining programmes. Large numbers of combatants have been demobilised, UNHCR has made a difference to refugee returns and there have been accomplishments in property restoration (in the Balkans, for example). But the key point is that the overall framing of peace by external agencies reinforces neoliberal prescriptions in the realm of political economy that neither take sufficient account of local needs and agency, nor reflect on the role of global capitalism and structural adjustment policies as drivers of conflict. As Ellen Moodie shows (2010), a narrative of 'successful peacebuilding' in El Salvador has been punctured by the persistence of actual and structural violence after the 1992 peace accords.

An alternative perspective derives from criticism of ambitious and intrusive peacebuilding *per se* that denies local sovereignty under the guises of 'capacity-building' and 'shared sovereignty'. From this perspective, peace-builders might heed the Greek myth of Erysichthon, an arrogant trespasser who felled trees in the sacred grove of Demeter, and who was condemned to suffer unending hunger. In spite of continually eating and selling his possessions, and even his daughter, to buy more food, Erysichthon could never satisfy his lust and was driven to eat his own limbs. The contention is that unaccountable ambition and irresponsible governance from above has no limits and permits an unending quest without local political roots. An alternative is to scale back international ambitions.

The question then arises: scaled back to what? It might be agreed, for example, that international involvement to support a peace process could be limited to emergency relief and the separation and demobilisation of armed groups, perhaps accompanied by disarmament schemes. Another strategy, evidenced in the delay in holding initial elections in post-NATO invasion Kosovo, has been to scale back democratisation until such time as social groups have learned to live in peace. Similarly, self-government can be delayed by the appointment of temporary and provisional authorities, sometimes arranged through the mechanism of holding national consultative conventions, as in Afghanistan. In practice, and according to geopolitical considerations, there has been a flexible application of many of these liberal peace governmentalities. Exceptionally, however, economic transition has been a core, non-negotiable objective of intervention, certainly in terms of macroeconomic policies, supporting private property rights, global integration and an ideal of state shrinkage in the economy. Scaling back this economic engineering would remove economic conditionalities from peace-building and divorce military peace operations, designed to stabilise peace, from integrated reconstruction packages. Military forces should not have the responsibility of buttressing a particular economic project or form of economic governance.

Another problem-solving construction offers a more measured approach to transition that would allow populations to produce development at their own pace. The ultimate goal is still an integrated global economy. The contentions of the 'lifeguards of capitalism' such as George Soros, Joseph Stiglitz, Jeffery Sachs and Amy Chua provide intellectual justification for global reforms that aim to promote order through what Paul Rogers (2000) terms 'liddism' (keeping a lid on disorder), rather than seeking a fundamental shift in the prevailing paradigm of global economy. If core capitalism is thereby saved from conflicts that threaten to disrupt the international system, this can also give a false impression that the affected populations are swimming towards development and waving rather than drowning. This level of problem solving does little to redress the dispossession of community resources and public goods by the constant process of capitalist accumulation (Harvey, 2003).

In summary, the above proposals have inherent weaknesses that invite more far-reaching ideas for interactions with war-torn societies. One of these involves revisiting the concept of human security and realising its potential. Human security, defined by Anuradha Chenoy and Shahrbanou Tadjbakhsh (2006) as 'the protection of individuals from risks to their physical or psychological safety, dignity and well-being', has emancipatory potential in its emphasis on rights. It can also be linked to tackling injustices in the global economy – particularly the issues of trade, aid and debt that galvanised the 'Make Poverty History' campaign in 2006. But human security is a malleable concept and despite its original radical promise, the human security discourse has been applied in ways that has meant the prioritisation and politicisation of some issues, and the depoliticisation of, and relative silence about, others. For instance, poverty reduction agendas in war-torn societies privilege macroeconomic discipline over welfare and distributive justice, as illustrated in several chapters in this book (Turner, Cooper and Pugh, 2010). The problem, however, is that the more emancipatory aspects of the human security agenda either are not followed through or have been captured to work in the interests of global capitalism, exemplified in the way that poverty reduction agendas in war-torn societies privilege macroeconomic discipline over welfare and distributive justice, as illustrated in several chapters in this book. Six key problems arise with re-energising 'human security'.

First, the language of human security has been adopted as a discursive framework within which to legitimise a range of Western military interventions from Kosovo to Afghanistan. It has also underpinned 'Responsibility to Protect' and counter-terrorism strategies that subordinate and securitise the interests of the 'other' to the imperatives of core capitalism (see Duffield, 2007). Human-security language has even been employed to legitimise new military technologies, such as unmanned aerial vehicles, by emphasising that their accuracy permits discrimination between combatant and civilian. Equally, this has created a discursive space for campaigns to restrict particular categories of arms such as landmines, cluster munitions and small arms that neither fit this representation nor underpin the defence strategies or arms industries of major powers. One consequence of the loud humanitarian discourse around such restrictions is that it has tended to obscure the main sources of global military expenditure and arms sales (Hynek, 2008; Cooper, 2010a).

Second, it represents a 'securitisation' of local political economy that serves to re-legitimise the neoliberal agenda after the failures of structural adjustment. As a development agenda, human security served two main purposes: alleviating threats to the world's poor and pre-empting post-Cold War threats to the advanced capitalist world in the form of unrest and war, migration and spread of diseases. However, strategies to protect the poor from the vulnerabilities of globalisation, as elaborated by Ha-Joon Chang (2008), for example, have been effectively sidelined by the core capitalist states, the IFIs and the World Trade Organisation. Despite the promise of human security and development through neoliberalism, global inequalities have gathered pace.

Third, the 'human security' paradigm has lent justification to externally directed projects of disciplinary control in the developing world with an emphasis on how human security requires law and order. As pointed out by Biljana Vankovska (2007), in the clash between versions of human security – freedom from want and freedom from fear – the latter is privileged, thus providing justification for the prioritisation of security sector reform and rule of law programmes and for greater involvement of the development community in security-related issues. War-torn societies receive an enormous amount of international attention, largely because of the supposed risks they pose to the advanced capitalist world. However, the current reform agenda problematises the domestic governance and transformation of the 'other' and focuses primarily on configuring the political economies operating *inside* post-conflict states. Such approaches ignore the gross inequalities of the global economy and offer only limited forms of global poor relief to contain potential revolts. In an attempt by the UN Trust Fund for Human Security (2009) to operationalise human security, there is no acknowledgement or discussion of global inequality and the practices of world economic institutions which have emptied out the original radical promise of the human security discourse. The effort to reform post-conflict economies is therefore akin to training goldfish in a desert – regardless of how good individual programmes are they are ultimately destined to fail (Cooper, 2010b).

Fourth, as illustrated in the preceding points, the human security project has lent credence to projects of military intervention and economic and social engineering that have *echoes* of imperialism. Of particular resonance is the way such feats of engineering combine a discursive emphasis on the protection and improvement of the 'other' with the neglect of local ownership or political roots (except as another feature of peacebuilding to be simulated, as David Chandler notes in this volume, through 'capacity building' and 'shared sovereignty'). Human security has become a popular discourse largely because of its *perceived* radicalism. It allows peacebuilding agencies to highlight some issues traditionally ignored in the state security discourse, while fending off critiques of the global structures of economic and political power. The language of 'peacebuilding from below' – replete in proclamations – is actually 'peacebuilding from below produced from above'.

Fifth, not only are such projects of engineering therefore inherently contradictory, but in neglecting local ownership and local political roots (see McGrew and Poku, 2006) their prospects for successful implementation are consequently limited. The end result tends to produce hybrid forms of the liberal peace, that reflect, while not necessarily meeting, everyday needs.

Sixth, the focus on the 'atomised individual' divorces humanity from its species life, that is the totality of social structures and relationships. An illustration of this is the way in which human security reinforces a binary divide between individual human rights and state rights, as well as neglecting class and community rights.

## Towards a paradigm shift?

Some commentators have, of course, outlined a radical emancipatory and empathetic version of human security that envisages genuine local empowerment based on the needs of everyday life (Richmond, 2007: 477). However, it can be argued that even such radical approaches are unable to escape many of the problems associated with 'human security', and its implementation that arise, in part, as an inevitable consequence of attaching the 'security' label to human life. There is a need, then, to develop a new, unsecuritised language and to contemplate a paradigm that takes local voices seriously, rejects universalism in favour of heterodoxy, reconceptualises the abstract individual as a social being and limits damage to planetary life – in short, a 'life welfare' perspective. Such a perspective would lead to a two-fold paradigm shift: from the 'liddism' of liberal peace to political economies of life welfare; and from universalist panaceas (which result in dysfunctional hybrid forms of political economy) to engaging with heterogeneity.

A life welfare paradigm would encompass alternative notions of life (the individual, community, the biosphere and planetary environment) and alternative understandings of the political economy of peacebuilding in war-torn societies. This is not, however, a prescription for resigned relativism but rather a prescription for a politics of emancipation in which the need for dialogue between heterodoxies is a core component (see below) – not least because there may be more than one means to reach the same ends. Such a politics of emancipation would therefore also incorporate the need to look beyond the human, to such issues as the environment and resources as well as connecting physiological and biological processes (often labelled 'bare life') to economic processes. While it would not be about abstract individuals, or about the imposition of liberal values on non-Western societies that do not subscribe to these, it would incorporate the goal of optimising the life potential of both individuals and diverse forms of community, recognising that the means to reach such a goal would be the object of serial negotiation. Furthermore, it would require researchers to focus on the archaeology and history of communities and their projected futures, rejecting the temporary, ameliorative interventions of international agencies and coalitions preoccupied with 'exits' that rely on quick, or technological, fixes. Nor would a life welfare paradigm take liberalism as the only normative construct. It would allow for the historically and spatially contingent transformation of varied societies. Indeed, it would embrace not only critiques of economic forces (finance capitalism, corporate power), but the 'economy of power' in different societies. The 'economy of power' can be expressed as different forms of governmentality (the techniques and technologies used by governments), so that varied energies are released to produce, for instance, either welfare liberalism or, indeed, neoliberalism.[1]

A paradigm shift would involve interrogation of the way in which the global system exacerbates the subaltern status of war-torn societies (already reinforced by overt violence) and advocate a commensurately greater focus on the outside of the post-conflict society, on the need for far-reaching transformation of the structures and institutions that determine what might be termed 'the limits of potential' for life security in war-torn societies as a whole.

This would involve more than simply equalising the 'free market' and enhancing global poor relief – as proposed by Sen, Soros and Stiglitz. While many of the technicist solutions proposed by such commentators may have merit as problem-solving approaches they nevertheless leave capitalism unproblematised. Such an approach – ignoring the limitations of reform within the status quo – is ultimately doomed to failure. Indeed, nothing announced the debility of the international economic system and this reformist approach quite so flamboyantly as the decision on 12 December 2007, by five central banks in the West, to bail out the 'free market' of finance capitalism to the tune of £50 billion – the same as the total global development aid, post-Gleneagles in 2006 (which included debt relief and spending on Iraq). While the promises of aid required lengthy highly visible worldwide campaigns, the rescue of what Keynes referred to as 'casino capitalism' was a precipitate response to the discreet lobbying power of the commercial banking sector.

As John Gray contends, '[a] reform of the world economy is needed that accepts a diversity of cultures, regimes and market economies as a permanent reality' (Gray, 1998 [2002]: 20). One step would be to at least allow post-conflict societies to adopt similar policies on issues such as industrial protection and social welfare to those on which developed economies based their original development (Cramer, 2006; Chang, 2008). Fundamental restructuring would also need to promote economic empowerment, redistribution and welfare, and a shift in the frameworks of ethical regulation from corporate voluntarism and unequal application of legislation to discrimination in favour of the disadvantaged. For David Harvey (2003: 209), this requires '[r]eformulating state power along more interventionist and redistributive lines, curbing the speculative power of finance capitalism, and decentralising or democratically controlling the overwhelming power of oligopolies and monopolies'. But as suggested earlier (Chapters 13 and 16, this volume), a statist framework does not always address the 'territories of difference' in ways that promote life welfare.

## Conclusion

There is, of course, a potential tension in achieving an emancipatory transformation of global economic structures *and* empowering local communities. Moreover, it would be erroneous to romanticise the 'local', because the local may include actors such as *genocidaires*, and because a focus on the local leaves the operations of the global economic structures unproblematised. Recognising this tension is the starting point for transforming global power structures through a 'willingness to engage in unscripted conversations' (Duffield, 2007: 234) and rejecting imposition in favour of negotiation over what type of 'peace' is being constructed and for whom. For example, societies that have had a tradition of cooperative capital accumulation may wish to persist with it.

This implies the production of new 'geographies of power' which foster social contracts at both the global level *and* the local level. These should be based on the core precepts of accountability, ownership and life welfare. The outcomes of 'unscripted conversations' are by definition unpredictable and open-ended. But it is to be hoped that initial contributions to that conversation are represented by this book.

## Note

1. We are grateful to Nikola Hynek of the Institute of International Relations, Prague, for his contributions to the ideas in these sections.

## References

Call, Charles T. and Vanessa Wyeth (eds), 2008, *Building States to Build Peace*, Boulder, CO: Lynne Rienner.
Chang, Ha-Joon, 2008, *Bad Samaritans: The Guilty Secrets of Rich Nations and the Threat to Global Prosperity*, London: Random House.
Chenoy, Anuradha M. and Shahrbanou Tadjbakhsh, 2006, *Human Security: Concepts and Implications*, London: Routledge.
Cooper, Neil, 2010a, 'From Motherhood and Apple Pie to UAVs in Afghanistan: Humanitarian Arms Control, NGOs and the Strategic Complexes of the Liberal Peace', in Jackie Smith and Ernesto Verdeja (eds), *Globalisation, Peacebuilding and Social Movements* (forthcoming).
Cooper, Neil, 2010b, 'Training Goldfish (in a Desert): Transforming Political Economies of Conflict Using Voluntarism, Regulation and Supervision', in Oliver P. Richmond (ed.), *Palgrave Advances in Peacebuilding: Critical Developments and Approaches*, Basingstoke: Palgrave Macmillan, pp. 307–26.
Cramer, Chris, 2006, *Civil War is Not a Stupid Thing: Accounting for Violence in Developing Societies*, London: Hurst.
Duffield, Mark, 2007, *Development, Security and Unending War: Governing the World of Peoples*, Cambridge: Polity.
Gray, John, 1998, *False Dawn: The Delusions of Global Capitalism*, London: Granta, 2002 edn.
Harvey, David, 2003, *The New Imperialism*, Oxford: Oxford University Press.
Hynek, Nikola, 2008, 'Conditions of Emergence and Their Effects: Political Rationalities, Governmental Programs and Technologies of Power in the Landmine Case', *Journal of International Relations and Development*, Vol. 11, No. 2, pp. 93–120.
McGrew, Anthony and Nana Poku (eds), 2006, *Globalization, Development and Human Security*, Cambridge: Polity.
Moodie, Ellen, 2010, *El Salvador in the Aftermath of Peace: Crime, Uncertainty, and the Transition to Democracy*, Philadelphia, PA: University of Pennsylvania Press.
Muggah, Robert, 2007, 'Great expectations: (dis)integrated DDR in Sudan and Haiti', London: Overseas Development Institute, Humanitarian Practice Network report, March.

Richmond, Oliver P., 2007, 'Emancipatory Forms of Human Security and Liberal Peacebuilding', *International Journal*, Vol. 62, No. 3, pp. 459–77.

Rogers, Paul, 2000, *Losing Control: Global Security in the Twenty-First Century*, London: Pluto Press.

Turner, Mandy, Neil Cooper and Michael Pugh, 2010, 'Institutionalised and Co-opted: Why Human Security has Lost its Way', in David Chandler and Nikola Hynek (eds), *Critical Perspectives on Human Security: Rethinking Emancipation and Power in International Relations*, London: Routledge, pp. 83–96.

UN Trust Fund for Human Security, 2009, *Human Security in Theory and Practice*, UN Office for the Coordination of Humanitarian Assistance, Human Security Unit, Geneva.

Vankovska, Biljana, 2007, 'The Human Security Doctrine for Europe: A View from Below', *International Peacekeeping*, Vol. 14, No. 2, pp. 264–81.

# Index

Adams, Dale, 252
Afghanistan, 40, 41, 184, 231, 234, 236, 237, 240–2, 300, 352
  drug production/trade, 80, 231
  women in, 41, 80
Afghanistan Expatriate Programme, 185
Africa, 73, 128, 212, 268–82, 343, 348, 350
Agamben, Giorgio, 296
agriculture, 21, 72, 73, 253–5, 259
  in developed world, 83
  women and, 41–3
aid conditionality, 251, 292, 343, 349
  *see also* international financial institutions (IFIs)
Alfa-5, 136
Algeria, 135, 296
al-Shahristani, Hussein, 61
Alston, Philip, 151
America–Israel Public Affairs Committee, 187
American Civil War, 130–1, 135
Amnesty International, 92, 94
Anderson, Benedict, 203
Angola, 131, 132, 135
Annan, Kofi, 50, 358, 366, 367, 369
Appadurai, Arjun, 235
Ashdown, Paddy, 5
Ashley, Richard, 2

Baku–Ceyhan–Tbilisi pipeline, 94
Balkans, 34, 247, 342, 349, 353
  and European integration process, 349–50
  *see also* Yugoslavia; *separate countries*
'bare life', 51, 53, 296, 398
Batatu, Hanna, 56
Bauman, Zygmunt, 271
Beijing Platform for Action (1995), 40
Bendaña, Alejandro, 307, 309
Beveridge, William, 291
biopolitics, 295
'blood/conflict diamonds', *see* diamonds and diamond mining

Bolton, John, 366, 368
Bonn Agreement (2001), 241, 242
Bonoli, Guiliano, 291
borderlands, 227–43, 247–8, 253, 255, 257, 258
  classical, 230
  and conflict, 275–6
  global, 231–2
  and identity, 271, 275
  internal, 230–1, 268–82
  and peacebuilding, 243
  Pelagonia, 258
  as sites of potential difference, 271–2
  and sovereignty, 270
  trade through, 79
borders and frontiers, 22–3, 229, 231
  Afghan–Pakistan, 238, Afghan–Tajik, 238, Croatian, 259, in Southeast Europe, 261
  colonial borders, 274–5, 277–8
  Rwanda–Congo, 272
Bornstein, Avram, 233
Bosnia and Herzegovina (BiH), 148, 149–50, 247, 251, 253–4, 261, 376–88
  corruption in, 381
  Dayton Peace Agreement for (1995), 352, 377
  Directorate for Economic Planning, 386
  economic development/dependency, 377, 385–7
  Economic Transition Unit (ETU), 150
  and EU association, 379–80, 384, 386, 388
  Federation, 378; canton powers, 382
  fiscal discipline, 383–4, 387
  industry, 257
  institutions, 378–9
  international aid/agencies in, 379, 380–1
  Jobs and Justice programme, 149
  as laboratory for technocratic experiment, 384–5

labour market, exploitation,
  unemployment in, 149–50, 153,
  382, 385–7
as microfinance model, 251, 253–4
neoliberalism and privatisation in,
  381, 383, 388
poverty reduction strategy, 386
revenue, taxation and public
  expenditure, 378–80, 383–5;
  Indirect Tax Agency, 379
social welfare in, 382, 387
state-weakening dynamics, 380–6
strikes in, 152
veterans, 382–3
boundaries, *see* borders and frontiers
Bremer, Paul, 141
Bretton Woods institutions, *see*
  international financial institutions
  (IFIs)
Briggs, Asa, 291
Burma, 233
Burundi, 211
Bush administration, 204, 368
Bush, George W., 2
business
  and conflict, 95–6, 101
  and peace, 19, 22, 23, 26
  women and, 44
Business Leaders' Initiative on Human
  Rights, 87, 88, 92

Cambodia, 35, 152
capacity-building, 343, 344, 345–8
capitalism and capital accumulation, 6,
  22, 24, 26, 52–4, 101, 124, 133, 239,
  262–3, 393, 395, 399
  'lifeguards' of, 395
CARE International, 146
Central American Human Rights
  Institute, 321
Central Intelligence Agency (CIA),
  240, 241
Centre for Transnational
  Corporations, 91
Chalabi, Ahmed, 184–5
Chapultepec Peace Accords, 321, 322
Chechnya, 142, 233
Cheney, Dick, 368
Chevron Oil, 97

children
  and labour, 151
  rights of, 36
  as soldiers, 36, 87
  trafficking of, 78–9
China and investment in Africa, 98–9
Christian Zionist groups, 181
citizenship, 235
'civil peace', 300–1
civil–political rights, 143, 147
civil society, 89, 290, 304–17, 362–3
civil society organisations (CSOs),
  304–17
  defined, 305
'clash of civilisations' thesis, 182
class structure, 25, 57, 123, 125
Clifford, James, 196
Coalition Provisional Authority, *see* Iraq
Collier, Paul *et al.*, 72, 180
Colombia, 21, 148, 152
  Plan Colombia, 25, 79
colonialism, 90
coltan, 125, 272, 277, 279
commodities, *see* extractive industries
  and mining
conflict, post-Cold War, 341
  and labour, 128–9
  legacies of, 3, 19
  and social resources, 132
conflict resolution, 14–15, 25
Congono, Mark, 133
Congo, *see* Democratic Republic of
  Congo (DRC)
cooperatives, 263
coping and survival economies, 149
corporate social responsibility (CSR),
  87–101
  and China, 99
  and communities, 91
  Draft Norms for, 87, 91, 92, 100
  and international law, 90, 97
  and voluntary/mandatory codes, 93–4,
    99
corporations, 149
cosmopolitanism, 18, 294
Côte d'Ivoire, 76–9, 110, 131
Cousens, Elizabeth, 361
Covenant on Economic, Social and
  Cultural Rights (1966), 145
Cox, Robert, 23, 154

Coyne, Christopher, 291
criminal economies/networks, 78, 79–80, 238–9, 321, 323, 326–8
see also shadow economies
Croatia, 247, 254, 255, 260
   war veterans in, 377–8

Darfur, see Sudan and Darfur
Davis, Danny, 199
Davis, Mike, 253
de-industrialisation, 247–8
demobilisation, 136
Democratic Republic of Congo (DRC), 125, 211, 268–70
   and decentralisation, 281–2
   infrastructure, 280–1
   Kivus, 232, 239, 271, 273, 277, 278
   political parties and movements, 269
   Sun City Peace Accords for, 280
   territories, 274–5, 278
democratisation and political reform, 40, 147, 292, 299
developing countries, 69–70, 71–3, 76, 127, 249, 258
   statistical profile of, 74–5 (table)
development/development studies, 25, 296
   see also inequalities and distributive justice
Dhanapala, Jayantha, 369
Diamond Area Community Development Fund, 114
Diamond Development Initiative (DDI), 110–1
diamonds and diamond mining, 81, 96–7, 105, 110, 135–6
   Kimberley Process Certification Scheme (KPCS), 81, 94, 96, 105, 109–11, 114, 115, 116–17
   Koidu Holdings, 111, 114, 115
   see also Sierra Leone
diasporas, 175–88, 195–7, 203, 212, 235–6
   Afghani, 178, 183, 184
   benefits to hostland, 201
   in Canada, 198, 199, 200, 201; in Germany, 186; in UK, 198
   and conflict, 180, 212
   Croatian, 178
   and development, 176–9, 186, 200–1, 212
   Eritrean, 177, 184, 186, 187
   Indian, 187
   Iranian, 202
   Irish–American, 184
   Jewish and Jewish–American lobby, 175, 181, 187
   Kurdish, 186
   Liberian, 178
   organisations and transnational networks of, 181, 183, 196–8
   Palestinian, 178, 181, 187
   and peace/peacebuilding, 183–5, 193–204, 212–15
   remittances by, 146, 176–9, 198, 200–1, 204
   Rwandan, 208–20
   and security, 179–82, 194
   Sierra Leonean, 183, 187
   Sinhalese and Tamil, 180, 196
   social impacts of, 201–2
   Somali, 179, 188
   and terrorism, 181, 182, 194, 204
   and women, 179
   see also refugees and returnees
disarmament, demobilisation and reintegration (DDR), 159–70
Docena, Herbert, 52
Doha Development Round, 72
domestic violence, 35
Donnelly, Jack, 143
Doyle, Michael, 295
drug trafficking, 237, 238, 240, 327–8
Dubey, Muchkund, 364–5
Duffield, Mark, 53, 57, 153, 177, 231
dumping, 73
Durkheim, Emile, 124
Durrand Line, 230, 241

East Asia, 70
East Timor, see Timor-Leste
Ebadi, Shireen, 202
Economic Community of West African States, 115
economic determinism, 2–6
   see also neoliberalism
economic integration, and conflict prevention, 81–2

economic protectionism, 72
Economic, Social and Cultural Rights Net, 93
economic survival, 34
'economism', 2
education, 43
El Salvador, 34, 39, 131, 320–32
  ARENA party, 328, 330
  civil society in, 320–1, 322
  conflict in, 320–1
  crime/criminality, 321, 323, 326–8
  employment in, 323
  everyday insecurity, 329
  forms of violence in, 323–4, 326–7, 330, 331
  government brutality, policing and *Mano Blanco* death squad in, 324–5, 328–31
  inequalities in, 322–3, 324, 325
  migration to US, 323
  Truth Commission, 324
  weapons in, 326
  youth gangs in, 325–8
emancipation and empowerment, 144, 308, 311, 393, 398
empires, 229, 233
  Ottoman, 233
employment, *see* labour
enclaves, 279, 280
Energoinvest (BiH), 257
Eritrea, 39, 43
Ethiopia, 236–7
ethno-nationalism, 377
European Payments Union, 83
European Union (EU), 17, 72, 145, 236
Evans, Tony, 143
'Everything But Arms' programme (EU), 72
ex-combatants, 146, 147–8
  and aggression, 168
  reintegration of, 159–70
  securitisation of, 160–70
extractive industries and mining, 71, 93, 98, 279
  *see also* diamonds and diamond mining
Extractive Industries Transparency Initiative, 88, 98

Fafo, 100
Falk, Richard, 147
Fanon, Franz, 296
Farabundo Martí National Liberation Front (FMLN), 131, 321
feminist studies, 45
Ferghana valley (Afghanistan), 234
Fields, Gary, 123, 127
'flexicurity', *see under* labour
food insecurity, 55, 277, 280
*Forces Nouvelles* (FN), 78
foreign investment, 21, 59, 87, 88, 95–6
Forest Law Enforcement Governance and Trade, 98
free trade, 20, 23
  US–German trade, 20
Free Trade Union of Cambodia (FTU), 152
Freire, Paulo, 306, 308
Friedman, Thomas, 18, 25
Frontiers, *see* borders and frontiers
*Front Populaire Ivoirien* (FPI), 77–8
functionalism, 17, 21
Fundamental Principles of Rights at Work (1998), 150

G77, 364–6
*gacaca* courts (Rwanda), 38
*garimpeiro* labourers, 136
Geertz, Clifford, 271
gender-based violence, 32–45
gender politics/narratives, 34, 35, 38–9
  *see also* women
Geuss, Raymond, 144
Ghani, Ashraf, 241
Giddens, Anthony, 291
global ethics, 144
global governance, *see under* governance
globalisation, 16, 17–18, 22, 23, 24, 144, 147, 196, 236, 250
Global Witness, 92
'Golden Arches theory', *see* Friedman, Thomas
Goma, 277
governance, 17–18, 88–95
  'chimeric', 53
  global, 375–6
  and international regulation, 349
  lack of accountability, 348, 350, 352–5

governance – *continued*
  liberal and top-down, 50–1, 298–9, 301, 352
  'metagovernance', 51
  and sovereignty, 346
Governance and Economic Management Assistance Program for Liberia (GEMAP), 166
*Gradjanska Platforma* (BiH), 150
Grameen Bank, 247, 248–9
  *see also* microfinance/microcredit
Gray, John, 398
Great Lakes region, 209, 211
'greed thesis', 81
Guatemala, 39, 42, 152, 305–6, 309–17
Guatemala, Agreement on Identity and Rights of Indigenous Peoples, 312
  civil society organisations, 310
  constitutional reform, 314
  *Mesas de Concertación*, 304–17
  peace agenda and peacebuilding in, 310, 312–17
  Peace Secretariat, 314
  San Antonio La Paz, 315
  Sololá department of, 314
  *Unidad Revolucionaria Nacional Guatemalteca* (URNG), 314
  violence in, 315
  women in, 315
Guinea, 110

Halliburton, 59
Hanlon, Joseph, 109, 116, 117
Harvey, David, 398
*hawala* systems, 178, 180, 188
health services, 41, 54
Helmand Valley Authority (Afghanistan), 237
Herceg–Bosna, 142
Hezbollah, 153
High Level Diamond Steering Committee, 107
High Level Panel on Threats, Challenges and Change (HLP), 358, 359, 361–4, 369–70
household surveys, 146
humanitarian agencies, 55
human rights, 36, 89, 93
Human Rights Watch, 92, 132

human security, 395–6
human/sex trafficking, 55, 239
Hunde people (DRC), 273–4

income generation, 147, 251
India, 21, 23, 24, 25, 249, 258
  and Peacebuilding Commission, 369
India–Pakistan conflict, *see* Kashmir
industrial sector, 91, 260
inequalities and distributive justice, 20–1, 73, 76, 144, 154, 250, 298, 322–5
  *see also* poverty
informal economies, 43, 236–9
  *see also* shadow economies
Ingushetia, 142
Institute for Multi-Track Diplomacy (IMTD), 19
insurance industry, 57
Integrated Diamond Management Program (IDMP), 113
International Alert, 92
International Business Leaders' Forum, 92
International Commission on Intervention and State Sovereignty (ICISS), 344
International Committee of the Red Cross (ICRC), 146
International Criminal Tribunal for Rwanda, 37
international financial institutions (IFIs), 71, 108, 145, 214, 248, 249, 251, 297, 343, 351, 372, 376, 394
  *see also* structural adjustment programmes
International Labour Organisation (ILO), 128, 143, 145, 147, 150–2, 154
International Monetary Fund (IMF), 71, 108, 384
International Organisation for Migration, 195
interventions, 276, 365
Iraq, 50–63, 52, 57, 141, 184, 300, 352–3
  academics, 57
  business in, 56–7
  children in, 55–6
  Coalition Provisional Authority (CPA) and Coalition in, 57, 59–60, 61, 63, 141, 353

constitution of, 52, 53
de-ba'thification, 56
economy, state role in, 56
education in, 56
foreign bases in, 58–9
industry in, 59, 63
insecurity, security forces and insurgency in, 52–3, 57–9, 60
insurance in, 57–8
labour and unemployment in, 55, 61–2, 63
and neoliberalism, 52
oil legislation, 60–2
peacebuilding, 62
Peace and Development Working Group, 51
Political Office for the Iraqi Resistance, 52
poverty, inequality and social exclusion in, 56–7
privatisation in, 61
Public Distribution System, 55
reconstruction and reconstruction funds, 58
and US policy, 20
US 'surge' in, 58–9
war economy in, 59
Iraq-Based Industrial Zone, 58
Iraqi Federation of Oil Unions, 61
Iraqi National Congress, 184
Islam, 234, 241
Israel, 20–4, 26, 135, 233
*see also* Middle East

Jabri, Vivienne, 231, 294
Jackson, Robert, 346
Jaffna peninsular, 237
Jeong, Ho-Won, 306
Jessop, Bob, 51
jobs, training and creation, 146, 148, 151–4, 161, 162, 166, 169
*see also* labour
Jordan, 55
justice, 36–7
traditional, 38

Kagame, Paul, 208, 211, 218
Kaldor, Nicholas, 134
Kashmir, 21, 22–4, 39, 234
Katanga, 90
Kaufman, Bruce, 127
Keen, David, 239
Kellogg, Brown and Root, 59
Kenya, 274
Keohane, Robert, 344, 353
Keynes, John Maynard/Keynesianism, 134, 290, 291, 399
Kharzai, Hamid, 184
Kimberley Process Certification Scheme (KPCS), *see under* diamonds and diamond mining
Kivus, *see under* Democratic Republic of Congo (DRC)
Koidu Holdings (Sierra Leone), *see under* diamonds and diamond mining
Kosovo, 34, 146, 147, 255, 261, 352, 353
agriculture in, 261
microenterprises in, 255–6
unemployment in, 148
Krasner, Stephen, 346–7, 352, 354
Kriger, Norma, 136
Kurdish Regional Government (KRG), 61
Kurdistan Workers Party, 239
Kurds, 240

labour, 49, 71, 79, 87, 124, 128, 129, 130, 252
conditions and rights, 112–13, 135, 137, 141–54, 252
'flexicurity' and, 151–2
forced, 132
markets, 123–37
relations, 128, 134
'segmented labour markets' theory, 127
standards, 133
*see also* trade unions
Laeken criteria, 145
land tenure and reform, 42–3, 216, 292
'In Larger Freedom', 364, 366
Latin America, 73, 79–80
Lebanon, 153
Lederach, Jean-Paul, 309
Levitt, Peggy, 202
liberal orthodoxy, *see* neoliberalism
liberal peace/peacebuilding, 15–16, 49, 50, 123–4, 148, 185, 217, 293–5, 297–9, 392, 397
defined, 3
liberal-realism, 295

liberal war, 231
Liberation Tigers of Tamil Eelam (LTTE), 198, 199, 200, 202, 227, 228–9, 236
Liberia, 110, 159–70
  crime in, 162
  and development, 166
  diamond sector of, 114
  Joint Implementation Unit, 160
  labour market in, 161, 163–4
  peacekeepers in, 168
  riots in, 160
  weapons collection in, 161
  youth in, 163
'liddism', 106, 107, 117, 395, 398
'life welfare', 8–9, 396–7
Lincoln, Abraham, 131
Loya Jirga, 40
Luck, Edward, 367

Macedonia, 258
*madrassas*, 241
'Make Poverty History', 396
Malloch Brown, Mark, 367–8, 369
Mani, Rama, 144
Mano River Union (MRU), 115
Marques, Rafael, 135, 136
Marshall Plan (1947), 82–3, 291, 301
Martin, Paul, 199
Marxism, 126, 310–11
microenterprises, 252, 258
  and technology, 256–8, 259–60
microfinance/microcredit, 247–64
  failures, 254–6, 260
  institutions (MFIs), 248–9, 254, 257, 261, 262–3, 264; DEMOS, 255
  saturation and displacement effects, 252–6
Middle East, 17, 18, 22
Migdal, Joel, 228, 234–5
migrants/migration, 124, 125, 135, 176, 178, 201, 235, 237
Millennium Development Goals (MDGs), 348, 350
Minna, Maria, 199
Mobutu, Sese, 233
Moldova, 237
Morocco, 179
Mozambique, 41, 42, 44, 124, 125, 132, 133, 148, 167
multinational companies, 91–2

Multi-National Force – Iraq, 58
Muslim mercantile networks, 131

Namibia, 39
neoliberalism, 16–19, 26–7, 49, 51, 52, 54, 62–3, 81, 91, 126–7, 134, 141, 144, 146–9, 154, 215, 249, 260, 292–3, 375, 376
  local, 248, 250
  open economies, 20, 71–2
  and peacebuilding, 293–8, 300–2
  post-Washington Consensus, 106, 137
  Washington Consensus, 52, 69, 134
Nepal, 81
Nicaragua, 34, 39
Niger Delta, 92, 97
Nigeria, 97, 128
Non-Aligned Movement (NAM), 364, 368
non-governmental organisations (NGOs), 51, 93–6, 98, 292
non-Western states, 340, 342–3, 348, 350
Noriega, Manuel, 34
Northern Ireland, 13, 17, 18, 20, 25
North–South relations, 20–2
Nyanga people (DRC), 273–4

Ocampo, Luis Moreno, 87
Ohrid (Macedonia), 258
oil industry, 88, 95
O'Laughlin, Bridget, 133
Organisation for Economic Cooperation and Development (OECD), 72, 145
Orientalism, 300
Orjuela, Camilla, 201
Ortega, Daniel, 34
Oslo peace process, 16, 23, 25, 135, 187
Ouattara, Allassan, 78
Ougadougou Agreement (2007), 78
Oxfam, 72

Paine, Thomas, 290–1
Pakistan, 22, 23, 25–6, 230, 234, 241
  Federally Administered Tribal Areas of Pakistan (FATA), 232, 234
Palestine, 21, 135, 143, 149, 187, 233
  Palestinian Expatriate Professional Project, 185
Panama, 34

para-states, 377
*Parti Démocratique de Côte d'Ivoire* (PDCI), 77–8
Partnership Africa Canada, 92
Pashtun people, 236, 241, 242
pastoralism, 236–7, 274
Patraeus, Gen. David, 58
peacebuilding, 5, 14, 49–63, 87, 147, 166, 198–9, 240, 290–2, 294–5, 360, 372, 376
 and culture, 297, 299, 301, 308–9
 and everyday life, 397
 and funding, 372
 gendered, 393
 local communities/ownership of, 392–3, 397, 399
 scaling back, 394–5
 UN strategic direction of, 361, 371
Peacebuilding Commission, *see under* United Nations
Peace Diamonds Alliance (PDA), 113
peacekeeping, 36, 78, 280
 MONUC, 280
 UN Peacekeeping Committee, 368
peace processes, 15–16, 134–5, 293
 constituencies, 305, 306, 312, 316
 and development, 124–6
 and interdependency, 20, 21
 simulations of, 27
 *see also* women
peace-to-war transitions, 232–9
Peres, Shimon, 17, 18, 19, 26
Peru, 37
Petronas Oil, 95, 96
Polanyi, Karl, 297
post-colonialism, 272–3, 297
poverty, 18–19, 25, 69–71, 73, 77, 256
 and conflict, 25
 reduction strategies/papers, 83, 106–7, 250, 350, 376, 396
 *see also* inequalities and distributive justice
Prebisch–Singer thesis, 71
privatisation, 89, 249–50, 276
problem-solving method, 294, 393–5
Pro-Credit Bank, 261
property rights, 141, 147
prostitution, 44

Przeworski, Adam, 292
Pupavac, Vanessa, 53

Quiché, 314

*Rassemblement des Républicains* (RDR), 78
Rawls, John, 143–4
realism, 15–16
refugees and returnees, 34, 55, 133, 147, 184, 259
 *see also* diasporas
regime change, 342, 351
regions and integration, 17, 21, 22, 231
remittances, 177, 180
 *see also under* diasporas
*Renamo* (Mozambique), 132
Reno, William, 233
Republika Srpska (BiH), 378, 385
'resource-mobilisation' theory, 311
resource wars, 80–1, 96
'responsibility to protect', 344–5, 396
retail and tertiary sectors, 146, 254
 *see also* microfinance/microcredit
Revolutionary United Front in Sierra Leone (RUF), 109, 132
Ricardo's theory, 70
'rights branding', 145
Rogers, Paul, 106, 395
Ron, James, 234
Rotberg, Robert I., 343
Ruggie, John, 92
Rupasinghe, Kumar, 203
Rwanda, 38, 40, 42, 81, 208–20, 239
 '59-ers' return to, 210–11
 *akazu* and neo-patrimonialism in, 214–15, 216–17
 colonial period, 210
 and development, 215–19
 diasporas in Belgium, US and South Africa, 218
 economic growth in, 219
 elections (2003), 213
 ethnicity in, 217
 flawed reconciliation in, 217
 inequalities in, 219
 investment in, 218–19
 justice system, 217–18
 land tenure, disputes and Land Law (2005) in, 42, 216–17
 liberal peace in, 217

Rwanda – *continued*
  poverty reduction strategy for, 216
  remittances to, 218
  villagisation, 216
  'Vision 2020', 216, 218, 220
Rwandan Diaspora Global Convention, 218
Rwandan Patriotic Front (RPF), 211, 213, 215

Said, Edward, 143, 297
sanctions, 99–100
Saravanamuttu, Paikiasothy, 203
Schumpeter, Joseph, 295
Second World War, 134
securitisation, defined, 165
securitisation of political economy, 396
security–development nexus, 19, 24, 26, 27, 69, 106–7, 109, 116, 182
security firms, 149
Sen, Amartya, 144
Serbia, 234
shadow economies, 79–81, 238, 240, 248, 270, 378, 385–6
Shell Oil, 97
Shue, Henry, 143
Sierra Leone, 37, 81, 105–17, 131
  capital flight from, 115–16
  cooperatives in, 113
  corruption in, 113
  diamond miners, 112–14
  diamond sector, mining and exports, 109–16; *see also* diamonds and diamond mining
  donor influence in, 107
  empowerment, 107–8
  government spending, 108–9
  human development in, 107
  Lebanese community in, 115
  neoliberalism in, 108, 109, 116–17
  peacekeeping in, 105
  poverty reduction strategy paper (PRSP), 108–9
  privatisation in, 108
  public sector salaries, 108
  security sector reform in, 107, 109
Sierra Leone Diamond Company (SLDC), 111
Sierra Rutile, 114
slavery, 130–1
Slovenia, 251
small and medium-sized enterprises (SMEs), 149, 256–8
smuggling, 238, 272
social capital, 148, 262–3, 291
social contract, 144, 153, 293, 298
social inclusion and exclusion, 53–4
social movements and theory, 145, 197, 311–12
social policy, protection and welfare, 25, 41, 51, 82, 142, 151, 289–302
  and state provision, 57, 291
social unrest, 250
socioeconomic rights, 143, 393
Somalia, 43, 54
Soro, Guillaume, 78
South Africa, 40, 124, 131
  Truth and Reconciliation Commission, 37
South Asia, 17, 18, 21
South Asian Association for Regional Cooperation (SAARC), 17, 21
Southeast Asia, 236
Southeast Europe, 247, 251–2, 257–60, 261, 262, 264
  *see also* Balkans *and individual states*
sovereignty, 18, 22–3, 229–30, 234
  and discursive construction of, 340–55
  forms of, 345–55
  legal, 351–4
  shared, 352
  states without, 345–55
  *see also* states
Soviet Union, 239
Sri Lanka, 199, 203, 227, 233, 235, 236, 237
Stammers, Neil, 142
statebuilding, 2, 5, 6, 186, 214, 230, 240, 275, 339–55, 375–88
State Investor Agreements, 94
states, 233, 235, 236, 239
  and coercion, 234, 240
  governance by, 375–6
  reconstruction of, 278–9
  regulation by, 89–95
  state weakening practices, 376–7
  'strong', 343
  'weak/fragile', 54, 88, 340, 343, 361
Statoil, 91
Stopler–Samuelson theorem, 70

## Index

structural adjustment programmes, 52, 70, 76, 77, 260
'subaltern geographies of political economy', 393
sub-nationalism, 18
Sudan and Darfur, 95–6, 124, 178, 185, 281, 394

Tajiks, 242
Taliban, 241
Talisman Energy, 95–6
Tanzania, 211
taxation, 237
territorial integrity, 234
Tilly, Charles, 228, 341
Timor-Leste, 37, 148
Titmuss, Richard, 291
trade, liberalisation and terms of, 69–84
trade unions, 134, 137, 142, 152
  United Mineworkers Union of Sierra Leone (UMU), 113, 114
Transdniestria, 237
transformative peacebuilding/conflict transformation, 304, 307, 308–9
transnationalism, 182, 235–6
Trepca complex (Kosovo), 148
Tripartite Declaration of Principles Concerning Multinational Enterprises and Social Policy (1978), 150
trusteeship/neo-trusteeship, 351, 352
truth commissions and reconciliation, 37
Turton, David, 236
Tutsi refugees, returnees and hegemony, 210, 211, 213, 214, 216–20
  *see also* Rwanda, *akazu*

Uganda, 40, 87, 211
  Lord's Resistance Army in, 87
UNCTAD, 301
UN Development Programme *Human Development Index*, 97
unemployment, 142, 250, 280
  youth, 146, 148
União Nacional para a Independência Total de Angola (UNITA), 132
'uninsured life', 57, 153, 393

United Kingdom (UK)
  Commission for Africa, 342, 351
  Department for International Development (DFID), 54, 107, 114, 290
  Overseas Development Institute (ODI), 347–8, 349
  social welfare in, 54
United Nations (UN), 358–72
  agencies, 370
  and civil society, 362–3, 370
  Convention on the Rights of the Child, 151
  Declaration on the Granting of Independence to Colonial Countries and Peoples (1960), 347
  Declaration on the Inadmissibility of Intervention in the Domestic Affairs of States and Protection of their Independence and Sovereignty (1965), 347
  Declaration on Principles of International Law Concerning Friendly Relations and Co-operation among States (1970), 347
  Economic and Social Council (ECOSOC), 365, 366, 369
  General Assembly, 370
  Global Compact (2000), 88, 90, 92, 150
  High Commissioner for Refugees, 55
  Integrated DDR Standards (2006), 164
  integrated missions, 362
  missions, 160, 360, 394
  Peacebuilding Commission, 50, 358–72, 394; Organising Committee of, 359, 369
  Peacebuilding Fund and funding, 358, 359, 363
  Peacebuilding Support Office (PSO), 359, 364
  reform of, 358, 359, 360, 367–8, 369, 371
  Secretariat, 370
  Security Council, 363, 366, 368, 369

United Nations – *continued*
  Security Council Resolution 1325 (2000), 40
  Universal Declaration of Human Rights (1948), 289
  US policy towards, 368
  Verification Mission in Guatemala (MINUGUA), 314, 315
United States, 50
  aid to El Salvador, 321
  Alien Tort Claims Act (1789), 93, 96
  Department of Defense, 59, 63, 371
  Institute of Peace, 50
  labour policy, 145
  military in Iraq, 58–9
  military spending, 60
  National Security Strategy, 339, 365
  USAID, 113
  war economy, 60
  welfare and healthcare, 54, 57
urbanisation, 43
Uzbekistan, 235

violence, forms of, 306–7
Voluntary Principles for Security and Human Rights, 88

war economies, 125, 130, 133
war-to-peace transitions, 229, 239–42
war on terror, 243
'Washington Consensus', *see under* neoliberalism
weak/fragile states, *see under* states
Weinstein, Jeremy, 132
welfare, *see* social policy, protection and welfare
West Africa, 78–9, 131
West Bank, 233

women, 32–45
  abuse of, 34, 36, 37, 55, 96
  and conflict, 32–45
  economic independence, 33
  and employment, 125
  ex-combatants, 43, 167
  in garment industry, 152
  and health, 41
  income generation, 148
  marginalised, 33, 38
  political representation, 40
  post-conflict backlash, 33–5
  and rights, 36, 39, 44
  in Second World War, 38
  socioeconomic discrimination, 40–44
  and truth processes, 37–8
  and unemployment, 55
World Bank, 70, 108, 128, 151, 177, 204, 376
  *see also* international financial institutions (IFIs)
World Bank Local Initiatives Project, 254–5
World Commission on the Social Dimension of Globalisation, 151
World Social Forum, 92
World Summit (2005), 358, 366–7, 371
World Trade Organisation (WTO), 72, 145

youth, 131–2
Yugoslavia, 81, 247
Yunus, Mohammad, 247

Zaire, 233
Zartman, I. William, 343
Zimbabwe, 39, 44, 136